Forensic Science

Visit the *Forensic Science, second edition* Companion Website at **www.pearsoned.co.uk/jackson** to find valuable **student** learning material including:

- Multiple choice questions to help test your learning
- Extension articles of interest
- Links to relevant sites on the web
- Glossary to explain key terms

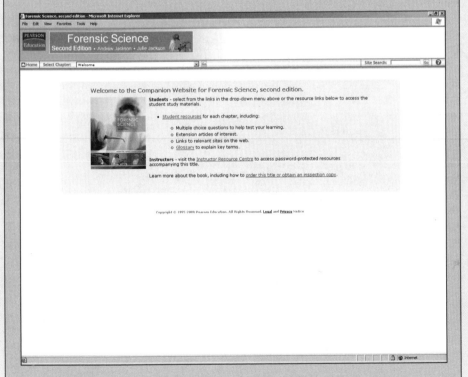

PEARSON
Education

We work with leading authors to develop the
strongest educational materials in forensic science,
bringing cutting-edge thinking and best
learning practice to a global market.

Under a range of well-known imprints, including
Prentice Hall, we craft high-quality print and
electronic publications which help readers to understand
and apply their content, whether studying or at work.

To find out more about the complete range of our
publishing, please visit us on the World Wide Web at:
www.pearsoned.co.uk

Forensic Science

2nd edition

Andrew R.W. Jackson

and

Julie M. Jackson

PEARSON

Prentice
Hall

Harlow, England • London • New York • Boston • San Francisco • Toronto
Sydney • Tokyo • Singapore • Hong Kong • Seoul • Taipei • New Delhi
Cape Town • Madrid • Mexico City • Amsterdam • Munich • Paris • Milan

Pearson Education Limited
Edinburgh Gate
Harlow
Essex CM20 2JE
England

and Associated Companies throughout the world

Visit us on the World Wide Web at:
www.pearsoned.co.uk

First published 2004
Second edition 2008

ISBN: 978-0-13-199880-3

British Library Cataloguing-in-Publication Data
A catalogue record for this book is available from the British Library

10 9 8 7 6 5 4 3
11 10 09 08

Typeset in 9.5/12pt Caslon 224 Book by 30
Printed and bound by Ashford Colour Press Ltd, Gosport

The publisher's policy is to use paper manufactured from sustainable forests.

Contents

Supporting resources

Visit **www.pearsoned.co.uk/jackson** to find valuable online resources

Companion Website for students
- Multiple choice questions to help test your learning
- Extension articles of interest
- Links to relevant sites on the web
- Glossary to explain key terms

For instructors
- Downloadable PowerPoint slides of all figures from the book

Also: The Companion Website provides the following features:

- Search tool to help locate specific items of content
- E-mail results and profile tools to send results of quizzes to instructors
- Online help and support to assist with website usage and troubleshooting

For more information please contact your local Pearson Education sales representative or visit **www.pearsoned.co.uk/jackson**

Preface

In preparing the second edition of this book, we have extended the coverage given to aspects of the discipline of forensic science that students seem to find particularly challenging. Most notably, the consideration that was given in the first edition to the use of statistics in forensic science has been considerably enhanced. There is now a whole chapter (Chapter 13) dedicated to statistics and the analysis, interpretation and evaluation of evidence.

Another aspect that has been augmented in the second edition is the characterisation of man-made fibres using polarized-light microscopy, which is the subject of an extensive new box in Chapter 3 (Box 3.5). This material is supported by the inclusion of a range of colour plates – a new feature of the second edition. Additionally, the book now includes boxes on the role of the forensic archaeologist in finding human remains (Box 12.1) and a case study concerning the law on double jeopardy (Box 14.3).

Naturally, since the publication of the first edition in 2004, there have been developments in the field of forensic science, and the book has been updated throughout to reflect these. Perhaps the area in which scientific development has been most rapid is that of DNA evidence, and the chapter on this (Chapter 6) has been enhanced accordingly.

Andrew R.W. Jackson
Julie M. Jackson
April 2007

Preface to the first edition

Forensic science is the application of science in the resolution of legal disputes. Science is valuable in this context because it has the potential to provide reliable, pertinent and often definitive information about a given case. Furthermore, the information that it supplies frequently cannot be obtained by other means. Science can be used to identify individuals, objects and substances. Importantly, it can provide evidence of contact between an individual and the items or people that he or she has encountered. It may also reveal other types of information that could be pivotal in a given case, such as the amounts or concentrations of particular substances present in a given sample, or details about the timing or sequence of events that occurred during an incident.

The role of the forensic scientist is to provide the justice system with impartial, scientifically rigorous information. Such information can be crucial in establishing whether a crime has been committed and, if so, by whom. It can be used, for example, to test eyewitness accounts of the events that occurred during a particular incident, or to provide the investigating authorities with new leads or intelligence information.

This book was written to provide a clear and authoritative introduction to forensic science. It strives to describe and explain the principal features of forensic science as it is applied at all stages of the process, from the collection of physical evidence at the scene to the presentation of scientific findings in court. The book includes a guest chapter on the rapidly developing technique of DNA profiling, written by Dr Harry Mountain, a geneticist and lecturer in forensic genetics. Through this text, the reader is introduced to the basic concepts and vocabulary necessary for an in-depth understanding of modern forensic science. However, although this book contains details of forensic methods, it does not contain specific information about risk and consequently it should not be used as an instruction manual. It should be noted that those parts of the book that are necessarily specific to a particular legal system are written from a UK perspective, with a particular emphasis on England and Wales. However, a conscious effort has been made to avoid allowing such jurisdiction-specific information to permeate throughout the book. Consequently, most of the text is equally valuable to all readers, irrespective of the legal system operated by their country.

This text will primarily be of use to first-year undergraduates studying forensic science, either as a single subject or in combination with another discipline. However, it will also be of value to students of related disciplines, such as law, and those who undertake forensic science as a subsidiary or elective subject. Furthermore, professionals, such as the police and lawyers, who routinely work with forensic scientists, may also find it useful as a reference book. The text is constructed in a concise and coherent manner, making extensive use of boxes to provide additional material on forensic techniques, further information and illustrative case studies. In order to enhance the reader's learning experience further, both chapter objectives and end of chapter problems are provided. In addition, there is a glossary giving definitions of more commonly used specialised forensic science terms. The book is also supported by a dedicated website, which is available at http://www.pearsoned.co.uk/jackson.

Andrew R.W. Jackson
Julie M. Jackson
September 2003

Acknowledgements

This book would not have been written without the help and forbearance of a number of people. We wish to acknowledge the role of Staffordshire University in this endeavour, especially in granting a semester of sabbatical leave for one of us (ARWJ) during the preparation of the first edition. We are indebted to Dr Harry Mountain of the Biology Department, Staffordshire University, for agreeing to write a guest chapter on DNA profiling and for producing an excellent and accessible account of the subject. We are particularly grateful to the following academic colleagues in forensic science at Staffordshire University for their support and help during this project: Mr David Flatman-Fairs, Dr Graham Harrison, Dr Andy Platt, Dr Mark Tonge and Dr John Wheeler. Thanks are also due to the helpful technical staff at Staffordshire University for their invaluable assistance, particularly Mr Graham Barlow and Mr Derek Lowe for their photographic expertise.

Our grateful thanks are due to Mr Andy Kirby, Scientific Support Manager for Staffordshire Police, who acted as consultant for the first edition and patiently answered our many questions. We wish to acknowledge the constructive criticism and helpful comments made by the following individuals who reviewed the first edition when in draft form: Dr Trevor F. Emmett (the entire manuscript), Dr Mark Tonge (Chapter 1), Mr Andy Kirby (Chapter 2), Dr Jo Bunford (Chapter 3), Mrs Esther Neate (Chapter 4), Dr Neil Jackson (Chapters 5 and 12), Dr Anya Hunt (Chapters 7 and 11), Mr Mike Allen (Chapter 8), Mr Philip Boyce (Chapter 9), Mr Dave Bott (Chapter 10), Professor M. Lee Goff (Box 12.1) and Ms Lisa Mountford (Chapter 13, now Chapter 14). We wish to acknowledge the constructive criticism and helpful comments made by Dr Niamh Nic Daéid, University of Strathclyde, Glasgow, UK, on the draft version of the new Chapter 13 and Dr Fritjof Korber, University of the West of England, Bristol, UK, who reviewed the new Box 3.5 when in draft form.

We are also indebted to a number of people who provided information or advice about specific aspects of the book, namely Dr Craig Adam, Mr Pat Griffin, Mr Graham Parker, Mr John Ross and Staffordshire University colleagues Dr Stephen Merry, Mr Hilton Middleton, Dr Andy Platt, Dr David Rogers and Dr Mark Tonge.

We would like to thank the following people for supplying us with photographic material: Mr Dave Bott, Mr Philip Boyce, Mr Philip Grocott (Leica Microsystems (UK) Ltd), Mr Andy Kirby, Mr Derek Lowe, Mrs Esther Neate, Mr Richard Neave, Mr John Ross, Mr John Rouse and Mr Joe Rynearson. Grateful thanks are also due to the following people who either supplied us with original material for illustrative purposes or provided experimental data: Ms Linzi Arkus, Mr Terry Barker, Ms Sarah Fieldhouse, Mrs Jayne Francis, Ms Alison Greenwood, Mr Hugh Jackson, Mr Tom Jackson, Ms Leanne Kempson, Ms Jennifer Lines, Dr Neil Lamont, Mr Derek Lowe, Mrs Stala Polyviou and Ms Jodie Stuart.

We wish to express our thanks to the staff of Alsager Library, Cheshire, UK, for invaluable assistance in information retrieval. Thanks are also due for the help given by members of staff at Pearson Education Limited, particularly Mr Owen Knight, Ms Mary Lince, Mr Julian Partridge and Ms Pauline Gillett. We are very grateful to the copy-editor Ms Colette Holden, the proofreader Ms Ros Woodward and the indexer, Mr Gary Hall, for their careful attention to detail. Thanks are due to Mr Tom Jackson for designing the cover of the second edition of the book and for the preparation of Plate 4. Also, we wish to thank all of those readers who took the time to inform the publishers of their impressions of the first edition and so helped to shape the second edition.

A special mention must be made of our family for their support and encouragement. In particular, we would like to thank our sons, Tom and Hugh, for their patience and understanding during the writing of this new edition.

Andrew R.W. Jackson
Julie M. Jackson
April 2007

Many people have helped me in the writing of Chapter 6. I would especially like to thank Julie and Andrew Jackson for inviting me to write the chapter, for their very positive and encouraging approach throughout its writing, and for inviting me to update it for the second edition.

I am very grateful for the critical and supportive reviews of the chapter from Kerry Brudenell (for the draft version) and from Sam Myers-Mills (for the second edition). Your suggestions and inputs are highly appreciated. I must also thank Carol Griffiths for directing me to Kerry.

My gratitude also to the staff of the Forensic Science Department, in particular Laura Walton, and Biological Sciences, who have been encouraging and forgiving of absences and missed deadlines during some of the writing.

My family I cannot thank enough: Gail for her patience, her reading of the numerous drafts, being critical with positive suggestions and overall life-support; and Rebecka and Natasha for welcome distractions and being understanding (in the main) of my frequent unavailability during the writing – paternity testing (see Section 6.4.3) should confirm to them who the stranger wandering around the house at a loose end is.

Harry Mountain
April 2007

Publisher's acknowledgements

We are grateful to the following for permission to reproduce copyright material:

Quote on p.9 reproduced from www.ukas.com with permission from the United Kingdom Accreditation Service; Figure 2.5 reproduced by kind permission of Jennifer Lines, Staffordshire University; Figures 2.7 and 5.1 reproduced by kind permission of Esther Neate, Wiltshire Constabulary, UK; Box 3.10 (figure (a)) from Whiston, C. (1987) *X-ray methods*. London: John Wiley & sons Limited © John Wiley & Sons Limited. Reproduced with permission; Figure 4.4 (fingerprint visualisation) reproduced by kind permission of Sarah Fieldhouse, Staffordshire University, UK; Figures 4.6 and 4.7 from Bowman, V. (ed.) (2005) *Fingerprint Development Handbook* (2nd edn). Reproduced under the term of the click-use licence; Box 7.1 (photograph) reproduced by kind permission of John Ross, Curator of the Crime Museum, New Scotland Yard, UK; Figure 7.8 from Timbrell, J. (2002) *Introduction to Toxicology* (3rd edn). London: Taylor & Francis, reproduced with permission from Thomson Publishing Services; Quote in Box 8.2 from *Annual Report of The Forensic Science Service 2001–02*, © Crown Copyright 2002, reproduced with permission from The Forensic Science Service; Figure 8.4 reproduced by kind permission of John Dickinson Stationery Ltd; Figure 9.5(a) and Box 11.1 (photograph) reproduced by kind permission of Andy Kirby, Staffordshire Police, UK; Box 9.1 (photograph (b)), Box 9.4 (photograph (a)), Figures 9.5(b), 9.6, 9.7(b), 9.7(c), 9.8 and 9.9 reproduced by kind permission of Philip Boyce, Forensic Alliance, UK; Figures 10.4(a), 10.7(a), 10.7(b), 10.8 and 11.1 reproduced by kind permission of Dave Bott, Staffordshire Fire & Rescue Service, UK; Figure 10.5(a) reproduced by kind permission of Gloucestershire Constabulary, UK; Figure 12.3 from Knight, B. (1996) *Forensic Pathology* (2nd edn). London: Arnold, reproduced by kind permission of Arnold; Box 12.6 (photographs (a), (b) and (c)) reproduced by kind permission of Richard Neave, University of Manchester; Figure 14.1 from Bond, C. *et al.* (1999) *The expert witness in court: a practical guide* (2nd edn, updated and edited by Suzanne Burn). Kent: Shaw & Sons Ltd. Reproduced with permission from Shaw & Sons Ltd; Figure 14.2 from Davies *et al.* (2005) *Criminal justice: an introduction to the criminal justice system in England and Wales* (3rd edn). Harlow: Longman, reproduced with permission from Pearson Education Ltd.

In some instances we have been unable to trace the owners of copyright material, and we would appreciate any information that would enable us to do so.

Information sources used in the preparation of case studies

Box 3.2: Deadman, H. A. 'Fibre Evidence and the Wayne Williams Trial' in Saferstein, R. (2001) *Criminalistics: An introduction to forensic science* (7th edn), Prentice Hall, New Jersey, USA, pp. 74–86; Nickell, J. and Fischer, J. F. (1999) *Crime Science: Methods of forensic detection*. The University Press of Kentucky, Kentucky, USA, pp. 75–81. Box 3.8: Evans, C. (1996) *The casebook of forensic detection: how science solved 100 of the world's most baffling crimes*. New York: John Wiley & Sons, Inc.; Owen, D (2000) *Hidden evidence: the story of forensic science and how it helped to solve 40 of the world's toughest crimes*. London: Quintet Publishing (Time Life Books), pp. 184–6. Box 4.1: Evans, C. (1996) *The casebook of forensic detection: how science solved 100 of the world's most baffling crimes*. New York: John Wiley & Sons, Inc., pp. 151–4; Owen, D. (2000) *Hidden evidence: the story of forensic science and how it helped to solve 40 of the world's toughest crimes*. London: Quintet Publishing (Time Life Books), pp. 172–3. **Box 4.2**: http://www.forensic.gov.uk/forensic_t/inside/news/list_casefiles.php?case=17; http://www.hmcourts-service.gov.uk/cms/144_9708.htm. Box 5.4: Evans, C. (1996) *The casebook of forensic detection: how science solved 100 of the world's most baffling crimes*. New York: John Wiley & Sons, Inc., pp. 51–5; Lane, B. (ed) (1992) *Encyclopaedia of forensic science*. London: Headline Book Publishing, pp. 111–14. Box 6.1: http://www.bbc.co.uk/science/horizon/2001/a6murder.shtml; http://news.bbc.co.uk/1/hi/uk/wales/1977508.stm; http://news.bbc.co.uk/1/hi/u/1257661.stm; http://news.bbc.co.uk/1/hi/english/uk/wales/newsid_1980000/1980731.stm. Box 6.2: http://www.forensic.gov.uk/forensic/news/press_releases/2002/2002-06-06_key.htm; http://www.forensic.gov.uk/forensic/news/casefiles/2002_09_fhn.htm. Box 6.3: Gill, P., Ivanov, P. L., Kimpton, C., Piercy, R., Benson, N., Tully, G., Evett, I., Hagelberg, E. and Sullivan, K. (1994) 'Identification of the remains of the Romanov family by DNA analysis' in *Nature Genetics* 6, pp. 130–5; Katzaman, J. (1998) in *Air Force News*, 10 June 1998 at http://www.af.mil/news/Jun1998/n19980630-_980961.html. Box 6.4: http://www.forensic.gov.uk/forensic/news/press_releases/2002/16-05-2002.htm; http://www.forensic.gov.uk/forensic/news/casefiles/2002_07_marion.htm; http://www.ananova.com/news/story/sm_563957.html; http://www.guardian.co.uk/uk_news/story/0,3604,713649,00.html; http://www.forensic.gov.uk/forensic/news/press_ releases/2002/23-08-2002.htm; http://uk.news.yahoo.com/020823/4/d82xk.html. Box 6.5: Modley, J. G. (1999) 'DNA identification of the victims of the Swissair Flight'. First International Conference on Human identification in the Millennium, 24–26 October 1999, London; news release from the Royal Canadian Mounted Police 'RCMP establishes DNA patterns from more than 142 victims of Swiss Air crash' at http://www.rcmp-grc.gc.ca/news/nr-98-12.htm. Box 7.1: Evans, C. (1996) *The casebook of forensic detection*. New York: John Wiley & Sons, Inc., pp. 246–8; Lane, B (1992) *The encyclopaedia of forensic science*. London: Headline Book Publishing, pp. 548–50. Box 7.2: Smith, Janet (2002) The Shipman Inquiry, first report. Great Britain: Shipman Inquiry, http://www.the-shipman-inquiry.org.uk. Box 8.2: http://www.bbc. co.uk/crime/caseclosed/ashiahansen.shtml, http://www.guardian.co.uk/uk_news/ story. Box 8.8: Evans. C. (1996) *The casebook of forensic detection: how science solved 100 of the world's most baffling crimes*. New York: John Wiley & Sons, Inc., pp. 48–51; Owen, D. (2000) *Hidden evidence*. London: Time Life Books, pp. 156–7. Box 9.5: Cathcart, B. (2001) *Jill Dando: her life and death*. London: Penguin Books Ltd; http://www.bbc.co.uk/crime/case-closed/jilldando.shmtl; http://www.guardian. co.uk/jilldando/story. Box 10.2: Yallop, H. J. (1980) *Explosion investigation*. Jointly published by Harrogate: The Forensic Science Society and Edinburgh: Scottish Academic Press Ltd. Box 11.4: Beveridge, A. (ed) (1998) *Forensic investigation of explosions*. London: Taylor & Francis, pp. 140–2; Evans, C. (1996) *The casebook of forensic detection: how science solved 100 of the world's most baffling crimes*. New York: John Wiley & Sons, Inc., pp. 87–9; Owen, D. (2000) Hidden evidence. London: Time Life Books, pp 140–2. Box 12.4: Evans, C. (1996) *The casebook of forensic detection: how science solved 100 of the world's most baffling crimes*. New York: John Wiley & Sons, Inc., pp. 187–90; Glaister, J. and Brash, J. C. (1937) *Medico-legal aspects of the Ruxton case*.

Churchill Livingstone; Goff, M. L. (2000) *A fly for the prosecution: how insect evidence helps solve crimes*. Cambridge, Massachusetts: Harvard University Press, pp. 12–13; Lane, B. (1992) *The encyclopaedia of forensic science*. London: Headline Book Publishing. pp. 191–205; Owen, D. (2000) *Hidden evidence*. London: Time Life Books, pp. 54–7. Box **12.5**: Evans, C. (1996) *The casebook of forensic detection: how science solved 100 of the world's most baffling crimes*. New York: John Wiley & Sons, Inc., pp. 147–9; Lane, B. (1992) *The encyclopaedia of forensic science*. London: Headline Book Publishing, pp. 181–2. **Box 14.3**: http://www.cps.gov.uk/ search.asp?mode=allwords&search=William+Dunlop&submit.x=13&submit.y=8; Box 14.4: Coghlan, A. (2002) 'Weighing up the odds' in *New Scientist* 2331, p. 13; http://www.guardian. co.uk/uk_news/story.

In its broadest sense, forensic science may be defined as any science that is used in the service of the justice system. Such a wide definition necessarily encompasses both civil disputes and criminal cases. However, in practice, forensic science is more likely to be involved in the investigation and resolution of criminal cases and it is with this aspect that this text is almost exclusively concerned.

This introductory chapter is designed to provide the reader with an insight into:

> the role played by forensic science in the investigation of crime (Section 1.1);
> the scientific investigation of forensic evidence (Section 1.2);
> the provision of forensic science services in England and Wales (Section 1.3);
> the accreditation of forensic science in the UK (Section 1.4);
> quality assurance issues within forensic science (Section 1.5).

Through the topics covered, the reader is introduced to the discipline of forensic science in general and to this book in particular.

1.1 The role of forensic science in the investigation of crime

Forensic science plays a pivotal role in most criminal prosecutions, especially those of a more serious nature. Three distinct phases may be recognised within the procession from the collection of physical evidence to the presentation of scientific findings in court, each of which is described briefly in the following sections.

1.1.1 The recovery of evidence from the crime scene

The involvement of forensic science in the investigation and resolution of criminal offences begins at the crime scene. Thus, the effective recovery of items of physical evidence is crucial to the success of the subsequent inquiry. In recent years, this task has normally been carried out by highly trained civilian specialists, usually known as Scenes of Crime Officers (SOCOs). Once recovered, items of physical evidence must be separately and appropriately packaged, labelled, stored and transported to the laboratory for the next stage, that of forensic examination (Section 1.1.2).

It is vitally important that a 'chain of custody' is established for each individual item of evidence from the point of its recovery at the crime scene through to its appearance as a court exhibit (Figure 1.1). If **continuity of evidence** (i.e. a complete documented record of the progress of a particular evidential object) cannot be adequately demonstrated, then that evidence may be deemed inadmissible in court because the possibility of contamination, or tampering, en route cannot be ruled out. The risk of contamination of evidence is minimised by applying the following precautionary steps:

Continuity of evidence

The provision of a complete documented account of the progress of an item of evidence since its recovery from a crime scene. If this cannot be adequately demonstrated, the evidence in question may be ruled inadmissible in court.

- ■ using chain of custody labels;
- ■ opening each package in an area other than where it was originally sealed;
- ■ assiduously using logging systems;
- ■ minimising the number of people handling the evidence;
- ■ storing packages in a dedicated secure area.

In addition, in serious incidents, the involvement of a dedicated exhibits officer will help to ensure continuity of the evidence.

Any significant deterioration in the condition of forensic evidence post-collection might also render it inadmissible as evidence in court. Therefore, exhibits must be treated and stored appropriately according to their type at every stage.

1.1.2 The forensic examination of evidence recovered from the crime scene

After recovery from the crime scene, evidential items of potential forensic importance are submitted for examination (although not every scene item collected necessarily proceeds to this next stage). Such analytical services may be obtained from a range of organisations, including the scientific support departments within the police service, the Forensic Science Service (FSS) and independent forensic practitioners (see Section 1.3 for more details).

Forensic analysis of items of physical evidence may provide answers to a number of important questions. In the first place, it may be necessary to establish whether a

Crime scene

↓

Scenes of Crime Officer (SOCO)

↓

Police Scientific Support Unit (SSU)

↓

Forensic laboratory

↓

Court

Figure 1.1 Typical route of an item of evidence recovered from a crime scene

crime has indeed been committed. Perhaps surprisingly, this is not always immediately obvious. For example, consider a case in which an individual is arrested and found to have packets of pale brown powder in his pockets, which he claims to be sugar. The police, however, suspect illegal possession of the drug heroin. In this particular example, identification of the packaged substance is key to determining whether a criminal offence has, in fact, taken place.

Much of forensic analysis is concerned with establishing whether any links exist between the suspect, victim and/or crime scene. According to Locard's exchange principle, 'every contact leaves a trace'. This means, in theory at least, that any physical contact between individuals, or between an individual and a place or object, invariably results in the transference of traces of physical evidence. Examples of **trace evidence** that may be transferred in this manner include hairs, fibres, glass fragments, body fluids and gunshot residues. A comparison between similar items of trace evidence recovered from two different locations may establish whether there is a connection between the two. For example, it may help to place a suspect at the scene of a particular crime (although this does not necessarily mean that the said individual was involved in the commission of that crime). Evidence that links two separate entities, be they people or objects, can be termed associative evidence.

In many cases, forensic science can provide information that either corroborates or refutes evidence from another source, such as supplied by eyewitnesses to a particular event. Furthermore, forensic evidence can facilitate intelligence gathering by the police. In the case of drugs, for example, the analysis of samples recovered from different locations may show that they have come from the same batch, or may help to pinpoint their country of origin (Chapter 7, Section 7.5.1). Forensic evidence may also reveal when an event occurred, or the order of a sequence of events. For example, it may be possible to determine the order in which two bullets struck a pane of glass (Chapter 3, Section 3.2).

Finally, the forensic analysis of particular types of evidence may help to establish the identity of an individual suspected of committing a crime. In cases where body fluids, such as blood or semen, are recovered from a crime scene, personal identification may be made through DNA profiling (Chapter 6). Similarly, a comparison of fingerprints left at a crime scene with those stored on the National Automated Fingerprint Identification System (NAFIS) may be successful in identifying the individual responsible (Chapter 4, Section 4.1.3).

Trace evidence
Minute amounts of materials (such as glass shards, paint chips, hairs or fibres) that, through transference between individuals, or between an individual and a physical location, may constitute important forensic evidence.

1.1.3 The presentation of scientific test results in court

The forensic scientist(s) responsible for the analysis of evidential items during a criminal investigation is required to write up his or her findings in the form of a report for use in court. As well as being comprehensive, the contents of such a report should be readily understood by non-scientists within the criminal justice system. In most cases, the forensic scientist's report is all that is seen by the court. However, on occasion, the forensic scientist is required to appear in court as an expert witness. In this capacity, he or she will give testimony of fact, and of opinion based on fact when required to do so, from within his or her own area of expertise (Chapter 14, Section 14.3).

1.2 The scientific investigation of forensic evidence

After recovery from a crime scene, items of potential forensic importance are sent to the laboratory for scientific investigation. The purpose of this process is to obtain information relevant to the case in question from the articles submitted. The type of approach used for any given piece of evidence will be determined by the type of information sought. An important distinction is between qualitative analysis and quantitative analysis. The former is concerned with information that can provide evidence about the identity of an entity, while the latter aims to establish the amount or concentration of a given substance. For example, qualitative analysis may establish whether a given sample of blood contains alcohol, but quantitative analysis will be required to determine whether the sample has an alcohol content that is above the legal limit for drink-driving (Chapter 7, Section 7.2).

1.2.1 The comparison of evidence

In the majority of cases, the scientific investigation of evidence will involve comparison. This may be performed in a number of different ways, each of which is discussed briefly below.

Comparison between an evidential object and a relevant database

Class characteristics
Characteristics that enable an object to be placed into a particular category, for example identifying a trainer as belonging to a certain brand.

In some instances, the purpose of this type of comparison is to identify the **class characteristics** of the evidential item concerned. For example, if footwear impressions or prints are recovered from a crime scene, these may be usefully compared with sole patterns held on a footwear database (Chapter 4, Section 4.2.2). Through this exercise, it may be possible to identify the manufacturer and, conceivably, the style of the shoe concerned. This type of footwear comparison is particularly relevant to trainers. Similarly, tyre marks left at an incident scene may be compared with an appropriate database of tread pattern designs.

With some specific types of forensic evidence, namely fingerprints and samples of body fluids or tissues used for DNA profiling, the object of comparison with a database is the identification of the individual concerned. In the case of fingerprints, this may be achieved by searching the National Automated Fingerprint Identification System (NAFIS) for possible matches (Chapter 4, Section 4.1.3). In a similar manner, DNA profiles may be compared with those held on the National DNA Database (NDNAD) (Chapter 6, Section 6.3.6).

Comparison between two pieces of evidence obtained from different places

This type of comparison seeks to determine whether two pieces of apparently similar forensic evidence, for example hairs, textile fibres, paint chips or glass fragments, share a common origin. Its purpose, therefore, is to determine whether any link exists between the two separate locations from which the evidence has been retrieved (Section 1.1.2). This may be between two individuals (as in the case of the victim of an attack and his or her assailant), between an individual and a crime scene, or even between two different crime scenes. This type of comparison may be usefully illustrated by the following hypothetical scenario.

Consider a case in which a car window is broken and the CD player stolen from the vehicle. A suspect is apprehended by the police and, although the CD player is not in the suspect's possession, there are splinters of glass adhered to the right-hand cuff of his jacket. A comparison is made between shards of glass taken from the car window and those recovered from the suspect. If these samples are found to be indistinguishable, this provides evidence that is consistent with the suspect being at the crime scene.

Comparison between questioned samples, both positive and negative controls, and reference collections

A crime scene sample that is to be tested to find its evidential value is usually referred to as a questioned sample (or sometimes a disputed sample). Such tests are designed to evaluate a hypothesis. A hypothesis is a supposition that is either true or false and that can be tested by experimentation. For example, if a suspect is detained and found to possess a packet containing a pale brown powder, then the hypothesis may be that the powder is heroin. In order to test this hypothesis, experiments may be carried out that compare the chemical characteristics of this questioned sample with those of a known sample of heroin. Known samples such as this are referred to as positive controls, knowns or standards. If the questioned sample and the positive control are shown to have characteristics in common, it might be concluded that the questioned sample is indeed heroin. However, this may not be the case. It is possible that the chemicals and/or equipment used in the test were contaminated with heroin. In order to eliminate this possibility, it is necessary to carry out the test in a way that is identical in all respects to the tests to be carried out on the questioned sample and the positive control sample, except that it contains neither of these materials. Such a test is known as a negative control or a blank. In some instances, it is necessary to go to considerable lengths when carrying out the negative control test. For example, when testing for trace levels of explosives, swabs from all surfaces that will come into contact with the sample will be obtained. These will then be tested to show that the equipment was free from explosives. Note that in many applications, the term 'control' is used to denote either positive or negative controls; the context makes it clear which type of control is being referred to. There are circumstances in which it is valuable to compare a questioned sample with a number of positive controls. For example, the properties of a liquid retrieved from a scene of suspected arson may be compared with those of a range of flammable liquids, such as different types of petrol, paraffin and diesel fuel. Through comparison, it may be possible to identify the questioned sample via elimination and positive matching. A collection of positive controls used for such a purpose is known as a reference collection.

Comparison between a scene impression and a test impression

Impressions made by recognisable objects, such as footwear, tyres and tools, are often detected during the examination of crime scenes (Chapter 4). If an object suspected of creating the impression(s) in question is subsequently discovered, then that object may be used to create a series of **test impressions**. A comparison of these test impressions with the **scene impression**(s) may reveal that both types were created by objects with the same class characteristics. However, in some cases, it may be possible to proceed beyond this stage and identify the suspect item as being the actual one used in the commission of a crime. This can occur when **individual characteristics**, i.e. those that are peculiar to a particular individual object, are shown to be visible on the scene impression(s), as well as on the test impressions. Such individual characteristics may be created by some aberration during the manufacturing process but are more likely to be acquired as a result of general wear and tear. Characteristics that are exhibited in evidence and that are capable of identifying a specific item are said to be individualising.

1.2.2 Establishing what occurred during a crime: crime reconstruction and simulation experiments

The forensic evidence left at a crime scene may also be used to establish at least some of the events that occurred before, during and immediately after the commission of a crime and, possibly, the order in which they took place. The partial or complete reconstruction of a crime may be very important in corroborating (i.e. supporting) or refuting an account of events given, for example, by an individual suspected of involvement, or an eyewitness. In cases of violent crime, expert interpretation of bloodstain patterns left at the scene may provide vital information about what actually happened (Chapter 5, Box 5.4).

In certain cases, **simulation experiments** may be performed to help ascertain what may have occurred during a given incident. This is best illustrated by an example. Consider a case in which a shotgun has been discharged during the commission of a crime. In such cases, it is valuable to know the distance from the muzzle of the gun to the target. As part of the investigation, a firearms examiner may conduct a simulation experiment in which the weapon concerned is test-fired at targets made of card, preferably using cartridges collected from either the crime scene or a suspect. During this experiment, the distance from the muzzle of the gun to the targets will be varied and recorded. This will enable a correlation to be established between the resultant damage patterns and the distance of firing. Thus, by comparison of the damage pattern at the scene with those produced during the simulation experiment, the distance over which the gun was fired during the commission of the crime can be established. This information may be important in corroborating or refuting a particular version of events given by an individual involved in the crime.

1.2.3 Intelligence information

Forensic evidence collected from crime scenes is potentially useful in gathering intelligence information on criminals and their activities. For example, it may help to establish that a given individual was responsible for a number of apparently

Test impression
An impression deliberately made using a suspect item in order to compare it with a scene impression.

Scene impression
An impression detected at the scene of a crime, which may be of potential forensic importance.

Individual characteristics
Characteristics that are unique to a particular object (e.g. a tool, tyre or shoe) and, as such, are potentially useful in the identification of scene impressions

Simulation experiments
A series of experiments designed to simulate a particular aspect of a crime, which, through a process of elimination, may help to pinpoint exactly what happened in that specific aspect.

unconnected crimes. It may also provide investigative leads to the police, for example when traces of paint found on the victim of a hit-and-run incident reveal the colour of the car involved.

The amount of information generated through the recovery of forensic evidence from crime scenes, together with that from other policing activities, is enormous. In order to maximise effective use of this resource, West Midlands Police in conjunction with the Forensic Science Service (FSS) have developed a computer software package known as **FLINTS** – the Forensic-Led Intelligence System. Since its first edition in 1998, FLINTS has undergone continual development, with FLINTS III being launched in April 2002.

FLINTS accesses a data warehouse, which holds many different types of information including crime reports, custody records, firearms registers, Automated Number Plate Recognition (ANPR), stop-and-search information, and forensic data such as fingerprints and DNA. Through the cross-reference and distillation of this stored information (which is automatically updated every few minutes), intelligence can be provided to the operator in response to the data/information that he or she inputs. FLINTS can be used to identify criminal networks, make connections between offenders and places, and establish patterns of crime (including, through geographical profiling, crime 'hotspots'). Although FLINTS concentrates mainly on current offenders, it can also provide information that may be useful in predicting future crimes. This intelligence system (nicknamed 'the digital detective') has already been adopted by other forces, such as Staffordshire Police.

FLINTS
Forensic-Led Intelligence System; a computer software package jointly developed by West Midlands Police and the Forensic Science Service (FSS).

1.3 The provision of forensic science services in England and Wales

Forensic science services in England and Wales are provided through scientific support within the police service, the Forensic Science Service (FSS) and other agencies, and independent forensic practitioners. Details of the accreditation of laboratories and individuals concerned with the provision of forensic science services are given in Section 1.4.

1.3.1 Scientific support within the police service

Within each police force, scientific support is typically organised into the following areas: the Scenes of Crime Department, the Fingerprint Bureau (or Department), the Photographic Services Department and the Chemical Enhancement Laboratory (CEL). Together these constitute the Scientific Support Unit (SSU), overseen by a Scientific Support Manager (SSM), or equivalent. The role of each of these scientific support services is discussed in detail in Chapter 2, Box 2.1.

1.3.2 The Forensic Science Service (FSS) and other agencies

The Forensic Science Service (FSS) is the biggest supplier of forensic science services in the United Kingdom. In 1991, it was established as an executive agency of the Home Office (formed from the regional government laboratories previously run by the Home Office Forensic Science Service). The FSS has six regional laboratories (at Birmingham, Chepstow, Chorley, Huntingdon, London and Wetherby) together with the National Firearms Unit (NFU) based in Manchester. It principally covers England and Wales. In Northern Ireland, forensic science services are provided by the Forensic Science Agency of Northern Ireland, while in Scotland there are four independent forensic laboratories – Strathclyde (based in Glasgow), Tayside (Dundee), Grampian (Aberdeen) and Lothian & Borders (Edinburgh) – which between them provide forensic science support to the eight Scottish police forces.

The main customers of the FSS are the regional police forces in England and Wales, other police forces (e.g. British Transport Police and Ministry of Defence Police), the Crown Prosecution Service (CPS), Her Majesty's Coroners and Her Majesty's Customs and Excise (HM C&E). In addition, the services of the FSS are available to other customers, both at home and abroad. It is worth emphasising that, within the criminal justice system, the services of the FSS are available to the defence, as well as to the prosecution.

The vast majority of the work undertaken by the FSS concerns the analysis of samples of forensic importance (e.g. body fluids, fibres, glass, paint, shoe marks and tool marks) and compiling reports for use in court (Chapter 14, Section 14.2). In a small percentage of cases, FSS scientists are required to appear in court in person as expert witnesses. For example, during 2004–05, when the FSS dealt with around 130 000 cases, scientists gave expert testimony in court on nearly 2500 occasions. They also attended approximately 1800 crime scenes during that same period. In addition, the FSS is responsible for running the National DNA Database® (NDNAD), which was established in 1995, and the National Firearms Forensic Intelligence Database (NFFID). The latter database was set up in partnership with the Association of Chief Police Officers (ACPO) in 2003.

There are a number of agencies other than the FSS itself that provide forensic services. For example, the Defence Science and Technology Laboratory (Dstl), an agency of the UK Ministry of Defence (formed when the Defence Evaluation and Research Agency (DERA) split into two organisations in July 2001) provides analytical services for explosives, firearms and ballistics. Dstl also provides a forensic service for the identification of chemical and biological warfare agents. Another example is the now-privatised LGC (formerly called the Laboratory of the Government Chemist), which offers a number of forensic services including the analysis of controlled drugs, DNA, ecological samples (such as diatoms, insects and pollen), questioned documents and toxicological samples (both ante-mortem and post-mortem), and the examination of mobile phones and computers. In September 2005, LGC acquired the UK's largest private sector supplier of forensic science services, Forensic Alliance Ltd (FAL), originally established in 1997.

1.3.3 Independent forensic practitioners

In addition to the services provided by the FSS and other agencies, there are many independent suppliers of forensic science services. These practitioners, working either alone or as part of, for example, a private practice, tend to be employed by the defence side in criminal prosecutions, although their services are equally available to the prosecution. In contrast, the prosecution side in a criminal case traditionally purchases its forensic services from the FSS. However, this dichotomy regarding the purchase of forensic services is gradually changing. Independent forensic practitioners tend to specialise in the type of forensic service that they supply, concentrating on one particular aspect, such as questioned document analysis. In common with other forensic scientists, independent forensic practitioners may be called to appear in court to give expert witness testimony (Chapter 14, Section 14.3).

1.4 The accreditation of forensic science in the UK

With regard to the provision of forensic science services in the UK, both laboratories and individual practitioners may be accredited (i.e. independently evaluated), provided that they fulfil the necessary criteria, by an appropriate third party.

1.4.1 Laboratory accreditation

Forensic laboratories may seek accreditation from the United Kingdom Accreditation Service (UKAS). The function of this government-recognised national accreditation body is 'to assess, against internationally agreed standards, organisations that provide certification, testing, inspection and calibration services'. UKAS accreditation demonstrates impartiality, competence and performance capability on the part of the organisation concerned.

The route to accreditation involves the following steps:

1. *Application.* First, a completed application form, prepared with reference to the appropriate Accreditation Standard, must be submitted. Following receipt, an assessment manager will be assigned to oversee the accreditation process of the applicant.

2. *Pre-assessment visit.* This visit will be carried out by the assessment manager. Its purpose is to verify that the company in question is ready to undergo the full accreditation process.

3. *Initial assessment visit.* A lead assessor (usually the assessment manager, see above), together with appropriate technical support, will undertake this second visit, during which those areas for which accreditation is sought are assessed. If, during this process, the laboratory is found not to comply with any of the requirements set down by UKAS, then these must be rectified before accreditation can be awarded.

4. *Maintenance and extension of accreditation.* Once granted, accreditation is maintained by yearly surveillance visits. A full reassessment is necessary every fourth year. If wished, an accredited laboratory may extend the scope of its assessment, for example to additional analytical tests.

Through the process described above, UKAS can provide accreditation to forensic laboratories in two main areas, testing and calibration, in both cases providing accreditation to ISO (International Organization for Standardization) 17025, which deals with the general requirements for the competence of testing and calibration laboratories. LGC Ltd is an example of a UKAS Accredited Calibration Laboratory, while UKAS Accredited Testing Laboratories include the laboratories of Forensic Alliance Ltd (now part of the LGC group), at Abingdon in Oxfordshire, Tamworth in Staffordshire and Risley in Cheshire, and those of the Forensic Science Service (see Section 1.3.2). More details of the requirements for compliance with ISO 17025 are given in Section 1.5.

UKAS also provides accreditation for organisations that themselves provide inspection and certification services. Among the services provided by such organisations are certification to ISO 9000 and ISO 14000 (two of the most commonly implemented ISO standards, and recognised worldwide). The ISO 9000 family of standards (including ISO 9001) concerns quality management, while that of ISO 14000 deals with environmental management issues. Either or both of these standards may be sought by businesses in the forensic science sector. For example, Dstl (see Section 1.3.2) has ISO 9001 certification awarded by Lloyds Register Quality Assurance Ltd, which itself has accreditation (for the provision of certification services) from UKAS.

1.4.2 Individual accreditation

Individual forensic practitioners may apply for registration with the Council for the Registration of Forensic Practitioners (CRFP), which was established in October 2000. The aim of this independent regulatory body was to set up and manage a register of competent forensic practitioners. Importantly, it enables the courts and judiciary to check the proficiency of an individual practitioner called to give evidence as an expert witness in court (Chapter 14, Section 14.3).

Forensic podiatry
A podiatrist is an individual trained in the care and treatment of the lower limb. Forensic podiatry concerns the application of the specialist knowledge of podiatrists within the forensic context, e.g. in the interpretation of footprints or gait.

Initially, individual practitioners came from within the areas of crime scene examination, laboratory science and fingerprint examination. However, since its inception, the CRFP register has grown to encompass new specialties, the latest of which – **forensic podiatry** – was added on 1 October 2006. Table 1.1 shows the different specialties covered by the CRFP register and the number of practitioners registered within each, as described in the CRFP Annual Review 2005/06.

In terms of numbers, the CRFP registered its 2500th forensic practitioner on 12 October 2006 and continues to expand its membership. In order to achieve registration with the CRFP, an individual forensic practitioner must undergo a rigorous independent assessment by a professional peer, including the examination of selected examples of his or her real-life casework. Successful applicants are entitled to use the initials RFP (Registered Forensic Practitioner) after their name. For continued inclusion on the CRFP register, individuals must undergo revalidation once every four years.

1.4.3 Course accreditation

Increasing interest in forensic science over the past decade has led to an expansion in the number of forensic science courses offered by UK universities, primarily at undergraduate level but also at postgraduate level. In response to this increase in provision, the Forensic Science Society (FSSoc) has introduced an accreditation system for forensic undergraduate and postgraduate courses. This system is based on three component standards, namely:

Table 1.1 The different specialties covered by the CRFP register and the number of practitioners registered within each*

Specialty	Number of registered practitioners
Scene examination	1001
Fingerprint examination	445
Human contact traces	213
Particulates and other traces	125
Drugs	115
Scene examination: volume crime	86
Fingerprint development	79
Marks	71
Toxicology	58
Road transport investigation	54
Questioned documents	49
Incident evaluation	40
Firearms	35
Medical examination	13
Odontology	12
Computers	10
Veterinary science	10
Anthropology	9
Fire scene examination	8
Archaeology	7
Imaging	7
Paediatrics	3
Telecoms	1

Source: CRFP Annual Review 2005/06

*An individual forensic practitioner may be registered in more than one of these specialties. Note also that this list is growing, with forensic podiatry added as a specialty after publication of the CRFP Annual Review 2005/06.

■ interpretation, evaluation and presentation of evidence;
■ crime scene investigation;
■ laboratory analysis.

In order to achieve accreditation for a particular course, institutions have to achieve the requirements of the first component standard (interpretation, evaluation and presentation of evidence) plus at least those of one of the other two component standards listed above. In the first wave, four universities (one Scottish and three English) had one or more of their courses accredited by the Forensic Science Society on 1 November 2006.

1.5 Quality assurance in forensic science

From the collection of items of evidence at the crime scene and their subsequent analysis in the laboratory, through to the presentation of scientific findings at court, it is of paramount importance that the quality of the processes involved at each constituent stage can be satisfactorily demonstrated. Quality assurance may be defined as those systems that are put in place to guarantee that quality control is carried out, while quality control may be described as those day-to-day operational procedures enacted to ensure that the products or services concerned meet the required standards.

There are a number of well-established means of quality assurance by which providers of forensic science services can ensure that they meet the exacting standards demanded of them. Police scientific support personnel (Chapter 2, Box 2.1) and forensic scientists must be appropriately trained, qualified, experienced and supervised for the tasks that they are required to undertake. For example, in the UK, fingerprint experts are trained and qualified by Centrex (Central Police Training and Development Authority), a process that takes several years. Fingerprint experts who report to the courts in England and Wales are on the National Register of Fingerprint Experts. Additionally, fingerprint experts may obtain individual accreditation from the Council for the Registration of Forensic Practitioners (Section 1.4.2).

As well as being experts in their own fields, laboratory personnel (whatever their specialist area, e.g. questioned documents or glass analysis) and crime scene investigators need a number of qualities in order to be fully effective. They must be able to work in an ethically and legally acceptable fashion, be impartial and objective in their work and proceed methodically, while keeping an open and enquiring mind at all times. Moreover, they must be able to communicate effectively, not only with members of the team involved in the same case as themselves but also to a wider audience, in the form of written reports of their findings and, where required, testimony in court (Chapter 14, Section 14.3).

As outlined in Section 1.4.1, laboratories involved in forensic analysis and examination may apply for accreditation from the UK Accreditation Service. This can be achieved by demonstration of compliance with all of the relevant criteria set down in ISO 17025. The requirements of this international standard include:

■ that laboratory personnel possess the necessary knowledge, skills and ability to carry out the tasks assigned, and that this competence is maintained by retraining, where necessary;

■ secure storage conditions for evidential samples (both pre- and post-examination) that are appropriate to the material concerned (i.e. to avoid any contamination, deterioration or loss of the evidence);

■ full validation of all technical procedures before use in casework or in-house verification of procedures that have been previously validated in another laboratory;

■ the proper use, maintenance and calibration of the equipment used in the forensic laboratory and, when necessary, its replacement;

- the full documentation and proper control of reference collections (e.g. drug samples or cartridges);

- the maintenance of a 'chain of custody' (Chapter 2, Section 2.4) to demonstrate that the integrity of evidential items has not been compromised;

- the use of appropriate quality control measures to assure the quality of test and calibration results. The measures available include alternative methods, independent checks, positive and negative controls, and repeat testing;

- the keeping of all necessary records of actions undertaken;

- the presentation of results in a form that is compliant with ISO 17025 requirements.

For further information, the interested reader is referred to ILAC-G19: 2002[1].

Finally, before closing this section on quality assurance in forensic science, it should be noted that, at the time of writing (March 2007), no single organisation exists to oversee the whole of the forensic process. To fill this perceived gap, the establishment of a Forensic Science Advisory Council (FSAC) has been recommended by both the Royal Commission on Criminal Justice (reported in 1993) and the House of Commons Science and Technology Committee (reported in 2005). The latter, in its publication *Forensic Science on Trial, Seventh Report of Session 2004–05*, advocated the setting up of a FSAC 'to act as a regulator of the forensic services market, and to provide a much needed overview of the process by which forensic science is used in the criminal justice system.'

---

1 ILAC-G19: 2002. *Guidelines for forensic science laboratories*. Rhodes, Australia: International Laboratory Accreditation Cooperation.

The crime scene | 2

Chapter objectives

After reading this chapter, you should be able to:

> List the information that may be provided by an examination of a crime scene.

> Describe how a crime scene may be preserved.

> Understand the reasons for recording a crime scene and describe the means by which this may be achieved.

> Review the general principles and processes involved in the search for items of physical evidence and their collection, packaging, labelling and storage.

> Understand and describe the principal roles of the key personnel involved in crime scene processing.

> Appreciate the pivotal importance of crime scene processing in the successful application of methods of forensic science to the solution of crime.

Introduction

As introduced in Chapter 1 (Section 1.1.2) Locard's exchange principle states that 'every contact leaves a trace'. From this it follows that the perpetrator of a crime will not only take traces of the crime scene away with him or her but will also leave traces of his or her presence behind. For this reason, all forensic science starts at the crime scene. It is from here that items of physical evidence that will be examined by forensic scientists are retrieved. The way in which scenes of crime are managed and recorded, and how the physical evidence is located, collected, packaged, labelled and stored are all fundamental to the success of subsequent forensic examinations. This chapter explores the principles, methods and procedures involved in the processing of crime scenes in general. More detailed information about the processing of fire scenes and explosion scenes is given in Chapters 10 and 11 respectively.

2.1 An overview of crime scene processing

The examination of any one crime scene seeks to answer a number of questions. It may provide pivotal information about:

- Who:
  - was the victim of the crime?
  - was the perpetrator of the crime?
  - witnessed the crime?
- When:
  - did the crime occur?
- Where:
  - did the key events that produced the crime scene take place? (For example, in the case of a body found in suspicious circumstances, there will be clues present that indicate whether the person died *in situ* or somewhere else)
  - and how did the people involved in the crime enter and, if applicable, leave the scene?
  - were those people who were involved in the crime located at the time of its commission, and were they standing, sitting, kneeling, etc. at that time?
  - did any inanimate objects that were involved in the incident originate from and where did they go to after the crime?
- What:
  - was the sequence of events that occurred during the commission of the crime?
  - was the motive?
  - was the **modus operandi (MO) of the criminal(s)** involved?
  - inanimate objects (tools, vehicles, weapons, etc.) were involved in the crime?
  - was placed at the scene during the crime?
  - was removed from the scene during the crime?
- Why:
  - did the crime happen where it did?
  - did the crime happen when it did?

> **Modus operandi (MO) of a criminal**
> *The way in which the perpetrator of a crime carries out the act.*

In order to obtain such information, it is necessary to carry out a number of actions. Key among these are those listed below:

1. The preservation of the scene in the state in which it was found by restricting access to trained, authorised personnel only and, where necessary, protecting it from the elements (Section 2.2).

2. The recording of the scene, in the state in which it was found, by notes and, where appropriate, photographs, video recording, sketches and the collection of data that will allow virtual scenes to be made using computer graphics (Section 2.3).

3. The construction of a systematic log of all actions taken at the scene and by whom these actions were taken (Section 2.3.1).

4. The systematic search for and recovery of physical evidence (Section 2.4).

5. The packaging and labelling of the physical evidence (Section 2.4).

6. The storage of the physical evidence (Section 2.4).

7. The subjection of the physical evidence to forensic examination (information on the methods used is given in Chapters 3 to 11).

Crime scene processing
The sum total of the activities that preserve and record the crime scene, find, recover, package and label physical evidence from the crime scene and log all actions taken at the crime scene.

Of these, actions 1 to 5 inclusive may be collectively referred to as **crime scene processing**. These occur at the scene, while actions 6 and 7 take place in specialised facilities housed either within police premises or in forensic laboratories.

Clearly, all crime scenes are different and the amount of time and effort that is expended in processing a given crime scene will depend on a number of factors. These include an assessment of the likely amount of useful evidence that can be retrieved from the scene, and the priorities of the government and the police force concerned. As would be expected, individual scenes of serious crime (such as murder or rape) receive more attention than do individual scenes of volume crime (such as car theft). Furthermore, within the area of volume crime, not all types of scene will necessarily be given the same priority. In England and Wales, each year, each police force will set its own targets that reflect the current policy set by Her Majesty's Government. For example, in 2002, Staffordshire Police targeted certain aspects of volume crime, specifically burglary, drugs offences and car crime, leading to a higher priority being given to scenes of these crimes compared with other types of volume crime.

Irrespective of the type of crime scene under examination, optimum effectiveness will only be achieved if each of actions 1 to 7 (outlined above) is carried out with due care, diligence and expertise, and in an ethically and legally acceptable fashion. These factors are also of paramount significance during:

■ the initial assessment of the scene (see Section 2.2);

■ the management of any risks to the health or safety of both the people working on the case and the public;

■ the interpretation of the scene in the light of the evidence gathered;

■ the communication between all individuals involved in the case;

■ the assessment of the intelligence value of the information obtained from the scene;

■ the maintenance of the integrity of the physical evidence collected from the scene (crucially, this includes the avoidance of the possibility of contamination of this evidence);

■ the preparation of reports and statements;

■ the presentation of evidence in court, when required (Chapter 14).

The requirement for expertise across such a broad spectrum of activities means that a number of specific roles have now been identified and there are professionals who specialise in these roles. In the United Kingdom, these may be grouped under the headings of police officers, police scientific support professionals (Box 2.1), forensic scientists and other specialist personnel.

Further information
Box 2.1

Police scientific support services in England and Wales

The police forces in England and Wales each employ expert scientific support personnel in each of the areas shown in the table below. Each force also has a Scientific Support Manager (SSM) or equivalent. In most forces, the SSM has overall responsibility for the management of all scientific support staff, which, as shown in the table, may be organised into four departments. Those departments that fall under the responsibility of the SSM are usually referred to as the Scientific Support Unit (SSU). The vast majority of scientific support personnel who work for the police forces of England and Wales are, in fact, civilians. There is a national training centre in Durham, where nearly all of the police forces in England and Wales send their scientific support personnel for training. This provision is supplemented by the Metropolitan Police, who have their own training school for their own staff but also offer places to the rest of the country.

In most UK police forces, and in this book, the staff who specialise in crime scene processing are denoted as Scenes of Crime Officers (SOCOs). However, this term is not universal. In the Kent Constabulary, they are given the title Crime Scene Investigators (CSI) whereas in the Greater Manchester Police they are called Crime Scene

Table 2.1   The range of expertise available in the Scientific Support Unit (SSU) (or equivalent) of a typical police force in England or Wales

Area of expertise	Most common managerial unit*
Crime scene examination	Scenes of Crime Department
Fingerprint comparison and identification	Fingerprint Bureau (or Department)
Specialist photography and video	Photographic Services Department
Laboratory-based chemical techniques	Chemical Enhancement Laboratory (CEL)

*Note that the names given to these units may vary from one force to the next

Examiners. The expertise of SOCOs lies in the assessment, protection, recording, examination and interpretation of crime scenes, the collection, packaging, labelling and storage of physical evidence, and in the communication of their findings both orally and in the form of written reports and statements. SOCOs are frequently required to give evidence in court.

Members of the Fingerprint Bureau identify people by comparing fingerprints. They also prepare written statements based on fingerprint evidence for use in court and, if necessary, attend court to present their findings. They work on the principle that no two people have fingerprints that match (Chapter 4, Section 4.1.1). Therefore, if a match can be found between a good-quality fingerprint taken from a crime scene and one obtained from a suspect, it is possible to say that the suspect had definitely left that mark and, by implication, that he or she had been at that scene. Similarly, the Fingerprint Bureau can look for matches between either fingerprints found at a crime scene or those taken from a suspect and the fingerprints held on the national database. In the former case, a match will produce investigative leads that could result in the arrest of a suspect, while in the latter, a match will allow the identity of the suspect to be confirmed. Finally, it is worth noting that fingerprints can be used to identify deceased people (Chapter 12, Section 12.4.1).

While SOCOs are skilled in the use of routine photography to record crime scenes (Section 2.3), they are not professional photographers. The Photographic Services Department gives expert support in this area. This provision allows images to be taken, for example, under specialised illumination conditions such as those involving the use of ultraviolet or laser light sources (Section 2.3.3). The Photographic Services Department also provides darkroom staff and facilities, allowing the rapid and secure development of scenes of crime photographs. Digital photography is currently under development as an alternative to traditional, film-based methods.

One of the most evidentially valuable activities that SOCOs undertake at crime scenes is the recovery of fingerprint

▶

Box 2.1 continued

evidence. In many cases, this is satisfactorily achieved by the application of fingerprint powder, followed by the photographic recording of the enhanced print and/or its lifting using a suitable adhesive-coated plastic film (Chapter 4, Section 4.1.5). This approach is often successful for the recovery of fingerprint evidence from smooth, non-porous surfaces but is not always the method of choice. The SOCO will frequently elect to send the entire object to the in-force chemical laboratory facility (usually called the CEL – see Table 2.1 above). Here, technicians can use a wide range of chemical enhancement techniques to visualise any latent (i.e. not visible) fingerprints present (Chapter 4, Section 4.1.5). Where appropriate, the CEL will also perform presumptive tests for blood (Chapter 5, Section 5.1.2) and, in certain circumstances (i.e. where the rules allow), may carry out presumptive tests for controlled drugs (Chapter 7, Section 7.5.3).

In addition to the roles of the CEL outlined in the previous paragraph, in-force laboratory facilities may also be used to:

■ recover marks made by footwear (Chapter 4, Section 4.2);
■ maintain and use a database of footwear marks;
■ carry out basic tyre examinations (Chapter 4, Section 4.5);
■ restore erased serial numbers (Chapter 9, Box 9.2);
■ perform basic document examinations (limited to the simple evaluation of indented writing and basic scrutiny of forgeries and alterations, see Chapter 8).

Finally, police scientific support also advises investigating officers about the potential value of forensic science in ongoing cases. It also provides a channel for the procurement of forensic science services, which in England and Wales are normally obtained from the Forensic Science Service (FSS) (Chapter 1, Section 1.3.2).

In England and Wales, police officers are responsible for the initial response to an incident (Section 2.2), the detective work involved in the investigation of any crime and the *overall* management of crime scene processing. Under certain circumstances, they may also be responsible for the collection of physical evidence, although this task is usually undertaken by **SOCOs** (Box 2.1). In complex cases of serious crime, such as murder or rape, other personnel with specialist knowledge are called to the scene as necessary. These may include:

SOCO
Scenes of Crime Officer (see Box 2.1).

■ police photographers (Box 2.1);

■ forensic scientists (e.g. personnel from the Forensic Science Service (FSS) with expertise in bloodstain pattern analysis, see Chapter 5, Section 5.2);

■ medical personnel (e.g. in the case of a suspicious death, a pathologist (Chapter 12, Section 12.3.3) or, in the case of a rape, a police surgeon (Chapter 5, Box 5.5));

■ fire investigation specialists from the fire service (where arson is suspected, see Chapter 10, Box 10.4);

■ a forensic entomologist (in the case of a partially decomposed body, see Chapter 12, Box 12.2);

■ a forensic anthropologist (when skeletal remains are found, see Chapter 12, Section 12.4.2);

■ bomb disposal experts;

■ engineers (e.g. to assess the safety of a damaged building or other structure).

The principles involved in the processing of a given crime scene do not alter with the seriousness of the crime concerned. However, there are important operational differences between the processing of the scenes of serious crime and those of volume crime. Actions by the law enforcement agencies that are reasonable at serious crime scenes are not necessarily so in the case of the scenes of volume crime. For example, consider the treatment of a bloody hand-print found on the wall of a house in which a murder by stabbing had been committed. In this case, after the print was properly recorded (Section 2.3), it would not be unknown for the portion of the wall on which it was found to be removed and then submitted for further examination in a forensic laboratory. Contrast this with the case of a tool mark found on a window frame, which is believed to have been made by a burglar while breaking and entering a domestic property. Typically, this would be photographically recorded, its impression would be made in silicone rubber and a small sample of paint from the frame would be taken. While there may be forensic benefit in doing so, it is highly unlikely that the whole window frame would be removed from the house for subsequent scrutiny in the laboratory. Certainly, any attempt to do this would normally prompt objections from the householder!

Other operational differences between the processing of serious and volume crime scenes originate from the finite resources that are available for this type of work. With these constraints in mind, the imperative given to the solution of a serious crime is generally greater than that warranted by any one incidence of volume crime. This difference in emphasis has led to the development of two different police management structures for the oversight of crime scene processing in England and Wales.

The management structure that is established for the investigation of each serious crime is summarised in Figure 2.1. Although the details of this structure vary slightly from one police force to the next, the main features remain essentially the same throughout England and Wales. Within this structure, responsibility for the management of the scientific support needed by the case concerned is given to the **Crime Scene Co-ordinator**, who is usually the force's **SSM** or a senior SOCO. Working under his or her supervision are a number of **Crime Scene Managers**. These are needed because the majority of serious crimes will have more than one scene and a Crime Scene Manager is allocated to each of these to see that it is properly processed. For example, in a kidnap and murder case, the scenes are likely to include:

- the body itself (all people, whether living or dead, who are associated with the crime may be considered to be crime scenes);
- the location in which the body was found;
- the place in which the murder took place (if different from where the body was found);
- the place in which the victim was held prisoner;
- the place where the kidnap occurred;
- any vehicles used by the kidnapper(s)/murderer(s);
- the suspects in the case;
- the home(s) and possibly the workplace(s) of the victim, and those of the suspects.

Crime Scene Co-ordinator
The person (usually the force's SSM or a senior SOCO) who is given the responsibility for managing the scientific support needs of all of the crime scenes of a given serious crime.

SSM
Scientific Support Manager (see Box 2.1).

Crime Scene Manager
In the case of a serious crime, this is the individual whose task it is to oversee the processing of a given crime scene.

(Information supplied
by Andy Kirby,
Staffordshire Police,
UK)

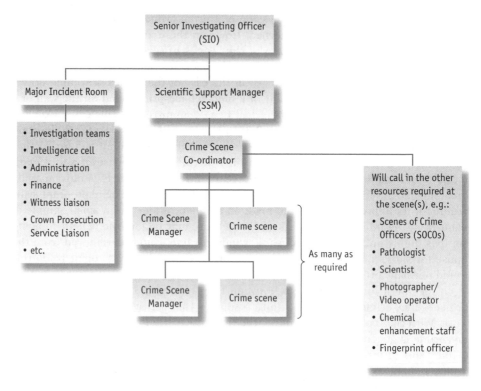

Figure 2.1 The management structure, as used in the investigation of a serious crime in England and Wales

Note that the SSM will provide the SIO with advice about the scientific aspects of the investigation. The SSM together with the Crime Scene Co-ordinator have responsibility for scientific strategy and resourcing. The Crime Scene Manager has the tactical role, ensuring that the scene is properly examined and that evidence is recovered. The Crime Scene Manager is responsible for conduct at the scene: for example, a pathologist may be required to visit the scene but he or she will not be allowed to enter it until the Crime Scene Manager agrees, having first considered all the circumstances at the scene.

It is vitally important that the possibility of cross-contamination between material from different scenes is avoided. For example, consider a case in which a suspected murderer has been arrested. On questioning, he emphatically denied ever having met the deceased. Forensic examination of his clothing revealed a hair that was shown by DNA evidence (Chapter 6) to have belonged to the victim and several fibres that matched fibres taken from the deceased's clothing. This would normally constitute strong associative physical evidence to link the suspect to the victim. Clearly, such physical evidence does not support his assertion that he had never met the victim. However, if, for example, it were shown in court that the same SOCO that had packaged the suspect's garments had also attended the scene of the crime earlier in the same day, then the associative implications of the evidence would be severely diminished.

Systems have been developed to minimise the opportunities for this type of occurrence. In England and Wales, it is part of the role of the SSM (Box 2.1) to ensure that, whenever possible, scientific support personnel do not each attend more than one of the scenes associated with a given crime. Furthermore, if, for example because of the finite number of personnel available, it proves necessary to send the same person to more than one such scene, the SSM must ensure that the person concerned goes through acceptable decontamination procedures between scenes. Finally, because of the pivotal importance of the avoidance of cross-contamination, the SSM must also ensure that a log is kept, for presentation in court if necessary, that shows which scientific support personnel attended each crime scene and when. It is common practice for the SSM to delegate responsibility for the tasks described in this paragraph to the Crime Scene Co-ordinator.

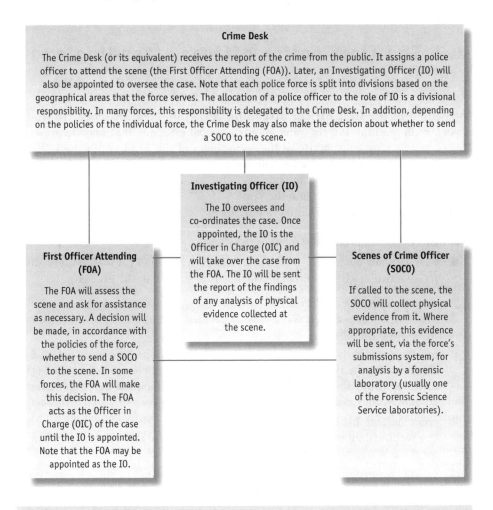

Crime Desk

The Crime Desk (or its equivalent) receives the report of the crime from the public. It assigns a police officer to attend the scene (the First Officer Attending (FOA)). Later, an Investigating Officer (IO) will also be appointed to oversee the case. Note that each police force is split into divisions based on the geographical areas that the force serves. The allocation of a police officer to the role of IO is a divisional responsibility. In many forces, this responsibility is delegated to the Crime Desk. In addition, depending on the policies of the individual force, the Crime Desk may also make the decision about whether to send a SOCO to the scene.

Investigating Officer (IO)

The IO oversees and co-ordinates the case. Once appointed, the IO is the Officer in Charge (OIC) and will take over the case from the FOA. The IO will be sent the report of the findings of any analysis of physical evidence collected at the scene.

First Officer Attending (FOA)

The FOA will assess the scene and ask for assistance as necessary. A decision will be made, in accordance with the policies of the force, whether to send a SOCO to the scene. In some forces, the FOA will make this decision. The FOA acts as the Officer in Charge (OIC) of the case until the IO is appointed. Note that the FOA may be appointed as the IO.

Scenes of Crime Officer (SOCO)

If called to the scene, the SOCO will collect physical evidence from it. Where appropriate, this evidence will be sent, via the force's submissions system, for analysis by a forensic laboratory (usually one of the Forensic Science Service laboratories).

Figure 2.2 A typical police management structure for the oversight of the processing of a scene of volume crime in England and Wales
In order to suit local policing needs, there is considerable variation in this structure from one force to the next and even between divisions in the same force

A typical management structure used in the processing of volume crime scenes in England and Wales is given in Figure 2.2. Usually, each such scene would be attended by a uniformed police officer, who would call for further assistance as required. A decision would be made as to whether the scene will be attended by a SOCO. This would be done in accordance with the policy of the individual force for which the officer worked. For example, in some forces, this decision is made by the first officer attending the scene, in others it is made by the staff of the Crime Desk. Some forces have a policy that all scenes of particular types of volume crime (especially domestic burglaries) are attended by a SOCO.

Further details of the roles of the first officer attending and the police scientific support professionals at scenes of both serious and volume crime are given in the following sections.

2.2 The first police officer attending and the preservation of the crime scene

First officer attending (FOA)
The first police officer to arrive at a given incident scene.

The actions of the **first officer attending (FOA)** an incident scene are vitally important in maintaining the value of any physical evidence that may be present. This is equally true irrespective of the seriousness of the incident involved. While the effort that is exerted by the law enforcement agencies at the scene of a serious crime will be greater than at any one scene of volume crime, the principles that underlie the actions taken remain the same.

At an incident scene, the FOA has a duty to:

■ carry out an initial assessment of the scene;

■ deal with any emergencies (the overriding duty of the FOA is to preserve life, irrespective of whether crucial evidence is destroyed in the process);

■ call for assistance as necessary;

■ preserve the scene (unless it has been decided that physical evidence will not be recovered);

■ make an appropriate record of his or her assessment and actions (included in this must be the times at which any key events took place, such as the FOA's arrival at the scene, and any estimated time of the incident that may be available from, for example, eyewitnesses);

■ communicate his or her assessment and actions to those who will take over the responsibility for the processing of the scene and/or those responsible for the investigation of the case;

■ provide *appropriate* information about the processing of the case to those members of the public who are directly involved.

The FOA's initial assessment will take into account any prior knowledge that he or she has about the incident that is believed to have occurred at the scene and is likely to start with an informal interview of the person who raised the alarm. This will enable the officer to obtain a first hand, although not necessarily reliable, account of the nature of the incident, and possibly the order of events and key timings. Given the often fragmentary, sometimes confusing and possibly misleading nature of the information that is obtained from a crime scene, it is vitally important that all law enforcement personnel, including the FOA, keep an open and enquiring mind throughout the processing of the scene.

One of the early tasks during the initial assessment is an evaluation by the FOA of whether it is likely that a crime has taken place. In making this evaluation, it is usually appropriate that the officer assumes the worst. For example, there have been instances in which murder has been initially assessed as suicide by the FOA, thereby losing valuable time in the early stages of the investigation.

In cases where it appears likely that a crime has been committed, the FOA must, during his or her initial assessment, ascertain whether any of the following are present or nearby:

- Injured persons.
- Victims.
- Eyewitnesses (who should be kept separate from one another, by the FOA, to avoid both conversation between them that could distort their memories of the incident and the possibility of the transfer from one to another of trace evidence, such as hairs and other fibres).
- Suspects (who must be kept separate from each other, and from witnesses). It should be borne in mind that seemingly innocent witnesses might, in fact, be suspects in the case.

In many instances, in order to carry out his or her initial assessment, the FOA will have to enter the scene. This must be done with great caution. In particular, due regard has to be paid to the health and safety of both the officer concerned and anyone else present. The avoidance of any unnecessary damage to the physical evidence present at the scene is also of crucial importance. This evidence is most likely to be found at the location(s) within the scene at which the crime(s) took place and along any path taken through the scene by the perpetrator(s) and, possibly, the victim(s).

It is not unknown for some attempt to have been made to clean up the scene before the arrival of the FOA. This may have been done by the perpetrator in an attempt to destroy evidence or by the victim out of a desire to return the situation to normality. In either case, the FOA must bring such activity to a halt, if it is still ongoing when he or she arrives. The officer should try to ascertain what has occurred during the cleaning processes (including the fate of any discarded objects) and in what ways the scene has been altered by it. It is quite possible that valuable evidence has been thrown in a waste bin or poured down a drain. This evidence may be retrievable even in the latter case as it is sometimes possible to recover valuable material (e.g. illicit drugs) from 'U-bend' traps within the plumbing system.

Many scenes contain a physical barrier through which anyone who had access to the location at which the crime took place must have passed. Typical examples include the outer walls, doors and windows of a property or the fence and gates of a field. Under these circumstances, the probability of finding physical evidence is particularly high at the points of entry and exit within this barrier that were used by the perpetrator(s). The FOA should therefore attempt to discover, from witnesses and direct observation, the most likely locations of these points and, if possible, avoid them when entering and exiting the scene. Note, in volume crime (burglary, car crime, etc.) the vast majority of evidence is recovered at the point of entry (POE).

While moving through the scene, the FOA should avoid the unnecessary disturbance of any part of it. He or she must take care not to leave his or her fingerprints at the scene. Also, any actions that might damage any pre-existing marks and impressions that might be present must be avoided if at all possible. As an aid to achieving this, the FOA should bear in mind the likely locations of evidentially valuable fingerprints – including door handles, light switches and any obviously disturbed items – and footprints. He or she should also note any details that might be evidentially valuable and that are likely to be transient in nature. These could include any discernible smell, the warmth of any cooked food or cooking equipment, and the locations and orientations of any objects that have to be moved by the FOA. An example of the last of these might well be a door that has to be opened to gain access to a room. Before doing this, the FOA should note whether the door was open or shut and, if shut, whether it was locked.

On completion of the initial assessment, the FOA must then deal with any emergencies. Most importantly, this will include the giving of first aid to anyone at the scene who needs it. If possible, it will also include the arrest of the likely perpetrator(s). When prioritising his or her actions, the FOA must remember that the saving of life takes precedence over both the arrest of a suspect and the preservation of physical evidence. It is, however, possible to give effective first aid while minimising the impact of this action on the value of any physical evidence present. To achieve this, the FOA should note such factors as:

- the original position and posture of the person being treated;
- the original direction of flow of any blood or other fluids present;
- the location, condition and spatial orientation of any objects – including clothing – that have to be moved in order to carry out the first aid;
- the presence of any objects in the hands (including fibres, such as hairs) or foreign material (e.g. skin) under the fingernails of the injured person.

If necessary, these notes may initially be made mentally. However, under these circumstances, they should be recorded in writing and sketches (as appropriate), as soon as the situation is under control.

After the initial assessment and while dealing with any emergencies, the FOA will call, usually by radio or mobile telephone, for any assistance needed. This may include the attendance of more police officers and, if there are any injured people present, ambulance(s) and paramedic staff.

Also, a decision must be made as to whether physical evidence will be collected from the scene. This will be made in line with the procedures, policy and priorities of the force concerned. The factors that will be taken into consideration during this decision will include the seriousness of the crime, the likelihood of the successful recovery of useful physical evidence and the disruption to the business of the public that evidence collection will cause.

If physical evidence is to be collected, this will, under some circumstances (particularly in the case of certain volume crimes), be carried out by the FOA or another uniformed officer. However, in England and Wales, this task is normally undertaken by SOCOs (Box 2.1). Irrespective of who carries out the recovery of physical evidence, it will be done once the scene has been preserved (see below) and the principles and processes involved remain the same (Section 2.4).

In order to maximise the efficiency and efficacy of the collection of physical evidence, it is important that an appropriate level of communication is established between the FOA and the personnel who will collect the evidence. In England and Wales, in cases of volume crime, there is likely to be a time interval between the departure of the FOA from the scene and the arrival of the SOCO. Under these circumstances, this communication may occur via radio or mobile telephone either directly or through the central control room of the force concerned. In contrast, the FOA will normally still be at the scene of a serious crime when the SOCOs arrive. Under these circumstances, the SOCOs will debrief the FOA before taking over responsibility for the processing of the scene. It should be emphasised that, in any event, serious crime scenes are always guarded by the police from the moment of the arrival of the FOA until the scene has been fully processed.

If physical evidence is to be recovered, the FOA must take immediate steps to preserve the scene as soon as the initial assessment of the scene has been completed, any emergencies have been dealt with and – if necessary – assistance called. At this point, a decision needs to be made as to whether the entire scene will be preserved or if there is to be a selective preservation of those parts of it that are most likely to yield physical evidence. Which of these two options is chosen will depend on the individual circumstances of the incident, particularly the severity of the crime. In the United Kingdom (and in many other nations), the former option will be adopted for the vast majority of scenes of serious crime.

In order to preserve a crime scene, there are two principal potential agents of damage from which the physical evidence present must be protected, namely people's inappropriate actions and the weather. In both cases, the approach used is to isolate the physical evidence from the potential cause of the damage.

At the scene of a volume crime, such as a domestic burglary, the exclusion of unauthorised people might be achieved by careful instructions to the householder concerning what may and what may not be touched before the arrival of the SOCO. However, in the vast majority of cases of serious crime and in some volume crimes, it is necessary to place a physical barrier (cordon) around the scene's perimeter in order to restrict access to it. In some cases, a suitable barrier is already present, such as the fence and gates that surround a house that is the location of a crime. However, in many cases such barriers are either absent or do not fully encompass the scene. Under these circumstances, a barrier made of plastic tape that is overseen by a police officer is usually sufficient to ensure that only authorised people enter the scene.

When considering where to place the cordon that will isolate the crime scene from its surroundings, it is important to remember that it is highly likely that the value of any physical evidence that is subsequently collected from outside the cordon will be low. This is because activities outside the cordon may physically degrade the evidence (e.g. a fingerprint may become smudged) or contaminate it (e.g. fibres from the investigator's clothing may become mixed with those from the perpetrator(s) and/or victim(s)). Furthermore, it is quite possible to decrease the area encompassed by the cordon, once it has been established. With these factors in mind, it is clear that the cordon should encompass as wide an area as is practicable. Certainly, it should include the location(s) in the scene where the crime(s) took place and the points of entry to and exit from the scene of the people involved in the incident.

In cases of serious crime, it is crucial that the cordon around the perimeter of the scene is policed at all times from the moment it is established until the scene processing is complete. The officer in charge of this cordon must rigorously exclude all people, including senior members of the police, who do not have a pressing and legitimate operational need to enter the scene. This officer must also keep a log of the names of all who enter the scene, the times at which each individual enters and leaves the scene and ensure that whoever enters the scene is wearing appropriate protective clothing (Figure 2.3).

(Photograph by
Andrew Jackson,
Staffordshire
University, UK)

Figure 2.3 Full protective kit as worn during the collection of physical evidence
The kit is worn in order to avoid contamination of the evidence with material (especially DNA) derived from the person who is collecting it. Note that this person is also wearing plastic overshoes of the type visible in Figure 2.4

In scenes that are either partially or wholly exposed to the elements, consideration needs to be given to whether aspects of the scene need to be protected from the weather. In making this decision, the following points will be taken into account:

■ an assessment of the susceptibility of the evidence to damage from the weather;

■ the prevailing weather conditions;

■ any likely changes in the weather before collection of the evidence will be possible;

■ the possibility of damage to, or contamination of, the evidence during any actions taken to protect it.

For some types of evidence, such as footwear marks or a small weapon, suitable protection may be afforded by placing a clean cardboard box over the evidence and/or redirecting any overland flow of water away from it. Large objects that are, nonetheless, easily moved may be placed in a sheltered area (e.g. a garden shed) to protect them from the weather. Before doing this, the position and orientation of the object should be recorded by notes, and sketches and/or photographs – as appropriate.

In the United Kingdom and in many other nations, in the case of serious crime, it is highly likely that further assistance will appear within a few minutes of the arrival at the scene of the FOA. The FOA must brief arriving law enforcement personnel as soon as practicable to convey his or her initial assessment of the scene and all of the actions that he or she has taken thus far. On arrival at the scene, the police scientific support personnel will assume responsibility for its preservation. They will do this under the supervision of a Crime Scene Manager, who will take charge of the scene as a whole. The scientific support personnel may use equipment such as stepping plates (Figure 2.4) or tents to protect specific locations within the scene and will review the position and security of the cordon. Indeed, in relatively large scenes, two cordons, one within the other, may be established. For example, if a body is discovered in the bedroom of a detached house that stands within its own grounds, an inner cordon may be placed around the house while an outer cordon may be positioned to encompass the limits of the grounds. In such cases, the inner cordon is usually directly controlled by the Crime Scene Manager, while a police officer keeps a log of all those who cross the outer cordon. Furthermore, those who are allowed to cross the inner cordon may well be required to wear more protective clothing than those who cross only the outer one.

In scenes of serious crime that contain a clear focal point, such as a dead body, there is a need to gain access to this point early in the investigation. In order to achieve this without damaging physical evidence present at the scene, a **common approach path (CAP)** from the cordon to the focal point will be created (Box 2.2). This will not be done until the responsibility for the scene has passed from the FOA.

Whenever possible, advice should be given to any emergency medical personnel attending the scene on how to minimise the impact of their actions on the physical evidence present. However, this advice, and the manner in which it is imparted, must not interfere with the effectiveness of any medical treatment given. The person issuing this advice will be the police officer in charge (who will be the FOA, at least until assistance arrives) or another law enforcement professional (police officer or SOCO). The identity of the medical personnel attending and, if possible, the impact of their actions on the scene must be noted by a police officer, often the FOA.

Common approach path (CAP)
A path that is made between the police cordon encircling a crime scene and the scene's focal point in order to gain early and controlled access to the focal point.

(Photograph by
Andrew Jackson,
Staffordshire
University, UK)

Figure 2.4 The use of stepping plates during the early assessment of a crime scene to avoid damage to items of physical evidence that might be on the floor (such as footprints)

Forensic techniques

Box 2.2

The common approach path (CAP)

In cases of serious crime (e.g. a murder), it is accepted practice in the UK to establish what is known as a common approach path (CAP). This runs from a point in the police cordon that surrounds the crime scene to the focal point of the scene (e.g. the body). This path is designed to allow early access to the focal point while minimising the impact on the scene as a whole. With this in mind, whenever possible, the course of the CAP is chosen such that it is unlikely to coincide with the path taken in or out of the scene by either the perpetrator(s) or the victim(s). During its establishment, the course of

the CAP is carefully photographed. Long and medium range shots are taken to record the scene's overall appearance from the CAP. In addition, close-up images of the scene's focal point are obtained from some distance away, using a telephoto lens, before there is any chance of its being disturbed by the approaching investigators.

During its creation, the course of the CAP is searched for items of physical evidence and its limits are marked with police plastic barrier tape. Any items of evidence that are located during this process are photographed *in situ* and then recovered in accordance with standard procedures.

In the United Kingdom, in the case of a violent incident, by the time the emergency medical personnel are ready to take any injured people to hospital it is highly unlikely that the FOA will be the only police officer at the scene. Under these circumstances, it is desirable that a police officer accompanies any injured person taken from the scene. In doing this, each officer concerned will be in a position to:

- listen to and note anything that is said by the injured person that might have a bearing on the case (such as the names of people involved in the incident) – declarations made by dying people are often taken as strong evidence in the belief that people are unlikely to lie in such situations;
- protect the victim from further attack, if necessary;
- detain the injured person if he or she is a suspect in the case;
- advise the medical personnel in the ambulance and at the hospital about how best to collect and package any physical evidence taken from the patient (Section 2.4) (such advice should only be acted on insofar as it is consistent with best medical practice);
- receive into custody any physical evidence taken from the injured person.

If, however, the ambulance is ready to leave before the FOA is joined by other police officers, then he or she will remain at the scene and allow the ambulance to leave without a police officer inside it.

Finally, it must be noted that the FOA needs to communicate effectively with members of the public present at the scene. Where appropriate, the officer should inform them about the steps that will be taken in the processing of the case and encourage their co-operation. Clearly, the FOA should neither divulge details to the public that might aid the perpetrator evade effective prosecution nor should he or she give information to the press unless asked to do so by the officer in overall charge of the investigation.

2.3 Recording the crime scene

Any crime scene from which physical evidence is to be recovered must be recorded; a process that is also known as 'documenting the crime scene'. This is done by making written notes that are augmented by photographs, video recordings and/or sketches, as appropriate. Also in England and Wales, in the case of a serious crime, accurate dimensional information will be taken using surveying equipment that will allow the subsequent use of computers to generate a virtual reconstruction of the crime scene.

In some cases, the investigator (whether SOCO or police officer) may initially produce an oral record of some or all of his or her notes using a portable audiotape machine and/or the soundtrack facility on a videotape recorder. If this is done, the oral record should be converted to written notes as soon as practicable. The products of all of the means used to record the scene (including any audio recordings used to assist note-making) must be stored in the case file for as long as required by the policies of the police force concerned.

Recording the crime scene
Taking notes, together with, as appropriate, photographs, video recordings, sketches and records of dimensions that record the crime scene as it was found, the processing of it and any fragile evidence that it contains.

There are a number of reasons for **recording the crime scene**, namely to:

■ provide a permanent record of the crime scene in the state in which it was found for use during the investigation (for example to act as a reminder to investigating officers and/or witnesses) and in court, if the case culminates in a trial;

■ produce an account of the steps taken during the processing of the crime scene;

■ record fragile physical evidence before it is recovered in case it is destroyed during the recovery process.

While the principles involved remain the same, the level of detail with which a given crime scene will be recorded will reflect the severity of the crime and the nature of the scene. For any one crime scene, this level will be determined by the priorities and policies of, and resources available to, the police force concerned. In the United Kingdom, and in many other nations, scenes of serious crime (especially murder) are recorded in great detail. The salient features of each of the means by which this is achieved are described in Sections 2.3.1, 2.3.2 and 2.3.3 below.

2.3.1 Note-taking at scenes of serious crime

To be fully effective, the notes taken at the scene must include the following:

■ A record of who reported the incident, the time and date at which it was reported and exactly where the incident scene is located (importantly, in England and Wales, the FOA must record that he or she *has made investigations* to establish not only the veracity of these records but also that any account of what happened during the incident, as given by the person who reported it, is a true reflection of what actually occurred).

■ An ongoing assessment, as far as is possible, of:
 – the likely nature of the incident (e.g. murder);
 – the events that took place during the incident (including their sequence and timings);
 – the roles and locations of the people involved in these events;
 – any material change that may have occurred to the scene between the time of the incident and the arrival of the FOA and/or factors that might have caused such change to have occurred (e.g. heavy rain that might have washed evidence away).

■ A log of the identities of all people who have been at the scene – including a record of the time and date at which each person entered and left the scene – from the moment of the arrival of the FOA (Section 2.2) to the time at which the processing of the scene is completed.

■ Detailed descriptions of the actions undertaken at the scene by each of the people referred to in the previous bullet point, including the chronology of events incorporating all key times and dates.

- A record of each item of physical evidence recovered from the scene, detailing the identity of the person who recovered it, the time and date at which it was recovered, the exact location from which it was taken and a description of the item involved.

- A log of all images taken of the scene (whether by still photography – conventional or digital – or video recording) describing for each image:
  - the exact location of the camera operator;
  - the identity of the camera operator;
  - the direction in which the camera was pointed;
  - the time and date at which the image was captured;
  - any special lighting or other conditions used;
  - the items and/or area of the scene from which the image was captured.

- A log of any sketches made of the scene.

- A detailed description of the surroundings of the crime scene.

- A record of the conditions of weather and light that prevailed during the processing of the scene.

- A thorough description of the crime scene itself in the condition in which it was found prior to the removal of any physical evidence, including details of any features that might be of evidential worth (such as the location and condition of any likely points of entry and/or exit used by the individuals involved in the incident).

Importantly, the notes made during the investigation of the scene should record the work undertaken and the order in which it was done. Such notes must be contemporaneous, that is they must be made at the time at which the activity being recorded took place. As mentioned previously, audiotapes may be used to record such notes at the scene, provided that these notes are then written up with the minimum of delay.

All notes must be sufficiently clear and detailed to be of value to someone reading them a long time after the scene was processed. In the United Kingdom, cases of unsolved serious crimes are periodically reviewed. Under these circumstances, the original notes may be re-read many years after they were made. If these notes are unclear, ambiguous or even physically difficult to read they may be insufficient for the needs of any re-opened investigation. Also, should a case result in a prosecution, the notes taken at the crime scene must be of sufficiently high quality to be presented in court, if required.

2.3.2 The sketching and virtual reconstruction of scenes of serious crimes

Until recently, **sketches** of serious crime scenes were frequently produced to show the locations and, as required, the dimensions and spatial orientations of salient objects and marks as they were found *in situ* (Figure 2.5). However, in England and Wales, such sketches have now been largely superseded by a combination of photographic images (both still and, where appropriate, video) and computer-generated **virtual reconstruction of the crime scene**. Such reconstructions are based on measurements taken at the crime scene using surveying techniques. Both sketches and virtual reconstructions have three significant advantages over photographs. These are that they provide a greater

Crime scene sketch
This is a drawing of the key features of a crime scene, including information about their dimensions and spatial orientations. A rough sketch made at the scene may be redrawn to produce a finished sketch.

Virtual reconstruction of the crime scene
A computer-generated image of the crime scene that is based on measurements taken at that scene.

(Reproduced by kind permission of Jennifer Lines, Staffordshire University, UK)

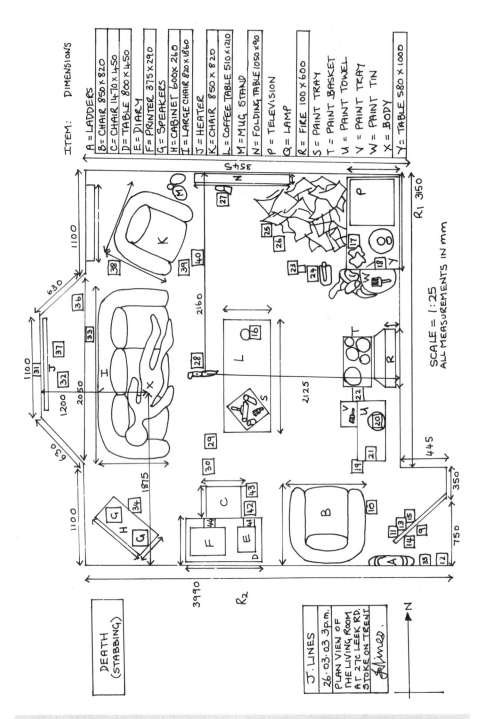

ITEM: DIMENSIONS

A = LADDERS
B = CHAIR 850 × 820
C = CHAIR 1470 × 450
D = TABLE 800 × 450
E = DIARY
F = PRINTER 375 × 290
G = SPEAKERS
H = CABINET 600 × 260
I = LARGE CHAIR 820 × 1860
J = HEATER
K = CHAIR 850 × 820
L = COFFEE TABLE 510 × 1210
M = MUG STAND
N = FOLDING TABLE 1050 × 90
P = TELEVISION
Q = LAMP
R = FIRE 100 × 600
S = PAINT TRAY
T = PAINT BASKET
U = PAINT TOWEL
V = PAINT TRAY
W = PAINT TIN
X = BODY
Y = TABLE 580 × 1000

SCALE = 1:25
ALL MEASUREMENTS IN mm

DEATH (STABBING)

J. LINES
26·03·03 3p.m.
PLAN VIEW OF
THE LIVING ROOM
AT 27C LEEK RD.
STOKE ON TRENT

N

Figure 2.5 A plan view sketch typical of those used in the recording of crime scenes
Note that the numbered squares show the positions of numbered labels placed beside items of evidence prior to close-up photography and item retrieval. Other types of sketch are also used as required, such as those that show the walls and, where necessary, the ceiling of a room

width and depth of field of view, they can eliminate distortion caused by perspective and they allow important features to be shown without the distraction of unnecessary detail. One advantage that virtual reconstructions have over conventional sketches is that they can be used to take the observer on a virtual tour of the scene in question.

Sketching is not entirely redundant, however. Sketches are still made if an object has to be moved before it can be photographed and in cases where dimensions are crucial to the case but in which virtual reconstructions are not to be made. Sketches may also be used to show the direction in which photographs were taken. Also, pathologists still routinely make sketches that show where a body was found and the sites of injury on that body. Finally, sketches may be used to accompany items that are submitted for forensic examination in instances where dimensions and/or spatial orientations will help the forensic scientist interpret the evidence. For example, the Forensic Science Service (FSS) requests that glass samples taken from a broken window are submitted with an accompanying sketch giving the height and size of the window concerned.

2.3.3 Recording photographic still and video images of scenes of serious crimes

Photographic images are taken to produce a permanent record of the appearance of the scene in the state it was in prior to the removal of physical evidence. Ideally, this record should be made while the scene is in exactly the form it was in on the arrival of the first police officer to attend. However, at some scenes, there is a pressing need to take emergency action – such as the attention to the medical needs of someone found injured at the scene. Under these circumstances, some disturbance of the scene may have occurred before it can be photographically recorded. The nature of any such disruption (for example, the movement of objects) should be noted and photographic images should then be taken without any further alterations being made to the scene. Certainly, objects that have been moved before they can be photographically recorded should *not* be moved back into their original positions prior to taking photographs.

Photographic images of the crime scene can be used to refresh the memory of crime scene investigators and, if appropriate, witnesses. They can also be used to corroborate or refute the statements of suspects and/or witnesses and they can be shown in court as an aid to the explanation of the nature of the incident. Unlike sketches, photographic images can, under certain circumstances, act as a substitute for items of physical evidence that either cannot be or have not been successfully recovered from the crime scene. In order to maximise the value of crime scene photography, it is important that the information recorded by it can be integrated with the other means by which the scene is documented. To this end, as noted in Section 2.3.1, a log should be kept of all images (whether still photographs or videotape) taken at the scene.

Crime scene photography is routinely carried out using conventional photographic techniques. However, specialised methods have also been developed to enhance features that might otherwise not be noticeable. For example, photography in subdued light of areas that have been sprayed with luminol reagent can reveal bloodstains that in their untreated state are invisible to the naked eye (Chapter 5, Section 5.1.2). Also, photographic images can be obtained using spe-

(Images by Andrew Jackson, Staffordshire University, UK)

(a)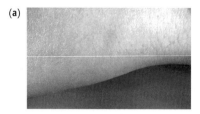

(b)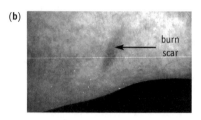

Figure 2.6 Images of a 6-week-old burn scar taken in (a) visible and (b) ultraviolet light

cialised illumination sources, such as those that provide ultraviolet or laser light. For example, the former may be used to enhance the appearance of injuries on human skin (Figure 2.6), while the latter can be of value in the recording of marks and impressions, such as fingerprints. In a similar vein, infrared photography can be used to visualise certain features, such as gunpowder marks on bloodstained garments and some types of ink. It should be noted that while specialised photographic techniques can be and are used at crime scenes, they are also employed in forensic laboratories, where lighting and other conditions may be more carefully controlled.

While the use of film-based still photography is well established, there is a recent trend towards the use of electronic means of image capture from the crime scene, whether in the form of digital photography or videotape. One of the advantages of digital still photography is that it allows rapid and effective image manipulation. This can, for example, enable overlapping photographs of a scene to be 'stitched' together to form a seamless panorama. Also, digital photography can facilitate image enhancement. For example, there are cases in which the clarity of an evidentially valuable mark, such as a fingerprint, is compromised by a repeating background pattern, such as the closely spaced security lines found on many bank-notes,

(Reproduced by kind permission of Esther Neate, Wiltshire Constabulary, UK)

(a)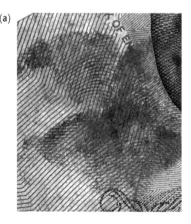

(b)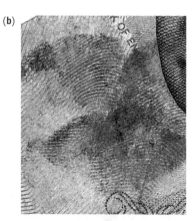

Figure 2.7 Images of a fingerprint on a banknote both (a) before and (b) after digital enhancement
Note that the background pattern of parallel lines apparent in (a) has been effectively removed in (b)

cheques, tickets, etc. Under such circumstances, it may be possible to digitally remove the underlying pattern from the overall image, thereby revealing the evidentially valuable mark (Figure 2.7). Note, however, that the ease with which digital images can be manipulated means that their credibility in court may be diminished compared with conventional photographs.

Videotape can be used to augment still photography in the recording of the overall appearance of a scene and the position of items of evidence within it. A narrative description may be added to the visual information at the crime scene by making use of the video camera's sound recording facility. However, the potential for recording unwanted noises means that this facility is often left unused. At present, video recording cannot replace still photography (whether film-based or digital) because of video's currently inferior resolution, and hence poorer ability to record details.

Wherever possible, crime scene photographic images should be free of any extraneous items, such as equipment brought to the scene by the investigators or indeed one or more of the investigators themselves. An important exception to this is the inclusion of a scale in the field of view of shots that are intended to record the size of a particular feature of the scene (this topic is returned to later on in this section).

The still photography of the scene of a serious crime should be comprehensive. As described below, it should include photographs that show the environment of the scene, those that record the overall appearance of the scene and shots of individual items of physical evidence.

Environmental still photographs

Pictures that show the environment of the scene should be taken in all directions. For example, if the incident took place in a suburban setting, then photographs of the street or streets involved should be taken from several angles, as should photographs of nearby properties (including gardens) and any alleyways or footpaths. Similarly, photographs of the scene should be made from its surroundings, again in all directions. For example, if the scene is a building, photographs of each of its walls, doors and windows should be obtained. Aerial photographs may also be taken, as these are particularly good at showing the extent of the scene and the scene within its broader environment.

Still photographs that show the overall appearance of the scene

It is normal practice to create a common approach path (CAP) early in the investigation of a scene that contains a clear focal point, such as a dead body. As described in Box 2.2, a full photographic record is made of the CAP and its creation.

Once the focal point of the scene has been examined, attention can be given to the scene as a whole. During this process, photographs that record the overall appearance of the scene will be taken. In particular, the paths through the scene that are likely to have been taken by the perpetrator(s) and/or the victim(s) will be photographed. Also, there is an option to take a series of overlapping pictures from one or more points within the scene so that they can be overlain to reveal a panorama of the entirety of the scene that is visible from the point or points concerned. If the scene is indoors, then photographs of the interior surfaces (walls, ceiling, floor) of the scene's constituent rooms will be taken, as necessary. Clearly, in doing this, particular attention will be paid to the room within which the focal point of the scene resides.

Unless there is a good reason to do otherwise, each photograph that is intended to provide a record of an aspect of the scene's overall appearance will be taken from eye height. Also, each such picture will normally be taken with a lens that minimises the distortion of the image (such as a standard 50 mm lens on a 35 mm camera). Furthermore, the scene will typically be photographed from a number of different angles, using both long and medium range shots. These measures will help to maximise the accuracy of the impression of the appearance of the crime scene in the eyes of those involved in the incident, those who witnessed it and those who investigated it.

Still photographs of items of evidence

Each item of physical evidence that is found at the scene of a serious crime should be photographed before it is recovered or otherwise moved. In many cases, more than one photograph of each such item will be required.

Long and/or medium range shots can be used to unambiguously record the location of the item concerned while it is *in situ* within the scene. Closer range photographs can be used to record its size. When taking such photographs, it is essential that a ruler or, better still, an L-shaped measure be added to the field of view near to the item of evidence (Figure 2.8). Also, to avoid distortions caused by perspective, it is important that the plane of the camera's film and those of the scale and the resting place of the object are all parallel. Under these conditions, it is possible to faithfully reproduce photographs of the object of known scale (including 1:1 images). Note, however, that it is not always absolutely necessary to include a scale in the field of view while photographing certain items *in situ* at the crime

(Photograph by Julie Jackson)

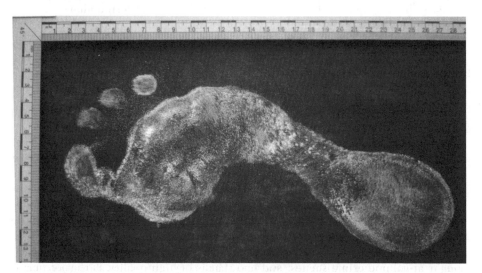

Figure 2.8 A photograph taken to show the size of an item, in this case a footprint
Note the presence of the L-shaped measure to allow the scale to be established

scene. This is only true of those items that can be easily recovered undamaged and that will not alter over time. If necessary, these objects may be photographed with scales at a later date or simply presented in court.

Photographs can also be used to preserve fragile pieces of evidence that might be damaged during their recovery. For example, consider a latent fingerprint that has been developed by dusting it with aluminium powder for subsequent recovery by lifting with adhesive tape (Chapter 4, Section 4.1.5). Photographing the fingerprint prior to lifting it provides a permanent image of the evidence that would be invaluable if the fingerprint were to become smudged during its recovery. Similarly, some or all of the evidential value of footprints and tyre marks in mud or snow can be recorded photographically prior to the recovery of the marks by casting techniques (Chapter 4, Sections 4.2 and 4.5 respectively).

When a dead body is present at a scene, it should be photographed from several different angles using medium range shots. Close-up photographs should also be taken of any injuries evident on the body. Once the corpse has been removed, the surface on which it rested should be photographed, as this may also contain valuable evidence. Indeed, this last point is a general one; whenever a piece of evidence is recovered from a scene it is wise to inspect the place from which it was removed for any traces of evidential value. If found, these traces should be photographed before they too are recovered.

2.4 The recovery of physical evidence

Any object, mark or impression that can provide information about the incident under investigation is an item of physical evidence. This section is concerned with an overview of the general principles involved in the search for, and collection, packaging, labelling and storage of, such items.

The underlying principles involved in the search for and handling of items of physical evidence is the same, irrespective of the crime being investigated. However, as with other aspects of crime scene processing, not all scenes that occur within a given police force's area will receive the same amount of attention. In England and Wales, the main difference between the recovery of physical evidence from scenes of volume crime and those of serious crime is in the methods used to search for evidence and, to an extent, the types of evidence recovered.

Consider the scene of a typical volume crime, such as a domestic burglary, from which physical evidence is to be sought. In England and Wales, the SOCO in attendance (or, more rarely, a police officer) will normally dedicate the bulk of his or her search efforts to the discovery of high-quality evidence in areas of the scene that have clearly been disturbed by the perpetrator. Such areas are to be found along the route taken through the scene by the criminal. They are most likely to occur at any points of entry or exit from enclosed parts of the scene (such as buildings, rooms, vehicles and areas of land surrounded by fences) and at the focal point(s) of the crime (such as the room(s) from which items were stolen).

Currently, in the United Kingdom, the type of physical evidence most frequently sought at volume crime scenes, and one that is of high quality, is that of fingerprints. There are several reasons why fingerprints are particularly valued by the police, notably:

■ the technology associated with the collection of fingerprints is well developed, reliable and, in most cases, easily applied;

■ fingerprints may be compared with those previously collected from known individuals, thereby, in the case of a match, allowing the identification of the person involved;

■ rapid results are possible as each police force in England and Wales has immediate access to the National Automated Fingerprint Identification System (NAFIS) (Chapter 4, Section 4.1.3);

■ fingerprint evidence is readily accepted in court.

It is noteworthy, however, that recent rapid developments in low copy number DNA techniques and the establishment of the National DNA Database (Chapter 6, Section 6.3.6) may mean that the collection of biological material for DNA profiling from scenes of volume crime will become more routine in the near future. Importantly, as demonstrated by the case highlighted in Box 2.3, it is now often possible to obtain a DNA profile from the skin cells that are left behind when an object

Case study

Box 2.3

A confidence trickster caught by low copy number DNA technology

In the late 1990s, Staffordshire Police was part of a consortium of police forces drawn from the Midlands area of the UK who were working together on what was named Operation Liberal. This campaign targeted crime perpetrated by people who stole from householders, having first gained their confidence by posing as official callers.

At this time, Staffordshire Police was also carrying out a pilot study to test the usefulness of the then emerging low copy number DNA technology. As explained in Chapter 6, this technology is *extremely* sensitive. It is quite capable of producing a profile from the DNA left behind when an object, such as a door handle, is used by someone with bare hands. Although this high sensitivity is clearly an advantage, it can also cause problems. This is because the profile will not only contain information derived from the last person to handle the object but, at least potentially, from all other people who have touched it. Therefore, it is best applied to objects that have been handled only by the suspect.

One of the cases being dealt with under Operation Liberal was that of an elderly lady who had had money stolen from her handbag while she was distracted by a man posing as a water company representative. This man called at the lady's door, stating that there was a problem with the water supply and that he would have to turn her water off for a short while. The lady showed the bogus official where the property's stopcock was and stayed with him while he turned it off. While the lady was so occupied, an accomplice of the bogus caller entered the property and stole cash from her handbag, which was in her bedroom. After a while, the self-styled water company representative indicated that he had heard from a workmate that the problem with the water supply was now fixed and he duly turned the stopcock on again. It was not until the next day that the lady realised that her money had been stolen. She called the police, who ascertained from her that the bogus caller had handled the water main stopcock.

Under the pilot study, it was decided to swab for DNA from the stopcock. From its condition, it was apparent that it had not been turned for some time prior to the incident in question. It was felt, therefore, that any profile obtained would be likely to be practically free of contamination. This proved to be the case. The DNA from the stopcock was shown to match one of the records held on the National DNA Database. On this basis, a suspect was arrested who was subsequently tried, found guilty and given a substantial prison sentence.

is touched by an individual. Other commonplace forms of evidence that are capable of forming strong evidential links with the perpetrator are footwear impressions (Chapter 4, Section 4.2) and tool marks (Chapter 4, Section 4.4).

While the types of physical evidence that are sought from scenes of volume crime are typically those that have the potential to individualise, types of evidence that can only reveal class characteristics (Chapter 1, Section 1.2) are also collected, particularly under circumstances in which they can corroborate other evidence. For example, consider the case of a man arrested shortly after he was seen breaking the side window of a car. The coat that he was wearing would be taken into custody and examined by a laboratory-based forensic scientist, as would a control sample of glass taken from that part of the broken window that was still held in the doorframe of the car concerned. Typically, glass fragments are not retained for long periods of time on garments that are being worn. In this case, the presence of fragments of toughened glass on the suspect's coat that match those taken from the broken car window could be particularly incriminating as they corroborate the account of the incident given by the eyewitness.

As would be expected, the process of physical evidence discovery and collection at the scene of a serious crime is typically more painstaking than at any one scene of volume crime. In the case of an outdoor murder scene, physical evidence recovery starts with a search of the strip of ground that is to become the common approach path (CAP) between the perimeter of the scene and the body of the deceased (Box 2.2). Once this path is established, a tent will usually be used to protect the body from the elements. Access to the body is then at the discretion of the Crime Scene Manager who will admit specialists in order of priority after the body has been photographed and videotaped. For example, in the case of a part-buried, skeletalised body, experts may examine the burial site and/or the remains according to the following sequence:

1. A forensic botanist (who may be able to establish how long the body has been buried on the basis of the vegetation growth that has occurred on the disturbed ground).

2. A forensic archaeologist.

3. A forensic entomologist (if there are insects feeding on the body, see Chapter 12, Box 12.2) or a forensic anthropologist if the remains are fully skeletalised (Chapter 12, Section 12.4.2).

4. A forensic pathologist (Chapter 12, Section 12.3.3).

Even if no other experts are called, a forensic pathologist will almost certainly attend the body of a murder victim, accompanied by a senior member of the police scientific support team (typically the Crime Scene Manager, who will be a senior SOCO or, in some cases, the SSM). Any item of physical evidence present on the body that might be readily dislodged and/or destroyed when the body is moved would then be removed and individually packaged. Typical items involved might be hairs held in a hand of the deceased. Where deemed appropriate, the entire body may be systematically covered in numbered strips of transparent plastic adhesive-coated tape. Items of recoverable trace evidence, such as fibres, will stick to the glue on the tape. Each of these strips – which are known as tape lifts – will then be removed along with adhering items of physical evidence. As with all types of trace evidence, the avoidance of contamination of these tape lifts is of paramount importance. This can be achieved if, as soon as each one has been removed from the body, it is adhered to a suitable surface (such as a piece of clear acetate film), sealed in place with further strips of adhesive tape and then sealed into a clean polythene bag.

The non-invasive part of the pathologist's post-mortem examination to establish the cause of death will start at the crime scene. Once this has been finished, and the search for trace items of physical evidence on the body (usually including swabs for DNA profiling, see Chapter 6) and the necessary records have been completed, the body will be removed to the mortuary. To prepare the body for removal, plastic bags are secured over its head, hands and feet (to stop the loss of any items of trace physical evidence that might still be present) and it is placed inside a clean plastic, zip-up body bag.

At the mortuary, items of physical evidence from the outside of the body (e.g. clothing and any items in pockets) that have not already been removed are collected and individually packaged. Where possible, samples of hair will be taken from the deceased, as these may be compared with any found in the possession of a suspect. During the invasive part of the post-mortem examination, samples of body fluids and tissues will be obtained. These can be used for pathological and toxicological assessments and as sources of control samples against which materials obtained from suspects can be compared. Throughout the processing of the body, it is treated as a crime scene in its own right, being documented with notes and sketches and photographic images as appropriate.

When the body has been removed from the scene of a murder, the search for evidence will continue in a systematic fashion. A number of different search patterns have been developed for this purpose, each of which is designed to ensure that the entire scene is thoroughly scrutinised (Figure 2.9). Indeed, it is common practice

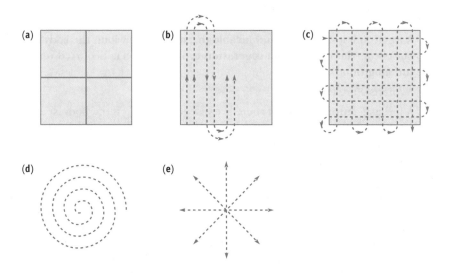

Figure 2.9 Examples of systematic patterns that can be used to search crime scenes
Dotted lines show the paths taken by officers engaged in the search. (a) Zone or quadrant, in which the scene is divided into portions of manageable size, each of which is then systematically searched in turn. (b) Lane, line or strip, in which a line of officers move forward side-by-side in a pattern that covers the entire scene. (c) Grid. (d) Spiral, which either starts at the epicentre of the scene and moves outwards to its perimeter or vice versa. (e) Wheel, in which officers start at the epicentre and move out, each in a straight line, until the perimeter is reached

to search the scene of a serious crime at least twice, with the last search being made immediately before the processing of the scene is deemed to be complete.

Once items of physical evidence have been discovered, the priority given to the recovery of each item must be decided. In doing this, due regard has to be paid to the value and fragility of different items of evidence. If all other factors are equal, evidence that is both capable of individualisation (Chapter 1, Section 1.2) and that is easily damaged (such as fingerprints) will be given a high priority and therefore will be collected at the earliest practicable opportunity.

During the collection of physical evidence, it must always be borne in mind that the retrieval of one type of evidence may destroy another. For example, the application of silicone rubber casting material to an area in order to collect an impression of a tool mark is likely to destroy any fingerprints present at the same location. This loss may be avoided by dusting the area with fingerprint powder prior to the application of the casting material.

When physical evidence is collected from a scene, adequate control samples should also be collected. These are taken for two reasons. Firstly, controls are needed to enable evidentially valuable information to be distinguished from the background. For example, in a case in which a paramedic covered a fatally injured person with a blanket just before the victim died, this blanket would, if possible, be taken as a control sample. This would be done so that any fibres found on the body that matched those from the blanket could be eliminated and not confused with any that might be of evidential value. Secondly, controls are needed to facilitate comparisons between known control samples and questioned samples taken from elsewhere. For example, a sample of carpet taken from a crime scene could be used to provide control fibres for comparison with fibres found on the shoes of a suspect.

Irrespective of the seriousness of the crime being investigated, it is imperative that as soon as any one piece of evidence has been recovered from the scene it must be appropriately packaged, labelled and stored. In order to avoid the possibility of cross-contamination between samples, all items must be packaged separately in previously unused containers. For similar reasons, and to avoid the loss of evidentially valuable material, the packages used for evidence should be completely sealed.

Different classes of material have different packaging requirements, for example:

- small items that may be easily lost (such as individual scalp hairs or chips of paint) may be wrapped in pre-folded paper (Figure 2.10) and held in fully sealed polythene bags;
- dry, cloth items and shoes may be sealed in paper bags/sacks;
- wet cloth items may be sealed in polythene bags and frozen;
- items that are believed to be contaminated with liquid hydrocarbon-based fuels (such as petrol) are packaged in nylon bags, closed with airtight swan-neck seals (Figure 2.11).

In many instances, it is wise to double-wrap items of physical evidence by placing the packaged item in a second, suitable, sealed container.

Each item of physical evidence must be labelled. As shown in Figure 2.12, the labels used convey identifying information about the item concerned and the case to which it relates. Each label also has spaces that are to be signed and dated by each person who has responsibility for the item, from the moment it is collected to

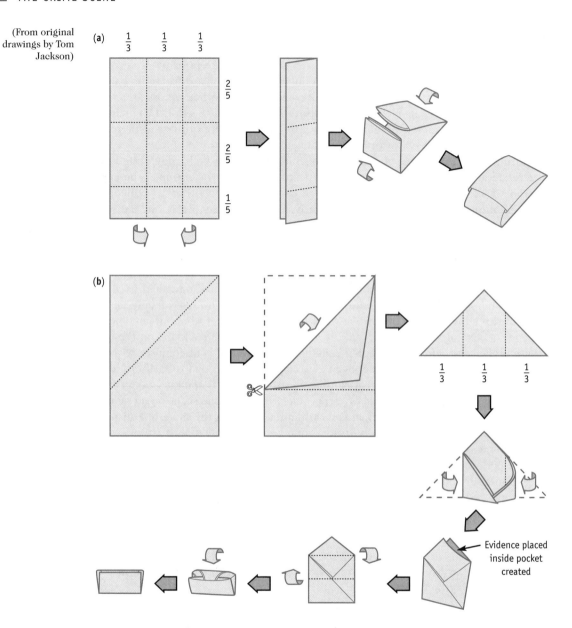

(From original drawings by Tom Jackson)

Figure 2.10 Folding paper to produce packaging suitable for small items of evidence *(a) The method recommended by the Forensic Science Service, England and Wales, and (b) an alternative, American (US) method. Note that once the evidence is wrapped in folded paper, it must be sealed into a suitable container*

the time at which it is destroyed. This produces what is known as a chain of custody. This is an uninterrupted series of identified individuals, each of whom can be asked to testify that the integrity of the item of evidence was not compromised while it was in his or her safe-keeping.

(Photograph by
Andrew Jackson,
Staffordshire
University, UK)

Figure 2.11 A nylon bag closed with an airtight swan-neck seal

Form 140 TAG
Rev. 12/96

Harlow 0191-485 4286   16053 dp

FOR COURT USE ONLY

Regina -v-..

....

Exhibit No. ....

Signed ....

Justice of the Peace/Clerk to

....

(Magistrate's Court)

Date..

FOR POLICE USE ONLY

Police Force: ....

Division...

Misc. Prop. No. ....

Description of Item

....

....

....

....

....

Identifying Mark.....................................

LAB. REF.

**C.J. Act 1967, s9;
M.C. Act 1980, s 102;
M.C. Rules 1981, r 70.**
I identify the exhibit described
overleaf as that referred to in the
statement made and signed by me.

Signature	Date

Figure 2.12 Both sides of an exhibit label

Items of physical evidence must be stored in secure facilities at all times. Also, the conditions under which such items are stored must be chosen with care, so as to minimise the rate of their deterioration. Different classes of item have different storage requirements. In the main, dry samples that are sealed in paper bags or cardboard boxes can be stored in cool, dry conditions, while wet samples kept in polythene bags need to be frozen to stop them mouldering. Biological samples usually need to be refrigerated or frozen and may require the addition of chemical preservatives.

Finally, it is important to note that there are usually a number of pressures that limit the amount of time that can be spent in the processing of a given crime scene. For example, deteriorating weather conditions may mean that physical evidence is likely to be destroyed unless it can be collected rapidly. Nonetheless, in order to be fully effective, the processes of physical evidence recovery must be carried out systematically, with an open and enquiring mind and a close attention to detail. As part of this, it should be borne in mind that not all scenes are as they first appear. For example, the use of specialist lighting techniques may reveal physical evidence that would otherwise remain hidden (e.g. in cases of sexual assault, semen stains may be more readily seen under ultraviolet light (in which they fluoresce) than under ordinary daylight). Importantly, any mistakes or omissions made in the collection, labelling and storage of physical evidence may well not be rectifiable by subsequent work on the recovered items. If an item of physical evidence is overlooked during the processing of a scene, it is usually impossible to return to collect it at a later date. This is because, even if the item is still present at the scene, it would not be possible to be sure that it had not been altered, or indeed placed at the scene, at some point after the scene had been processed. Clearly, during the processing of a given crime scene it is better to err on the safe side when collecting items of physical evidence, taking more items and in larger amounts than the bare minimum.

2.5 Summary

■ The crime scene is often the source of information that is crucial to the solution of the case concerned. Importantly, recovered items of physical evidence may help to establish key aspects of the case, including whether a crime has been committed and, if so, the type of crime concerned, how it was carried out, when it was committed and the identity of the perpetrator(s) and victim(s).

■ Key to the effective processing of a crime scene are the actions of the police officers involved (notably the First Officer Attending (FOA)) and the police scientific support professionals (in particular, the Scenes of Crime Officer (SOCO)). Principal actions undertaken during the processing of a crime scene are the preservation of the scene, the recording of the scene, the logging of all actions taken at the scene and the systematic search for and recovery of items of physical evidence. These items, which may be subjected to laboratory-based forensic examination, must be properly packaged, labelled and stored.

■ The principles involved in the processing of any crime scene remain the same irrespective of the seriousness of the case.

However, it is important to realise that, within this framework, the exact sequence of events involved in crime scene processing will vary considerably from one incident to the next, reflecting the unique nature of each individual scene. In essence, there is no 'right way' to process the crime scene. The nature and scale of the crime, the police authority and investigating team in charge, and the resources available to them, will all have a bearing on the processing of the crime scene. Notwithstanding this, the scene of a serious crime (such as murder) will typically receive a much higher level of scrutiny than will one of a volume crime (such as burglary).

■ A crime scene is a changing environment. Therefore, in order to ensure that the maximum amount of information is retrieved from it, the crime scene should be processed without unnecessary delay. However, in order to be fully effective, actions taken during crime scene processing need not only to be timely but must also be scientifically and ethically sound, and legally acceptable.

Problems

1. The duties of the First Officer Attending (FOA) at a crime scene have been summarised as 'to assess, protect and communicate'. Do you agree that this is an accurate synopsis? Justify your answer.

2. Early one summer's morning, a man who is walking his dog along a public footpath bordered by fields discovers a dead body. The weather is fine, warm and sunny, but there has been recent rain and further heavy rain is forecast. A very rough plan sketch of the scene is shown in Figure 2.13. A brief inspection reveals that the victim is quite clearly dead, and appears to have suffered multiple stab-wounds. The man makes a 999 call using his mobile phone to request police attendance. The first police officer to attend the scene is logged in at the police control room as the First Officer Attending (FOA). Shortly after the arrival at the scene of the FOA, further police officers, together with scientific support personnel, arrive and take over responsibility for the scene. How may the scene be preserved, recorded and searched? Once items of physical evidence have been recovered, what steps should be taken to avoid cross-contamination between them?

3. Consider a case in which the body of a stabbing victim was found smeared in her own blood. The investigator noticed that there was also an approximately circular bloodstain with scalloped edges on the body that, because of its characteristic shape, appeared to have fallen onto the body from above. What samples do you believe need be taken, from the scene and/or elsewhere, in order to use DNA profiling to test the hypothesis that the circular stain originated from the attacker? Do you believe that DNA profiling in this case has the potential to prove beyond all doubt who the attacker was? Note that very small samples of blood can be used to reveal profiles based on nuclear DNA and that such samples can be obtained by rubbing a bloodstain with a sterile medical swab moistened, if necessary, with sterile water. Before answering this question, you might find it useful to read Chapter 6.

4. When obtaining control samples of glass from a broken window that was unlatched and opened in a case of suspected burglary, the SOCO took several pieces of glass that were still retained in the frame. Why do you think that several pieces of glass were taken? Do you think that it would have been better to have taken the samples from the ground beneath the window? If the investigating officer had reason to believe that this case was not a burglary but an insurance fraud perpetrated by the householder, might there be any benefit in unscrewing the window and submitting it in its entirety for forensic examination? You might find it useful to read Section 3.2 in Chapter 3 before answering the last part of this question.

5. When packaging dry non-trace items of physical evidence, it is common to use brown paper bags, each of which has a transparent plastic window incorporated in its construction. Why do you think that these bags are often preferred over either plain brown paper bags or plain transparent plastic bags?

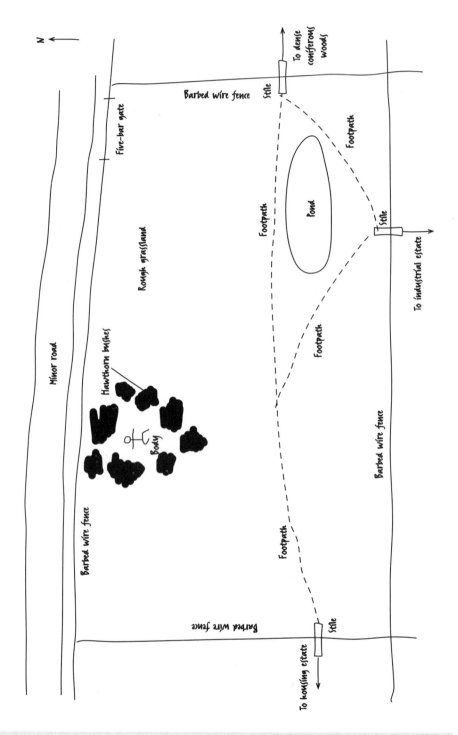

Figure 2.13 A very rough plan sketch of a crime scene

6. A laboratory-based forensic scientist needs to gain access to a piece of physical evidence that is packaged in a brown paper bag. To do this, the scientist carefully inspects how the bag is sealed and then makes a clean incision through one side of the bag in an area that is distant from both the contents of the bag and any of the original seals. Once the analysis of the item of evidence is completed, the scientist returns it to its original package through the incision made earlier. This incision is then immediately sealed with clear plastic adhesive-coated tape. The scientist then signs across the seal and covers the signature with another piece of adhesive tape. Explain, as far as you are able, why the scientist carried out these operations.

Further reading

Fisher, B. A. J. (2000) *Techniques of crime scene investigation* (6th edn). Boca Raton, FL: CRC Press LLC.

Forensic Science Service (2004) *The scenes of crime handbook*. Chorley: Forensic Science Service.

Lee, H. C., Palmbach, T. and Miller, M. T. (2001) *Henry Lee's crime scene handbook*. San Diego, CA: Academic Press.

Redsicker, D. R. (2000) *The practical methodology of forensic photography* (2nd edn). Boca Raton, FL: CRC Press LLC.

Trace and contact evidence
Part I: Recoverable materials

3

Chapter objectives

After reading this chapter, you should be able to:

> List the common types of material that are encountered as trace physical evidence that is recovered from incident scenes.

> Describe the specialised processes that are used to collect both questioned and control samples of at least one common type of trace recoverable evidence.

> Outline the means by which trace recoverable materials may be characterised to obtain both class characteristics and points of comparison.

> Appreciate the investigative, associative, corroborative and, where applicable, individualising value of recoverable trace evidence.

Introduction

Much of forensic science is firmly rooted in Locard's exchange principle that 'every contact leaves a trace'. This trace may be in the form of a specific recoverable material, such as a chip of paint, or that of a mark or impression, such as a fingerprint. This chapter will deal with each of the main types of recoverable trace materials found at crime scenes, with the exception of body fluids (dealt with in Chapter 5), drugs of abuse (Chapter 7), gunshot residues (Chapter 9), those materials (known as fire accelerants) used by arsonists to promote combustion (Chapter 10) and explosives (Chapter 11). Marks and impressions are discussed in Chapter 4.

The topics covered in this chapter are hairs and other fibres, glass, soils, vegetable matter and paint, together with a review of the other types of trace recoverable materials of forensic value. In each case, emphasis is given to an overview of the methods that are used to characterise the materials concerned. While specialised evidence recovery techniques are dealt with in this chapter (especially those used to recover fibres), the more general principles and methods used in the recovery of physical evidence are described in Chapter 2. As with all types of physical evidence, it is vitally important that the significance of recoverable trace evidence is properly evaluated.

3.1 Hairs and other fibres

The term **fibre** (spelt fiber in the United States) is used to denote any solid object that is thin, flexible and elongate, having a high length to transverse cross-section area ratio. As shown in Figure 3.1, fibres of forensic interest can be classified on the basis of their origin and composition. Many of the types of fibre referred to in this figure are common objects. These include hairs, especially those of human origin, and those man-made and natural fibres that are formed into textile products (Chapter 4, Section 4.6) that are used in the manufacture of clothing and household fabrics.

Many of these common fibres are readily transferred from one object to another during physical contact. Indeed, a given fibre may be transferred more than once (Box 3.1). Interestingly, in most environmental conditions, these common types of fibre are resistant to biological, physical and chemical degradation and therefore persist intact for long periods of time. Furthermore, their examination provides multiple points of comparison that can enable them to be identified to the class level. For example, it is possible to determine the type of polymer (e.g. polyester) from which a particular man-made fibre is formed.

The achievement of this class-level of identification, coupled with the comparison of the characteristics exhibited by a questioned fibre obtained from an incident scene and a control fibre (such as that taken from the belongings of a suspect), can provide useful information. Importantly, such information is frequently enough to enable the fibre examiner involved to conclude that the two fibres are either different or, alternatively, sufficiently similar that they may have originated from the same source.

Fibre
Any long, thin, flexible solid object with a high length to transverse cross-section area ratio.

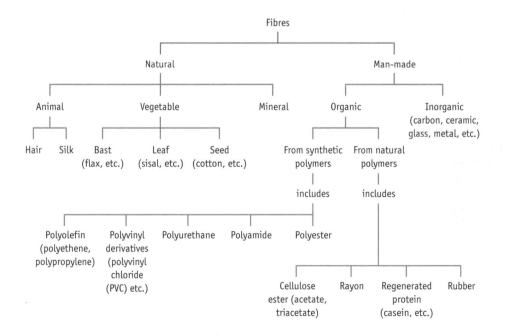

Figure 3.1 A classification of fibres of interest to forensic science

Further information

Box 3.1

The re-transfer of trace evidence

Many kinds of trace evidence, including fibres, are materials that are readily transferred from one object to another. This fact forms the basis of their ability to provide evidence of association. For example, a suspect might be associated with the scene of an incident by the presence on his or her clothing of traces of fibres, soil, glass, oil, paint and/or vegetation that match those found at the scene.

The fact that many types of trace evidence can be readily transferred once means that, in the main, they may easily be transferred again. This has four important implications, as outlined below.

■ Great care has to be exercised in order to avoid the possibility of the cross-contamination of one item of evidence (e.g. a garment worn by a complainant in the case of an alleged assault) with items of trace evidence from another (e.g. fibres from a garment worn by the alleged assailant). The avoidance of cross-contamination is crucial in all forensic work and is reviewed in Chapter 2, Section 2.4.

■ Under certain circumstances, items of trace evidence may be readily lost. Some such items, for example human hairs, are large enough to be observed either with the naked eye or with the aid of a magnifying glass. Such an individual item of trace evidence may be found at a crime scene on a larger piece of physical evidence (e.g. a bed sheet). If it is likely that the trace item will be lost from the larger item during transit from the crime scene, then it is prudent to document the trace item *in situ* before its recovery (Chapter 2, Section 2.4). The trace and larger items will then be separately packaged and labelled at the scene for subsequent laboratory examination. Also, the everyday actions of an individual will typically cause the majority of any transferred items of trace evidence (such as fibres, glass fragments or particles of gunshot residue) to be rapidly lost from his or her hair, skin and/or clothes. Therefore, in order to maximise the probability of finding such transferred trace evidence on a person, it should be looked for with the minimum of delay. Furthermore, it should be noted that the action of looking for one type of trace evidence could cause the loss of another. For example, glass fragments of forensic value are routinely searched for by shaking the garment on which they are believed to have alighted (Section 3.2). This action may well also dis-

lodge, and lose, evidentially valuable fibres that have been transferred to the garment. To avoid this loss, fibre samples can be obtained from the garment before it is shaken, by means of tape lifts (Section 3.1.1).

■ It is quite common for items of trace evidence from one object to be transferred to another via an intermediary object, a process known as secondary transfer (direct transfer from one object to another is called primary transfer). For example, the presence of fibres from the fabric of a chair found on a person's jacket might indicate that their jacket had been in contact with the chair. However, it might also be possible that the fibres from the chair were transported to the jacket via clothing worn by someone who had been in contact with the chair and then the jacket. Indeed, it is possible that there were two, three or even more intermediary objects involved, thus producing tertiary, quaternary, etc. transfers. Clearly, it is important that the possibility that items of trace evidence arrived on an object of interest by transfer *subsequent* to the primary transfer is taken into account during the interpretation of trace evidence.

■ The everyday actions of people tend to quickly dislodge items of trace evidence that have been transferred to them and the clothing that they are wearing. However, it should be noted that there are circumstances under which transferred trace items may not be rapidly lost from a recipient object. Importantly, the death of an individual is typically accompanied by a dramatic decrease in the rate of loss from the deceased's body and clothing of transferred fibres. Consequently, it is likely that the clothing of a murder victim that has come into contact with his or her killer will retain fibres from the everyday environment of the murderer, even after several weeks of exposure to the elements. Indeed, in the case of the murders for which Wayne Williams was successfully prosecuted, it was argued that such fibres were retained on the bodies of the two victims concerned, even though they had both been retrieved from a river (Box 3.2). Significantly, the abrupt slowing in the loss rate of transferred fibres that accompanies death means that, under many circumstances, a high proportion of such fibres present on a murdered corpse are likely to have originated from the environment of the murder.

Occasionally, the presence of highly unusual fibres and/or an unusual combination of fibre types can provide extremely strong evidence that links a suspect to a crime or series of crimes. This is well illustrated by the case of Wayne Bertram Williams (Box 3.2). Furthermore, fibre evidence can sometimes yield information of such high resolution that identification of the individual is possible. This can occur when the fibres concerned are actively growing human hairs that have been pulled out of the skin. If the roots of such hairs have cells from the hair follicles still adhered to them, there may be sufficient nuclear DNA available for the individual to be identified through DNA profiling. Although it is possible to extract DNA from the hair shaft irrespective of whether or not the hair was actively growing when it was detached from the skin, this is rarely done. This is because hair shaft DNA is mitochondrial and this is of lower evidential value than nuclear DNA. Finally, it is worth noting that the recent development of low copy number DNA techniques means that it is now possible to obtain a DNA profile from the nuclei of the few skin cells that may be adhered to the hair shaft as a consequence, for example, of dandruff. DNA profiling is dealt with in detail in Chapter 6.

In many cases, the likelihood of the transfer of fibres is heightened by violent contact. As a consequence, this type of physical evidence is often of particular value in cases of violent crime, such as assault, rape or murder. However, this is by no means exclusively the case. For example, a burglar may leave incriminating fibres from his or her clothing on reaching through a broken window in order to unlatch it.

Fibre evidence can be of value in crime scene reconstruction. Also, it may be instrumental in the furtherance of an investigation. For example, the presence of several similar, long, scalp-hairs of human origin at the scene of a crime could

Case study
Box 3.2

The conviction of Wayne Bertram Williams

Wayne Bertram Williams was convicted in 1982 of the murder of two men, both then aged in their 20s and both found in the Chattahoochee River. He was also linked in court to the murder of a further ten young males. These 12 murders, together with the killing or disappearance of each of another 18 young African American people, all took place between the summers of 1979 and 1981 in Atlanta, Georgia, USA.

This was an extremely high-profile case and one in which fibre evidence played a very significant role. Importantly, the case against Williams included the presence on the bodies of victims of many different and, in most cases relatively uncommon, types of fibre that were linked to the defendant. For example, the victims of both

of the murders for which Williams was convicted were found to have fibres on them that matched control fibres taken from each of four items (i.e. a bedspread, a carpet, a blanket and a dog) that were known to be in Williams' everyday environment. Furthermore, the bodies of these two victims also had fibres on them that, while not present on both bodies, nonetheless matched further items in Williams' environment. In one case there were three such further matches, while in the other case there were two.

Importantly, it was argued in court that the combination of different fibre matches meant that it was highly unlikely that their origin was other than that of the defendant's environment. Williams was sentenced to two consecutive life terms.

strongly suggest that a person with, or who had, long hair has at some time been present at that scene. This information may prove to be important in assisting the police in their search for a victim or perpetrator of the crime or an eyewitness of the incident. However, as with most types of physical evidence, fibre evidence is most commonly used to help corroborate or refute a previously proposed link between an individual and a scene. In such cases, it is the job of the forensic scientist to compare the characteristics of fibres found at the scene (the questioned fibres) with those of control fibres taken from the individual concerned, or his or her belongings. Descriptions of the methods used to collect fibre evidence and those of fibre characterisation are given in Sections 3.1.1 and 3.1.2 respectively.

3.1.1 The recovery of fibre evidence

Consider a scenario in which there was a violent struggle during which a jumper worn by an assailant was brought into contact with a jacket worn by the victim. Under these circumstances, trace amounts of fibres from the jumper would normally be transferred to the jacket and vice versa. If, shortly after the incident, the victim were to report the crime to the police and a person who is suspected of being the assailant were to be detained, then fibre evidence taken from the jacket and the jumper could be of significant evidential value.

In order to obtain this evidence, two different types of sample would be taken from each of the jumper and the jacket. The first of these types is designed to obtain any trace level fibres that were transferred during contact (the questioned fibres), while the second is intended to provide adequate control fibres from each of the garments.

During the forensic examination of the four samples so produced, the characteristics of the fibres of the control sample taken from the jumper would be compared with those of the questioned fibres obtained from the jacket in order to see if any of the fibres match. Similarly, a comparison would be made between the control samples taken from the jacket and the questioned fibres taken from the jumper – again to ascertain whether there are any matches.

The presence of matches would normally allow the investigator to state that their findings were consistent with an exchange of fibres between the two garments. Clearly, this information could constitute useful evidence that may, for example, be of value in testing the likely veracity of conflicting accounts of the incident as provided by the complainant and the suspect. On the other hand, the absence of matches is likely to lead the scientist to an inconclusive finding; that is one that neither supports or refutes any claim that the two garments had been in contact.

The techniques used to obtain trace and control samples of the types alluded to above are quite different from each other, and are discussed below.

The recovery of trace-level fibres

Any technique used to obtain trace-level fibres should ideally sample all of the types of fibre that have been transferred to the object being sampled without taking fibres from the object itself. Also, in many instances, it is desirable to obtain only those types of fibre that have been transferred to the object in the recent past. There are a number of approaches that can be adopted in order to attempt to achieve these objectives. These include hand picking with tweezers, using a vacuum cleaner fitted with a specialist attachment that directs the stream of air onto a paper or fabric filter, scraping, combing (of hair) and making tape lifts. All of the approaches have advantages. However, for the majority of work, **tape lifting** is usually the method of choice.

To create a tape lift, sticky tape is brought into contact (sometimes once, sometimes more than once) with the area to be sampled. Specialist tapes with different degrees of tackiness can be purchased for this purpose. The tape is then stuck to another suitable surface, such as a sheet of clear acetate plastic film, in order to keep it free from contamination. The tape lift is then systematically searched for fibres of interest (known as the target fibres). This is done by eye, with the aid of a low-power microscope, or by using one of the commercially available automated fibre finder systems. Once a target fibre has been identified, the dissection of the tape and the application of a small quantity of solvent (e.g. xylene) to dissolve the tape's adhesive can enable it to be removed. The target fibre can then be mounted on a microscope slide for subsequent examination.

Tape lifting
A method for recovering trace materials (such as hairs and other fibres) in which sticky tape is brought into contact with the area to be sampled and then adhered to a plastic sheet.

The recovery of control samples of textile fibres and human hair

The means by which control samples are taken should ideally obtain fibres that are representative of those that might have been transferred *from* the object being sampled while excluding any fibres that have been transferred *to* that object. The method used varies depending on whether the fibres to be sampled are those of a textile product or hair.

In the case of a textile product (most commonly a garment), the recovery of control samples can be achieved by teasing out individual fibres from those areas of the product that are least likely to be contaminated with foreign fibres (e.g. the seams). In doing this, it is important to bear in mind that there may well be several different types of fibre present in the product, any one of which has the potential to be evidentially valuable.

The procedures to be adopted when obtaining control samples of human hair for microscopic comparison with questioned hair should be founded on an understanding of the variation exhibited by the properties to be examined. An important consideration is that human hair not only varies from person to person but also it varies from location to location on the same person. For example, the scalp hair of any one adult is different from his or her pubic hair. This means that control samples need to be obtained from all body locations that may have a bearing on the case.

Even the hairs of a single body location of a given individual (e.g. his or her scalp) show significant levels of variation in their physical characteristics when compared with the variation seen from individual to individual in the population. This means that, in order to obtain the maximum amount of value from a macroscopic and microscopic comparison of hairs recovered from the scene of an incident and those taken as a control sample, the number of hairs taken in the control sample should be fairly large. While there is no consensus about the exact number that is required, 30–50 hairs from each body location to be sampled would typically be considered to be enough. Also, as many of the characteristics of a given hair show variation along its length, from a scientific point of view it is best if the control hairs are taken by pulling them out of the skin, rather than cutting them.

It is worth noting that the circumstances of a case can sometimes aid the investigator in deciding from where on the body control samples of hair should be taken. For example, consider a case in which scalp hairs are found on a club that is suspected to have been used to hit someone on the head during an assault. Under these circumstances, it would be prudent to take control samples from the head of the victim in the area of the damage caused during the assault. This is because it is this area that is most likely to have been 'sampled' by the weapon used.

Finally, it must be noted that the collection of control samples must be undertaken with due regard to the legal rights of the people involved.

3.1.2 An overview of the examination and characterisation of hairs and other fibres

The forensic examination of fibres is primarily carried out in order to identify the individual fibre types (i.e. whether human scalp hair, nylon textile fibre, etc.) and to provide descriptions of characteristics that can be used as points of comparison between the fibres of interest. Much of this work is based on microscopic examination. However, the starting point is the inspection of the macroscopic features of the specimen, firstly with the unaided eye and then using a low-power stereomicroscope. In many cases the specimen, which might be a garment from which control fibres are to be taken or a tape lift on which questioned fibres are held (see Section 3.1.1), will be made up of multiple and various fibres. In such cases, the inspection of macroscopic features facilitates the selection and isolation of specific fibres for more detailed examination. In the case of tape lifts, this process may now be aided by the use of one of several commercially available automated fibre finder systems.

Once individual fibres have been isolated, they can be examined with a compound microscope, using visible and/or ultraviolet light. Such microscopes are capable of producing images at higher levels of magnification than the stereomicroscopes referred to above. In order to facilitate this higher magnification examination, each fibre is typically held in a mounting medium between a microscope slide and a thin glass cover slip. The mounting medium may be one that will eventually set solid (such as DePeX) to produce a permanent mount, or one that will not set (such as a mixture of glycerol and water) thus producing a temporary mount.

Whether permanent or temporary mounts are to be prepared, a mounting medium with a fairly similar refractive index (Box 3.3) to that of the fibre will be chosen. This will facilitate the penetration of light into the fibre, allowing internal features to be observed. However, this approach means that surface details are often difficult to see. Such details are particularly important in the examination of hairs, all of which have scales on their outermost surface. Therefore, to allow images of these surface details to be obtained with a light microscope, **scale casts** are made prior to the preparation of any permanent mounts. To prepare one of these casts, the hair concerned, except for a small portion at its root end, is embedded in a thin layer of a suitable varnish (such as clear nail lacquer), which has been freshly painted onto a surface of a microscope slide. Once the varnish is dry, the hair is then held by the protruding end and pulled out, leaving a cast of the scale pattern in the varnish (Figure 3.2).

Scale cast
A cast made by embedding a hair in a suitable varnish and then retracting it once the varnish has dried, to show the pattern of scales on the surface of the hair.

Further information

Box 3.3

Refractive index, optical isotropy, optical anisotropy and birefringence

Light does not travel at the same speed in all media through which it can pass. It moves fastest in a vacuum, as it is slowed down by interactions between it and the matter that makes up all other transparent media. The refractive index of a medium (symbol n) is the ratio of the speed of light in a vacuum to the speed of light in that medium. Therefore the value of n is exactly 1 for a vacuum and more than 1 for all other transparent media (although it very nearly equals 1 for air). Note that for a given transparent material, the value of n is dependent on both its temperature and the wavelength of the light that is passing through it.

All gases (including air), all liquids (except liquid crystals), unstressed glasses and unstressed crystals of cubic symmetry show no directional dependence on their interaction with light that is transmitted through them. Each example of any of these classes of materials therefore has only one refractive index for any given temperature and wavelength of light. These materials are said to be optically isotropic and are described as exhibiting optical isotropy. All other transparent substances are said to be optically anisotropic and to exhibit optical anisotropy.

In the forensic context, silicate glass (Section 3.2) is the most frequently encountered class of optically isotropic materials. The refractive index of fragments of glass is routinely measured as it provides a valuable point of comparison between questioned samples and controls.

The refractive index of any anisotropic substance depends not only on its temperature and the wavelength of the light passing through it but also on both the light's direction of travel through the material and the light's direction of vibration (see Box 3.5 for a description of what is meant by vibration direction). Included among the optically anisotropic substances are the vast majority of man-made fibres and most of the minerals that are made

visible in soils by light microscopy. Both of these classes of material are commonly encountered in the forensic context, as discussed in Sections 3.1 and 3.3 respectively.

An important property of optically anisotropic materials is that they are doubly refracting. That is, a beam of plane-polarized light that is made to pass through such a material appears to be resolved into two component beams, both travelling in the same general direction but with mutually perpendicular directions of vibration. The properties of any given specimen of optically anisotropic material coupled with the direction in which the light is shone through it will dictate the relative speed of these two beams. In every anisotropic material, there is either one or two such directions in which the two beams travel at identical speeds to one another. These directions are called optic axes. Thus all doubly refracting media have either one or two such axes and are therefore referred to as being either uniaxial or biaxial respectively. In all directions other than that of an optic axis, the two beams travel at different speeds; that is, they experience different refractive indices. Birefringence is the name given to the numerical value of the difference between these two refractive indices; the maximum value of which is characteristic of the material concerned. This maximum is often referred to as *the* birefringence of the material. Once it has been determined, the birefringence of a material can be compared with typical values, such as those given for man-made fibres in Appendix 1, in order to help to establish the class of material being observed. Birefringence can also act as a point of comparison between questioned and control samples.

The birefringence, and a number of other useful optical properties, of fibres and minerals, is routinely established using polarized-light microscopy. The application of this technique to man-made fibres is expanded upon in Box 3.5.

(Photomicrograph by
Andrew Jackson,
Staffordshire
University, UK)

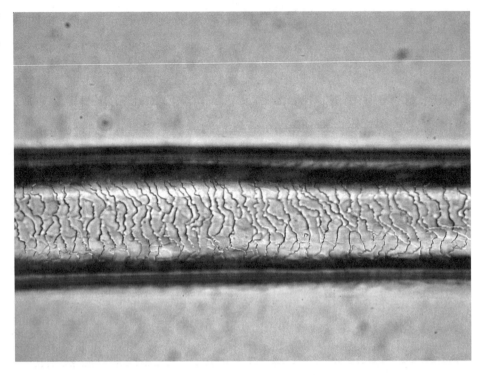

Figure 3.2 A scale cast obtained from the shaft of a human scalp hair

The procedures described in the preceding paragraph allow longitudinal images of fibres to be observed. Slides that enable transverse cross-sections to be inspected can be prepared by placing thin slices of the fibre concerned in a suitable mounting medium between a glass slide and cover slip. For some applications, the alternative view that is offered by these slides can be informative. For example, human beard hairs are frequently triangular in transverse cross-section, whereas human scalp hairs are rarely so. Also, some carpet fibres are seen to be characteristically trilobate (i.e. three lobed) in transverse cross-section.

During the forensic examination of fibres using light microscopy, their morphological features are described (see Box 3.4 for information on the morphology of hair), as are their optical properties (e.g. colour, any fluorescence under ultraviolet light and, as described in Boxes 3.3 and 3.5, birefringence). In order to ensure that these examinations are thorough, they are often carried out with the aid of protocol sheets that prompt the examiner to look for specific characteristics. Where appropriate, numerical parameters are used to quantify the observed attributes (such as thickness and birefringence). When considered together, the set of characteristic properties possessed by any one fibre, as revealed by light microscopy, is usually sufficient to allow its type to be identified. For example, polyester fibres are readily distinguished from acrylic ones (Box 3.5). Moreover, the set of characteristics exhibited by one fibre (e.g. a questioned fibre) can be compared with those observed in another (e.g. a control fibre) to see whether they match.

Further information

Box 3.4

The forensic study of the shape (i.e. morphology) of hair

A hair is a fibre that grows out of a hair follicle in the skin of a mammal. At one end of any one hair is its root. Unless the hair has been pulled out, this is found within the skin. At the other end is the hair's tip. The hair shaft is the main portion of the hair that lies between the root and the tip.

A longitudinal view of a mature hair shaft, as seen using a light microscope (see figure (a) overleaf), shows it to contain up to three main morphological features, namely:

■ the cuticle (the outer layer of the hair shaft, made up of tough, flattened cells called scale cells);

■ the cortex (made up of spindle-shaped (i.e. fusiform) cortical cells, which are cemented together);

■ the medulla (made up of collapsed cells, and intercellular and intracellular air-filled voids).

The first two of these features are present in all cases but the medulla may be absent.

The morphological study of hair has revealed a number of forensically valuable observations, in particular those listed below.

■ There are species-to-species variations in the structural detail observable within hair. This means that it may well be possible to identify from which species a given sample of hair originated on the basis of its morphology alone. Forensically, a fundamental distinction of this type is that between human and non-human hair. In order to make this distinction, the examiner can make use of the following observations:

 – The colour of a human hair typically shows relatively little variation along the length of the shaft, whereas that of a non-human will often show dramatic changes in colour and/or banding.

 – The width of the medulla (where present) divided by the width of the shaft (a parameter known as the medullary index) is typically less than 1/3 in human hair and greater than 1/3 in non-human hair.

 – The appearance of the medulla (where present) is different in human and non-human hairs. In the former, it is typically not continuous and shows little structure when observed using light microscopy, whereas in the latter it typically has a well-defined structure (e.g. like a ladder), is continuous but varies in its appearance along the length of the shaft.

 – Where seen, the pigment granules in human hair (which are nearly all in the cortex) tend to be evenly distributed across the width of the shaft – with a slightly greater density towards the cuticle. In non-human hair, the pigment is typically either centrally located or has a greater granule density towards the medulla.

 – The scale pattern of human hair typically does not vary greatly along the length of the shaft (although the level of damage to the scale margins may well increase from the root end to the tip). In contrast, the scale pattern of non-human hairs often varies significantly from hair root to tip.

■ It is often possible to use morphology to deduce from which part of the body a given human hair originated (e.g. scalp hair is morphologically distinguishable from pubic hair).

■ Human hair morphology carries indications of racial type. For example, the scalp hairs of Negroid peoples typically have a more flattened shape in transverse cross-section compared with the scalp hairs of Mongoloid peoples.

■ The root of a human scalp hair that was pulled out while the hair was actively growing (i.e. in the anagen phase of the growth cycle) is characteristically flame-shaped (see figure (b) overleaf) or broken, and may have follicular material attached to it. In contrast, a human scalp hair that was detached from the skin after the hair had ceased growing (i.e. it was in the telogen phase of the growth cycle when it was removed) has a root with a characteristic club-like appearance (see figure (c) overleaf). Hair in the anagen phase is much harder to pull out of the scalp than that in the telogen phase. Hence, the presence of an anagen phase root is symptomatic of a hair that has

▶

Box 3.4 *continued*

been pulled out with a significant amount of force. (Note that there is a phase in the growth cycle of human scalp hair between those of anagen and telogen. This is called the catagen phase, in which growth is slowing down. Catagen hairs are relatively rare and their roots, when pulled out, are typically club-shaped and often have follicular material attached.)

■ Morphology can reveal differences between hairs taken from the same body location on different individual humans. For example, the scalp hairs of one person might be significantly thicker than those of another. Unfortunately, there is also considerable variation in the morphological characteristics of the hairs of any one individual. To give an extreme but common example, people with grey hair actually have a mixture of colourless (or nearly colourless) hairs and coloured ones. This has implications for both the collection of

control hairs for forensic purposes and the interpretation of evidence based on morphological comparisons. It also means that, in order to maximise the possibility of resolution between individuals, a wide range of morphological features should be observed and described in each hair examined. The main morphological points of comparison used to evaluate associative evidence based on human hair include:

- the colour, length, waviness and diameter of each individual hair;
- the size, shape, density and distribution of observable pigment granules in each hair shaft;
- cosmetic alteration of each hair;
- damage to each hair, including any caused by disease or dietary deficiency;
- the presence or absence of nits or fungal infection;
- the shape of the cross-section of the hair shaft.

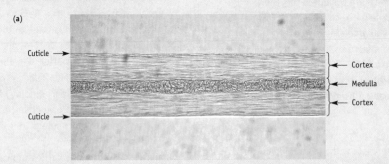

(a)

Cuticle →

Cuticle →

← Cortex
← Medulla
← Cortex

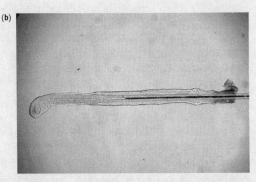

(b)

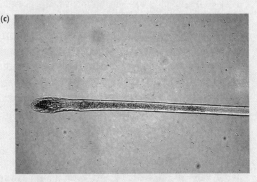

(c)

(a) A longitudinal view of a portion of the shaft of a human mature scalp hair (87 μm wide)

(b) A longitudinal view of the root of a human scalp hair in the anagen phase of the growth cycle (note that the shaft is approximately 75 μm wide) (c) A longitudinal view of the root of a human scalp hair in the telogen phase of the growth cycle (note that the shaft is approximately 75 μm wide)

(Photomicrographs by Andrew Jackson, Staffordshire University, UK)

Box 3.4 continued

Note that the morphological comparison of questioned and control samples of human hair will only very rarely enable the examiner to identify the individual who provided the questioned sample as being the same person who supplied the control sample. In other words, with very few exceptions, hair morphology is not capable of individualisation. However, it may well enable the examiner to conclude that either two hair samples are sufficiently similar to have originated from the same person or that they are significantly different and therefore did *not* come for the same individual. In either case, this can be highly valuable information.

Forensic techniques

Box 3.5

Observations of man-made fibres using polarized-light microscopy

Natural and plane-polarized light

In order to appreciate the value of polarized-light microscopy, it is first necessary to understand the difference between natural and plane-polarized light. To do this, it is best to picture light as being made up of waves. By way of an analogy, consider a rope that is held taut between an eyebolt in a wall and someone's hand. Each wave of light has some similarity with the travelling wave that can be produced in that rope when the hand is moved up and down or side to side, or indeed in any other imaginable direction that is across the direction of travel of the wave along the rope. The direction in which the hand is moved is called the vibration direction. In this analogy, natural light would be represented if waves with very many vibration directions were created and superimposed. If the rope were made to pass through a gap in closely spaced railings made up of vertical bars, then only waves with a vertical vibration direction would be propagated beyond the railings concerned, as all other waves would crash into the bars. Consequently, on the far side of the railings, only light with a vibration direction in the vertical plane would exist. This is analogous to plane-polarized light as this too has only one vibration direction plane. Polaroid is a commercially available plastic sheet material that only allows light with one vibration direction plane to pass through it. That is, if natural light is shone upon one side of it, plane-polarized light emerges from the other side. In the analogy discussed above, a sheet of Polaroid does to light what the railings did to the waves passing down the rope.

Polarized-light microscopes

The defining characteristic of polarized-light microscopes is that each contains both a polarizer and an analyser. Each of these is a device, usually a sheet of Polaroid, that will produce plane-polarized light when it is illuminated with natural light. There are polarized-light microscopes that can be used to view specimens in reflected light; however, it is normal to observe fibres in transmitted light (i.e. light that is passed through the specimen). The description given here is that of the essential features of a polarized-light microscope designed to be used with transmitted light. As shown in Plate 1, in such microscopes the polarizer and analyser are situated below and above the stage on which the specimen is placed, respectively. This means that the specimen is illuminated in plane-polarized light.

As illustrated in Plate 2, the top of the image seen when looking down the microscope is labelled as north. Similarly, the bottom is labelled south, the right-hand side east and the left-hand side west. It is possible to rotate the polarizer so that the vibration direction of the plane-polarized light that it produces is between any two opposite points of the compass. However, it is conventional to position the polarizer such that the light that shines on the specimen vibrates in the east–west direction.

The normal orientation of the analyser is such that it will only allow light to pass through it that is vibrating north–south. The analyser can be moved in or out of the light path. When it is out of this path, the sample is being

▶

Box 3.5 *continued*

observed in plane-polarized light. In contrast, when it is in this path and the polarizer and analyser are in their conventional orientations, the specimen is said to be viewed under crossed polars.

Other important characteristics of polarized-light microscopes are that:

■ the stage can rotate freely in the plane that is perpendicular to the path taken by the light that is made to travel through the specimen;

■ there is an accessory plate slot between the polarizer and the analyser (see Plate 1).

The optical properties of man-made fibres

The vast majority of man-made fibres are optically anisotropic (see Box 3.3); these are uniaxial, with the optic axis running down the length of the fibre. As expected, an optically anisotropic fibre will apparently split light that passes through it in any direction other than along its optic axis into two plane-polarized beams travelling at different speeds. As the refractive index (see Box 3.3) experienced by a beam of light is inversely proportional to its speed, the slow beam experiences a higher refractive index than the fast one. The difference between the speeds of the beams is maximal, as is the difference between the refractive indices that the beams experience, when the light that passes through the fibre does so at right-angles to the fibre's optic axis. The birefringence value (Γ) of the fibre is the maximum absolute value of the numerical difference between the two refractive indices, thus:

$$\Gamma = |n_{\parallel} - n_{\perp}|$$

In which, respectively, the subscripts $_{\parallel}$ and $_{\perp}$ represent the beam that vibrates parallel to the fibre's optic axis and the other that vibrates perpendicular to this axis.

For most types of fibres $n_{\parallel} > n_{\perp}$, but for some (e.g. those made of acrylic) $n_{\parallel} < n_{\perp}$. Those fibres with $n_{\parallel} > n_{\perp}$ are said to have a positive sign of elongation, whereas those in which $n_{\parallel} < n_{\perp}$ have a negative sign of elongation.

The optical path difference and polarization colours

As described in Box 3.3, each optically anisotropic object appears to split light that is shone through it into two plane-polarized beams, which travel in essentially the same direction as each other. Unless travelling along the direc-

tion of an optic axis, these beams travel at different speeds through the object concerned. This means that the front of one draws ahead of the front of the other. When the beams emerge from the anisotropic material into an optically isotropic material (such as air, unstressed glass or the mounting medium used to make the microscope slide), unless they enter another optically anisotropic object, the distance between these fronts does not alter. This distance is called the optical path difference (OPD). An optically anisotropic object that is observed under crossed polars will appear to be black in specific orientations to the incoming plane-polarized light. These are when the incoming light travels along an optic axis or when the vibration direction of the incoming light is coincidental with the vibration direction of one of the two beams. In all other orientations, the object will appear to be brighter than the background and, in many instances, highly coloured.

To understand the origin of these colours, it is necessary to appreciate that white light is made up of all of the colours of light's spectrum (that is, the colours of the rainbow). Each wavelength of light has its own colour, for example light with a wavelength (λ) of 410 nm is violet, whereas that with $\lambda = 710$ nm is red. If light with specific wavelengths is removed from white light, the remaining mixture of wavelengths is perceived by the eye as being a particular colour.

The colours that are seen when an optically anisotropic object is viewed under crossed polars are called polarisation colours (also known by the more general term interference colours). These occur because, depending on the OPD, interactions in the analyser remove, to varying extents, light of specific wavelengths from the white light that illuminated the specimen. What is left is light of a mixture of wavelengths, which is seen as a specific colour.

Therefore when a colourless specimen is illuminated in white light and viewed under crossed polars, the exact polarisation colour seen will be determined by the OPD of the specimen. This, in turn, is dependent on the thickness of the specimen (t) and its birefringence (Γ), thus:

$$OPD = t \times \Gamma \qquad \text{Eq 1}$$

Consider an object of constant birefringence, e.g. a piece of quartz, that has been cut to form a wedge such that the vibration directions of its two beams are parallel and

Box 3.5 continued

perpendicular to the direction in which the wedge alters in thickness. The OPD produced by this object will start at zero when its thickness = 0 and will increase as it becomes progressively thicker, such that at all locations its OPD accords with Equation 1 given above. Therefore, if this object is viewed in crossed polars, all of the polarisation colours up to that of the maximum OPD produced by the wedge will be seen. This is shown in Plate 3.

Determining the birefringence and sign of elongation of a man-made fibre

Plate 2 shows a dye-free (i.e. colourless) man-made fibre viewed in crossed polars. It is a cylindrical fibre and so its width (w) equals the thickness (t) that is experienced by light travelling through the centre of the fibre, as shown in the following diagram:

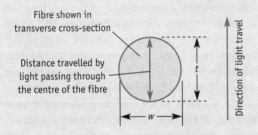

The width can be determined using, for example, a calibrated scale in the eyepiece of the microscope. In order to find the birefringence (Γ), Equation 1 is rearranged to give:

$$\Gamma = \frac{OPD}{t} \qquad \text{Eq 2}$$

As t can be found readily, all that is required is the value of the OPD, which should be available from the colour in the centre of the fibre. Plate 4 shows how the polarisation colours change with increasing OPD. Noting that the centre of the fibre is blue, all that should be required is to look along Plate 4 from left to right until the colour blue is found and then read the OPD that corresponds to this colour from the scale at the bottom. However, there is a problem: there are two blue colours on Plate 4, one with an OPD of 580 nm and the other with an OPD of 1150 nm.

Fortunately, there is a solution to this difficulty. Consider what happens if a second optically anisotropic material, known as an accessory plate, is placed into the light path between the polarizer and the analyser, such that the vibration directions of its two beams are coincidental with those of the fibre. There are two possible outcomes:

■ the OPD of the accessory plate will add to that of the fibre and the polarisation colour on Plate 4 that corresponds to that seen when looking down the microscope will be further to the right than before; or

■ the OPD of the accessory plate will subtract from that of the fibre and the polarisation colour on Plate 4 that corresponds to that seen when looking down the microscope will be further to the left than before.

The first of these, which will be referred to here as an addition, will occur if the vibration direction of the slow beam in the accessory plate is coincidental with that of the slow beam in the fibre. The second (i.e. subtraction) will happen if the vibration direction of the slow beam in the accessory plate is coincidental with that of the fast beam in the fibre.

If a subtraction occurs such that the OPD of the accessory plate is exactly the same as that of the fibre, then the total OPD will be zero and, in accordance with Plate 4, the centre of the fibre will be black. So, one approach would be to have a series of accessory plates made, all identical except that each would have a different but known OPD. One of these would be placed in the accessory plate slot of the microscope and its stage would be rotated to the position in which subtraction was seen to occur. Then each plate would be tested in turn until the centre of the fibre went black. The OPD of the fibre would then be known, as it would be the same as that of this plate.

However, an alternative, and more convenient, method would be to insert a wedge of the type described previously into the accessory plate slot, with the stage rotated to the subtraction position as described above. This wedge will be wider than the fibre, so that it can be seen either side of the fibre. If the wedge is pushed into the field of view, the polarisation colours outside the fibre will be those of the wedge alone and will move

▶

Box 3.5 continued

progressively to the right as shown on Plate 4. At the same time, because the OPD of the plate is subtracting from that of the fibre, the polarisation colours in the fibre will move progressively to the left, as shown on Plate 4. The colour in the centre of the fibre will go black (called compensation black) once the point has been reached where the polarisation colour of the wedge when viewed alone is the same as that of the centre of the fibre in the absence of the wedge. This situation is shown in Plate 5. In the case of the fibre shown in Plate 5, in order to achieve the position shown, the wedge had to be pushed in until the second blue produced by the wedge alone was seen. This is now known to be the polarisation colour of the centre of the fibre in the absence of the wedge. From Plate 4, it can be seen that this equates to an OPD of 1150 nm. Notice that the scale on Plate 4 is divided into what are called orders. Each colour on Plate 4 is known by its name and the order in which it appears. As the second blue appears in the third order, it is called third-order blue. The width of the fibre is 19.6 μm. As this is a cylindrical fibre, its width equals the thickness (t) of its centre, in nanometres (nm). This equals 19.6 × 1000 = 19 600 nm. These figures for OPD and t can be used in Equation (b) to find the birefringence of the fibre (note that it is crucially important that OPD and t are in the same units before this is done):

$$\Gamma = \frac{OPD}{t} = \frac{1150 \text{ nm}}{19\,600 \text{ nm}} = 0.059$$

From tables such as that provided in Appendix 1, it can be seen that this value is consistent with the fibre being made of nylon 6.6, which in fact it is.

This process has also provided the information necessary to establish the fibre's sign of elongation. This is possible because, as indicated in Plate 5, the vibration direction of the wedge's slow beam is known (it is marked on the wedge by the manufacturer). In this case, it is perpendicular to the direction in which the wedge becomes thicker, and as indicated in Plate 5, it runs northeast–southwest. As subtraction has occurred, it is known that the vibration direction of the wedge's slow

beam is coincidental with that of the fibre's fast beam. The fibre's fast beam is therefore vibrating at right-angles to the fibre's optic axis. As the fast beam is the one that experiences the lower refractive index, in this case this must be $n_\perp$ and so it is known that $n_\parallel > n_\perp$, which is a positive sign of elongation (as expected for nylon).

There are a number of other means by which the sign of elongation of a birefringent fibre may be established. These include the use of a first-order red tint plate, as discussed below. It is commonly the case, however, that the sign of elongation of the fibre will not have been established before the quartz wedge is placed into the accessory plate slot. Under these circumstances, it is not possible to tell whether the fibre should be aligned northwest–southeast or northeast–southwest in order for subtraction to occur. However, this is not a problem. If the fibre is aligned northwest–southeast and the quartz wedge is inserted in the accessory plate slot, then the polarisation colours in the centre of the fibre will be seen to move either to the right or to the left on Plate 4. If they move to the left, then subtraction is occurring. However, if they move to the right (i.e. the colours become progressively higher in their order) as the thickness of the quartz wedge increases, then addition is happening. If the latter is observed, then the wedge is removed from the microscope and the stage is then rotated through 90 degrees, so that the fibre now runs northeast–southwest. When the wedge is now reinserted in the accessory plate slot, subtraction will be observed.

In addition to the quartz wedge, there are other accessory plates that are of value. Included in these is the first-order red tint plate. This is a piece of optically anisotropic material (e.g. gypsum) that is cut such that it is of uniform thickness and has a OPD that is near to 550 nm and is either known (e.g. 530 nm) or assumed to be 550 nm. The vibration directions of its slow and fast beams are known and marked on the plate by the manufacturer. This type of plate is particularly useful in estimating the OPD of fibres with first-order grey polarisation colours. Plates 6, 7 and 8 show such a fibre. In Plate 6, it is shown as it appears under crossed polars. In

Box 3.5 *continued*

Plate 7, a first-order red tint plate has been placed into the accessory plate slot. The fibre and plate together are second-order turquoise in colour and from Plate 4 this can be seen to be due to a total OPD of approximately 650 nm. Plate 8 is the same as Plate 7, except that the stage has been rotated by 90 degrees. Now the polarisation colour is first-order orange, which from Plate 4 can be seen to be the result of a total OPD of approximately 410 nm. The image in Plate 7 has occurred because the OPD of the first-order red tint plate (530 nm in this case) has added to that of the fibre. Hence, the fibre's OPD is 650 − 530 = 120 nm. In contrast, the image in Plate 8 shows a polarisation colour that is due to the OPD of the fibre subtracting from that of the plate (530 − 120 = 410 nm). This has confirmed that the estimated OPD of 120 nm derived from the observed colour seen in Plate 7 is a reasonable number. From this and the knowledge that this cylindrical fibre is 30 600 nm (i.e. 30.6 μm × 1000) wide, the birefringence can be estimated as:

$$\Gamma = \frac{OPD}{t} = \frac{120 \text{ nm}}{30\,600 \text{ nm}} = 0.0039 \qquad \text{Eq 3}$$

Note that the sign of elongation of this fibre can be deduced from the information provided by either of Plates 7 or 8. Using Plate 7 to show how this can be done, note that the direction of vibration of the slow beam of the first-order red tint plate is northeast–southwest. Addition has occurred to create the colour seen in the fibre in Plate 7. Therefore, the direction of vibration of the slow beam of the fibre must also be northeast–southwest. As the optic axis of the fibre runs northwest–southeast, the slow beam is the one that moves under the influence of $n_\perp$ (i.e. not $n_\parallel$). As the slow beam experiences the higher refractive index, $n_\parallel < n_\perp$, which is a negative sign of elongation.

This, coupled with a comparison between the data given in Appendix 1 and the estimate of the birefringence given by Equation 3, suggests that this fibre is acrylic. This indeed is the case.

As can be seen from the descriptions provided above, both the quartz wedge and the first-order red tint plate provide means by which man-made fibres can be rapidly characterised. Furthermore, in many instances, the information that is provided by these means can lead to the identification of the polymer type from which the fibre has been made. For these reasons, these devices are in common use in the forensic examination of man-made fibres. However, they do have limitations. Quartz wedges produce their best results with undamaged cylindrical fibres, the centres of which exhibit polarisation colours somewhere between and including first-order yellow and third-order red. Arguably, first-order red tint plates are most useful for colourless, undamaged cylindrical man-made fibres that exhibit first-order polarisation colours in their centres.

Note also that there are more accurate ways of establishing the OPD than those described above (including the use of tilting compensators or Senarmont compensators) and the estimation of the thickness of non-cylindrical fibres is more challenging than that of the cylindrical fibres described above. However, these topics are beyond the scope of this book.

Furthermore, although birefringence measurements and sign of elongation determinations are frequently carried out for man-made fibres, they are rarely determined for natural fibres. This is despite the fact that natural fibres are optically anisotropic. The reason for this is that other features of natural fibres (such as their morphologies) are more discriminating than are birefringence and sign of elongation.

For further information on polarized-light microscopy the interested reader is referred to the references below.

Further reading

Gaudette, B.D. (1988) 'The forensic aspects of textile fiber examination' in Saferstein, R. (ed.) *Forensic science handbook*, Vol. II. Upper Saddle River, NJ: Prentice Hall, pp. 209–72.

Palenik, S. J. (1999) 'Microscopical examination of fibres' in Robertson, J. and Grieve, M. (eds) *Forensic examination of fibres*, 2nd edn. London: Taylor & Francis, pp. 153–77.

Robinson, P. C. and Bradbury, S. (1992) *Qualitative polarized-light microscopy*. Oxford: Oxford University Press and the Royal Microscopical Society.

The direct comparison, in the same field of view, of two fibres can provide the examiner with an extremely powerful aid in the confirmation or refutation of a match between the fibres concerned. This is facilitated by the use of a comparison microscope. As can be seen from Figure 3.3, instruments of this type have two identical stages on which the slides of the two fibres can be placed and may have both visible and ultraviolet light sources. Crucially, they have carefully balanced optics, enabling both fibres to be viewed under identical conditions.

An electromagnetic spectrum of an object is an expression of the intensity of the absorption or emission of electromagnetic radiation by that object as a function of the energy or frequency of that radiation. A range of microspectrometers can be used to obtain a variety of electromagnetic spectra from single fibres. Using these, it is now possible to obtain ultraviolet, visible, Raman and infrared spectra that not only provide additional points of comparison between questioned and control fibres but may also yield information about the chemical composition of the fibres and/or any dyes or pigments present. Such spectroscopic techniques can be particularly useful in the examination of man-made fibres. A description of ultraviolet and visible spectroscopy is given in Box 3.6, while infrared and Raman spectroscopies are described in Box 3.9 later in the chapter.

There are a number of other techniques that can be used to further characterise fibres and to produce additional points of comparison. Among these are the following:

- Dye extraction from questioned and control fibres, followed by thin-layer chromatography (Chapter 11, Box 11.5).

- Microchemical tests that can be carried out on the dyes and/or pigments of small sections of fibre that have been placed on microscope slides beneath cover slips. Under these circumstances, the fibre sections can be exposed to liquid reagents (such as bleach (sodium hypochlorite solution) or concentrated sulphuric acid) by placing a small drop of the reagent concerned on an edge of the cover slip. Capillary action will then draw the reagent under the cover slip and around the fibre. Any observable colour changes can then be viewed with a compound light microscope and used as points of comparison.

- Scanning electron microscopy (SEM), which is particularly good at providing details of surface morphology (Chapter 9, Box 9.6).

- Melting point determination, which is applicable to many man-made fibres.

- Pyrolysis-gas chromatography (Chapter 11, Box 11.5) of man-made fibres.

- The ashing of natural fibres followed by microscopic examination of the residues.

While the presence of matches between fibres obtained from different sources (e.g. a suspect and a crime scene) can provide valuable associative evidence, the interpretation of the significance of such evidence must be carried out with great care. This is because due regard has to be paid to such issues as the rate of transfer of fibre evidence, the persistence of fibres on garments and other items, the potential for secondary and even tertiary transfer, and the frequency of different fibre types in the environment.

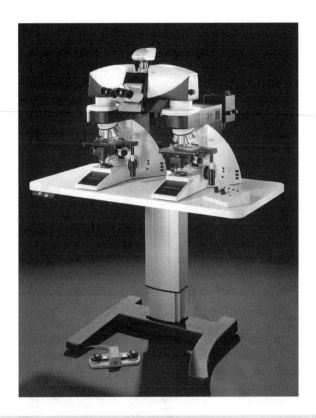

(Leica Microsystems (UK) Ltd)

Figure 3.3 The FS4000 comparison microscope

Forensic techniques

Box 3.6

Ultraviolet–visible spectroscopy and microspectrophotometry

The study of how electromagnetic radiation interacts with matter is called spectroscopy. This study reveals that the energy states that molecules, atoms or ions can possess are quantised. That is, while a given atom, ion or molecule in a given chemical environment can exist in any one of an infinite number of energy states, it cannot reside in an energy state that is intermediate between two adjacent states. To illustrate this with an approximate analogy, a ball bouncing down a flight of stairs can alight on any one of the treads, each one being analogous to an energy state. However, it cannot come to rest at a point in space between two treads.

A molecule, atom or ion can absorb energy from incident electromagnetic radiation if Bohr's frequency condition is satisfied:

$$\Delta E = h\nu \qquad \text{Eq 1}$$

where h is Plank's constant, ν is the frequency of the incident radiation and ΔE is the difference in energy between two quantised energy states E and E' (higher energy), i.e.

$$\Delta E = E' - E$$

The molecule, atom or ion can be excited from E to E' by absorbing radiation and then revert from E' to E by

Box 3.6 *continued*

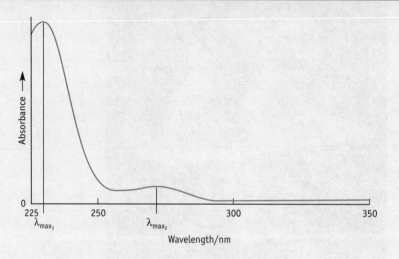

The aqueous ultraviolet absorption spectrum of cocaine hydrochloride
(Spectrum recorded by Andrew Jackson, Staffordshire University, UK)

emitting radiation. The frequency of the radiation concerned is determined by Equation 1 and, when travelling in a vacuum, its wavelength (λ) is given by:

$$\lambda = \frac{c}{\nu} \qquad \text{Eq 2}$$

where c is the speed of light in a vacuum, which to three significant figures is $3.00 \times 10^8\,\text{m s}^{-1}$. Note that the speed of light (or other electromagnetic radiation) and its wavelength are both decreased when it passes through a material (e.g. air or glass), such that the ratio of the speed of light to its wavelength remains constant. The frequency of the radiation remains unaltered by the medium through which it travels. This means that Equation 2 will also yield the correct wavelength of radiation with a given frequency that is passing through a material, provided that the speed of light in that material is substituted for c. Note that the speed of light is little altered when it passes through air; consequently, to a very good approximation, Equation 2 holds true for electromagnetic radiation passing through air.

With rare exceptions, atoms, molecules and ions each contain electrons. In each case, these electrons reside in a defuse, yet ordered, cloud. This is located around the atomic nucleus or (in the case of a molecule) nuclei, in which the remainder of the matter of the atom, ion or molecule resides. Furthermore, these electrons are located in what are known as orbitals, each of which is capable of holding up to two electrons. If electromagnetic radiation of suitable frequency, ν, is absorbed by an atom, ion or molecule, this can excite it via the promotion of one of its electrons from the orbital in which it is found (of energy E) to one that is either unoccupied or partially occupied and that has an energy of E'. By undergoing this electronic transition, the energy of the atom, ion or molecule will increase by $E'-E$. As described earlier in this box, in order for this to occur, Bohr's frequency condition must be satisfied, i.e.

$$E' - E = \Delta E = h\nu$$

For such electronic transitions, the values of ν that satisfy this condition correspond to electromagnetic radiation in the ultraviolet–visible region of the spectrum. This region extends over the frequency range of approximately 3.85×10^{14} to 3.00×10^{15} Hz, that is radiation with wavelengths, when measured in air, in the approximate range 780 to 100 nm. Standard ultraviolet–visible spectrophotometers[1]

---

[1] Instruments that are designed to monitor light absorption by samples are called spectrophotometers.

Box 3.6 continued

that are used in the laboratory do not operate over exactly this range but from 190 to 900 nm.

Many molecules of forensic interest, including textile dyes and drugs, absorb in the ultraviolet–visible region and so show one or more typically broad absorption bands in their ultraviolet–visible spectra. For transparent materials, the spectrum of the sample under test can be obtained by using a scanning spectrometer that can plot the absorbance (defined by Equation 3, given below) of the sample as a function of wavelength. This spectrum provides class characteristics of the sample under study. As shown in the figure opposite, these include the value of the wavelength of maximum absorbance (λ_{max}) for each of its absorption bands.

In some cases, quantification of a known analyte that absorbs in the ultraviolet–visible region is conveniently achieved using spectrophotometric methods. In these methods, the absorbance (defined below) of a solution of the analyte, or a derivative of the analyte, is measured at one or more wavelengths and used to establish the concentration of the chemical species of interest. In the vast majority of cases, the Beer–Lambert law (defined below) is complied with when a solution of the analyte or its derivative is illuminated with monochromatic (i.e. single wavelength) radiation of an energy that is absorbed by the chemical species concerned. This law states that:

$A = kcb$

where:

■ A is the absorbance of the solution at the wavelength that is being used. Absorbance is defined by the following equation:

$$A = \log\left(\frac{I_0}{I}\right) \qquad \text{Eq 3}$$

in which I_0 is the intensity of the radiation before it has passed through the sample and I is the intensity of the radiation after it has passed through the sample;

■ k (a constant) is the absorptivity of the solution at the wavelength that is being used;

■ c is the concentration of the analyte or derivative under study; and

■ b is the distance that the radiation passes through the absorbing medium (b is called the path length).

Note that A has no units and the units of k are such that they will cancel out with those of c and b. Commonly used units for c and b are $g\,dm^{-3}$ and cm respectively; in which case, the units of k are $dm^3\,cm^{-1}\,g^{-1}$.

If a series of standard solutions, each containing a known but different concentration (c) of the analyte (or its derivative) is prepared and the value of A is determined for each of these then, according to the Beer–Lambert law, a plot of c (horizontal axis) against A will produce a straight line. If the value of A is then determined for the solution under test, the concentration of the analyte (or its derivative) within this solution can be determined by the interpolation of this calibration plot.

There are ultraviolet–visible spectrophotometric methods that are effective in the analysis of mixtures that contain more than one chemical species that absorb in this region of the spectrum. However, complex mixtures of such species will usually have to be separated, to produce samples of greater purity, prior to quantification by ultraviolet–visible spectrophotometry. In many cases, this separation can be achieved by high-performance liquid chromatography (HPLC) (Chapter 11, Box 11.5).

In many forensic applications, the samples of interest have microscopic dimensions. For example, a synthetic fibre will typically be thinner than 20 μm. Similarly, a paint chip that is made up of multiple coats of different paints will contain layers of microscopic thickness. Microspectrophotometers, which are microscopes combined with spectrophotometers, have been developed that can establish the ultraviolet–visible spectroscopic properties of such microscopic samples. Unsurprisingly, the use of these instruments is known as microspectrophotometry.

3.2 Glass

Glass is the name given to a class of hard, brittle materials that are manufactured by cooling melts consisting of silica (SiO_2) mixed with varying amounts of other oxides. These other oxides are most commonly those of sodium or potassium (or both), together with those of calcium, magnesium, aluminium and/or lead(II).

The most frequently encountered type of glass is soda-lime glass, which is used to produce windows and containers such as bottles and drinking glasses. It is made by fusing silica (in the form of sand) with sodium carbonate and either calcium carbonate or calcium oxide. More specialised glasses include pure fused silica and the heat-resistant borosilicate glasses (such as Pyrex) which are made with significant levels of boron oxide (B_2O_3). Lead(II) oxide is included in the formulation used to make decorative 'lead crystal' tableware as it gives glass attractive optical properties. All glasses also contain low levels of other elements owing to impurities introduced in the raw materials. Many also contain trace constituents that have been deliberately added, for example to impart colour, and/or that have contaminated the glass during manufacture or use.

Toughened glass
Glass that has been heat-treated to introduce internal stresses within its fabric.

Toughened glass (also called tempered glass) is that which has been heat treated to introduce internal stresses within its fabric. Such glass is used for the side and rear windows of cars. When broken, it does not tend to produce sharp shards but, instead, forms cuboid fragments. **Laminated glass**, used for windscreens and 'bullet proof' glass, is made by sandwiching plastic film between sheets of ordinary glass. This material is much less likely to shatter completely when struck compared with glass without the integral plastic.

Laminated glass
Glass made by sandwiching plastic film between sheets of ordinary glass.

The breakage of glass frequently occurs during the commission of crimes, particularly those of theft from and of vehicles, burglary and crimes against the person. The types of glass involved are typically those used to make windows (including the side and rear windows of cars), containers and the windscreens and headlamps of cars. Both the patterns of fragmentation and the glass fragments themselves are valuable sources of evidence.

3.2.1 Information from patterns of glass fragmentation

There are a number of scenarios in which it is of considerable evidential value to know from which side a particular sheet of glass was broken. For example, if a shot was fired through the window of a house, it might be of great importance to know whether the person firing the shot was standing inside or outside the house at the time. If the damage is due to a small, fast-moving object (such as a flying stone or, as in this case, a bullet), then the direction in which the projectile was travelling at the time of impact can be readily established. This is possible because such damage is characterised by a crater-shaped hole in the vicinity of the impact that is narrowest on the impact side of the glass.

However, not all breakages result in the formation of these symmetrical crater-shaped holes. Indeed, as the velocity of the projectile decreases, the shape of the hole tends to become less regular and is ultimately no longer useful in establishing the side of impact.

Fortunately, in the case of non-toughened glass, it is frequently possible to decipher the direction of impact, even in the absence of such crater-shaped holes. In order to appreciate how this can be done, it is necessary to understand the sequence of events that happens when a sheet of non-toughened glass is broken by an impact. During this process, the glass first bends. This bending action causes the glass on the side of the sheet opposite to that of the impact (i.e. the far side) to stretch and then to break. This produces a series of cracks, called radial fractures, to radiate across the sheet from the point of impact, thereby forming a number of V-shaped portions of glass. If the impact is sufficient to cause each of these portions of glass to bend far enough, the stretching effect that this induces on the near side of the glass will be enough to cause the glass to crack again. This time, however, the cracks occur across the V-shaped portions to produce ∇-shaped fragments. These secondary cracks – called concentric fractures – typically occur at approximately the same distance from the point of impact in each of the V-shaped portions and therefore form a rough circle about this point. If the impact causes sufficient distortion in the sheet of glass, then the point of impact will be encircled with another ring of concentric fractures, which is of larger diameter than the first.

The bending and subsequent fracture of a piece of glass frequently produce what are termed stress marks that are readily visible on its edge with the aid of low-power magnification. As can be seen from Figure 3.4, these take the form of nested, J-shaped curves. One end of each of these is approximately at right angles to one side of the glass, while the other end of the same curve is asymptotic with the other side of the glass. Importantly, the curves form a right angle to the side of the glass that was stretched during the bending process and in which the crack started. This means that the right angle appears on radial cracks on the side opposite to that where the impact occurred. For identical reasons, concentric fractures exhibit stress marks that form right angles with the side of the sheet of glass on which the blow impacted. It is therefore possible to tell from which side a window has been broken, provided that it is glazed with non-toughened glass and that sufficient glass remains in the frame in order to establish the identity of at least one radial crack or one concentric crack.

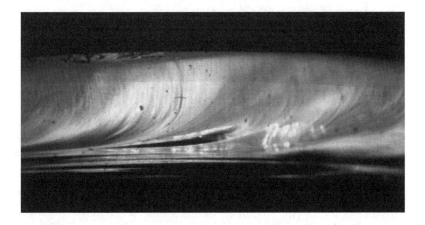

(Photomicrograph by Andrew Jackson, Staffordshire University, UK)

Figure 3.4 Stress marks on the edge of a fractured piece of glass
Note that the glass is 4 mm thick

If a sheet of glass is broken by two successive impacts but nonetheless remains intact, then it is often possible to deduce which impact occurred first. This is because those cracks produced by the second impact will terminate if they meet any of the fractures caused by the first impact. This termination will occur at the intersection of the fracture lines (Figure 3.5).

Finally, it is occasionally possible to fit together fragments of glass found at a scene with those in the possession of a suspect in much the same fashion as the pieces of a jigsaw puzzle. For example, such a fit may occur between shards of headlamp glass recovered from the scene of a hit-and-run road traffic accident and those that remain in the front of a car driven by the suspect. Such evidence is extremely strong as it is believed that no two pieces of glass will shatter in exactly the same fashion.

(Photograph by
Andrew Jackson,
Staffordshire
University, UK)

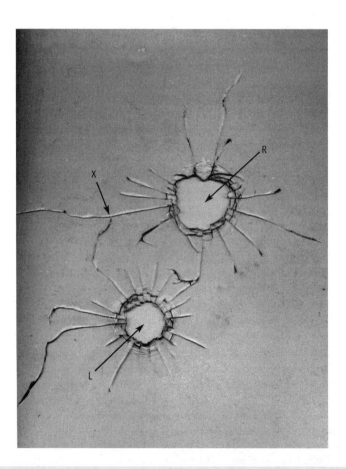

Figure 3.5 Fracture patterns produced by two successive impacts on the same sheet of glass
Note the termination of one of the cracks created by the impact on the left (L) on intersection with one of the cracks created by the impact on the right (R) (at point X). This clearly shows that impact R occurred before impact L. Note that the glass was not flexed between the time of impacts and the photograph being taken, thus ensuring that all cracks were due to the impacts

3.2.2 Information from glass fragments

If large fragments of glass are available, then features such as their colour, thickness and degree of curvature can be readily observed. These observations can provide both points of comparison between questioned and control samples and information that may lead to the classification of the glass and/or its intended use. For example, curved container glass may be distinguished from flat window glass.

When a piece of glass shatters, shards of it are distributed over a considerable area. This is particularly true of the smaller fragments. Clearly, someone breaking a windowpane with a blow from a heavy object will cause fragments to be propelled from the pane in the direction of the blow. However, tiny particles will also be ejected for up to three metres in the general direction from which the blow originated. It is almost inevitable that some of these back-scattered particles will become caught in the hair and/or clothing of the person breaking the pane. Indeed, somebody who smashed a window violently (e.g. with a hammer) would commonly have more than 400 particles of glass on their person immediately after the event. However, most of these fragments, which typically have sub-millimetre dimensions, are lost fairly rapidly. Inevitably, the rate of loss will depend on the activity of the person and the properties of the garments that the person is wearing. However, under normal circumstances, the majority will be lost within one hour of the incident and virtually all will have gone after 24 hours. It is noteworthy that a typical person will have at most two fragments of glass found on the entirety of their clothing (excluding pockets). Therefore, if more than two fragments obtained from a suspect's clothes are indistinguishable from a representative control sample taken from the broken pane of glass, this is likely to be considered as significant.

Tiny particles of glass may be collected from a suspect's hair (by combing) and/or his or her clothing. The latter is best achieved by a combination of hand searching and vigorously shaking the garment over a clean sheet of paper or purpose-designed sampling funnel. Typically, pockets will also be brushed out but little significance is usually attributable to any glass found in them. This is because glass fragments can lodge in pockets for protracted lengths of time which may well make it difficult to be certain whether the fragments concerned were present before the incident in question took place.

The particles obtained from the suspect can then be examined to reveal class characteristics that will help to identify the type of glass involved and that will provide points of comparison with control samples taken from the scene. **Refractive index** (Box 3.3) and density are two characteristics that are routinely determined. Both of these have the advantages that they are readily observed, discriminating and non-destructive.

The density of a questioned glass fragment (which typically will be about $2.5 \, \text{g cm}^{-3}$) can be established by placing it in a medium made of two miscible liquids of different densities. For example, tribromomethane ($CHBr_3$, density 2.89 g cm^{-3}, also called bromoform) and bromobenzene (C_6H_5Br, density $1.50 \, \text{g cm}^{-3}$) may be used for this purpose. The density of the medium is then adjusted by the addition of one or other of the liquids until the fragment remains suspended in the medium, neither rising nor falling. At this point, the density of the medium is identical to that of the glass fragment. After the questioned fragment has been removed and kept safe for further testing, a fragment of control glass can be

Refractive index
(of a medium)
The ratio of the speed of light in a vacuum to the speed of light in that medium. Symbol n.

added to the medium. If it floats or sinks then its density is not the same as that of the questioned fragment, thereby establishing that the two glasses do not have the same origin. Additionally, if a sample of the medium of known volume is weighed to find its mass, its density can be established (density = mass/volume), thereby establishing the density of the questioned glass. Note that the bromine-containing compounds referred to above are toxic. A relatively non-toxic polytungstate salt dissolved in water can be used as an alternative. Water can be added to this liquid to lower its density until it reaches that of the glass. After use, water can be evaporated from the solution, thereby increasing its density and making it ready for reuse.

The refractive index of a glass fragment is usually determined by immersing it in a thermally stable, transparent, colourless liquid that has a high boiling point – such as a silicone oil. The glass particle and the liquid that surrounds it are then illuminated with a monochromatic (i.e. single wavelength) light. The most commonly used light is sodium D radiation, which has a wavelength of 589 nm and is readily provided by a sodium lamp. The boundary between the fragment and the liquid is then observed through a microscope while they are slowly heated. As the temperature rises, the refractive index of the glass changes very little but that of the liquid drops at an appreciable rate. At a certain temperature, when the refractive indices of these two materials match, the boundary between them disappears. This event can be detected by eye or, in automated systems, electronically. The refractive index of the oil at the temperature of this event, and hence that of the glass, can then be found from a calibration graph prepared by conducting similar experiments using different reference glasses, each of known refractive index. Once established, the refractive indices of questioned and control fragments of glass can be compared. Any questioned fragments that do not have refractive indices that are sufficiently close to those of control fragments can then be eliminated as potential matches. Note that it is wise to compare the refractive indices of the questioned fragments with those of several control samples taken from the piece of glass that was broken at the crime scene. This is because there is a discernible variation in the refractive index of different fragments taken from the same piece of glass.

Refractive index measurements, when used in conjunction with the process of **annealing**, can also be used to readily distinguish between ordinary and toughened glass. To anneal a fragment of glass, it is heated to a high temperature for a prolonged period of time (typically 550 °C for between 1 and 24 hours) after which it is slowly cooled to room temperature. This process removes the stresses within the glass and is therefore accompanied by a change in its refractive index. As stress is deliberately introduced into toughened glass during its manufacture, a fragment of this type of material will undergo a significantly greater change in its refractive index on annealing than will ordinary glass.

Annealing (of glass) *The process whereby glass is heat-treated in order to remove the stresses within it.*

There are other tests and processes that can be employed to provide both further class characteristics of questioned glass fragments and additional points of comparison between these fragments and control samples. Prominent among these is the establishment of the elemental composition of the glass. This is often routinely carried out on questioned and control samples that are indistinguishable on the basis of their refractive indices. It can be achieved by a number of techniques, including energy dispersive X-ray analysis (EDX) coupled with scanning electron microscopy (SEM) (Chapter 9, Box 9.6).

3.3 Soils

Soils are those materials that are naturally developed at the interface between the Earth's crust and the atmosphere by the combined action of biological, chemical and physical processes. These materials are made up of naturally occurring mineral matter, organic matter, soil atmosphere and soil water, in various proportions. In the forensic context, a fifth component is usefully recognised, that of fragments of man-made materials such as concrete or brick.

Soils are of interest to the forensic scientist for a number of reasons. Under most moisture conditions, they are either friable or sticky. In either case, they are readily transferred from a scene to individuals and objects present at that scene and then possibly, by secondary transfer (Box 3.1), to other objects such as the inside of vehicles. Also, soil varies significantly from one location to the next and, at any one location, with depth. Note that a vertical section through a soil is called its **profile**. This normally consists of horizontal bands (termed soil horizons), each of which has different characteristics from its neighbours. There are many tests that can be used to provide class characteristics of a soil and thereby reveal this variation. Furthermore, many soils exhibit plastic properties over a wide range of moisture contents and may therefore retain the impression of objects pressed into them, such as footwear and tyres (Chapter 4, Sections 4.2 and 4.5 respectively).

The tests referred to in the previous paragraph reveal class characteristics that may be used to corroborate or refute other evidence. For example, the presence of soil on the seat of a suspect's trousers that matches soil found at a crime scene may be found to be consistent with an eyewitness account of the commission of the crime. Furthermore, the evidence of an association between the suspect's trousers and the scene would be even stronger if an imprint was found in the soil at the scene of textile fabric that matched that of the trousers.

The choice of tests employed in the characterisation of given samples of soil will depend on the circumstances of each individual case. However, these tests would normally include colour comparisons. When doing this, the samples to be compared must be viewed under identical conditions. In particular, it must be remembered that soils change colour with their moisture contents. Consequently, the samples should be dried (or moistened) to the same degree prior to comparison. Questioned samples are often presented to the laboratory in the form of smears, for example on a garment, for comparison with much larger control samples taken from the scene. Under these circumstances, a good colour comparison may be achieved if the scientist smears the control sample onto a clean portion of the same garment prior to examination.

Other tests that may usefully be carried out include:

- ■ *low-power light microscopy*, which may reveal features of **soil structure** and the presence of unusual materials, whether manufactured or of plant or animal origin;

- ■ *high-power polarized-light microscopy* to determine the identity of observable minerals (Box 3.3 gives further information on the optical properties of minerals), fragments of rock and possibly soil microstructure;

- ■ *establishment of the particle size distribution of the soil* by passing it through a stack of nested sieves of decreasing mesh size and quantifying each of the fractions so produced;

Soil profile
A vertical section through a soil showing the different horizons from the surface to underlying parent material.

Soil structure
The arrangement of voids, individual soil particles and aggregates of these particles within a soil.

■ *X-ray powder diffraction* to identify the crystalline phases present (Box 3.10);

■ *differential thermal analysis* (Box 3.7).

One of the main challenges in the interpretation of the significance of soil evidence is the difficulty in assessing the degree of natural variation in soil characteristics, both within a given location and between different locations. With this in mind, due regard must be given to the collection of control samples. In particular, multiple samples should be taken from and around the incident scene and any possible alibi locations. As soils vary in their characteristics with depth, care needs to be exercised to ensure that control samples are taken from each part of the profile that may have produced the questioned sample.

In addition, the interpretation of soil evidence that involves matching points of comparison between a questioned sample and a control sample should take into account the number of points used and the discriminating power of these points. In the main, as with any trace evidence, the confidence that the examiner has that the two samples may have a common source increases with the number of points of comparison that have been established *and* that produce a match between the samples. It should be noted that, with the current state of knowledge of soil distribution characteristics, it is only under very unusual circumstances that an examiner will be able to unequivocally individualise a given questioned soil to a particular location.

As well as providing associative evidence, soils can, under certain circumstances, provide investigative leads. In particular, the identification of the type of soil found on an object or a person may be useful in locating the area in which the object or person came into contact with that soil. Under these circumstances, maps that show the distribution of soil and/or rock types can be consulted to narrow down the search area.

3.4 Vegetable matter

There are a number of ways in which an individual and/or his or her belongings can become contaminated with traces of vegetable matter. These include:

■ the inadvertent collection of soil that contains decaying vegetable matter;

■ the collection of plant fragments (e.g. leaves, petals, stems and/or pollen) while moving through a vegetated area and/or as a consequence of deliberately damaging plants;

■ the drilling, cutting or breaking of wood or wood products (as might occur during breaking-and-entry).

The microscopic examination of such fragments of vegetation can reveal class characteristics, which may allow the plant to be identified, often to species level. Pollen and spores, with their immense diversity of shape and intricate surface ornamentation, are particularly useful in this respect.

Information from vegetation might be of value in providing investigative leads. For example, fragments of vegetation found on the body of a murder victim might

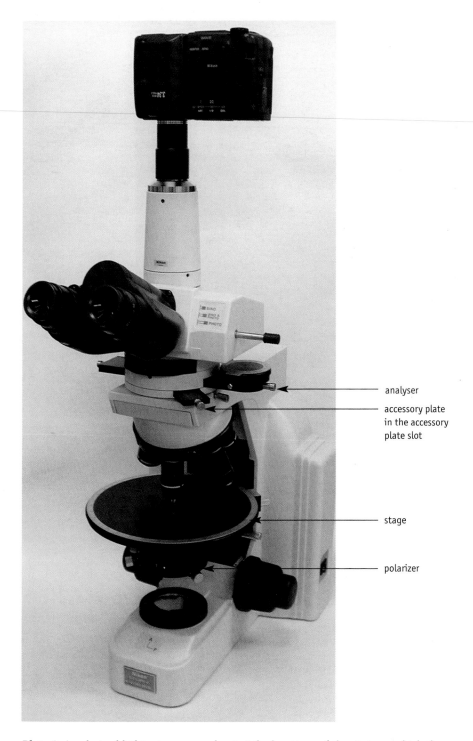

analyser

accessory plate
in the accessory
plate slot

stage

polarizer

Plate 1 A polarized-light microscope, showing the locations of the stage on which the specimen is placed, the polarizer, the analyser and the accessory plate slot. *Photograph by Andrew Jackson, Staffordshire University, UK.*

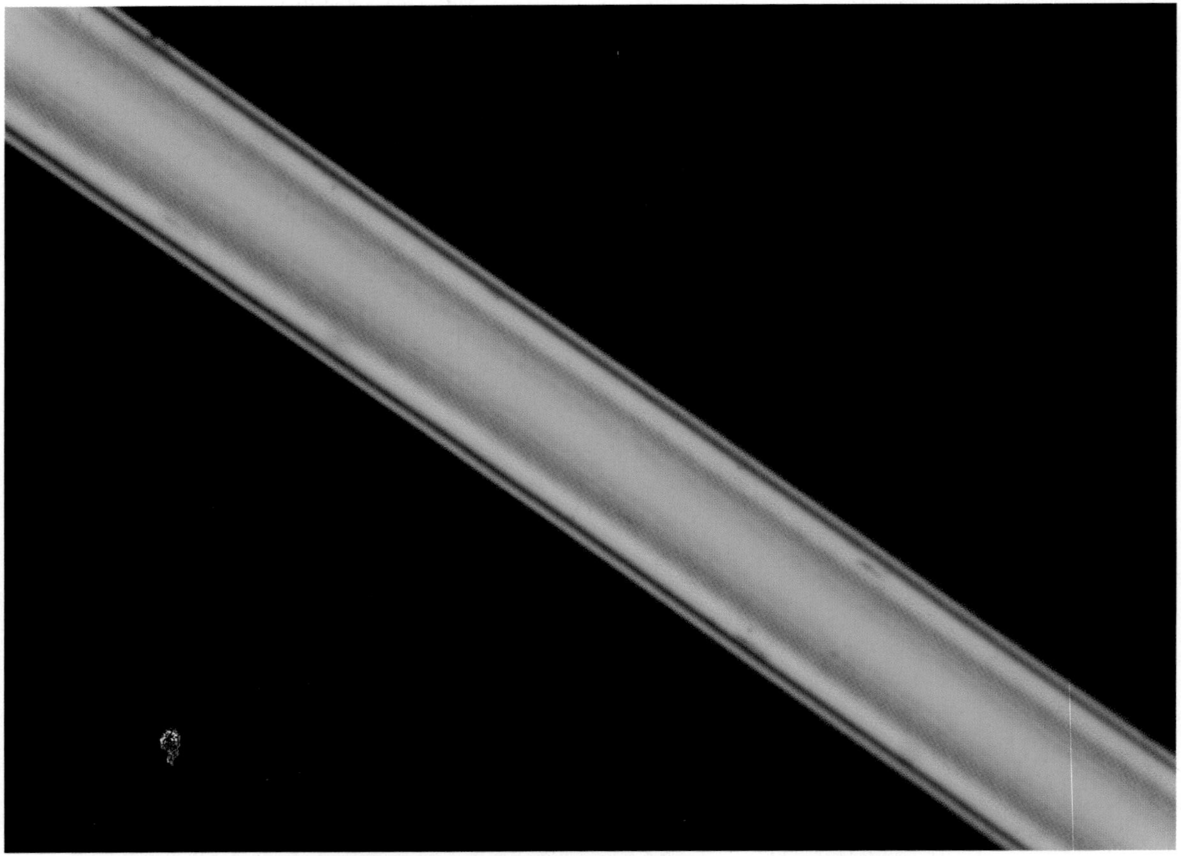

EAST

NORTH

SOUTH

WEST

Plate 2 An image of a fibre seen in crossed polars. Note that the colours in this plate may not be exactly the same as those viewed down the microscope. This is due to the reproduction process and any variation from the true colours is likely to be relatively small. *Photograph by Andrew Jackson, Staffordshire University, UK.*

Plate 3 The polarization colours seen when a quartz wedge is viewed under crossed polars. Note that it is not possible to make a quartz wedge that gradually becomes infinitely thin. For this reason, the wedge is made to become thinner and then end abruptly. Therefore, those polarization colours that would be generated by the very thinnest portion of the wedge are absent. If these were present, they would be seen to be grey tending towards black as the wedge becomes thinner. *Photograph by Graham Barlow, Staffordshire University, UK.*

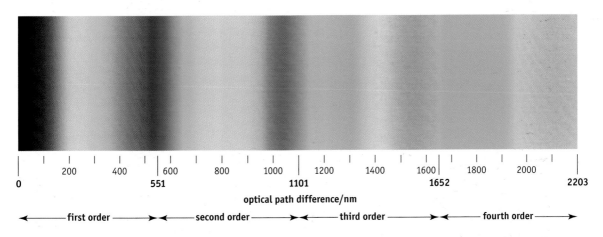

Plate 4 The correlation between polarization colour and optical path difference (there are commercially available charts based on this, called Michel–Levy charts, which convey the information shown here and other details besides). *Generated from a photograph by Graham Barlow, Staffordshire University, UK, by Tom Jackson.*

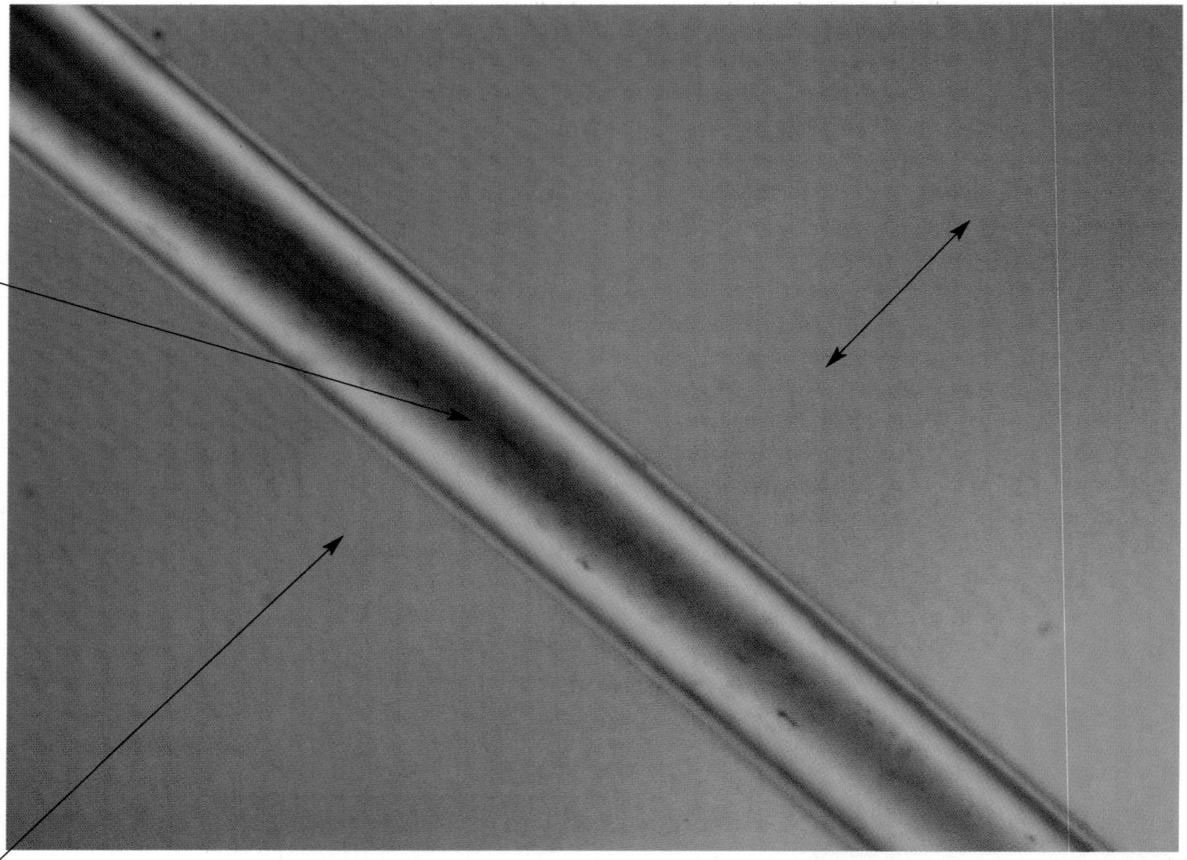

NORTH

EAST

WEST

SOUTH

Plate 5 Compensation black (visible in the centre of the fibre) as seen when a quartz wedge is superimposed on the fibre shown in Plate 2. Note that the vibration direction of the wedge's slow beam is northeast–southwest, as indicated by the double-headed arrow, and that the wedge becomes increasingly thick from northwest to southeast. Note also that the colours in this plate may not be exactly the same as those viewed down the microscope. This is due to the reproduction process and any variation from the true colours is likely to be relatively small.

Photograph by Andrew Jackson, Staffordshire University, UK.

Compensation black seen in the centre of the fibre when the area outside the fibre is third-order blue.

Third-order blue seen running southwest–northeast (i.e. along the direction of the arrow) in that region of the image that is outside the fibre. Note that third-order blue is the second blue encountered when the colours of Plate 4 are looked at in turn from left to right.

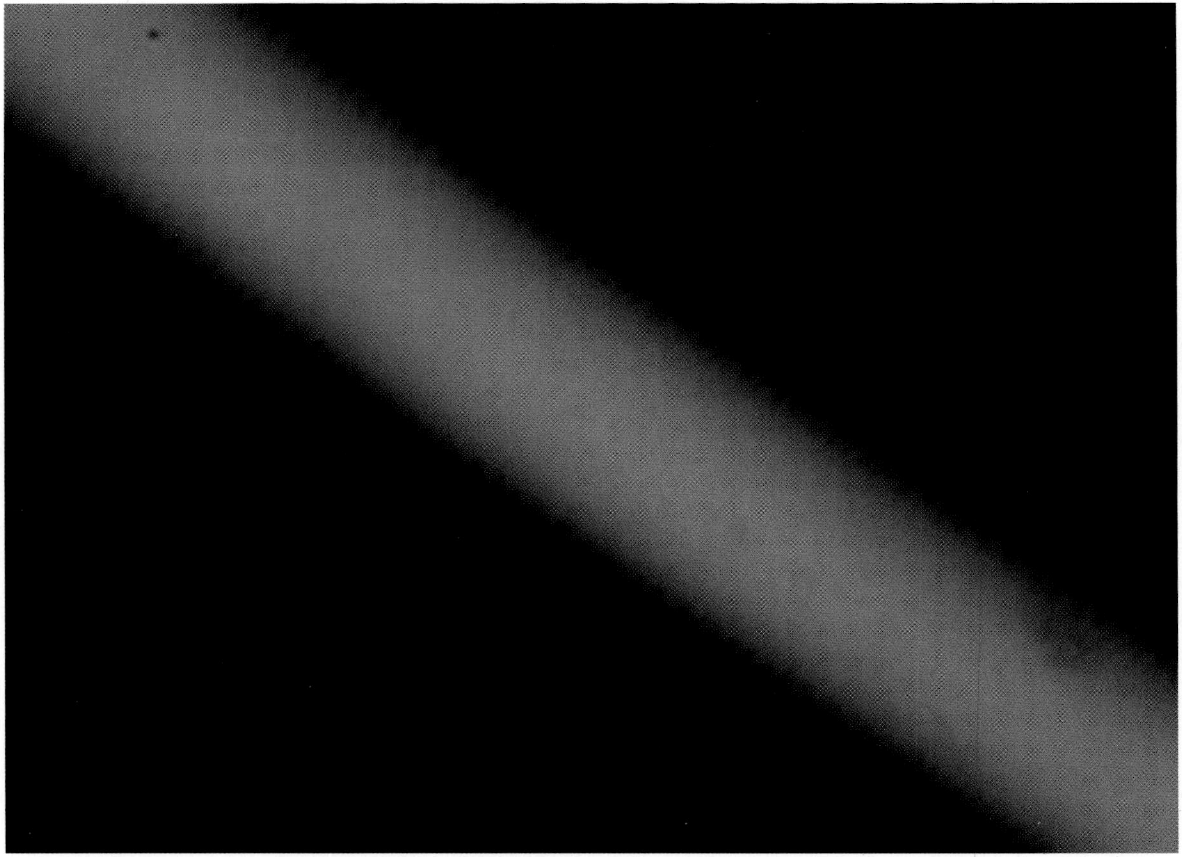

NORTH

EAST

SOUTH

WEST

Plate 6 An image of a fibre seen in crossed polars. Note this fibre is 30.6 μm wide. Note also that the green spots visible on the fibre in the southeastern area of the image are due to a contaminant and should be ignored.
Photograph by Andrew Jackson, Staffordshire University, UK.

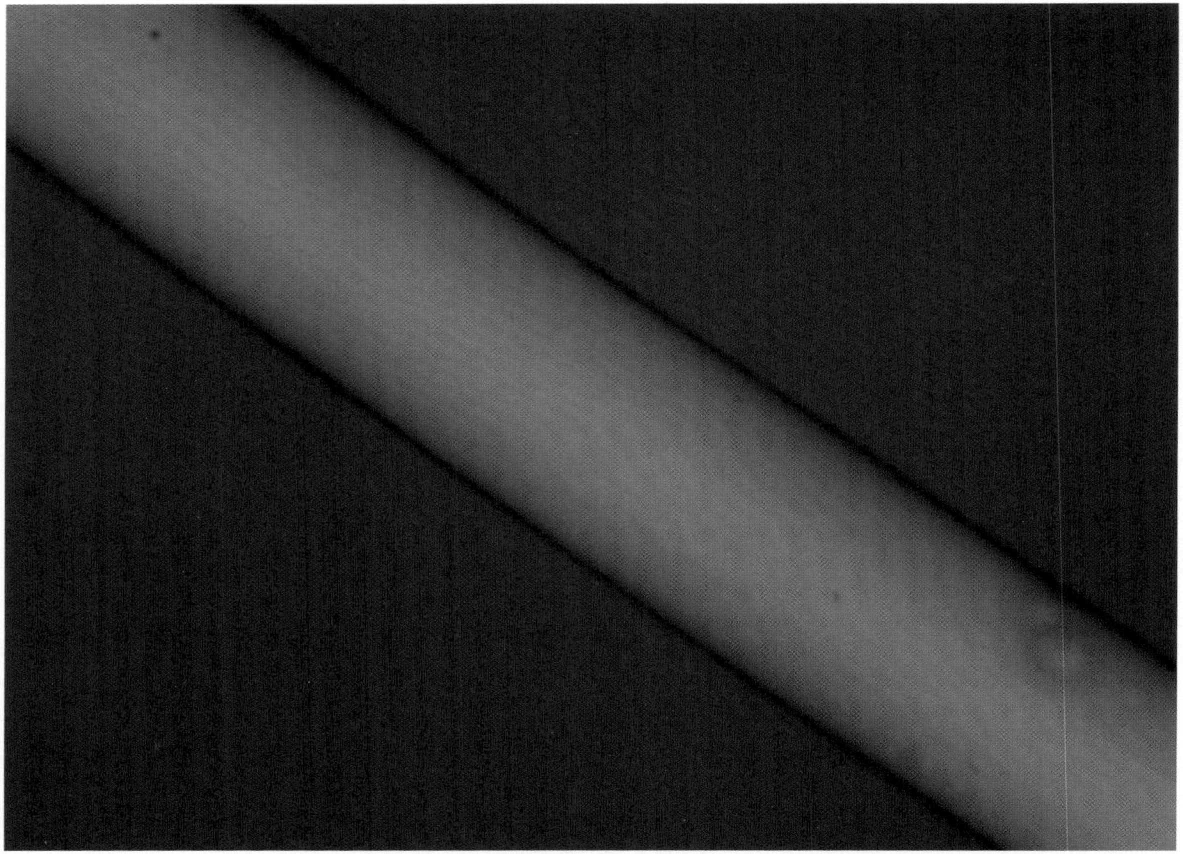

Plate 7 The fibre shown in Plate 6 viewed under crossed polars in the presence of a first-order red tint plate. As in Plate 6, the green spots visible on the fibre in the southeastern area of the image are due to a contaminant and should be ignored. *Photograph by Andrew Jackson, Staffordshire University, UK.*

Plate 8 As Plate 7 but with the stage, and hence the fibre, rotated by 90° about the centre of the light path of the microscope at the point where this path passes through the specimen. *Photograph by Andrew Jackson, Staffordshire University, UK.*

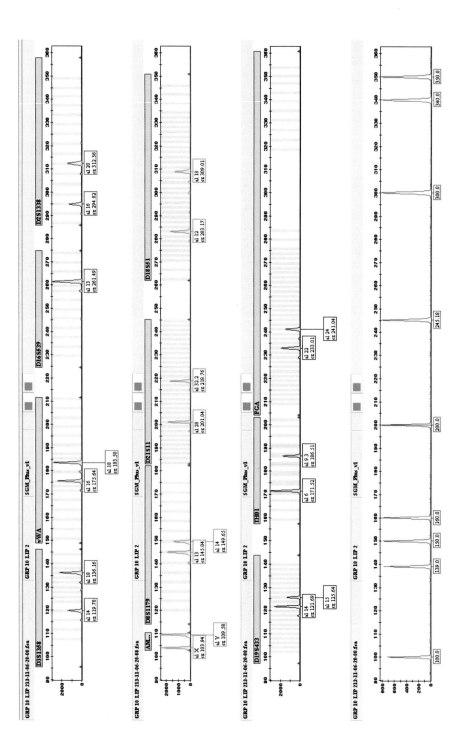

Plate 9 This picture shows a full DNA profile obtained from a lip-print on a glass using the AmpFL STR® SGM Plus™ (SGM⁺) system. Aspects of this type of profiling are discussed throughout Chapter 6. The DNA profile shows the genotype of the source individual at 11 genetic loci. The range in size of the alleles at each locus is indicated by the shaded bar above the peaks, which also gives the locus name. Each peak is labelled with the size of the peak in base-pairs (sz) and the corresponding allele number (al). For example, at the D3S1358 locus there is a peak of size 119.78 bp, of allele 14, and also a peak of size 136.16 bp, of allele 18. At this locus the genotype of the source individual is 14,18. The grey lines under each locus indicate the size of every allele that could be present in a profile. The uppermost panel, with the peaks in blue, shows the loci D3S1358, vWA, D16S539 and D2S1338; the panel with green peaks shows the loci Amelogenin (alleles here are labelled X and Y), D8S1179, D21S11 and D18S51; the panel with black peaks shows the loci D19S433, THO1 and FGA. The red panel shows the molecular size standards that allow the calculation of the peak sizes in the other panels above.

Forensic techniques

Box 3.7

Thermal analysis

During thermal analysis, a small sample (typically <200 mg) of the material to be characterised is subjected to a carefully controlled temperature programme (usually a steady increase in temperature) while one or more of the physical properties of the sample are monitored.

One such property that is commonly utilised in thermal analysis is mass, in which case the technique is known as thermogravimetry (TG). In another common technique of this type, called differential thermal analysis (DTA), the property that is monitored is the temperature difference between the sample and an inert reference material that is subjected to the same temperature programme as the sample. DTA detects changes undergone by the sample in which it gives out heat (termed exothermic events) and those in which it absorbs heat (known as endothermic events). For example, during the differential

thermal analysis of soils, the combustion of organic matter and the evaporation of water are, respectively, examples of exothermic and endothermic events that are commonly observed.

Differential scanning calorimetry (DSC) is a thermal analytical technique that, like DTA, can detect both endothermic and exothermic events. During DSC analysis, both the sample and an inert reference material are subjected to the same temperature programme. During this process, the amount of energy that must be provided to each of the sample and the reference in order to maintain a zero temperature difference between them is measured. This is then displayed as a function of temperature. As can be seen from the figure shown below, this can be used, for example, to readily differentiate between butter and margarine.

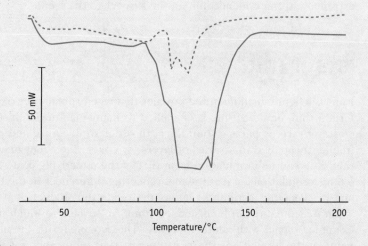

DSC traces of butter, shown as a dashed line, and margarine
In traces such as these, endothermic events appear as troughs whereas exothermic ones are shown as peaks. This experiment used 2.53 mg of butter and 3.80 mg of margarine. The amplitude of the features in the butter trace have been increased to compensate for the difference in sample sizes to allow the two traces to be compared on the same vertical scale. Both samples were heated at a rate of 10.0 °C per minute

(Supplied by Terry Barker, Staffordshire University, UK)

help to narrow down the area that is to be searched in an attempt to find the scene of the murder. In the case of cannabis or another illegal herbal drug, the presence of identified fragments of the plant concerned on a person or on his or her possessions could, in themselves, be incriminating.

Vegetation can also be used to provide associative evidence. For example, while it is common to be contaminated with the pollen of wind-pollinated (anemophilous) plants just by being in their vicinity; this is not true in the case of insect-pollinated (entomophilous) plants. Indeed, physical contact is normally required in order for pollen transfer to occur between an object and a blooming entomophilous plant.[1] Consequently, the presence of pollen from a ground-level entomophilous plant on the upper parts of a person's body would, under most circumstances, *not* be consistent with that person merely walking through an area in which such plants were common. Evidence such as this could then be used to test, for example, the likely veracity of two conflicting accounts, one given by the complainant in the case of an alleged assault and the other by the suspect. The identification of different pollen types (and of other microscopic entities, such as plant spores and algal cysts) and the application of this knowledge to the resolution of crime is the domain of the **forensic palynologist**.

Occasionally, fragments of vegetation taken from the scene of an incident can be shown to physically fit with those obtained from the person or belongings of someone believed to have been at that scene. Such jigsaw fits may occur, for example, in a burglary case in which a door was broken open to gain access to the premises. Under these circumstances, a direct physical fit between wood fragments found in the possession of a suspect and wood remaining in the door frame could provide extremely strong evidence linking the suspect to the scene.

Forensic palynologist
A botanical ecologist who specialises in the study of microscopic entities (palynomorphs), primarily pollen grains and plant spores, and their distribution, and whose expertise is utilised in the investigation of crimes.

3.5 Paint

Paint is a liquid, manufactured product that when spread over rigid surfaces dries to form a thin, hard coating. It is applied to many man-made objects, including vehicles and various parts of buildings, in order to decorate and protect them. It is frequently applied in a series of layers, or coats. Each coat may consist of a paint that differs in its formulation from that of the underlying coat. There are many different formulations of paint made, reflecting differences in the technical, aesthetic and/or economic attributes that are desired in the product.

Hardened paint can be dislodged from the surface to which it is adhered by, for example, impact with another surface. This, coupled with the ubiquitous nature of paint in the human environment, means that chips and smears of paint are frequently-encountered forms of trace physical evidence. This is particularly true in cases involving road traffic accidents or breaking-and-entering.

In cases where only questioned samples are available, such as might occur if the victim of a hit-and-run incident has been found but the culprit has yet to be appre-

---

1 Such pollen may then be collected by a forensic examiner from the object concerned by vacuuming or tape lifting in much the same fashion as used to collect trace levels of fibres (Section 3.1.1).

hended, then paint can provide investigative leads. Clearly, under these circumstances, the appearance (especially the colour) of the paint involved will help the police in their search for the vehicle involved in the incident. In some cases, the comparison of the attributes of the sample with those of paint samples kept on record may lead to the identification of the possible make, model and/or an age range of the vehicle concerned. This approach played a significant role in the apprehension of Malcolm Fairley (Box 3.8).

Case study
Box 3.8

The part played by paint evidence in tracking down the serial rapist known as 'The Fox'

In 1984, a series of violent sex attacks were carried out in Buckinghamshire and Bedfordshire by a hooded man armed with a sawn-off shotgun. Prior to this, the man, who became known as 'The Fox', had perpetrated a number of burglaries in the area. Through interviewing the victims of his crimes, the police were able to establish two important facts – that he spoke with a northern accent and that, as he wore his watch on his right wrist, he was apparently left-handed.

On 17 August 1984, The Fox struck again but this time in the village of Brampton, Yorkshire. In this incident, he broke into a house in the early hours of the morning, tied up the couple living there and, while the children slept in another room, raped the wife. Before leaving the scene, he removed traces of himself from his victim and cut out a section of the bottom sheet that was soiled with his semen. However, despite his attempts to remove any incriminating evidence from the scene itself, The Fox left behind a trail of forensic clues outside the house.

During their search of the surrounding area the next day, the police discovered several pieces of evidence including:

■ a trail of footprints leading to a spot where a car had been hidden;
■ tyre tracks;
■ the square of semen-soaked bed linen;
■ an improvised hood made from part of a pair of overalls;
■ a sawn-off shotgun (hidden under a pile of leaves); and
■ minute specks of yellow paint adhered to a tree branch, at a height of 45 inches (1.1 m) from the ground.

The tiny flakes of paint were subsequently identified in the laboratory as a car paint known as 'Harvest Gold' used only by the British Leyland Company. Further enquiries revealed that this particular paint had been used on a single model – the Austin Allegro – between May 1973 and August 1975. As a result of their investigations, the police knew several facts about the man dubbed The Fox, including his blood group, accent, build and shoe size. Now they knew the colour and model of the car he had driven that night and that its paintwork was likely to be scratched.

Further break-ins and assaults by The Fox continued, both in the north and south of England, while the police continued to eliminate individuals from their list of suspects. On 11 September 1984, two policemen were sent to an address in north London to check out one such suspect. On their approach, they saw a bright yellow Austin Allegro parked outside and a young man in the act of cleaning it. The officers noticed scratches to the car's paintwork at a height of about 45 inches from the ground. When asked by one of the officers to put on a watch lying in the car, the man, whose name was Malcolm Fairley, complied. When he fastened the watch to his right wrist, he revealed that he, like The Fox, was left-handed. Furthermore, the officers discovered overalls whose material matched that used to make the improvised hood worn by The Fox in the Brampton incident.

Malcolm Fairley was arrested. He was tried and found guilty of a number of charges, including counts of rape, indecent assault and burglary with intent to commit rape. On 26 February 1985, Malcolm Fairley, alias The Fox, was sentenced to six life sentences.

In the majority of cases, paint is used to provide associative evidence, either as well as or, more commonly, instead of investigative leads. In order to achieve this, both questioned and control samples must be available. (A paint chip found on the tip of a screwdriver suspected of being used to force a window open and a sample of paint taken from the window frame concerned would, respectively, constitute examples of questioned and control samples.) Under these circumstances, the comparison of the characteristics of the two samples of paint will normally allow the examiner to decide whether they are sufficiently similar to be consistent with their having the same source.

During the forensic examination of paint, physical and chemical attributes of the sample are ascertained to provide class characteristics and points of comparison. Many of these attributes, such as the paint's colour, apparent layer thickness, surface texture and the appearance and pattern of occurrence of embedded particles, can be determined by microscopic examination using reflected light. Sometimes this examination is aided by the use of specialised light sources that provide specific colours of light or ultraviolet radiation.

Other attributes may be established by the use of:

■ *microspectrophotometry* (Box 3.6), to provide a graph that is a quantitative expression of the colour of each layer evident in a given paint sample;

■ *pyrolysis gas chromatography* (Chapter 11, Box 11.5), to reveal a pattern that reflects the chemical composition of the organic components of the paint;

■ *infrared or Raman spectroscopy*, to provide graphs each made of peaks and troughs that not only can act as a pattern which may be used for comparative purposes but that can also be interpreted to reveal information about the chemical composition of the paint (Box 3.9);

Forensic techniques

Box 3.9

Infrared and Raman spectroscopies

The atoms that make up molecules vibrate and the energy with which a molecule vibrates is quantised. This means that the molecule can reside in one of many vibrational energy states but not in a vibrational energy state that is between two such states that are adjacent to one another. Bohr's frequency condition was introduced in Box 3.6 in the context of electronic transitions. This is just as valid for transitions between the vibrational states of a molecule. According to this, a molecule can be promoted from a vibrational energy state E to a higher vibrational energy state E' by absorbing electromagnetic radiation with a frequency that accords with the following:

$$E' - E = \Delta E = h\nu$$

in which h is Plank's constant and ν is the frequency of the radiation.

One means of expressing the frequency of electromagnetic radiation is wavenumbers. The wavenumber of radiation is

Box 3.9 continued

the number of wavelengths that fit into a unit length. In the context of infrared and Raman spectroscopies, the unit length used is usually one centimetre, in which case the units of wavenumbers are cm^{-1}. If E and E' are vibrational energy levels, then the absorption of electromagnetic radiation will fall in the range 1×10^2 to 1×10^4 cm^{-1}, which is within the infrared portion of the electromagnetic spectrum. This means that infrared (IR) spectroscopy can be used to monitor transitions between the vibrational energy states of a molecule. In this technique, the sample's reflectance or transmittance of electromagnetic radiation in the infrared region is monitored as a function of wavenumber. In these plots, the absorption of radiation due to such a vibrational transition appears as a trough in an otherwise horizontal background. Most molecules exhibit many such troughs (confusingly referred to as peaks), as exemplified by the IR spectra of aspirin and phenobarbitone shown in Chapter 7, Figure 7.10.

It is also possible to monitor transitions between the vibrational energy levels of molecules by Raman spectroscopy. The physical basis of this is quite different from that of infrared spectroscopy. Raman spectra originate from the inelastic scattering of light, a phenomenon that is also termed Raman scattering. Consider a molecule that is struck by light of energy $h\nu_0$. It may elastically scatter this light, in which case the energy of the light will remain unchanged after the collision. Alternatively, the light may be Raman scattered in one of two ways. In one of these, the energy of the light becomes $h(\nu_0 - \nu_v)$, while in the other it becomes $h(\nu_0 + \nu_v)$. In both cases, ν_v is the frequency corresponding to the energy needed to excite the molecule from E to E'. Of the two types of Raman scattered light, that with an energy of $h(\nu_0 - \nu_v)$ is more intense and is generally used for recording the spectrum. The spectrum is normally obtained using monochromatic laser light as the exciting radiation. As exemplified by the spectra of paint samples shown below, these spectra are usually shown as a plot of the variation in Raman intensity as a function of wavenumber, the inelastically scattered portion of the exciting radiation being designated as 0 cm^{-1}. As can be seen from these examples, Raman spectra consist of a series of peaks on a more or less horizontal background.

Vibrational spectroscopy, whether IR or Raman, has a number of applications in the field of forensic science. The position of the troughs in IR spectra and the peaks in

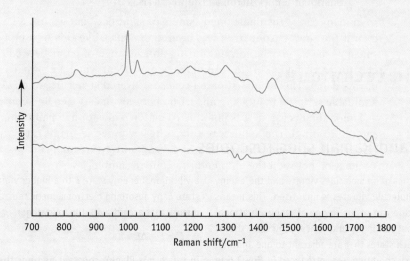

Raman spectra from the surface of a paint flake from a silver Mercedes car (upper trace) and silver refinish paint sprayed from an aerosol can (lower trace)

(Spectra recorded by Andrew Jackson, Staffordshire University, UK)

Box 3.9 continued

Raman spectra generally differ from one type of molecule to the next. This means, in principle at least, that either such spectrum can be used as a means of establishing the identity of an unknown pure compound by comparing its spectrum with those held on a database. For example, IR can often successfully identify the type of polymer from which an individual man-made fibre is made. This provides an important class characteristic of the fibre concerned. Indeed, the spectrum itself can be used as a class characteristic, allowing comparisons to be made between questioned and control samples, even if the chemical identity of the two samples is unknown, as in the case of the spectra of the two paints shown below. Clearly, great care is required in the interpretation of such comparisons. For example, while there clearly is a difference between the spectra shown opposite, it is possible that this is, to some degree at least, attributable to differences in any polishes applied to the two samples. Finally, both IR and Raman spectra contain information about the chemical composition of the sample. This is because specific functional groups absorb IR and/or produce Raman scattering in known regions of the spectrum. For example, the −O−H group found in alcohols typically absorbs IR in the region 3200 to 3600 cm^{-1}. Great care and considerable expertise is needed in making interpretations based on observations of this type. Finally, it is worth noting that it is often possible to obtain IR and/or Raman spectra from samples of microscopic dimensions and that both techniques are non-destructive. Both of these are valuable attributes within the forensic context, where samples are often small and irreplaceable.

■ *X-ray powder diffraction*, to reveal the identity of the crystalline components of the paint and to provide a pattern that can be compared with the diffraction patterns of other paints (Box 3.10);

■ *elemental analysis* by, for example, energy dispersive X-ray analysis (EDX) coupled with scanning electron microscopy (SEM) (Chapter 9, Box 9.6). SEM-EDX is capable of differentiating between different layers of paint on the basis of their elemental compositions.

In many cases, the questioned sample of paint does not exhibit a layered structure, even if the source paint itself was layered. Samples like this may be in the form of a smear (such as may be formed during an exchange of paint between colliding vehicles) or a crushed chip (for example, as may occur when a crowbar is used to break open a door). This is unfortunate because a layered structure, when evident, provides a valuable series of points of comparison between questioned and control samples.

Finally, on occasion, it is possible to match a questioned paint chip with a control sample in much the same way that a jigsaw piece is fitted into a partly finished jigsaw puzzle. When this occurs, it is frequently extremely strong evidence of an association between the chip and the control sample.

3.6 Others

Any material that may be transferred in small amounts from one object to another has the potential to be of trace evidential value. This includes the materials covered so far in this chapter, body fluids (Chapter 5), illegal drugs (Chapter 7), gunshot residues (Chapter 9), fire accelerants (Chapter 10), explosives (Chapter 11) and many others.

Materials that fall into this last category include oils, waxes (including polishes), inks (discussed in Chapter 8, Section 8.5, in the context of questioned documents), cosmetics, tobacco and other smoking materials, food and drink, and even macro-invertebrate animals (e.g. insects, spiders and slugs). All of these are capable of revealing class characteristics that may provide investigative leads or, more commonly, associative evidence. The techniques used to reveal these characteristics will depend on the materials concerned and the circumstances of the individual case. However, those that may be usefully employed include:

- *microscopic examination*;
- *spectroscopic methods* such as ultraviolet and visible spectroscopy (Box 3.6), infrared and Raman spectroscopy (Box 3.9), and mass spectrometry;
- *chromatographic techniques* such as thin-layer chromatography and gas chromatography (Chapter 11, Box 11.5);
- *elemental analysis* by such methods as EDX analysis coupled with SEM (Chapter 9, Box 9.6) and atomic absorption and emission spectroscopies (Chapter 7, Box 7.5);
- *thermal analysis* (Box 3.7);
- *X-ray powder diffraction* (Box 3.10).

In the main, trace evidence is useful in the corroboration or refutation of other evidence. However, there are situations in which it can provide extremely powerful evidence that is, arguably, individualising. As discussed in the sections on glass (Section 3.2), vegetable matter (Section 3.4) and paint (Section 3.5), this can occur when jigsaw puzzle-like fits can be produced between questioned and control samples. It also can occur when the trace evidence allows DNA profiling (Chapter 6) or when there are multiple forms of trace evidence that link together people and/or places.

It is noteworthy that there are forms of trace evidence that, although not necessarily frequently encountered, are associated with particular types of crime. Examples of these include condom lubricants found in some rape cases and, in safe-breaking cases, the specialised materials from which strong-boxes are constructed.

Forensic techniques

Box 3.10

X-ray powder diffraction

Many materials of interest to forensic scientists, such as paint, many drugs and soil, contain components that are present as microscopic crystals. X-ray powder diffraction can be used to identify these components (i.e. provide qualitative information). In order to do this, at least a few milligrams of the sample must be available and each of the components concerned must represent at least a few per cent by mass of the total material present. X-ray powder diffraction can also be used to find out how much of each crystalline component is present. However, such quantitative work is not commonly carried out using this method.

▶

Box 3.10 continued

For the vast majority of materials, sample preparation for qualitative analysis by this method simply requires the grinding of the sample to a fine powder, although even this simple step can be omitted in many cases. One of the advantages of X-ray powder diffraction is that the sample is not destroyed during analysis, although some materials will be damaged by the X-ray beam used and, clearly, the physical condition of the sample will be altered if it is ground.

X-ray powder diffraction is possible because each crystal is made up of a regular array of atoms and/or ions. In each case, it is convenient to think of this array as being constructed on the basis of a three-dimensional lattice made up of points. The points all lie on lattice planes. The perpendicular spacing between successive parallel planes (i.e. the d-spacing of that family of planes) is a characteristic of the crystal concerned. Any one crystal contains many such families of parallel planes, each with specific d-spacings. For example, crystals of the drug diamorphine (i.e. the main active component of heroin, see Chapter 7, Section 7.2.2) all have, among many others, families of planes with d-spacings of 5.281, 6.996, 6.567 and 5.078 Å (note that 1 angstrom, symbol Å = 1×10^{-10} metre).

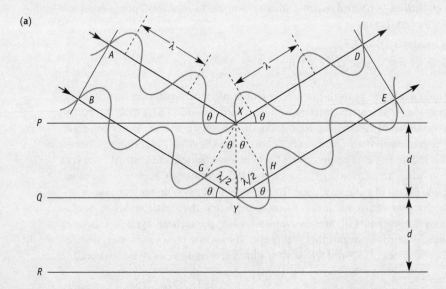

(a)

(a) Derivation of the Bragg equation

A schematic illustration showing an incident monochromatic X-ray beam (represented by AX and BY) of wavelength λ impinging at an angle of θ with a family of lattice planes, three members of which are shown (labelled P, Q and R). These are perpendicular to the plane of the paper. In this case, the conditions of the Bragg equation are met as the distance GY plus YH is a whole number of wavelengths (1 in this case). This means that the emerging X-rays are in phase (i.e. the peaks and troughs along XD and YE are in step with each other). Therefore, the X-rays constructively interfere and emerge as what appears to be a reflected beam. The Bragg equation can be derived from this diagram. Note that the angles $X\hat{G}Y$ and $X\hat{H}Y$ are both 90°. It can be shown that the angles $G\hat{X}Y$ and $Y\hat{X}H$ are both θ. Furthermore, they are both opposite the side of a right angle triangle that is nλ/2 long (n=1 in this case but constructive interference will occur when n is any whole number from 1 to ∞). Therefore, as the hypotenuse (XY) of each of these triangles = d, in each case d sin θ = nλ/2, therefore nλ = 2d sin θ

(From Whiston, 1987 © John Wiley and Sons Limited. Reproduced with permission.)

Box 3.10 continued

During X-ray powder diffraction analysis, a fine beam of X-rays is shone on the sample. Families of lattice planes within the crystalline components of the sample behave as if they reflect this beam whenever the conditions of the Bragg equation are met. This equation takes the form:

$$n\lambda = 2d\sin\theta$$

in which n is a whole number with a value between 1 and ∞, λ is the wavelength of the X-rays, d is as described earlier and θ is the angle of incidence and the angle of diffraction (see figure (a)).

In a typical X-ray powder diffraction experiment, as far as is practicable, the X-rays used all have the same wavelength. This wavelength is known and the angle 2θ is measured for each reflection observed. From this information, the d-spacing of the family of planes that is responsible for a given reflection can readily be calculated on the assumption that $n = 1$, in which case $d = \lambda/2\sin\theta$. The relative intensity of each reflection is also measured. Comparison of the d-spacings of the families of planes that led to each of the observed reflections and the relative intensities of these reflections with those held on a database allows the identity of the crystalline component(s) of a sample to be identified. For example, as shown in figure (b), by use of this method, both the diamorphine and sucrose present in a batch of street heroin cut with cane sugar can be recognised.

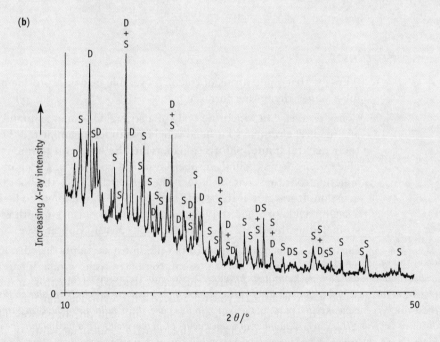

(b) The X-ray powder diffraction pattern obtained from a few milligrams of a sample of street heroin cut with cane sugar

Note the crystalline materials that are responsible for the main peaks have been labelled D and S, standing for diamorphine (the principal active component of street heroin) and sucrose (a sugar) respectively

(The pattern was recorded and interpreted by Derek Lowe, Staffordshire University, UK)

3.7 Summary

■ Trace materials that may be recovered from an incident scene, individuals believed to be associated with that scene and/or the belongings of those individuals can be of significant evidential value. These materials may include hairs and other fibres, glass, soils, vegetable matter, paint and many other substances.

■ Each of these materials can be characterised by the methods outlined in this chapter to reveal class characteristics. These characteristics can be used to provide investigative leads. They can also provide points of comparison between questioned samples taken from an incident scene and control samples taken from an individual or his or her belongings. Comparisons based on these points provide associative evidence that may enable the corroboration or refutation of incident scenarios suggested by other pieces of evidence.

■ In the main, the examination of trace recoverable evidence enables the type of object to be identified. For example, the examination of a sample of hair may well allow the species from which it originated to be established. Furthermore, the comparison of two samples of trace recoverable evidence will frequently allow the examiner to state whether their similarities are sufficient to be consistent with them having a common origin.

■ Under certain circumstances, trace recoverable evidence can also lead to the identification of the source of that evidence (i.e. it can individualise). This can occur when there is a jigsaw puzzle-type physical fit between questioned and control samples, where a DNA profile match is possible (Chapter 6), or in cases where there are multiple types of matching recoverable trace evidence linking an individual to a place or to another individual.

Problems

1. Why is it that some forms of trace recoverable evidence provide more powerful evidence than other forms?

2. Consider a case in which the body of a strangled woman is found by the side of a road. The woman's husband is believed to have committed the murder, in their marital home, before transporting the body in the family car to the place where it was found. Inspection of the body reveals a number of fibres adhering to it that match those of the carpet that lines the boot of the car in question. It was noted that some of these fibres were found to be adhering to a small trickle of blood that emanated from the victim's mouth when she was strangled. Is this detail of evidential value? Justify your answer.

3. Dusting a surface for fingerprints will almost certainly dislodge and lose any evidentially valuable fibres present. Similarly, using a tape lift to recover the fibres will probably destroy the fingerprints. Bearing this in mind, if, as a crime scene examiner, you were faced with a surface that might reveal both fingerprint and fibre evidence, what would you do? In answering this question, take time to weigh up the relative evidential value of fingerprints (Chapter 4, Section 4.1) and fibres (Section 3.1).

4. A knitted balaclava helmet that was believed to have been used to hide the identity of an armed robber during a bank raid, was found and examined. On the inside of the helmet, two 30 cm long, brown coloured, human scalp hairs were found. On this basis, would it be reasonable for the police to be told that the wearer had brown hair of at least shoulder-length?

5. It is a common defence for a suspect to claim that he or she was a bystander at the time and scene of a crime. Consider a case in which someone was caught running from the direction of a car that had just had its front passenger window smashed in an aborted attempt to steal the car's radio. The police submitted the jacket worn by the suspect concerned for forensic examination. Do you think that it would be possible, on the basis of glass evidence alone, to establish whether the suspect was a bystander or the person who broke the window? Fully justify your answer and, if you believe that it would be useful to do so, suggest experiments that might be carried out in order to test your thoughts on this matter.

6. List the types of recoverable trace materials that could be used as evidence to link the victim of a hit-and-run incident with the vehicle that was involved.

7. Consider a case in which a householder has complained that his house has been burgled, resulting in several valuable pieces of jewellery being stolen, and that the burglar broke a window in order to gain access to his property. Why, in such a case, might it be very important to differentiate between radial and concentric fractures in the glass that remains in the window frame?

8. Consider a jacket, a jumper and a textile fabric-covered chair. The jacket and the jumper both have fibres on them that match those of the chair. Fibres that match both those of the jacket and those of the jumper are found on the chair. Fibres that match the jumper are found on the jacket. How might this situation have arisen?

Further reading

Caddy, B. (ed.) (2001) *Forensic examination of glass and paint: analysis and interpretation*. London: Taylor & Francis.

Curran, J. M., Hicks, T. N. and Buckleton, J. S. (2000) *Forensic interpretation of glass evidence*. Boca Raton, FL: CRC Press LLC.

Murray, R.C. and Tedrow, J. C. F. (1992) *Forensic geology*. New York: Prentice Hall.

Ogle, Jr, R. R. and Fox, M. J. (1999) *Atlas of human hair: microscopic characteristics*. Boca Raton, FL: CRC Press LLC.

Robertson, J. (ed.) (1999) *Forensic examination of hair*. London: Taylor & Francis.

Robertson, J. and Grieve, M. (eds) (1999) *Forensic examination of fibres* (2nd edn). London: Taylor & Francis.

Robinson, P. C. and Bradbury, S. (1992) *Qualitative polarized-light microscopy*. Oxford: Oxford University Press and the Royal Microscopical Society.

Saferstein, R. (ed.) (1988) *Forensic science handbook,* Volume 2. Englewood Cliffs, NJ: Prentice Hall.

Trace and contact evidence

Part II: Fingerprints and other marks and impressions

4

Chapter objectives

After reading this chapter, you should be able to:

> Understand those characteristics of fingerprints that enable them to be used as a means of personal identification and allow them to be systematically classified.

> Distinguish between latent, visible and plastic fingerprints and outline the main techniques used to develop the first of these.

> Describe the methods used to recover footwear impressions from an incident scene and discuss how they may be subsequently compared with suspect footwear.

> Appreciate the significance of any bite marks present at a crime scene and their potential role in the identification of the individual responsible.

> Discuss the evidential value of tool marks connected with an incident scene and the means by which suspect tools may be identified as the instruments involved.

> Outline the valuable forensic evidence that may be afforded by recording and preserving any tyre marks left at an incident scene.

> Understand the role of textile products both in the creation of impressions and as the recipients of damage marks.

Introduction

This chapter examines the valuable evidence that can be provided by the different types of marks and impressions left at a crime scene. Of these, fingerprints[1] may be considered to be the most important type as they are unique to the individual and can therefore be used as a means of personal identification. Furthermore, they are frequently present at crime scenes and typically form an essential part of the evidential material gathered.

---

1 In this book, the term 'fingerprint' is used for both those found at the crime scene and those taken from an individual under controlled circumstances. It should be noted, however, that within the field a distinction is sometimes made between the former (finger marks) and the latter (fingerprints).

Other marks and impressions that may be found at an incident scene include footwear impressions, bite marks, tool marks and tyre marks. In all four of these types, it may be possible to match scene impressions with suspect items (or, in the case of bite marks, directly with suspect individuals) through the creation of test impressions. Textile products are another means by which marks and impressions may be left at an incident scene, as exemplified by the imprints made by gloved hands. Moreover, they may themselves show signs of damage, which can be used, in some cases, to identify the type(s) of implement involved in the incident. Note that for information about impressions made by indented writing, the reader is referred to Chapter 8, Section 8.7.6.

4.1 Fingerprints

4.1.1 The basis of fingerprints as a means of identification

In humans, the surface of the palms of the hands and the fingers, and the soles of the feet and the toes, are covered with a special type of thickened skin known as **friction ridge skin**. This has evolved in primates to provide a gripping surface and also, through the greater concentration of nerve endings present, to facilitate an enhanced sense of touch. As the name suggests, friction ridge skin has a ridged appearance, rather like that of a ploughed field in miniature, with furrows separating the individual ridges. However, these ridges are not arranged in straight lines but form complex patterns on the surface of the skin. Contact between an area of friction ridge skin and another surface may result in the creation of a characteristic print or impression on that surface (Section 4.1.4). Furthermore, a set of prints, for example of the fingers and thumbs, can be reproduced deliberately using inks or similar substances to produce a permanent record. Such prints can be used as a means of personal identification that is based on the following premises:

Friction ridge skin *In primates, including humans, the thickened skin that covers the plantar surfaces of the feet (i.e. the soles) and the palmar surfaces of the hands.*

■ *The fingerprints of an individual stay unchanged throughout life.* The friction ridge pattern of an individual is formed in the foetus, at about 28 weeks after conception. The exact arrangement of the ridges is determined by the dermal papillae, a layer of cells that separates the outer layer of skin (the epidermis) from the underlying dermis. This pattern endures throughout life, although it may be marred, for example, by deep scarring. Moreover, it persists for some time after death and may therefore prove useful in post-mortem identification (Chapter 12, Section 12.4.1).

■ *No two fingerprints are identical.* Support for this principle came first from Sir Francis Galton's theoretical calculations presented in his landmark publication, *Finger prints*, in 1892. In this, he demonstrated that the odds against two individual fingerprints being exactly the same was 64 billion to 1. Perhaps even more compelling is the actual evidence accrued from fingerprinting individuals over the past 100 years. Of the many millions classified to date, no two fingerprints have yet been found to be the same, even those of identical twins.

4.1.2 The classification of fingerprints

The presence of recognisable ridge pattern types has allowed fingerprints to be systematically classified. The fingerprint classification system adopted in most English-speaking countries (including England and Wales from 1901) was the Henry System. This ten-print classification system was developed by Sir Edward Richard Henry (1850–1931), based on the observations made by Sir Francis Galton (1822–1911) of three basic types of fingerprint patterns – loops, arches and whorls. Each of these three types, and their subtypes, are described below and illustrated in Figures 4.1–4.3.

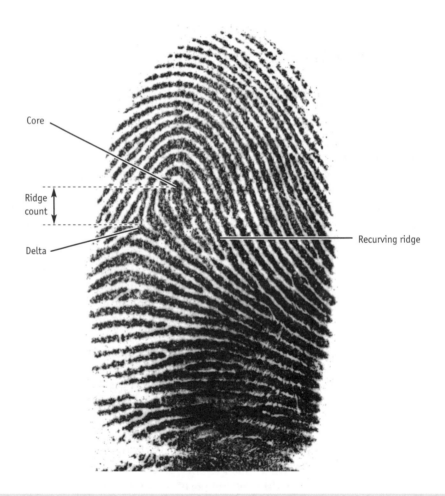

Figure 4.1 Fingerprint patterns: the radial loop, showing the four features used in its classification

Note that the ulnar loop pattern (not illustrated) differs from the radial loop pattern in only one respect, i.e. the loop opens in the direction of the little finger and not in the direction of the thumb

Loops

Approximately 60 per cent of all fingerprints fall into the loop pattern category, making it the commonest of the three basic types. In this pattern, at least one ridge must enter from one side, curve around and then exit at the same side (Figure 4.1). Two subtypes are recognised – the *radial loop* and the *ulnar loop* – depending on the direction of flow of the ridges. In simple terms, if the loop opens in the direction of the thumb (i.e. towards the radial bone of the forearm), it is termed a radial loop and if it opens in the direction of the little finger (i.e. towards the ulnar bone of the forearm) it is known as an ulnar loop.

To be classified as a true loop pattern, *all* of the four features listed below, and illustrated in Figure 4.1, must be present:

■ a single delta (an area where the ridges diverge);

■ a core (the pattern's centre);

■ a minimum of one recurring ridge that flows between the delta and the core;

■ a minimum **ridge count** of one.

Ridge count
In fingerprint patterns categorised as loops, the number of ridges that traverse an imaginary line connecting the core with the delta.

Arches

The arch pattern accounts for about 5 per cent of all fingerprint patterns. Two subtypes are recognised: the *plain arch* and the *tented arch* (Figure 4.2). In the plain arch, which is the simplest fingerprint pattern of all, the friction ridges flow from one side to the other rising smoothly in the centre, like a wave. In contrast, the tented arch, which may be considered as an intermediate between an arch and a loop, usually has either a central upthrusting ridge or ridges meeting at an angle of 90° or less at the apex of the arch. However, as may be expected, there are also tented arches that show some, but not all, of the four characteristics of the loop pattern.

Whorls

The whorl pattern accounts for about 35 per cent of all fingerprint patterns. The situation regarding the classification of whorl patterns based on the Henry System is complicated because different ways of subdividing whorl patterns are used. One categorisation that is in common usage, and is recognised by the Federal Bureau of Investigation (FBI), places whorls into the following four types – plain, central pocket, double loop and accidental. The simplest of these is the *plain whorl*, which has two deltas and a minimum of one ridge that completely encircles the core, describing the shape of a circle, oval or spiral in so doing (Figure 4.3a). If an imaginary line connecting the two deltas encounters at least one ridge circling the core, then the pattern belongs to the plain whorl subtype. However, if it does not, the pattern is distinguished as a *central pocket whorl* (Figure 4.3b). A more complicated whorl pattern is the *double loop whorl*, which consists of two loop patterns in combination (Figure 4.3c). The fourth and final subtype, the *accidental whorl*, is applied to fingerprints that either consist of a combination of two or more pattern types (with the exception of the plain arch) or whose pattern does not fit into any of the recognised categories previously described.

(a)

(b)

Figure 4.2 Fingerprint patterns: (a) plain arch and (b) tented arch

(a)

(b)

(c)

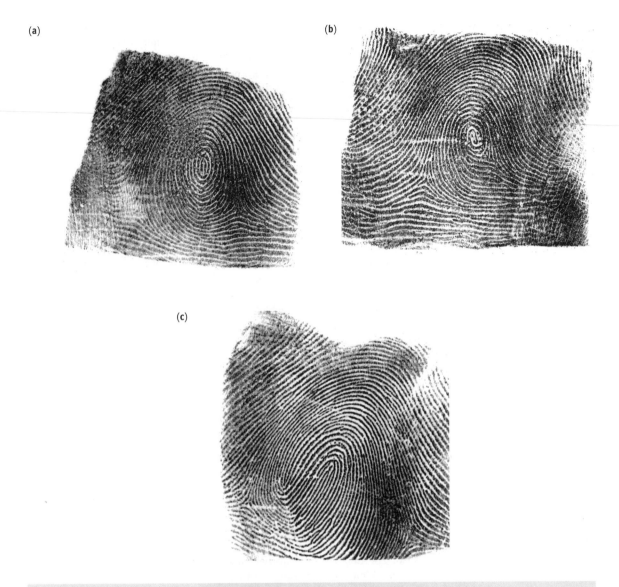

Figure 4.3 Fingerprint patterns: (a) plain whorl; (b) central pocket whorl; and (c) double loop whorl

4.1.3 The comparison and identification of fingerprints

Within each police force in England and Wales, the comparison and identification of fingerprints are carried out by highly trained fingerprint experts within the Fingerprint Bureau (Chapter 2, Box 2.1). In the past, fingerprint information was held on a series of card indices that had to be filed, searched and retrieved by hand – a long and laborious process. Each individual police force maintained its own locally based fingerprint collection, while a 'national collection' was kept at New Scotland Yard for further reference. However, this situation was revolutionised by the development of the Automated Fingerprint Recognition (AFR) system – a

NAFIS
National Automated Fingerprint Identification System: the national fingerprint database used by police forces in England and Wales.

computerised system introduced in 1992 that was taken up by most (but not all) of the forces in England and Wales. This AFR technology was then incorporated into its successor, the National Automated Fingerprint Identification System (**NAFIS**), which, by 2001, had become available to all police forces in England and Wales. The benefits of using NAFIS are enormous and include improved matching accuracy, an increase in the speed of search times and improved communication between police forces, to name but a few.

The national fingerprint collection held on NAFIS is the only definitive database that allows the identification of individuals. Every person who has been arrested and charged, reported or summonsed for a recordable offence has his or her fingerprints taken. In some cases, these fingerprints may be electronically scanned using the Livescan system and the captured images transmitted to NAFIS. This recently developed technique has been adopted by over two-thirds of police forces. If not already on file to confirm the identity of the individual concerned, these fingerprints are added to the national database. It is worth noting that *in the past* only fingerprints taken from individuals who were subsequently convicted were kept on the database as a permanent record of identity. However, following the implementation of the Criminal Justice and Police Act 2001, fingerprints from arrested individuals who are not subsequently cautioned for, or convicted of, a criminal offence need not be eliminated from the NAFIS system, although they are held separately within it.

The comparison of fingerprints recovered from a crime scene with those held on the national database may lead to the identification of an individual present at that scene (see below). Persons who have a legitimate reason to be at a particular crime scene (such as a householder in the case of a domestic burglary) may well provide the police with their fingerprints for elimination purposes. Fingerprints taken in these circumstances are not added to the national fingerprint database.

National Automated Fingerprint Identification System (NAFIS)

The NAFIS database holds approximately five million 'ten-print' sets of fingerprints and can be used to carry out a number of different types of searches, details of the two main kinds of which are given below.

First, it can be used to unequivocally establish the identity of an individual by comparing a set of ten-prints taken from the suspect with any held for that person on the database. The majority of searches carried out using NAFIS are of this type. Currently, the individual in question would have to be arrested and taken to a custody suite for his or her prints to be taken. However, in November 2006, trials of hand-held electronic fingerprinting devices (used to scan the subject's index fingers) began in a year-long pilot scheme that will ultimately involve ten police forces (known as Operation Lantern). These mobile devices facilitate access to NAFIS and will allow police officers on patrol to check, within a matter of minutes, the identity of individuals suspected of committing an offence.

The second most-used type of search involves the comparison of fingerprints left at a crime scene with those held on NAFIS. Fingerprints recovered from a crime scene are scanned into NAFIS[2] (these must be 1 : 1 in size). In each case, the finger-

---

2 Note that images with white ridges and black furrows, produced by some latent fingerprint development techniques, are usually colour-inverted so that ridges appear black on a white background before identification is carried out.

print expert marks up the individual characteristics of the scene fingerprint and the computer searches through the stored images held on the database for likely matches. As a result of this process, the NAFIS computer system generates the 15 best matches, providing the fingerprint expert with a list of possible suspects. However, it should be emphasised that the decision over the identification, if any, of a scene print rests with the fingerprint experts.

In making a comparison between a scene print and one held on file, the fingerprint expert looks at the following features, whenever these are identifiable in the scene print:

- the type of fingerprint pattern (i.e. loop, arch or whorl);
- the finger type (left or right hand, thumb, etc.); and
- the **ridge characteristics**, especially the ridge endings and bifurcations (where a ridge branches into two) (Figure 4.4).

Ridge characteristics
Recognisable features of the friction ridges that may be used in the comparison and identification of fingerprints. Also known as minutiae or Galton details. Examples include ridge endings and bifurcations.

(Fingerprint visualisation by Sarah Fieldhouse, Staffordshire University, UK)

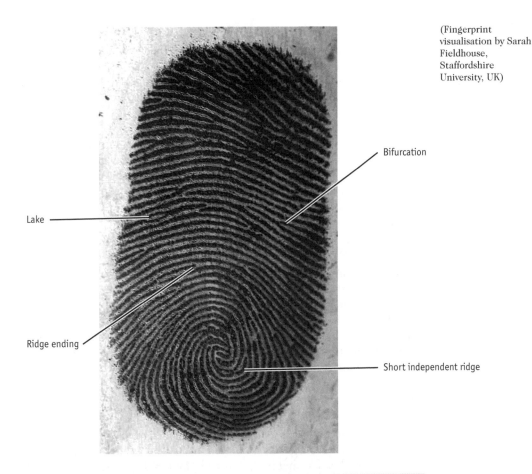

Bifurcation

Lake

Ridge ending

Short independent ridge

Figure 4.4 The ridge characteristics used in the comparison and identification of fingerprints
Note that the fingerprint shown is a negative image of one that was visualised using superglue fuming, hence the ridges appear in black

If there are enough ridge characteristics in the same positions on both the scene print and that held on file, the fingerprint expert can make an identification. Until recently, in the United Kingdom, the minimum number of matching characteristics required for a full identification was 16. However, today, there is no minimum quantitative standard and the decision over identification rests with the fingerprint expert concerned, whose opinion must then be validated by two other fingerprint officers.

4.1.4 The different types of fingerprint

Fingerprints recovered at an incident scene can usually be placed into one of the three categories outlined below, although sometimes the distinction is a fine one. As such fingerprints are normally transient in nature, categorisation into type enables them to be quickly and appropriately processed.

Latent fingerprints
Fingerprints that are invisible to the naked eye. These need to be visualised using appropriate development techniques before comparison and possible identification.

Latent fingerprints

Latent fingerprints cannot be seen with the naked eye. They consist mainly of perspiration exuded from the sweat pores, which occur in single rows along the ridges of the friction ridge skin. Perspiration is composed mainly of water (~95 per cent) with the remaining 5 per cent made up of other substances such as salt and amino acids. Some body oil or grease may also be present in latent fingerprints, transferred to the fingertips by touching other parts of the body such as the hair. Latent prints require visualisation before identification (Section 4.1.5). The chemicals used in their development react with the different chemicals present in the perspiration. In some instances, *negative* latent fingerprints may be formed when an individual touches a surface that is either covered in dust, for example, or that is sticky for some reason.

Visible fingerprints
Clearly discernible fingerprints formed by the deposition of substances such as ink or blood.

Visible fingerprints

As the name suggests, this type of fingerprint contrasts well with its substrate and is therefore easily visible to the naked eye. **Visible fingerprints** are formed when an appropriate substance is transferred by the fingertips onto a suitable surface. Examples of such materials are paint, blood, grease, ink, faeces, cosmetic materials and soot. It should be noted that the nature of the surface upon which a print is deposited might be the only factor that determines whether a print is classified as latent or visible.

Plastic fingerprints
Three-dimensional fingerprints formed when the fingertips are pressed into a suitable material such as putty or clay.

Plastic fingerprints

The third type of fingerprint does not involve the deposition of substances, visible or otherwise, onto a surface but is formed when a negative ridge impression is made into some suitably soft material. These are known as **plastic fingerprints** and may be found, for example, in fresh paint, clay, soap, candle wax, chocolate or putty. Being three dimensional, they are often reasonably visible to the naked eye.

4.1.5 The development of latent fingerprints

Latent fingerprints may be defined as fingerprints that are invisible to the naked eye. In contrast to visible prints and plastic impressions (Section 4.1.4), latent prints need to be developed in order to make them visible. In the early years of fingerprint collection, the availability of visualisation techniques was restricted largely to the application of various powders. However, over recent years, this situation has changed dramatically with many more new techniques (many of them chemical in nature), together with variations or refinements of existing techniques, becoming available. A brief description of the main techniques is given below.

Acid black 1, acid violet 17 and acid yellow 7

The reagents acid black 1, acid violet 17 and acid yellow 7 are used in the development of fingerprints contaminated with blood. The first two can be used on any type of surface, while the effective use of acid yellow 7 is confined to the enhancement of lightly contaminated fingerprints on non-porous surfaces. These blood reagents must be used as part of the sequential processing of blood-contaminated latent fingerprints (Figure 4.6), as they are not effective in developing those parts of a latent fingerprint in which only the usual constituents of sweat are present.

In the presence of proteins from blood or other body fluids, acid black 1, acid violet 17 and acid yellow 7 produce blue-black, vivid violet and yellow fluorescent images respectively. It should be noted that the blood reagent acid violet 17, but not acid black 1, may be used after the application of acid yellow 7 on non-porous surfaces. One or more of these blood reagents can be used for fingerprint enhancement at crime scenes if necessary (i.e. in those situations where it is not possible to send the evidential item or structure to the laboratory).

Fluorescence examination: the use of lasers and high-intensity light sources

Latent fingerprints may occasionally be observed to fluoresce when viewed, with appropriate viewing filters, under a laser or high-intensity light source. This inherent fluorescence is usually due to the presence of contaminants (such as grease, urine or coffee) in the sweat that forms the latent print (Section 4.1.4). Furthermore, latent fingerprints can be made to fluoresce by subjecting them to certain chemical treatments, for example spraying with zinc chloride solution after ninhydrin treatment and then viewing the prints under laser light. In some cases, it may be possible to make the background material fluoresce, thus showing up the fingerprint as a darker image. Iron arc lasers are still widely utilised for fingerprint visualisation but in more recent years a number of non-laser high-intensity light sources have been developed. These have some advantages over lasers, including greater portability.

Gentian Violet

Gentian Violet (also known as crystal violet) is a purple dye that stains the fatty components of sweat. It is particularly useful for developing latent fingerprints present on the adhesive surface of good-quality sticky tape, although it does not work well on Sellotape. It is also very effective on latex gloves.

Iodine fuming

Iodine fuming is one of the oldest techniques used to develop latent fingerprints but is currently used only rarely. It can be applied to practically any surface, both porous and non-porous (although the results usually show up best against a light-coloured background). When heated, iodine crystals undergo a process called sublimation whereby they change directly from the solid state to a gaseous one, without forming a liquid first. When latent prints are exposed to iodine vapour, a reaction may take place between the fumes and some component of the latent print to produce a yellowish-brown print. Importantly, the use of iodine fuming is not detrimental to the use of other, subsequent, visualisation techniques. Note that iodine-developed fingerprints are prone to fading but can be fixed with α-naphthoflavone solution, which gives a blue image.

Ninhydrin and/or DFO application

Ninhydrin (triketohydrindene hydrate) is an extensively used reagent for developing latent prints on porous surfaces, such as paper, cardboard, plasterboard or Artex. It is also effective in developing bloody fingerprints on most porous surfaces. A solution is made by dissolving ninhydrin crystals in a suitable solvent. In the United Kingdom, the recommended solvent from the Home Office is HFE 7100 but a number of other solvents have been developed for this purpose. The resultant solution is applied to the evidential object, often as a fine spray. The ninhydrin reacts with amino acids present in the perspiration component of the latent print to give a bluish-purple colour, known as 'Ruhemann's Purple'. This coloration can take up to several days, or possibly more, to develop but heat and increased humidity can accelerate the chemical reaction. Such conditions may be effectively provided by a humidifying oven, in which fingerprints can be developed in approximately two minutes. However, this treatment is not suitable for Artex, bare wood or plasterboard. These substrates are usually wrapped in black plastic and left until the fingerprints develop fully (usually after about ten days).

Once developed, ninhydrin-treated prints *may* be subjected to further enhancement, such as spraying with a zinc chloride solution, which makes the prints highly fluorescent, and then viewing them under an argon laser.

Another reagent that reacts principally with the amino acids present in fingerprints is the ninhydrin analogue DFO (1,8-diazafluoren-9-one). This produces a red-coloured fluorescent product, which needs to be viewed with a laser or high-intensity light source (thus necessitating the extra step of fluorescence examination). DFO may be applied to similar types of surface to those that may be treated with ninhydrin. If both reagents are used during the sequential processing of fingerprints, it is recommended that DFO be used first.

Physical developer (PD)

In the PD technique, a sequence of aqueous solutions is used to visualise latent prints on porous surfaces, especially paper, that have been wet. This procedure involves the immersion of the evidential object in a prewash solution of maleic acid (i.e. *cis*-butenedioic acid), followed by submersion in the PD working solution. This latter solution is composed of a mixture of a redox solution (an aqueous solution of ammonium ferrous sulphate, ferric nitrate and citric acid), surfactant solution and silver nitrate solution. After thorough rinsing in water and drying, the developed prints are photographed. The application of PD can often achieve results where other visualisation techniques have failed. As mentioned earlier, it is especially useful for paper that has been wet but is also effective on chip wrappers and materials soaked in petrol.

Powders

The application of powder to latent fingerprints is the most common visualisation technique in use today. It is suitable for hard, relatively smooth, non-porous surfaces, e.g. tiles and mirror glass, and works by adhering to any grease and/or dirt present in the print. In the United Kingdom, fingerprint powders are usually used at the crime scene when the objects under test cannot be submitted to the laboratory for appropriate treatment. In this situation, grey aluminium powder is generally applied, although black or white powder may sometimes be used instead. In the laboratory, coloured powders are used to enhance fingerprints that have been previously developed using superglue fuming (see later); they are very rarely used on undeveloped latent prints. Once an appropriate fingerprint powder has been selected for the surface under test, it is most commonly applied with a brush; synthetic fibre ones having largely superseded those composed of natural bristles.

As well as the various coloured powders, there are a number of other types of fingerprint powder available. For example, in some instances, e.g. on human skin and finished leather, the use of magnetic fingerprint powder is more appropriate for print development. A special device, known as a magnetic powder applicator, is used to apply magnetised powder to the surface in question without the need to touch it (Figure 4.5). The integral magnet removes excess powder from the print, leaving it clearly visible.

(Photograph by Andrew Jackson, Staffordshire University, UK)

Figure 4.5 The application of magnetic fingerprint powder

Fluorescent and phosphorescent powders (known collectively as luminescent powders) constitute another type of fingerprint powder. These are often applied to prints after they have been developed using other visualisation techniques. When exposed to laser or ultraviolet (UV) light, the luminescent powder emits light, thus enhancing the appearance of the developed print.

Radioactive sulphur dioxide

This technique has some use in detecting latent fingerprints on a number of different surfaces, including clean, fine fabric, adhesive tape and paper, although it is used very rarely. Briefly, radioactive sulphur dioxide gas (SO_2) is applied to the surface under test and reacts with the water component of any latent fingerprints present. These prints may be subsequently detected by autoradiography.

Small particle reagent

This reagent is composed of molybdenum disulphide (MoS_2) particles suspended in a solution of detergent. Small particle reagent may be applied to exhibits either by dish or spray application. The molybdenum disulphide particles adhere to the fatty components of any latent fingerprints present, forming a grey deposit. Small particle reagent is principally recommended for use in wet conditions outdoors or on waxy or polystyrene surfaces but, in practice, is usually not as effective as other appropriate development processes.

Solvent black 3 (Sudan black)

Solvent black 3 may be used to develop latent fingerprints on a number of non-porous substrates, such as metals and plastics, and is especially effective when these surfaces are covered with a film of grease or oil. The images produced by the reaction of this dye with the fatty constituents present in the latent fingerprints are blue-black in colour. In the laboratory a formulation of this dye based on ethanol is used, but for the crime scene a new formulation (based on methoxypropanol) with lower flammability has been developed.

Superglue fuming

Fuming with superglue vapour (ethyl cyanoacrylate) is a relatively recent technique that is suitable for use on a variety of non-porous surfaces, such as rubber, metals and electrical tape. It is simple to perform but potentially very hazardous. It must therefore be carried out in a chamber fitted with a suitable extraction system, such as internal carbon filters. Although originally a laboratory-based technique, a portable version of superglue fuming has been recently developed by Foster and Freeman Limited for use at the crime scene itself.

Treatment with superglue vapour causes the development of a hard white polymer on some latent fingerprints. Note that the negative image is usually used for identification purposes, so that the ridges appear in black (Figure 4.4). This polymerisation of the superglue, believed to be catalysed by the water content of the fingerprint, is effective in conditions of 80 per cent relative humidity, atmospheric pressure and room temperature (taking only a few minutes to develop). The rate of development can be accelerated further by heating the superglue to approximately 120 °C to encourage its evaporation. The active circulation of the air within the chamber used for fuming will also speed this process up. Most items subjected to superglue fuming are subsequently stained with a fluorescent dye, such as Basic Yellow 40, followed by fluorescent examination. This further enhancement helps to maximise the number of fingerprints developed.

Vacuum metal deposition

Vacuum metal deposition involves the evaporation of a metal, usually zinc or gold (or a combination of both), and its deposition, under vacuum, as a thin film on the latent print. It is particularly useful for the detection of latent prints on non-porous surfaces that are smooth, such as plastic packaging materials, e.g. polythene, glass, and photographic prints and negatives.

During the processing of a crime scene (Chapter 2), small items suspected of bearing latent fingerprints, which are suitable for chemical treatment, are packaged by SOCOs and sent to the in-force chemical enhancement laboratory (CEL). Here, highly trained, specialist laboratory staff select the most appropriate visualisation technique for each of the items submitted. In some cases, it may be necessary to apply more than one technique before a print is adequately developed. Therefore, the operator must be aware of the sequence in which different techniques can be applied in order to maximise the chances of success. Illustrative flow charts for the sequential processing of latent fingerprints on different types of surfaces are given in the *Fingerprint development handbook* (see Further reading), two examples of which are shown in Figures 4.6 and 4.7. Consideration must also be given to the possible effects of the different visualisation techniques on other types of forensic evidence that may be present. After suitable development, photographic images are sent to the Fingerprint Bureau for comparison and identification.

There will be items at the crime scene that are too large or otherwise unsuitable for submission to the CEL. If these have appropriate (ideally non-porous, smooth and reasonably flat) surfaces, they may be dusted *in situ* with aluminium powder to reveal any latent fingerprints present. Any developed fingerprints may then be photographed before being lifted either with special adhesive tape or with gelatine lifters. Gelatine lifters are flexible pads, approximately 1 mm thick, composed of a layer of low-adhesive gelatine sandwiched between a backing sheet and a plastic cover sheet. In use, the cover sheet is removed and the gelatine pad applied to the surface in question. Once the print is lifted, it is preserved either by replacing the cover sheet or by covering the gelatine with clear sticky-backed plastic. Gelatine lifters can be cut to the required size and are particularly useful where the surface bearing the print is uneven. After labelling, lifted prints are sent to the in-force Fingerprint Bureau, where they are input into NAFIS (Section 4.1.3). It should be noted that it is not possible for lifted fingerprints to undergo any further chemical enhancement. However, their clarity may be improved by the use of digital imaging.

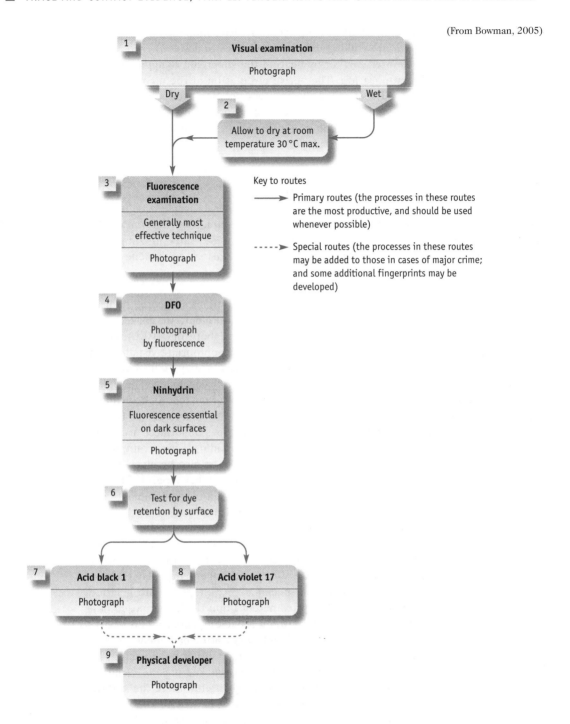

Figure 4.6 The sequential processing of latent fingerprints in blood on porous surfaces
Note that these recommendations were made based on best possible documented trials available at the date of publication

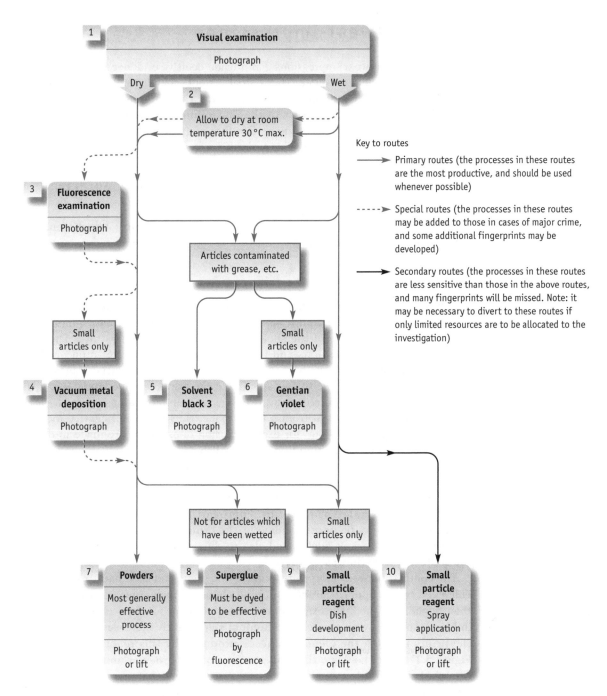

(From Bowman, 2005)

Figure 4.7 The sequential processing of latent fingerprints on smooth, non-porous surfaces (e.g. glass, paint or varnish and hard plastic mouldings)
Note that these recommendations were made based on best possible documented trials available at the date of publication

4.2 Footwear impressions

In some cases, footwear impressions can provide decisive evidence linking a suspect with a particular incident scene. They can also yield valuable information about, for example, the number of individuals involved and their movements at or near the scene of the crime. The recovery of the maximum possible number of footwear impressions from an incident scene is therefore of great importance, notwithstanding the often-laborious nature of this task.

4.2.1 Types of footwear impression, and their detection and recovery

Footwear impressions may be divided into two basic groups: two-dimensional impressions and three-dimensional impressions.

Two-dimensional footwear impressions

This type of impression is made when the undersole of a shoe[3] encounters a hard, flat surface such as a linoleum floor or a counter top. In many cases, material is transferred from the sole of the shoe and deposited on the substrate. These are known as positive impressions and include those made with wet mud or blood. Positive impressions are usually readily visible, at least in the initial stages before the material adhering to the sole wears off and the prints become latent (i.e. invisible to the naked eye). Less frequently, two-dimensional impressions are made by the removal of residual material from a flat surface, thus creating negative footwear impressions. These may occur, for example, when impressions are made in dust or on a surface covered with a thin film of wax polish.

As many two-dimensional impressions are virtually impossible to detect with the naked eye, a useful first step is to illuminate suspect areas with a high-intensity light shone from an oblique angle. This simple technique helps to show up a variety of different types of latent footprint. Footwear impressions (accompanied by a scale) should always be photographed at the crime scene, with shots taken from directly above, at various angles, and also to show the position of the prints within the context of the crime scene itself.

The contrast between footprints found at the scene and their background may be enhanced by the application of a suitable chemical technique and the footprints then re-photographed. For example, in the case of faint footwear impressions made in blood, spraying with the reagent luminol significantly increases the visibility of the prints through the chemiluminesce produced by this reaction (Chapter 5, Figure 5.1). Note, however, that this reaction must be viewed under conditions of total darkness. In other cases, enhancement techniques that are suitable for developing latent fingerprints are also applicable to footwear impressions. Examples include dusting with aluminium or Magna Black powder, superglue fuming (usually

---

3 Note that throughout Section 4.2 the word 'shoe' is used to indicate any type of footwear.

followed by the application of a suitable powder or dye) and ninhydrin treatment (Section 4.1.5).

Enhancement may take place either *in situ*, or in the forensic laboratory if the object bearing the print is easily transferable. If it is not feasible or appropriate to remove a print-bearing object from the incident scene, it may be possible to 'lift' the footprints in some way for further forensic examination in the laboratory. In the case of dust impressions, which are particularly prone to disturbance, this may be accomplished by using a portable electrostatic lifting apparatus (ESLA), such as the pocket-size Pathfinder, to transfer the impression onto a Mylar sheet and thus preserve it. As with fingerprints, footwear patterns that have been enhanced by dusting with aluminium or Magna Black powder may be lifted with gelatine lifters (as described in Section 4.1.5). It is worth noting that indented footwear impressions on paper surfaces may be successfully detected using the Electrostatic Detection Apparatus (ESDA), which is used primarily for the detection of indented writing (Chapter 8, Box 8.9).

Three-dimensional footwear impressions

This type of footwear impression is formed when the shoe is impressed into a soft, plastic material such as earth, sand or snow. As is the case with two-dimensional footprints, these are initially photographed at the crime scene in order to obtain a permanent record. They are then preserved, if possible, by taking casts. Plaster of Paris and dental stone are both used for **casting** three-dimensional footwear impressions.

To cast a footwear impression in soft soil, a mixture of dental stone and water is made using about 300 ml of water to 800 g of dental stone. This gives a thin pouring consistency. Before casting, the footwear impression is sealed with hairspray to prevent the casting material from damaging the finer details of the impression. After about half an hour, the cast (previously inscribed with details for identification purposes) can be removed from the impression but should be allowed to air dry for a further day or two before cleaning with suitable brushes and subsequent examination. Care must be taken when cleaning soil from the cast, as too much cleaning will remove important fine detail. Ideally, this task should be done by an expert in footwear identification.

Casting
A technique in which a suitable material is poured into an impression, for example of a shoe print, tool mark or tyre, and allowed to set hard before removal.

4.2.2 The creation of test impressions and their comparison with scene prints

Footwear impressions recovered from a crime scene can yield useful information, not only about the type of footwear worn by an individual but also about its make. This is particularly true of trainers (training shoes), which are currently the most popular type of footwear worn. Typically, these have elaborate undersole patterns that are usually peculiar to a particular brand, if not to a particular style (or even size of a certain style) within that brand. These may be identified by searching databases of different sole patterns, such as 'Solemate' created by Foster & Freeman Limited. This particular footwear database holds over 3500 sole patterns and covers

220 brands of work wear, casual wear and sportswear. Moreover, standardised sole pattern codes within the database allow it to be searched using SICAR (Foster & Freeman's shoe print management system). Using this system, unknown scene prints may be matched and the make of shoe identified.

On 15 February 2007, the Forensic Science Service launched its new online system for footwear mark identification know as Footwear Intelligence Technology (FIT). This computer database holds thousands of footwear impressions and will enable footwear impressions from crime scenes to be rapidly identified and, possibly, linked to suspects and to other crime scenes.

Footwear impressions may also give information about other aspects of a suspect's shoe such as size (although that of the sole does not necessarily accurately reflect that of the actual upper shoe), degree of wear and, very importantly, any random damage characteristics present on the undersole.

In order to link an individual with a crime scene through footwear impression evidence, it is naturally necessary to get hold of the suspect's shoes. Once acquired, these are used to produce test prints for comparison with the scene prints. In the case of two-dimensional impressions, test prints can be produced using a variety of methods. For example, the soles of the shoes may be covered with a layer of water-based ink and then imprinted, while worn, onto an acetate sheet. If test prints for three-dimensional footwear impressions are required, the suspect's shoe is used to create another such print, in as similar a fashion as possible to that found at the crime scene. The resultant impression is then cast as previously described.

When comparing test impressions with scene impressions, the pattern of the undersoles must first agree. The size of the undersole and the degree of wear present are also significant in matching a particular shoe with footwear impressions found at or near a crime scene. However, in order to establish an incontrovertible link between the test and scene prints, it is necessary to demonstrate that the random damage characteristics, acquired by shoes during general wear, clearly match (Figure 4.8). It is only these features that impart a degree of individuality to a particular shoe. As well as establishing a link between a crime scene and an individual (as demonstrated in the case study outlined in Box 4.2), footwear impressions may also be important in linking separate crime scenes together. This type of evidence enables the police to gather intelligence on the activities of the criminals involved.

(a)
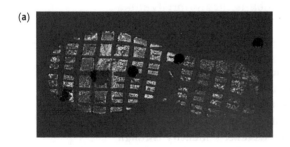

(b)

Figure 4.8 The comparison of footwear impressions: (a) a scene print and (b) a test print taken from a suspect shoe

4.3 Bite marks

In the collection of evidence from a crime scene, the significance of bite marks should not be overlooked. For example, these may be apparent on a victim's skin when the crime is one of rape or some other form of assault. However, bite marks may also be present on a variety of inanimate objects connected with the crime scene. These may be food items, such as apples, chocolate, cheese or chewing gum, or non-food items, e.g. bottle tops and pencils. In such cases, awareness and observation by scenes of crime officers are crucial to their successful recovery.

Bite marks are potentially important as evidence because it may be possible, in some cases, to make a match between them and the teeth of a suspect. Typically, an individual's teeth show a number of characteristics that can help impart individuality to them. These include features such as gaps between the teeth, the ridges on their biting edges, their relative positions within the mouth, and whether any of the teeth are rotated, missing or broken. The chances of making a match are improved with the number of these distinguishing characteristics identifiable in the bite mark, the number of individual tooth marks that make up the impression and its clarity. Such comparisons are the realm of the **forensic odontologist**.

The initial stage in the preservation of bite marks is to take photographs using oblique lighting. If the bite marks are sufficiently deep, this is usually followed by casting in an appropriate medium. Rubber-based dental impression creams, for example, are applicable to dental impressions on both human skin and water-soluble food items. In the many cases where the material bearing the bite marks is perishable, it is important that the treatment of bite marks is not unduly delayed as decomposition and/or desiccation processes will inevitably alter their appearance.

In order to make a comparison between the bite marks found at a crime scene and the teeth of a suspect, it is first necessary to make a cast of his or her teeth. This is then used to create an outline of the biting edges on a transparent overlay. Various methods are employed by forensic odontologists to achieve this, e.g. tracing from a photocopy of the cast, or impressing the cast into wax and then outlining the resultant cavities. A more recent method, and one that has been shown to improve the accuracy of the result, involves the use of computer technology. The cast of the suspect's teeth is scanned into a computer and used to produce a detailed outline of the biting edges, only one pixel thick, which is then printed onto a transparent sheet. This sheet bearing the outline image of the suspect's teeth is then carefully positioned over a photograph of the crime scene bite marks and the two compared.

The evidence provided by bite marks has, on occasion, proved highly significant in securing a conviction. In a number of notable cases, bite marks and bruises found on the body of the victim have been found to correspond with the teeth of a suspected attacker (Box 4.1). Moreover, recovery of saliva from the vicinity of the victim's injuries may lead to the confirmation of the attacker's identity through DNA profiling (Chapter 6).

Forensic odontologist *An expert whose knowledge of dental anatomy is made use of within a legal context, for example in matching a human bite mark to the teeth of a suspected individual.*

Case study
Box 4.1

The importance of bite mark evidence in the conviction of Theodore 'Ted' Bundy

On 15 January 1978, a savage attack took place in the Chi Omega sorority house (a female students' social club), Florida State University, Tallahassee, that left two young female students dead and two others seriously injured. Another student was attacked nearby, about 90 minutes later, but she survived and was able to describe her attacker.

A month later, on 15 February 1978, a young man driving a stolen car was stopped in Pensacola, Florida. He was identified as Theodore 'Ted' Bundy, an escaped prisoner who had been serving a 15-year jail sentence for the aggravated kidnapping of Carol DaRonch. Her attempted abduction took place in Salt Lake City, Utah, in November 1974. After his recapture, Ted Bundy was put on trial in June 1979 for the Chi Omega murders; a trial in which the former law student conducted his own defence.

Pivotal among the evidence presented at the trial by the prosecution was an enlarged photograph of a bite mark found on the left buttock of one of the murdered students, Lisa Levy. Importantly, the inclusion of a ruler beside the injury at the time the picture was taken provided the necessary scale. It was demonstrated in court by dentist Dr Richard Souviron that the outline of Ted Bundy's front teeth, created on a transparent overlay, and appropriately enlarged, exactly matched that of the photographed bite mark.

Ted Bundy was found guilty of the murders of the two Florida State University students and sentenced to death. After ten years on Florida's Death Row, he was finally executed on 24 January 1989. Before he died, he indicated that the number of young women he had murdered was in the region of 40–50 individuals. These sexually motivated killings had taken place in a number of American states apart from Florida, including Washington, Utah and Colorado, during the decade prior to his arrest in 1978 for the Chi Omega murders.

4.4 Tool marks

Tool marks are frequently present at crime scenes, particularly when the crime is one of burglary. Such marks or impressions may provide evidence that can, on occasion, lead to the positive identification of a tool, and, by association, to the identity of a suspect. Even when a suspect tool is not available, tool marks left at one crime scene may be found to match those found at others, thus establishing a vital intelligence link between separate crimes.

Tool marks may be made by a variety of different instruments. Some, such as screwdrivers and crowbars, are used as levers, while others, for example drills and wire cutters, are used as cutting implements. The marks and impressions left behind by tools may provide only general information about their shape and size. However, much more important in terms of tool identification are any striations that are detectable in the tool mark. These are caused by irregularities present on the edges of the tool itself (be it chisel, crowbar, screwdriver, knife, etc.), which have been acquired during the manufacturing process and/or during subsequent usage. These random damage characteristics mean that any striations they reproduce in a tool mark are uniquely identifiable with that tool. It is therefore possible, in some cases, to make a positive match between a particular tool mark and the instrument that made it.

When tools have obviously been used in an incident, the crime scene should first be searched for any fragments that may have broken off the tool during use, particularly in the vicinity of a forced entry. It may be possible to demonstrate that a particular piece of a tool recovered from a crime scene fits perfectly with a damaged tool found in a suspect's possession and was therefore originally part of it. It should be noted that manufacturing marks may also be significant when matching fragments of a tool together. As well as tool fragments, it is important that valuable trace evidence associated with the use of tools is not overlooked at the scene of a crime. This may consist of substances, such as oil or even blood, deposited in the tool mark by the tool, or, conversely, material, e.g. wood or paint, that has been transferred from the damaged surface onto the tool.

The first stage in the recovery of tool marks from a crime scene is usually to take photographs. The tool marks are first photographed to show their context in relation to the wider crime scene and then close-ups are taken. The correct positioning of the camera (i.e. with the plane of the film parallel to that of the tool mark), the use of oblique lighting and the inclusion of a scale are all vital elements in producing close-up photographs of acceptable quality. However, although important as a back-up method, photography in itself is not the best recovery method for tool marks found at a crime scene, since much of the fine striation detail of the tool mark is not reproduced in the resultant print. If possible, it is much better to physically remove the area of damage for later examination in the laboratory. Great care must be taken in the packaging and transportation of objects bearing tool marks, in order to prevent any damage or contamination. It is also necessary that any suspected tools recovered from the crime scene should be treated in a similar fashion. They should never be placed into tool marks to test for fit, since such an action could lead to contamination and/or damage of the evidence. If it is not feasible to remove the tool impressions from the crime scene, it is possible, in some cases, to take casts of them using a suitable casting material such as silicone rubber or dental impression cream. However, like photography, this is very much a secondary method, as casting will usually result in the loss of a considerable amount of fine detail

If a suspect tool is found, it can be used to create a number of test impressions for direct comparison with the scene tool mark(s). This is done by impressing the instrument into a suitably soft medium such as a rubber-based compound. When making test impressions, it is important to try to imagine how the tool might have been used at the crime scene and to recreate this type of action as near as possible. A series of test impressions made at slightly different angles and under different amounts of pressure will help maximise the chances of obtaining a test impression that replicates how the tool was used in the commission of the crime, thus allowing it to be realistically compared with the scene tool mark. Comparison of test and scene tool marks is usually performed using the comparison macroscope. In the example illustrated in Figure 4.9, a scene impression made with a screwdriver is compared with a test impression created with a suspect screwdriver. Note that, in this case, the extremely close match observed between the striations of the two images shows a unique match, thereby demonstrating that the two marks were made by the same tool. Tool mark evidence has been crucial in a number of cases in connecting a suspect with a crime scene, as exemplified in the murder of Kevin Jackson outlined in Box 4.2.

(Leica Microsystems
(UK) Ltd)

Figure 4.9 Tool marks viewed under the comparison macroscope
The left-hand photograph shows a scene impression made with a screwdriver while the right-hand photograph shows a test impression made using a suspect screwdriver

Case study
Box 4.2

The murder of Kevin Jackson

On 30 December 2001, 31-year-old Kevin Jackson was fatally wounded when he intercepted a gang of car thieves attempting to steal the Toyota RAV4 jeep belonging to his father-in-law, parked outside his house on the outskirts of Halifax, West Yorkshire. Two days later, on 1 January 2002, the father of two died in hospital. He had received repeated wounds with a screwdriver-type implement, culminating in a fatal blow to the left side of his head.

Launching their investigation, the police focused their attention on known car criminals. This led to the arrest, a few days later, of Rashad Zaman (aged 21). Examination of his car by a Forensic Science Service (FSS) scientist led to the discovery of a screwdriver in the boot. DNA analysis of minute amounts of blood found at the blade–handle junction of the screwdriver revealed a match with that of the victim, Kevin Jackson. Furthermore, examination by a tool-mark specialist of the damage marks present inside the lock of the RAV4 showed that the screwdriver found in Zaman's car boot was the implement used in the attempted theft.

In the ensuing weeks, two further suspects, Raees Khan (aged 21) and Rangzaib Akhtar (aged 20) were arrested. Searches of the residences of the three suspects led to the recovery of a number of evidential items. Key among these was a pair of Rockport boots from Rashid Zaman's house that were spattered with blood. Again, DNA analysis revealed a match with that of the victim, the pattern showing that the wearer of the boots must have been in close proximity to the attack. A further piece of evidence, and one of immense importance to the case, was the recovery of skin fragments from beneath the victim's fingernails that were used to procure a full DNA profile. This DNA profile was found to match that of one of the suspects, Raees Khan. Another type of evidence linking the suspects with the crime scene concerned footwear impressions left in the snow. Examination by a footwear specialist from the FSS showed that some of the scene prints matched a pair of Nike trainers recovered from the home of Rangzaib Akhtar, while others matched the Rockport boots mentioned previously.

On 20 December 2002, at Leeds Crown Court, all three defendants were found guilty of murder. Zaman and Khan were sentenced to life imprisonment, while Akhtar was given custody for life. On 26 November 2004, Khan's appeal against conviction was dismissed by the Court of Appeal. Applications by Zaman and Akhtar for leave to appeal against conviction were also dismissed on that date.

4.5 Tyre marks

The majority of major crimes involve the use of a motor vehicle of some description and, in some cases, this vehicle will leave tyre marks at the scene. It is important that any such evidentially valuable marks are accurately recorded by photography and preserved. Tyre marks are largely formed by the tyre tread (i.e. that part of the tyre that normally makes road contact), of which there is a multitude of different designs. This type of forensic evidence can give valuable information about the make and specification of the tyre(s) involved in an incident and, if a suspect vehicle is available, may be used to make a positive identification.

Tyre marks found at a crime scene may be categorised into one of the three following groups:

■ *Latent tyre prints*. This type of print is invisible to the naked eye and, as such, is easy to miss during a search of the incident scene. Latent prints are commonly found on smooth substrates and may be formed, for example, when a dust-laden tyre runs over a cardboard box. In this particular example, the tyre print would usually be lifted with a black gel lift and photographed. In other instances, appropriate chemical enhancement techniques may be used for latent tyre prints. For example, if a latent tyre track is contaminated with grease, Sudan black may be applied, while for those containing protein, ninhydrin or DFO may be effective (Section 4.1.5).

■ *Visible tyre prints*. This type of print may be positive or negative, depending on how it is made. *Positive* visible tyre prints are formed when a substance, such as blood or mud, is picked up by a tyre and then deposited onto a comparatively uncontaminated surface. *Negative* visible tyre prints are created when the tread of a tyre removes material from a substrate. This may occur, for example, when a vehicle is driven over a thin layer of snow.

■ *Plastic tyre prints*. Prints belonging to this group are three-dimensional, negative prints formed when the tread of a tyre is impressed into a suitably soft substrate, such as deep snow or soft earth.

There are many similarities between the treatment of tyre prints and that of footwear impressions (Section 4.2). As with three-dimensional footprints, the next stage in recording plastic tyre prints, after photography, may be to make casts using an appropriate casting material. Dental stone, for example, is suitable for casting impressions made in soft earth or sand (see Section 4.2.1 for technique details). It is usually only practicable to cast a short portion of a tyre mark (of approx. 60 cm in length), whereas, with photography, the entire tyre track can be recorded by taking sequential photographs that slightly overlap. Casting is probably best viewed as an important secondary method that may show details not apparent from photographs.

Once recovered, scene prints can provide valuable information that leads not only to the identification of the type of tyre, but also to the makes, and even years of manufacture, of motor vehicles on which such tyres were originally used. As mentioned previously, tyre tread designs are hugely variable and complex. They can be used to identify the tyre manufacturer and, through this, possibly, the makes of vehicle that could have been involved in an incident. Such information can help narrow the field when searching for a suspect vehicle. In some instances, details from the sidewall of a tyre may be found impressed on a surface, e.g. on the clothes of a victim involved in a hit-and-run accident. The sidewall, as the name suggests, stretches from the tread of the tyre to the wheel rim and typically contains specific data, e.g. of tyre size designation, as well as characteristic design detail. Such impressions can also help lead to the identification of the type of tyre concerned. If a suspect vehicle is found, test impressions can be prepared of all four tyres (and the spare) for comparison with the scene tyre prints (Figure 4.10).

(Photographs by
Andrew Jackson,
Staffordshire
University, UK)

(a)  **(b)**

Figure 4.10 The comparison of tyre marks: (a) a tyre mark left at the incident scene and (b) a test tyre mark made using a suspect tyre

4.6 Textile products

Strictly, the term textile refers to anything that may be or has been woven. However, as fibres (i.e. thin, flexible, highly elongated objects) are the fundamental unit of textile products, the term textile is also used in a broader sense to include most non-woven products that are principally made from fibres, including ropes.

Textile products can be of highly significant evidential value. Not only can they provide information based on the characteristics of their constituent fibres (Chapter 3, Section 3.1), they can also be examined to reveal details of their construction, mode of manufacture and, in some cases, patterns of wear and damage. Such information can be used to provide multiple points of comparison between, for example, a sample of textile fabric recovered from an incident scene and that found on a suspect or victim.

Under certain circumstances, impressions of textile products may be left at an incident scene. These may be found in a variety of media including dust, oil, blood and plastic materials such as mud and putty. It has even been known for the nose of a bullet that has passed through a person to carry an imprint of the fabric worn by that person (Chapter 9, Figure 9.8). Impressions of textile products that are more commonly encountered include imprints of gloves (as may be worn by a criminal to avoid leaving his or her fingerprints) and imprints of the clothing of a hit-and-run victim on the vehicle involved in the incident.

In many cases, examination of a textile product (or its impression) found at a scene is sufficient to allow class characteristics to be determined. These will enable the examiner to state whether or not it is *possible* that two samples have a common origin or, indeed, whether a given sample of textile product could have produced a particular impression. Less frequently, the presence of patterns of wear or damage have allowed examiners to make an unequivocal link between textile evidence found at an incident scene and that recovered from the belongings of a victim or suspect.

4.6.1 Damage to textile fabrics

A textile fabric is a manufactured product with useful mechanical strength that has a large area to thickness ratio and that is composed of fibres or, more commonly, yarns. (A yarn is a long, thin textile product made up of fibres.) Textile fabrics are used to manufacture clothing and a wide range of household products, including towels, tablecloths, bed sheets and carpets. The examination of patterns of damage to textile fabrics can reveal information about the way in which the damage occurred.

Violent crimes, such as physical assault, rape and murder, frequently result in damage to objects made from textile fabrics, usually clothing. The systematic examination of such damage, both with the naked eye and with the aid of magnification, will reveal features that are evident at three different levels, namely:

■ the garment and fabric, such as the position of the damage relative to any body fluid staining;

■ the yarn (where present), such as whether the ends produced by a severance are neat or frayed;

■ the fibres, such as the shape of each severed end.

Taken together, these features reveal patterns that can be useful in crime scene reconstruction and as sources of corroborative evidence.

Commonly encountered forms of damage include those caused by stabbing or slashing with a knife, cutting with scissors, tearing and, in many parts of the world, the discharge of firearms. In any one case, the pattern of damage produced is a function of not only the manner in which the damage was inflicted but also the properties of the textile fabric that was damaged. As the number of permutations of variables that this combination produces is essentially infinite, it is reasonable to suppose that each pattern of damage will be unique. Furthermore, actions such as washing the fabric after the damage was inflicted may have modified the pattern before it can be subjected to forensic examination. In addition, the pattern may have been complicated by, for example, further damage made by medical personnel in the course of the treatment of a wound.

Bearing all of this in mind, it would appear that it is extremely difficult, if not impossible, to draw any conclusions about the cause of a given example of textile damage by an examination of its pattern. However, this is not generally the case. This is in part due to the fact that a given class of cause of damage tends to produce characteristic damage features in a given class of textile fabric (e.g. a knitted fabric). On this basis, it is usually possible to distinguish between, for example, a severance caused by tearing and one produced by a slash cut (Table 4.1).

Table 4.1 Some commonly observed features that allow discrimination between tears and slash cuts in woven and knitted textile fabrics

Feature	Woven fabric		Knitted fabric	
	Tear	Slash cut formed by a sharp implement	Tear	Slash cut formed by a sharp implement
Direction of severance	Exhibits a preference to be parallel to either the weft or warp threads	Shows no directional preference	Exhibits a preference to be parallel to features evident in the construction	Shows no directional preference
Marked stretching associated with severance	Often evident	Not usually seen	Often evident	Not usually seen
The formation of curved or tubular portions of fabric at the severance edges, the axes of these curves or tubes being parallel to the severance	Often present	Not seen	Often present	Not seen
Ability to match patterns formed in or on the fabric during manufacture, yarn ends or fibre ends across the severance	Rare	Common	Rare	Common
Ends of yarns	Frayed	Neat	Frayed	Neat
Presence of short lengths of thread held within the fabric in the proximity of the severance line	Not seen	Not seen	Not seen	May be present (caused when a loop of thread is severed twice)
Cuts on the surface of the fabric at both or one of the ends of the severance	Not seen	Often seen	Not seen	Often seen

Once a hypothesis has been formulated regarding the cause of a given damage pattern, it can be tested by performing carefully controlled simulation experiments. These involve using a suspect implement, or implements, to cause damage to the textile fabric in order to establish the characteristic damage features that they form. These features can then be compared with the characteristics exhibited by the damage in question. In such tests, the greatest comparative value can be obtained by using the crime-damaged textile fabric in the simulation experiment. However, it is important that any other necessary forensic tests are carried out both on the questioned sample of textile fabric and the suspect implement before conducting any simulation experiments. Otherwise, valuable evidence, for example latent fingerprints on the suspect implement, may be destroyed.

4.7 Summary

■ Evidence gathered from an incident scene may take the form of recoverable items (see Chapter 3) or it may involve the recording and preservation of various marks and impressions left at the scene (dealt with in this chapter). Within this latter group, fingerprints are of particular importance, not only because they are commonly associated with crime scenes, but because they can be used to identify the individual(s) involved. In a restricted number of cases, bite marks, either on a victim's body or on inanimate objects such as food items, may be significant in identifying the perpetrator of a crime.

■ As well as marks and impressions made directly by parts of the human body, others may be left by items of clothing worn by individuals, such as footwear and gloves. Yet other marks and impressions may be left by objects used by, or associated with, individuals engaged in criminal activities. Tool marks and the tyre marks of vehicles both fall into this last category. Textile products may also be of evidential value, not only as the causal agent of scene impressions, but as the bearers themselves of damage marks.

Problems

1. Latent fingerprints are detected on a beer glass used in an attack in a public house. Describe the different types of technique that may be used in order to make the fingerprints sufficiently visible for subsequent comparison and identification. Why is the order in which these techniques are applied important to their successful recovery?

2. Write an essay describing the challenges involved in using footwear impressions recovered from an incident scene to identify a suspect individual.

3. A Scenes of Crime Officer notices an apple core on the dashboard of a crashed stolen vehicle. Is this particular object of any evidential value to the investigation? Give reasons for your answer.

4. During a forced entry into the back of an off-licence, impressions in the wood of the doorframe indicate that a chisel has been used. Two weeks later, a tool of this type is found in the garage of a suspect. Discuss the steps that need to be taken in order to establish whether this particular instrument could have been used in the break-in.

5. Tyre tracks from a getaway vehicle are found in a snowy coniferous wood. Discuss the information that may be obtained from this type of impression if (a) no suspect vehicle is found and (b) a suspect vehicle is located. In the

latter case, expand your answer to include the potential value of any soil and/or vegetation traces found on the recovered vehicle (you may wish to refer to Chapter 3, Sections 3.3 and 3.4).

6. With reference to marks and impressions, explain the potential evidential value of textile products associated with an incident scene.

Further reading

Bodziak, W. J. (2000) *Footwear impression evidence: detection, recovery and examination* (2nd edn). Boca Raton, FL: CRC Press LLC.

Bowman, V. (ed.) (2005) *Fingerprint development handbook* (2nd edn). London: Home Office Scientific Development Branch.

Cowger, J. F. (1993) *Friction ridge skin: comparison and identification of fingerprints*. Boca Raton, FL: CRC Press LLC.

Gaensslen, R. E. and Lee, H. C. (eds) (2001) *Advances in fingerprint technology* (2nd edn). Boca Raton, FL: CRC Press LLC.

McDonald, P. (1993) *Tire imprint evidence*. Boca Raton, FL: CRC Press, Inc.

Robertson, J. and Grieve, M. (eds) (1999) *Forensic examination of fibres* (2nd edn). London: Taylor & Francis.

The examination of body fluids

5

Chapter objectives

After reading this chapter, you should be able to:

> Outline the composition and biological function of each of blood, semen and saliva.

> Describe the presumptive tests used to determine whether a body fluid found at a crime scene is blood, semen or saliva.

> Explain the basis on which serological tests work, with particular reference to their use in various types of blood testing.

> Understand the importance of bloodstain pattern analysis in the investigation of scenes of violent crime.

Introduction

The scene of a violent crime is often characterised by the presence of certain types of body fluids. Those most commonly encountered are blood, saliva and, in the case of sexual assault, semen. Such materials can be used to establish crucial links between the victim and the perpetrator of a particular crime.

In this chapter, blood, saliva and semen are examined in turn. In each case, the composition and biological functions of the fluid concerned are described, followed by an exploration of the traditional methods used in their forensic analysis. This chapter does not cover DNA analysis, which is dealt with in Chapter 6.

This chapter also includes a section devoted to bloodstain pattern analysis. The interpretation of this type of evidence can yield valuable information about the events that took place during a violent assault and, possibly, give some indication of the order in which these events occurred.

5.1 Blood

5.1.1 The composition and function of blood

Cardiovascular system
In mammals, the system comprising the heart and the blood vessels. Through the pumping action of the heart, blood is distributed to all parts of the body.

Blood is a fluid medium, which in humans, and in other vertebrates, is found within the **cardiovascular system**. This system consists of the heart, which performs as a muscular pump, and the blood vessels, which serve to circulate the blood to different parts of the body. Blood has numerous functions. It acts as an internal transport system carrying, for example, waste products for excretion and nutrients for metabolism. It is also plays an important role in maintaining body temperature, defending against infection and protecting the body from the consequences of injury.

Human blood, in common with that of other mammals, consists of 55 per cent (by volume) blood plasma and 45 per cent (by volume) cellular material (i.e. blood cells and platelets). Blood plasma is a pale yellow fluid composed of approximately 90 per cent water and 10 per cent dissolved materials, including antibodies, enzymes, hormones, blood proteins, waste products (e.g. carbon dioxide), and nutrients such as amino acids and glucose. Substances, for example drugs (including alcohol), can also be found in blood plasma and may be tested for as part of a criminal investigation (Chapter 7, Section 7.5). **Blood serum** is blood plasma minus its protein content. This clear liquid is exuded when whole blood or plasma is clotted. The clotting process involves the use of blood proteins, such as fibrinogen, which, as a result, are removed from the plasma, thus producing the serum.

Blood serum
The clear fluid that remains after blood proteins have been removed from blood plasma by the clotting process.

The cellular components of blood may be divided into the three main types listed below.

■ *Erythrocytes* (red blood cells). These are the commonest type of blood cell and account for over 44 per cent of the total blood volume. They occur in concentrations in the following ranges: $3.8–5.8 \times 10^{12}$ cells l^{-1} of blood in women and $4.5–6.5 \times 10^{12}$ cells l^{-1} in men. They contain haemoglobin, an iron-containing protein, responsible for the carriage of oxygen (and carbon dioxide) in the blood. In contrast to most other mammalian cells, erythrocytes lack nuclei.

■ *Leucocytes* (white blood cells). These cells together with thrombocytes (see below) constitute less than 1 per cent of the total blood volume. They occur in concentrations of $4.0–11 \times 10^{9}$ cells l^{-1} of blood in healthy adults. White blood cells are involved in protecting the body from infection. They may be further subdivided into phagocytes and **lymphocytes**, which are responsible for the capture and ingestion of foreign substances (such as bacteria) and the production of antibodies respectively.

Lymphocytes
White blood cells responsible for the production of antibodies in response to the presence of antigens (foreign substances) in the body.

■ *Thrombocytes* (platelets). These are non-nucleated cell fragments, which are formed from the fragmentation of very large cells called megakaryocytes in the bone marrow. Adult humans normally have $1.5–4.0 \times 10^{11}$ platelets l^{-1} of blood. Thrombocytes are involved in the process of blood clotting.

5.1.2 Presumptive tests for blood

At the scene of a crime, presumptive tests may be used to detect the presence of blood that might otherwise be overlooked, either because it occurs in minute amounts or because it merges well with its background. In some cases, attempts may have been made to clean up the blood at a crime scene prior to the arrival of the investigating authorities. Even under these circumstances, however, traces often persist, for example in cracks in the walls and floors. Presumptive tests may also be employed to indicate whether a particular stain is probably composed of blood (and not of some other substance, such as ink, rust or chocolate) before other, more complicated, blood-specific tests are carried out (Section 5.1.3). Presumptive tests, with the exception of the luminol test (see below), are not usually carried out directly on the objects bearing, or suspected of bearing, bloodstains. Instead, they are performed on filter paper, or another suitable absorbent material, that has been rubbed either over a designated search area or over the stain itself.

The presumptive tests used for blood are based on the ability of the haemoglobin present in red blood cells (Section 5.1.1) to catalyse the oxidation of certain reagents. In most cases, the oxidising agent used is a solution of hydrogen peroxide ($H_2O_{2(aq)}$). Many of these tests use reagents that change colour as a result of oxidation. One example that is widely used is phenolphthalein, which is colourless in its reduced form but bright pink when oxidised. The stain to be tested may be prepared in the following manner: a small circular piece of absorbent card or paper (~25 mm in diameter) is folded in half and then in half again to form a point. A small amount of the stain is then scraped onto this point and the chemicals administered in the correct order. In the phenolphthalein test (also known as the Kastle–Meyer or 'K–M' test), a drop of the dye in its reduced form is added to the test material. The presence of blood is indicated by the development of a pink coloration when a drop of hydrogen peroxide solution is subsequently added. Another reagent that is used for this purpose is leuco-malachite green (LMG), which is also colourless in its reduced state but blue-green when oxidised.

Colour-change tests are capable of detecting tiny amounts of blood present at a crime scene. However, caution should be applied in the interpretation of their results as some vegetable materials, such as horseradish and potatoes, which contain the enzyme peroxidase, may give positive results. Such results are known as false positives. Moreover, it should be noted that, as colour-change tests give positive results in the presence of haemoglobin, they do not distinguish between human blood and that of other animals. This discrimination requires the application of specific tests, notably the precipitin serological test (Section 5.1.3) or the analysis of blood DNA (Chapter 6).

In some circumstances, the application of the luminol test for blood may be more appropriate than the colour-change tests described above. The luminol test is particularly useful when, for example, the surrounding surfaces have been washed down in order to eradicate any obvious bloodstains. It can also be used to reveal the presence of, for example, bloody footwear impressions (Figure 5.1 and Chapter 4, Section 4.2). Another advantage of luminol is that it does not adversely affect any subsequent ABO or DNA profiling (see Section 5.1.3 and Chapter 6 respectively).

(a)

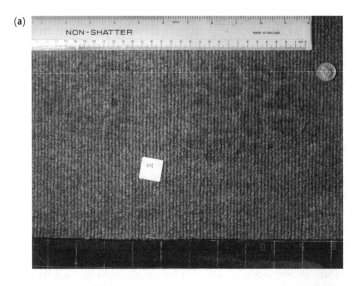

(b)

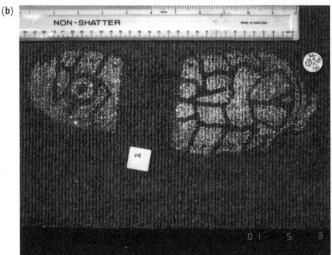

Figure 5.1 A bloody footwear impression (a) before and (b) after treatment with the reagent luminol

To perform the luminol test, an alkaline solution containing both luminol and an appropriate oxidising agent, such as hydrogen peroxide or sodium perborate, is prepared and sprayed onto the search area. Where blood is present, the luminol is catalytically oxidised and, as a consequence, a distinct glow is produced. This luminescence may be viewed and photographed under darkened conditions. Again, caution needs to be exercised in the interpretation of results from the luminol test as false positives may be produced by substances such as household bleaches, metals and vegetable peroxidases.

5.1.3 Serological tests for blood

If presumptive testing indicates that a particular stain is composed of blood, the next logical step is to ascertain whether that blood is of human origin. This can be done by:

- using the precipitin serological test to identify the presence of proteins specific to humans (see below, and also Box 5.1 for further information on serological tests);
- analysing for DNA sequences specific to humans (Chapter 6).

The precipitin test for species of origin

The precipitin test for species of origin is based on antigen–antibody complex formation, which produces a clearly visible, cloudy precipitate. This **serological test** was developed by the German biologist Paul Uhlenhuth in 1901. In his experiments, he injected rabbits with protein extracted from the egg of a chicken and afterwards harvested the rabbits' serum. He then introduced this antiserum into the white of a chicken's egg and observed the formation of a cloudy precipitate (precipitin). This work was further developed to produce antisera capable of identifying (by the formation of a precipitate) the blood protein of humans, and a number of other different animals.

The precipitin test may be applied to bloodstains in a number of different ways. For example, it may be conducted in a capillary tube, with a layer of human antiserum (i.e. serum containing antibodies specific for human antigens) overlain by a layer containing an extract of the bloodstain under investigation. The formation of a

Serological test
A test that involves the use of specific antibodies to detect the presence of specific antigens.

Further information

Box 5.1

Serological tests

Serological tests are based on the interaction between antibodies and antigens. Antibodies are proteins produced by the lymphocytes (a type of white blood cell) in response to the introduction of foreign substances (known as antigens) into the body. Antigens are generally proteins or complex carbohydrates. The interaction between an antibody and its antigen is highly specific and, consequently, the diversity of antibodies produced as part of the body's immune response is immense. In the normal course of events, the resultant antigen–antibody complexes are removed from the body by the scavenging activities of another type of white blood cell, the phagocytes.

In the past, antibodies required for serological testing were produced in the following manner. First, the antigen for the required antibody was injected into the body of a mammal, such as a rabbit. This caused the production of the corresponding antibody in that animal's blood. The blood serum containing the specific antibody (known as the antiserum) was then harvested and used in serological tests to detect the presence of the original antigen. However, this practice has been superseded by a technique that facilitates the production of monoclonal antibodies. Essentially, this involves the cloning of the lymphocytes of a sensitised animal to produce a pure solution of the desired antibody.

cloudy precipitate at the interface between the two layers indicates a positive result for human blood. In another method, known as cross-over electrophoresis, a gel-coated slide containing twin wells is used. A liquid extract of the bloodstain is placed in one depression, while human antiserum is placed in the other. The application of an electric current to the slide induces the antibodies (from the antiserum) and the antigens (from the blood sample) to move towards each other. If a line of precipitation forms where the two meet, then the bloodstain is human in origin (Figure 5.2).

Clearly, human antiserum is used first to establish whether the blood sample is human in origin. However, if the result is negative, and if it is deemed necessary to search further for the species of origin, the precipitin test can be repeated using antiserum prepared for other animals. These are commercially available for a number of animals including farm beasts and domestic pets. It should therefore be possible to determine the species from which a particular non-human bloodstain originated, if a suitable antiserum is available. The precipitin test is highly sensitive, needing only tiny samples of blood. Furthermore, it has been found to be effective for testing dried bloodstains more than a decade old.

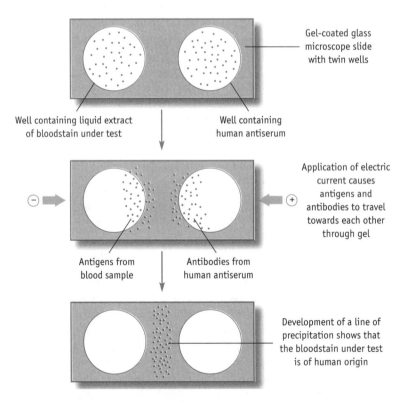

Figure 5.2 The application of the precipitin test using the cross-over electrophoresis technique

Blood typing

After a bloodstain has been identified as being of human origin, further forensic analysis can be used to establish whether it can be associated with a particular individual and, if so, to what extent. Traditionally, this involved the use of a number of blood typing systems; some based on serological techniques (in this case, the reaction of antisera with blood antigens) and some based on variant types of protein. However, this type of approach has been superseded by DNA profiling, which has a much greater ability to individualise biological evidence (Chapter 6). For this reason, only a brief outline of blood typing is included here.

Serological techniques have been used in the identification of a number of different blood group systems. The first of these systems – the ABO system – was identified by the Austrian biologist Karl Landsteiner in 1901. He categorised human blood into four broad groups based on the presence or absence of either or both antigen 'A' and antigen 'B' on the surface of red blood cells (Table 5.1). Figure 5.3 shows the approximate percentage distribution of the ABO blood groups in the populations of the United Kingdom and Western Europe. It should be noted that non-blood body fluids, such as saliva and semen, can also be used for the establishment of ABO blood groups, if the individual concerned belongs to that portion of the population classified as '**secretors**' (Box 5.2).

Secretors
Individuals in whom blood group antigens are present in non-blood body fluids, such as urine, semen and saliva.

Table 5.1 The ABO blood groups (where ✓ denotes presence and ✗ denotes absence)

Blood group	Antigen A	Antigen B
A	✓	✗
B	✗	✓
0	✗	✗
AB	✓	✓

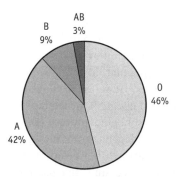

Figure 5.3 The percentage distribution of ABO blood groups in the populations of the UK and Western Europe

Further information

Box 5.2

Secretors and non-secretors

The term 'secretors' is given to those individuals who have significant concentrations of their A and/or B antigens not only in their blood but also in other body fluids, such as gastric juice, perspiration, saliva, semen and urine. The blood group of secretors can therefore be established from non-blood body fluids using traditional serological techniques. Approximately 80 per cent of the population are classed as secretors, while the remaining 20 per cent are referred to as 'non-secretors'.

The status of an individual as a secretor or non-secretor can also provide important information to an investigation. For example, if a saliva sample taken from the vicinity of a bite mark revealed that the individual responsible was a secretor but that taken from a suspect showed that he or she was a non-secretor, this indicates that the suspect did not inflict the bite mark in question.

However, the importance of the secretor/non-secretor status of individuals is now essentially of historical interest only. This approach has been made redundant by DNA profiling (Chapter 6), which can be used to identify individuals from any type of available biological evidence containing nuclear DNA.

Since the discovery of the ABO system, a number of other systems based on blood groups have been identified. Notable among these is the Rhesus system discovered by Landsteiner and the American immunologist Alexander Wiener in the late 1930s. They originally identified the Rhesus antigen in Rhesus monkeys (*Macaca mulatta*). Subsequent serological testing demonstrated that approximately 85 per cent of the human population contain the Rhesus antigen in their red blood cells. Such individuals are said to be Rhesus positive. Individuals who lack the antigen are termed Rhesus negative.

In addition to the use of blood groups, other systems have been developed based on certain proteins (including enzymes) found in the red blood cells. These proteins occur in more than one form within the population and hence are termed polymorphic. The variant types of a particular protein can be identified and, as their percentage occurrence in the population is known, this information can be used to help characterise blood samples. However, to be of forensic use, the proteins must be able to withstand drying and ageing. One example of a polymorphic protein suitable for forensic analysis is phosphoglucomutase (PGM).

The greater the number of independent factors (both blood groups and polymorphic proteins) that can be identified in a given bloodstain, the smaller will be the percentage of the population possessing that particular combination. This can be determined by multiplying together the frequency of occurrence in the population of the different factors identified by the serologist. This information can be used to associate, or disassociate, a particular bloodstain with a given individual.

5.2 Bloodstain pattern analysis

Much of the physical evidence present at crime scenes can be used to help establish the identity of the individual(s) involved. For example, fingerprints, footwear impressions and trace materials such as hairs and other fibres can all be used to connect an individual, or individuals, with a particular crime scene, albeit with varying degrees of certitude. In contrast, the analysis of bloodstain patterns, a form of physical evidence frequently found at violent crime scenes, may provide valuable information about *what* occurred during the course of a crime, and the order in which these events took place. It may therefore play a pivotal role in crime scene reconstruction (Chapter 1, Section 1.2.2). The interpretation of bloodstain patterns requires particular expertise, which is acquired, to a large extent, through direct experience. However, the bloodstain pattern analyst should be aware of all aspects of crime scene investigation so that any information concerning **bloodstain pattern analysis** can be placed in context.

When it is considered that adult human males contain approximately 5–6 litres of blood, and adult human females about 4–5 litres, it is not surprising that, in many instances of violent crime, copious amounts of blood are found at the scene. If the crime is committed indoors, the floors, walls and even ceilings may all show evidence of bloodstains. This type of evidence may occur in several rooms within a house and therefore the search of the scene, carried out with the aid of a good light source, should be both extensive and thorough. As with all types of physical evidence, it is essential that all bloodstains present at a crime scene are recorded by an appropriate combination of notes, sketches, photographs and/or video footage (Chapter 2, Section 2.3) before they are disturbed by the investigators.

For the purposes of this book, the patterns made by bloodstains present at a crime scene are grouped into three basic categories: active, passive and transfer. These are discussed in turn below.

Bloodstain pattern analysis *The interpretation of bloodstain patterns present at violent crime scenes to help reconstruct the events that occurred during the commission of a crime.*

5.2.1 Active bloodstains

Active bloodstains are defined here as those caused by blood that has been made to travel by a force other than that of gravity. Bloodstains of this type may arise in a number of different ways. For example, they may occur as a result of impact to the body of a victim with some part of an assailant's body, such as a fist, and/or a weapon, such as a hammer or baseball bat. Bloodstains caused by impact usually take the form of a spatter pattern, in which numerous small droplets of blood are dispersed over the target surface.

Another type of active bloodstain is caused by the projection of pressurised blood onto a surface. This occurs most notably when an artery is breached and the heart continues to pump. The volume of blood issuing from a punctured artery under pressure may be large (known as gushes) or relatively small (termed spurts). The overall pattern of these projected bloodstains may clearly reflect the rise and fall of blood pressure in the arteries (Figure 5.4). The presence of spines (i.e. linear stains) is also characteristic of this type of active bloodstain and is caused by the volume of blood involved and the pressure under which the blood is projected.

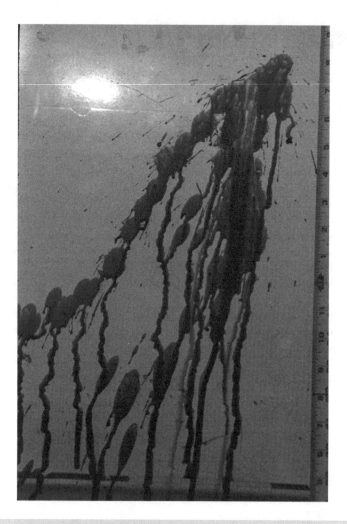

Figure 5.4 Bloodstain pattern produced by arterial spurting

A further example of an active bloodstain is one that emanates from a secondary object that is soaked with blood, such as the weapon used in an attack. Blood may be flung off the object as it is moving or as a result of a sudden cessation in its motion. Stains created in this fashion are sometimes referred to as cast-off stains (Figure 5.5). The pattern produced is characteristically composed of individual drops of blood distributed along a line. This line may be curved or straight depending on the circumstances of its deposition. By examining such bloodstain patterns, it may be possible to deduce the minimum number of times that a victim has been struck, as each line corresponds to at least one strike.

In addition to general information about the way in which particular bloodstain patterns have arisen, the experienced analyst may be able to deduce further valuable information from the bloodstain evidence available. For example, in the case of active bloodstains, it may be possible to ascertain the direction in which droplets of blood were travelling when they hit a target surface (such as a wall). If, on impact,

Figure 5.5 Cast-off stain traversing the ceiling

individual drops create tear-shaped stains, the direction of travel may be discerned from the direction in which the tails of the individual stains point. This is usually the same as the direction of travel of the blood droplets (Figure 5.6). The one exception to this rule concerns the stains created when a larger droplet of blood impacts on a surface throwing off smaller droplets. The tail portion of these smaller, 'satellite' stains point towards the parent drop (Figure 5.7). It is therefore important to distinguish between parent and satellite stains when interpreting the direction of travel.

(Image by Julie Jackson)

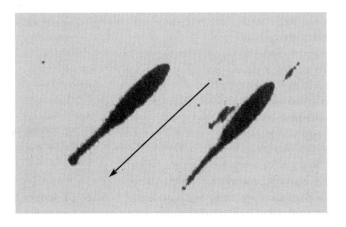

Figure 5.6 Bloodstains showing direction of travel

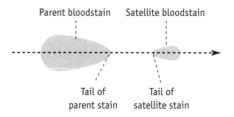

Parent bloodstain   Satellite bloodstain

Tail of
parent stain

Tail of
satellite stain

Figure 5.7 Parent and satellite bloodstains
The dashed arrow shows the direction of travel of the blood droplet on impact

Detailed examination of bloodstains, whether active or passive, may also yield information about the angle at which the blood has hit the surface. This is known as the angle of impact. It refers to the acute angle between the trajectory of the drop and the target surface when viewed at right angles to the plane of the trajectory that is perpendicular to the target's surface. For example, it is known that an essentially circular bloodstain on a hard, smooth, flat surface occurs when the angle of impact is approximately 90°. In general, as the angle of impact decreases, the shape of the resultant bloodstain becomes progressively more elongated. Use can be made of this to obtain information about the trajectory and point of origin of drops of blood (Box 5.3).

Forensic techniques

Box 5.3

Information from bloodstains obtainable by trigonometry

Consider a crime in which blood is caused to pass through the air and land on a planar surface, such as a wall, floor or ceiling. In such cases, trigonometric calculations based on measurements taken at the scene can often allow important elements of the crime to be reconstructed. In particular, it is often possible to calculate the angle at which each drop impacted with the surface. Also, it may well be feasible to establish the location of the origin of any two drops of blood that came from the same place and then impacted with the same surface in different locations.

These calculations are based on the fact that a drop of blood passing through the air will rapidly assume a spherical shape. When this hits the surface, it will produce a stain that is more or less oval. As shown in figure (a), the width of this stain (W) is the same as the diameter of the drop before impact (i.e. AB). The length of the stain (L), however, is not only related to the drop's diameter but it

is also dependent on the angle of impact (θ). As can be seen from the diagram, AB (which equals W) is the length of the side of the right-angled triangle ABC that is opposite to θ. Also, $L = BC$, the hypotenuse of ABC. Therefore:

$$\sin \theta = \left(\frac{AB}{BC}\right) = \left(\frac{W}{L}\right)$$

and

$$\theta = \sin^{-1}\left(\frac{W}{L}\right)$$

So, for example, if a bloodstain was 5 mm long and 3 mm wide, its angle of impact, θ, would equal:

$$\sin^{-1}\left(\frac{3}{5}\right) = \sin^{-1}(0.600) = 36.9°$$

Identical reasoning leads to the conclusion that a second bloodstain that is 4 mm long and 3 mm wide was formed by a drop that impacted at an angle of 48.6°.

Box 5.3 continued

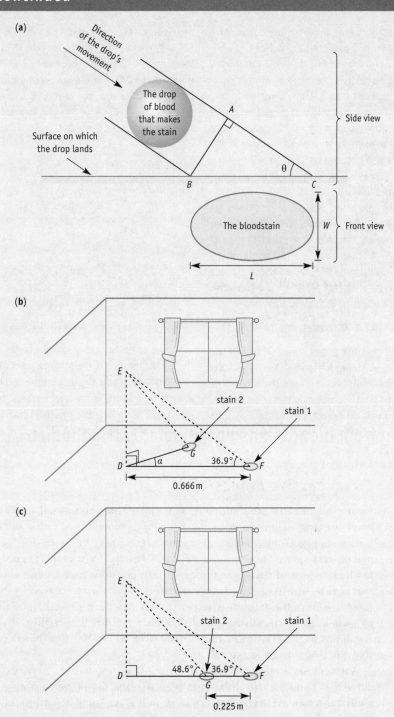

(a)

Direction of the drop's movement

The drop of blood that makes the stain

Surface on which the drop lands

A

B

θ

C

Side view

The bloodstain

W

Front view

L

(b)

E

stain 2

stain 1

D

α

G

36.9°

F

0.666 m

(c)

E

stain 2

stain 1

D

48.6°

36.9°

G

F

0.225 m

(a), (b) and (c) Information from bloodstains obtainable by trigonometry

Box 5.3 *continued*

If both of these stains were caused by drops that came from the same place, it is possible to calculate the position of their origin. As shown in figure (b), an imaginary straight line extrapolated from the long axis of the first of these stains will intersect with a similar line drawn from the second stain. The point of intersection of these lines (D) will lie on the surface. An imaginary line that passes through this point of intersection and that is drawn at 90° to the surface will also pass through the place where the drops came from (E). As shown in figure (b), two right-angled triangles are therefore created that share DE as one of their sides. The length of the side adjacent to the angle of impact can be readily measured in each of these. Therefore, either triangle can be used to calculate the distance from D to E and thereby locate the origin of the drops of blood. Take triangle DEF for example. The side adjacent to the angle of impact (36.9°) is 0.666 metres long. Therefore, the length of DE is given by:

$$\tan 36.9° \times 0.666 = 0.500 \text{ metres}$$

It is even possible to locate E if the lines DG and DF are coincidental (i.e. a as shown in figure (b) is 0°). Under these circumstances, points D, E, F and G all lie in the same plane (figure (c)). The problem is that the distances from the stains to point D cannot be measured as D no longer lies on the intersection of two lines. The strategy

now is to measure the distance between the stains (i.e. GF) and use the sine rule in triangle EFG to establish the length of EF. Then the distances DE and DF can be found from triangle DEF. If it is assumed that the stains of interest are identical to those described above, $E\hat{G}F = 180° - 48.6° = 131.4°$, $G\hat{E}F = 180° - (36.9° + 131.4°) = 11.7°$.

According to the sine rule,

$$\frac{GF}{\sin G\hat{E}F} = \frac{EF}{\sin E\hat{G}F}$$

If $GF = 0.225 \text{ m}$,

$$EF = \frac{(GF) \times (\sin E\hat{G}F)}{\sin G\hat{E}F} = \frac{0.225 \sin 131.4°}{\sin 11.7°} = 0.832 \text{ metres}$$

From this,

$$DE = EF \times \sin 36.9° = 0.832 \times 0.600 = 0.500 \text{ metres}$$

and

$$DF = EF \times \cos 36.9° = 0.832 \times 0.800 = 0.66 \text{ metres}$$

It should be noted that the methods described above for finding the location of the common point of origin of drops of blood assume that the drops move through the air in a straight line. This is rarely true, not least because of gravity. Clearly, therefore, the results of such calculations are estimates of the true position of the point of origin.

5.2.2 Passive bloodstains

Passive bloodstains are defined here as those that are formed solely under the influence of gravity. They include such features as blood flows, pools and drops.

Passive blood flows found at a crime scene may be extensive, covering surfaces and objects, as well as areas of the victim's body. However, this is not always the case as the position of the body, under certain circumstances, can prevent the gravitational flow of blood. The interpretation of patterns created by blood flows may provide information about whether a body has been moved since death. For example, changes in the direction of flow that cannot be attributed to other factors (such as characteristics of the surface over which the flow has occurred) indicate that the body has been moved.

An examination of other types of passive bloodstains may reveal information about the length of time that has passed since the bloodshed occurred. For example, in the case of drops and pools, drying times may be estimated by comparison with the results of experiments that take into account the surface conditions and environmental factors present at the crime scene. Another important aspect

(Photograph by Julie Jackson)

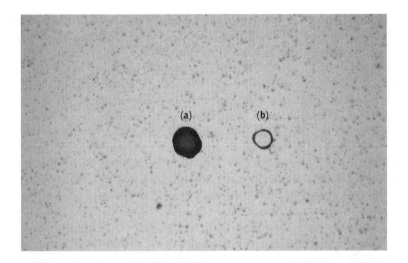

Figure 5.8 Standing drop of blood on a smooth, non-absorbent surface *(a) Left to dry undisturbed and (b) wiped five minutes after being shed*

concerning the drying of pools and standing drops of blood is the initial formation of an outer ring of dried blood within a very short time period. This has been demonstrated to occur within 50 seconds of the blood being shed. Attempts to remove such drying bloodstains after this time, for example by wiping, usually fail to eradicate the encrusted outer ring. It is therefore possible to observe whether drying bloodstains have been disturbed after their creation (Figure 5.8).

Observation of the shape of a passive bloodstain caused when a drop of blood drips onto a surface can reveal information about the angle of impact of the drop. This phenomenon is also relevant to the creation of certain active bloodstains and is described earlier in Section 5.2.1.

5.2.3 Transfer bloodstains

Transfer bloodstains are those that have been deposited on surfaces as a result of direct contact with objects contaminated with wet blood. The ease with which wet blood can be transferred means that this type of bloodstain is commonly present at bloody crime scenes. Close examination of transfer bloodstains may yield valuable information about the points of contact made between individuals and objects during the course of a crime. It may also help to establish the movement of the individuals involved.

Transfer stains may be created by any object that is wet with blood, including weapons used in an attack (e.g. knives or scissors) and parts of the body of the victim or assailant, such as the hands, feet or hair. To give a particular example, transfer stains may be left when a weapon is wiped on a piece of cloth. The pattern of the resultant transfer stain may be detailed enough to enable the bloodstain analyst to discern the class characteristics of the weapon that created it. In exceptional circumstances, it may be possible to proceed even further and identify the actual weapon responsible for a particular stain.

As exemplified previously, the pattern of a transfer stain is of primary importance in establishing the type of object that caused it. However, if a particular pattern occurs repeatedly, then the movement of the object in question may also be followed. In many cases, this type of repetitive pattern is caused by bloodstained shoes, feet or hands. After initial contamination, the amount of blood deposited decreases with each successive contact until it is eventually depleted and the trail of the individual responsible disappears. It is noteworthy that even when a trail of transfer stains becomes so faint as to be invisible to the naked eye, it may be possible to visualise the prints by the use of the luminol reagent (Section 5.1.2).

Bloodstain pattern analysis can be used to help establish the events that took place during the course of a violent attack and, to a varying degree, the probable sequence in which those events occurred. Included in this type of analysis are the location of any bloodstains present at a crime scene and the quantification of the amount of blood involved. The interpretation of bloodstain patterns requires considerable expertise and experience. For example, the texture of the surface receiving the bloodstain will influence the appearance of the pattern and therefore needs to be taken into account. The evidence provided by bloodstain pattern analysis may be used to refute or corroborate a particular version of events as given by a suspect or witness, as in the case of Graham Backhouse outlined in Box 5.4.

Another important point that needs to be considered is that not all of the blood present at a violent crime scene necessarily belongs to the victim. Some of the bloodstains may have resulted from injury to other individuals present, especially the assailant(s). If appropriate samples are submitted for analysis, DNA profiling (Chapter 6) can be used to identify the different types of blood present. Consequently, the decisions made by the person responsible for crime scene investigation as to which bloodstains should be sampled for analysis may be pivotal to the solution of a particular crime.

Case study
Box 5.4

The role of bloodstain pattern analysis in the conviction of Graham Backhouse

On 9 April 1984, Margaret Backhouse, wife of farmer Graham Backhouse, suffered severe leg injuries when her husband's Volvo car exploded as she turned the key in the ignition. Subsequent investigations revealed that the cause of the explosion was a crude bomb, made out of metal piping and containing numerous shotgun pellets, planted under the driver's seat. It was believed that the intended target was Graham Backhouse, who had previously complained to the police that he was the subject of a hate campaign. Before the explosion, this campaign had taken the form of threatening phone calls and letters and a bizarre event in which the decapitated head of a sheep was left on the couple's farm accompanied by a sign warning 'You Next'.

Box 5.4 continued

As a consequence of the events at the Backhouses's farm in Horton, near Chipping Sodbury, Gloucestershire, Graham Backhouse received round-the-clock police protection. However, this was ended, at his request, after nine days had passed and replaced by an alarm button linked to the local police station. On the evening of 30 April 1984, the sounding of this alarm summoned the police to the farm. There, they found the body of neighbour Colyn Bedale-Taylor with shotgun wounds to the chest and a Stanley knife gripped in his hand. Also present was Graham Backhouse, with several knife wounds to his chest and face, including a deep one that ran diagonally downwards from his left shoulder across his body.

According to Backhouse, 63-year-old Bedale-Taylor had come to his farm that evening and they had argued. He alleged that Bedale-Taylor had confessed to planting the car bomb that seriously injured Margaret Backhouse and then attacked him with a Stanley knife in the kitchen of the farmhouse. After a violent struggle, in which Backhouse received several knife wounds, Backhouse stated that he ran down the hall to get his shotgun, with Bedale-Taylor in pursuit. When Bedale-Taylor failed to heed a verbal warning, Graham Backhouse shot him.

However, forensic investigation of the murder scene revealed a number of factors that were not consistent with the story told by Graham Backhouse. Several of these anomalies concerned the analysis of bloodstain patterns, including:

■ the relatively small amount of blood found in the kitchen (where the violent struggle between the two men was purported to have taken place);

■ the absence of 'splash-type' bloodstains (usually associated with violent struggles) on the kitchen furniture and walls;

■ the presence of drops of Backhouse's blood on the kitchen floor (a pattern consistent with the dripping of blood from a stationary individual);

■ the discovery that some of the overturned chairs *covered* drops of blood on the floor (suggesting that the furniture had been upset after the struggle and not during it);

■ the presence of Backhouse's blood smeared along the top of one of the overturned chairs, yet the lack of any blood on the gun used subsequently by Backhouse to shoot Bedale-Taylor;

■ the absence of a trail of blood following the route allegedly taken by the wounded Backhouse from the kitchen to the end of the hall, where he kept his shotgun;

■ the discovery that Bedale-Taylor's hand that held the knife was *entirely covered* with his own blood (from his shotgun wounds), indicating that the knife had been placed in his grasp *after death*.

In addition, the pathologist involved in the case stated that the deep knife wounds suffered by Backhouse could only have been inflicted by another individual *if* Backhouse had remained still and made no attempt to ward off the attack.

The evidence provided by bloodstain pattern analysis was used to reconstruct the events that took place at the farmhouse during the evening of 30 April 1984. It was postulated that Graham Backhouse shot Colyn Bedale-Taylor and then attempted to cover up his crime by self-inflicting several deep knife wounds and disarranging the kitchen furniture to simulate the scene of a fight. By killing Bedale-Taylor, Backhouse sought to implicate him further in the attempted murder of his wife, Margaret (he had already implied Bedale-Taylor's guilt in this respect earlier in the police investigation) and therefore divert suspicion away from himself.

Graham Backhouse was tried in February 1985 at Bristol Crown Court for the attempted murder of his wife, Margaret, and the murder of Colyn Bedale-Taylor. He was found guilty on both counts and given two life sentences. His alleged motive in killing his wife was to claim the insurance money on her life, which was doubled to £100 000 in the month prior to the attempt on her life (he had debts totalling £70 000). It also transpired that the hate campaign directed at Graham Backhouse (see first paragraph) had been orchestrated by Backhouse himself.

5.3 Saliva

5.3.1 The composition and function of saliva

Saliva is 99 per cent water and has a pH of 6.8–7.0. It is produced by three main pairs of salivary glands (the parotid, submaxillary and sublingual glands), which open into the mouth region via ducts. Saliva performs a number of different functions. It cleanses the mouth and provides necessary lubrication. It enables partly broken-up food to be formed into a ball (known as a bolus) in preparation for swallowing. This process is assisted by the glycoprotein mucin, which is secreted by the sublingual glands located on the floor of the mouth beneath the tongue. Saliva also contains the digestive enzyme salivary amylase (also known as alpha (α) amylase), which is responsible for the breakdown of starch into maltose and dextrins. Cast-off cheek cells are also usually present in the saliva.

5.3.2 Presumptive test for saliva

Adults make about 1.0–1.5 litres of saliva per day. It is not unusual for this type of body fluid to be present at violent crime scenes, especially in association with bite marks. The presumptive test used in the identification of saliva is based on the presence of the digestive enzyme salivary amylase and its role in the breakdown of starch.

To perform the test, a sample of the suspect stain is added to a soluble starch solution. The reagent iodine, which reacts to the presence of starch, is then added to the mixture. If the iodine turns a blue-black colour, starch is present in the solution. No digestion of the starch has taken place, owing to the absence of salivary amylase, and the body fluid tested is not therefore saliva. If, however, the iodine undergoes no reaction and remains a yellow-brown colour, this indicates that starch is no longer present in the solution. Breakdown by salivary amylase has occurred and the result of the presumptive test for saliva is therefore positive.

In common with other types of biological evidence, saliva can be used to identify an individual through DNA profiling (Chapter 6). This is made possible by the presence of cells that have been shed into the saliva from the inside of the mouth.

5.4 Semen

5.4.1 The composition and function of semen

Semen is a fluid produced by the testes (male reproductive glands) and accessory sex glands, such as the prostate gland and seminal vesicles. The pH of semen (also referred to as seminal fluid) is slightly alkaline, ranging between pH 7.2 and 7.4. Semen usually contains a high concentration of sperm cells (also known as spermatozoa), which are the male sex cells or male gametes. The density of sperm cells normally ranges between 5.0 and 15×10^7 cells ml^{-1}. However, in some individuals, the density of spermatozoa is abnormally low. If this falls below a threshold of 2.0×10^7 cells ml^{-1}, the condition is known as oligospermia. In some cases, sperm may be entirely absent from the seminal fluid; a condition termed **azoospermia**. This occurs, for example, in males who have undergone a vasectomy for sterilisation purposes. Under these circumstances, azoospermia is usually a permanent condition.

Both sperm cells and egg cells (i.e. female sex cells or female gametes) contain half the normal chromosome complement. The full chromosome complement is restored when fusion occurs between a sperm cell and an egg cell (sexual reproduction). The sole function of the sperm cell is to reach the female egg cell and fertilise it. This is reflected in its structure, which is adapted to give it high motility. In human males, the seminal fluid provides a medium in which the spermatozoa can be transferred into the body of a female during sexual intercourse. The volume of the ejaculate (i.e. emitted seminal fluid) normally ranges between 2 and 6 ml. The average ejaculate is 3 ml in volume and carries in the region of 3.0×10^8 sperm cells.

Azoospermia
A condition characterised by the absence of sperm cells from the seminal fluid.

5.4.2 Tests for semen

In cases of sexual abuse and rape, the presence of semen at the crime scene provides highly important forensic evidence. As might be expected, semen can be recovered from the body of the victim in many cases. In addition, semen may also be collected from, for example, used condoms, bedding, clothes, furniture and carpets. For further information on the collection of samples from individuals involved in rape cases, the reader is referred to Box 5.5.

Further information
Box 5.5

The collection of samples from individuals involved in rape cases

In many cases of rape, there are no witnesses to the actual assault, other than the individuals directly involved. The presence of physical and biological evidence is therefore extremely important in establishing links between the victim and perpetrator. Traces of semen, in particular, are relevant in demonstrating that sexual contact has occurred and can be used to help establish the identity of the perpetrator through DNA profiling.

When a rape has been reported, the victim will usually be seen by a police surgeon (note that this traditional title is being replaced in more and more forces in England and Wales by the term 'forensic medical examiner' or FME). This role is often performed, on a part-time basis, by a general medical practitioner. He or she will have been specially trained to deal with cases of sexual assault in a sensitive manner. The examination of the victim (e.g. for injuries and bruising) and the collection of evidence

samples are carried out according to strict procedural guidelines. In the United Kingdom, medical examination kits are available for the collection of evidence samples in cases of sexual assault.

Please note that the information about essential and non-essential samples given below concerns female rape victims and male rape suspects. Those that are classified as 'intimate samples' are given in blue in the lists below, and both victim and suspect are entitled to refuse to supply them. However, both victim and suspect would usually be particularly encouraged to give blood samples for the purpose of drug and alcohol analyses, as detection of any such substances could have an important bearing on the case.

Essential samples from rape victims are:

■ clothing (to be removed over a clean sheet of paper, which is also submitted for analysis);

▶

Box 5.5 continued

- combings from pubic hair (for 'foreign' hairs);
- mouth swab (also known as a buccal scrape) (for DNA analysis; note that previously a blood sample was taken for this purpose);
- urine;
- vaginal swabs (for the recovery of semen).

Samples from rape victims that may be required, depending on case circumstances, include:

- blood samples (for alcohol and drug analysis);
- cervical swab (if more than two days have elapsed since the alleged rape);
- pulled or cut head hairs (control sample);
- cut pubic hairs (control sample);
- samples of body fluids found on skin.

If an individual is taken into police custody on suspicion of carrying out a rape, he will also be examined by a police surgeon and items of physical evidence collected.

Essential samples from rape suspects are:

- clothing (to be removed over a clean sheet of paper, which is also submitted for analysis);
- combings from pubic hair (for 'foreign' hairs);
- mouth swabs (for DNA analysis; note that previously a blood sample was taken for this purpose);

- penile swabs;
- cut pubic hairs (control sample);
- urine.

Samples from rape suspects that may be required, depending on case circumstances, include:

- blood samples (for alcohol and drug analysis);
- pulled or cut head hairs (control sample);
- samples of body fluids found on skin;
- traces of cosmetics on skin.

In addition to the essential samples listed above, a medical examination form must be completed for each victim and suspect. All samples, whether taken from the victim or the suspect, must be collected in accordance with prevailing procedures, designed to take into account ethical, legal, medical and scientific considerations.

Reference

The majority of the information on the types of sample taken from rape suspects and victims was obtained from:
Forensic Science Service (2004) *The scenes of crime handbook 2004.* Chorley: Forensic Science Service.

There are a number of tests that can be used for the detection of semen. A search of the crime scene using ultraviolet light may reveal the presence of semen, although many other materials including body fluids such as urine, also fluoresce under these conditions. Moreover, not all semen fluoresces, and, for this reason, this type of search tends to be used later in the search process rather than as a primary tool. Direct observation of semen under a high-powered microscope will reveal the presence of spermatozoa. If sperm cells are present, this is the most definitive test for semen available. However, in conditions of azoospermia, where no spermatozoa are present (Section 5.4.1), this test will give a false negative result.

There are presumptive tests used for the detection of semen that, unlike microscopic examination, are not dependent on the presence of sperm cells. For example, the acid phosphatase (ACP) test is used both in the search for seminal stains and in their presumptive identification. ACP is an enzyme secreted by the prostate gland. It is found in very high concentrations in seminal fluid compared with other body fluids. In the presence of diazotized *o*-dianisidine, acid phosphatase will react with α-naphthyl phosphate to produce a purple colour. If a body fluid is semen, a positive reaction to the acid phosphatase test will occur in less than half a minute. A purple colour may also be given by other body fluids (e.g. vaginal fluid). However, as the levels of ACP are much lower in these other body fluids, compared with those found in seminal fluid, the reaction time will be distinctly longer. False positive results may also be obtained from other substances such as plant phenols.

Another test used for the identification of semen that is unaffected by the absence of spermatozoa is the p30 test. This uses serological methods to detect the presence of p30, a protein produced by the prostate gland. Among body fluids, p30 is found almost exclusively in seminal fluid. Hence, this test for the presence of semen may normally be considered to be definitive.

Once a stain has been identified as semen, its sperm cells can be used to establish whether a particular suspect was involved in a specific attack, through the technique of DNA profiling (Chapter 6). It is noteworthy that recent developments mean that even in rape cases where spermatozoa are absent, limited DNA profiling may now be carried out. This is based on the analysis of Y-chromosome DNA obtained from skin cells left behind in the body of the female victim by the male perpetrator. This test can be used to help to establish that rape has occurred. The limitations of Y-chromosome analysis mean that the profiles produced are not unique and this test cannot therefore definitively identify the perpetrator. However, it can be used to exonerate any suspect whose DNA profile does not match that produced by the male skin cells found lodged in the victim.

5.5 Summary

■ Body fluids, particularly blood, saliva and semen, are commonly found at scenes of violent crime, providing valuable items of physical evidence. Presumptive tests are available for the initial detection of these three common types of body fluid; some of which may also be used as search techniques.

■ Blood, saliva and semen are all examples of biological materials and as such may be used to link an individual with a specific crime scene using the technique of DNA profiling (Chapter 6). This approach has effectively replaced the more traditional method of blood typing, which uses serological techniques to test blood, and other body fluids, to help identify individuals through blood group information.

■ The patterns created when blood is shed during the course of a violent assault can provide valuable information about the events that took place. In some cases, it may be possible to place these events in a probable sequence, based on the evidence available, in order to reconstruct a crime. The interpretation of bloodstain patterns is therefore an important aspect of body fluid analysis and one that requires considerable experience and expertise on the part of the analyst.

Problems

1. A body fluid stain found at a crime scene is identified (by presumptive testing) as blood. The next stage is to establish whether the blood is of human origin. Describe the underlying principles of the serological test that is used for this purpose and outline two of the methods by which this test may be applied.

2. A match is made between the blood of a suspect and bloodstains found at a violent crime scene. Traditionally, this would have been done by blood typing but this method has largely been superseded by DNA profiling. With reference to this chapter and to Chapter 6, compare and contrast these two different approaches.

3. Expert interpretation of the bloodstain patterns present at a violent crime scene can help to establish the events that took place. Using specific examples, discuss how bloodstain patterns can provide pertinent information regarding their creation and the probable state of the victim at the time.

4. A stain found on the clothing of a victim of sexual assault is suspected of being semen. Describe the different tests available for semen identification, including their advantages and disadvantages. Once it has been established that a stain is indeed semen, how can this be linked to a specific individual?

Further reading

Baechtel, F. S. (1988) 'The identification and individualization of semen stains' in R. Saferstein (ed.) *Forensic science handbook*, Volume II. Upper Saddle River, NJ: Prentice Hall.

Bevel, T. and Gardner, R. M. (2002) *Bloodstain pattern analysis: with an introduction to crime scene reconstruction* (2nd edn). Boca Raton, FL: CRC Press LLC.

Fisher, B. A. J. (2000) *Techniques of crime scene investigation* (6th edn). Boca Raton, FL: CRC Press LLC.

James, S. H. and Eckert, W. G. (1999) *Interpretation of bloodstain evidence at crime scenes* (2nd edn). Boca Raton, FL: CRC Press LLC.

Lee, H. C. (1982) 'Identification and grouping of bloodstains' in R. Saferstein (ed.) *Forensic science handbook*. Englewood Cliffs, NJ: Prentice Hall.

MacDonnell, H. L. (1997) *Bloodstain patterns* (revised edn). Elmira Heights, NY: Golas Printing.

Wonder, A. Y. (2001) *Blood dynamics*. San Diego, CA: Academic Press.

The analysis of deoxyribonucleic acid (DNA): DNA profiling

Guest chapter by Harry Mountain

6

Chapter objectives

After reading this chapter, you should be able to:

> Understand the nature of DNA and its relationship to genes.

> Appreciate that genetic differences between individuals can be revealed by examining their DNA.

> Comprehend the technology of DNA analysis.

> Understand the application of the technology to produce DNA profiles.

> Conduct a basic analysis and interpretation of a DNA profile.

> Appreciate the impact of DNA profiling on forensic investigations.

Introduction

In 1984, research and insights by Dr Alec Jeffreys at the University of Leicester, UK, led to the development of a procedure initially known as DNA fingerprinting. Its impact on forensic science cannot be overstated. Its application to criminal cases was rapid and, through some famous cases, was soon brought into the public eye.

Under the pressure of the adversarial legal system and with technical advances in genetics, the original DNA fingerprinting procedure has undergone numerous modifications and refinements. Modern methods and procedures are more precisely called DNA profiling or DNA typing, but in news reports and on the numerous crime programmes on television they are still commonly referred to as DNA fingerprinting. DNA profiling is almost taken for granted nowadays, but occasionally the elucidation of high-profile and dramatic cases based on improved sensitivity and precision reminds us that DNA profiling is a remarkable and revolutionary technology.

As introduced in Section 6.1, DNA profiling is one of the most powerful tools in forensic science. This chapter aims to describe the background and application of the technology. The topics covered are key material for introductory-level DNA profiling; extension material can be found on the website associated with this book.

To understand how DNA can be so useful forensically, the nature of DNA and genes and their relationship to individuality will be discussed in Section 6.2. The technology of DNA analysis and its application to modern DNA profiling is described in Section 6.3. Interpretation of the data generated is covered in Section 6.4. A second type of forensic DNA analysis using mitochondrial DNA is described in Section 6.5. Concluding the chapter in Section 6.6 is a discussion of potential future developments in the forensic use of DNA.

6.1 The forensic value of DNA profiling

DNA profiling has not displaced other important analytical procedures described elsewhere in this book; rather, it is used in conjunction with other procedures, depending on the nature of the investigation. A DNA profile is rarely the sole piece of evidence; it is not allowed to be in the UK. Its development, however, has been genuinely revolutionary for forensic science and when applied in its most powerful form, allows a biological sample at a scene of crime or accident to be linked very strongly to the individual from whom it originated. Before the development of DNA profiling, with the exception of fingerprints (Chapter 4, Section 4.1), this was not usually possible.

Depending on the events, evidence of biological origin at a scene of crime could be hairs, fingerprints, lip-prints, blood, semen, saliva, tissue samples, bone, urine, faeces, etc. Successful DNA analysis from these samples produces a profile that has the potential to identify a possible source of the evidence, whether the victim or the suspect. DNA profiling has progressed to such an extent that, excepting identical twins, it is extremely unlikely that two unrelated people could have the same profile. Hence, if evidence generates a profile and a suspect's profile matches it, then it is highly unlikely that any other random person could be the source. This contrasts with the forensic use of blood type (Chapter 5, Section 5.1.3) or hairs (Chapter 3, Box 3.4), which might allow elimination of a suspect but only rarely leads to the unambiguous identification of an individual.

Technical developments, partly related to sensitivity, have led to wider use of DNA profiling beyond that of rape and assaults, with which the first applications were associated. Reduced cost of DNA profiling, due to automation and expanded provision, has led to its being most commonly used in volume crime cases such as burglary and vehicle theft. DNA profiling evidence from biological samples greatly increases the chance of finding the perpetrators when there is often a lack of witnesses or other evidence in such cases. In accidents and disasters, DNA profiling can be used to identify the dead by assigning body parts to an individual. Badly degraded, old bodies can be DNA typed to identify the remains when DNA is available from possible relatives or from samples of the deceased's artefacts, perhaps a hairbrush, for the purposes of comparison.

The forensic use of DNA is not only possible but is widely applicable because:

■ within the DNA of an individual there are detectable patterns that are repeated a number of times that are characteristic of her or him;

■ DNA, being a relatively robust molecule, survives well under a wide range (but not all) of environmental conditions; if it was labile, its use would be limited. DNA is naturally broken down as the cells in biological samples age, but if the conditions are appropriate, such as following rapid desiccation or freezing, DNA can survive for centuries;

■ DNA can be isolated from any of a wide variety of biological samples likely to be left at a crime scene or incident;

■ the source of the DNA (blood, sputum, semen, etc.) does not matter and will usually produce the same pattern for any one individual. Exceptions to this are known but are rare;

■ sophisticated, precise and extremely sensitive techniques are available, which allow the detection of the above patterns in very small samples (a miniscule blood spot, a single hair follicle, lip-prints on a glass, physical fingerprints and even old, degraded samples can give useful DNA profiles);

■ the techniques are relatively cheap and rapid to carry out;

■ the data generated are readily assembled into databases in computers, which can be searched for a given DNA profile and thereby identify an individual from the available pool of information. In the UK, the National DNA Database is a huge repository of DNA profiles from individuals and crime scenes (Section 6.3.6);

■ a strong and widening range of scientific support from the fields of molecular and population genetics exists, enabling the appropriate interpretation of DNA profiling data to be made (Section 6.4).

Forensic applications of genetics are likely to increase in the future as they are undergoing development partly related to other dynamic aspects of the study of human genetics such as the Human Genome Project.

Before exploring detailed aspects of DNA profiling, it is useful to examine the nature of the data it produces and some simple but important points regarding their interpretation.

6.1.1 DNA profiles

A full DNA profile of an individual generated by modern technologies is shown in Plate 9. There is a large amount of complicated information on this profile, and its interpretation occupies much of this chapter. To introduce the topic of DNA profiling, it is easier to discuss a simplified version of a DNA profile. Figure 6.1a shows a DNA profile (from a different individual from that in Plate 9) in a diagrammatic form. The profile is a series of peaks arranged along a baseline resembling a graph. The upper panel shows the full profile. For clarity, in the lower three panels the full profile has been separated according to the colour of the peaks as they appear on a computer screen (as shown in Plate 9). In Figure 6.1a, these different colours are represented by solid lines, dotted lines and dashed lines (blue, green and black, respectively, in Plate 9). Note that, with the exception of those labelled X and Y, each peak is designated with a number. Basically, a profile from another individual would differ in the position of some of the peaks along the horizontal axis. The pattern of peaks is likely to be unique to a given individual. Simplified, diagrammatic examples of DNA profiles are shown in Figure 6.1b. If asked whether the profile from suspect 1 or 2 best matches the evidence, it seems trivial to reach a conclusion by comparing the patterns and answer suspect 2. It is tempting to conclude that the

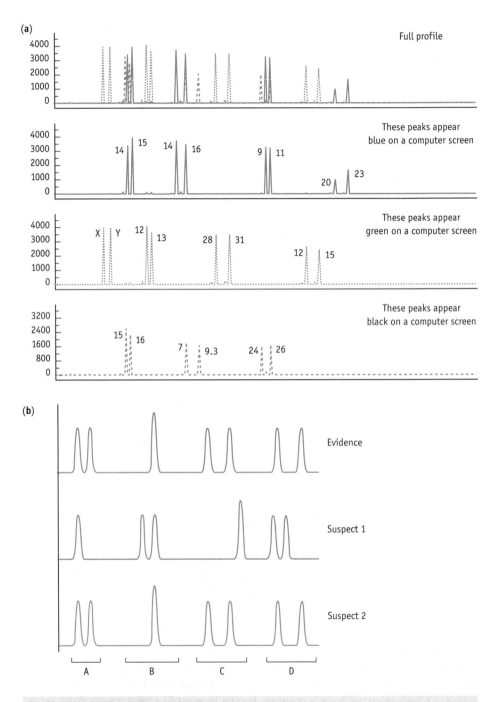

Figure 6.1 Examples of DNA profiles

(a) A modern DNA profile. The upper panel shows the full profile; for clarity, the lower panels show the same data separated according to the colour of peaks as they appear on a computer screen. (b) Simplified diagrammatic examples of DNA profiles from a sample of evidence and two suspects

evidence must be from suspect 2. Nevertheless, this may not be the case: there is more to analysing DNA profiles than simply matching the patterns. To interpret the pattern, you must understand how it is derived and what the peaks labelled A, B, etc. represent on Figure 6.1b. Also, one needs to know how common particular patterns are in the population. Before addressing these issues in Sections 6.3 and 6.4, it is worth considering why DNA is related to individuality.

6.2 DNA, genes and their relationship to individuality

DNA profiling works by looking at personal individuality at the genetic level, by examining differences between people in their DNA. The aim of this section is to explore, in a forensic context, aspects of individuality that have a genetic basis that can be revealed by analysing DNA structure.

6.2.1 Individuality and genes

A person displays his or her individuality in many ways that are often immediately apparent – facial characteristics, hairstyle, posture, height, voice, accent, style of dress, etc. Such features are in part the result of complex factors, including social and family environments, but some also have a genetic basis, e.g. height, fingerprints, eye and skin colour, and sex.

If everybody were genetically the same (as in identical twins), they would still be individuals and appear different because of environmental influences. DNA profiling would be pointless, as there would be no difference genetically between people. DNA profiling is, however, immensely powerful because, at the level of genes and DNA, people are unique (except identical twins). A person's unique **genotype** is produced at conception and remains with and dies with that individual. His or her children will carry parts of it but combined with another's DNA. No matter how the appearance of a person may change throughout life, their genotype does not change. The term genotype refers to the genes and their **alleles** that the person carries.

DNA profiling attempts to examine the DNA of an individual to produce a unique, unalterable pattern that will be a characteristic of any tissue or body fluid that originates from him or her.

Genotype
The combination of genes and alleles of those genes carried by an individual; his or her genetic make-up.

Allele
A particular gene can have a number of forms, each of which is an allele.

6.2.2 Genes and DNA

Genes are information; they are biochemical instructions that determine, along with environmental factors, the characteristics of humans and all other organisms. Familiar examples of such characteristics are blood type and eye, hair and skin colour, which are all, at least in part, under the control of genes. These instructions are passed from parents to child – the child obtains half his or her genes from the mother and the other half from the father. Eye colour, at least in its basic form of blue and brown, shows a simple pattern of inheritance. Skin colour is more complex: a number of different genes are involved, and colour can also be influenced by the environment, e.g. a pale skin can become brown after sunbathing.

Information can be written and stored in many forms such as on paper, on a CD-ROM or on audiotape. For each format, the information might be the same, but it is stored and transmitted differently. In each case, the information is written in a language. Genetic instructions are written and transmitted as information on DNA molecules.

The information carried by most genes constitutes an instruction to make a particular protein – it is the protein that influences the characteristic of the person. A gene is therefore said to encode a particular protein. For example, the human *HBB* gene encodes the β-globin protein, which is a component of haemoglobin, the oxygen-carrying red pigment of blood. As discussed in Section 6.2.4, the genetic instructions can be altered in an infrequent but important process called **mutation** to produce different forms of the gene. These different versions of the same gene are referred to as alleles.

Using the ABO blood type as an example (Chapter 5, Section 5.1.3), there is one gene involved. The gene encodes a protein that alters the surface of red blood cells, conferring on them the property known as blood type. Different alleles of the gene encode different versions of the protein, each altering the surface of red blood cells in a characteristic way and resulting in the different types A, B and O. There is a different allele of the gene for type A, type B and type O.

A useful analogy here is that of a written recipe for a cake: the recipe (genes) is present as paper and ink (DNA); it is the cook (proteins), reading the information, mixing the ingredients in the correct order and following the baking instructions, that makes the cake (body). To push the analogy, if the recipe is copied from person to person, mistakes (mutations) might be introduced in amounts or ingredients, and the cakes produced would become slightly different (they would have different characteristics because the instructions have been altered).

DNA, the material out of which genes are made, is a long complex molecule. Its key features are illustrated in Figure 6.2. DNA is a polymer of simpler molecules called **nucleotides** (Figure 6.2a). There are four different nucleotides, which can be joined together in any order and for enormous lengths. Each of the four nucleotides differs from the others in the type of base that it contains. The bases are adenine, cytosine, guanine and thymine. These (and, less formally, the nucleotides that contain them) are abbreviated to A, C, G and T, respectively. The language of genes is written in an alphabet of these four bases. A specific gene will have a particular sequence of bases. This sequence is read by the machinery of the cell, in complex processes called transcription and translation, to direct the synthesis of the particular protein encoded by the gene.

DNA has the structure of the well-known double helix (Figure 6.2b), which consists of two strands, each a polymeric chain of nucleotides, wound around each other. The strands consist of sugar molecules, in the nucleotides, linked by phosphate groups, forming the sugar–phosphate backbone. If the molecule is untwisted, it resembles a ladder, the rungs being the **base pairs** (Figure 6.2c). Each strand has a 5' end and 3' end (so-called because of the detailed molecular structure). This gives polarity or direction to the strands called the 5' to 3' direction. Note that in the double helix, the strands are in opposite directions and are said to be anti-parallel. Attached to the sugars are the bases; hydrogen bonds between the bases hold together the two strands of the double helix. Note that A can pair only with T, and G only with C: these are the base-pairing rules. Hence, if you know the sequence of one strand, that of the other is also known by applying the rules of base pairing. The information contained in a DNA molecule is its sequence, i.e. the order of bases along the molecule (Figure 6.2d).

Mutation

A change in a gene; an alteration in its DNA sequence. This process generates new alleles.

Nucleotides

The building blocks of the nucleic acids DNA and RNA.

Base pairs

An association between the bases of the nucleotides on opposite strands of the DNA double helix. Hydrogen bonds link the bases. There are two types of base pairs: A–T and G–C. The length of DNA molecules and genes is usually measured in base-pairs.

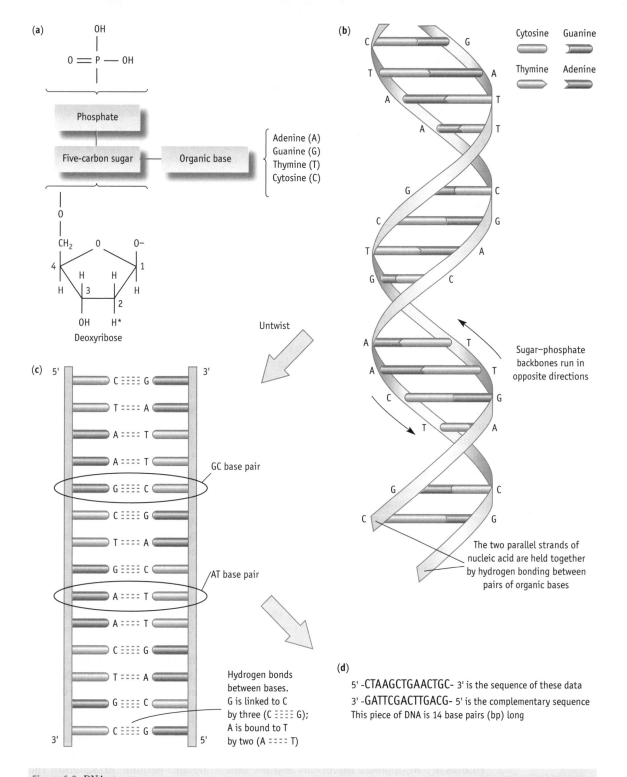

(a)

OH
|
O = P — OH
|

Phosphate

Five-carbon sugar — Organic base — Adenine (A)
Guanine (G)
Thymine (T)
Cytosine (C)

Deoxyribose

(b)

Cytosine   Guanine
Thymine   Adenine

Sugar–phosphate backbones run in opposite directions

The two parallel strands of nucleic acid are held together by hydrogen bonding between pairs of organic bases

Untwist

(c)

5'   3'

C :::: G
T ==== A
A ==== T
A ==== T
G :::: C   GC base pair
C :::: G
T ==== A
G :::: C
A ==== T   AT base pair
A ==== T
C :::: G
T ==== A
G :::: C
C :::: G

3'   5'

Hydrogen bonds between bases. G is linked to C by three (C :::: G); A is bound to T by two (A ==== T)

(d)

5' -CTAAGCTGAACTGC- 3' is the sequence of these data
3' -GATTCGACTTGACG- 5' is the complementary sequence
This piece of DNA is 14 base pairs (bp) long

Figure 6.2 DNA structure

The diagrams show the key features of the DNA molecule. (a) The general structure of a nucleotide consisting of a base, sugar (deoxyribose) and phosphate group. (b)The double helical structure of DNA consists of two polynucleotide strands wound around each other and held together by hydrogen bonds between complementary bases. (c) A simplified diagram of DNA. (d) A short sequence of DNA

Each gene is made up of a specific sequence of thousands of the four nucleotides (A, C, G and T). The length of the sequence depends on the gene itself and the size of the protein it encodes. The length of a section of DNA or a gene is measured in base pairs (bp). Figure 6.2d shows a short sequence of DNA 14 bp long, but note that DNA molecules can be very long from thousands (10^3) to hundreds of millions (10^8) of base pairs.

In early 2001, the draft sequence of the human genome was published. This is the complete DNA sequence of human DNA and the total length is 3.2×10^9 base pairs. The organisation of this huge amount of DNA and genetic information is discussed in the next section.

6.2.3 The hierarchy of DNA organisation

DNA is organised into distinct structures within the cells of an organism. Figure 6.3 shows its various levels of organisation. The short DNA molecule, discussed in Figure 6.2, is a section of a longer sequence called a gene (Figure 6.3b). A gene sequence contains the information to direct the synthesis of another type of nucleic acid called RNA. RNA is also a polymer of nucleotides, but it differs from DNA in three main features: the structure of the sugar; a base called uracil replaces thymine (Figure 6.2a); it is not usually in a double-stranded helical form. The gene sequence in Figure 6.3b contains the information to direct the synthesis of messenger RNA (mRNA), which encodes a particular protein that influences the phenotype of the organism. Curiously, in the majority of human genes, the genetic information encoding a protein is split up into sections called **exons**. The DNA sequences between the exons are called **introns**; an important point here is that not all DNA is involved in encoding proteins. The role of this non-coding DNA is not always clear and it is sometimes referred to as 'junk DNA'.

Figure 6.3c shows an even longer DNA molecule carrying several different genes. Between the genes is intergenic DNA; in common with intron DNA, this does not encode proteins. **Chromosomes** (Figure 6.3d) are very long DNA sequences carrying hundreds or thousands of genes. Each chromosome consists of a single, very long DNA molecule wound around and packaged with proteins. Along the chromosomes, written in the DNA sequence, are genes. The exact total number of human genes is as yet uncertain. Initial estimates of the gene number after the genome was sequenced in 2001 were in the order of 30 000–35 000 but since then this has been revised to between 20 000 and 25 000.

The total set of chromosomes is called the karyotype (Figure 6.3f). In humans this consists of 22 chromosome pairs and two sex chromosomes (XX for a female, XY for a male), giving a total of 46. One chromosome in each pair comes from the mother and one comes from the father. The 44 non-sex chromosomes are called autosomes; when arranged in approximate order of size, they are designated 1, 2, 3 to 22, with chromosome 1 being the largest (Figure 6.3f). Most cells carry two copies of each autosome and two sex chromosomes and are said to be **diploid**. **Gametes** are the exception to this; they have half the chromosome number and are said to be **haploid**. Each egg carries each of the 22 autosomes and a single chromosome X. Each sperm carries the 22 autosomes and either an X or a Y chromosome. So, during fertilisation, an egg fuses with a sperm to create a cell containing 22 pairs of autosomes and two sex chromosomes – the diploid number. If the sperm carries chromosome X, then the child will be female; if it carries chromosome Y, the child will be male.

Exons

The parts of genes that carry protein information.

Introns

DNA sequences within genes between exons.

Chromosome

A thread-like structure consisting of a long strand of DNA, carrying many genes, in a complex with protein.

Diploid

Having two sets of chromosomes, one from each parent.

Gametes

The sex cells: sperm in males, eggs in females.

Haploid

Having only one set of chromosomes. Usually applies to gametes.

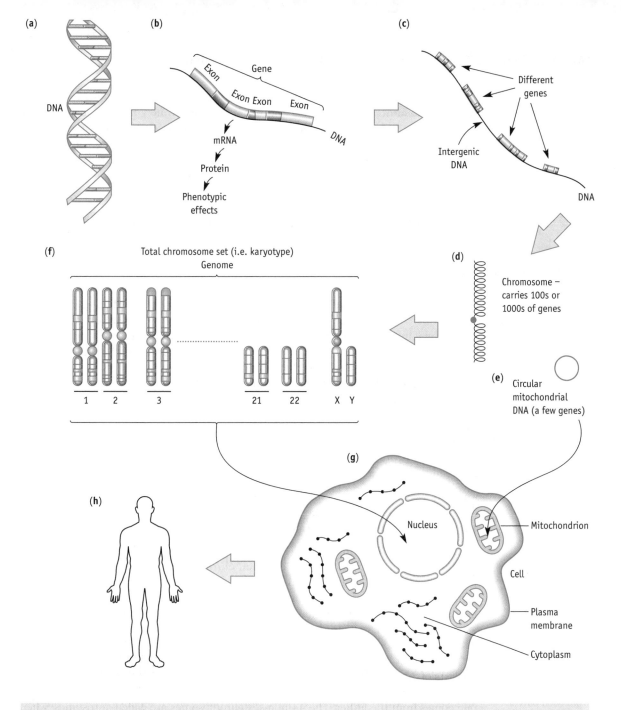

Figure 6.3 A hierarchy of organisation of DNA and genes

(a) The DNA segment (from Figure 6.2b) is part of a longer DNA molecule called a gene. (b) Simplified structure of a human gene. (c) Very long DNA molecules can carry numerous different genes separated by intergenic DNA. (d) Very long DNA sequences carrying hundreds to thousands of genes form chromosomes. (e) The DNA in the mitochondrion is a circular molecule 16 569 bp long, which carries only a few genes. (f) In the cell nucleus of humans are 22 chromosome pairs and two sex chromosomes (XX for a female, XY for a male). The total set of chromosomes is called the karyotype. (g) In the cell, the 46 chromosomes (f) are present in the nucleus, while the small circular mitochondrial DNA (e) is present in large numbers in the mitochondria. (h) A human adult contains in the order of 10^{14} cells of about 200 different types

An important point here is that each autosome is present twice – one is a maternal chromosome, the other a paternal chromosome. For example, both chromosomes 1 carry the same set of genes, whether from the father or mother, *but* the form of each gene may be different; that is, they may be different alleles – this is very important and is discussed below in Sections 6.2.4–6.2.6. Note, though, that in males there is only a single Y chromosome and a single X chromosome; in males, these chromosomes are haploid.

The 46 chromosomes of the human karyotype contain a total length of DNA of about 2 m, which is packed into a microscopic cell nucleus, about 5μm diameter, in each cell of the body (Figure 6.3g). As this DNA is located exclusively in the cell nucleus, it is referred to as **nuclear DNA**.

Nuclear DNA
DNA present in chromosomes in the cell nucleus.

Another distinct type of DNA is present in most cells. The cell organelle called the mitochondrion (Figure 6.3g), of which some cells have thousands, contains DNA called **mitochondrial DNA** (mtDNA). Unlike nuclear DNA, which is linear and 10^7–10^8 bp long, mtDNA is a DNA circle that is very much smaller, being only 16 569 bp long (Figure 6.3e). Also unlike nuclear DNA, a child receives mtDNA only from its mother. Normally the father's mtDNA is not present in the child. mtDNA has forensic uses, which are described in Section 6.5.

Mitochondrial DNA
A small DNA circle located in the mitochondrion.

The human adult (Figure 6.3h) contains about 10^{14} (i.e. 100 trillion) cells. The majority of these are diploid and carry identical DNA. Exceptions are sperm and egg cells, which are haploid, and the red blood cells, which are unique in carrying no DNA. Any sample from a person that contains cells, intact or damaged, is a potential source of DNA for forensic analysis – DNA from any part of the person will usually generate the same profile. Exceptions are known; for example, in people who have received transfused blood, the donors' DNA will be detected for a time; people who have received a transplanted organ or bone marrow will produce a profile of the donor in tissue derived from the transplant; a sufferer of mouth cancer may produce a DNA profile from an oral sample different from one from other tissues; rare individuals, called chimaeras, who are made up of two genetically distinct groups of cells, may produce a different profile from different tissues. All of these interesting exceptions are considered to be rare.

6.2.4 Genetic differences: mutations and alleles

As discussed in Section 6.2.2, an alteration (mutation) in the DNA sequence of a gene can alter the encoded protein. Sometimes the alteration in the DNA results in a non-functional protein. If the protein is very important for the correct function of the cell or organism, then the result may be lethality or, if not so severe, a genetic disease. Sometimes the changes have only minor consequences, for example the gene for the ABO blood type. Alleles are variants of the DNA sequence of the gene. In a population, a gene can have many alleles (hundreds in some cases), but each individual carries only up to two alleles for a particular gene. This is because each gene is present in two copies, as each chromosome that carries the gene is present twice in a diploid cell, one copy from the mother and the other from the father (Section 6.2.3).

Locus
The position of a gene or section of DNA on the chromosome.

The position of a gene or sequence of DNA is called its **locus**. This is like a co-ordinate of the gene or section of DNA – it says on which chromosome it is present and where along that chromosome it is found. Just as a gene can have alleles, so a locus can be said to have alleles if there are variations of its DNA sequence. Often, the term 'locus' (plural loci) is used rather than 'gene' because it can describe a region of a chromosome that might not be part of a gene (e.g. the intergenic DNA, Figure 6.3c).

Although each gene or locus is present twice, on each chromosome it can have a different allele. **Heterozygous** is the genetic term describing this state. The **homozygous** state is when the alleles are the same.

Mutations in DNA that create new alleles can occur as a consequence of the presence of certain environmental factors, e.g. mutagenic chemicals, radioactivity and certain radiations. However, most mutations are introduced into the DNA by errors in the natural cellular processes of DNA replication and repair.

Various types of mutation are shown in Figure 6.4. Note that all the sequences in the figure are variations formed by mutation of the original sequence, and hence all these sequences are alleles of the same gene or sequence. Mutations can be small, altering a single base pair to another one, so-called point mutations (Figure 6.4a); these are indicated by asterisks. Insertion or deletion mutations add or remove base pairs to or from the sequence (Figure 6.4b). The size of insertion or deletion can be as small as a single base pair or as large as tens of thousands of base pairs. An important point here is that insertions increase the length of the DNA and deletions reduce it. Point mutations do not alter length.

Figure 6.4c illustrates a type of sequence called a **tandem repeat**. Tandem here means 'one after the other': a sequence of DNA (CTAG in the example in Figure 6.4c) is repeated several times, one following the other. The number of repeats can vary; the more repeats, the longer the DNA sequence. Figure 6.4c shows examples containing 2, 3, 8 and 11 repeats; these are all alleles of the sequence. In the example, the repeat CTAG is 4 bp long; repeats can be shorter or much longer than this.

Techniques employed to analyse DNA in forensic science (Section 6.3) depend on the separation of DNA molecules according to their length. Hence, alleles that differ in length, because they have an insertion or deletion or because the number of repeats is different, are easily analysed. Modern DNA profiling is based largely on the analysis of tandem repeats.

Terminology relating to tandem repeats is complex and is not always consistent among authors of different texts, but basically they are classified according to the length of the repeat:

- *Short tandem repeats (STRs)*: the length of the repeat is short by definition, between 1 and 4 bp. These are extremely important in modern DNA profiling.
- *Variable number tandem repeats (VNTRs)*: the length of the repeat is not strictly defined but is often taken to be 6–100 bp.
- *Satellite DNA*: this is a general term referring to any type of tandem repetitive DNA.
- *Microsatellite DNA*: this has very short repeats of 2–4 bp (the repeat in Figure 6.4 is a microsatellite); these are the same as STRs.
- *Minisatellite DNA*: this has repeat lengths of 6–100 bp and is often equated with VNTRs.

In Sections 6.3 and 6.4, we consider mainly STRs as they are the most widely used forensically.

Heterozygous
Having two different alleles for a given gene or sequence.

Homozygous
Having two identical alleles for a given gene or sequence.

Tandem repeat
A short sequence of DNA repeated consecutively a number of times. These have important forensic applications.

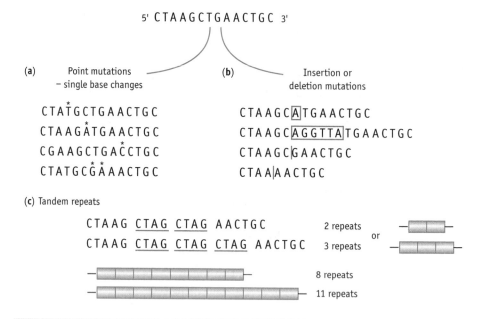

Figure 6.4 Variation in DNA sequences: mutation and alleles

Any change in a DNA sequence is referred to as mutation. (a) Point mutations are a change in a single base pair of the sequence. (b) Insertion or deletion mutations add to or remove base pairs from the sequence. (c) Tandem repeats – here, the sequence inserted or deleted is a sequence that is repeated one after the other, a number of times

6.2.5 DNA sequence variation among individuals

Genetically, individuals differ because they contain different combinations of alleles at some of the numerous, between 20 000 and 25 000, gene loci in the human genome. It is estimated that randomly selected individuals will differ in their DNA sequence at about a million positions. This large number corresponds to, on average, one difference every 1000 bp. Most of these will be point mutations, but all the types of mutation discussed above are represented.

The word 'mutation' often carries negative connotations. If most mutations damaged genes, then the million or so DNA sequence differences between individuals might be thought to mean that most people will carry many deleterious mutations. However, work on the human genome has revealed that, surprisingly, most of the genome is not involved in coding for proteins – in other words, genes are only a small part of the genome (only about 3 per cent of DNA is involved in coding directly for proteins), (see Figure 6.3 and Section 6.2.3). This has led to the unscientific term 'junk DNA' for the parts of the genome whose function is unclear. Whether it is actually junk is a source of debate – it may have a role, but we do not know what it is; it clearly is not obviously to do with genes. More correct terms are 'non-genic DNA' and 'non-coding DNA'. Most of the million DNA differences between individuals will, purely by chance, fall into non-coding regions of the genome and so will not affect protein function. They are not, therefore, likely to have effects on the **phenotype** of the individual.

The importance of this for forensic work is that the 'junk DNA' can accumulate mutations that do not affect how well the organism can survive. For example, a mutation forming an allele that resulted in an altered protein leading to fatality in childhood would mean that the allele is unlikely to become very abundant in the population, as people with the mutation will die before they have children and the allele will be lost. Most serious genetic diseases are rare. Mutation in non-genic 'junk DNA', however, will have no effect on the phenotype of the person, and the alteration can be passed on to his or her children. The mutation, an allele of the DNA region, is said to be selectively neutral because the survival of the individual carrying it is not compromised by its presence.

In DNA profiling, the loci examined are thought to exhibit **selective neutrality**. The importance of this is that alleles can become abundant in the population; they are not so rare as to be of very limited use for forensic purposes. This may seem counter-intuitive: surely a rare allele would be highly characteristic of a given individual carrying it? This is true. However, because it is rare, most criminals will not have it and it will not be deposited at a crime scene.

Phenotype
The observable characteristics of a person or organism.

Selective neutrality
A term used to denote a genetically inherited characteristic that confers neither benefit nor harm to the individual's ability to reproduce successfully.

6.2.6 Inheritance of alleles

The types of mutation discussed in Sections 6.2.4 and 6.2.5 are inherited according to the standard rules of genetics. Figure 6.5 summarises the important points. In this example, a single region (locus) of a chromosome is being followed; this region has a number of alleles that differ in the number of repeats – the locus is an STR. For simplicity, only the chromosomes carrying the locus are shown (remember that there would be another 44 chromosomes in the cells). The father has three repeats on one chromosome and six repeats at the same locus on the other, and so he can be designated as having the genotype 3,6. Similarly, the mother has genotype 2,8. In the parents, the complex process of meiosis reduces the chromosome number by half, producing the haploid number in the gametes. Each gamete has only one of each chromosome and hence only one allele of the STR. Hence, the father's sperm will be a mixture of cells carrying the three-repeat allele or the six-repeat allele. The mother's eggs will carry either a two- or an eight-repeat allele. At conception, the haploid sperm fuses with the haploid egg, producing the diploid fertilised egg, which can have one of four possible combinations of alleles, as shown; a given child will have one of these. This is all normal genetics, but note that genetics terms such as 'dominance' and 'recessiveness' are irrelevant in this case, as the phenotype is not being considered. All that matters is the combination of alleles in the individual.

As discussed, individuals differ at the level of DNA by containing different combinations of alleles at the numerous loci in the human genome. To study differences at the genetic level – the basis of DNA profiling – we need to be able to examine DNA and identify the alleles at certain loci that can be used to distinguish between people. The techniques that allow this are discussed in the next section.

For simplicity, only one chromosome is shown.

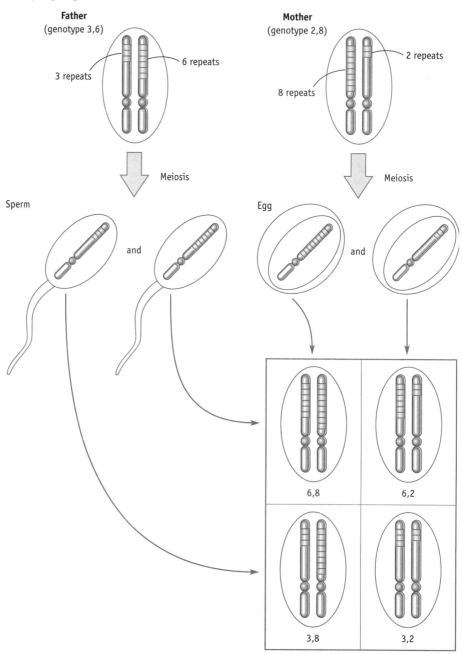

Father
(genotype 3,6)

6 repeats

3 repeats

Mother
(genotype 2,8)

2 repeats

8 repeats

Meiosis

Meiosis

Sperm

and

Egg

and

6,8

6,2

3,8

3,2

This couple's children could have genotypes of
3,2, 3,8, 6,8 or 6,2 with equal likelihood

Figure 6.5 Inheritance of alleles
In this example, the inheritance of the alleles of a single region (locus) of a chromosome is being followed. This region has a number of alleles that differ in the number of repeats; it is an STR. For simplicity, only the chromosomes carrying the locus are shown; remember that there would be another 44 chromosomes in the cells. The repeats do result in differences in chromosome length, but in the diagram this is greatly exaggerated; in reality, the difference is so small that the chromosomes would appear identical

6.3 Forensic DNA analysis and DNA profiling

From its origins in 1984, forensic DNA analysis has undergone rapid development, improving its precision, sensitivity and speed. In this section, the main techniques that underpin modern DNA profiling will be described. Readers interested in its historical development are referred to the website associated with this book.

The forensic use of DNA samples begins with their collection from the crime or incident scene and ends with the presentation of the data at court or enquiry. As with the collection and storage of other evidence, strict procedures are adopted and must be followed rigidly in order for the evidence to be robust.

An outline of the procedure is as follows:

1. Collect and store evidence from the scene.
2. Extract DNA from the sample.
3. Quantify the DNA.
4. Amplify the genetic loci to be examined.
5. Separate the amplified DNA according to size using electrophoresis.
6. Interpret the pattern of alleles produced.
7. Compare one or more DNA samples for a match.
8. Present the data in the context of other evidence.

6.3.1 Collection and storage of DNA samples

General aspects of sample collection from a scene are dealt with elsewhere in this book, particularly in Chapter 2 (see, in particular, Section 2.4). In most respects, the collection of samples for DNA analysis is simply that of taking any biological samples. Blood and other tissue samples from unknown people are potentially hazardous (if, for example, sources are infected with hepatitis B, tuberculosis or HIV), and safety procedures must be followed. Another important issue is contamination: because the techniques of DNA analysis can detect very low amounts of material – as low as a single cell using certain methods – potential contamination by material from the Scenes of Crime Officers (SOCOs) must be avoided. Use of barrier clothing addresses these issues. An officer should wear a face mask and cover their hair when collecting DNA evidence. Material can be transmitted on gloves, so the officer must avoid touching his or her face while wearing gloves. Staff involved in the retrieval and processing of DNA evidence have their DNA profiles stored on an elimination database. DNA profiles from the scene are compared with the database to ensure that accidental contamination has not occurred.

DNA is a fairly stable molecule under a range of conditions. Correct storage is important to prevent degradation that could result in poor-quality profiles. How DNA is preserved depends on the nature of the evidence. Dry samples (e.g. hairs, or dried stains of blood or semen) can be stored at normal temperatures in paper bags, as these maintain the dryness of the material. Wet samples (e.g. clothing stains) can be allowed to dry out naturally at normal temperatures or the samples can be frozen to prevent the degradation of the DNA by microbes and through breakdown by chemicals in the cell. Tissue samples from the scene and fresh reference samples from people involved or potentially involved in the incident (e.g. blood, mouth scrapes, oral, vaginal and rectal swabs) are frozen rapidly prior to DNA extraction.

Further to this, collection of control samples must be made. These are samples of the background material near the stain but untouched by it. The importance of this is to control for any contamination of the sample and to test whether there is anything in the background that might interfere with the DNA profile.

Forensic DNA analysis has become so sensitive that at the extreme a small blood-stain of about $3\,mm^2$, a single hair with a good root or a used cigarette butt can give a DNA profile. Only about $1\,ng$ $(10^{-9}\,g)$ of DNA is required for an optimum DNA pro-filing result, but note that a modified procedure called LCN DNA profiling can produce profiles from less material than this (Section 6.6.1).

6.3.2 Extraction of DNA

Sources of DNA evidence cover a wide range of biological material. As discussed in Section 6.2, DNA is present in the nuclei and mitochondria of cells and so any sample of biological origin, containing cells, is a potential source of DNA. Table 6.1 summarises potential sources of DNA. These sources are commonly found at crime scenes, but note that often the sources may be in combinations, for example in rape and sexual assault cases, and not separate as listed in the table. In a sample of mixed material, one source of DNA may be detected and the other not.

Most internal organ tissues can be a source of DNA. Bone and tooth pulp contain DNA, which can survive a long time beyond that of many other tissues and have proved useful as DNA sources from old or badly decomposed bodies (Box 6.1).

The method of extraction of DNA from the evidence depends on the particular sources; clearly a different procedure is needed to extract DNA from bone than from hair and blood. Generally, cellular material may be concentrated by centrifugation followed generally by agitation, to loosen cells into solution, and then the cells are broken open to release the DNA and other cellular components into solution. Subsequent steps remove the proteins, lipids and RNA, leaving a solution of DNA. If required, a further purification process can be included that removes contaminants that could interfere with the reactions involved in producing a DNA profile. For example, the blue dye in denim can inhibit the reactions, as can large amounts of haem and related compounds from blood samples.

After extraction, the DNA is usually quantified to determine its concentration in order to ensure that the amount of DNA to be typed is a standard amount for optimal DNA profiling. The amount of DNA can be measured using the fluorescence of stained DNA or by estimating the depth of colour produced in a colorimetric reaction.

6.3.3 The polymerase chain reaction (PCR)

Most modern DNA profiling is based on the polymerase chain reaction (PCR). DNA obtained by extraction of biological evidence (Section 6.3.2) is often present in insufficient amounts to detect or analyse it directly. PCR enables the specific gener-ation of large amounts of the DNA of interest (in this context, short tandem repeats

Table 6.1 Evidence as sources of DNA

Evidence	Source	Comments
Blood	White blood cells	Good source of DNA
Semen	Sperm cells	Rich source of DNA
Hair with roots	Hair follicle cells	Good source of DNA
Skin, dandruff	Skin cells	Not good sources of DNA for routine analysis
Shed hair shafts	Adhering dead skin or follicle cells	Not usually a good source of nuclear DNA; mtDNA can be obtained
Sweat stains	Skin cells rubbed off into the sweat	Can be a good source of DNA
Vaginal fluid	Mainly liquids that may contain cells sloughed off mucosal surfaces	Good source of DNA
Nasal secretions	Mainly liquids that may contain cells sloughed off mucosal surfaces	Good source of DNA
Urine	Mainly liquids that may contain cells sloughed off mucosal surfaces	Contains few cells; not profiled routinely but may be used for serious offences
Faeces	Cells sloughed off the intestinal surfaces	Not usually a good source of nuclear DNA; mtDNA can be obtained

Case study

Box 6.1

DNA evidence in old cases: James Hanratty

James Hanratty was hanged on 4 April 1962 for the so-called A6 murder, a notorious case of the early 1960s. In August 1961, an armed man forced Michael Gregsten and his lover Valerie Stone to drive from Dorney Reach in Berkshire along the A6 in Bedfordshire. On parking at a site called Deadman's Hill, Michael Gregsten was shot twice in the back of the head, killing him. Valerie Stone was raped, shot five times and left for dead, although remarkably she survived. Various pieces of evidence led to James Hanratty being arrested, charged and ultimately convicted of the murder and rape. From his arrest to his death, James Hanratty strongly defended his innocence. Subsequently, his family have maintained that the case was a miscarriage of justice and over the years the case has attracted great scrutiny from legal experts, journalists and politicians. Innocence was argued on the basis of potential alibis that

were found for James Hanratty, and the conduct of some of the police officers during the investigation was brought into question. A Court of Appeal for the case was granted in 1999. Application of DNA profiling had produced evidence from the underwear of Valerie Stone and a handkerchief that was found wrapped around the gun. A comparison of the profile with the DNA of James Hanratty's relatives showed matches to the evidence. In March 2001, DNA from his exhumed body, from tooth pulp, also matched the evidence. In the Appeal, the DNA evidence carried great weight and the decision of the Court of Appeal was that the original conviction was safe. This judgment may be challenged on the argument that the DNA may be a result of contamination. At the time, long before DNA profiling, evidence was not necessarily collected and stored in such a way that cross-contamination would be avoided.

– STRs) from the extracted DNA, to such a level as to allow them to be analysed by gel electrophoresis (Section 6.3.4).

Invented in 1983 by Kary Mullis, PCR has become one of the most powerful techniques of molecular genetics; its impact has been revolutionary. At its simplest, PCR is a means of amplifying or copying a particular region of DNA (forensically, this would be an STR locus of interest) to produce a large amount of it. It does this by mimicking DNA replication that occurs in cells prior to cell division. Only the genes/regions of interest are amplified (in this case, the STR loci); all other DNA present is ignored: this is called the specificity of the reaction. PCR is specific, fast and extremely sensitive.

Figure 6.6 outlines the basis of PCR. The primers are short sequences of DNA that are designed and synthesised to base pair to the ends of the region to be amplified; in this case, to unique sequences either side of the repeat sequence. Also attached to the primers are fluorescent molecules (tags), which allow the amplified DNA to be visualised in electrophoresis (Section 6.3.4 and Figure 6.7). Note that there are two primers needed per locus, and only the DNA between the primers is amplified. The reaction consists of temperature cycles conducted in a programmable heating block called a thermocycler. The first temperature, called the denaturation stage, of 95 °C breaks the hydrogen bonds of the double helix; the DNA becomes single-stranded, exposing the bases in order that the primers can bind. Reducing the temperature to typically 50–60 °C allows hydrogen bonds to reform, permitting the primers to base pair to the complementary sequences at the ends of the STR to be amplified. At 72 °C the heat-stable enzyme *Taq* polymerase extends the primers, synthesising new DNA as it makes the two strands fully double-stranded. At this point, the amount of target DNA has doubled. This is then put through another cycle of temperatures, resulting in a further doubling of the region of interest. Each cycle doubles the amount of target DNA, in this case an STR. A cycle may take 5 minutes and 30 cycles will give a 2^{30} or about 10^9 increase in the amount of target DNA, so in 2.5 hours the DNA of interest has been increased in amount about a thousand million-fold. This degree of amplification makes the methods very sensitive. At its absolute limit, a single DNA molecule can give an easily detectable amount of DNA in a few hours. This extreme sensitivity, though, does come at a price: very great care must be taken to avoid contamination with other material – the method, if carried out carelessly, is very sensitive to artefacts.

As little as 0.2 ng of DNA or even that from a single cell (6 pg) can give a DNA profile based on PCR. Re-examination of old, stored evidence where the DNA may be degraded and present in very small amounts is possible only because of PCR. Box 6.1 summarises a case where DNA data were generated from 40-year-old evidence. Subsequent boxes in this chapter all describe evidence generated by PCR.

In Figure 6.6b an example of PCR on an STR is shown. One allele has four repeats and the other has six repeats; hence, after the reaction, two fragments are produced, which when separated by gel electrophoresis (Section 6.3.4 and Figure 6.7) produce the pattern shown in Figure 6.6b. When compared with the DNA standards, the genotype of the source is determined to be 4,6 for this STR. In this example, only a single genetic locus is being examined.

PCR is used for STR analysis and mitochondrial DNA analysis (Section 6.5) and hence underpins all modern forensic DNA analysis.

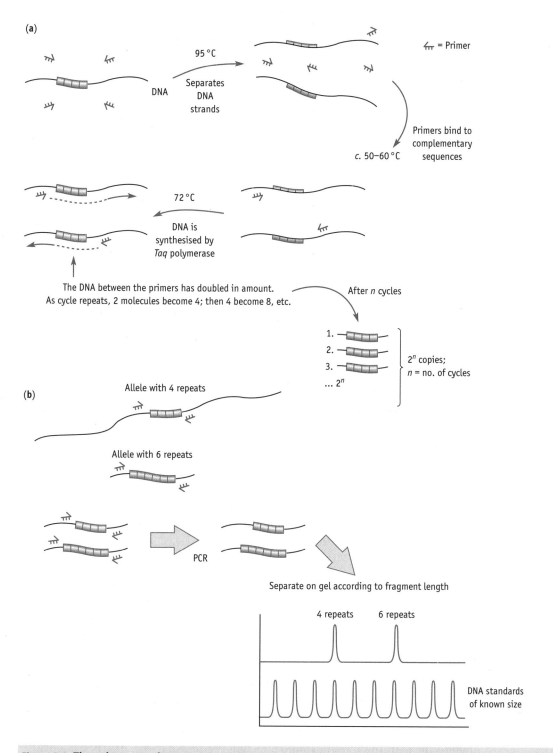

(a)

95 °C

Separates DNA strands

DNA

$\twoheadleftarrow$ = Primer

c. 50–60 °C

Primers bind to complementary sequences

72 °C

DNA is synthesised by *Taq* polymerase

The DNA between the primers has doubled in amount. As cycle repeats, 2 molecules become 4; then 4 become 8, etc.

After *n* cycles

1.
2.
3.
... 2^n

2^n copies; n = no. of cycles

(b)

Allele with 4 repeats

Allele with 6 repeats

PCR

Separate on gel according to fragment length

4 repeats   6 repeats

DNA standards of known size

Figure 6.6 The polymerase chain reaction (PCR)

This figure shows the basics of the PCR reaction when being used to amplify a short tandem repeat (STR). (a) The primers, shown as short half-arrows, are designed to bind to the regions of DNA just outside the STR. The reaction is put through a series of temperature cycles, each with 95 °C, 50–60 °C and 72 °C stages. At each cycle, the amount of target DNA doubles. Thirty cycles will increase the amount of target DNA about 10^9 times. (b) The amplified STRs are then analysed using gel electrophoresis (see Section 6.3.4 and Figure 6.7) and compared with standards in order that the number of repeats can be estimated, the alleles for the STR identified and the genotype of the individual determined

6.3.4 Measuring the length of DNA molecules: gel electrophoresis

After the PCR described above, the amplified DNA fragments are analysed to determine the number of repeats present. This analysis is based on a technique called gel electrophoresis, which underpins almost all DNA analysis, forensic or otherwise. Gel electrophoresis separates DNA molecules according to their length and allows their measurement, usually in base pairs (bp). In the discussion of mutations and tandem repetitive DNA in Section 6.2.4, it was mentioned that STRs are often used in forensic DNA analysis and that the alleles of these STRs alter the length of the DNA. By measuring the length of DNA-containing STRs using gel electrophoresis, the number of repeats can be determined, ultimately establishing the genotype for an individual at that locus.

Figure 6.7 summarises important aspects of gel electrophoresis. Figures 6.7a and 6.7b illustrate a simple version of gel electrophoresis used to discuss its principles. In forensic DNA laboratories a variation of gel electrophoresis called capillary electrophoresis is used (Figure 6.7c); this is considered later in this section. The gel is moulded from a jelly-like material. For simple analyses a material called agarose is used, but for more precise work polyacrylamide or derivatives of this are used. In either case, the basis of the method is the same. DNA samples (generated by PCR) to be analysed are loaded into wells formed in the gel (Figure 6.7a). Not shown, for clarity, in Figure 6.7 is the buffer solution in which the gel is immersed. This buffer solution maintains the pH and carries the electric current. A voltage is applied across the gel, and because DNA carries a negative charge on its phosphate groups (Figure 6.2), it migrates towards the positive pole (the anode) and moves through the gel. The gel is a loose network of molecules that act like a molecular sieve. Long molecules of DNA have difficulty moving through the network as they frequently become caught in it, whereas shorter molecules migrate through the gel more rapidly. Hence, the DNA separates in the gel according to the size of the fragments; small fragments migrate faster than larger ones.

After the gel has run for an appropriate time, the DNA, which is not immediately visible, must be visualised. A common method for the type of gel electrophoresis shown in Figure 6.7b is to stain the gel with a dye called ethidium bromide, which binds to the DNA. Under ultraviolet light, the dye fluoresces orange and the DNA appears as bright-orange bands on the gel. A fluorescent dye allows very small amounts of DNA to be detected. Each band of DNA corresponds to a population of DNA molecules of all the same base pair length.

The example in Figure 6.7 shows the analysis of an STR. Apart from the PCR-amplified DNA samples from individuals A and B loaded into wells 1 and 2 respectively, in lane 3 a set of known DNA size standards are loaded, effectively to calibrate the gel in order that the sizes of the DNA fragments from the individuals can be determined easily. In the example, the DNA standards are called an **allelic ladder** as each fragment represents a number of repeats at the locus, in other words its allele.

After staining the gel (Figure 6.7b), lane 1 shows two bands of DNA visible as does lane 2, although the sizes are different, since the DNA bands have migrated to different positions on the gel. Comparison of the bands in lanes 1 and 2 with the allelic ladder molecules in lane 3 allows numbers of repeats for the STR (its allele

Allelic ladder
A set of DNA molecular size markers that correspond in length to the known alleles for the locus.

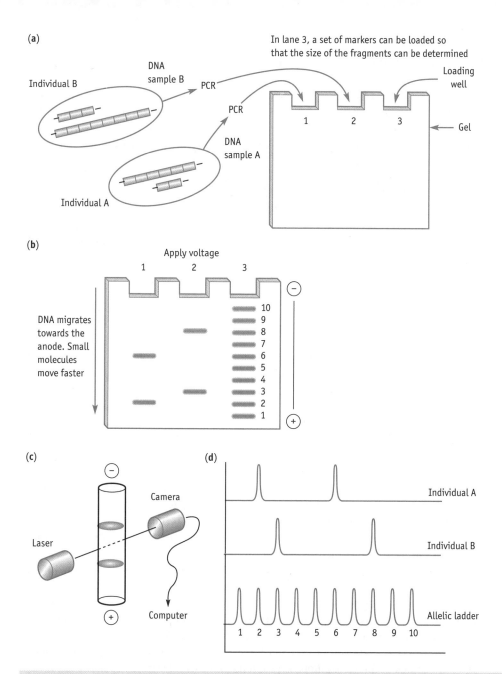

Figure 6.7 Separating DNA molecules according to their length: gel electrophoresis

(a) DNA samples containing fragments of DNA are loaded into wells on the gel. In this example, the DNA fragments are from an STR, repeat mutation; sample A is from individual A with 2 and 6 repeats, and sample B is from individual B with 3 and 8 repeats. Also on the gel are loaded, into well 3, DNA standards of known size: this allows the size of unknown fragments to be determined by comparison.

(b) Application of a voltage across the gel causes the DNA to migrate towards the anode and separate according to the length of the molecules. In the gel, the DNA is visualised by staining with coloured dyes that bind to it. The DNA appears as bands of colour: each band consists of a very large number of DNA molecules of the same length. (c) Capillary electrophoresis (CE): in modern methodology, the gel material is in a very fine capillary tube; the DNA is labelled by having fluorescent molecules (tags) attached to it during the PCR reaction and is visualised when the laser, shone through a clear section of the capillary tube, causes the migrating DNA to fluoresce – this is detected by a CCD camera and the information passes to a computer. (d) Data from capillary electrophoresis are shown as an electropherogram. Note that the three samples shown would have been run separately along the capillary

number) to be determined. Hence, the DNA in lane 1 has its smallest band corresponding to a size of two repeats and the larger band is six repeats; for this STR locus, the genotype of individual A is 2,6, and so he or she is heterozygous. Similarly, individual B's DNA in lane 2 has the genotype 3,8 for this locus, and so he or she is also heterozygous.

The discussion above aims to give the general principles of gel electrophoresis, how DNA molecules are separated according to length and how the length can be determined using DNA size standards, allowing the allele of the STR to be established. The main modern separation technique used in forensic DNA analysis is capillary electrophoresis (CE). CE is a type of gel electrophoresis that gives great accuracy of measurement and also allows for automation. Figure 6.7c illustrates the principle of CE. The gel is contained in a fine capillary tube. DNA, which had been labelled with fluorescent molecules as part of the PCR reactions, migrates through the gel along the capillary towards the anode. Small DNA molecules migrate faster than longer molecules. At a certain point along the capillary, the DNA passes a fine laser beam, which excites the label and causes the DNA to fluoresce. A camera detects the fluorescence and the data are fed directly into software on a computer. Here the DNA bands appear on the computer screen as peaks on a graph, called an electropherogram (EPG) (Figure 6.7d; see also the example of a full DNA profile in Figure 6.1 and Plate 9). As in Figure 6.7b, the size of the peaks is determined by comparison with the standard DNA allelic ladder; here, the peaks confirm that individual A is of genotype 2,6 and that of individual B is 3,8.

With CE, only one sample can be run on the capillary at a time; the electropherograms in Figure 6.7d would be from three separate runs. To ensure consistency and to enable the data from separate runs to be compared, internal DNA size standards are added to every sample before electrophoresis, but for clarity these are not shown in Figure 6.7c. Size standards are labelled with a red tag and cannot be confused with the DNA from the evidence. Figure 6.8d and the red panel in Plate 9 show the internal size standards, which are controls for any variation in the rate of migration between different runs on the capillary. This control is extremely important; for example, without it DNA from a crime scene might migrate slightly differently compared with that of the perpetrator who was the source of the evidence. Hence, the DNA evidence would not match, leading to his or her elimination as a potential suspect.

In forensic DNA laboratories, CE is carried out by a piece of equipment called a genetic analyser, which may have multiple capillaries, allowing simultaneous analysis of a number of samples. The genetic analyser also allows automation of the process; a large number of samples can be loaded on to it and the machine will work through them. For all its sophistication, though, at the heart of it is the fairly straightforward process of capillary gel electrophoresis.

6.3.5 Modern DNA profiling

In current practice, DNA profiling is based on the PCR amplification of a number of STRs (microsatellite) loci. This approach has the following advantages over earlier methods:

■ Application of PCR amplification of alleles increases the sensitivity of the technique and is also more rapid and simple to execute.

■ STRs are rather short alleles that are readily amplified by PCR, further increasing the sensitivity of detection (long sections of DNA generally do not amplify so well). Several loci can be examined in the same PCR reaction.

■ Simultaneous examination of several well-characterised loci in the same reaction allows for automation, improved resolution, improved standardisation and ease of comparison and assembly of DNA profile databases.

In the UK, the current standard profile is made using a system called AmpF*l* STR®SGM Plus™ (Applied Biosystems), hereafter referred to as SGM+, which was developed from a system of the Forensic Science Service of England and Wales. This system is not used throughout the world; other countries have systems that differ in the number of STR loci and the particular loci examined, although there is usually some overlap between the loci. The general principles are the same for all the systems.

In the SGM+ system, the extracted and quantified DNA (Section 6.3.2) is subject to PCR. In the simplest form of PCR (Section 6.3.3), two primers are used to amplify one locus (Figure 6.6). The SGM+ system, however, simultaneously amplifies 11 different loci. Essentially, there are 11 PCR reactions taking place in the same tube; there are two specific primers for each of the 11 loci. A reaction containing several amplifications at once is said to be a multiplex PCR. The reason for examining 11 loci is that it increases the discrimination of the analysis; the more loci that are examined, the less likely it is that two people will share the same combination of alleles (this point is discussed further in Section 6.4). After the PCR stage the products of the reaction are separated according to size by capillary electrophoresis (Section 6.3.4) and the data are presented as an electropherogram; this is the DNA profile.

Table 6.2 gives the names of the 11 loci amplified in the SGM+ system. Except for amelogenin, all the loci are STRs with a repeat length of 4 bp. For example, the repeat at the THO1 locus is the sequence AATG repeated many (up to 19) times. Loci vWA, THO1, FGA and amelogenin are genes; they encode proteins and are given the correct gene nomenclature.

The loci beginning with 'D' are not parts of genes and are named according to rules for naming DNA segments. 'D' stands for DNA, and the number following indicates the chromosome on which the particular sequence is found. 'S' indicates a unique sequence and the number identifies the particular sequence. For example, locus D3S1358 is the unique DNA sequence (it is not found anywhere else in the genome) number 1358 on chromosome 3.

Note that all 11 loci are on different chromosomes. This is to ensure that the alleles of a particular locus are inherited independently of the alleles of the other loci; in genetic terms, they are not linked. Without going into detail, this is important as linkage would complicate the analysis further. Most of the loci have a large number of alleles.

Alleles are generally named according to the number of repeats present in the STR. For example, for TH01, allele 5 consists of five repeats of the sequence AATG, while allele 6 consists of six repeats. In the case of a designation such as THO1 allele 5.3, this means that there are five repeats but with an insertion of 3 bp; it is not a perfect simple repeat.

The amelogenin locus is not an STR and has two alleles. The gene, which encodes a protein in tooth pulp, is unusual in that it is present on both the X and Y chromosomes. Curiously, the gene on the Y chromosome is 6 bp longer than that on the X. This can, therefore, be used for determining the sex of the source of the DNA. A female source in the SGM$^+$ system generates a PCR product from each X chromosome of 103 bp; this produces a single band in electrophoresis. From a male, the X chromosome still produces a 103 bp band but the Y chromosome produces a 109 bp fragment and so the profile will have two bands. The alleles of the amelogenin locus are, therefore, a strong indicator of the sex of the person who left the evidence. They are not an absolute indicator of sex, however, as there are a number of interesting but rare conditions in which the sex of a person is not in agreement with the combination of sex chromosomes.

At this point, we will discuss a DNA profile in detail. In Figure 6.1a, a DNA profile using the SGM$^+$ system was shown as an introductory example. Figure 6.8 shows a profile generated by this system, but for clarity the profile has been split over four

Table 6.2 Loci amplified by the SGM$^+$ kit

Locus name	Chromosome carrying locus	Protein encoded	Number of alleles*
D3S1358	3		15
vWA	12	von Willebrand factor	20
D16S539	16		9
D2S1338	2		14
D8S1179	8		16
D21S11	21		43
D18S51	18		41
D19S433	19		18
TH01	11	Tyrosine hydroxylase	19
FGA	4	Fibrinogen	65
Amelogenin	X and Y	Amelogenin	2

*The number of alleles for each locus is likely to increase as more people have their profiles determined.

panels. On the electropherogram, each panel would appear as a different colour, which can be overlaid without confusion; in a single-colour representation, it is clearer to separate the colours into different panels. Plate 9 shows a full SGM⁺ profile in colour as it would appear on a computer screen.

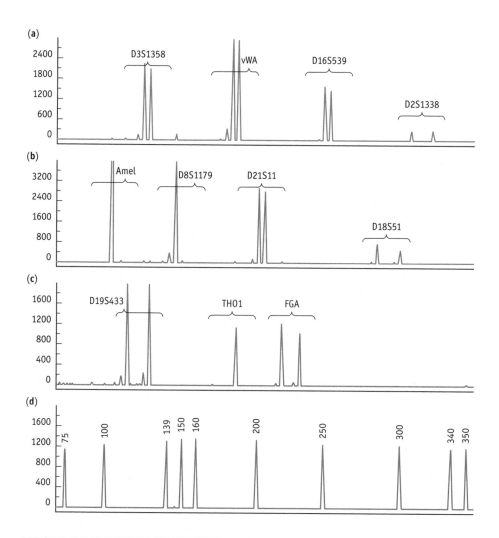

Figure 6.8 A modern DNA profile

An SGM⁺ profile is shown. For clarity, the profile has been split into four panels. PCR amplified loci are shown and labelled in panels (a), (b) and (c). Panel (d) shows the molecular size standards; the size of each standard in base pairs is indicated. The numbers on the vertical axes are in fluorescence units; the higher this value, the more labelled DNA is present in the sample

The DNA profile consists of a series of peaks along a baseline. Each peak is a DNA molecule generated in the PCR amplification stage, and its position on the graph along the horizontal axis relates to the length of the DNA molecule. The shortest molecules are to the left-hand edge of the panel. The lowest panel (Figure 6.8d) of ten peaks shows the DNA molecular size standards that were added after the PCR. Each peak is labelled with its size in base pairs. Using these size standards, the size of the peaks in the other panels can be found with a high degree of precision. From the size of the PCR product (the peak), the particular locus being examined is clear and the particular alleles of that locus can be established. The nine labelled red peaks of Plate 9 are the size standards on this profile. As discussed in Section 6.3.4, these standards are added to all samples before electrophoresis and are extremely important in allowing comparisons between different samples and ensuring consistency.

Figure 6.8a shows a set of eight strong peaks. On the computer screen these peaks appear blue, as the primers used to amplify them in PCR were labelled with a particular coloured fluorescent tag. The intelligent design of the PCR allows the separation of the four loci, as shown in this panel, and their alleles. The left-hand pair of peaks have sizes of 124 and 128 bp. From data tables for the SGM$^+$ system, products of these sizes belong to the locus D3S1358 on chromosome 3. Further, the 124 bp product is generated by allele 15 of D3S1358 and the 128 bp product by allele 16. Hence, the genotype of the person at locus D3S1358 is 15,16. Remember that the loci being detected here are STRs, the alleles of which differ by the number of times the repeat is present (Section 6.2.4). Here, it can be seen that the repeat for D3S1358 is 4 bp long because allele 16 is 4 bp longer than allele 15.

The next pair of peaks have sizes of 183 bp and 187 bp, which according to the tables correspond to alleles 18 and 19 of the locus vWA; the genotype at vWA is therefore 18,19. The four loci of Figure 6.8a were labelled with a 'blue' fluorescent tag. These are shown in colour on Plate 9. On this plate, the grey bar over the peaks is the locus name and the range of size for the alleles of the locus. Figure 6.8b, and the equivalent section of Plate 9, shows the 'green panel'; the loci were labelled with a 'green' fluorescent tag. As for the 'blue' panel, the size of each peak gives the corresponding allele.

This type of analysis is continued for all the peaks on the electropherogram. Figure 6.8 shows the locus names and approximate range. Figure 6.1a shows the allele designations for this profile. The data from Figure 6.8 are summarised in Table 6.3, with data from Figure 6.1a. First, using the amelogenin locus, the sex of the DNA source can be determined. The single peak of 103 bp in Figure 6.8 indicates that the source was female. In Figure 6.1a, the two peaks of 103 and 109 bp indicate a male. With regard to the other loci, the genotypes are all different, although some alleles of particular loci are in common, e.g. at D16S539 both people carry allele 10, although the other alleles are different.

The designation of alleles can be carried out automatically. Computer programs identify the alleles and label them according to interpretation rules, which also remove artefact peaks and assess the quality of the profile. For commercial forensic laboratories, this means that hundreds of samples can be analysed in minutes. Plate 9 is the result of such an analysis; the alleles at each locus have been identified and labelled. Note that there are some smaller peaks present, which the computer has ignored according to the interpretation criteria. In some instances, these peaks may be of significance and could be analysed. Also shown on Plate 9 are a number of grey stripes under each locus; these represent the expected sizes for each allele known for a given locus. If a peak falls in a grey stripe, it will be identified; if not, it may represent a new allele or an artefact.

Consistency and repeatability of DNA profiling is paramount in forensic work. Apart from the internal size controls added to each sample, another control called the allelic ladder is run separately. This consists of an artificial mixture of DNA fragments, containing nearly all known alleles of each of the 11 loci of SGM⁺. After electrophoresis, a complicated profile is produced (again in four colours), but with very many peaks (not a maximum of 22 from an individual). If the system is working correctly, all the peaks should be identified correctly as their corresponding, known alleles.

DNA profiles such as Plate 9 and Figures 6.8 and 6.1a and their associated genotypes (Table 6.3) are readily isolated from suspects and from biological evidence at crime scenes. A match of evidence and suspect links the suspect to the scene extremely strongly.

6.3.6 The National DNA Database™ (NDNAD)

A major advantage of modern DNA profiling is that the data generated can be readily presented and collected in databases that can be searched with new DNA evidence from a crime scene. In April 1995 the Forensic Science Service (FSS) of England and Wales set up the National DNA Database™ (NDNAD), the first database of its kind in the world. Many countries now have or are starting to develop such databases; in the United States, the FBI Laboratories are responsible for a database called the Combined DNA Index System (CODIS).

NDNAD is a collection of DNA profiles from unsolved scene of crime evidence and DNA profiles from suspects and convicted criminals. At the time of writing in 2007, there are over 3.1 million personal profiles (about 5 per cent of the UK population) on the database, as well as about 250 000 profiles from evidence at crime scenes. Typically, DNA evidence from a crime scene will be used to interrogate the database

Table 6.3 Allele designation of the loci shown in Figures 6.8 and 6.1a

Locus name	Allele designation from Figure 6.8	Allele designation from Figure 6.1a
D3S1358	15,16	14,15
vWA	18,19	14,16
D16S539	10,11	9,10
D2S1338	19,23	20,23
D8S1179	Homozygous 13	12,13
D21S11	28,29	28,31
D18S51	13,16	12,15
D19S433	12,15.2	15,16
THO1	Homozygous 9.3	7,9.3
FGA	19,22	24,26
Amelogenin	Homozygous X	X,Y

to identify a potential source of that profile. It can also compare the evidence with that from other crimes and perhaps link incidents to a common person.

In the UK, non-intimate samples (buccal cells from a mouth scrape or hairs with roots) for DNA profiling can be taken from people charged or reported for record-able offences and now, through new legislation, from volunteers who wish their DNA to be retained. Famously, former prime minister Tony Blair provided a voluntary sample for the database, to which his profile is now a permanent addition. Formerly, profiles of people found innocent were deleted from the database, but now they are retained following a change in the law. Since April 2005, in the UK reference DNA samples from suspects who are not charged can also be preserved and used as evidence in any and all cases.

The database matches of a suspect to a crime scene along with supporting non-DNA evidence can be now be used to charge the suspect with the crime, leading to legal proceedings. A recent demonstration of the power of database analysis is described in Box 6.2, but numerous other examples could be given. NDNAD is fundamental to all DNA profiling work in forensic science. There is more to interpreting DNA profiles than simply identifying matches, and this is discussed in Section 6.4.

Case study

Box 6.2

The importance of the National DNA Database (NDNAD): the Joseph Kappen case and the Craig Harman case

A dramatic example of the use of the NDNAD relates to the rape and murder of three 16-year-old girls in 1973 in the Neath area of South Wales, UK. The body of Sandra Newton was found in a ditch at Tonmawr in June; Pauline Floyd's and Geraldine Hughes' bodies were found in woodland at Llandarcy in September. At the time there was no evidence to identify the killer. With the improved technology of Low Copy Number DNA (Section 6.6.1), a profile from 28-year-old clothing evidence was obtained and used to search the database. No match was found; the killer's DNA was not on the database. A novel search of the database was then employed. Instead of looking for perfect matches, the search revealed profiles with some similarities to the DNA evidence from the bodies, with the intention of identifying potential relatives of the murderer. About 100 candidates were identified with the search. With this information and existing intelligence from the South Wales Police, a relative of the probable killer was identified (it was fortunate the relative's profile was on the database) and this led to a strong suspect, Joseph William Kappen, who had died of lung cancer in 1991. DNA samples from other relatives confirmed their similarities to the DNA profile from the evidence, resulting in the exhumation of Joseph Kappen's body in May 2002. The DNA profile from the body matched that of the evidence from the girls' bodies. In the absence of a trial, it cannot be said conclusively that Kappen was guilty of the three murders, but the case is now closed.

In March 2003, a brick thrown from a footbridge over the M3 motorway crashed through the windscreen of a lorry. It struck the driver Michael Little on his chest, causing heart failure and killing him. Partial DNA evidence from the brick and other complete DNA evidence from a nearby attempted car theft did not match profiles on the DNA database. Familial searching was carried out on the database, producing 25 possible relatives of the person whose DNA was found on the brick and the car. Discovery of a close relative led to the identification of Craig Harman, who was convicted of the manslaughter of Michael Little in 2004. This is the first case where familial searching led to a prosecution.

6.4 Interpretation of DNA profiles

Clearly the two profiles in Table 6.3 do not match. If the data in Figure 6.8 were evidence at a crime scene and the profile in Figure 6.1a was a potential source, then it is easy to exclude the individual. There is a very important point here: DNA evidence can be exclusive – it can absolutely discount a person as being the source if the profiles display differences.

Suppose, however, that the DNA profiles of evidence (Figure 6.8) and suspect appear identical. Neglecting accidental contamination, then the obvious conclusion is that the suspect is the source. However, if the profile shown is fairly common in the population, the match could be coincidence and the conclusion may not be valid. Modern DNA profiling attempts to determine the chance that two people will share the same profile; that is, it tries to approach individuality for the profile, improving the confidence in the conclusion that there is extremely strong support that the suspect was the source if a match is shown with the evidence. Remember, though, that DNA evidence cannot conclusively identify its source as the perpetrator of a crime; in the legal system, it is the jury that decides.

To address how common a particular profile is in a population requires the application of some principles of population genetics. Before tackling the full profile of Figure 6.8, it is useful to consider a simple case.

6.4.1 Single locus data: simple population genetics

Figure 6.7c shows a study using PCR amplification of a single STR locus on two suspects. Individual A (lane 1) has a genotype of 2,6, and individual B (lane 2) has a genotype of 3,8. If, from a crime scene, DNA evidence of genotype 3,8 is found, what relevance does this have regarding the suspects? First, suspect A can be excluded absolutely as the source, as he or she does not have either of the alleles present in the evidence. Suspect B carries both alleles that are found in the evidence, 3 and 8. Does this mean that he or she is the source of the evidence? Not necessarily – if there is other evidence such that only A or B can be the source, then the DNA evidence indicates it must be B. However, if the source could be anybody in the population, then how likely is it that B was the source? The source must have the genotype 3,8, and so it depends how common this genotype is in the population: if it is a very rare combination, then this is supportive of B being the source but not necessarily proof. If 3,8 is a very common genotype, then it is meaningless with regard to the guilt of B.

To try to resolve this issue, we need to know how common the genotype 3,8 is in the population. This can be found only by experiment, isolating the DNA from many individuals and genotyping them for the STR of interest. These data give a table of allele frequencies, i.e. how common certain alleles are in the population. For example, Table 6.4 shows allele frequencies for the STR discussed above. Here, the 2 repeat allele has a frequency of 0.36, which means that out of 100 alleles (from 50 people, as each person carries two alleles) sampled randomly, 36 would be expected to be the 2 repeat. The maximum value is 1.00, in which case no other alleles are present. The lowest value is 0; in other words, the allele is not found in the population. In Table 6.4, alleles of 1, 5 and 7 repeats are not found, and so their allele frequencies are 0. Note that the sum of all the allele frequencies is 1.00.

Table 6.4 Allele frequencies for the alleles of the STR

Allele (number of repeats)	Allele frequency
2	0.36
3	0.01
4	0.39
6	0.09
8	0.15

Table 6.4 still does not tell us how frequent the genotype 3,8 is in the population. To estimate this requires the use of one of the basic theorems of population genetics – the Hardy–Weinberg principle. This describes a mathematical relationship between allele frequencies and genotype frequencies. The simplest case considers a gene or STR with two alleles, P and Q, with respective allele frequencies p and q. If certain conditions are met or assumed, then the Hardy–Weinberg principle states that the genotype frequencies will be $(p + q)^2 = p^2 + 2pq + q^2$ where p^2 is the frequency of the homozygous genotype PP, q^2 is the frequency of the homozygous genotype QQ and $2pq$ is the frequency of the heterozygous genotype PQ.

This can be extended to any number of alleles for a given locus, as in Table 6.5, which, although it appears very complicated, has a simplicity to it. The frequency of a particular homozygote is the particular allele frequency squared. For a given heterozygote, its expected frequency is two times the product of the two allele frequencies.

Using the data from Table 6.4, we can now address how common the genotype 3,8 is expected to be in the population. From Table 6.4, the frequency of allele 3 repeats (p) is 0.01 and that of 8 repeats (q) is 0.15. Applying the Hardy–Weinberg principle, the expected frequency of the 3,8 heterozygote is $2pq$ or $2 \times 0.01 \times 0.15 = 0.003$. This means that three people in a thousand would be expected by chance to have the 3,8 genotype. This seems a low chance, but it is not proof that individual B is the source if many other people could have been. If only a limited number of people could have been the source and B is the only one with genotype 3,8, then the evidence is stronger.

Table 6.5 Hardy–Weinberg principle applied to loci with multiple alleles

Number of alleles	Name of alleles	Allele frequencies	Genotype frequencies
2	P,Q	p,q	$(p + q)^2 = p^2 + 2pq + q^2$
3	P,Q,R	p,q,r	$(p + q + r)^2 = p^2 + 2pq + 2qr + 2pr + q^2 + r^2$
4	P,Q,R,S	p,q,r,s	$(p + q + r + s)^2 = p^2 + 2pq + 2qr + 2pr + 2ps + 2rs + 2qs + r^2 + q^2 + s^2$
5	P,Q,R,S,T	p,q,r,s,t	$(p + q + r + s + t)^2 = p^2 + 2pq + 2qr + 2pr + 2ps + 2rs + 2qs + 2qt + 2rt + 2rs + r^2 + q^2 + s^2 + t^2$

6.4.2 Interpreting full, multiloci DNA profiles

Using the Hardy–Weinberg principle outlined previously, the profile of Figure 6.8 can be analysed using data from tables of allele frequencies for the loci in the SGM$^+$ system. Basically, the expected genotype frequency for each locus is calculated as above. This generates Table 6.6. The allele frequencies shown are obtained from tables of population data for the loci. There is a range of genotype frequencies. That for D19S433 is expected to be found in only 4 out of 1000. For D3S1358, D8S1179 and THO1, 123 people in 1000, i.e. more than 1 in 10, can be expected to have the particular genotype. Individually, these genotypes are not very discriminating.

These values show how common the observed genotype of the particular locus is expected to be in the population. To estimate how common the entire profile is likely to be, the genotype frequencies for all the loci are simply multiplied together. This is valid because the loci are all on different chromosomes and the inheritance of one genotype has no influence on the inheritance of other alleles at different loci.

Hence, for the profile in Figure 6.8, its frequency in the population is expected to be $0.123 \times 0.057 \times 0.024 \times 0.029 \times 0.123 \times 0.067 \times 0.042 \times 0.004 \times 0.123 \times 0.020 = 1.66 \times 10^{-14}$. This represents a remarkably low frequency. The chance that two unrelated people selected at random would have the same profile (the probability of identity) is $1/1.66 \times 10^{-14} = 6 \times 10^{13}$; this is also called the **match probability**. Effectively, this means that one person in 6×10^{13} would be expected to have the profile. The match probability in this case greatly exceeds the population of the Earth. Such impressively large numbers must be treated with some caution, however. The statistics do not consider relatives in the population. As discussed below in Sections 6.4.3 and 6.4.4, relatives are much more likely than non-relatives to share alleles and hence the likelihood of a profile match between relatives is greater. Also, the profile of everyone on the Earth is not known and although it may be statistically unlikely that two people could share the same profile, it does not prove the profile is unique.

These data related to the profile in Figure 6.8 can also be presented as a **likelihood ratio**, where the probabilities of alternative events are compared. In this case,

Match probability
The likelihood that two unrelated people selected at random could have an identical profile.

Likelihood ratio
How much more likely an event is compared with the alternative event.

Table 6.6 Genotype frequencies of the loci in Figure 6.8

Locus name	Genotype P,Q	Allele frequencies		2pq	p²	Genotype frequency
		p	q			
D3S1358	15,16	0.28	0.22	0.123		0.123
vWA	18,19	0.26	0.11	0.057		0.057
D16S539	10,11	0.04	0.30	0.024		0.024
D2S1338	19,23	0.13	0.11	0.029		0.029
D8S1179	13,13	0.35	0.35		0.123	0.123
D21S11	28,29	0.16	0.21	0.067		0.067
D18S51	13,16	0.15	0.14	0.042		0.042
D19S433	12,15.2	0.07	0.03	0.004		0.004
THO1	9.3,9.3	0.35	0.35		0.123	0.123
FGA	19,22	0.06	0.17	0.020		0.020

with the DNA profile evidence observed, one hypothesis, which would be the prosecution argument, is that the suspect left the evidence and that is why the profiles match. If the hypothesis is true, then the probability for this match is 1.0. The alternative possibility is that the evidence is from another person, the defence case. This probability from the STR data is 1.66×10^{-14}. The likelihood ratio is thus equal to $1/1.66 \times 10^{-14} = 6 \times 10^{13}$, which has the same value as the match probability, but its meaning is different; it means that the hypothesis that the evidence originated from the suspect is 6×10^{13} times more likely than the alternative. (For more on likelihood ratios, see Chapter 13, Section 13.6.)

The reason for using ten loci is that even though each individual locus is not very discriminating, as some of their alleles are very common, the whole profile becomes very discriminating because of the multiplication of many low probabilities. Hence, it is more likely, but not certain, that the profile is found only in the source individual. For several reasons discussed in Section 6.4.4, the probability calculated may be an underestimate, but the system is still very powerful in its resolution.

6.4.3 DNA profiling in paternity testing

DNA profiling has an important use in paternity testing and, more broadly, establishing familial relationships among a group of people. A wide variety of issues revolve around familial relationships; where these might be in question, for whatever circumstances, DNA profiling is a powerful tool allowing their resolution. Cases are often civil, but there are also applications in criminal cases; for example, a body may be identified as that of a missing child by comparing its DNA profile with that of the parents.

The inheritance of alleles follows the basic pattern of inheritance discussed in Section 6.2.6 and Figure 6.5. A child can receive only one of the father's alleles and one of the mother's alleles. By looking at the DNA profiles of mother, father and child, there should be a clear relationship.

Table 6.7 gives summarised profile data for a hypothetical paternity case where there are two alleged fathers. Comparing the daughter's genotypes for each locus with those of the mother and the alleged fathers allows a decision to be made. Consider just locus D3S1358, where the child has genotype 16,17. Allele 16 must be from the mother as neither alleged father has this allele. Allele 17 of the child must be from the father, and only alleged father 2 has allele 17. This effectively excludes alleged father 1 as being the father. Applying the same analysis for all the other loci confirms this. For each allele that is not maternal in origin, alleged father 2 can be the source and so the evidence favours alleged father 2 as being the father.

As discussed above, however, this is not necessarily proof of paternity; it depends on how common the alleles donated by the father are in the population. For reporting evidence, a statistic called the combined paternity index is calculated. For the data above, this has a value of about 540 000, which means that it is 540 000 times more likely that father 2 is the father than a random male in the population. This statistic is rather unwieldy and is often converted to the probability of paternity (PrP). The closer this value is to 1, the more certain is paternity. The data in Table 6.7 give a PrP value of 0.999 98, very strongly supporting the hypothesis of the paternity of father 2. The calculation of these statistics is beyond the scope of the chapter; extension information is available on the accompanying website.

Table 6.7 Paternity case

Locus	Genotype of			
	Mother	Child	Alleged father 1	Alleged father 2
D3S1358	15,16	16,17	14,15	13,17
vWA	18,19	18,18	14,16	13,18
D16S539	10,11	9,10	9,10	9,12
D2S1338	19,23	23,24	20,23	19,24
D8S1179	13,13	13,14	12,13	14,18
D21S11	28,29	28,30	28,31	30,33
D18S51	13,16	13,14	12,15	14,17
D19S433	12,15.2	15.2,16	15,16	16,16
THO1	9.3,9.3	7,9.3	7,9.3	7,10
FGA	19,22	22,22	24,26	22,22
Amelogenin	XX	XX	X,Y	X,Y

Statistical analysis sounds very convoluted and becomes more complicated than perhaps the initial matching of maternal and paternal alleles would seem to warrant. In paternity, clearly other evidence of associations and sexual relationships would be relevant. The use of statistics attempts to introduce objectivity into the interpretation of the DNA profiles.

6.4.4 Familial testing

Just as parents and their children can be identified by DNA profiling because of the pattern of shared alleles as described above (Section 6.4.3), so other relatives are also expected to share some of their alleles. DNA profiles from relatives are likely to show a higher proportion of shared alleles than unrelated people. Non-relatives may share alleles in a profile, as described above (Sections 6.4.1 and 6.4.2). Some alleles are very common in the population and hence are likely to be shared, but this is by chance and not by genetic descent. The more distant the relatives, the fewer alleles expected to be shared by them and the lower the confidence in establishing relatedness using DNA profiling. The use of more loci in DNA profiling would allow greater reliability in establishing distant relatedness.

Using DNA profiling to identify relatives is proving a powerful application of the NDNAD by the police. As described earlier (Section 6.3.6), DNA profile evidence from an incident or crime scene is compared with all the profiles in the NDNAD with the intention of finding a match over the whole profile. The success of this depends on the profile of the source individual being on the database. If this was not the case, the DNA evidence could lead nowhere. However, by searching the database for profiles that share a higher proportion of alleles with the evidence, relatives of the source may be identified; this is then intelligence for the police investigation and may lead to the individual who left the evidence. In familial searching, where only partial matches are being searched for, it is expected that a fairly large number of profiles in the database might meet the criteria. This does not mean that all these profiles are from relatives to the source individual; some will be partial matches by chance. Other evidence related to the incident will eliminate many of the chance matches, and ultimately a true relative may be found and lead to the actual source of the evidence. This is a use of the database beyond searching for simple matches. The first high-profile example of familial searching was the cold case review that led to Joseph Kappen described in Box 6.2. Familial searching first led to a conviction in the case of Craig Harman, jailed for manslaughter in 2004 (Box 6.2).

6.4.5 Quality control and complications in DNA profile data

From the earliest days of DNA evidence being presented in court, it has been put under intense scrutiny. DNA evidence has been dismissed on highly technical grounds related to conduct in the laboratory. A DNA profile must be produced according to quality assurance systems, from the collection to presentation of DNA evidence, aimed at ensuring data are robust enough in order to withstand the rigour of courtroom challenges.

The following are examples of conduct related to quality management:

- At every stage of processing, the track of the evidence is documented to ensure continuity of evidence is maintained.
- Throughout the procedures, great care is taken to avoid contamination because of the great sensitivity of PCR-based techniques.
- Positive and negative controls are included in the tests.
- Attributing peaks on the electropherograms to alleles requires accurate sizing and must be controlled carefully.
- Objective standards for analysing the data are employed.
- Laboratories undertaking the work carry out trials, both declared and blind, to test the systems and are subject to inspections by standard monitoring organisations.

The DNA profiles discussed in Section 6.4.2 are full profiles because information is obtained for all 11 loci. In practice, the quality of the profile may be compromised by the quality and quantity of the DNA from the scene of crime evidence. Hence, interpreting a profile may not be so straightforward as described previously:

- *Partial profiles*: these occur when not all alleles amplify, and a full DNA profile is not obtained. They are often encountered when the DNA evidence is badly degraded or is found in very low amounts. Interpretation may still be possible based on the successful amplifications, but the discriminating power may not be so high, as fewer matches can be observed. Having fewer matching peaks reduces the match probability, with consequent impact on the strength of the DNA evidence.
- *Mixed profiles*: in these cases, the extracted DNA is from two or more people. Bloodstains in assaults may be from more than one person. In the case of rape, evidence may contain the DNA of the victim and the perpetrator. The mixed

profile can be compared with that of the victim and, by subtraction, a profile of the rapist be made, although this may not be complete. Sperm in semen can be separated from cells of the victim, thereby increasing the proportion of the sample's DNA originating from the rapist. Multiple rape may give mixed profiles that are very complex but that can still be unravelled, depending on other evidence. Commonly, the victim has a partner whose DNA is also present in the mixture. Mixed profiles are apparent by there being more than two alleles for some, although not necessarily all, of the loci. Mixed profiles can be a challenge to interpret, and it may be best not to use them as evidence if they can be avoided; however, they may be the only evidence. The problem of mixed profiles is considered in Figure 6.9, which for simplicity considers two contributors (A and B), and the alleles of just one locus; remember that in a full SGM$^+$ profile another nine loci would be present. When the peak heights are similar (Figure 6.9b, c) there are no criteria by which the alleles can be paired to give the genotypes of the contributors to the mixed profile. Hence, a set of possible genotypes can be made but the true genotypes of the contributors cannot be determined. From a mixed profile at all ten STR loci of SGM$^+$, the number of possible permutations of the genotypes is large. At the time of writing, a pilot study is taking place in some police forces of a computer-based analysis that attempts to interpret mixed profiles (see Section 6.6.2).

Analysing and interpreting DNA profile data as described in Sections 6.4.1 and 6.4.2 uses the Hardy–Weinberg principle. This principle is of great importance in population genetics but is founded on some assumptions. The relevant assumptions here are:

- mating is random within the population;
- the mating population is large;
- mating between closely related individuals does not occur;
- there is no immigration into or emigration out of the population.

The assumptions are unlikely to be met in real human populations: populations on islands and in remote regions may be quite small; migration has occurred widely throughout history and is very important today; and within populations mating is not random, as people often tend to have children with partners from the same social class and racial or cultural groups.

A consequence of this is that alleles do not flow freely in the population and groups may differ in the alleles they contain or show certain alleles at different frequencies to other groups. If an allele occurs in one group, it will remain within that group unless matings take place with members outside the group. In multicultural and multiracial societies such as the UK, much of Europe and the United States, the populations are not uniform for allele frequencies. Data are available for subgroups in the population. The DNA profile in Section 6.4.2 was analysed using US Caucasian allele frequencies. In the UK, the racial groups usually considered are: White European, Afro-Caribbean, Indian Subcontinental, South-East Asian and Middle Eastern. Clearly, these are very broad groups and within them are likely to be further subpopulations. Assigning populations to groups is not without problems

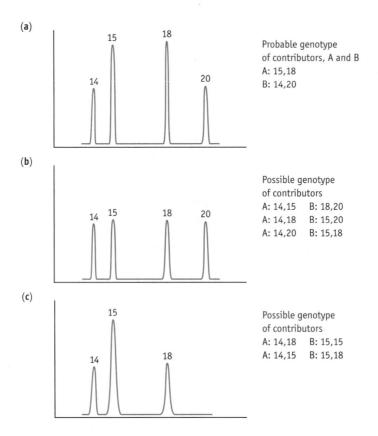

Figure 6.9 A mixed profile at a single locus

Mixed profiles are manifest by there being more than two alleles present for a given locus on the electropherogram. For simplicity, here a single locus is shown but note that the pattern of there being more than two alleles is likely to be repeated at each locus in the profile. (a) Four alleles of 14, 15, 18 and 20 repeats are shown at this locus, and therefore it is likely that there are two contributors to the DNA mixture. Alleles 15 and 18 have similar peak heights and, since peak height is related to the amount of DNA, it is probable that the genotype of one contributor, the major one, was 15,18. The other, minor contributor was probably 14,20. The difference in peak height allows the separation of the profiles with some confidence. (b) This diagram shows the same alleles as in (a), but here the peak heights are similar and the genotypes cannot be separated. There are a number of possibilities for the genotypes of the two contributors, known here as A and B. (c) Three alleles are shown and the peak height of 15 is greater than the other two. Here a 15,15 homozygote is possible, or both contributors could carry allele 15

and is not always consistent between different countries. The populations of Spanish and southern European origin in the United States are grouped as Hispanics for a subset of allele frequencies. The original populations in Europe are classified in the general Caucasian group.

Families have more genes and alleles in common with each other than with the unrelated population. This has a bearing on DNA profile interpretation. If close relatives could be the source of evidence, then the discrimination of the profiling is different, as we are considering not random population members but a family population. The extremely high discrimination of the SGM$^+$ system does allow resolution of individuals (except for identical twins) and the likelihood ratios and other evidence favour one conclusion over others. For example, a suspect may claim that he is not the source of the matching DNA evidence and that the evidence is his brother's. The likelihood that two siblings could have an identical SGM$^+$ profile is in the order of 1 in 10 000 (note the much lower discrimination value here compared with the match probabilities in Section 6.4.2, which assume unrelated people). Even if the brother refuses to provide a sample for DNA analysis and elimination, the 1 in 10 000 match probability argues strongly that the source was the original suspect.

That the assumptions of the Hardy–Weinberg principle are not met fully does not negate analyses carried out using it; it can be considered as presenting the simplest ideal case upon which complicating factors can be introduced. Population substructures and inbreeding have predictable consequences, which with sufficient data can be taken into account when interpreting the DNA profile. Detailed treatment of these factors is beyond the scope of this chapter.

Although it is straightforward to calculate a match probability, as described in Section 6.4.2, the points discussed above, about assumptions in the analysis, do question the accuracy of the value. Is it really, say, 6×10^{13}? This is difficult to address, and in the UK the value usually quoted in court for a full matching SGM$^+$ DNA profiles is one in a billion (1 in 10^9). This is clearly a conservative estimate compared with the calculated match probability, but it is considered not to overestimate the statistical significance of the match. In other countries, the full value of the match probability may be quoted.

6.4.6 Y chromosome analysis

The DNA profiles considered above are based on the analysis of STRs present on autosomes (Table 6.2). The only marker on the sex chromosomes is amelogenin. Only males (usually) carry a Y chromosome. As the greater proportion of serious crime is carried out by men, there is an interest in examining DNA found only in this gender. The Y chromosome is a small chromosome with few genes; unlike other chromosomes, it does not have a homologue (see Section 6.2.3) and is not subject to the processes of recombination that assort the alleles on the autosomes, generating new combinations. A Y chromosome is altered only by the process of mutation, which is infrequent. Numerous (over 200) STRs are present on the Y chromosome and multiplex PCR systems are available to analyse some of these; one system, Yfiler™ of Applied Biosystems, allows the determination of the alleles and number of repeats present at 16 loci on the Y chromosome. A DNA profile produced by such an analysis would superficially resemble a SGM$^+$ profile, but more careful examination would show that at each locus only a single allele is present; this is because the Y chromosome is present only once in a cell. A Yfiler profile hence would consist of 16 peaks, and the genotype would consist of a column of numbers, one for the repeat number (allele) at each locus.

Since the Y chromosome cannot recombine, a father's combination of alleles (his haplotype, since the Y chromosome is haploid) is expected to be passed to his sons unaltered (unless mutation occurs), and they will then pass on the haplotype, unchanged, to their sons down the paternal line. A Y chromosome is not expected to be unique to an individual: his father, paternal grandfather, brothers and sons will all share the same Y chromosome alleles, unless mutation has altered some. The discrimination of Y chromosome analysis is low compared with STR profiling on autosomes; a match probability of about 0.003 might be expected for 11 Y chromosome STRs. Note that as Y chromosomes are haploid, they cannot recombine or show independent assortment, and the approach used to calculate expected genotype frequencies for SGM$^+$ profiles in Sections 6.4.1 and 6.4.2 is not appropriate.

In many cultures, the surname is passed down the paternal line and hence should follow the Y chromosome. This has led to the suggestion that a given pattern of Y chromosome alleles might be associated with a surname. Imagine a forensic scientist examining DNA evidence and being able to give the surname of the source. The principle has been demonstrated with some names, but for general application it is probably rather far-fetched; certainly for common surnames with multiple origins. Illegitimacy and cases where the accepted father is not the biological father may complicate paternal lines.

In mixed profiles from males and females, Y chromosome analysis provides genetic links solely to the male. In multiple rape, a mixed Y chromosome profile might be easier to separate to its components and link to suspects than autosomal STR data.

Y Chromosome analysis has been exploited widely in studies of human populations and migrations. Its application to forensic work is a topic of discussion. It has been used in special circumstances but is not used routinely.

6.4.7 Summary

Sections 6.3 and 6.4 have covered the basis of modern DNA profiling, describing the techniques of DNA analysis and their application to the study of STRs, currently the most powerful type of forensic DNA analysis. The SGM$^+$ system has been used as an example of a system of multiplex PCR-based STR analysis, and the nature of the data generated and its basic interpretation has been considered. Further, the application of STR analysis to the Y chromosome and its potential was covered. The impact of the technology on forensic science has been revolutionary.

6.5 Analysis not involving STRs: single nucleotide polymorphism analysis

Standard DNA profiling as described above is currently based on STR analysis. There are a large number of STR loci in the human genome; they have large numbers of alleles and, because alleles differ in the number of repeats, the length of each allele differs. It is relatively easy to measure the length of DNA molecules, and hence the analysis of STR loci is straightforward. However, as described in Section 6.2.4, there are other types of variable DNA in the human genome. Indeed, it was mentioned that the majority of mutations in the human genome are point mutations, i.e. single base changes. Ninety per cent of human genetic variation is in the form of point mutations, and such mutations are very abundant. If a particular base (at a precise location in the human genome) can be more than one of the four bases (A, C, G or T, or a subset of these), it is said to be a single nucleotide polymorphism (SNP). An SNP can be found every 100–300 bp throughout the human genome, which hence contains literally millions of SNPs. A change of base from, say, A to G does not alter the length of the DNA, and determining which base is present at a SNP needs techniques in addition to those used in STR analysis. This section covers one approach to SNP analysis and considers forensic applications in the context of mitochondrial DNA analysis. Further applications related to predicting physical appearance are considered in Section 6.6.5.

6.5.1 Analysis of single nucleotide polymorphisms (SNPs)

A given SNP can have a maximum of four alleles: it can be A, C, G or T. Many SNPs have only two alleles, A or G for example. Compare this with the number of alleles for STR loci in Table 6.2. To determine the allele of a given SNP, the particular base present has to be established. The technique used to do this is called DNA sequencing, one of the most important procedures in genetics.

DNA sequencing allows the precise base sequence (Section 6.2.2) of a section of DNA to be determined. All mutations and different alleles are initially characterised using DNA sequencing, which is capable of revealing all types of mutation. This is a complex but important technique that was, until fairly recently, technically demanding. For routine analysis, however, DNA sequencing is usually avoided, and assays are developed that are simpler and can be automated, for example SGM$^+$ for STR analysis. DNA sequencing is not used routinely in forensic science. Its main forensic use is for mtDNA analysis, where it is needed to reveal point mutations. The interested reader is directed to books listed at the end of this chapter, as it is inappropriate to cover the technique in detail here.

For routine analysis of SNPs, a much simplified version of DNA sequencing, called minisequencing, was developed. This method is illustrated in Figure 6.10. The aim is to establish which base is present at the SNP site (Figure 6.10a). A primer is made that is complementary to the sequence next to the SNP. After allowing the primer to base pair to the target sequence (Figure 6.10b), the DNA is incubated in the presence of DNA polymerase and four modified nucleotides (Figure 6.10c). These nucleotides, called dideoxynucleotides, can be added to the end of the primer; which one is added is determined by the base at the SNP (Figure 6.10d), but its addition prevents any other nucleotides being added. Each of the four types of dideoxynucleotides is labelled with a different fluorescent tag and hence the colour of the fluorescence after electrophoresis establishes the base at the SNP (Figure 6.10e).

By using different-length primers for different SNPs, several SNPs (at different loci) can be examined in the same reaction, and a profile, not unlike a DNA profile, is produced. For a sample of DNA evidence, the base at each SNP can be determined, which gives a genotype for each SNP locus. As with other types of variable DNA, an individual can be homozygous at the SNP if both their alleles have the same base, for example G,G, or heterozygous if the alleles are different, for example G,T. Using allele frequencies for each SNP, a likelihood of two people sharing the same profile can be estimated. The small number of alleles (maximum of four) means that a larger number of SNPs (about 50) are needed in order to achieve the same discrimination as current STR-based profiling.

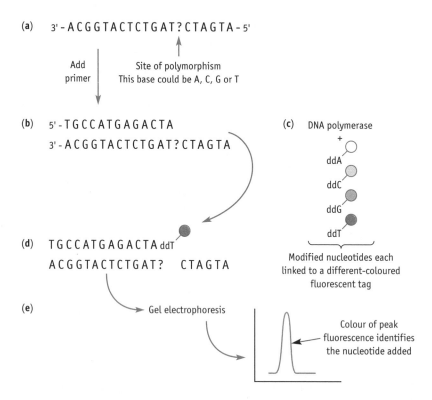

Figure 6.10 Minisequencing for SNP analysis

(a) At the SNP site the base can be of up to four types, A, C, G or T. (b) A primer is designed that binds to the sequence adjacent to the SNP. (c) After allowing the primer to base pair to the target sequence, it is incubated in the presence of DNA polymerase and four modified nucleotides, called dideoxynucleotides. When a dideoxynucleotide is added to the end of the primer by the DNA polymerase, no further nucleotides can be added; the extension of the DNA is blocked. Each dideoxynucleotide has a different-coloured fluorescent tag linked to it. (d) The polymerase adds the next complementary nucleotide on to the primer; in the example this is ddT. No further reaction takes place. (e) After electrophoresis, the colour of the peak, due to the fluorescent tag, identifies the nucleotide added; in the example this is a T, and hence the unknown base at the SNP in (a) is found to be an A

Minisequencing illustrated in Figure 6.10 is just one of a number of techniques that allow the allele of a SNP to be determined. It is inappropriate to cover them all here. One method called microarray hybridisation analysis avoids using gel electrophoresis to separate SNP products and has the potential to examine a very large number of SNP loci simultaneously.

In principle, a DNA profiling system based entirely on SNPs could be developed and might have some advantages in that SNP analysis can give profiles with badly degraded DNA. Whether such a system could ever displace STR analysis remains to be seen. It seems unlikely, as the SNP data are not compatible with the current DNA database. SNP data may be added to STR data. Where SNP analysis is likely to become important is in predicting features of the person who left the sample, as discussed in Section 6.6.5.

6.5.2 Mitochondrial DNA analysis

Most of the forensic DNA analysis discussed earlier has been based on STR loci present in DNA in the cell nucleus. Despite its remarkable power and sensitivity, in some cases it may not be possible to obtain an STR profile because of the degradation of the nuclear DNA in the sample. Badly decomposed or charred bodies, old bones and hair shafts without roots are often poor sources of nuclear DNA. One course, in these circumstances, is to examine mitochondrial DNA (mtDNA). As explained briefly in Section 6.2.3, mtDNA is much more abundant – there may be tens or hundreds of thousands of copies of mtDNA per cell. mtDNA is not resistant to degradation, but its abundance means that some intact copies may survive longer. mtDNA analysis is essentially a comparison of SNPs in the mtDNA; it is not based on STR analysis.

6.5.3 Mitochondrial DNA (mtDNA)

Human mtDNA is a circular molecule of DNA, 16 569 bp in circumference (Figure 6.11a). Unlike nuclear DNA, it has no 'junk' DNA; nearly every base pair has a function. The genetic information in the mitochondrion is essential and most of it does not vary between individuals – it is said to be highly conserved. When mutations are present, they are often associated with disease. Most of the mtDNA circle therefore has no forensic value because it varies very little between individuals. An exception to this is in the D-loop (or control region, in some texts). This section of the molecule, which is involved in replication of the mtDNA, is about 1000 bp long and contains two regions called hypervariable regions 1 and 2 (HV1 and HV2), which can vary in sequence. The sequence variation is mainly point mutations (single base changes, SNPs), which do not alter the length of the DNA and are detected easily only by determining the base sequence of the DNA. Uncommon single base insertions and deletions have been found. There are no STRs in mtDNA.

Mitochondria lack the DNA repair systems of the nucleus and, as a consequence, the mtDNA mutates at a higher rate and is likely to show sequence differences between individuals. In the hypervariable regions, a difference of 1–3 per cent may be expected between unrelated individuals; in other words, in a stretch of 100 bp up to 3 bp might be different.

To investigate mtDNA, a procedure similar to the early stages of standard STR analysis is followed. DNA is extracted from the sample and PCR (Section 6.3.3) is then used to amplify the regions HV1 and HV2 using specific primers designed to base pair to their ends (Figure 6.11a). The base pair sequence of the amplified HV1 and HV2 is then determined using a technique called DNA sequencing.

The DNA sequences of the hypervariable regions are then compared with a reference sequence, which is the first mtDNA to be sequenced, referred to as the Anderson sequence. Differences are noted and can be compared with other samples (from suspects or victims) relevant to the particular case (Table 6.8).

In comparing the mtDNA sequences, it must be borne in mind how mtDNA is inherited. An individual inherits his or her mtDNA only from the mother. Although the father's sperm have mitochondria, these are not usually maintained in the fertilised egg. The consequence is that all the brothers and sisters in a family will share the same mtDNA as the mother but not the father. This pattern is called maternal inheritance. They will also share the same mtDNA as the mother's siblings and the grandmother. Figure 6.11b shows an example of this. In the first generation, the children of the original couple all inherit their mother's mtDNA. One of the daugh-

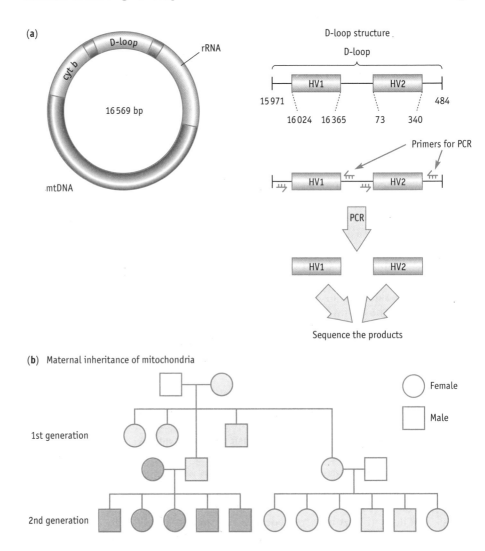

Figure 6.11 Mitochondrial DNA (mtDNA)

(a) Aspects of mtDNA structure. Only the approximate portions of the D-loop and the cytochrome b gene (cyt b) are shown, as these sections have most forensic value. Within the D-loop, the positions and sizes of the hypervariable regions 1 and 2 (HV1, HV2) are shown. The molecules are not to scale. (b) A pedigree illustrating mitochondrial inheritance. Blue shading indicates people who have inherited the same mitochondrial DNA from the female at the start of the pedigree

ters has children (generation 2) and these all share the same mtDNA. A son in generation 1 also has children but, being male, he does not pass on his mtDNA to them; all his children will have the mtDNA of their mother.

An individual should have just one type of mtDNA – that from his or her mother and the sequences of his or her hypervariable regions of only one type. This is the usual case and is termed homoplasmy. More rarely, in sequencing HV1 and HV2 of a person, it appears that two bases are present at a particular location. In this case, the person has two types of mitochondria, which differ in the base they carry at that position. This state is called heteroplasmy.

mtDNA data are simply DNA base sequence data. HV1 and HV2 both generate DNA sequences of about 300 bp. For a given sample or individual, the base sequences are compared with the Anderson reference sequence and the differences noted. Each base on the mtDNA is identified by a number according to its position on the DNA circle, from 1 (agreed by convention) to 16 569. Table 6.8 shows an example of mitochondrial DNA data.

In the example, the mtDNA of the living relative has an identical sequence to that of bodies 2, 3 and 5. The bodies could be siblings, a mother and children, or more complicated relations sharing a common maternal source for the mtDNA. Other forensic evidence would help to judge the relationships, and this could be supported by STR analysis. Bodies 1 and 4 have different sequences and are not maternally linked to the bodies or to each other. Body 4 at position 16 296 apparently has a T and an A, i.e. heteroplasmy. As with STR data, to put the interpretation on a firmer footing requires the application of more complex statistics than those used for STR analysis and are not appropriate at this level.

mtDNA analysis is not as discriminating between unrelated individuals as is STR DNA profiling. The advantage of mtDNA is that it can be applied successfully to samples that fail to produce STR data. Until fairly recently, DNA sequencing was slow, technically difficult and labour-intensive. It has become easier with automated approaches developed from the genome sequencing projects, but it is still not as straightforward as STR profiling.

Table 6.8 mtDNA sequence data from a communal grave compared with a living relative*

Source of DNA	Base pair position on mtDNA															
	HV1												HV2			
	16 111	16 126	16 169	16 261	16 264	16 278	16 293	16 294	16 296	16 304	16 311	16 357	73	146	195	263
Anderson sequence	C	T	C	C	C	C	A	C	C	T	T	T	A	T	T	A
Body 1			T		T	G					C				C	G
Body 2	T										C					G
Body 3	T										C					G
Body 4		C	T					T	T/A				G			G
Body 5	T										C					G
Living Relative	T										C					G

Only sequence differences are shown; blank cells indicate identity with the Anderson sequence.

Another approach to analysing mtDNA utilises minisequencing (Figure 6.10 and Section 6.5.1). Although the HV1 and HV2 regions are variable in sequence by definition, certain bases in them are more likely than others to mutate. Minisequencing selects 12 of these bases in the D-loop and determines the bases at those particular sites. Comparison is made of the data from evidence with the reference sequence and with data of suspects, victims or relatives. Mismatches between samples enable suspects to be excluded. Matched sequences may then have to be re-examined by full sequencing of HV1 and 2. Minisequencing is rapid, and technological advances may allow more sites to be examined.

6.5.4 Applications of mtDNA analysis

One application has been in the identification of old, badly degraded bodies. Box 6.3 gives two examples, the identification of the Romanov remains and the identification of the remains of a US airman from Vietnam. mtDNA has also been employed in identifying bodies from air disasters.

mtDNA can be employed to study non-human remains. If it is necessary to demonstrate the source animal for a product suspected to be made from a protected species, then the cytochrome b gene on the mtDNA can be PCR amplified and sequenced. This well-studied gene is used widely in taxonomy, and the sequence should identify the species.

As mtDNA is not as discriminating as STR analysis, it is often used forensically only when standard profiling has failed. Nevertheless it does have niche applications within the field.

Case study

Box 6.3

Applications of mitochondrial DNA: the Romanov case and identification of missing servicemen

A classic case involving mitochondrial DNA (mtDNA) was the confirmation of the remains of the Russian imperial family. In the course of the Russian Revolution, the Tsar and his family were captured by the Bolsheviks and were executed in July 1918. The graves were rumoured to be in a wood near Ekaterinburg, Russia. DNA isolated from bones excavated from the site in 1991 revealed by STR analysis that a family group was present but this evidence did not say anything about the bones being those of the Romanovs. To address this, use was made of mtDNA: since this is inherited only down the maternal line, any maternal descendants of the Romanovs should show the same sequence of mtDNA. Prince Philip, Duke of Edinburgh, is a living maternal descendent of Tsarina Alexandra's sister. His mtDNA sequences were identical to those from the bones of the three children and their mother on the basis of the STR analysis, essentially proving they were the bones of the Romanovs.

mtDNA has been used in the identification of old and badly degraded bodies. The US Army Central Identification Laboratory has used it to identify the remains of American servicemen lost overseas, for example in Vietnam. In 1998, the unit identified remains interred in the Tomb of the Unknowns as those of Air Force Lieutenant Michael J. Blassie, 26 years after he was shot down in Vietnam.

6.6 Current and future developments

It has been the aim of this chapter to describe the genetic and technical background to current DNA profiling. Such an important technology does not remain stagnant. This section intends to briefly outline developments that have taken place since the establishment of the basic technology and those that are occurring or may occur in forensic DNA analysis.

6.6.1 Low Copy Number DNA and sensitivity

There is a strong motivation to try to increase the sensitivity of DNA profiling in order to enable the analysis of a wider range of evidence. Very low levels of DNA and degraded DNA can result in poor-quality or completely negative results using standard DNA profiling. Research at the FSS of England and Wales has led to the development of an extremely sensitive technique called low copy number DNA profiling (LCN), which is an extension of the SGM$^+$ technology. The increased sensitivity is achieved in part by increasing the number of cycles in the PCR stage (Section 6.3.3) from 28 to 34, thereby increasing the amount of product about 100-fold. LCN is often capable of producing a profile from amounts of DNA that are too small to quantify, even from a single cell. Application of this technique has allowed DNA profiles to be made and used successfully as evidence from incredibly small samples, e.g. the few skin cells left in a physical fingerprint or a lip-print. A flake of dandruff can give a full profile, as can a single hair. Surfaces likely to have been touched may be sources of DNA, even though there may be no obvious stain or sample.

LCN is now used routinely. It is employed in situations where standard SGM$^+$ profiling has produced a partial or negative result and when insufficient DNA has been produced from the sample for standard profiling. The quality or amount of sample itself, from previous experience, may suggest that a normal DNA profiling reaction would fail.

Old stored evidence from unsolved cases and from resolved cases that predated DNA profiling or previously failed to give DNA profiles can be re-examined using LCN, with some dramatic results (see Box 6.4).

Increased sensitivity inevitably means a greater risk of contamination and generation of artefacts in the data. The extreme sensitivity of LCN readily produces mixed profiles and partial profiles (Section 6.4.5). Nevertheless, it has proved to be a very powerful technique. LCN requires rigour in the laboratory in order to avoid contamination and also at the crime scene where the evidence is collected.

LCN is so sensitive that it has raised issues about transfer of DNA from the site where the evidence was deposited to another location. It could be imagined that person A shakes hands with person B; some of A's skin cells are transferred to B, who then touches an object at a crime scene, depositing A's cells and hence DNA at the scene. Similarly, B might touch an object previously touched by A and transfer A's cells to another location (note, however, that it is also likely that B's cells would be present, producing a mixed sample). Such inadvertent transfer probably occurs all the time but would be difficult to detect normally as the amount of material transferred will be extremely small. However, LCN can detect extremely small amounts of evidence. Such transfer of material can be demonstrated in laboratory

Case study

Box 6.4

Applications of low copy number DNA profiling (LCN): the Tony Jasinskyj case and the John Anthony Cook case

Marion Crofts, a 14-year-old schoolgirl cycling near her home in Fleet, Hampshire, UK, was raped and murdered in June 1981. With the development of LCN in the late 1990s, evidence stored 20 years before could be re-examined. A DNA profile was obtained from Marion's clothing and also from a microscope slide containing evidence from Marion's body. A decision had been made to leave the slide untouched until DNA technology had advanced sufficiently in order to be confident of producing a profile from such an old, small sample. A search of the National DNA Database revealed a match to a sample taken from the body and the slide. The probability of someone unrelated having the same profile was one in a billion. Tony Jasinskyj had been arrested on suspicion of assault, and hence his profile was on the database. In May 2002, he was con-victed for the rape and murder of Marion Crofts.

Another example where improved methods are expanding the potential for DNA analysis is a case from August 2002. John Anthony Cook was convicted for the murder of Monica Jepson, a pensioner, at a nursing home in Birmingham, UK, in 1995. A DNA profile was produced using LCN on a faecal sample left at the scene of the crime. Faeces can be a good source of mitochondrial DNA, but standard profiling is not usually successful. The profile obtained matched that of John Cook, whose DNA profile was on the database because of his arrest in an unrelated incident. This evidence and that of a partial fingerprint led to his conviction. Excrement is frequently deposited at crime scenes, and hence this development may prove very important.

experiments, but its relevance in the real world is unclear; it may provide a case for the defence.

Although it may not be used as routinely as SGM$^+$ profiling due to the associated difficulty in anti-contamination and interpretation of the DNA profile, the fact that LCN might prove useful as the investigation progresses has an impact on the collection of material from the scene of crime. Contact traces may be sampled from areas likely to have been touched by the offender. Evidence can be collected and stored with appropriate precautions in case it is necessary to apply LCN in the future. It is difficult to imagine that the system could become more sensitive than that of LCN procedures. LCN is now used widely, despite its higher costs, as it has had a great impact in improving detection rates in volume crime such as burglary and vehicle theft, making it cost-effective. Wider use and provision will lead to cost reductions, and it is expected that LCN will be carried out in all cases where it can be used.

6.6.2 Technical developments

Automation

To be effective in a wide variety of forensic work, large numbers of samples need to be processed. Single cases could be imagined to generate numerous samples and, if local population screening is undertaken, this will run into thousands. Certain cases will be given priority over others, but ideally the processing time of any sample would be as rapid as possible. The costs of the tests will be an issue for the police force requesting them. Automation, and the expansion of the technical provision, are allowing the processing of very large numbers of DNA samples. With current technology, up to 80 samples of potential DNA evidence can be processed rapidly, taking as little as 8 hours from crime scene to court statement.

Portability

Hand-held equipment that would allow a profile to be generated very rapidly after sampling the evidence directly at the crime scene has been proposed and is being developed. Technical developments in these fields can be incredibly fast, and 'real-time' DNA profiling could occur at scenes in the not too distant future.

Modifications to STR analysis

PCR is more efficient when amplifying shorter fragments than longer fragments. In forensic applications, badly degraded DNA may not give a profile at all or may give only a partial profile. To improve the success rate of STR analysis on problematic DNA samples, one approach is to reduce the size of the fragments to be amplified. This can be achieved by redesigning the primers to be closer to the repeat sequence (Figure 6.6 and Section 6.3.3); hence, for each locus the range of allele size will be smaller and more likely to be amplified by PCR on degraded DNA. Such a system called Minifiler™ by Applied Biosystems is available; on poor-quality DNA, where SGM⁺ gives partial profiles or fails, this can give good-quality full profiles.

Mixed profiles

The problem of mixed profiles was discussed in Section 6.4.5 and Figure 6.9. The Forensic Science Service in the UK has piloted a potentially very powerful system called DNAboost™, which aims to determine the genotypes present in the mixture. This is achieved by generating all possible permutations of genotypes from the data and using these to interrogate the database. Matches provide intelligence leads for the police to further their investigation. To date, the pilot study in four UK police forces has shown that over 50 per cent of DNA samples that were unable to be interpreted, because they were complex mixtures, partials or minor components, resulted in useful leads after analysis using DNAboost. Clearly, this development is of potentially great importance.

Ageing the evidence

DNA profiles give no information about the timing of the deposition of the evidence. Certainly older samples may have only degraded DNA, but this depends on the evidence's environment. The time at which the evidence was left, though, could be crucial to an investigation in the inclusion and exclusion of suspects. Research on the question of sample age has examined not DNA, which is relatively stable, but RNA. RNA is labile; by looking at the rate of decay of certain RNAs in blood, predictions could be made about how long the evidence was deposited before being collected by the forensic scientist. Such work is in the research stage. It might be imagined that the rate of RNA decay would alter dramatically under different environmental conditions and in different cell types, and hence a general test to age evidence based on nucleic acid analysis is currently difficult to envisage.

Identifying the evidence

With LCN the nature of the evidence might be unknown: yes, DNA evidence was found, but what type of tissue was the source? Was it a very small spot of blood, saliva or semen? This could be highly relevant to an investigation. Most cells from an individual contain the same genomic DNA. To address this question, RNA analysis has been proposed because each cell type produces a different set of RNAs. Testing evidence for certain tissue-specific RNAs could help establish its source tissue if the RNA survives in the evidence. Again, this is still a research question and is not yet applied in forensic work.

6.6.3 Wider application of DNA profiling

Originally, DNA profiling was associated with serious crimes of murder, rape and assault, but increasing sensitivity and automation have led to it being applied to a wider range of crimes, for example car crime and burglary. Box 6.5 gives an example of its use in accident investigations.

Every DNA profile requested has a financial cost to the police. In the past, the relatively high cost influenced judgements about whether to use DNA evidence in a particular investigation. The cost had to be balanced with the high success rate using DNA evidence, which ultimately reduced the time of the investigation. Expanding provision, automation and competition among agencies providing DNA profiling services has reduced the cost of standard DNA profiling to between £30 and £300. Along with fingerprinting, DNA profiling is considered as the first choice of evidence in criminal cases.

6.6.4 Increasing the number of STR loci analysed

The more STR loci that are examined in DNA profiling, the more unlikely it becomes that two people could share the same profile. The SGM$^+$ system described in Section 6.3.5 with 11 loci and analysed in Section 6.4.2 already has such a high discrimination that it is thought to be highly unlikely, but not certain, that two unrelated people (except identical twins) could have the same profile. Clearly, more loci could be added to further reduce the likelihood of fortuitous matches, and a 16-loci system has been developed. This is not yet used forensically in the UK but is applied in population genetic studies. There is a discussion about whether to move to a 16-loci system in the UK; the argument is that the NDNAD is now so large that the chance of accidental matches occurring is becoming significant. The match probabilities achieved with SGM$^+$ are extremely low, but the value assumes the likelihood of a match among non-relatives. If a match for relatives is considered, then the probability over the 10 loci is still low but significantly higher than the figures calculated earlier. There are numerous relatives in the NDNAD, and the likelihood of obtaining a chance match is approaching a significant level, although an accidental match has never occurred to date. Moving to a 16-loci system would make this less likely. More loci would also give greater confidence in establishing relatedness in familial searching of the database (Section 6.4.4). The counter-argument is that ten loci are adequate, and the possibility of relatives, and not the actual perpetrator, being identified in a database search is always considered when the strength of the evidence is being addressed.

As mentioned in Section 6.4.5, the figure routinely quoted in court for full matching SGM$^+$ DNA profiles is one in a billion. If more loci were added to the profiling system in the UK it would not necessarily alter how the data are presented in court, unless the procedures were reviewed to take account of the modified system. It remains to be seen whether the UK will move to a 16-loci system.

Perhaps some loci could be changed or incorporated if some of these are associated with specific traits (Section 6.6.5). Such changes, though, would have implications for the DNA database.

6.6.5 Interpreting DNA: predicting phenotypic features

With the exception of the amelogenin locus from which the sex of the DNA source can be determined, the other loci examined in DNA profiling are STRs, and the alleles, as far as is known, are not associated with any physical features of a person carrying them. There could clearly be some advantage in crime investigations if the DNA evidence could be read to give clues to the physical appearance of a suspect. This work is in its early stages.

The melanocortin I receptor gene (*MCIR*) encodes a protein involved in the control of the pigmentation of hair. Along the gene are 12 SNPs, and certain alleles of these are associated with red hair colour. A person having one of these alleles from

Case study

Box 6.5

Use of DNA profiling in accidents and catastrophes: Swissair Flight 111

Swissair Flight 111 flying from New York to Geneva, in September 1998, crashed into the sea off the coast at Peggy Cove near Halifax, Nova Scotia, Canada, killing all 229 passengers and crew. On impact, the plane underwent severe fragmentation. Only one body could be identified visually. Identification of many of the bodies and body parts (exceeding 2500) was only possible using DNA analysis, although other evidence was also employed, e.g. fingerprints, and dental and radiological details. STR DNA profiling was carried out on over 1200 samples at several sites in Canada. The majority of tests were successful, even on material that was retrieved three months after the accident. To make positive identifications, the profiles had to be compared with those of relatives (about 300 were used, from 20 different countries). In some cases, DNA profiles were obtained from personal effects at the homes of the deceased (hairbrushes, razor blades, etc.). Clearly, the identification of the remains was an enormous effort, but through good organisation and procedures (based on experience of other air crashes) within just over two months all the victims had been identified.

mtDNA (Section 6.5.2) has also been used widely in body identification in accidents and catastrophes (see Box 6.3).

each parent is highly likely to have red hair. This forms the basis of a genetic test for red hair, which can be carried out on DNA evidence. The allele of each SNP can be determined using minisequencing (Figure 6.10). The test is not absolute; with the appropriate genotype, it is about 96 per cent likely, but not certain, that the suspect would have red hair. Such a prediction of hair colour could be of use in particular investigations, but generally red hair colour is not very common in the population and a crime is more likely to be committed by a non-redhead. Red hair colour is much more common in certain ethnic groups, and markers for red hair could be incorporated into genetic ethnicity tests. The genetics of more common hair colours and types are not simple but are being researched with the intention of analysing DNA for predictive purposes. Regardless of the predicted genetic hair colour or type, the actual hair characteristics of the person may be very different, as hair is readily and commonly modified, for example by the use of hair dyes and straightening, or naturally through baldness and greying.

Research on a gene called *OCA2* on chromosome 15 has given us some understanding of the genetic basis of eye colour. The gene is involved with broader aspects of pigmentation in hair and skin as well as eyes, and some mutations in it result in a form of albinism. Three SNPs close to, but not actually in, the coding part of the gene were found to be associated strongly with eye colour in terms of brown and blue. Other SNP alleles were associated with green eyes. Further work is needed, but it is suggested that for blue and brown eyes the difference is in the amount of the protein made while for green eyes the structure of the protein is altered. Eventually such research could lead to a forensic minisequencing assay to predict eye colour and perhaps skin characteristics.

Studies of the frequency of various STR alleles in different ethnic groups have shown that some are more frequent in certain groups. From this, the ethnicity of the individual leaving DNA evidence can be predicted, not with certainty but with a certain probability. It has proved very difficult to define ethnic groups genetically, as the majority of markers STRs or SNPs are found in most populations, although the individual population frequencies may vary significantly. From a DNA profile, a likelihood of ethnicity can be made; it is not absolute, but it may be a useful lead. In the UK, the Forensic Science Service offers an ethnic inference test, which gives the likelihood of a DNA sample originating from each of five groups – white-skinned European, Afro-Caribbean, Indian Subcontinental, South East Asian and Middle Eastern.

Predicting the age of the person leaving the DNA evidence could also be useful information, but currently there is no way to address this with any degree of precision using DNA analysis.

Research is under way into the genetics of many physical features (e.g. skin type and colour, height, facial characteristics). Forensically, an ideal outcome of such research would be the generation of a 'photofit' of a suspect from the DNA evidence, although currently this seems a long way off, if it is possible at all. Although this does seem somewhat fanciful at present, the pace of developments in the understanding of human genetics is very rapid, and predicting the timing of envisaged outcomes difficult. As discussed in Section 6.2.1, factors other than a person's genes can influence their appearance. There is also some ethical concern that some features may be associated with diseases and, hence, medical aspects of the person would be revealed in the analysis of some characteristics.

6.6.6 DNA databases

In the future, there may be more international sharing of database information. Not all countries examine the same loci in their DNA profiles, but most systems have some in common, allowing comparisons to be made across borders.

The power of the NDNAD in the UK (Section 6.3.6) is constantly being demonstrated and is likely to become greater with more use of familial searching and applications, involving new developments, for example DNAboost™. As mentioned earlier, at the end of 2006 there were over 3.1 million DNA profiles on the database representing about 5 per cent of the UK population. This is the largest DNA database in the world, with the highest proportion of the population in it. It is predicted to eventually rise to about five million samples. In 2006, about 20 000 people were convicted with the help of DNA evidence. From the point of view of solving crime, the bigger the database, the more effective it will be. However, legal and ethical concerns regarding the database and its use are expressed strongly by a number of groups. The debate about whether everybody in the UK should have their profile on the database recurs occasionally. Such a complete database would certainly be a powerful resource in terms of criminal detection. Clearly, then, a profile from evidence would be seen to link directly to a suspect. It has been argued that this would be a great deterrent to criminal activity. Currently, there is a high chance of an evidence profile matching a database profile, and there might be thought to be some deterrent aspect to the database, but whether this is demonstrated by crime figures is debatable. A complete DNA database of the UK population would contain sensitive information not related to crime, for example cases of illegitimacy and cases where the accepted father is not the biological father. Should this information be available to people with no connection to the families concerned? The database also contains a huge number of profiles from people who have been acquitted; they have not committed a crime but their DNA will remain on the database for life. In the UK, DNA profiles can be taken and kept from a person arrested for an offence that could lead to a prison sentence, even if they are not subsequently charged. In some countries it is illegal to retain samples from people who have been acquitted. Concern has also been expressed at the proportion of ethnic groups on the database: 37 per cent of black men have their profile on the database, while the figures for Asian men and white men are 13 per cent and 9 per cent, respectively. A DNA database of the entire population would at least be representative of the population. Some advocates of such a database argue that because of the sensitive nature of some of the information, it should be administered by a body with no connection to the police. Currently, NDNAD is run by an independent body and is contracted to the Forensic Science Service, but it is owned by the Association of Chief Police Officers. There is also the concern that the database, by including many unconvicted people, is altering the state's perception of its population, relegating them to potential suspects in the future. There is no question of the value, importance and power of the NDNAD in the investigation of crime and other incidents, but anything that touches upon the nature of individuality and its application is bound to raise important ethical concerns.

From its origins in the mid-1980s, DNA profiling has become established as a major tool of forensic science. Over the coming years, the continuing and astonishing progress in human genetics related to the human genome sequence will certainly have implications for forensic DNA analysis, both technically and in terms of the information that can be gleaned from the DNA evidence left at an incident or scene of crime.

6.7 Summary

■ Linking a biological sample, found at a crime scene or other incident, to the individual from which it originated with a high degree of confidence has been possible only since the development of DNA profiling (or DNA typing). DNA profiling analyses the DNA present in biological material, producing a pattern called a profile that ideally would be unique to that individual.

■ Differences between individuals at the level of DNA are of a number of types. Of particular interest in forensic DNA analysis are tandem repeat alleles, in particular, in modern procedures, short tandem repeats (STRs). Based around a genetic technique called the polymerase chain reaction (PCR), modern DNA profiling allows the generation of an STR profile from incredibly small amounts of material (as are often found at crime scenes) and samples that may be decades old. The data generated by the procedures can be analysed using established principles of population genetics to produce an estimate of the likelihood that two unrelated people could show the same profile or the likelihood that a sample of evidence originated from a given suspect. DNA profiling is the basis of modern paternity testing.

■ Its remarkable sensitivity and discriminating powers have led to DNA profiling becoming a major technique in forensic science; its impact cannot be overstated. A number of countries have set up DNA databases that store the profiles from suspects or criminals as well as profiles from crime scenes. As new evidence becomes available, it can be searched against the databases, perhaps linking people to crimes or linking two unsolved crimes.

■ Mitochondrial DNA analysis is based on DNA sequencing rather than STR analysis. It has had many forensic applications and tends to be used if STR analysis has failed.

■ Such a powerful technology as DNA profiling does not remain stagnant; it is being developed in a number of ways, allowing improved sensitivity, robustness, precision and speed. The remarkable rapid progress in human genetic research will undoubtedly impact on aspects of DNA profiling as well as having other profound future forensic applications.

Problems

1. An STR locus from 10 individuals was amplified using PCR. The results are shown in Figure 6.12.

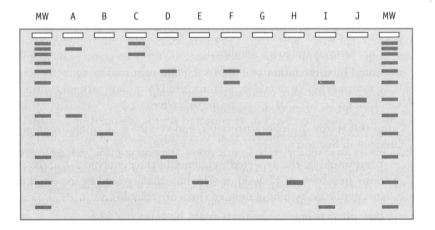

Figure 6.12 Agarose gel electrophoresis of PCR amplifications of an STR from individuals A to J MW are molecular size standards corresponding to repeat numbers of 15, 16, 17...26

(a) Describe how the PCR reaction could be used to amplify an STR locus, explaining how its specificity and extreme sensitivity are achieved.

(b) Explain the meaning of STR. Why are STRs so useful in forensic DNA analysis?

(c) Why do most of the individuals in the figure produce two DNA bands as a result of the PCR?

(d) From the figure, give the genotypes of the individuals A to J.

2. Explain how DNA profiling can be used to establish familial relationships. Figure 6.13 shows a gel on which three PCR reactions (B, C and D) were electrophoresed, along with molecular size standards A. The samples B, C and D were amplified from DNA from man B and woman C, who was the mother of child D. The genetic locus amplified is an STR. The molecular size standards in lane A correspond to repeat numbers of 10, 11, 12, 13, 14, 15 and 16 repeats.

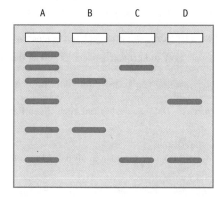

Figure 6.13 Agarose gel electrophoresis of PCR amplifications of DNA from three individuals B, C and D. Lane A carries the molecular size standards

(a) Give the genotypes of the three people in terms of the number of repeats they carry at the locus amplified.

(b) Could B be the father of child D? Explain your reasoning.

(c) If B and C did have children together, what would be their possible genotypes for the genetic locus studied here?

3. Using the Hardy–Weinberg principle and the data on allele frequencies in Table 6.4 in Section 6.4:

(a) What would be the expected frequency of the genotype 2,4 in the population? In a town of 150 000 people, how many would be expected to have this genotype assuming none of them are related?

(b) How many people in the town might be genotype 6,6?

(c) If evidence at a crime scene produced a genotype for this locus of 4,6 and this matched that of a suspect, calculate the match probability and the likelihood ratio.

4. Why are the calculations of frequencies of genotypes or DNA profiles based on the Hardy–Weinberg principle likely to be underestimates?

5. Discuss aspects of modern DNA profiles that may complicate their interpretation, both in technical aspects and in the statistical analysis of them.

6. Discuss the advantages and limitations of mitochondrial DNA compared with STR DNA analysis with regard to:

   (a) the types of data that are generated;

   (b) the discrimination of the methods;

   (c) the circumstances in which they are employed;

   (d) the interpretation of information regarding familial relationships.

Further reading

For a more general background to genetics from a DNA point of view and more detailed treatments, which are remarkably clear, of the technology of DNA analysis, the following book is highly recommended:

Brown, T. A. (2001) *Gene cloning and DNA analysis* (4th edn). Oxford: Blackwell Science.

Two excellent treatments of DNA profiling that cover legal and ethical aspects as well as the technical and historical are:

Krawczak, M. and Schmidtke, J. (1998) *DNA fingerprinting* (2nd edn). Abingdon: BIOS Scientific Publishers.

Rudin, N. and Inman K. (2001) *Introduction to forensic DNA analysis* (2nd edn). Boca Raton, FL: CRC Press LLC.

A superb review of all modern aspects of forensic genetics is:

Jobling, M. A. and Gill, P. (2004) 'Encoded evidence: DNA in forensic analysis', *Nature Reviews: Genetics* **5**, pp. 739–751.

The original article describing the identification of the Romanov remains is an accessible, interesting account:

Gill, P., Ivanov, P. L., Kimpton, C., Piercy, R., Benson, N., Tully, G., Evett, I., Hagelberg, E. and Sullivan, K. (1994) 'Identification of the remains of the Romanov family by DNA analysis', *Nature Genetics* **6**, pp. 130–135.

There are numerous popular texts that cover specific cases and that may include applications of DNA profiling. One of these, which details the Narborough murders and the early application of DNA fingerprinting, is:

Wambaugh, J. (1989) *The blooding* (paperback reissue). London: Bantam Books.

Forensic toxicology and drugs of abuse | 7

Chapter objectives

After reading this chapter, you should be able to:

> Describe the main groups of poisons.

> Outline the legal classification of drugs of abuse within the UK system, including examples.

> Discuss the main types of commonly abused drugs, with particular reference to their chemical nature, physical forms and effects.

> Explain the different factors that influence the toxicity of a substance.

> Appreciate the different routes of uptake of toxic compounds into the human body and the means by which they are subsequently eliminated.

> Review the information sought during the analysis of samples for drugs and other poisons and recognise the means by which such analyses may be carried out.

Introduction

Forensic toxicology may be defined as the scientific study of poisons in relation to the law. The creation of this discipline is credited to the Spanish physician Mathieu Orfila (1787–1853), who published his landmark treatise on poisons, *Traité des poisons*, in 1813. A poison is any substance that produces an injurious or lethal effect when administered to, or otherwise taken up by, an organism in a sufficiently high quantity.

An individual may be exposed to toxic (i.e. poisonous) substances by accident (e.g. in the workplace or the environment, or through ingesting contaminated food). Poisons may be administered as a means of suicide or murder. Many potentially harmful substances are deliberately taken by individuals for the mood- and mind-altering effects that they induce. These substances are known collectively as drugs of abuse.

This chapter begins with a description of the main groups of poisons, with the exception of those used as drugs of abuse, which are considered separately in the following section (Section 7.2). The factors affecting the toxicity of a substance, and the routes of uptake and elimination of toxic compounds are considered in Sections

7.3 and 7.4 respectively. The chapter concludes with a review of the means by which poisons, including drugs of abuse, may be analysed within the forensic context.

7.1 Common poisons

Poison

Any substance that has an injurious or fatal effect when introduced into, or taken up by, a living organism.

Poisons may be classified in many ways, for example according to their chemical structure, the effect that they have on the physiology of the human body or the methods used for their extraction prior to analysis. Each system therefore emphasises a particular facet of toxicology.

In this book, the following broad groups of poisons are explored: anions, corrosive poisons, gaseous and volatile poisons, metal and metalloid poisons, pesticides, toxins and drugs of abuse. Each of these groups is examined in turn within this section, with the exception of drugs of abuse, which are dealt with separately in Section 7.2. It should be noted that, in some cases, a particular poison may be placed in more than one of the broad categories given above. For example, strychnine is an extremely poisonous toxin that has been used as a pesticide, especially against mammalian pests. Hence, although placed in the section dealing with toxins, it could also be categorised as a pesticide.

7.1.1 Anions

An anion is a negative ion. Many compounds used in the home and/or workplace contain toxic anions, for example some weedkillers, bleaching agents and insecticides. One of the most toxic anions is cyanide (CN^-). For example, a lethal dose of its potassium salt (KCN) when taken by mouth can be as little as 2.8 mg per kg of body mass. Examples of other, less poisonous, toxic anions include fluoride (F^-), bromide (Br^-), iodide (I^-), chlorate(I) (ClO^-, also called hypochlorite), nitrite (NO_2^-), nitrate (NO_3^-), oxalate ($C_2O_4^{2-}$) and sulphite (SO_3^{2-}).

7.1.2 Corrosive poisons

Corrosive poisons are those that cause destruction of the body tissues upon contact. The severity of the resultant damage is determined by the concentration and nature of the substance concerned, and the length of contact time. Corrosive poisons are often ingested, causing surface damage to the mouth and intestinal tract. On occasion, they may penetrate deeper into the tissues, causing perforation of the gut wall. Without appropriate and rapid treatment, corrosive poisons may prove fatal. The use of corrosive poisons as a means of murder or suicide in developed countries is now relatively unusual compared with the past. However, in less-developed countries incidents involving such poisons are still encountered fairly frequently.

Common corrosive poisons include both acids and alkalis. The acids concerned may be strong mineral acids, such as hydrochloric acid (HCl), nitric acid (HNO_3) or sulphuric acid (H_2SO_4), or organic acids, for example acetic acid (CH_3COOH) and oxalic acid $(COOH)_2$. Among the alkalis that may be used as corrosive poisons are potassium hydroxide (caustic potash, KOH) and sodium hydroxide (caustic soda, NaOH). There are also corrosive poisons that are neither acids nor alkalis, for example heavy metal salts and some strong detergents.

7.1.3 Gaseous and volatile poisons

There are several unrelated gases that may be placed in this category, the most important of which, in a forensic context, are carbon monoxide (CO) (described in more detail below) and hydrogen cyanide (HCN). This group also includes the volatile poisons, which are substances that easily vaporise at normal temperatures and pressures to produce toxic vapours. Some volatile substances are used recreationally for the 'high' feelings that they induce (Section 7.2.2). Circumstantial evidence at a scene may indicate the presence of a particular toxic gas or vapour, while careful examination of the scene will often help to establish the manner of death.

Carbon monoxide is a colourless, odourless gas, which is extremely poisonous to humans. Haemoglobin, the principal oxygen carrier in vertebrate blood, has a much higher affinity for carbon monoxide than it does for oxygen and preferentially combines with it to form carboxyhaemoglobin. This reaction reduces the oxygen carrying capacity of the blood and may therefore lead to death by asphyxia.

Carbon monoxide is formed from the incomplete combustion of fossil fuels, which may occur, for example, when domestic appliances (e.g. gas fires and water heaters) are faulty and/or ventilation is restricted, or during fires. It is often, therefore, a cause of accidental death. Carbon monoxide is also present in the exhaust gases of motor vehicles, a source that is frequently used in suicide.

The post-mortem examination of individuals who have died as a result of gas poisoning might reveal the likely identity of the gas responsible. For example, the unusual cherry-pink appearance of any post-mortem lividity indicates carbon monoxide poisoning while a deeper red coloration of this feature is sometimes observed in cases of cyanide poisoning (Chapter 12, Section 12.1.2).

7.1.4 Metal and metalloid poisons

There are a number of metals and metalloids that are poisonous to humans; the most common of these are arsenic (As) and antimony (Sb) (both metalloids), and the metals lead (Pb), lithium (Li), mercury (Hg) and thallium (Tl). Symptoms of poisoning with such elements include vomiting and diarrhoea (possibly bloody), cramps and paralysis. Death may take place within 24 hours but more usually occurs after several days or even many weeks. Individuals may ingest toxic metals or metalloids as a means of suicide, or accidentally come into contact with them through, for example, industrial or environmental exposure.

Historically, the deliberate administration of certain metals and metalloids has frequently been used as a means of murder, especially before the introduction of appropriate legislative controls and the development of suitable detection techniques. Arsenic, in the form of compounds such as arsenious oxide (As_2O_3) (a tasteless, white powder), was particularly popular in this respect. It could be found in a variety of man-made products such as weedkillers and insecticides (e.g. in flypapers). A major advantage of using metals or metalloids to kill was the similarity of the symptoms they produced to those caused by food poisoning or common diseases such as dysentery and cholera. Moreover, such poisons could be administered in small quantities over time, for example in food or as a substitute for necessary therapeutic drugs; a tactic that could only help to avoid suspicion when death eventually came. However, the use of potentially toxic metals and metalloids as agents of murder is now relatively rare in developed countries. It should be noted that such poisons, like many others, persist in the body after death. Arsenic, for example, may be detected in the hair, nails and bones many years after the individual has died.

7.1.5 Pesticides

Pesticide

Any chemical agent that is used to kill pest organisms.

A **pesticide** may be defined as any chemical substance that kills organisms regarded as pests. This general definition encompasses more specific terms that reflect the type of target organism concerned, such as fungicide, insecticide, herbicide (kills weeds) and rodenticide (kills rats, mice, etc.). Pesticides are widely used in agriculture, horticulture and, to some extent, in the home environment. Humans may become accidentally exposed to pesticides, for example during the manufacturing process, through inappropriate application techniques, by contact with coated seeds or in contaminated foodstuffs. Pesticides are also used as a means of suicide, especially in less-developed countries and, on occasion, as an agent of murder. The main symptoms of pesticide poisoning are convulsions and vomiting.

There are a number of different groups of pesticides that are potentially toxic to people. For example, the organophosphorus compounds (also known as organophosphates) were developed as more selective and less persistent alternatives to organochlorine insecticides such as DDT (dichlorodiphenyltrichlorethane). Unfortunately, accidental exposure to organophosphates has proved to be more toxic to humans than exposure to the organochlorines. Examples of organophosphates include malathion and parathion. Among the herbicides, paraquat stands out as being particularly toxic to humans. Oral ingestion of this contact herbicide, either as a means of suicide, an act of murder or as a result of accident, results in a painful and lingering death.

7.1.6 Toxins

Toxin

Any poisonous substance that is naturally produced by an organism, be it animal, plant, fungus or microorganism.

Alkaloid

Any of a group of nitrogen-containing organic bases that occur in plants and fungi; many have potentially toxic effects.

A **toxin** may be defined as any poisonous substance that is naturally produced by an organism, whether plant, animal, fungus or microorganism (Table 7.1). Thus, natural toxins constitute an extremely diverse group; in terms of both their chemical structure and the way in which they act upon biological systems. They may be taken accidentally (e.g. in contaminated food or due to mistaken identity) but have also been used as the means of suicide or as an agent of murder (Box 7.1).

One important subgroup, which is described in a little more detail here, is the plant alkaloids. An **alkaloid** may be defined as any of a group of nitrogen-containing organic bases found in plants and fungi. Many of the compounds belonging to this group have medicinal or toxic properties (depending on their type and/or dosage). Some, such as cocaine and the morphine-derivative heroin, are used as drugs of abuse (Section 7.2.2).

Among the alkaloids that are highly toxic to humans, and other animals, are aconitine (from monkshood, *Aconitum napellus*), atropine (found in deadly nightshade, *Atropa belladonna*) and strychnine (from the poison berry, *Strychnos nux vomica*). Death by alkaloid poisoning is agonising. In the case of strychnine, the main effect is muscle over-stimulation, which progressively worsens from twitching to spasms and convulsions; the victim being fully conscious throughout. The process includes contraction of the facial muscles, which pulls the victim's face into a characteristic grin known as the *risus sardonicus*. The convulsive attacks increase in frequency until the victim eventually dies during one of them as a result of respiratory failure.

Table 7.1 The diversity of natural toxins

Type of toxin	Examples
Plant toxin	Alkaloids, e.g. atropine (from deadly nightshade, *Atropa belladonna*) and coniine (from hemlock, *Conium maculatum*); ricin (from castor oil plant, *Ricinus communis*); digitalin (from foxglove, *Digitalis purpurea*); fluoroacetate (first isolated from leaves of *Dichapetalum cymosum*).
Animal toxin	Physalitoxin (from the Portuguese man-of-war jellyfish, *Physalia physalis*); tetrodotoxin (found in pufferfish); venom (from poisonous snakes such as rattlesnakes, *Crotalus* spp., and spiders such as the black widow, *Latrodectus mactans*); formic acid (found in ants)
Microbial toxin	Botulinum toxin (produced under anaerobic conditions by the bacterium *Clostridium botulinum*); alpha toxin (produced by the bacterium (*Clostridium perfringens*)
Fungal toxin	Aflatoxins (from the mould *Aspergillus flavus*); phallotoxins and amatoxins (e.g. from the death cap mushroom, *Amanita phalloides*)

Case study

Box 7.1

The assassination of the Bulgarian dissident Georgi Markov

Georgi Markov, an acclaimed writer in his native Bulgaria, defected to Britain in 1971. Subsequently, he worked as a broadcast journalist for a number of radio stations, including the BBC World Service, and used this as a platform to criticise the communist regime then operative in Bulgaria.

On 7 September 1978, while walking to join a bus queue on Waterloo Bridge in London, Markov felt a sharp jab on the back of his right thigh. Turning, he saw a stranger in the act of picking up a dropped umbrella. The man apologised (in a voice with a foreign accent), summoned a taxi and left. Markov continued on his journey to work at the BBC. That evening, he became ill with a high temperature and vomiting and the next morning was taken to hospital. Four days later, on 11 September 1978, Georgi Markov died. It was found that his white blood cell count was more than three times the normal value. The cause of his death was initially given as septicaemia (infection of the blood).

The circumstances of Markov's death resulted in an investigation by Scotland Yard. Following post-mortem examination, the area of skin bearing the puncture wound found on his right thigh was sent to the Chemical Defence Establishment at Porton Down, Wiltshire (now called the Defence Science and Technology Laboratory, Porton Down). There, a tiny metal pellet (approx. 1.5 mm in diameter) was retrieved from the sample (see figure). The pellet had two minute holes drilled into it at 90°, creating an X-shaped cavity capable of holding a minute amount of poison ($< 500 \mu$g). Although no poison was found within this recess, the presence of the pellet and its construction indicated that the dissident had not died of natural causes.

▶

Box 7.1 continued

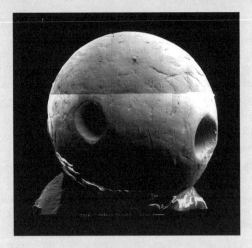

Photomicrograph of the recovered metal pellet (approx. 1.5 mm in diameter)

(Reproduced by kind permission of John Ross, Curator of the Crime Museum, New Scotland Yard, UK)

It was thought that the pellet had been implanted into Markov's thigh through the tip of the umbrella, which must have been specifically modified for that purpose. The next task was to establish the probable identity of the poison (no trace was detected in the pellet or in Markov). To be effective, the poison had to be extremely toxic in the minute quantity that the implanted pellet was capable of delivering. By a process of elimination, it seemed likely that ricin, one of the most deadly known toxins, had been used to murder Markov.

Ricin is a glycoprotein obtained from the waste material that remains after the seeds of the castor oil plant (*Ricinus communis*) are processed for their oil. The symptoms caused by ricin poisoning (such as dizziness, high temperature, vomiting and diarrhoea) concurred with those suffered by Markov. Moreover, administration of ricin to a pig (in the quantity thought to have been used for Markov) caused its death within 24 hours. A post-mortem examination of the pig revealed the same patterns of damage that were observed in the Markov case.

The evidence pointed to the murder of Markov by ricin poisoning, administered in the form of a pellet implanted by a suitably modified umbrella. It was widely thought that his assassination was carried out on behalf of the communist regime in his native Bulgaria in order to silence his vocal criticism of its activities. Indeed, after the fall of communism in Bulgaria, the incoming government admitted as much. However, no one has yet been brought to trial for the assassination of Georgi Markov.

7.2 Drugs of abuse

Drugs of abuse
Drugs either produced illegally or diverted from licit sources that are taken by individuals for recreational purposes.

There is an extensive variety of **drugs of abuse**, which are either produced illegally or diverted from licit sources. In England and Wales, the primary source of information concerning the extent of drug misuse, especially among young adults (aged 16–24 years), is the British Crime Survey (BCS). This survey has been performed every two years 1994–2000, and annually thereafter. The latest available BCS (2005–06) reports that rates of drug use in the previous year were higher among young adults (i.e. the age group 16–24 years) compared with the general adult population (i.e. aged 16–59 years). The 2005–06 BCS states that, when questioned, 25.2 per cent of young people in England and Wales had used one or more illicit drugs, 21.4 per cent had used cannabis (the most widely abused drug), 5.9 per cent had used cocaine and 4.3 per cent had used ecstasy within the past year. For further information on the current and changing patterns of drug use in England and Wales, the interested reader is referred to *Drug misuse declared findings from the 2005/2006 British Crime Survey (England and Wales)* (see Further reading section).

7.2.1 The legal classification of drugs of abuse within the UK system

The main piece of legislation controlling drugs in the United Kingdom is the Misuse of Drugs Act 1971. This act is primarily aimed at preventing the unauthorised use of specific substances. The term **controlled drug** is used for any drug that is subject to this act. Under this legislation, drugs are placed in one of three different categories (A, B or C), depending on the harm engendered by their misuse. Thus Category A drugs are most dangerous, while those in Category C are considered least harmful (and include many prescription drugs). The penalties that apply to offences concerning particular drugs are governed by the category to which they belong (Table 7.2).

Controlled drug
In the UK, any drug that is subject to the Misuse of Drugs Act 1971.

Another important piece of legislation concerning drugs is the Misuse of Drugs Regulations 2001, which, to quote, 'revoke and re-enact, with amendments, the provisions of the Misuse of Drugs Regulations 1985, as amended'. Under the 2001 Regulations, controlled drugs are placed into five different schedules. These Regulations stipulate the requirements concerning, for example, the legitimate distribution, production, record keeping and storage of controlled drugs, as well as determining whether such drugs may be made available on prescription or not.

7.2.2 Commonly abused drugs

Drugs may be broadly categorised into stimulants, depressants and hallucinogens, according to their impact on the **central nervous system**, especially on the activity of the brain (Table 7.3). It should be noted that, as well as the risks ascribed to the drugs themselves, there are secondary risks associated with drug abuse. In particular, the injection of drugs using unclean needles can introduce viral infections, such as hepatitis B and HIV, and certain bacterial diseases. For an individual addicted to a particular drug (or drugs) funding the habit is expensive. For example, the estimated annual cost for a heroin addict is £10 000, while a cocaine addict may need to find as much as £20 000 per annum. Drug users frequently turn to other criminal activities, such as theft and prostitution, in order to fund their habits.

Central nervous system
In vertebrates, the system consisting of the brain and spinal cord.

Table 7.2 The classification of controlled drugs under the Misuse of Drugs Act 1971

Category of drug	Examples	Penalty for possession and dealing	
		Possession	Possession with intent to supply, or supplying
Class A	Amphetamines (if prepared for injection); cocaine; crack cocaine; ecstasy; heroin; lysergic acid diethylamide (LSD); magic mushrooms*	Up to seven years' imprisonment and/ or an unlimited fine	Up to life imprisonment and/or an unlimited fine
Class B	Amphetamines (powder form); barbiturates[†]; codeine	Up to five years' imprisonment and/ or an unlimited fine	Up to 14 years' imprisonment and/or an unlimited fine
Class C	Anabolic steroids; benzodiazepines[†] (such as temazepam and diazepam); cannabis; gamma hydroxybutyrate (GHB); ketamine	Up to two years' imprisonment and/ or an unlimited fine	Up to 14 years' imprisonment and/or an unlimited fine

*Under the Drugs Act 2005, the Misuse of Drugs Act 1971 is amended so that *fresh* magic mushrooms (i.e. fungi that contain the drugs psilocybin or psilocin) are now classified as Class A drugs. Note that *prepared* magic mushrooms already belong to Class A.
[†] Controlled under the Misuse of Drugs Regulations 1985.

Table 7.3 A categorisation of drugs based on their impact on the activity of the brain

Category	Impact on brain activity	Examples
Stimulants	Primarily stimulates brain activity	Amphetamines Cocaine
Depressants	Primarily inhibits brain activity	Alcohol Barbiturates Benzodiazepines Heroin
Hallucinogens	Induces alterations in perception and mood (without either stimulating or inhibiting brain activity)	Ecstasy Lysergic acid diethylamide (LSD) Cannabis (mild effect)

In this section, the most commonly abused drugs are each described in turn. Those drugs that are subject to the Misuse of Drugs Act 1971 are grouped together according to the class to which they belong (Table 7.2). Alcohol and volatile substances, which are not subject to this Act, are considered separately. It should be noted that although volatile substances are not – strictly speaking – drugs, they are included here as they are commonly abused for recreational purposes.

Class A drugs

Amphetamines Under the Misuse of Drugs Act 1971, amphetamines are classified as Class A drugs when prepared for injection, but categorised as Class B drugs when in powder form. They constitute a group of synthetic **stimulants** that include the following compounds:

> **Stimulant**
> *Any drug that arouses and stimulates the central nervous system.*

■ amphetamine;

■ methamphetamine;

■ 3,4-methylenedioxyamphetamine (MDA);

■ 3,4-methylenedioxymethamphetamine (MDMA) (known as 'ecstasy', see separate section).

The chemical structure of these examples is given in Figure 7.1. Amphetamines may be synthesised from a number of different precursors, either commercially available chemicals or plant derivatives. For example, with reference to plant-derived precursors, isosafrole and safrole may be used to produce MDA and MDMA while ephedrine (a natural stimulant) may be utilised as a starting material for methamphetamine.

Amphetamines are legitimately produced for use as medicines, which are available only on prescription. In the United Kingdom, their clinical use is currently confined to the treatment of hyperactivity in children and narcolepsy (a pathological disorder of sleep) in adults. However, in the past, amphetamines have had other uses, e.g. as appetite suppressants and cold treatments. As a prescribed medicine, amphetamines are taken orally. However, when abused, they may be self-administered in a number of different ways, namely through swallowing, injecting, snorting

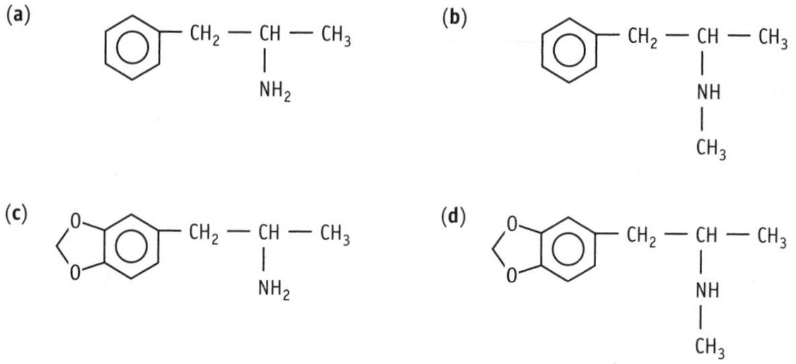

Figure 7.1 The chemical structure of (a) amphetamine; (b) methamphetamine; (c) 3,4-methylenedioxyamphetamine (MDA); and (d) 3,4-methylenedioxymethamphetamine (MDMA)

or smoking. The latter route is used in particular for smokable methamphetamine; a clear crystalline compound commonly referred to as 'ice'.

The general impact of amphetamines on the body is to stimulate and arouse the central nervous system (CNS), thus giving rise to street names such as 'speed' and 'uppers'. The effects produced by amphetamine abuse are similar to those of cocaine but of longer duration. Their effects include an increase in energy, heart rate, blood pressure and body temperature, euphoria and a loss of appetite. As with other drugs, the risks associated with amphetamine abuse are influenced by the level of the dose, the frequency of repeated doses, the length of use and the method of administration. To give just two examples, intravenous administration of amphetamines may cause delusions and paranoia, while long-term use can lead to heart strain.

Cocaine and crack cocaine Cocaine is one of a number of naturally occurring alkaloids found in the leaves of the coca plant (Figure 7.2). This evergreen shrub is cultivated at high altitudes primarily in South America, especially in Bolivia, Peru and Columbia, but is also grown in parts of tropical Asia such as Java and Sri Lanka. Of the four varieties of the coca plant, *Erythroxylon coca* var. *coca* (ECVC) is the source used for the illegal manufacture of cocaine. The extraction and isolation of this alkaloid from the coca leaf can be readily performed by a series of relatively unsophisticated techniques.

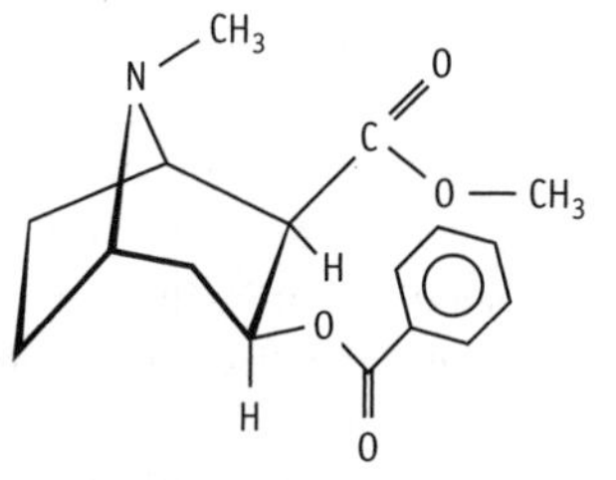

Figure 7.2 The chemical structure of cocaine

It should be noted that it is also possible to synthesise cocaine by chemical means. However, this method of production is costly both in financial terms and in the level of expertise required, compared with the extraction of naturally occurring cocaine from suitable plant material. Furthermore, it can result in a product of low purity that contains undesirable by-products.

Cocaine hydrochloride is usually available as a white crystalline powder (often adulterated) and is known by various street names such as C, coke, Charlie and snow. It is usually snorted, becoming absorbed via the mucous membranes of the nose, but may be injected or swallowed. It can be converted into the free base form, known as 'crack' cocaine, by, for example, heating together equal weights of cocaine hydrochloride and sodium bicarbonate in water. Crack, also known as stone or rock, has become an increasingly popular drug of abuse in recent years. It is usually smoked in a glass pipe; a method of administration that, like the intravenous injection of cocaine hydrochloride, leads to a rapid onset of its effects.

Cocaine is a powerful stimulant, similar in its effects to amphetamines. Chewing the dried leaves of the coca plant is, in fact, a traditional method of appeasing hunger, suppressing fatigue and stimulating the central nervous system. It has also been used as a local anaesthetic. Its stimulatory properties were recognised by, among others, Sigmund Freud who, in the 1880s, described euphoria and exhilaration among the effects occasioned by its use. The effects induced by crack are the same but of greater intensity and shorter duration compared with cocaine hydrochloride. There are many medical complications associated with cocaine intoxication and abuse, including stroke, renal failure and respiratory arrest.

Ecstasy Ecstasy is the name given to the compound 3,4-methylenedioxymethamphetamine (MDMA) (Figure 7.1d). This synthetic drug is the N-methyl analogue of the amphetamine derivative 3,4-methylenedioxyamphetamine (MDA). Ecstasy became popular in the mid-1980s among young people and is particularly associated with the 'rave' scene. It is known by a number of other street names including Adam, disco biscuits, doves, E, hug drug, M&M and XTC. Another recreational drug, MDEA (3,4-methylenedioxyethylamphetamine), is an analogue of MDMA. Commonly known as Eve, its effects on the individual are similar to those described below for ecstasy.

Ecstasy is available in capsule or tablet form (of various sizes, shapes and colours) and is usually swallowed, although it may be smoked, or crushed and snorted. It is an **hallucinogen** and as such is capable of producing changes in the conscious mind. Among the psychological effects experienced by users are a heightened sense of emotion and awareness and an increased empathy with their companions. Under the influence of ecstasy, users are often able to dance for hours without stopping. Other, less welcome, psychological effects include depression, aggressive outbursts, panic attacks and paranoia. There are numerous medical effects associated with ecstasy use including nausea, muscle tension, blurred vision, trismus (involuntary clenching of the jaw) and an increased heart rate and blood pressure. Furthermore, the use of ecstasy can lead to potentially fatal complications such as cardiovascular collapse, seizures, dehydration, hyperthermia (overheating) and hyponatraemia. The last is a condition in which low sodium levels in the blood cause a reduction in its osmotic potential. This causes excess fluids in the body tissues, most notably in the brain, which can lead to seizures and death.

Hallucinogen
Any drug that alters the perception and mood of an individual, without either stimulating or inhibiting brain activity.

Heroin Heroin is mixture of compounds synthesised from opium. Opium is the dried latex collected from the field poppy *Papaver somniferum* L. by slitting the unripe seed capsules and allowing the bitter, milky liquid to exude, dry and oxidise in the sun. It is estimated by the United Nations Drug Control Programme (UNDCP) that almost 80 per cent of the global illicit cultivation of *P. somniferum* occurs in just one country – Afghanistan. However, the opium poppy is also clandestinely cultivated in a number of other Southwest Asian countries (e.g. Pakistan and Iran) and in other regions of the world, namely Southeast Asia (especially Burma (Myanmar)), Central America (primarily Guatemala and Mexico) and South America (Columbia).

To produce heroin, morphine is isolated from opium and then reacted with an acetylating agent, preferably acetic anhydride but sometimes acetyl chloride. The main active component of heroin is diacetylmorphine, commonly known as diamorphine (Figure 7.3). Note that in the United States, the terms heroin, diacetylmorphine and diamorphine are used synonymously.

Heroin is available on the street as a powder, which may be white or brown in colour depending on its purity and the type(s) of other substances present. It may be diluted with one or more of a number of **cutting agents** such as milk powder, various sugars, caffeine and other drugs, e.g. barbiturates or the non-barbiturate **depressant** methaqualone. Heroin has a number of street names including brown, gear, H, horse, junk and smack. The percentage by weight of diamorphine in street heroin varies considerably. Average values are 35 to 41 per cent but levels range from 1 to 98 per cent. Pharmaceutical grade diamorphine has a purity value greater than 99.5 per cent.

Heroin is highly soluble in water, which makes it particularly suitable for intravenous or intramuscular injection. Other routes of administration are smoking or snorting (correctly termed nasal insufflation). Whatever route is employed, the onset of the effects of heroin abuse is rapid.

Heroin is a powerful analgesic (i.e. painkiller), which exerts a depressing effect on the CNS. Individuals usually feel relaxed, drowsy and lethargic as a result of heroin use and, sometimes, experience feelings of euphoria. Other effects include suppression of the cough reflex, respiratory depression, sweating, nausea and blurred vision. An overdose can induce coma, which may consequently lead to death. Box 7.2 describes the case of Dr Harold Shipman, a general practitioner who used injections of pharmaceutical grade diamorphine to murder his victims.

Heroin is a highly addictive drug that causes both psychological and physical dependence. The main treatment for heroin addicts trying to break their habit, and overcome the symptoms associated with withdrawal, involves the use of methadone as a heroin substitute. This synthetic opiate is actually more addictive than heroin but as its route of administration is oral (either taken in a syrup or in tablet form), the dangers associated with heroin injection are removed.

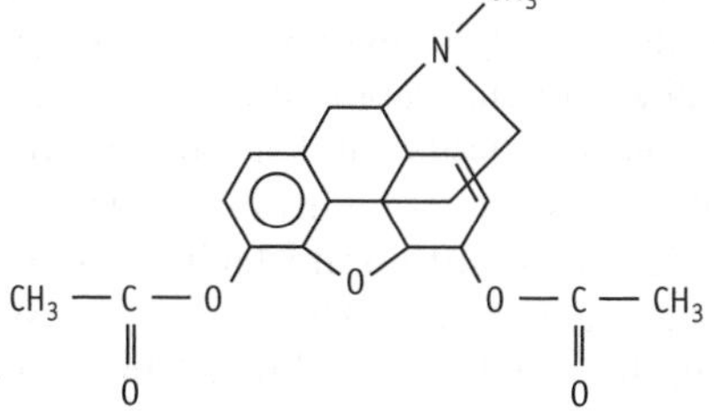

Cutting agent
Material deliberately mixed with drugs of abuse in order to increase the apparent amount offered for sale.

Depressant
Any drug that has a depressing effect on the central nervous system, including the inhibition of brain activity.

Figure 7.3 The chemical structure of diamorphine

Case study
Box 7.2

The case of Dr Harold Frederick Shipman

Harold Frederick Shipman (born 14 January 1946) graduated from Leeds University Medical School in 1970 and began work at Pontefract General Infirmary. In 1974, he left to join a group practice in Todmorden, Lancashire, UK, as a general practitioner. It was during this time that he began to suffer from blackouts. His colleagues at the practice discovered that he was addicted to pethidine (an opiate used as a painkiller) and had been falsifying prescriptions in order to obtain it for his own use. Although he was fired by the practice and heavily fined, he was not struck off by the General Medical Council (GMC). In the last quarter of 1975, Harold Shipman was treated for his addiction to pethidine at The Retreat, York. In 1977, Shipman joined another group practice, this time in Hyde, a suburb of Manchester. Five years later, in 1992, he left to set up his own single-handed GP practice in Market Street, Hyde. His list of patients exceeded 3000, attesting to his popularity as a doctor and the high regard in which he was held.

However, there was growing concern, from a number of different quarters, about the high number of deaths among Shipman's patients, compared with those of other local general practitioners in Hyde. These concerns were expressed to the Coroner in March 1998 by a local GP. Many of the deaths were of elderly women and many of these lived alone. It was the unexpected death of another of Shipman's patients, Kathleen Grundy, a fit and active 81-year-old widow, on 24 June 1998 that finally brought matters to a head. The emergence of a new will, sent on the day of Mrs Grundy's death to a local firm of solicitors, aroused the suspicions of her daughter, who was herself a solicitor (and whose firm usually handled Mrs Grundy's legal affairs). In this document, which was poorly typed and phrased, Kathleen Grundy bequeathed her entire estate (valued at nearly £400 000) to Shipman and not, as in her original will, to her family. Mrs Grundy's daughter contacted the police about her suspicions that the newly amended version of her mother's will was a forgery.

A decision was taken to exhume the body of Kathleen Grundy in order to perform a post-mortem examination. Toxicological tests revealed the presence of morphine; a metabolite of diamorphine formed almost instantly when diamorphine enters the bloodstream. As a consequence of this discovery, Shipman was arrested on 7 September 1998 for the murder of Kathleen Grundy. In the wake of his arrest, other people came forward to say that they too were concerned about the circumstances surrounding the deaths of their relatives, who were Shipman's patients. Certain patterns began to emerge. The deceased individuals were frequently described as being fit and active in life. Death had been sudden or unexpected. Furthermore, Dr Shipman was usually reported to be present on the day of death (either attending the patient before or even at the time of death) or discovering the body afterwards. The number of potential victims continued to grow and the evidence against Shipman began to mount, including the discovery at his practice of the typewriter used to produce the supposed last will of Mrs Kathleen Grundy.

On 5 October 1999, the trial of Harold Shipman for the murder of 15 elderly patients, including Kathleen Grundy, began at Preston Crown Court. On 31 January 2000, Shipman was convicted of killing all 15 with lethal injections of diamorphine and of forging the will of Mrs Kathleen Grundy. He was sentenced to life imprisonment. In June 2001, a public inquiry, chaired by the High Court judge Dame Janet Smith, began into the circumstances surrounding the deaths of 493 of Shipman's patients between 1974 and 1998. The first report of this inquiry, published on 19 July 2002, concluded that Shipman had murdered 215 of his patients (including the 15 for which he was convicted) and was strongly suspected of being responsible for the deaths of 45 more. A series of reports followed, culminating in the sixth report of the Shipman Inquiry (published on 27 January 2005), in which Dame Janet Smith focused mainly on Shipman's time as a junior doctor at the Pontefract General Infirmary (1970–74). At the end of this final report, she gave the following overall conclusion 'that Shipman killed about 250 patients between 1971 and 1998, of whom I have been able positively to identify 218'.

Meanwhile, on 13 January 2004, Dr Harold Shipman was found hanging in his cell at 6.20 a.m. and was pronounced dead after attempts to resuscitate him failed.

For further information, the interested reader is referred to the official website of the Shipman Inquiry at www.the-shipman-inquiry.org.uk.

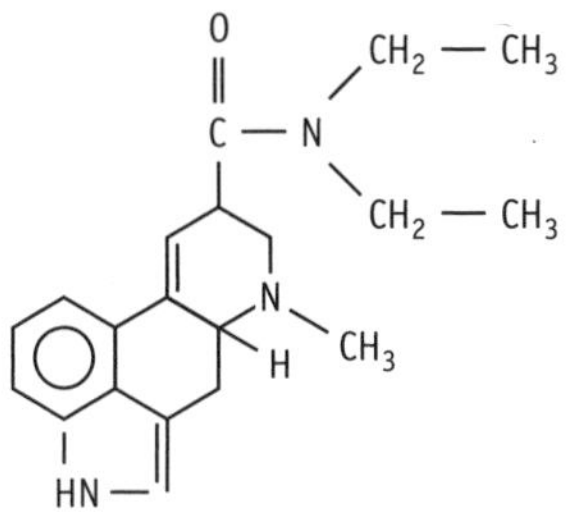

Figure 7.4 The chemical structure of lysergic acid diethylamide (LSD)

Lysergic acid diethylamide (LSD) Lysergic acid diethylamide (LSD) is an extremely potent hallucinogen. It may be synthesised from lysergic acid (a naturally occurring alkaloid found in the ergot fungus *Claviceps purpurea*) or lysergic acid amide (a closely related alkaloid found in the seeds of the morning glory (*Ipomoea* spp.) and the Hawaiian baby wood rose). Its chemical structure is shown in Figure 7.4.

The hallucinogenic properties of LSD were first discovered in 1943. In the 1950s and 1960s, LSD found some use as a therapeutic drug in, for example, the treatment of alcoholism, but is no longer used medically in any capacity. Its popularity as a drug of abuse has declined and it is currently encountered with relative infrequency. LSD may be supplied illegally in a number of different forms, including microdots (small, vividly coloured tablets) and blotter acids (small squares of absorbent paper impregnated with LSD, often carrying imprinted designs).

Dosage units vary between 50 and 300 µg but even 20–25 µg is sufficient to induce its hallucinogenic effects. LSD is usually taken orally and absorption occurs very quickly. On an LSD 'trip', which can last for up to 12 hours, characteristic effects experienced by the user will usually include an alteration in his or her visual perception and time distortion. The physical and psychological effects of LSD abuse are related to the size of dose taken. If this is very high, the potential life-threatening risks include respiratory arrest and hyperthermia (i.e. overheating). Some LSD users may experience 'flashbacks' up to several years after they have discontinued use of the drug.

Class B drugs

Barbiturates Barbiturates are derivatives of barbituric acid (2,4,6-trioxohexahydropyrimidine), which was first synthesised in 1864. They were prescribed for use as anaesthetics, anticonvulsants, sedatives and hypnotics. However, their use, particularly in the latter two capacities, has been replaced almost completely by the benzodiazepines, following the high rate of barbiturate abuse in the 1960s. Currently, the only licensed use of barbiturates is thiopental, used as a general anaesthetic, and phenobarbitone (also known as phenobarbital) and primadone for the control of epilepsy. Consequently, barbiturate abuse is now very rare.

Barbiturates are usually encountered in the form of capsules or tablets. Those available on the illicit market have almost invariably been legally manufactured and subsequently diverted for illicit use. Barbiturates are depressants, i.e. they have a depressing effect on the CNS. In general, users feel relaxed and sleepy as a consequence of taking barbiturates. Individual members of this large family of drugs may be short-acting (e.g. secobarbital), medium-acting (e.g. butobarbitone) and long-acting (e.g. phenobarbitone). Prolonged barbiturate use, especially at levels higher than prescription levels, can cause physical dependence. Withdrawal symptoms, experienced after barbiturate use has ceased, may include convulsions, delirium and insomnia.

Class C drugs

Cannabis Cannabis is the most commonly used illegal drug in England and Wales, in the United States and indeed throughout the world. It is derived from the annual plant *Cannabis sativa* L., which has a worldwide distribution. *Cannibis sativa* is grown commercially as hemp and its fibres used for the production of rope and cloth. In this form, it consists predominantly of stalks with only a small amount of foliage present compared with wild plants and those cultivated illegally for cannabis production.

Cannabis is a mild hallucinogen. The active components of cannabis responsible for its hallucinogenic properties are the tetrahydrocannabinols (THCs), especially Δ^9-tetrahydrocannabinol (Δ^9-THC) (Figure 7.5). These are concentrated in the leaves and flowering tops of the cannabis plant. As far as cannabis for illegal use is concerned, the concentration of THCs present (usually expressed as a percentage by weight) is determined by the form in which it is supplied (see below):

■ *Herbal cannabis* (also known as *marijuana*). In this form, the dried, crushed leaves are mixed with other parts of the cannabis plant such as the flowers and seeds. Herbal cannabis has the lowest concentration of THCs compared with other commonly encountered preparations.

■ *Cannabis resin* (also known as *hashish*). The surface of the cannabis plant is covered in resin, which can be obtained by processing the herbal material in some way. For example, the seeds, leaves and resin can be separated from the rest of the plant material by threshing and the mixture then sieved to yield its resinous component. Cannabis resin is usually supplied in the form of compressed slabs or cakes. In terms of THC concentration, it is intermediate between the herbal and oil forms.

■ *Cannabis oil* (also known as *hashish oil* or *hemp oil*). This dark-coloured oil or tar-like substance is obtained by solvent extraction from either cannabis resin or the crude plant material. It is often potent, with the highest concentration of THCs of the three forms listed.

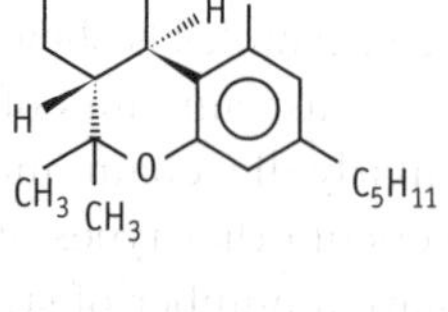

Figure 7.5 The chemical structure of Δ^9-tetrahydrocannabinol (Δ^9-THC)

It should be noted that there are other forms of cannabis than those given above, e.g. sinsemilla (the unfertilised flowering tops of female *C. sativa*) and Thai sticks (marijuana leaves wrapped around bamboo stems).

Cannabis products are usually smoked either on their own or in combination with tobacco but may be self-administered in other ways; for example, cannabis resin may be consumed with food. The effects of smoking cannabis usually commence within 10–20 minutes and last for between two and three hours. They include a feeling of relaxation, sleepiness and a lack of concentration. There are a number of risks associated with **chronic** cannabis use such as apathy and low energy levels while high doses can induce hallucinations, panic attacks and psychosis.

Cannabis and its preparations were originally classified as Class B drugs. However, in a report sent to the Home Secretary in March 2002, the Advisory Council on the Misuse of Drugs (ACMD) recommended the reclassification of all cannabis preparations to Class C under the Misuse of Drugs Act 1971. This reclassification came into effect in January 2004.

Chronic
Occurring over a long period of time.

Anabolic steroids Anabolic steroids are synthetic compounds, the majority of which are chemically similar to the male sex hormone, testosterone. This naturally occurring steroid hormone is responsible in males for the differentiation of the male sexual organs, the development of secondary sexual characteristics at puberty and for the maintenance of sexual function in adults. Testosterone also promotes muscle growth.

Anabolic steroids are legally available on prescription and are used, for example, in the treatment of anaemia. Many are manufactured for use as veterinary drugs. The illegal use of anabolic steroids occurs primarily among individuals involved in sport, athletics or bodybuilding (at both amateur and professional level). These drugs, in combination with a specific diet and a programme of intensive training, help to accelerate muscle growth and increase body mass, thus enhancing the performance, or appearance, of the individual. Anabolic steroids are available as tablets or capsules but are more usually administered, in liquid form, as an intramuscular injection.

Anabolic steroids have a number of unwanted adverse effects. Among the harmful effects reported in males are liver damage, impotency, sterility and heart attack, while females may develop masculine characteristics, such as deepening of the voice and facial hair growth. There is also risk of miscarriage or stillbirth for women. In teenagers, the use of anabolic steroids may prevent normal bone growth. In addition, mood-swings, aggression, depression and memory effects are all associated with anabolic steroid abuse.

Benzodiazepines Benzodiazepines are manufactured legally as prescription drugs, usually as tablets or capsules. They are used as anticonvulsants, hypnotics and tranquillisers. This large group of lipophilic acids includes chlordiazepoxide, diazepam (Valium), temazepam, flunitrazepam, lorazepam and nitrazepam. The chemical structure of the first three examples is shown in Figure 7.6.

In the United Kingdom, there are vast amounts of illegal benzodiazepines available on the black market, particularly diazepam and temazepam. Illegal users of benzodiazepines may also be abusers of other types of drugs, such as heroin and/or amphetamines. Benzodiazepines have a number of street names, including moggies and, with reference to specific jelly capsules (usually temazepam), jellies.

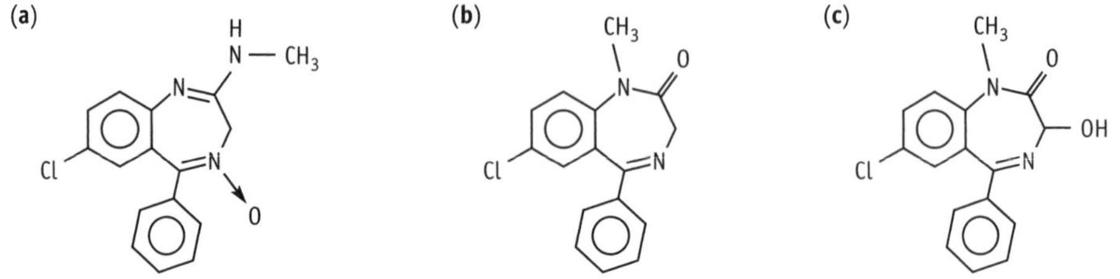

Figure 7.6 The chemical structure of (a) chlordiazepoxide, (b) diazepam and (c) temazepam

Benzodiazepines are usually administered orally but, when abused, are sometimes dissolved and injected, which is a highly dangerous practice. The effects of their use are dependent on their type (benzodiazepines, like barbiturates, act for different lengths of time), the amount used and the administration route involved. Benzodiazepines are depressants and users usually experience a reduction in tension and anxiety, and feelings of lethargy and drowsiness. One in particular, flunitrazepam, has been associated with instances of 'date rape', where the drug is surreptitiously slipped into the drink of the intended victim. The metabolism of this short-acting benzodiazepine is rapid, therefore making subsequent detection difficult.

There are a number of risks associated with benzodiazepine use; for example, overdose may induce convulsions. Benzodiazepines can cause physical and psychological dependence. Long-term users may experience withdrawal symptoms, such as panic attacks, tremor and insomnia, after cessation of benzodiazepine use.

Alcohol

An alcohol is an organic compound with the general formula ROH, where R is an alkyl group. In common usage, and for the purposes of this book, the term alcohol refers to ethanol (Figure 7.7), which is the alcohol present in alcoholic drinks. The concentration of ethanol in alcoholic beverages varies according to the production process. This concentration is usually expressed as a volume/volume percentage (%v/v). Those produced by fermentation alone appear at the lower end of the scale, for example beer and cider usually fall in the range 3–6% v/v, while table wines normally have alcohol contents of 9–12% v/v. Fortified wines (e.g. port and sherry) have higher concentration, typically 17–21% v/v. Finally, those drinks produced by distillation of the liquid produced by fermentation (e.g. spirits such as vodka, whisky and gin) typically have alcohol concentrations of about 40% v/v in the United Kingdom. Alcohol is the most widely used, and abused, drug in the world.

Alcohol is a depressant, i.e. it has a depressing effect on the central nervous system. Its effects on the behaviour of an individual can be *roughly* correlated with the level of alcohol present in the body, as measured by blood-alcohol concentration (BAC) (Table 7.4). However, it should be emphasised that there is a wide variation

$$CH_3 - CH_2 - OH$$

Figure 7.7 The chemical structure of ethanol

in the behaviour of individuals at different BAC levels, depending on the rate of absorption, tolerance to alcohol and even the time of day. Alcohol misuse is known to increase the risk of accident (especially involving motor vehicles) and to be a significant contributory factor in many cases of assault and murder. Furthermore, excessive and/or long-term consumption can lead to alcohol-induced disease, especially of the liver.

After consumption, alcohol is absorbed through the stomach and small intestine into the bloodstream. The rate of alcohol absorption is influenced by a number of different factors, such as the concentration and amount of alcohol consumed, and the presence, or otherwise, of food in the stomach. Once absorbed, it is circulated by the blood to all parts of the body. The elimination of alcohol from the body takes longer than its absorption. This occurs principally via metabolism in the liver, with a small percentage excreted unchanged in the urine, sweat and breath.

There are strict legal limits for the maximum concentration of alcohol that is allowed in the breath, blood or urine of drivers. Current UK limits for these parameters are $35 \mu g/100 \, ml$, $80 \, mg/100 \, ml$ and $107 \, mg/100 \, ml$ respectively. In cases of suspected drink-driving, there may be some delay between the possible offence and samples being taken for analysis. Under these conditions, it may be necessary for back-calculations to be performed in order to establish whether the individual was over the limit at the time of driving (Box 7.3).

Volatile substances

Volatile substance abuse (sometimes referred to as solvent abuse or glue-sniffing) is mainly associated with adolescents. A variety of different substances are used for this purpose including aerosol propellants (found, for example, in aerosol deodorants and hairsprays), butane and propane (gases used in cigarette lighters and their refills), paint, paint thinners, glue and correction fluids.

Volatile substances may be self-administered in a number of different ways, depending on type. For example, they may be inhaled through the nose or mouth

Table 7.4 A rough guide to behaviour at different blood-alcohol concentrations

Blood-alcohol concentration (measured in mg of alcohol per 100 ml of blood)	Effects on behaviour
< 50	Little or no apparent effect
50–100	Inhibitions reduced, resulting in increased talkativeness, friendliness or aggression; some degree of sensory disturbance; slight loss of muscular co-ordination
100–150	Further loss of muscular co-ordination; slurred speech; possibly slight nausea
150–200	Obvious drunkenness; nausea
200–350	Stupor; vomiting; danger of coma
>350	Increasing risk of death from respiratory paralysis

Forensic techniques

Box 7.3

The back-extrapolation of alcohol concentrations in blood

In cases in which an individual is suspected of drink-driving and in which a blood sample is to be taken for analysis, there is an inevitable delay between the time of the suspected offence and the collection of the sample. In some cases, this delay will be sufficient for a significant alteration to have occurred in the concentration of alcohol in the blood. However, under such circumstances it is normally possible to estimate what the concentration was at the time of the incident by back-extrapolation.

The process of absorption of alcohol from the gut into the blood is relatively rapid. While the time taken to complete this process is altered by a number of factors, such as the amount of food taken with the alcoholic drink, it is likely to have ceased once more than two hours have passed since the last alcoholic drink was consumed. If the incident in question occurred after this time, it is likely that the alcohol concentration in the blood will have passed its peak before the incident. Consequently, the concentration that is found in any blood samples subsequently taken for analysis would be lower than at the time of the incident. However, if, at the time of the incident, alcohol was still being absorbed into the blood from the gut, it is likely that the blood alcohol concentration will have risen after the incident, although it may have fallen from its maximum level before the samples for analysis were taken. Clearly, back-extrapolation in cases in which the absorption process was occurring at the time of the suspected offence is likely to be more difficult than in cases in which it may safely be assumed that absorption had ceased by the time of the incident. This box will only be concerned with calculations for straightforward cases in which such an assumption can be made and where no alcohol was consumed between the incident and the time at which the blood sample was taken.

In most cases, the rate of elimination of alcohol from the blood (β) is essentially constant in any one individual. Therefore, once the alcohol absorption process has ceased, the blood ethanol concentration at some initial time (C_0) can be calculated from its concentration at a later time (C_t), provided that both β and the time interval (t) that has elapsed between the initial and later times are known, thus:

$$C_0 = C_t + t\beta$$

in which C_0 and C_t are measured in mg of ethanol per 100 ml of blood, t is in hours and β is measured in mg of ethanol per 100 ml of blood per hour.

Unfortunately, β varies significantly from one person to the next. There have been a number of studies that have examined this variation. From these, it has been estimated that the lowest likely rate of elimination is 12.5 mg of ethanol per 100 ml of blood per hour, whereas the highest likely rate is 25 mg of ethanol per 100 ml of blood per hour, and the average rate is 18.7 mg of ethanol per 100 ml of blood per hour (Ferner 1996).

In order to illustrate how use may be made of this information, consider a hypothetical case in which a man is arrested after driving a car that was involved in a road traffic accident at 3.00 a.m. Assume that there are reliable eyewitnesses that confirm that the driver last drank an alcoholic drink at least two hours earlier. A blood sample was taken at 5.00 a.m. that same morning which showed a blood alcohol concentration of 70 mg of ethanol per 100 ml. Was the driver likely to be over the limit of 80 mg of ethanol per 100 ml of blood at the time of the accident?

Given the length of time between the last alcoholic drink and the accident, an assumption can be made that the ethanol absorption process from the gut to the blood has ceased. At the lowest likely elimination rate, the blood alcohol concentration at the time of the accident (C_0) would be:

$$C_0 = C_t + t\beta = 70 + 2 \times 12.5$$

$$= 95 \, \text{mg/100 ml}$$

Using identical reasoning, at the highest rate of elimination it would be 120 mg/100 ml; while at the average rate it would be 107.4 mg/100 ml.

Therefore, it is likely that the man was above the legal limit for drink-driving at the time of the accident.

Reference

Ferner, R. E. (1996) *Forensic pharmacology: medicines, mayhem and malpractice.* Oxford: Oxford University Press, p. 123.

from a plastic bag, sniffed from a piece of cloth or clothing, or sprayed directly into the back of the throat. In any such case, after inhalation, the substance concerned is absorbed through the lungs and reaches the brain very quickly. The initial effects usually experienced by the user are of euphoria and exhilaration. However, these substances are essentially depressants of the CNS and the initial 'high' is followed by, for example, dizziness, blurred vision and slurred speech, and, eventually, stupor. Other effects, such as nausea, blackouts and vomiting, may also occur.

The abuse of volatile substances is not thought to cause physical dependence. However, there are many risks associated with this practice. These include an increased risk of accident while intoxicated, permanent liver and kidney damage (through chronic abuse) and brain damage (through long-term abuse, i.e. over a decade). Moreover, fatalities may occur, for example, through choking on own vomit or heart failure.

As can be seen from the list given at the beginning of this section, those volatile substances that are commonly abused are items that have legitimate use in every-day life. However, under the Intoxicating Substance (Supply) Act 1985, it is illegal for such products to be sold to anyone under the age of 18 if it is suspected that the intended purpose of the purchase is abuse. More recently, the Cigarette Lighter Refill (Safety) Regulations 1999 have made the sale of butane gas lighter refills to any individual under the age of 18 an offence.

7.3 Factors affecting toxicity

The toxicity of a substance is related to its dose, a fact recognised by the Swiss chemist, physician and natural philosopher Paracelsus (1493–1541). He stated that 'All substances are poisons; there is none that is not a poison. The right dose differentiates a poison from a remedy.' Thus, virtually all substances are poisonous if taken in sufficiently large amounts; even water, imperative for the maintenance of life, can be harmful if several litres are drunk in rapid succession.

The level of dose required to elicit a response in an organism is dependent on the toxic properties of the substance in question. Responses may be classed as graded, i.e. measured by a parameter such as the level of some type of pathological damage (e.g. necrosis of the liver cells) or 'all-or-none' as in death. In the latter case, plotting the percentage response of a group of animals (or cells) against the log of the dosage (i.e. the dose per unit weight or surface area of the target organism) produces a typical S-shaped (or sigmoid) curve (Figure 7.8). This is known as the dose–response curve and can be used to determine the LD_{50}. This measure may be defined as the dose at which 50 per cent of the test organisms die. It may be used, for example, to examine the effect of different administration routes on the toxicity of a particular substance, or to compare the relative toxicity of different substances (although alternative measures, such as fixed dose testing, are currently being considered). The results from toxicity testing on laboratory animals may be used to gauge, by extrapolation, the likely effects that exposure to such substances will have on humans, although there is a wide variation in the susceptibility of people to toxic substances.

It is important to realise that the toxicity of a substance is determined not only by its inherent toxic properties but also by a number of factors relating to the individual

(From Timbrell, 2002)

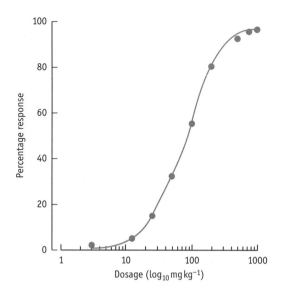

Figure 7.8 A typical dose–response curve where the percentage response is plotted against the log of the dosage

exposed to it. For example, poor health and advanced years are both factors that might be expected to increase a person's vulnerability to toxic substances. Also, previous exposure to a particular substance can have a significant effect on how an individual reacts to the next dose. This may lead to one of the three following scenarios.

◼ *Sensitisation.* Prior exposure to a particular substance may lead to the development of sensitisation when an individual encounters it for a second time. This is characterised by an enhanced immune response. If the immune response is excessive or inappropriate, the condition is termed hypersensitivity and is exemplified by anaphylactic shock, which may result in the death of the individual.

◼ *Tolerance.* This condition may develop when an individual is repeatedly exposed to a particular substance. Consequently, the dose must either be increased or given more frequently in order to have the same effect as when it was first administered. Drugs such as amphetamines, barbiturates, benzodiazepines and opiates, e.g. heroin and morphine, can all lead to the development of tolerance. Tolerance may be lost after abstention from the substance in question and resumption of the drug habit at levels previously tolerated may have serious or even fatal results. Heroin users returning to old habits after a period in prison are particularly vulnerable to this risk.

◼ *Accumulation.* The time taken for the concentration or amount of a poison in the body (or a given part of the body) to halve is called the half-life, $t_{1/2}$. Some poisons, known as cumulative poisons, have values of $t_{1/2}$ that are long enough to allow chronic exposure to sublethal doses to lead to the accumulation of the poison within the body. If, in a given case, both the rate of intake is sufficiently high and $t_{1/2}$ is long enough, the amount of poison in the body will eventually become large enough to cause ill health and, possibly, death. Heavy metals such as lead and mercury, and the metalloid arsenic, are well known cumulative poisons.

It should be noted that some substances, for example aspirin, cocaine, heroin and penicillin, may elicit an idiosyncratic response in a few individuals. Idiosyncrasy may have fatal results and is due to the genetic makeup of the individual concerned. Finally, the dose of a toxin that will cause the death of an individual may be lowered if another toxic substance is present in the body. It is known, for example, that the presence of alcohol exacerbates the toxic effects of benzodiazepines.

7.4 Routes of uptake and elimination of drugs and other toxic substances

The toxic effect of a potentially poisonous substance is not exerted until that material encounters a biological system. Such substances may enter the body by one or more of the routes of uptake outlined below:

- ■ *Ingestion.* In this route of uptake, potentially toxic materials are taken into the gastrointestinal tract through the mouth. Examples include the many drugs that are administered orally (during either abuse or therapeutic use) and toxins present in foodstuffs (as a result of either accident or design).

- ■ *Inhalation.* This process involves the intake of gases, vapours and/or particles into the lungs. This may result from accidental exposure, e.g. to carbon monoxide in the ambient environment, or deliberate activity, as exemplified by the abuse of solvents (Section 7.2.2).

- ■ *Skin contact.* The skin forms an effective barrier against many potentially toxic materials. However, some poisonous substances, for example phenol and organic mercury compounds, are capable of penetrating this barrier.

- ■ *Mucous membrane contact.* Substances may be deliberately introduced into the body via contact with those mucous membranes that are externally accessible. Such sites are present at several locations in the body and include the eyes, ears, mouth, nose and rectum. In drug abuse, one of the ways of administration used for amphetamines, cocaine and heroin is that of snorting the material up the nose or, as it is more correctly termed, nasal insufflation.

- ■ *Injection.* Injection involves the deliberate introduction of a compound directly into the body, generally by means of a hypodermic syringe. The substance may be administered into a vein (i.e. intravenously) or into a muscle (i.e. intramuscularly). It may also be administered under the skin (i.e. subcutaneously) or into the skin (i.e. intradermally). Injection is commonly used for therapeutic purposes or during the abuse of drugs such as heroin or cocaine. On rare occasions, however, the injection of a poison or a drug has been used as a means of murder, as exemplified by the assassination of Georgi Markov (Box 7.1) and the killings committed by Harold Shipman (Box 7.2) respectively.

In toxicological terms, the absorption of a substance is considered to have occurred when it enters the general blood circulation of the body. In the case of intravenous injections, administration occurs directly but in other routes of uptake, the process involves transference of the substance concerned across cell membranes into the surrounding blood vessels. The **bioavailability** of a particular substance may be described as the proportion of the original dose that is absorbed and the rate at which this absorption takes place. This is influenced, for example, by the chemical and physical attributes of the substance concerned and the route of uptake used. Importantly, substances absorbed from the intestine have to encounter the liver (the key metabolic organ) before entering the general circulation. Numerous drugs are rendered inactive by the liver and consequently their bioavailability tends to be low. This process is known as first-pass metabolism.

After absorption, compounds are distributed around the body by the circulation of the blood. Distribution is followed by elimination. The nature of the poison concerned will dictate how this may occur. Water-soluble substances can be removed from the body in the urine (after passing through the kidneys) and in the bile (after processing by the liver). Volatile compounds can be removed in expired air from the lungs. However, fat-soluble poisons must first be metabolised into water-soluble species before they can be lost from the body in urine or bile. Note that bile is discharged into the gut for elimination with the faeces. However, a proportion may be reabsorbed in the gut, carried back to the liver and discharged once more into the gastrointestinal tract. This recycling (known as enterohepatic recirculation) can result in the retention of certain substances such as cannabis metabolites within the body for extended periods, which may have important implications for toxicological analysis.

Bioavailability
The proportion of the original dose that is absorbed and the rate at which this absorption takes place.

7.5 The analysis of drugs and other poisons

7.5.1 The information sought by analysis

The analysis of a sample for drugs of abuse and/or other poisonous substances aims to provide information about one or more of the following: the chemical identity of any poisons present, the concentration of such substances and/or their amounts. In the forensic context, this information can be used in a variety of ways. Importantly, it can establish the following:

■ Whether a particular sample contains a controlled substance or other poison.

■ Whether the concentration of a particular substance within given samples of body fluids and/or tissue is consistent with therapeutic administration (in the case of drugs that have medicinal applications), intoxication or death by poisoning with the substance concerned. For example, it can establish whether the concentration of ethanol in a given sample of breath, blood or urine, exceeds the legally permissible limit for driving (currently $35\,\mu g/100$ ml, $80\,mg/100\,ml$ and $107\,mg/100\,ml$ respectively in the United Kingdom).

Hence, the analytical results can help the courts to establish whether a crime has been committed, the nature of that crime and whether the accused is guilty of the offence(s) for which he or she is being tried. For example, **qualitative analysis** may reveal that a powder is heroin (Section 7.2.2). If the courts are convinced that this powder was confiscated from the accused, he or she may be convicted of the illegal possession of a controlled substance. Furthermore, **quantitative analysis** may help the courts to establish whether the amount of heroin seized was consistent with personal use by the individual concerned or with the intent to supply the drug to others. In the latter case, the accused may be convicted of a more serious offence and consequently be given a more substantial sentence.

Analytical data can also corroborate or refute the account of events as given by the accused, an eyewitness or a victim. For example, in a murder trial, the accused may claim he had been drinking with the victim and that the victim had consumed large quantities of alcohol prior to attacking the accused, who then killed the victim while acting in self-defence. In order to help test the accuracy of this account of the incident, post-mortem analysis of the blood-alcohol level of the victim may be compared with the level expected on the basis of the scenario described by the accused.

Post-mortem analysis of body fluids and/or tissues for drugs and other poisons can help establish the cause of death and, in some cases, the sequence of events that occurred immediately before death. This is exemplified by the post-mortem analysis of blood for carbon monoxide in apparent fire victims. High levels of this poison, coupled with smoke blackening of the airways, indicate that the deceased was alive and breathing when the fire was under way. However, low levels of carbon monoxide in the blood, together with a lack of smoke blackening of the airways, *may* indicate that death occurred prior to the fire. Post-mortem analysis may also reveal the presence of drugs at therapeutic levels within the deceased. Such information may help to establish the chain of events that occurred before death and, possibly, assist in the identification of an unknown body. The interpretation of the results of post-mortem analysis requires great care, however. For example, someone who dies in a very rapidly developing fire may do so before inhaling significant quantities of smoke or carbon monoxide. Also, biochemical changes that occur in the body after death can result in the redistribution of substances between different biological materials. For example, drugs and/or their metabolites can be transferred from the tissues to the blood, leading to elevated levels in the latter. Thus, therapeutic doses may lead to levels in post-mortem blood samples that would be potentially lethal if present in the blood of a living person. Clearly, it is also important to be mindful of the biochemical changes that occur to a drug or other poison once it is in the body. For example, once in the blood, diamorphine (the principal active component of street heroin) is very quickly hydrolysed to 6-monoacetylmorphine. This, in turn, is more slowly metabolised to morphine. Hence, the post-mortem analysis of blood is unlikely to find diamorphine, even in cases of death by heroin overdose. However, in such cases, high levels of 6-monoacetylmorphine and morphine in the blood will indicate the true cause of death.

Samples taken from living people can be analysed to screen for the presence of banned substances. Such screening is used to test athletes, employees whose contracts of employment stipulate that they are prohibited from using certain drugs, people undergoing substance abuse rehabilitation programmes and prisoners.

Significantly, the analysis of the chemical composition of seized illicit drugs can reveal intelligence information. This is because these street drugs are not chemically

Qualitative analysis
Chemical analysis concerned with establishing the identity of the analyte.

Quantitative analysis
Chemical analysis concerned with establishing the concentration and/or amount of the analyte.

pure but are mixtures of different components. One or more of these components will have the drug action desired by the user. However, others will be present as impurities that have originated in the raw materials from which the drug was formed, have been created as part of the isolation or synthesis of the drug, or have been deliberately added as diluents. The last of these categories of impurity are collectively known as cutting agents. They are added in order to increase the apparent quantity of the drug being sold. In many cases, the nature and concentration of the impurities present in any one type of drug and/or the concentration of its active component are known to vary with both the geographical region of origin and from batch to batch. Hence, chemical composition information can be used to probe supply routes and link seized drug batches together. Also, similarities in the wrapping materials used to contain different portions of illicit drugs may be able to show that two or more samples have the same source. For example, individual doses of powdered drugs may be sold wrapped in paper torn from a page of a magazine. Jigsaw fits between the wrappings of such doses recovered by the police will provide conclusive evidence of a common point in their supply chain. In a similar vein, entomological techniques can be used to establish the geographical region of origin of seized herbal cannabis from the types of arthropod it contains. The sum total of the characteristics of a sample of illicit drugs as revealed by means of the forensic analysis of both the drugs and their wrappings is known as a drug profile. Clearly, drug profiling can provide valuable information about the operation of illicit drug supply networks.

7.5.2 The types of sample that are analysed

Bulk sample
One that is large enough to weigh.

Trace sample
An amount so small that it cannot be weighed (although it may well be possible to establish its weight by means of quantitative chemical analysis).

Both **bulk samples** (i.e. those large enough to be weighed) and **trace samples** are subjected to forensic analysis for drugs and other poisons. For the purposes described in Section 7.5.1, such samples are analysed to establish the identity, composition and/or quantity of one or more of their constituents. A review of the principal methods used to do this is given in Section 7.5.3.

Examples of bulk materials that are analysed include samples of seized illicit drugs, legal drugs in the form of tablets, capsules, etc., and samples of poisons or suspicious materials (e.g. liquid that is suspected of being a pesticide that has been stored in an old soft-drink bottle).

Many types of samples are analysed for trace levels of drugs or other poisons. Notable among these are biological samples taken from people; suspected drug-taking paraphernalia (syringes, wrapping materials, the contents of ashtrays, etc.); laboratory glassware, solvents, etc. from clandestine drug synthesis or purification operations; food or drink that may have been adulterated; and items (crockery, cutlery, containers, clothing, etc.) that have been in contact with such food or drink. The first of these include those samples that can be obtained from living persons, in particular breath, blood, urine, stomach contents, hair, nail clippings, saliva and sweat, and those tissues and body fluids that can be obtained during post-mortem examinations. The specimens taken during such examinations and submitted for toxicological analysis may include samples of blood from different points in the body, urine, liver, bile, vitreous humour (i.e. the transparent jelly-like material of the eye's inner chamber), lung, brain, cerebrospinal fluid (liquid that surrounds the brain and spinal cord and fills the cavity within these organs), hair and nail clippings. The biological samples chosen for analysis will vary from case to case and will reflect:

■ those that are available (e.g. it may well not be possible to obtain urine or blood from a decomposed body);

■ those in which the **analyte** can readily be identified and/or quantified (e.g. samples of lung and/or brain are frequently used in the detection and identification of volatile substances, while, in many cases, the liver is of use in the analysis for drugs);

■ those for which there is an extensive literature to aid the interpretation of the analytical results (blood has a particularly comprehensive literature and for each of many drugs and other poisons there is a known correlation between concentration in blood and biological response);

■ those that are acceptable for legal and ethical reasons (e.g. samples of breath, blood and urine are all acceptable from a legal perspective for the determination of alcohol levels in cases of possible drink-driving);

■ whether information about chronic or **acute** exposure to the analyte is being sought (e.g. while blood may provide information about acute poisoning, a history of chronic or past exposure will be revealed in samples of hair if the poison and/or its metabolites were introduced into this tissue when it is formed and are retained within it).

Analyte
The chemical species that is being analysed for in the sample under test.

Acute
Occurring within a short time period.

7.5.3 Methods of analysis

The methods used to analyse for drugs and other poisons all exploit the chemical, physical and/or biochemical properties of the analyte of interest that allow it to be identified and/or quantified. Except in those cases in which the analyte is the only material present in the sample, the method will also have to be capable of using these properties to distinguish the analyte from the **matrix** of the sample.

Matrix
All of the sample except the chemical species being analysed for.

Readily made observations

In all cases, analysis will start with the observation of those physical properties that can readily be ascertained. Normally, these will include the colour and morphology of the sample that may be seen with the naked eye and/or with the aid of a microscope. These characteristics can be highly informative. For example, shape, dimensions, colour and manufacturer's marks can be used to establish the identity of commercially produced tablets and capsules. However, even in cases in which these observations lead to apparent identification, care needs to be exercised. This is especially true in the case of capsules, as their contents may be tampered with easily. Also, the items, whether tablets or capsules, may be counterfeit goods. Although it should be noted that experts in this field can normally readily detect counterfeit tablets from their appearance, this task can be made easier by intelligence information about trends in drugs counterfeiting.

Certain street drugs may, to varying degrees of certainty, be identified by their appearance. In some cases (e.g. herbal cannabis and 'magic mushrooms'), an examination of morphology alone may be sufficient to unambiguously identify the material concerned. However, in most instances this is not possible. For example, while the fact that a sample is a pale brown powder is consistent with its being heroin, this is clearly not proof of its identity as these characteristics are shared by many other substances. The common visible characteristics of the more frequently encountered street drugs are described in Section 7.2.2. It is noteworthy that even in cases in which appearance is not sufficient to identify the material, valuable information can be obtained from visual examination. For example, the use of a low-power microscope may readily reveal that a given sample of powder is made up of two or more morphologically distinct constituents.

Visual examination of the packaging of both legal and street drugs can also yield important information. Naturally, the packaging of any legal drug will contain written details of the nature and original quantity of its contents. However, such information must be treated with caution. This is because the contents of the packaging may have been altered in some way, the packaging and/or its contents may be counterfeit or mistakes may have occurred when the drug was being packaged. Consequently, in order to identify the contents without doubt, confirmatory information based on its appearance and/or its chemical composition is needed. As mentioned in Section 7.5.1, in the case of street drugs, packaging has the potential to provide evidence that links different samples together, thereby demonstrating that they have a common source.

The physical appearance of food and drink that is suspected of being tampered with, as well as that of body fluids submitted for toxicological analysis, can also be informative, as can any unusual odour associated with these materials. For example, poisonous rat-bait is frequently coloured red, green or blue, and the presence of such colours in food may alert the analyst to the possibility of its contamination with such bait. A number of poisons have characteristic odours, in which case smell may be a useful indicator of their presence; whether in food, drink or stomach contents. Examples of such poisons include cyanide and many volatile organic compounds. Clearly, smell alone will not be sufficient to identify unequivocally the material concerned.

Presumptive tests

Once their readily observed physical characteristics have been noted, bulk samples will, in many cases, be subjected to presumptive tests. These tests are designed to quickly and cheaply indicate the presence of certain analytes (i.e. they provide qualitative but not quantitative information). They most commonly take the form of colour tests. During these, a small amount of the sample is treated with reagents that are known to produce characteristic colours on reacting with the analyte of interest, thereby indicating a positive result. These tests are rarely completely specific. That is, most will produce a positive result with any one of a range of different **chemical species**. Nonetheless, it may be possible to narrow down this range, as, in many cases, the exact colour produced will vary from one chemical species to another. However, the interpretation of the colour of the reaction remains somewhat subjective and is not always straightforward. For example, the presence of impurities in the sample may mask the colour produced or even produce their own colour reactions.

Typically, colour tests will produce a positive result with about 1 mg of the analyte and are carried out in a test tube or on the surface of a white, glazed ceramic tile or via the use of commercially available 'dipstick' kits. Irrespective of the equipment and reagents used, a blank test and a positive control test may be carried out alongside the test of the sample. The blank test consists of the reagents only (i.e. with no

Chemical species *Any collection of atoms, ions or molecules which share an identical set of chemical properties (e.g. ethanol is a chemical species as all ethanol molecules are chemically identical).*

sample present), while the positive control contains both the reagents and a pure portion of the analyte that is being tested for. The appearance of these blank and positive control tests may then be compared with the colour produced by the sample under investigation and thereby aid the interpretation of this colour. The blank test also helps to confirm that contamination of the equipment used has not occurred and the positive control serves to prove that the reagents do indeed lead to colour production with the analyte of interest.

It is important to realise that presumptive tests cannot unequivocally identify the drug or other poison present in any sample. However, they provide valuable information that guides the analyst in the selection of further tests that will confirm or refute the indications provided by the presumptive tests. Table 7.5 lists some of the presumptive tests commonly employed in the analysis of drugs.

Thin-layer chromatography

Both bulk samples and samples that contain trace levels of drugs or other poisons may be analysed by thin-layer chromatography (TLC, Chapter 11, Box 11.5). Often those reagents that are employed in colour tests may also be used to locate (i.e.

Table 7.5 Some common presumptive tests used in the analysis of bulk samples of drugs

Drug	Marquis test (formaldehyde mixed with concentrated sulphuric acid then added to substance under test)	Mandelin's test (ammonium metavanadate in concentrated sulphuric acid added to substance under test)	Cobalt isothiocyanate test (cobalt isothiocynate in water added to substance under test)
Diamorphine	Dark purple	Blue–grey	Blue
Morphine	Mauve or purple	Blue–grey	No change
Codeine	Blue–purple	Olive green	No change
Cocaine	Slight pink or orange	Orange	Blue
Amphetamine and methamphetamine	Orange	No change	No change
MDA, MDMA and MDEA*	Purple–blue	No change	No change
Benzodiazepines	No change	No change	Temazepam gives blue, other benzodiazepines produce no change

* MDA is 3,4-methylenedioxyamphetamine, MDMA is 3,4-methylenedioxymethamphetamine and MDEA is 3,4-methylenedioxyethylamphetamine.

Note that barbiturates do not produce a colour change with any of the above tests. However, they do form a blue-violet colour when assayed using the Dillie–Koppanyi test (in which cobalt acetate in methanol that has been acidified with acetic acid is first added to the substance under test, followed by isopropylamine in methanol). Also, benzodiazepines produce a pink or red-purple colour when exposed to the Zimmerman test (in which 2,4-dinitrobenzine in methanol is first added to the substance under test, followed by potassium hydroxide in water).

visualise) the analyte(s) on TLC plates after development. TLC is a separative technique and one that provides numerical data about the chemical species present in a sample (in the form of R_f values). Furthermore, in many cases, different compounds appear as different coloured spots after they have been visualised. For these reasons, TLC is often more able to discriminate between different analytes than are colour tests. For example, as indicated in Table 7.5, both amphetamine and methamphetamine produce an orange reaction when assayed using the Marquis test. These compounds can be readily differentiated, however, by TLC. This may be done by dissolving the solid in methanol, spotting it onto a silica gel TLC plate together with both positive and negative control samples and developing the plate using a 25/6/0.4 by volume mixture of methanol, propanone and ammonia. The spots on the plate can then be visualised by a number of techniques. These include spraying with dilute (0.5 M) sodium hydroxide, allowing the plate to dry and then spraying with an aqueous solution of Fast Black K (0.5% wt/vol). Where present, the amphetamine spot will appear purple, while the methamphetamine will be rendered orange or red. Furthermore, the R_f values of these two compounds will be quite different (0.62 for amphetamine and 0.26 for methamphetamine; Figure 7.9).

It should be noted, however, that although TLC can refine the indications provided by presumptive tests, confirmatory tests (such as gas chromatography–mass spectrometry, GC–MS, Chapter 11, Box 11.5) will usually have to be performed before the identity of the analyte can be unequivocally determined.

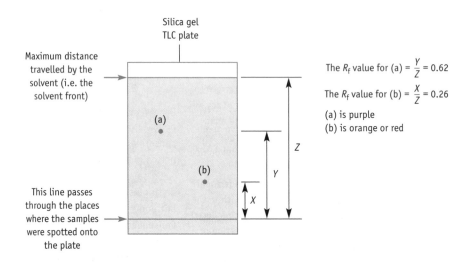

Figure 7.9 TLC of (a) amphetamine and (b) methamphetamine
This TLC plate has been developed with a 25/6/0.4 by volume mixture of methanol, propanone and ammonia, and visualised by spraying with dilute (0.5 M) sodium hydroxide, allowing the plate to dry and then spraying with an aqueous solution of Fast Black K (0.5 % wt/vol)

Immunoassay

Immunoassay techniques (Box 7.4) are of significant value in the analysis of both trace and bulk samples for drugs and other poisons. In some cases, it is possible to devise immunoassays that are highly specific, thereby allowing the concentration of an individual compound to be established – even in a complex mixture. For example, a highly specific and sensitive radioimmunoassay has been devised to analyse plasma for the herbicide paraquat. This is capable of quantifying this poison even when chemically related herbicides are also present in the sample. Also, immunoassays can be devised that are deliberately intended to detect the presence of a range of chemically related compounds. Thus, for example, immunoassay techniques have been developed that allow the detection of any one of several barbiturates and their metabolites.

Forensic techniques

Box 7.4

Immunoassays for drugs and other poisons

In a forensic context, immunoassays are widely used in the analysis of body fluids (such as urine and blood) for the presence of drugs and other poisons, in both ante-mortem and post-mortem samples. Such techniques may be highly specific, i.e. tailored to recognise an individual compound (e.g. methamphetamine), or may be designed to react with a group of chemically related compounds. In the latter case, a positive result requires confirmation of the identity of the analyte by the application of another suitable analytical technique, such as gas chromatography–mass spectrometry (GC–MS). Immunoassay techniques have a number of advantages: they are highly sensitive, well suited to the analysis of high numbers of samples (an obvious advantage when screening for banned substances in body fluids) and do not require a preliminary extraction stage.

Immunoassay is based on the antibody–antigen reaction. This is a natural process that occurs within the mammalian immune system. A specific antibody is produced by the immune system in response to the introduction of a specific 'foreign substance' (termed the antigen) into the body of the mammal concerned. The antibody selectively binds with the antigen to form an antigen–antibody complex. This natural phenomenon is exploited in immunoassays. In these techniques, specific antibodies are used to detect (and, often, quantify) the analyte of interest. The analyte, which, in this context, is a drug or another poison, acts as the antigen to the antibody used in the test. *Note* that for the purposes of this box, the term poison is used to denote both drugs and other poisons.

In immunoassays used to test for poisons, fixed quantities of both the antibody specific for the analyte being tested for and a labelled form of that substance are added to the sample under test. Both the labelled molecules and, if present, the unlabelled analyte molecules in the test sample competitively bind with the antibody in numbers that are inversely proportional to each other. Thus, measuring the labelled poison (either bound to the antibody or free in the solution) can give information concerning the original concentration of the unlabelled poison in the sample.

In some types of immunoassay, it is not possible to distinguish between the labelled poison bound to the antibody and that remaining free in solution. Consequently, physical separation of the two phases is required before measurement. Immunoassays that require such separation are known as heterogeneous immunoassays. Examples include radioimmunoassay. In other systems, the bound, labelled poison can be discerned from that which is free in solution and, therefore, no separation stage is needed. Immunoassays that do not require a separation stage are termed homogeneous

▶

Box 7.4 continued

immunoassays. An example of this type is fluorescence polarisation immunoassay (FPIA).

There are a number of different methods of immunoassay used in the analysis of poisons. These vary in the nature of the substances used to label the poison molecules and, consequently, the methods employed to make the required measurements. Two of the main methods are described briefly below.

Radioimmunoassay (RIA)

In this type of immunoassay, the poison molecules are labelled with an appropriate radioisotope, such as iodine-125 (^{125}I) or tritium (^3H), and measurements are of radioactivity. RIA is a heterogeneous immunoassay and thus the two phases containing the radiolabelled poison (i.e. bound to the antibody and free in solution) require separation before measurements can be made. The concentration of unlabelled poison molecules in the test mixture may be determined by reference to a standard curve. This graph is produced by adding increasing concentrations of the unlabelled poison to a fixed quantity of radiolabelled poison and the antibody specific to the poison concerned. The percentage of radiolabelled poison bound to the antibody is then plotted against the concentration of unlabelled poison.

Fluorescence polarisation immunoassay (FPIA)

In this type of immunoassay, a suitable fluorescent substance (such as fluorescein, an organic dye) is used to label the poison concerned. It is possible to distinguish between the fluorescence-labelled poison bound to the antibody and the fluorescence-labelled poison free in solution. This is because the former produces polarized fluorescence while the latter generates unpolarized fluorescence. FPIA is therefore an example of homogeneous immunoassay.

One of the great benefits of immunoassay techniques is that, because of their high specificity and sensitivity, they can be used to analyse for trace levels of substances in complex matrices. Therefore, unlike many chromatographic methods, they do not have an inherent need for a prior extraction stage. Immunoassay techniques are particularly well suited to the analysis of samples in high numbers. They are used to screen samples of body fluids for the presence of banned substances, followed by confirmatory analysis by GC–MS (Chapter 11, Box 11.5) of any positive findings.

Instrumental methods

While presumptive tests and TLC are valuable in indicating the likely nature of any drug or other poison present in a sample, definitive analysis is normally carried out by instrumental means. The techniques chosen will depend on a number of factors including the nature of the analyte and its matrix, the concentration of the analyte and the amount of sample available.

For organic analytes at trace levels, the most commonly used methods are based on either gas chromatography (GC) or high-performance liquid chromatography (HPLC) (Chapter 11, Box 11.5). These techniques have the advantage that they separate the analyte from the mixture it is held in while simultaneously providing both qualitative and quantitative information about it. In many instances, the GC or HPLC is linked to another instrument, such as a mass spectrometer (MS), to produce so-called hyphenated techniques (Chapter 11, Box 11.5).

In some cases, quantification is conveniently achieved using ultraviolet–visible spectrophotometric methods (Chapter 3, Box 3.6). These work well in cases in which the analyte is the only chemical species present that absorbs light in the ultraviolet–visible part of the electromagnetic spectrum. Unfortunately, complex mixtures of such species will usually have to be separated, to produce materials of greater purity, prior to quantification by such methods. This disadvantage limits their use in the analysis of drugs and other poisons, which are frequently present in combination with many other species. Note, however, that detectors that rely on the absorbance of light in the ultraviolet–visible region are routinely used in the analysis of drugs and other poisons by HPLC (Chapter 11, Box 11.5). This is possible because the separation of the sample into its component parts that is afforded by the chromatographic column means that, in many cases, only one light-absorbing species is present in the detector at any one time.

As described in Chapter 3, Box 3.9, virtually all molecules absorb electromagnetic radiation in the infrared region of the electromagnetic spectrum to produce a series of peaks (seen as troughs in the transmittance spectrum), the positions and number of which are characteristic of the molecule concerned. Therefore, by comparing the positions of the peaks in the infrared spectra of an unknown compound with those of known compounds until a match is found, the likely identity of the unknown can be established (Figure 7.10). Hence, infrared spectroscopy can provide valuable qualitative information about *pure* compounds. Unfortunately, most samples that are

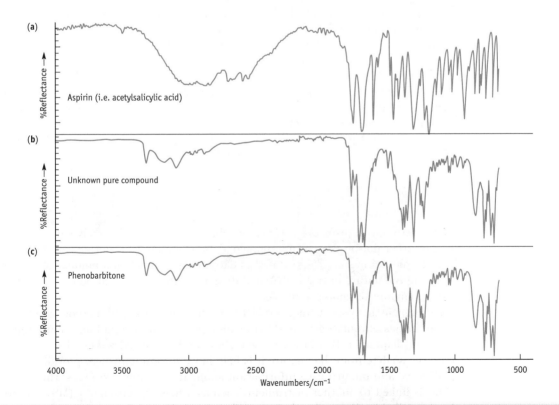

Figure 7.10 The infrared spectra of (a) aspirin, (b) an unknown pure compound and (c) phenobarbitone
From a comparison of the positions of the peaks (seen here as troughs) in these spectra, it is evident that the unknown is not aspirin but could well be phenobarbitone

(Recorded by Jayne Francis, Staffordshire University, UK)

analysed for the presence of drugs and other poisons are complex mixtures, thereby limiting the applicability of this technique. However, relatively recently, affordable infrared microscopes (Figure 7.11) have been developed. These are capable of obtaining this type of qualitative information from the individual particles of powders that are made up of physical mixtures of two or more pure compounds.

There are a number of methods that can be used to identify and quantify metallic poisons. Notable among these are atomic absorption spectroscopy (AAS) and inductively coupled plasma atomic emission spectroscopy (ICP-AES) (see Box 7.5). These are capable of analysing liquids, giving both qualitative and quantitative information about the elements they contain with great selectivity, high sensitivity and low limits of detection. This means that they can be used to analyse body fluids with the minimum of sample pre-treatment. Solid samples can also be analysed. However, this is normally done after they have been chemically treated to bring their component elements into solution.

Factors influencing the choice of analytical methods

The methods used to analyse a given sample will vary depending on a number of factors. Important among these is how much is already known about the sample. For example, consider a case in which it is believed that a person died as the result of ingesting the herbicide paraquat. In such an instance, the purpose of a toxicological analysis may be to establish whether there was a lethal concentration of this substance in the plasma of a blood sample taken from the deceased during post-mortem examination. Such an analysis would be conducted using a proven method that will allow the quantification of this substance within plasma. A number of such methods exist, including the highly specific and sensitive radioimmunoassay mentioned earlier in this section (Box 7.4). Owing to the specificity of this method, it could not be expected to reveal the presence of poisons other than paraquat. Hence, while it may

(Photograph by Andrew Jackson, Staffordshire University, UK)

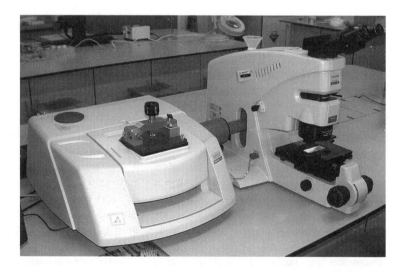

Figure 7.11 An infrared microscope

Forensic techniques

Box 7.5

Atomic absorption and emission spectroscopies

As explained in Chapter 3, Box 3.6, an atom, ion or molecule can absorb light in the ultraviolet–visible region of the electromagnetic spectrum, resulting in the promotion of an electron from the orbital in which it is residing to one of higher energy that is either empty or partially full. In order for this absorption to occur, the difference between the energy state of the atom, ion or molecule concerned at the start of the process (E) and at the end (E', which is of higher energy than E) must satisfy Bohr's frequency condition, i.e.:

$$E' - E = \Delta E = h\nu; \text{ in a vacuum this} = \frac{hc}{\lambda}$$

where h is Planck's constant and ν is the frequency of the incident radiation.

Note that in a vacuum, ΔE also $= \frac{hc}{\lambda}$, in which c is the speed of light in a vacuum, and λ is the wavelength of the incident radiation.

As described in Box 3.6, the ultraviolet–visible absorption spectra of molecules each typically consists of one or more broad bands of elevated absorbance. As exemplified by the spectrum of aqueous cocaine hydrochloride, shown in Box 3.6, each such band typically extends over a range of wavelengths that is tens of nanometres (nm) wide. In contrast, gaseous atoms have ultraviolet–visible absorption spectra that consist of very narrow peaks (known as lines), which extend over a wavelength range in the region of 0.002 to 0.005 nm wide. Atomic absorption spectroscopy (AAS) takes advantage of this phenomenon to allow the concentration of each of a large number of the elements to be determined, even in complex mixtures.

In common with other types of absorption spectrometers, AAS machines contain a radiation source and a radiation detector, between which are a sample holder and wavelength selector. The last of these components is used to select and restrict the range of wavelengths that reach the detector at any one time. However, in the case of AAS, the radiation source and sample holder are somewhat specialised.

Let us consider the sample holder first. In order to observe the line absorption spectra exhibited by atoms, the sample must be atomised. This means it must be broken into its constituent atoms so that each is in a chemically isolated environment in the gas phase. For most elements of forensic interest (e.g. toxic metals such as lead and cadmium), atomisation can only be achieved at high temperatures. The most convenient way of achieving these temperatures is in a flame. In flame AAS (FAAS), the sample in the form of a solution is sprayed into a stream of a flammable mixture of fuel and oxidant gases that is burnt to produce a flame that acts as the sample holder. As an alternative to a flame, a small graphite furnace can be used as a sample holder. This is made to heat up rapidly to a high temperature by passing an electrical current through it, thereby atomising the sample.

Irrespective of the means by which the analyte is atomised, the radiation source used makes use of the fact that Bohr's frequency condition also applies to atoms emitting radiation. Consider an atom in an excited state E' that relaxes to a lower energy state E by the emission of electromagnetic radiation. The frequency of the emitted radiation will accord with Bohr's frequency condition, i.e. $E' - E = h\nu$, which, in a vacuum $= hc/\lambda$. Therefore, an atom of an element that has relaxed from E' to E by emitting electromagnetic radiation will have produced radiation with exactly the right frequency to promote another atom of the same element from E to E'. The radiation source used in AAS is therefore a cloud of excited atoms of the element that is to be analysed for. If the intensity of the radiation produced by this cloud were to be plotted as a function of wavelength, it would be seen to consist of a series of extremely sharp peaks (called lines) that have identical wavelengths to the lines in the absorption spectrum of the element concerned. Furthermore, the exact wavelengths at which these lines occur are unique to a given element. It is for this reason that AAS is capable of analysing for one element, even in mixtures that contain many elements.

In most cases, the cloud of excited atoms is formed in a hollow cathode lamp. This consists of a sealed glass tube that has a Pyrex or quartz window at one end. This

▶

Box 7.5 continued

tube is filled with an inert gas, such as argon, at a low pressure and contains two electrodes – an anode and a cathode. The surface of the cathode is made of the element that is to be analysed for. A direct current potential difference of several hundred volts is applied across the electrodes. This ionises the inert gas, producing electrons that move towards the anode and positively charged ions that move to the cathode. These ions strike the cathode with sufficient force to knock atoms from its surface. This cloud of atoms contains some that are in excited states and acts as the source of radiation for the instrument.

Excited atoms are also produced in high-temperature gases. As in a hollow cathode lamp, these atoms can relax by emitting radiation that is characteristic of the elements involved. This phenomenon is exploited in atomic emission spectroscopy (AES) to identify and/or measure the concentration of a wide range of elements that might be present in a sample. To do this, the sample is heated to a very high temperature and the radiation that is emitted is passed through a wavelength selector and into a radiation detector. The high temperatures required are generated either in a flame or high-temperature plasma. In this context, a plasma is a gas that contains a high concentration of ions and electrons. During inductively coupled plasma atomic emission spectroscopy (ICP–AES, often known simply as ICP), the plasma is maintained in a flow of argon. To start the plasma, an electric spark is passed through the argon. This causes enough of the argon to lose electrons and become ions for the gas to interact with a fluctuating magnetic field. This is provided by an induction coil that is wrapped around the gas stream. The coil is supplied by a radiofrequency generator that is sufficiently powerful to heat the gas and generate the plasma.

The quantification of specific elements within a sample may be achieved by either AAS or AES by establishing a calibration graph. In most instances, this is achieved by passing a series of solutions of known analyte concentra-

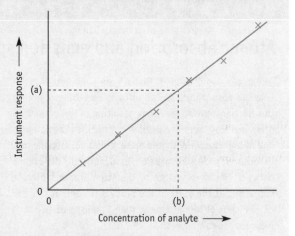

A typical calibration graph as used to find the concentration of an unknown AAS or AES

Point (a) represents the instrument response obtained from the sample of unknown concentration and point (b) shows the concentration of this sample as established by interpolation

tion through the instrument in turn. In each case, the instrument response is noted. A graph is then plotted with the concentration of the analyte on the x-axis and the instrument response on the y-axis. Quantification is now possible by passing the solution of unknown analyte concentration through the instrument and noting its response. As shown in the figure above, interpolation will now allow the concentration of the unknown to be established.

The great advantages of both AAS and AES are their element specificity (meaning that complex mixtures can be analysed without the need to separate them first), their high sensitivity and low limits of detection. However, they do require the destruction of the portion of the sample that is analysed and they give no direct information about the chemical form of the analyte element(s) present.

well be fit for this application, it would not be particularly useful in a case in which the presence of a wide range of poisons needs to be tested for.

Also of importance is the amount of material that is available. In the case of a bulk sample, there may well be enough material to conduct presumptive tests, TLC and instrumental methods. In contrast, it would not be possible to carry out all of this work on a small sample that is believed to contain trace levels of the analyte. In such instances, a judgement would have to be made, based on the circumstances of the case, about which method(s) to use. Compared with presumptive tests and TLC, many instrumental methods of analysis (notably those based on GC, HPLC, AAS and ICP) provide high levels of sensitivity and selectivity with low limits of detection and yield reliable qualitative and quantitative results. Consequently, when trace samples are all that are available, such instrumental methods will be the ones of choice.

The optimisation of both the analyte's concentration and the chemical form of the sample

Most samples that are analysed for the presence of drugs or other poisons are complex mixtures. Furthermore, in many cases, the concentration of analyte within the sample is low – this is especially true of samples of biological materials taken from people, whether ante-mortem or post-mortem. These two factors mean that most samples cannot be analysed without some form of pre-treatment. The purpose of such pre-treatment is to:

- simplify the matrix within which the analyte is held in order to remove substances that will interfere with the signal produced by the analyte when it is analysed;
- concentrate (or, rarely, dilute) the analyte so that it is present at a concentration that is within the working range of the instrument to be used to analyse for it; and/or
- alter the physical state or chemical form of the sample to make it compatible with the analytical technique to be employed (e.g. most techniques require samples in solution form, while GC furthermore requires volatile and thermally stable analytes; therefore, prior to GC analysis, chemical derivatisation is sometimes needed).

Naturally, the form and extent of the pre-treatment will depend on the nature of:

- the sample (especially its physical form – solid, liquid or, rarely, gas; its purity and the likely concentration range of the analyte within it);
- the analyte (especially important is whether the analyte is a molecule or an element);
- the analytical technique that is to be employed after the sample pre-treatment has been completed.

In the main, pre-treatment methods that are employed when the analyte is a molecule must be less destructive than when it is an element.

In many cases in which biological samples are being analysed for trace levels of molecular analytes, the pre-treatment centres around the extraction and concentration of the analyte. Prior to this, additional pre-treatment may be required. This may involve, for example, removing part of the sample by physical means (e.g. filtration or centrifugation), changing the physical form of the sample (e.g. the maceration of tissue) or adjusting the sample's level of acidity. After this stage, the sample is usually present as a water-based solution or slurry and is ready for extraction. During extraction, the sample is brought into contact with a material that has an affinity for the analyte but that will not mix with the sample as a whole. Materials used for this purpose are commonly organic solvents which are not miscible with water but which will dissolve the analyte. Mixing the sample with the solvent will therefore result in the transfer of the analyte to the solvent. If the resulting mixture is left to stand or centrifuged, the organic and aqueous phases will usually separate, thereby allowing the analyst to remove the organic phase, which now contains the analyte. If the solvent has a higher affinity for the analyte than does water, and if the volume of the organic solvent is sufficiently lower than that of the aqueous phase, the concentration of the analyte will be increased by extraction. Note that in order to maximise the efficiency of extraction, the same aqueous phase sample may be mixed sequentially with multiple batches of organic solvent. These batches will then be combined. Irrespective of the number of batches of organic solvent used, the analyte's concentration can subsequently be increased by reducing the volume of the solvent by evaporation. The extraction stage not only pre-concentrates the analyte but, importantly, it also isolates it from many of the impurities present in the original sample.

Note that many drugs and other poisons are either weak acids (e.g. phenobarbitone) or weak bases (e.g. cocaine). Both ionised and un-ionised forms of these substances exist. The organic solvents that are used to extract these from aqueous solution have a much higher affinity for them when they are un-ionised than when they are ionised. In order to suppress the formation of the ionic form in the aqueous phase, and thereby promote extraction, the level of acidity of the solution is manipulated by the addition of an acid (e.g. hydrochloric acid) or a base (e.g. ammonia), as appropriate. Weak acids are extracted from suitably acidic aqueous solutions, in which they are in the un-ionised form. In contrast, weak bases are un-ionised when in suitably alkaline aqueous solutions and it is from these that such substances are extracted.

Solid-phase extraction (SPE) is an alternative to the liquid–liquid extraction outlined above. During SPE, a liquid sample is passed through a bed of finely divided solid adsorbent that is designed to selectively remove the analyte of interest from solution in the sample. The adsorbent may then be washed to purify the analyte further. Finally, the analyte is desorbed with a small volume of a suitable solvent. This process can both isolate the analyte from impurities and increase its concentration.

In the main, samples that are to be analysed for metals or other elements are treated somewhat differently. This reflects the fact that while it is necessary to present the analyte in a form that is suitable for the technique to be used in the ultimate analysis, it is not normally necessary for the analyte to retain its original chemical form. For example, the analysis of a food sample for a heavy metal poison may be attempted by AAS. To achieve this, the food may first be heated in a furnace until it turns to ash. This will simultaneously concentrate the metal (provided that it does not vaporise during ashing) and may alter its chemical form to make it readily soluble in a suitable acid. The metal can then be extracted into the acid and analysed by AAS (Box 7.5).

Finally, it is important to note that, in all cases, the analyst should keep the number of pre-treatment steps to the minimum. This is because each such step either decreases the total amount of analyte present and/or introduces new materials to the sample, thereby increasing the possibility of sample contamination. Also, each additional step adds to the time and cost of the overall procedure and may expose the analyst to unnecessary risk owing to the additional use of hazardous chemicals, etc.

7.6 Summary

■ Toxicology is the scientific study of poisons; the addendum 'forensic' referring to its application within a legal context. A poison may be defined as any substance that exerts a toxic effect when it encounters a biological system. In this chapter, the following broad groups of poisons are described: anions, corrosive poisons, gaseous and volatile poisons, metal and metalloid poisons, pesticides, toxins and drugs of abuse. Any exposure of an individual to potentially toxic substances may be accidental or the result of a deliberate act of, for example, attempted suicide or murder.

■ In addition, many substances are deliberately self-administered for the effects they induce. These are known collectively as drugs of abuse and are generally considered separately from other groups of poisons as a special case. The vast majority of these are subject to the Misuse of Drugs Act 1971 and therefore may also be referred to as controlled drugs. Such drugs may be produced illegally and/or diverted from licit sources. Examples include amphetamines, benzodiazepines, cannabis, cocaine, heroin and lysergic acid diethylamide (LSD). However, some abused drugs, such as alcohol, are available legally.

■ The toxicity of a potentially poisonous substance is determined by the dose that is administered, although other factors related to the recipient, such as weight, age, state of health and previous exposure, are also important. Poisons may be taken into the body via a number of different routes; namely ingestion, inhalation, skin contact, mucous membrane contact and injection. After absorption into the general blood circulation and subsequent distribution around the body, toxic substances are then eliminated from the body. Understanding the nature and dynamics of these processes is fundamental to the qualitative and quantitative analysis of blood or tissue samples taken from individuals for toxicological analysis.

■ The analysis of a sample for drugs and other poisons may be qualitative and/or quantitative. The information obtained may help the courts to establish whether an offence has been committed, the nature of that offence and whether the accused is guilty. It can also provide intelligence information by linking different samples to the same source. The analytical procedures used will normally include the recording of readily made observations (e.g. shape, colour and dimensions) and will often employ presumptive tests, thin-layer chromatography (TLC), immunoassay and/or instrumental methods such as gas chromatography (GC) or atomic absorption spectroscopy (AAS).

Problems

1. Explain what is meant by the term 'drugs of abuse'. With reference to specific examples, describe the different routes of administration that may be employed by drug users.

2. Under the Misuse of Drugs Act 1971, controlled drugs are classified as Class A, Class B or Class C. Using an example from each class, discuss their effects on the individual and the potential risks associated with their use.

3. 'The toxicity of a substance is determined not only by its inherent toxic properties but also by a number of factors relating to the individual exposed to it.' Discuss. (Include in your answer, an explanation of the following conditions: sensitisation, tolerance and idiosyncratic response.)

4. Discuss the uptake of potentially toxic substances into the human body, their distribution and subsequent elimination. Within this context, explain what is meant by the terms 'absorption' and 'bioavailability'.

5. Consider a case in which an individual has been arrested on suspicion of supplying drugs to users. At the time of the arrest, the person concerned was found to be in possession of 12 individual doses of what appeared to be heroin, each wrapped in brown paper. A subsequent search of the arrested person's house revealed a roll of brown paper, from which some paper had apparently been torn, a quantity of off-white powder in a strong plastic bag and several packets of caffeine tablets. Shortly after the arrest, a known drug user, who lived in the same town as the arrested person, was caught in possession of what appeared to be a dose of heroin wrapped in brown paper. Review the potential that forensic science has to help the investigation of this case and the types of forensic analysis that may be used in such an investigation.

6. When carrying out a colour test for a particular drug, the method used may prescribe that a positive control test is carried out using a known sample of the drug concerned. Furthermore, it may stipulate that this control test must not be carried out until after the test on the sample under investigation has been completed. Why might such a stipulation be made?

7. During an analysis of a bulk sample for illegal drugs, the analyst working on the case performs the presumptive tests named in Table 7.5. She observes that the material in question produces each of purple, red-brown and blue coloured products when subjected, respectively, to the Marquis test, Mandelin's test and the cobalt isothiocyanate test. Which drug will she suspect is present? The analyst then decided to subject the sample to GC–MS in an attempt to confirm the identity of any drug present. She also analysed a cotton swab that she had wiped over her gloves, the bench top, and all of the surfaces of the equipment to be used in the presumptive tests before these tests were carried out. Why did she do this?

8. A sample of blood taken from a driver one hour after he had been involved in a road traffic accident was analysed for ethanol by gas chromatography with a flame ionisation detector (GC–FID), using propan-1-ol as an internal standard. The results obtained from this analysis are given in Table 7.6. Was this person above the drink-drive limit at the time of the accident?[1] Assume that:

■ the person had not drunk any alcohol in the two hours immediately prior to the accident;

■ the sample of blood was 5.0 ml in volume and that, prior to analysis, this was diluted with 5.0 ml of an alcohol-free preservative and 5.0 ml of water that contained the internal standard (i.e. making a total volume of 15.0 ml);

■ other than the dilution referred to in the previous bullet point, the sample was not pre-treated in any way prior to analysis.

Table 7.6 The analytical data required to answer question 8 (data supplied by Dr M.D. Tonge, Senior Lecturer in Forensic Science, Staffordshire University)

Sample	[Ethanol]/ mg dm^{-3}	[Propan-1-ol]/ mg dm^{-3}	Peak areas/µV s	
			Ethanol	Propan-1-ol
Standard 1	250	250	6 235	10 560
Standard 2	500	250	12 196	10 225
Standard 3	750	250	18 266	10 363
Standard 4	1000	250	24 672	10 401
Sample analysed*		250	15 193	10 697

*i.e. made up of 5.0 ml of blood, 5.0 ml preservative and 5.0 ml water that contained a total of 3.75 mg of propan-1-ol.

Further reading

Cole, M. D. (2003) *The analysis of controlled substances*. Chichester: John Wiley & Sons Ltd.

Ferner, R. E. (1996) *Forensic pharmacology: medicines, mayhem and malpractice*. Oxford: Oxford University Press.

Karch, S. B. (ed.) (1998) *Drug abuse handbook*. Boca Raton, FL: CRC Press LLC.

Karch, S. B. (2001) *Karch's pathology of drug abuse* (3rd edn). Boca Raton, FL: CRC Press LLC.

King, L. A. (2003) *The Misuse of Drugs Act: a guide for forensic scientists*. Cambridge: Royal Society of Chemistry.

Moffatt, A. C. (ed.) (1986) *Clarke's isolation and identification of drugs: in pharmaceuticals, body fluids, and post-mortem material* (2nd edn). London: The Pharmaceutical Press.

Roe, S. and Man, L. (2006) 'Drug misuse declared: findings from the 2005/2006 British Crime Survey (England and Wales)', *Home Office Statistical Bulletin*. London: Home Office Research, Development and Statistics Directorate.

Rubinson, J. F. and Rubinson, K. A. (1998) *Contemporary chemical analysis*. Englewood Cliffs, NJ: Prentice Hall.

Timbrell, J. A. (2002) *Introduction to toxicology* (3rd edn). London: Taylor & Francis.

Timbrell, J. A. (2005) *The poison paradox: chemicals as friends and foes*. Oxford: Oxford University Press.

Trestrail, J. H. (2000) *Criminal poisoning: investigational guide for law enforcement, toxicologists, forensic scientists, and attorneys*. New Jersey: Humana Press, Inc.

Questioned documents | 8

Chapter objectives

After reading this chapter, you should be able to:

> Describe the procedure for comparing questioned handwriting with specimen handwriting, including the means by which the latter are routinely obtained.

> Outline the different methods used to forge signatures and explain how a forensic document examiner can distinguish between genuine and forged signatures.

> Appreciate how the technological production and reproduction of documents in the office environment has changed dramatically over the years and, with it, the type of expertise required of the document examiner.

> Understand the threat to mass-produced printed documents from counterfeiting and the measures that can be taken to combat this illegal activity.

> Discuss the different analytical techniques used in the comparison of inks.

> Explain how those characteristics of paper used in paper analysis are determined by the paper manufacturing process.

> Appreciate how the document examiner can glean useful information from the analysis of any tears, folds, holes, obliterations, erasures or indentations present on a questioned document.

Introduction

The term 'questioned document' is a wide-ranging term applicable to any document over which there is some dispute or query and to which the skills of a document examiner may be brought as part of the investigative process. Document examination is a very important and highly skilled area of forensic science, requiring thorough training of its practitioners and access to suitably equipped laboratories. In the United Kingdom, there are forensic document examiners in both the public sector, notably the Forensic Science Service, and the private sector, for example Document Evidence Ltd of Birmingham and London.

Examples of questioned documents include disputed wills, forged cheques, altered receipts, ransom notes and anonymous letters. To give a clearer idea of the

Further information

Box 8.1

Some examples of typical questions addressed to forensic document examiners

- Was the sample of questioned handwriting created by a particular person?
- Is the signature forged?
- Is the date that appears on the disputed document compatible with its age?
- Has the receipt been altered?
- Have the entries in this diary been written over a period of months or all on one occasion?

- Were a number of different documents written by the same individual?
- What writing appears beneath the obliterated portion of text?
- What type of machine was used to produce the text of a questioned document?
- Is the document genuine or counterfeit?
- Can you tell us about the origin of this anonymous document?

variety of work encompassed within this specialist area, some examples of the types of questions that may be put to forensic document examiners are listed in Box 8.1.

In this chapter, the key aspects of the analysis of questioned documents, including handwriting and signature investigation, the examination of typed, word-processed and photocopied documents, printed documents and counterfeiting, and ink and paper analysis, are systematically examined. Throughout the chapter, emphasis is placed on the techniques employed by forensic document examiners to reveal information contained within questioned documents.

8.1 Handwriting investigation

Generally, the largest part of the work undertaken by forensic document examiners is connected with the analysis of handwriting. Fundamental to this analysis is the principle that the writing of each person is unique to them. Further, that each piece of writing from a given individual is in itself unique, but that the writings of that individual vary over a natural range of variation, which is another feature of that person's writing. As a consequence, handwriting can be used as a means of individual identification, provided that sufficient quantities of specimen material (preferably non-request) are available for comparison with the questioned handwriting (Section 8.1.2). It should be noted that the scientific analysis of handwriting undertaken by forensic document examiners is entirely different from the work of graphologists, who scrutinise the handwriting of individuals in an attempt to infer their personality traits. Confusion may arise because graphologists are also often referred to as handwriting experts.

8.1.1 The development of handwriting

Handwriting is a complex motor task, which must be learnt. In the United Kingdom, this process usually begins when the child is about 4 years of age. In the early stages, the child consciously copies the different letters presented to him or her. As these are usually in a standard form, the handwriting of the child is similar at this stage to that of his or her classmates (and to that of other children taught using the same writing system). Such features in common are known as *class characteristics*. However, as the child increases in skill, the act of handwriting becomes less demanding and his or her construction, and other aspects (such as shape and proportion), of character forms becomes more individualised. Such distinctive features are known as *individual characteristics*, and taken in the context of class characteristics, it is these that are used by document examiners to identify handwriting. The main period during which these individual characteristics are developed is during the adolescent years. After this, the handwriting of a mature individual usually stays basically the same with only minor changes until the lack of pen control associated with advancing years causes it, once again, to alter significantly.

8.1.2 The comparison of handwriting

Cursive writing
Joined-up handwriting in which the individual letters appear in lower case.

Script
Unjoined handwriting in which the individual letters appear in lower case.

A number of different basic types of handwriting are recognised. In the United Kingdom, these are designated as block capitals (i.e. upper-case unjoined writing), **cursive writing** (i.e. lower-case joined-up writing) and **script** (i.e. lower-case unjoined writing) (Figure 8.1). Two other terms should be mentioned in this context, namely connected writing and disconnected writing. In the United Kingdom, forensic handwriting experts usually consider these terms to be synonymous with cursive writing and script respectively.

In practice, the normal handwriting of most individuals is somewhere between cursive writing and script. In such cases, handwriting experts will normally use the term cursive writing to denote handwriting in which the letters within words are predominantly joined and, conversely, use the term script for handwriting in which the majority of the letters within words are not joined. Signatures are a specialised form of handwriting, which are examined separately in Section 8.2.

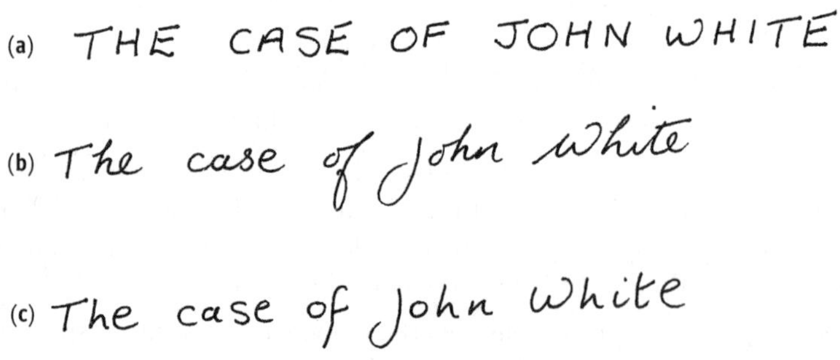

(a) THE CASE OF JOHN WHITE

(b) The case of John White

(c) The case of John White

Figure 8.1 The three basic types of handwriting recognised in the UK: (a) block capitals; (b) cursive writing and (c) script

It is crucial that any comparison between questioned and specimen handwriting is carried out on a 'like for like' basis. This means that in order to make a meaningful comparison, the type of handwriting must be the same in each of the two samples. Furthermore, individual letters that are compared in the two samples must also be the same as each other. For example, the letter 'b' in one document written in cursive style must be compared with the letter 'b' written in cursive style in the other. Groups of letters and words that are compared in the two samples *ideally* will also be the same as each other. However, this is not always possible in cases where the specimen handwriting used in the comparison is of the non-request variety (the nature of non-request specimens of handwriting is described later in this section).

When analysing handwritten questioned documents, the forensic document examiner compares all characters present, deciding on the basis of his or her experience which are those handwriting traits that help make it uniquely identifiable. This examination is best carried out using a low-power stereoscopic microscope. Under magnification, the construction, proportions (both internal and relative to each other) and shape of the individual characters are clearly visible. In the case of the construction of characters, it is necessary to ascertain both the directions in which the constituent pen strokes have been made and the order in which they have been laid down. (The direction of pen movement can also reveal the difference between right- and left-handed individuals. For example, circular pen strokes, as seen in the letter 'o', made in an anticlockwise direction indicate right-handedness whereas those made in a clockwise direction attest to left-handedness.) Other handwriting features such as the connections between letters (if any) and the slope of the writing may contribute to individualising the content, as can general writing features, such as word and letter spacing, and date style and arrangement.

It is important to realise that the handwriting of an individual shows natural variation. This means that it is never exactly the same on any two occasions. When making a comparison with questioned handwriting, it is therefore necessary for the document examiner to have access to sufficient quantities of specimen handwriting in order to assess this natural variation and take it into account. The forensic document examiner is also aware that handwriting may show variation because of other factors. These may be associated with the mental and physical state of the writer, for example whether a person is ill, stressed or under the influence of alcohol or other drugs, or it may be caused by the writing surface or writing instrument used. In some cases, variation occurs because the writer is attempting to disguise his or her own natural handwriting.

The **specimen handwriting** required for comparison with questioned handwriting falls into one of two categories:

■ *Non-request specimens.* This type of specimen is preferable as it consists of documents that the author, at the time of writing, had no notion would be used for the purpose of an enquiry. Ideally, such documents should originate, as near as possible, from the time at which the questioned document was written.

■ *Request specimens.* In this case, as the name suggests, the suspect is asked to produce handwriting samples especially for the purpose of the enquiry (Box 8.2). This differs from non-request specimens in that the conditions under which this task is carried out can be more controlled. The same type of paper and pen can be provided and the individual may be requested to write out

Specimen handwriting *Handwriting samples obtained from an individual suspected of authorship of a piece of questioned (disputed) handwriting for the purposes of comparison.*

Case study

Box 8.2

The role played by handwriting comparisons in the Chris Cotter case

On 21 March 2000, Chris Cotter, the white former boyfriend of the black Olympic triple jumper Ashia Hansen, was attacked outside her home in Birmingham. In the assault, Mr Cotter was stabbed three times in the back and slashed across his forehead. He claimed that he had been set upon by a number of white men, possibly as many as five, who expressed their objections to his relationship with Ms Hansen. The police launched an extensive enquiry into this apparently racially motivated attack. Shortly afterwards, hate mail was received by Ms Hansen, and a number of other black international athletes including Dwain Chambers and Tony Jarrett.

On 19 May 2000, Chris Cotter himself was arrested, together with two friends, Craig Wynn and Surjit Singh Clair. All three were charged with conspiring to pervert the course of justice. At their trial at Birmingham Crown Court, an integral part of the prosecution's case concerned the findings of a senior document examiner from the Forensic Science Service (FSS). He had compared the handwriting on the envelopes of the hate letters with request handwriting samples given by the three defen-

dants at the time of their arrest. When asked by the court, he said, 'The disguised nature of this handwriting was a severe limitation, but I could say that there was moderate evidence to support the view that Clair was the writer. In places, the disguise had lapsed and distinctive similarities with the specimen were found.'*

On 8 June 2001, all three defendants were found guilty of conspiring to pervert the course of justice. Cotter and Wynn received prison sentences of two years each. However, Clair, who had entered negotiations with the *Express* newspaper to sell the story for several thousand pounds, was also found guilty of attempting to obtain property by deception and received an additional sentence of 12 months. The court was told that Cotter's motivation in staging the attack upon himself was primarily concerned with winning back Ms Hansen's affection, but that the prospect of financial gain from selling the story also played a part.

*Quote taken from the *Annual Report of The Forensic Science Service 2001–02*, © Crown Copyright 2002.

exactly the same text as in the questioned document. However, this type of specimen material has its limitations. It will lack the natural variation that can be provided by non-request specimens, assuming that the latter type is available in sufficient quantities. Moreover, the suspect may attempt to disguise his or her handwriting or it may change as a result of stress, or other factors. Dictating the text and doing so repeatedly with breaks in between can help overcome the problem of disguised or unnatural handwriting.

In practice, it is best if both request and non-request handwriting specimens are available to the forensic document examiner. He or she uses the material to make a comparison between the specimen and questioned handwriting, systematically comparing characters (individually and in groups), physical features (such as the appearance of ink lines under a microscope) and general writing features (such as line position and punctuation). As a result of this process, the document examiner is able to make an assessment of the similarities and differences between the specimen and questioned handwriting. This necessitates considerable experience on the part of the document examiner, who must determine the significance of the similarities and differences observed. On this basis, he or she will be able to reach one of the following conclusions, each of which constitutes an expert opinion:

- ■ There is conclusive evidence that the writer of the specimen and questioned handwriting is one and the same person.

- ■ There is supporting evidence that the writer of the specimen and questioned handwriting is one and the same person but the possibility that different individuals wrote the specimen and questioned handwriting cannot be ruled out.

- ■ The evidence is inconclusive either because it is contradictory (i.e. both similarities and differences are of approximately similar significance) or there is very little evidence, for example a few letters in a name.

- ■ There is supporting evidence that different individuals wrote the specimen and questioned handwriting but the possibility that the writer of the specimen and questioned handwriting is one and the same person cannot be ruled out.

- ■ There is conclusive evidence that different individuals wrote the specimen and questioned handwriting.

8.2 Signature investigation

Signatures differ significantly from bulk handwriting in that they are highly stylised portions of writing. So much so that in some cases, they are completely illegible! They are used as a means of personal identification and, as such, are produced on numerous occasions, for signing cheques, letters, etc. This repeated usage means that their production becomes essentially automatic to the individual. However, because of natural variation, a person's signature is never identical on two separate occasions.

Signatures are often the subject of fraudulent reproduction (i.e. forgery). Interestingly, in some instances, individuals may even try to give the impression that their own signatures have been forged on particular documents, with the express intention of later denying authorship. For example, in credit card transactions, an individual may use this 'self-forgery' when purchasing goods or services and then later claim that the card was stolen and their signature forged by another person. The aim of this deception is to avoid paying the credit card bill. In order to be successful, self-forged signatures must be similar enough to the individual's normal signature to avoid arousing suspicion and yet be different enough so that claims of fraudulent use by another are subsequently upheld.

8.2.1 Methods of signature forgery

In order to produce a credible **signature forgery** that will stand up to comparison with the genuine signature, the forger must have access to at least one example of an authentic signature. He or she may fraudulently reproduce this by either tracing or freehand simulation.

Signature forgery
The fraudulent reproduction of the genuine signature of another individual.

Tracing method

There are two methods of tracing a signature. In the *trace-over method*, the sheet of paper on which the forged signature is required is positioned below one bearing the genuine signature. The signature's outline is then traced over and appears as a faint indentation on the sheet below. This impression is then inked in order to produce the forged signature. In the *light box*, or *window*, method, the document bearing the genuine signature is placed on a light box, or against a window, and the sheet of paper on which the forgery is to be written is positioned over it. Illuminated from behind, the target signature becomes sufficiently visible through the overlying sheet to be traced. This is usually done directly by pen but, in some cases, the signature is first traced by pencil and then inked.

Freehand method

This forgery technique tends to produce a smoother and more fluent signature than can be achieved by using one of the tracing methods described above. The degree of success achieved will usually depend on the amount of practice undertaken by the forger in producing the desired signature and the level of skill he or she acquires.

8.2.2 The detection of forged signatures

In forging another's signature, the forger attempts to both copy the genuine signature accurately *and* to maintain the fluency of the writing. In practice, however, these two aims tend to work in opposition to each other. If the writing is speeded up in order to improve its fluency, then accuracy will suffer as a result. Conversely, if the writing is slowed down in order to obtain greater accuracy, then some of the fluency will be lost. The result is necessarily a compromise between the two. Box 8.3 lists some of the characteristics that indicate to the document examiner that a signature, or longer piece of handwriting, may be forged.

The comparison of signatures has much in common with the comparison of handwriting (Section 8.1.2). In order to assess the range of natural variation, it is necessary for the document examiner to have access to sufficient specimen signatures to allow him or her to assess their natural variation. Often this is in the region of 6–12 signatures. Ideally, these should be non-request specimens that are, as far as possible, contemporaneous with the questioned signature. It should be noted that questioned signatures can be compared only with specimen signatures of the same name; it is not usually feasible to make comparisons between signatures of different names.

The document examiner makes an assessment of the similarities and differences between the two types of signatures – questioned and specimen – and their significance. The relatively small amount of information contained within a signature means that every aspect of it must be minutely examined. Based on this comparison, the document examiner may be able to state definitely whether a particular signature is genuine or forged, or it may only be possible to give a qualified conclusion (Section 8.1.2). It is not normally possible to identify who wrote a forged signature since the act of forgery necessarily involves the suppression of the forger's natural handwriting.

Forensic techniques

Box 8.3

Characteristics of forged signatures

There are a number of handwriting characteristics associated with forged signatures that will alert the experienced document examiner to the fact that they may not be genuine. A selection of these is given below (usually, more than one of the following signs are present):

- ■ 'Shaky' handwriting (apparent when viewed under magnification). This occurs when the forger concentrates on copying the genuine signature very accurately by writing slowly (thus resulting in a loss of fluency).
- ■ Unnatural pen lifts. This shows that the forger has paused to check progress.
- ■ Pen strokes with blunt ends where the pen has been lifted from the paper. This indicates that the pen strokes of the writer have been made slowly and deliberately, while in fluent writing, such pen stroke ends tend to be tapered. Low-power microscopy is needed to view this particular feature.
- ■ Evidence of retouching. This indicates that the forger has attempted to patch up 'less good' parts of the signature in an effort to make it more realistic.
- ■ Difference in scale. The writing is noticeably smaller or bigger than the genuine writing.
- ■ Incorrect proportioning of the letters.
- ■ Unnatural similarity between two (or more) signatures. (Such close correspondence between signatures would not occur if the signatures were genuine because of the range of natural variation shown in an individual's normal handwriting.)

In addition to the handwriting characteristics listed above, there may be other features that differ from the victim's normal practice, e.g. the positioning of the signature relative to the rest of the document. Moreover, there may be physical evidence present that has its origins in the type of forgery method used. For example, the trace-over method produces an impression of the signature, which is subsequently inked in (Section 8.2.1). However, it may be possible to detect minute areas of indentation that the pen has missed, by examining the questioned signature under an oblique light source (figure (a)).

(a)
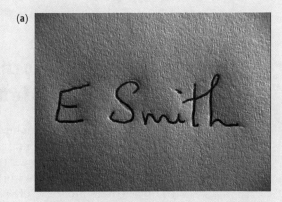

(a) An example of a signature produced using the trace-over method
Note the areas of indentation apparent under the signature, especially under the letters 'S' and 'h', when viewed under oblique light

(b)
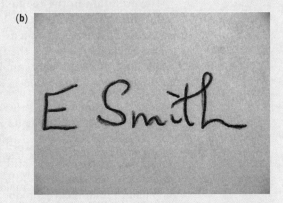

(b) An example of a signature produced using the light box method, first using pencil and then redone in ink
Note the pencil marks apparent underneath the ink when the signature is viewed under infrared light

(Images by Andrew and Julie Jackson)

▶

Box 8.3 *continued*

In the light box method, in those cases where the genuine signature is traced first in pencil and then redone in ink, viewing the signature under infrared light can reveal the pencil marks underneath the ink (figure (b)).

Much of the information presented in this box is equally applicable to longer pieces of forged handwriting. However, it is worth noting that, in such instances, the act of forgery becomes harder with each additional word. This can be explained by the fact that the imitation of another's writing style necessitates the suppression of the forger's own natural handwriting. Inevitably, these suppressed characteristics begin to surface as the amount of writing increases, becoming ever more apparent in the forged material.

8.3 Typed, word-processed and photocopied documents

The technology used to produce documents in the office environment, and indeed in the home, has changed dramatically over the last 40 years. From their advent at the end of the nineteenth century until the 1960s, manually operated typewriters were prevalent in the office workplace. However, during the 1960s and 1970s, electric typewriters progressively replaced the old-style manual typewriters. From the 1980s onwards, further advances were made with the progressive introduction of computer-based word-processor systems. This development in the production of original single documents has been paralleled by significant improvements in the technology used to produce copies of documents, to the photocopiers and facsimile (fax) machines commonly used today.

The evolution in the technological production and reproduction of documents within the office environment has necessitated a concomitant development in the expertise of forensic document examiners. The questions most frequently asked of them are likely to concern the type of machine used to produce a questioned document (and, if possible, its make and model) and whether a particular suspect machine was used to produce a specific questioned document or documents.

8.3.1 Typed documents

Although computer-based word-processor systems effectively dominate the modern workplace, typewriters are still used by a substantial number of individuals. In the recent case of the serial killer Dr Harold Shipman, a typewriter was used by Shipman to fraudulently produce the will of one of his victims (Chapter 7, Box 7.2) The investigation of typed documents, therefore, still forms an important part of the document examiners' repertoire. Typewriters, as mentioned previously, may be either manually or electrically operated.

Manual typewriters have fixed typebars, which means that the style of their typeface cannot be changed except by a typewriter mechanic. Their mode of operation involves the depression of character keys on the keyboard, which, in turn, causes the corresponding typebars to swing up and the typeface to strike on an inked ribbon, thus transferring an image of the typeface onto the paper beneath. With continued use, manual typewriters become progressively more worn and damaged and this deterioration may become apparent in the appearance of the typed material. For example, individual characters:

- may appear out of alignment (i.e. they are too much to the right/left and/or too high/low);
- may not be uniformly inked;
- may show evidence of a damaged typeface; and/or
- may show evidence of a typeface that has accumulated dirt in a characteristic fashion.

Such defects, in combination, help to individualise a particular machine and may make it possible to identify it as the source of a particular typed document (or documents). They can also be used to show if two different typewritten documents were produced on the same machine. It should be noted that the evidential value of damage defects is greater than that of misalignments.

Single element electric typewriters differ from manual typewriters in that their typeface is not fixed but carried on a single element that can easily be replaced. This element may be in the form of a 'golfball' (where the characters cover the surface of the ball and are made to strike the paper by the ball's rotation) or a 'daisywheel' (where the characters are carried individually at the end of spokes radiating from a central hub). Whatever the type, these single elements inevitably show signs of wear with increasing use and develop characteristic faults, which may help to make them uniquely identifiable. However, any such individualising features will be lost when the operator replaces the deteriorating element with a different one (although their transitory existence may still be useful in dating documents). As well as replacement for reasons of dilapidation, typing elements may also be interchanged when a different style of typeface is required.

Identification of the type of typewriter

Familiarity with the different typefaces used by typewriter manufacturers will assist the document examiner in identifying the make and, possibly, the model of the typewriter that has been used to produce a particular document. To this end, several classification systems based on differences in spacing and typeface are available, for example that constructed by Interpol (the International Criminal Police Organization). Such information will obviously be helpful in the search for a particular suspect machine.

Comparison of typescripts

In order to investigate possible links between a questioned typewritten document and a specific typewriter, it is necessary to gather specimen typewriting for comparative purposes. Ideally, the forensic document examiner will have access to the suspect machine itself and use this to produce multiple specimen copies of the questioned typewriting. As well as being identical in content, copies should be as near as possible in appearance to that of the disputed document and take into account, for example, the state of the ribbon used. In the absence of the suspect machine itself, similar material that has been typed on it in the past must be collected, ideally from around the time on which the questioned typewriting was produced.

In many instances, a careful side-by-side examination of the questioned and specimen typescript is sufficient to ascertain whether both were produced on the same machine. During this process, similarities and differences between individual characters, together with correspondence, or otherwise, between other distinctive features such as obvious misalignments are duly noted. However, sometimes, it is necessary to scrutinise the documents more closely before a conclusion can be reached. In these cases, specially designed grids, whose line spacing equates to the spacing used by typewriter manufacturers, can be useful in detecting less obvious misalignments in the placing of individual characters.

As well as comparing the questioned and specimen typescript, the document examiner will also carefully examine the typewriter itself, and, in the case of single element electric typewriters, any relevant typing elements, if these are available. Typewriting ribbons (both inked and correction types) associated with the suspect machine may also yield important evidential material and should be included in the investigation.

8.3.2 Word-processed documents

In the modern office environment, computer-based word-processor systems have almost totally eclipsed typewriters as the means of document production. In essence, keyboard operators use word-processor programs in order to compose documents, which are then usually stored electronically on computer file. These files may be printed out as and when required, using any of the several types of computer printers available on the market. Box 8.4 describes the three main types that are currently in common use.

In modern word-processor systems, the keyboard operator can easily change the font size, style and spacing of the typeface by selecting these parameters from a menu that is predetermined by the word-processing software. Importantly, the same software may be used on many word-processing computers. As a consequence, it is not possible, by the examination of any one document, to establish whether a particular computer was used to compose it. This is in marked contrast to the situation in which a typewritten document may be linked to the machine on which it was typed (Section 8.3.1).

It is also difficult to link a document with a specific computer printer beyond the level of its class characteristics. For example, in the case of ink-jet printers (described in Box 8.4), the printed text has a slightly blurred outline, which is characteristic of documents produced by this type of printer. However, identification beyond this level is much more challenging. In contrast, in laser printers (Box 8.4), it may be possible to link a particular document with a suspect printer, or show that two or more documents have been printed on the same machine, if there are faults present on the drum that are transferred to the printed page. In such cases, the appearance of more than one mark per page is usual and is due to the fact that the drum circumference is generally less than the length of an A4 piece of paper.

Further information

Box 8.4

The three main types of computer printer

Dot-matrix printers

This is the oldest type of printer. It incorporates a printer head that contains and controls a series of electromagnetically operated pins. Specific configurations of these pins correspond to individual printed characters. When the configured pins strike the paper through an inked fabric ribbon, they transfer a series of ink dots onto the paper to produce the desired character in printed form.

Ink-jet printers

In ink-jet printers, ink is forced through a nozzle to form the printed characters. The exact mechanism by which the ink is delivered depends on the type of ink-jet printer used. Briefly, in 'continuous stream' printers, ink is delivered in a continuous stream and forms droplets that are subsequently charged. Those charged droplets needed to form the printed character are deflected towards the paper, while the remainder are ultimately returned to the ink reservoir. In contrast, 'drop on demand' printers have a grid of minute nozzles through which only those ink droplets needed to make up the printed character are forced.

Laser printers

Laser printers are capable of producing text characters of a consistently high standard. Their operation is based on the same principle as that used in photocopiers (Section 8.3.3). They contain a photosensitive, positively charged, rotating drum. Acting on information received from the computer, a laser beam selectively discharges the drum so that a positively charged image of the document is left behind on its surface. The next stage involves the application of a negatively charged toner (i.e. a black or other coloured powder), which adheres to the positively charged document image. The toner is then transferred to a sheet of paper that is made to pass over the rotating drum. Finally, the toner is fused to the paper's surface by the application of pressure or heat to produce the finished print.

8.3.3 Photocopied documents

In the past, photocopiers required paper of a special type but modern photocopiers use plain paper. Plain paper photocopiers are extensively used in the office workplace for the reproduction of documents, as well as being widely available to the general public, for example in shops (newsagents, post offices, etc.) and libraries. They operate on the same principle as the laser printer (described in Box 8.4), using light to facilitate the creation of an image of the original document. This image is formed using toner (a coloured, usually black, powder) that is fused to the surface of the paper, thereby making the copy. The forensic document examiner may be able to identify the model of photocopier used to produce a disputed document by the examination of certain features of the photocopy. Such features may include any characteristic marks caused by the mechanism used to handle the paper during copying, and the morphology and chemical composition of the toner used.

The document examiner may also be able to link a particular copy to a specific photocopier. As was the case with laser printers (Box 8.4), this may be facilitated by the appearance of regularly spaced marks on the photocopy that correspond to damage features present on the rotating drum. More transitory in nature, but often of great significance, are those marks appearing on the copy as specks or dots,

Trash marks
Random marks present on photocopied documents that originate from the photocopier used for their reproduction.

either singly or collectively, often referred to as '**trash marks**'. These are caused by the presence of, for example, dust or dried correction fluid, on the glass sheet on which the original document is placed for copying (known as the platen). As well as being important in identifying the machine used to reproduce a disputed document, trash marks can sometimes provide evidence to link together several photocopies and show that they have been produced using the same photocopier.

8.4 Printed documents

Mass-produced printed documents are an integral part of modern society. There are a wide variety of different types in common use, each fulfilling a particular function. Examples include banknotes, passports, chequebooks, vehicle registration documents, MOT test certificates and tax discs. Each of these types has an intrinsic value, for example, as a means of personal identification, as proof of ownership, or in monetary terms. As a result, many types of printed documents are prone to fraudulent reproduction.

Further information

Box 8.5

Traditional printing methods

Screen printing
This printing method involves the use of a mesh screen made, for example, of silk or nylon, which is masked by a stencil. Ink is forced through the screen, thus transferring the stencilled design onto the surface of the material to be printed.

Letterpress
In this method (also known as *relief printing*), the printing design stands proud of its background. Only this raised area is inked and, when this is brought into contact with the surface of the paper, the design is printed. This method is used extensively for the production of newsprint.

Gravure
In gravure (also known as *intaglio*), the image to be printed is incised into the surface of the printing plate. This engraved area consists of hundreds of tiny sunken cells. The entire printing plate is inked and then the surface ink scraped off by means of a metal blade. When the paper is pressed against the plate by roller, the ink left

behind in the printing cells is transferred to the paper in the desired pattern.

Lithography
Lithography has been practised for over two hundred years and is currently the most widely used of the printing methods. In this method, the printing plate, which is usually composed of aluminium, is first treated with a greasy substance to form an image of the desired design. The plate then comes into contact with a roller that moistens the non-printing area of the plate, followed by contact with an inked roller. As the grease attracts the ink but the moisture repels it, ink is taken up *only* by the greased printing image. The plate next makes contact with a 'blanket' cylinder (composed of rubber) onto which the inked design is transferred (i.e. offset). The image on the blanket cylinder is then printed onto the paper. The term '*offset lithography*' is sometimes more accurately used to describe this method of printing where there is no direct contact between printing plate and paper.

The scrutiny of counterfeit documents is a routine part of the work of forensic document examiners. For this reason, it is necessary for practitioners to be familiar with the different methods used to produce printed documents. The four main types of traditional printing method are outlined in Box 8.5. All of these conventional methods involve the use of pressure to transfer ink to create the image on the paper. In contrast, modern computer printing technologies involve minimal or no contact. These are termed non-impact printing methods and include ink-jet and laser printing (Box 8.4).

Further information

Box 8.6

The use of anti-counterfeiting measures in the euro currency

On 1 January 2002, the euro currency (consisting of seven different banknotes and eight different coins) was introduced into 12 European countries. At a stroke, the individual currencies of these participating countries were replaced by a new currency. The sudden circulation of vast numbers of new banknotes and coins (14.5 billion and 50 billion respectively), together with a general public unused to handling the new currency, potentially provided an exceptional opportunity for counterfeiting, particularly with regard to the euro banknotes.

In order to minimise this risk, each euro note, printed on pure cotton paper, includes a combination of five different, easily visible security features within each banknote (see table).

In addition to those features that are designed to be easily recognised by the general public, the euro notes incorporate further security devices designed to be detected by equipment routinely used by money-handling organisations such as banks and shops. Examples of these include fluorescent materials, observable under specialised lighting conditions, and microprint, which can be seen under magnification.

Reference

Sample, I. (2002) Making a mint. *New Scientist* 19 January, pp. 36–9 (this gives further information on inbuilt security features used in bank notes).

The security features of different denominations of euro banknotes (indicated by ✓ where present)

Security feature	Mode of detection	Denomination of euro banknote						
		5	10	20	50	100	200	500
Raised print	By touch	✓	✓	✓	✓	✓	✓	✓
Watermark	By sight using transmitted light	✓	✓	✓	✓	✓	✓	✓
Security thread	By sight using transmitted light	✓	✓	✓	✓	✓	✓	✓
Hologram foil stripe	By sight with banknote tilted under reflected light	✓	✓	✓				
Iridescent stripe	By sight with banknote tilted under bright reflected light	✓	✓	✓				
Hologram patch	By sight with banknote tilted under reflected light				✓	✓	✓	✓
Colour changing ink feature on the value numerals	By sight. Colour change is from purple to olive-green or brown				✓	✓	✓	✓

If a particular document is suspected of being counterfeit, a comparison with examples (preferably several) of the genuine article will help establish whether or not it is authentic. This comparison may involve the examination of a number of different aspects. These include the process used to produce the document (i.e. printing or photocopying), the presence, if any, of in-built security measures, the types of inks or toners used, and the properties of the paper. If a printed document is shown to be counterfeit, it may be possible, in some cases, to trace it back to those responsible. For example, trash marks present on a photocopied counterfeit document may be used to link it with a suspected photocopying machine (Section 8.3.3).

The quality of the printing of a counterfeit document, and therefore its potential to be passed off as genuine, will depend on the skill, experience and resources of the individual(s) involved. In order to combat the widespread threat posed by counterfeiting, most genuine printed documents include one or more inbuilt security features. Box 8.6 describes the anti-counterfeiting measures taken with respect to the recently introduced euro banknotes.

8.5 The analysis of handwriting inks

There are a number of different types of writing implement that may be used in the preparation of handwritten documents and with each of these is associated a particular kind of ink. Currently, the most popular type of pen is the ballpoint, which was introduced in the 1940s, and which has now largely replaced the more traditional fountain pen. Other modern types include felt-tipped, fibre-tipped and roller-ball pens. A visual examination of the writing on a document, using low-powered microscopy, may provide general information on the type of ink, and therefore the type of writing instrument, used. For example, text written using ballpoint ink is readily identifiable, being thick and glossy in appearance, often with characteristic striation marks. These striations originate from incomplete inking of the ball that is used to transfer the ink to the page.

8.5.1 Comparison of inks

Beyond the broad identification of the type of writing implement used, analysis of the ink itself can yield valuable information about whether any alterations or additions have been made to the original document. Much of the work carried out by forensic document examiners in this area therefore involves a comparison of the inks found on a particular document to establish whether they are different. The discovery of more than one ink on a single document might suggest that it has been altered at some stage.

The tests used for ink analysis fall into two broad categories: non-destructive and destructive. Non-destructive tests are used preferentially before destructive ones and mainly concern the examination of the inked text under different lighting conditions (Figure 8.2). Furthermore, infrared and Raman microscopes have now been developed that make it possible to obtain both infrared and Raman spectra of inks *in situ* on documents. The theoretical basis of each of these non-destructive techniques is described in Chapter 3, Box 3.9.

(a)

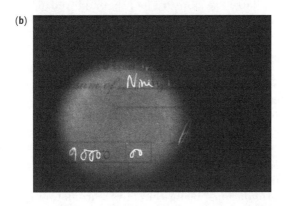

(Images by Andrew
and Julie Jackson)

(b)

Figure 8.2 A portion of a receipt written in black ink viewed under the Video Spectral Comparator (a) in normal lighting conditions and (b) illuminated with light of wavelengths 440–580 nm and viewed through a filter that removes light with wavelengths shorter than 645 nm
Note that in (b) it becomes apparent that two different black inks have been used and the receipt has been altered

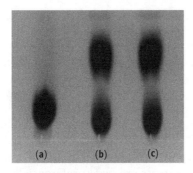

(Image by Andrew and
Julie Jackson)

Figure 8.3 A thin-layer chromatography (TLC) plate of a questioned black ink (b) and two control black inks, (a) and (c), observed using the Video Spectral Comparator (VSC)
This image was created by illuminating the plate with light of wavelength 530–660 nm and observing the radiation emitted by the plate at wavelengths of approx. 665 nm and above. The colours of the image were inverted for clarity prior to printing. Note that the questioned ink (b) clearly matches control (c) but not control (a)

If the application of various non-destructive techniques is unsuccessful in detecting the presence of different inks on a disputed document, then the next step is to apply the so-called destructive tests. The term 'destructive' is, in fact, somewhat misleading in this context as these types of test necessitate the removal of only minute amounts of ink. Nonetheless, it is advisable to make a permanent record of a questioned document at this stage, either by taking a photograph or photocopying, before any destructive tests are carried out. Once samples have been taken, the usual means of discriminating between them is to separate their constituent dye components using **chromatography**, and then to compare the results (Figure 8.3). There are two chromatographic methods that are suitable for ink samples – high-performance liquid chromatography (HPLC) and thin-layer chromatography (TLC) – and, of these, the latter is more frequently employed. These techniques are described in Chapter 11, Box 11.5.

Chromatography
A technique in which the constituents of a substance are separated by their differential migration through an appropriate medium.

8.5.2 Dating of inks

Although techniques for the comparison of inks are relatively well developed, there are, as yet, no reliable methods for accurately ageing the inks used on documents. However, in some cases, a piece of written text may be exposed as fraudulent, if, for example, it can be demonstrated that the ink used only became commercially available *after* the date on which the document purports to have been written. In the United States, the US Treasury Department (Bureau of Alcohol, Tobacco and Firearms) has built up an extensive, and apparently unique, reference library of commercial ink formulations, using thin-layer chromatograms to facilitate the dating of inks. Moreover, this department has also been instrumental in encouraging a number of US manufacturers to chemically 'tag' their inks on an annual basis, in order to pin-point their year of manufacture.

8.6 Paper analysis

Currently, the majority of documents are produced on paper and, consequently, paper analysis forms an important part of the work undertaken by forensic document examiners. Although much talked about, the 'paperless office', where most, or all, information is stored and communicated electronically, has become a reality only in a few specialist areas. The use of paper still represents the preferred option for many types of documentation.

8.6.1 Comparison of paper

Much of the work undertaken by forensic document examiners skilled in paper analysis involves a comparison of the characteristics of two (or more) pieces of paper to ascertain whether or not they may have a common origin. Essentially, the properties of paper are determined by what happens during the various stages of the manufacturing process (Box 8.7). This process involves many variables, such as the type of raw fibres used, the choice of sizing agent and the decision whether or not to bleach the fibres. The paper manufacturer can alter these variables to optimise

Further information

Box 8.7

The manufacture of paper

Paper is composed primarily of cellulose – a polysaccharide that forms the main structural material in plant cell walls. In general terms, paper quality is positively correlated with the percentage of cellulose that it contains. Paper can be made from almost any type of fibrous material. For example, cotton, linen, hemp and sisal are all sources of cellulose that may be utilised by the paper manufacturing industry. However, the most commonly used material is wood, usually from coniferous trees.

Prior to their use in paper manufacture, the fibres, whatever their origin, must be treated, either mechanically and/or chemically, to form pulp. The pulped fibres are then combined with copious amounts of water. At this stage, the pulp is usually bleached and other materials, such as whiteners, dyes and kaolin (china clay), may be added, depending on the properties desired in the finished product. A suitable sizing agent, e.g. starch or gelatin, is added to help bind the fibres together.

In the next stage, the prepared mixture is introduced onto a moving frame, which retains the fibrous material, while allowing most of the water to escape. The resultant fibrous mat is pressed to remove yet more water and finally dried. During these final stages of treatment, a watermark – a patterned area containing fewer fibres per unit area – may be introduced into the paper by a raised design present on a special type of roller known as the 'dandy roll'. In some cases, the final product is given a special coating if, for example, a glossy finish is required.

the efficiency of their production process, while producing paper of the desired type and quality.

The forensic document examiner makes use of these properties when searching for similarities and differences between two (or more) pieces of paper. There are basically two categories of tests available, namely non-destructive and destructive. Non-destructive tests are applied first, as these do not entail any damage to the documents. Such tests usually involve a visual comparison of features, such as the colour, size and shape of the sheets of paper, while thickness may be measured using a micrometer. Another non-destructive test that may be applied in this regard is a comparison of the fluorescent properties of the pieces of paper when viewed under ultraviolet (UV) light.

If it is deemed necessary to proceed further with the comparison, then there are a number of destructive tests that can be applied. However, it should be noted that the amount of paper required for such tests is very small and therefore the damage to the document limited. Destructive tests can yield information on a number of different properties of the paper, which can be used for comparative purposes, including:

■ the types of raw fibre used (established by microscopic examination);

■ the type of pre-treatment used to prepare the pulp, i.e. whether chemical or mechanical;

■ the nature of the surface coating (established by X-ray powder diffraction, see Chapter 3, Box 3.10).

8.6.2 Dating of paper

Another important aspect of paper analysis is the dating of paper as this may yield valuable information about the authenticity of disputed documents. In this respect, the **watermarks** used by paper manufacturers are particularly useful. Watermarks contain fewer fibres per unit area than the rest of the sheet of paper and, as such, are usually visible when the paper is held up to the light (Figure 8.4). If the watermark is obscured by text or other marks, various techniques can be employed to reproduce a clearer image of the design. For example, sandwiching the questioned document between a radioactive source and a sheet of photographic paper may clearly reveal the pattern of the watermark on the photographic paper once it has been developed.

The design of a watermark can be used to identify the paper manufacturer responsible. Furthermore, if the design used by a particular manufacturer has been

Watermark
A recognisable design incorporated into paper during the manufacturing process by reducing the number of fibres present within the patterned area.

Case study
Box 8.8

The Hitler diaries

In this classic case of publishing fraud, the Hitler diaries were eventually exposed as forgeries through an examination of the types of materials used to produce them. However, this revelation did not occur until after the diaries had been accepted, on the basis of handwriting examination, as the genuine diaries of Adolf Hitler.

In February 1981, a set of three, black-bound diaries, purportedly handwritten by Adolf Hitler, were brought to the attention of the German publishing company Grüner and Jahr by Gerd Heidemann, a journalist on its news magazine *Stern*. The source of the diaries, according to Heidemann, was a collector of Nazi memorabilia. On the basis of this sample, the publishing company agreed to purchase 27 volumes of the Hitler diaries and also a previously unknown third volume of his autobiography, *Mein Kampf*, for just under 2.5 million German marks.

Three separate document examiners made comparisons between the handwriting in the diaries and specimen samples of what was believed to be Hitler's handwriting. As a result of their independent examinations, they each concluded that the diaries and the handwriting samples had been written by the same person. On the basis of these results, the diaries were accepted to be authentic. However, later investigations into the case revealed that the supposedly genuine handwriting samples provided for comparison purposes had in fact been written by the same forger (Konrad Kujau) who had been responsible for producing the diaries.

It was due to subsequent investigations by the West German police (at the behest of the publishing company Grüner and Jahr) that the Hitler diaries were eventually revealed as fraudulent. The police focused their attention, not on the handwriting itself, but on the paper used in the diaries and the inks used to write the entries. They discovered that a paper-whitening substance had been used to treat the paper; a finding that was subsequently confirmed by scientists from the German government. As this chemical was not in use until after 1954, the author of the handwritten diaries could not possibly have been Adolf Hitler, who committed suicide in 1945. Other types of material used in the diaries provided additional evidence that the diaries had a more recent origin. For example, the polyester and viscose threads used to attach seals to the diaries were not available until after the Second World War. Furthermore, scientists demonstrated that the writing in one of the diaries (that for 1943) was less than 1 year old at the time of their examination.

As a result of this case, both Heidemann, the staff journalist, and Kujau, the forger, received prison sentences; the former for misappropriating money from his employer.

(Reproduced by kind permission of John Dickinson Stationery Limited)

(Image by Andrew and Julie Jackson)

Figure 8.4 The Basildon Bond watermark viewed using transmitted light

altered periodically and such changes have been recorded, then it should be possible to date the paper bearing the watermark, at least to within a given time period. In addition, there are other aspects of the production process that can be used to ascertain the authenticity of a questioned document. If certain materials are identified in the paper used for a disputed document that were not available at the purported time of writing, then this provides compelling evidence that the origin of these documents is more modern and that they are not, in fact, genuine. This type of evidence was brought to bear in the case of the Hitler diaries (Box 8.8).

8.7 Tears, folds, holes, obliterations, erasures and indentations

In addition to those aspects of document examination previously discussed in this chapter, there are a number of other features that can yield important information concerning the history, origin and/or authenticity of questioned documents. These are examined in turn in this final section.

8.7.1 Tears

It may be possible to demonstrate that two or more pieces of paper were originally part of a larger sheet by mechanically fitting the torn pieces together. However, it should be borne in mind that there is a very real possibility that similar tear patterns have arisen as a result of two or more sheets of paper being superimposed on one another and torn simultaneously. Further evidence for the common origin of torn pieces of paper can be provided if other features, such as watermarks and/or writing, are present on both sides of the divide and can be clearly shown to match. An interesting historical example occurred in Lancashire, UK, in 1794. At this time, firearms were muzzle-loaded, which necessitated holding the projectile in place with wadding. In the case in question, a piece of paper wadding was recovered from the gunshot wound of a murder victim during autopsy. By the process of matching, this fragment was subsequently found to have been torn from a ballad sheet found in the pocket of an apprehended suspect. The suspect was found guilty and sentenced to death. In more recent times, the matching of torn sheets of paper can have particular relevance with regard to drug dealing, where portions of drugs may be wrapped in scraps of printed paper torn from newspapers or magazines. In such cases, it may be possible to match individual fragments and even to trace the torn pieces to the original newspaper or magazine from which they were taken.

Some types of document are designed to incorporate a line of weakness, such as a series of short cuts in the paper or a line of perforations (either elliptical or circular), so that part of the document is more easily torn off. A common example is the chequebook, where cheques are torn out when required, each leaving behind a stub in the chequebook. Such tears are often irregular in nature, leaving pieces of paper of uneven length on either side of the tear. In these cases, it may be possible to make a match between two parts of a document torn along perforations. Other examples include books of matches, as may be found in arson cases, and perforated sheets of stamps.

8.7.2 Folds

If a document shows evidence of folding, this may indicate that it has been contained within an envelope. If two or more separate sheets of paper show a similar pattern of folds, this may be consistent with them having been folded together in the same bundle at some time.

The presence of folds on a document may yield significant information about the order in which ink lines have been made and, consequently, the order of writing. This is possible because the nature of the ink mark at the point of fold is different depending on whether it was made before or after the document was folded. Essentially, those ink marks made after folding contain comparatively more ink, partly because the surface of the paper acquires damage along the fold line.

8.7.3 Holes

Holes present in documents are often the result of stapling; a method used for fastening two or more separate sheets of paper together, usually in the vicinity of the top left- or right-hand corner. In stapling, the open ends of the staple are forced to pierce through the sheets of paper and then bent towards each other under the final sheet, thus holding them all together. The position, number and even appearance of staple holes may provide useful information to the forensic document examiner. A close match between the position and size of staple holes on two, or more, separate sheets of paper is consistent with them having been previously attached together. If patterns of distortion around the staple holes on separate sheets are also similar, then this provides a further indication that they were once held to one another.

Obliterations
Segments of writing that have been obscured by the application of an appropriate substance such as a correction fluid.

8.7.4 Obliterations

During the course of their work, it is likely that document examiners will encounter portions of text that have been deliberately obliterated by the application of certain substances. These **obliterations** may have been made using the same ink that was used to create the original text, or a different substance such as another ink or a correction fluid. Different approaches may be taken to decipher the writing hidden beneath the obliterating medium. In some cases, it may be possible to interpret the original writing by simply examining the reverse of the document. Naturally, under these circumstances, any writing apparent will appear as a mirror image.

If the previous approach is not successful, examination under specialist lighting conditions will often enable the original writing to be read. There are several pieces of equipment commercially available for this purpose, such as the Video Spectral Comparator (VSC) built by Foster & Freeman Limited (Figure 8.5) and the Docucenter 3000 made by the Swiss firm Projectina AG. Among the features of this type of apparatus are a variety of light sources, including different wavelength bands of visible light, ultraviolet and infrared in reflectance mode, and transmitted white light. These features can be used to help distinguish between the different types of inks, if more than one is present (Figure 8.6), and can also be used to reveal writing obscured by correction fluid. It is worth noting that these types of apparatus can be used to examine objects other than questioned documents, including thin-layer chromatography (TLC) plates (Figure 8.3). In the case of typewritten material obliterated by correction fluid, the application of a suitable solvent may be successful. This renders the dried fluid translucent, for a brief period of time, thus enabling the typewriting underneath to be read.

(Photograph by Andrew Jackson, Staffordshire University, UK)

Figure 8.5 The Video Spectral Comparator (VSC) made by Foster & Freeman Ltd

(Images by Andrew
and Julie Jackson)

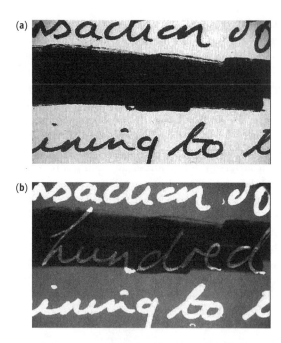

Figure 8.6 A portion of obliterated handwriting viewed under the Video Spectral Comparator (a) in normal lighting conditions and (b) illuminated with light of wavelengths 580–700 nm and viewed through a filter that removes light with wavelengths shorter than 735 nm

8.7.5 Erasures

Erasures
Portions of writing that have been removed by either mechanical or chemical means.

In some texts, the term 'erasure' is used to include the application of correction fluids. However, in this book, correction fluids are considered under the heading 'obliterations' (see previous section) while **erasures** are interpreted as those instances where writing is actually *removed* from a document, using either mechanical or chemical means. The mechanical erasure of writing may involve the use of a suitably abrasive medium, e.g. hard rubber, or the removal of slivers of paper by means of a sharp instrument such as a knife. Chemical methods of erasure include the application of bleaching agents, which convert the dye into colourless materials, and the use of certain solvents. Whatever the method of erasure, it may be possible to detect minute traces of the original writing material, by, for example, inducing them to luminesce.

8.7.6 Indentations

Indented writing
Writing that appears in the form of an impression on a surface below that originally written on.

In forensic document analysis, indentations are primarily associated with writing. Indented writing has already been mentioned in this chapter with reference to the 'trace-over' method of forging signatures (Box 8.3). However, there are other circumstances under which **indented writing** may appear. This phenomenon commonly occurs when an individual writes on one document while it is resting on another. In a similar manner, if, for example, a diary or pad of paper were used, indentations of the handwriting may be apparent, albeit with increasing faintness, on several subsequent pages. As well as direct impressions resulting from the act of writing itself, 'secondary impressions' may be created under certain circumstances. For example, impressions of writing may be transferred by contact between documents when they are stored together in close proximity.

The method selected for the detection of indented writing is influenced by the depth to which the impression has been made. If the indented writing is sufficiently deep, it may be possible to read what is written by illuminating the document with an oblique light source. However, a more sensitive method, suitable for shallower impressions, is the application of the electrostatic detection apparatus (ESDA) (Box 8.9). It is noteworthy that ESDA does not always reveal the presence of some deep impressions that are nonetheless visible in oblique lighting. Thus, these two methods complement each other.

Forensic techniques

Box 8.9

The electrostatic detection apparatus (ESDA)

The electrostatic detection apparatus (ESDA) is a piece of equipment produced by Foster & Freeman Limited. The technique of electrostatic detection, which has been routinely used by document examiners over the past 20 years, is mainly employed for the visualisation of indented writing. However, newer applications have been developed for this non-destructive technique within the area of forensic document analysis. These include the examination of torn edges of paper for possible matching and the determination of the sequence of writing impressions and inkstrokes. ESDA may also be used to detect indented footwear impressions on paper surfaces (Chapter 4, Section 4.2).

Method of use
The piece of paper[*] bearing the indented writing is placed on the porous bronze plate of the ESDA and a thin Mylar® film positioned on top. Air is drawn downwards through the plate by a pump, thus holding the paper and transparent plastic sheet securely in position. The Mylar film is then given an electrostatic charge by moving a highly charged wire (known as a corona) backwards and forwards across its surface, at a height of approximately 2 cm (Figure (a)).

The potential of this electrostatic charge on the plastic sheet is determined by the dielectric properties of the paper, which, in turn, are influenced by the presence of indented writing. Essentially, those areas corresponding to the indentations will have the greatest opposite charge.

The next stage involves the application of photocopy toner powder to the Mylar sheet. This may be applied either in the form of a cloud of powder or by mixing it with glass beads. In the latter case, the mixture is poured over the surface of the sheet and the beads and excess powder collected in a trough by tilting the plate (Figure (b)). Whatever the method of application, the toner adheres selectively to those areas of greater potential which correspond to the indented writing. The clarity of the image produced on the Mylar sheet is positively correlated to the depth of the indentation. This grey or black image is temporary in nature but can be preserved for future use by the application of 'sticky-backed' transparent plastic.

[*]Prior to ESDA examination, submitted documents must not have been treated with any solvent (such as used in the visualisation of latent fingerprints) or the technique will not work.

▶

Box 8.9 continued

(a)

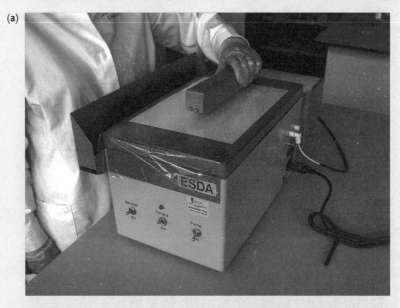

(b)

(a) Charging the film using the corona and (b) applying the photocopy toner powder

(Photographs by Andrew Jackson, Staffordshire University, UK)

8.8 Summary

■ The term 'questioned document' may be applied to any document over which some query has been raised (usually concerning its authenticity or origin) and which may, as a result, be submitted for forensic investigation. Much of the work of the forensic document examiner is concerned with the comparison of questioned handwriting with specimen handwriting, with the aim of identifying the individual concerned. Signatures suspected of being forged also form a regular part of the document examiner's caseload. If genuine signatures are available, then a comparison can be made between them and the suspect one, in a similar manner to that used for handwriting comparisons. However, it is not usually possible to identify the person responsible for forging a signature.

■ In addition to handwriting and signature investigation, the forensic document examiner may be asked to scrutinise disputed office documents, such as those produced by typing or word-processing, or reproduced by photocopying. Information sought may include the type of machine used, whether several documents have been generated on the same machine and/or whether a particular document can be shown to have originated from a given machine.

■ In the case of printed documents that are suspected of being counterfeit items, the primary concern of the document examiner is to establish whether they are authentic, by comparison with examples of the genuine article. In this respect, the analysis of ink and paper may supply significant information, although these types of analysis have a much wider applicability within document examination. For example, a comparison of ink samples taken from a document can be used to ascertain whether or not it has been altered. Finally, the examination of any tears, folds, holes, obliterations, erasures or indentations present on questioned documents may yield valuable information concerning their authenticity, origin and/or history.

Problems

1. With reference to the development of handwriting within the individual, discuss the difference between class and individual characteristics and explain how the latter are used by document examiners in handwriting comparisons.

2. The specimen handwriting required for comparison with questioned handwriting may be obtained in two different ways, namely request and non-request specimens. Discuss the relative merits of these two options.

3. Describe those characteristics of forged signatures that indicate to the document examiner that they may not be genuine. Where appropriate, make reference to the type of forgery method used.

4. (a) Outline the main types of traditional and modern printing technologies.

   (b) With reference to a particular example, describe the inbuilt security features that have been incorporated to combat the threat of counterfeiting.

5. A comparison of inks used on a particular questioned document revealed the presence of more than one type of ink. Discuss the different methods that could have been used to obtain this information and the possible implication of these results for the authenticity of the document concerned.

6. The characteristics of paper are influenced by what happens during the manufacturing process. With reference to specific characteristics, describe how these may be used in (a) the comparison of paper and (b) the dating of paper.

7. Several separate typed sheets, all showing evidence of both stapling and folding, are submitted for forensic examination. Describe what types of comparative analysis the document examiner could use to ascertain whether these separate sheets share a common origin.

8. This case concerns a disputed letter. The alleged recipient of this letter claimed that the reason that the signature appeared on a different portion of paper from that of the text is because the two were separated by the action of an automatic letter-opener, which not only cut the envelope but also severed the letter along a fold. The purported sender of the letter claimed that she had never signed the document concerned and that the supposed recipient must have fabricated the excuse outlined above. Given the two portions of paper, how would you proceed to establish whose explanation is more likely to be the truth?

Further reading

Ellen, D. (1997) *The scientific examination of documents* (2nd edn). London: Taylor & Francis.

Hilton, O. (1992) *Scientific examination of questioned documents*. Boca Raton, FL: CRC Press, Inc.

Levinson, J. (2001) *Questioned documents: a lawyer's handbook* (revised edn). London: Academic Press.

Morris, R. N. (2000) *Forensic handwriting identification: fundamental concepts and principles*. London: Academic Press.

Nickell, J. (2005) *Detecting forgery: forensic investigation of documents*. Lexington, KY: The University Press of Kentucky.

Firearms 9

Chapter objectives

After reading this chapter, you should be able to:

> Recognise the forensic value of the examination of firearms and firearms-related physical evidence.

> Describe the essential characteristics of the common types of firearm and ammunition encountered during forensic investigation.

> Understand the terms internal, external and terminal ballistics.

> Discuss the key types of information that may be obtained by the examination of suspect firearms, spent cartridge cases, projectiles and other ejecta, and appreciate how such information can be gained.

Introduction

Under English law, a firearm, as defined in Section 57 of the Firearms Act 1968 (as currently amended) is 'a lethal barrelled weapon of any description from which any shot, bullet or other missile can be discharged...'. Also, included in this legal definition are all prohibited weapons, any component of these prohibited or lethal barrelled weapons, and any accessory adapted or designed to deaden the sound or decrease the flash produced by the weapon being fired.

Criminals use firearms to shoot and beat people, resulting in injury and death. They also employ these weapons to intimidate and to cause damage to property. Although it is little comfort, as indicated by the data presented in Figure 9.1, by international standards, the availability of firearms is relatively low in the United Kingdom, as is the level of firearms-related death. Furthermore, the proportion of crime that involves firearms is relatively small. Home Office statistics reveal that for England and Wales, all notifiable offences in which the use of firearms was reported and that the police recorded remained at a level of 0.2–0.4 per cent of all notifiable offences throughout the period 1992 to 2004. Moreover, if air weapons are excluded, the percentage drops significantly, e.g. in the reporting year 2004–05, the figure decreases from 0.4 to 0.2 per cent. Nonetheless, the criminal use of firearms remains a significant issue. The Home Office reports that for England and Wales, in the year 2004–05, there was a total of 22 789

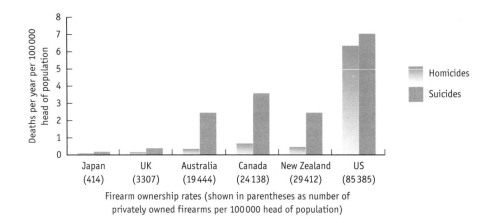

Figure 9.1 The incidence of suicides and homicides in which firearms were involved and firearm ownership rates for six 'first world' countries
The statistics are taken from Warlow, T. A. (1996) Firearms, the law and forensic ballistics. London: Taylor & Francis Ltd. They are based on a Canadian report published in 1995 that cited then recent data

notifiable offences in which the use of firearms was reported and that the police recorded (of which 11 825 involved an air weapon). Included within these were 78 homicides (one of which was due to the use of an air weapon) and 1378 acts endangering life (of which 165 were attributable to air weapons).

In cases in which the criminal use of firearms is suspected, the examination of any recovered firearms and/or related artefacts (spent cartridge cases and bullets, clothing, wounds, trace materials, etc.) is an extremely important part of forensic science. It can be crucial in establishing that a crime has been committed. In cases of wounding or murder, it can frequently be used to help link the victim with the weapon and the weapon with the assailant. Furthermore, such examination can also form a pivotal part of crime scene reconstruction. In order to facilitate the efficient storage and retrieval of information obtained during the forensic examination of firearms and ammunition, the National Firearms Forensic Intelligence Database (NFFID) was established in 2003. This database has two parts: one, known as IBIS, is an automated system that allows comparisons to be made of the characteristics of spent ammunition from unsolved crimes and weapons that have been recovered; the other part is a database of the characteristics of individual weapons (e.g. make, model, calibre) and information from ammunition.

This chapter will introduce the reader to the salient aspects of the forensic study of both firearms and the consequences of their discharge. It opens with a description of the types of firearms and ammunition that are more commonly encountered in forensic work (Section 9.1). This is followed by an exploration of what happens when a firearm is discharged (Section 9.2) and the information that may be obtained from an examination of firearms and spent ammunition (Sections 9.3 and 9.4 respectively). The chapter closes with an overview of the information that can be gained from the analysis of the material that is vented from a firearm other than the projectile and any wadding (Section 9.5).

9.1 Types of firearm and ammunition

This section is concerned with a brief description of the most common types of firearm and ammunition that are encountered in forensic casework in mainland United Kingdom. The meaning of the key technical terms used in this and following sections is given in Box 9.1.

Further information

Box 9.1

Key firearms-related technical terms

Below is given an alphabetical list of key terms that are frequently encountered in the field of forensic firearms examination, together with their normal meanings in this context. Words or phrases shown in *italics* within the meanings given are listed as key terms elsewhere in this box.

ammunition: that which is, or may be, fired in a gun. Also, that which is, or may be, discharged from an air weapon.

assault rifle: a *rifle* designed for military use that can be fired in either an *automatic* or a *self-loading* (i.e. *semi-automatic*) manner.

automatic: when fired, will discharge repeatedly either until the trigger is no longer pressed or until the weapon's magazine runs out of ammunition.

barrel: a tube which directs the projectile.

black powder: *gunpowder*

bolt-action firearm: a firearm in which, after firing, the manual pulling back and pushing forward of a bolt is required to cause the empty *cartridge* case to be ejected from the weapon and a live *cartridge* to be placed in the firing chamber.

bore of a shotgun: the *gauge* of the weapon concerned.

breech: the end of the *barrel* or, where present, the *chamber* that is furthest from the muzzle.

bullets: this word has several meanings: (1) those *small arms* projectiles fired one at a time from the barrel of a gun; (2) small spheres; (3) projectiles used for a small *calibre* gun. (It is the first of these meanings that is used in this book.)

calibre: in its simplest meaning, this is the nominal and approximate internal diameter of a given firearm's barrel. For guns with *rifled barrels*, the units of this are either inches, expressed as decimals (as in .45"), or millimetres (as in 9 mm). When used as a designation for cartridges, this diameter information is supplemented by letters, other numbers and/or words that signify something specific about the cartridge. For example, these supplementary characters might indicate the date of the adoption of the cartridge by an army, the length of the cartridge or the weight of propellant that it contains. In this form, it can be thought of as a 'short-hand' that is used to specify the cartridge type that a firearm is designed to fire and an attempt to give a unique designation to this cartridge type. In the case of most shotguns, the calibre of the weapon concerned is indicated by its *gauge*; a parameter that is more commonly referred to in the United Kingdom as its bore.

cartridge: the defining characteristic of any *small arms* cartridge is that it contains a measured amount of *propellant*. However, as shown in figure (a), the vast majority of such cartridges also have a case to hold the propellant, a primer and a projectile (i.e. *bullet*) or projectiles (i.e. *shot*).

chamber: that part of a firearm designed to hold the cartridge while it is fired.

double-action revolver: a revolver that, when the trigger is pulled with the *hammer* in the uncocked position, will rotate its *magazine* to bring a new cartridge into the firing position, cock and fire. Note, however, in the strictest use of this term it refers to a revolver that in addition to functioning as described in the previous sentence will also function as a *single-action revolver*.

double-base propellant: *smokeless powder* based on cellulose nitrate and glyceryl trinitrate.

▶

Box 9.1 continued

(a)

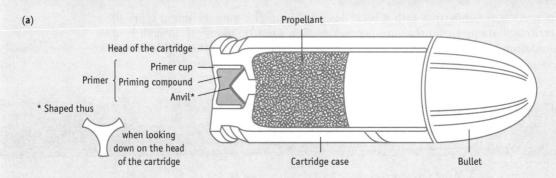

(a) An example of a cartridge

gauge of a shotgun: a measure of the *calibre* of the weapon concerned. It refers to the number of solid lead spheres, each of which has a diameter that will just pass along the inside of the barrel of the gun, that make one pound (lb) in weight. In this context, the term bore is synonymous with gauge.

gunpowder: a mixture of saltpetre (potassium nitrate), charcoal (carbon) and sulphur used as a firearms *propellant*; now almost wholly replaced for this purpose by *smokeless powder*.

hammer: a device that is common to the design of many firearms, which are collectively known as hammer guns. In such guns, the hammer is spring-loaded when in the cocked position. When the trigger is pulled, the hammer flies from the cocked to the uncocked position. At the end of this movement, depending on the details of the gun's design, either the hammer's impact causes a firing pin to strike the cartridge or the hammer strikes the cartridge directly. In either case, the portion of the cartridge that is hit is that which contains the *primer* and, consequently, the gun is made to fire. In most hammer guns, the upper part of the rear of the hammer ends in a spur, by which the shooter can pull the hammer to the cocked position. Note that guns without hammers, or without visible hammers, are referred to as hammerless. Semi-hammerless guns only have the spur of the hammer showing.

handgun: a *pistol*.

lever-action: see *manual firearm*.

magazine: a store for *ammunition*. Many firearms have inbuilt magazines.

manual firearm: a firearm in which the shooter actuates a fairly sophisticated mechanism using, e.g., a manually actuated bolt-action rifle, a lever (lever-action) or sliding handle (pump-action) to load a live *cartridge* into the firing chamber in place of any spent *cartridge* case present.

muzzle: that end of the *barrel* of the firearm from which the projectile(s) exit(s) the weapon.

pistol: this has two common meanings: (1) a firearm designed to be held in and discharged from one hand, whether *single-shot*, *self-loading* or *revolver* in design; (2) as in sense 1 but restricted to *single-shot* and *self-loading* firearms. (In this book, it is the first of these definitions that is used.)

primer: consists of a primer cup, priming compound and anvil (figure (a)). When struck by the firing pin, the cup is indented, causing the priming compound to explode by compressing it against the anvil. The flash of this explosion passes through a hole in the head of the *cartridge* and ignites the *propellant*.

propellant: material that undergoes a chemical reaction resulting in the rapid production of gas that is used to force the projectile or projectiles along and out of the *barrel* of a firearm when the weapon is discharged.

pump-action: see *manual firearm*.

revolver: a firearm designed to contain multiple *cartridges* within a cylindrical magazine and that has a mechanism that, by the progressive partial rotation of this cylinder, brings each cartridge in line with the *barrel* so that it can be fired. In order to replenish the ammunition within the cylinder, the spent cartridge cases must be manually replaced with live cartridges.

Box 9.1 *continued*

rifle: a firearm with a *rifled barrel*, which fires *bullets* and that is designed to be discharged while held in both hands and, in most cases, while held against a shoulder.

rifled barrel: a gun barrel featuring a series of spiral grooves and lands along the length of its interior surface (see figure (b)).

round: a military term for a *cartridge*.

safety catch: a system that is under the control of the shooter via the movement of a lever, or similar device, such that when the lever is in one position pulling the trigger will not discharge the weapon, whereas, when it is in another, the gun will fire when the trigger is pulled.

self-loading firearm: a firearm that utilises some of the energy of one discharge to extract the case of the spent *cartridge* from the firing chamber, eject the empty case

from the gun, re-cock the firing mechanism and load a live *cartridge* from the weapon's *magazine* into the firing chamber ready for the next discharge, which must be actuated by renewed pressure on the trigger.

semi-automatic: *self-loading*.

shot: the pellets that are designed to be fired many at a time from a *shotgun*.

shotgun: a firearm, the *barrel* or barrels of which have a smooth (i.e. not rifled) interior and which is designed to fire *shot*, and to be discharged while held in both hands and, in most cases, while held against a shoulder.

single-action revolver: a *revolver* that must be cocked by pulling the *hammer* back with the thumb in order to be able to fire the next shot by squeezing the trigger (for comparison, see *double-action revolver*).

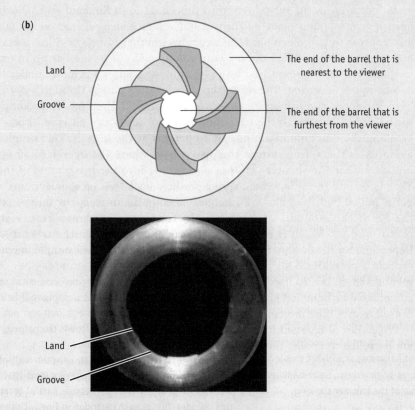

(b) A schematic drawing and a photograph of a rifled barrel
Note that the depth of rifling grooves is typically 0.1 mm

(Drawing reproduced from an original by Tom Jackson; photograph reproduced by kind permission of Philip Boyce, Forensic Alliance, UK)

Box 9.1 continued

single-base propellant: *smokeless powder* based on cellulose nitrate.

single-shot firearm: a firearm that, once discharged, requires the shooter to manually extract the spent *cartridge* case and replace it with a live *cartridge* before the weapon can be fired again.

small arms: firearms that are small and light enough to be hand carried.

smokeless powder: firearms *propellant* that is based either on cellulose nitrate or a combination of cellulose nitrate and glyceryl trinitrate (forming single-base and double-base propellants respectively).

sub-machine gun: a compact, *self-loading* or *automatic* weapon that is designed to be discharged while held in both hands and to fire self-loading pistol ammunition.

While a forensic examiner working in this field will meet a wide range of weapons, most of them will fall into one of four categories, namely: handguns (including air pistols), shotguns, rifles (including air rifles) and sub-machine guns. Among the others encountered will be blank firing guns and **deactivated firearms** that have been converted to fire live cartridges, and imitation firearms.

Deactivated firearms
Firearms that have been deliberately rendered incapable of firing projectiles, so that they can be sold as non-firearms.

As indicated in the introduction to this chapter, in England and Wales offences involving air weapons make up the vast bulk of notifiable offences in which firearms are reported to have been used. Air weapons, whether pistols or rifles, use a pulse of high pressure air to force the projectile along and out of the barrel. In most such weapons, the air is pressurised by a piston moving down a cylinder under the force of a compressed spring. The air in the cylinder then passes through a port into the barrel to force the projectile to move. The shooter then has to recompress the spring manually prior to the next shot. In many designs of air rifle, this is done by breaking the gun around a hinge that operates at the breech. This simultaneously compresses the spring, forces the piston back along the cylinder and opens the breech so that the shooter can load a projectile into the breech end of the barrel. The piston and the compressed spring are held back by a mechanism until the trigger is pulled and the gun is discharged. Pneumatic air weapons do not pressurise the air at the moment of discharge. Instead, they contain a reservoir of pre-pressurised air, which is released by means of a valve when the trigger is pulled. Depending on the design, this reservoir is replenished by, for example, a hand pump or from a pressurised air bottle of the type used by an underwater diver. A closely related system is also used in some weapons, known as gas-powered guns, in which compressed or liquefied gas (usually carbon dioxide) held in a replaceable reservoir is used to expel the projectile when the trigger is pulled.

Projectiles discharged from air weapons are capable of killing; therefore, as these are barrelled weapons, they can be considered as firearms under English law (see the Introduction to this chapter). However, with the exception of air weapons that are declared by the Secretary of State to be especially dangerous and those that discharge projectiles with energies greater than 8.1 J (6 ft lb) for pistols and 16.3 J (12 ft lb) for rifles, these weapons are less tightly controlled in this country than are other firearms.

Although air weapon offences form the bulk of firearms offences in England and Wales, they rarely lead to death. For this reason, the remainder of this chapter deals almost exclusively with firearms other than air weapons. However, it should be noted that the kinds of information that can be gained from the examination of marks on lead pellets that have been discharged from air weapons (Figure 9.2a) are the same as those which can be obtained from the examination of bullets fired from other types of small arm. The information available from the examination of spent projectiles is described in Section 9.4.

As indicated in Figures 9.3 and 9.4, handguns are of particular importance. Home Office statistics reveal them to be the most common category of non-air weapon firearm to be identified as being involved in offences recorded in England and Wales. Indeed, according to a Home Office statistical bulletin published in 2006 (see Coleman, Hird and Povey (2006) in the Further reading section), in the year 2004–05 handguns were identified as being involved in 40 per cent of such cases. However, it should be noted that although the overall proportion of notifiable offences involving non-air weapon firearms in England and Wales in the year 2004–05 in which firearms were discharged was 44 per cent, handguns were fired in only 13 per cent of notifiable offences in which they were used. In the year in question, handguns caused death or serious injury in 32 per cent of the offences in which they were fired, compared with 34

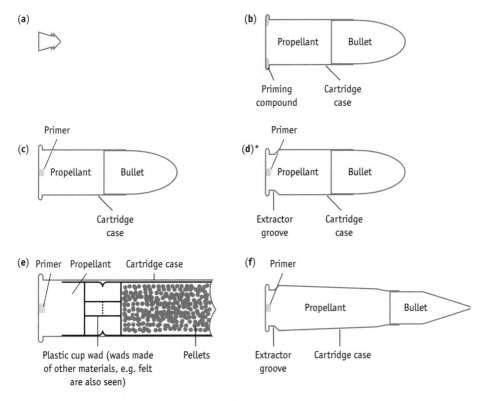

* For a more detailed drawing of a typical cartridge of this type, see Box 9.1.

Figure 9.2 The essential features of typical (a) lead air weapon pellets, (b) rim-fire and (c) centre-fire ammunition designed for use in revolvers, and cartridges to be fired in (d) self-loading pistols and sub-machine guns, (e) shotguns and (f) rifles
Note that while these are the common types of ammunition, there are other forms which are encountered by firearms examiners

(a)

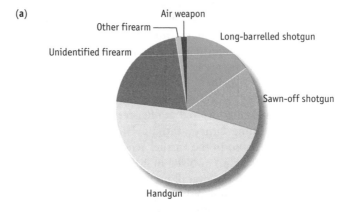

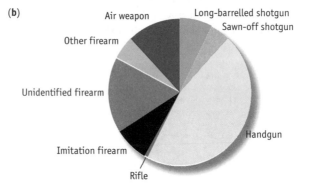

(b)

Figure 9.3 The proportions of the (a) 78 homicides and (b) 1378 attempted murders and other acts (including wounding) endangering life in England and Wales in which the use of firearms was reported and that the police recorded in the year 2004–05 that were carried out by different category of weapon

per cent in the case of shotguns and 4 per cent in the case of other non-air weapon firearms. There is evidence that homicide using firearms among people engaged in drug and/or organised crime is most often perpetrated with handguns. A recent study has been carried out on the homicides involving firearms that were committed in England and Wales in both of two periods, namely 1992 to 1994 and 1995 to 1998 (see Home Office 2001). This showed that a total of 417 relevant homicides had occurred during these periods and that of the firearms used in the 118 of these killings that were connected with drug-related or organised crime, 72 per cent were handguns.

Some handguns encountered in the forensic context are single shot weapons. However, most are either revolvers or self-loading firearms. Weapons that can be accurately described as automatic pistols are a rarity (the term automatic is sometimes erroneously applied to self-loading weapons).

The majority of all handguns have rifled barrels and are designed to fire bullets. Typical ammunition of the types designed to be fired in each of revolvers and self-loading pistols are shown in diagrammatic form in Figure 9.2. Note that a revolver cartridge is rimmed (that is, its case has a projecting rim that extends all around its closed, i.e.

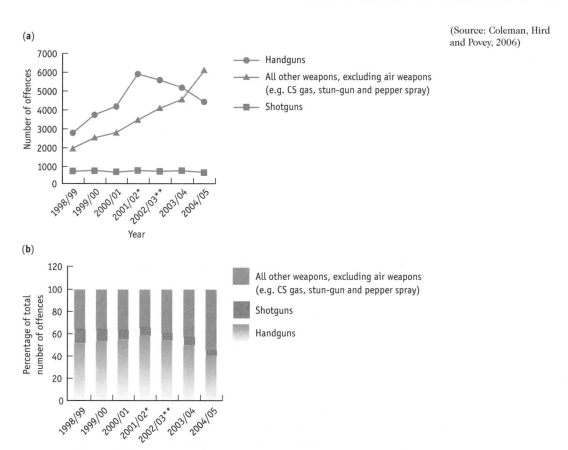

(Source: Coleman, Hird and Povey, 2006)

Figure 9.4 Crimes in England and Wales in which the use of firearms other than air weapons was reported and that the police recorded, categorised by the type of principal weapon involved

(a) The number of offences within each category for each of the years indicated. (b) On a year by year basis, the percentage of the total number of these offences that each category represents. Note in some instances, the identification of the type of weapon used is based solely on descriptions provided by witnesses or victims. Additionally, unless a firearm is discharged or recovered, it is not possible to be sure whether the weapon was an imitation or a real firearm.

* Before 1 April 2002, some police forces implemented the principles of the National Crime Recording Standard, and this may have inflated some of these figures.

** On 1 April 2002, the National Crime Recording Standard was introduced; consequently, some crime category figures may have been inflated.

head, end) but does not have an extractor groove. In contrast, cartridges intended for use in self-loading pistols do have extractor grooves and, depending on design, may or may not have a rim (the cartridge illustrated in Figure 9.2 is rimless).

It is worth noting that although revolvers retain the spent cartridge cases until they are manually removed, self-loading pistols eject the spent cases a fraction of a second after the cartridge has been fired. This means that spent cartridge cases are more likely to be found at a shooting incident involving a self-loading pistol than one in which a revolver was used.

As shown in Figure 9.4, over recent years there has been a sustained decline in the use of shotguns in the commission of crime in England and Wales. However, shotguns are still involved in a significant proportion of those domestic homicides that are committed using firearms. Of the 417 homicides that were examined in the study referred to earlier in this section, 96 were classified as domestic, of which 64 per cent involved shotguns.

Shotguns that are encountered in forensic casework include both single- and double-barrel models; of the two, the latter is more common in the United Kingdom. The single-barrel models may be classified as single-shot, bolt-action, lever-action, pump-action (more common than either bolt- or lever-action) or self-loading. Note, however, that single-barrel shotguns that can be used in either pump-action or self-loading mode are also now available and that revolver shotguns also exist. Double-barrel sporting shotguns in the UK have traditionally been of the hinged barrel design. By virtue of this hinge, the shooter can open the gun to have access to its chambers; thereby allowing the exchange of spent cartridges with live ones.

In most cases, the muzzle-end of a shotgun barrel contains a tapered section, such that the internal diameter of the barrel concerned is slightly smaller at the **muzzle** than elsewhere along its length. The purpose of this constriction, which is referred to as the choke, is to decrease the natural tendency of the pellets to disperse during flight. It is the norm for the two barrels of double-barrel weapons to have different degrees of choke. Some shotguns have screw-in choke tubes, which may be replaced, allowing the degree of choke to be altered, while others have devices that allow the shooter to even more readily alter the degree of choke. In many cases, shotguns used by criminals have had their barrel(s) deliberately shortened so as to make the firearms concerned easier to conceal. Such guns, which are called sawn-off shotguns, will have had their chokes removed when their barrels were shortened.

Among both single-barrel and double-barrel shotguns, 12-bore firearms are the most common. The designation 12-bore (also called 12-gauge) is in fact a proxy measure of the internal diameter of the gun's barrel. It refers to the fact that 12 spheres of solid lead with this diameter weigh one pound (1 lb = 0.454 kg).

Other than size, the essential features of modern shotgun cartridges remain the same irrespective of the bore of the weapon in which they are intended to be fired. They have a metal base, in the centre of which is the primer cup, and plastic or paper sides which are crimp sealed at the top. Shotgun cartridges contain one or more wads between the propellant and the shot. These may be made of a number of materials, including felt, cardboard or plastic. They are disc-shaped and are there to make a more-or-less gas-tight seal with the barrel and to cushion the shot while it is accelerated out of the gun during firing. In modern cartridges, a plastic cup holds the shot so as to keep it away from the inside of the barrel during discharge. In cartridges with plastic cup wads (Figure 9.2), this cup is designed to also serve as the wad.

Rifles and sub-machine guns are briefly described in Box 9.1. As in the case of shotguns, rifles may be single-shot, bolt-action, lever-action, pump-action or self-loading, and there are some revolver rifles. Additionally, automatic rifles are available; a variant of which is the assault rifle. Typical rifle ammunition is illustrated in Figure 9.2. Sub-machine guns are designed to fire self-loading pistol ammunition, the essential features of which are also shown in Figure 9.2.

Muzzle
That end of the firearm's barrel from which the projectile(s) exit(s) the weapon.

9.2 Internal, external and terminal ballistics

Ballistics is the scientific study of projectile motion. When considering small arms, distinction is drawn between internal ballistics (also called interior ballistics), external ballistics (also known as exterior ballistics) and terminal ballistics.

Internal ballistics considers the processes by which the propellant's chemical energy is transferred to the kinetic energy possessed by the projectile(s), the efficiency of this transfer and, importantly, what happens to the projectile(s) as it/they move along the barrel of the firearm. It is during this time that the rifling (if present) and imperfections within the interior wall of the barrel impart marks onto the bullet or, in some instances, shotgun wadding (as appropriate). As described in Section 9.4, such marks have the potential to provide both class and individualising characteristics to aid the identification of the weapon that fired the projectile concerned.

The behaviour of the projectile(s) once they have left the barrel and before they impact with their target is the domain of **external ballistics**. This is of importance to the firearms examiner who is concerned with crime scene reconstruction. A knowledge of external ballistics will help to establish where the perpetrator of a given shooting could possibly have been located when the firearm was discharged.

Terminal ballistics is the study of what occurs when projectiles strike their targets. There are a number of reasons why this is of value to the forensic firearms examiner. For example, when a bullet strikes a person with sufficient energy, it will create an entry wound. In cases in which such a projectile does not lose all of its kinetic energy within the body of the individual concerned, it will also create an exit wound. A knowledge of the characteristics of these types of wound will allow one to be distinguished from the other, enabling, for example, examination to reveal whether a bullet that killed someone by passing through his or her chest did so from front to back or back to front. Clearly, such information may be valuable in crime scene reconstruction and in the corroboration or refutation of the account of the incident given by those who witnessed it.

The patterns of damage caused by the discharge of a firearm are influenced by each of internal, external and terminal ballistics. Clearly, therefore, there are multiple variables that control these patterns. However, many of these are held constant if the same gun, firing the same ammunition, is used for each shot discharged at a fresh target. Under these circumstances, in the case of shotguns, the damage pattern is largely a function of the distance from the muzzle to the target (i.e. the range). Using this knowledge, the firearms examiner may conduct a series of test firings with the shotgun believed to have been involved in a given shooting. Each such firing will be at a card target, set at a known range and will, ideally, use cartridges recovered from the scene or the suspect, or identical ammunition. The ranges of these firings will be varied, allowing correlations to be drawn between range and each of pellet spread and, where range permits, wadding strikes, blackening and the impact of unburned powder (wadding and, to a greater extent, unburned powder and the materials responsible for blackening are not able to travel as far as the pellets). The correlations can then be used to establish the likely minimum and maximum distances from the gun's muzzle to the target in the shooting incident under examination.

Internal ballistics
The study of what occurs in the span of time between the firing pin striking the primer and the projectile(s) leaving the firearm.

External ballistics
The study of projectile behaviour after discharge from the firearm but prior to impact with the target.

Terminal ballistics
The study of the behaviour of projectiles when they strike their targets.

Obviously, in cases involving bullet discharge, pellet spread information is not available for the establishment of the range of firing. However, in such cases, at ranges of less than one metre, the effects of muzzle flash, gas ejection, blackening and the impact of unburned powder can be used to estimate muzzle-to-skin distances. In contact or near contact shots, unburned powder will be found within the wound and muzzle flash may have caused charring around the wound's exterior (unless there is a fully gas-tight seal between the gun and the skin). Also, large volumes of gas ejected from the gun may have entered the wound. The high pressures that are thereby produced in the wound cavity frequently result in the formation of radial splits in the skin around the entrance wound; resulting in a characteristically stellate (i.e. star-shaped) pattern (Figure 9.5). They may also press the skin against

(Reproduced by kind permission of Andy Kirby, Staffordshire Police, UK)

(a)

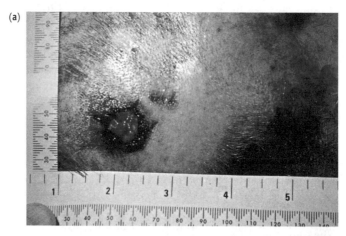

(Reproduced by kind permission of Philip Boyce, Forensic Alliance, UK)

(b)

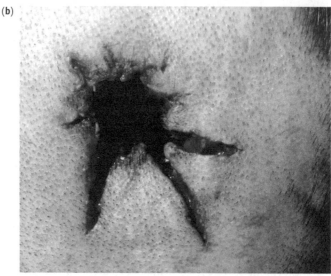

Figure 9.5 Examples of stellate entrance wound patterns that are characteristic of contact or near contact between the muzzle of the gun and the skin at the time of firing

the muzzle of the gun with enough force to cause bruising in the form of an image of the muzzle of the gun. This image may be sufficiently clear and characteristic to allow the probable model of the gun to be established. Gas escaping from the high-pressure zone along surfaces that are approximately at right angles to the direction of the shot may leave blackening between layers of clothing, the clothing and the skin and/or, within the wound, across the surface of substantial bones. At ranges greater than 5 cm, the direction travelled by some of the materials ejected along with the bullet deviates sufficiently from the line of fire to blacken the skin and 'tattoo' the victim with unburned particles of propellant (Figure 9.6). As range increases, the area covered by these marks increases, their intensity decreases and the ability of the particles to puncture and thereby tattoo the skin decreases. The test firing of the weapon involved, at card targets set at known distances from the muzzle of the weapon, will allow the examiner to interpret the spread and intensity of the patterns found around the wound of the victim in terms of the likely minimum and maximum range of the shot. As the effects seen alter significantly with the type of ammunition used, such tests should ideally be carried out using cartridges recovered from the scene or suspect or identical ammunition.

Whatever the type of weapon involved, establishment of the range over which it was fired can have significant evidential value. It may help to corroborate or refute accounts given of the incident by those present at the scene and it can help in the reconstruction of the incident. As explored in Box 9.3 later in the chapter, it may be of particular value in establishing whether a particular fatal shooting could have been the result of suicide.

Another aspect of projectile motion that is of significant forensic importance is that of **ricochet** (i.e. the deviation in the flight-path of a projectile as a consequence of impact). If death has occurred due to ricochet, rather than a shot aimed at the victim, this information is of evidential value. It is known that the propensity for ricochet is not the same for all projectiles. For example, low-velocity, heavy bullets are

> **Ricochet**
> *The deviation in the flight-path of a projectile as a consequence of impact.*

(Reproduced by kind permission of Philip Boyce, Forensic Alliance, UK)

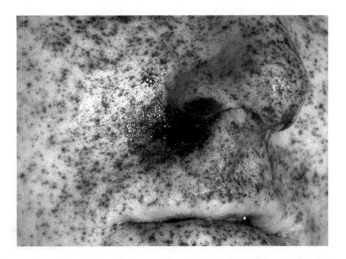

Figure 9.6 The area around a gunshot wound showing 'tattooing' caused by unburned propellant particles

more likely to ricochet than are high-velocity ones that are both light and designed to expand within the intended quarry (which, rather than ricochet, are likely to break up on impact). The examination of the scene may reveal evidence of the incidence of ricochet, in the form of damage at the impact site(s) concerned. Also, recovered bullets may have been marked in a fashion that provides evidence of the surface from which ricochet has occurred. Furthermore, particles (e.g. of soil, paint, glass or plaster) derived from the impact site that led to ricochet may be found on the bullet's surface.

9.3 The examination of suspect firearms

For safety reasons, it is vitally important to ensure that any firearm that is to be stored or examined is first inspected by a competent person to make sure that it is not loaded. There are a number of reasons why a firearms examiner may need to load and, in many instances, test fire a suspect weapon. For example, this will be required if spent cartridge cases, known to have been test fired with the suspect firearm, are to be collected for the purposes of comparison with spent cartridge cases recovered from the scene of a shooting incident. Clearly, after any such occasion during which the firearm concerned is loaded, checks must be carried out to ensure that it is no longer loaded before it is stored or examined.

To achieve its full potential, the examination of any given firearm must be carried out in a planned, systematic and logical fashion. There are actions that if carried out in the wrong order may destroy valuable information and may even place the firearms examiner in danger of injury. For example, if a weapon is test fired before the inside of its barrel has been inspected, this will preclude the detection of small particles of material of potential evidential value (such as **gunshot residues**) that were lodged within it prior to the test firing. Furthermore, the presence of obstructions within the barrel that make it unsafe to be fired may be missed, possibly leading to the bursting of the weapon upon test firing.

The types of observation that an examiner will make will, to some extent, be determined by the circumstances of the case. However, routine observations recorded during the examination of a firearm will typically include:

Gunshot residues
The heterogeneous mix of finely divided particles that is expelled alongside the intended projectile(s) when a firearm (other than an air weapon) is discharged.

- its type (e.g. shotgun, self-loading pistol);
- its condition as received (recorded with the aid of photographs, where practicable);
- the number of cartridges that it (or its magazine) can hold;
- its manufacturer, make and model, bearing in mind that there have been instances in which:
  - unscrupulous gunsmiths have been known to produce counterfeit goods that are designed to appear to be those of a well-reputed brand,
  - guns designed to be able to fire only blanks have been adapted to fire projectiles,
  - individual amateur gunsmiths have produced 'home-made' guns;
- its serial number (serial numbers are frequently removed by criminals but, in many such cases, may still be rendered legible (Box 9.2));

Forensic techniques

Box 9.2

Erased serial numbers

Among the products habitually stolen by criminals are certain types that are routinely stamped with identifying serial numbers during the manufacturing process. Such groups include metal items, such as firearms and motor vehicle engines, and plastic products, for example mobile phones. When such stolen goods are recovered, it is often the case that the thief has erased, or attempted to erase, the serial number in order to conceal the identity of the object. However, it is possible, in some cases, to restore the original serial number to a state in which it can be read.

Serial numbers are impressed into objects during manufacture, either using steel dies, where the receiving surface is metallic, or heat stamps, where the product is plastic. However it is applied, it is the changes induced by this stamping process in the substrate *below* the impression that are key to the restoration of erased serial numbers.

In the case of metallic objects, the metal crystals below (and around) the impressed number are placed under strain by the stamping process and consequently become more electrochemically reactive. Erasure of the serial number, for example by grinding or filing, may not go deep enough to remove this underlying layer completely. If an appropriate etching reagent is then applied, the areas of stress react more readily with it and, consequently, the serial number may reappear. To give an example, Fry's Reagent is the one most commonly used for the recovery of serial numbers on iron and steel firearm components. This is composed of a mixture of hydrochloric acid (80 ml), water (60 ml), copper(II) chloride (12.9 g) and ethanol (50 ml). Another example of an etching agent, which is suitable for aluminium alloys, is Vinella's solution. This is composed of glycerol (30 ml), hydrofluoric acid (20 ml) and nitric acid (10 ml). In the case of aluminium alloys which may contain silicon, Hume–Rothery solution (copper(II) chloride (200 g), hydrochloric acid (5 ml) and water (1000 ml)) may be used, applied between stages of application of Vinella's solution.

In the case of plastic items, the impression of serial numbers using a heat stamp causes shrinkage of the surrounding polymers. If a serial number is erased from a plastic surface, it may be restored by the application of an appropriate solvent. This causes preferential swelling in those areas affected by heat, which underlie the original serial number.

- its calibre (this information is normally embodied in the make and model of the gun concerned; however, it is quite possible that the weapon concerned has been altered since manufacture – this is particularly likely in the case of illegally **reactivated guns** that had been previously legitimately deactivated and sold as non-firearms);

- if it has a rifled barrel, the class characteristics of its rifling (e.g. the number of lands and grooves and the direction of twist, i.e. whether the direction of the rifling spiral is right- or left-handed);

- if it has a smooth bore and is a shotgun, the degree of choke of the barrel(s) and whether this degree of choke can be readily altered by the shooter;

- its weight (if required), overall length, barrel length and the distance from the muzzle to the trigger(s);

- the positions of the safety catch (where present) and any levers that allow the shooter to select specific features of the gun (e.g. switch between self-loading and automatic modes of firing).

Reactivated guns
Legitimately deactivated firearms that have been illegally converted back into a state in which they are capable of firing projectiles again.

The examination of a given suspect firearm may help to answer a number of important questions. Unfortunately, space does not permit an exhaustive description of the means by which this may be done. However, a selection of such questions is given below, along with an indication of some of the key means by which firearms examination may help to answer them.

9.3.1 Whom or what has this firearm been in contact with?

During the commission of a crime, any firearm involved will have been brought into contact with a number of surfaces and substances. Each time this occurs, such contact may well mark the gun and/or transfer material to the weapon that is of evidential value. Examples of these types of contact and the evidence that they may well produce are given in Table 9.1. From this, it is apparent that the careful and systematic search for and evaluation of such evidence may be able to help establish links between the weapon and with whom or what it has been in contact. However, it must be borne in mind that the strength of the link varies with the ability of the evidence to yield individualising characteristics and the availability of appropriate

Table 9.1 Examples of trace and contact evidence that may be recovered from a suspect firearm

Examples of contact types	Typical evidence of the contact that may be discovered during firearm examination	Cross-reference to other parts of the book where further information on the evidence type concerned can be found
Between the firearm and the skin of anyone handling it	Fingerprints	Chapter 4, Section 4.1
	DNA-containing skin cells	Chapter 6
Between the firearm and the pocket (or other parts of clothing, in particular gloves) of the person carrying it	Textile fibres	Chapter 3, Section 3.1
Between the firearm and body fluids/ tissue from the victim (may happen during close range shooting or if the weapon is used as a club)	Blood	Chapter 5, Section 5.1.2 (gives information on presumptive tests for blood)
		Chapter 5, Section 5.1.3 (gives information on blood typing)
		Chapter 6 (gives information on DNA profiling, which can be carried out using blood-derived DNA)
	Saliva (may be found on the barrel of the gun if it has been placed inside the victim's mouth, e.g. as occurs in some suicides)	Chapter 5, Section 5.3.2 (gives information on presumptive tests for saliva)
		Chapter 5, Section 5.1.3 (gives information on blood typing which, in some people, can be established from their saliva)
		Chapter 6 (gives information on DNA profiling, which can be carried out using the buccal cells (i.e. cells of the inside of the mouth) which may be found in saliva)
	Tissues (e.g. skin, fat)	Chapter 6 (gives information on DNA profiling, which can be carried out using the cells of such tissues)
	Hair	Chapter 3, Section 3.1

Table 9.1 Continued

Examples of contact types	Typical evidence of the contact that may be discovered during firearm examination	Cross-reference to other parts of the book where further information on the evidence type concerned can be found
Between the firearm and any object (e.g. a windowpane) that it has been used to break	Fragments of the broken object	Chapter 3 examines, in general terms, the value of recoverable trace materials (e.g. fragments of glass) that provide evidence of contact.
Between the firearm and ammunition that has been fired in it	Lacquer from the cartridge on the face of the breech or inside the barrel Gunshot residues inside the barrel	Note that because firearms are constructed of harder materials than is ammunition, marks made by the ammunition on the firearm are much less likely than marks made by the firearm on the ammunition. The evidential value of such marks made on ammunition is discussed later in this chapter (Section 9.4), as is that of gunshot residues (Section 9.5)
Between the firearm and any tools that may be used to alter or repair it	Machine-tool and/or hand-tool marks on those parts of reactivated weapons that have had to be made to render the weapon functional Saw marks on the end of the barrel(s) and, possibly, stock (i.e. wooden portion, or equivalent) of a sawn-off shotgun or rifle (may be accompanied by paint from the saw) Punch, drill or milling marks made in an attempt to erase serial numbers	The evidential value of tool marks in general is discussed in Chapter 4, Section 4.4; whereas that of paint is described in Chapter 3, Section 3.5

control samples. For example, a good-quality fingerprint found on a gun will provide unequivocal evidence that the person who left the print had indeed touched the firearm concerned, provided that a control print is available for comparison (Chapter 4, Section 4.1.3). However, if gunshot residues were found within the barrel of a gun they may reveal class characteristics that, while consistent with the firing of a particular cartridge, could not prove that the cartridge in question was fired in that particular gun. For more on the analysis of gunshot residues, see Section 9.5 and for a discussion on the difference between class and individualising characteristics, see Chapter 1, Section 1.2.1.

9.3.2 Could this firearm be responsible for firing the shots that were discharged at a given shooting incident?

Evidence recovered from the scene of a shooting incident may include spent cartridge cases, projectiles and/or gunshot residues. Depending on the type of weapon involved, the projectiles may be bullet(s) or shot and wadding. Also, the characteristics of any damage or injury caused by the shooting will normally be known.

Early in the inspection of the suspect weapon, its type will have been established. If, for the sake of argument, it is found to be a pistol designed to fire .22" rim-fire cartridges, this would not be able to produce the damage caused by a 12-bore shotgun. If such damage is known to have been caused by the only weapon used in the incident, then, clearly, the pistol could not have been the gun concerned. Similarly, if on the basis of recovered spent ammunition, the incident was known to have involved the firing of a single .45" centre-fire cartridge, this is compelling evidence that the suspect pistol described above could not have fired the shot. While this type of reasoning is apparently obvious, care does need to be taken in many cases. This is because, as discussed in Section 9.4, it is often possible to fire a weapon, either with or without adaptation, using a range of cartridge types. To give an extreme example, shotguns can be adapted to fire pistol cartridges.

If a cleaning patch is passed down the barrel of a suspect weapon before it is test fired, any gunshot residues present will be sampled. If such residues are found, this is evidence that the gun has indeed been fired (although it is generally not possible to say when this occurred). Furthermore, such residues may reveal class characteristics that agree with those of gunshot residues found at the scene (Section 9.5) or even particles of unburned propellant that can be compared with propellant found in unused ammunition known to be in the possession of the suspect.

Swarf
Shavings of metal.

In the case of sawn-off weapons, inspection of the barrel(s) may reveal small particles of metallic **swarf** with a composition that matches that of the barrel. Such evidence would be consistent with the weapon *not* having been discharged since it was shortened.

The test firing of the suspect weapon will provide control samples of spent cartridge cases. Similarly, spent bullets may be collected if the gun concerned is test fired into a bullet recovery system designed to capture the fired projectile in an undamaged state. This consists of a large container filled with a readily deformed material (e.g. water or cotton waste) that will, nonetheless, slow the bullet to a standstill within a relatively short distance. The items collected during test firing can then be compared with used cartridge cases and projectiles retrieved from the crime scene. As discussed in Section 9.4, the information that such comparisons can reveal is frequently individualising, allowing a given weapon to be unambiguously linked to a given incident.

9.3.3 Could this firearm have been unintentionally discharged?

Those accused of perpetrating an illegal shooting incident in which someone has been killed or injured rarely admit to intentionally firing the weapon involved. For example, it may be claimed that the safety catch malfunctioned, or that the firearm was discharged:

- ■ while it was being uncocked to make it safe;
- ■ when the spur of the hammer of the gun in an uncocked position was accidentally struck from behind or caught on clothing; or
- ■ when the cocked gun hit the floor during a scuffle.

All of these are indeed possible, at least with some guns, and the firearms examiner will wish to provide as much information as possible to assist the jury in establishing whether, in the particular case under consideration, such an explanation is credible. Also, in cases in which it is believed that a fatal shot was self-inflicted, the examination of the firearm concerned may be of value in establishing whether the death was suicide or the result of an accident (see Box 9.3 below).

In either of the scenarios outlined previously, the examiner will carry out investigations and mechanical tests on the weapon concerned. The exact nature and number of which will be determined by the case under consideration. However, typical among these investigations and tests are the following:

- An evaluation of the weight of the trigger pull (a parameter that is also known as the trigger pressure) of the weapon concerned. This is tested because firearms with light trigger pulls are prone to accidental discharge. Typical trigger pulls for various classes of firearm are given in Table 9.2. It would be normal for a firearms examiner to include in his or her report a comparison of the trigger pull found on the suspect weapon with that expected for the type of weapon concerned. It should be noted that the weight of a trigger pull for a given firearm will depend on the exact location on the trigger that the load is placed and the direction relative to the long axis of the weapon in which it is applied. Therefore, it may be of value to the jury to know the minimum trigger pull achievable, as well as that obtained when the load is applied directly away from the muzzle and in the centre of the trigger as would occur in normal use. Also, it should be noted that some rifles and pistols have mechanisms that enable the shooter to choose between a normal trigger pull and a very light set trigger (also known as a hair trigger), which is adjustable. Rifles fitted with these devices can typically be adjusted to give a pull of ≤ 0.3 kg. Clearly, the examiner should report if such a device is fitted and, if so, the setting to which it was adjusted when the examiner received the firearm.

- An examination of the firearm to establish the operation of any safety catch and the presence and operation of any other internal safety devices present. For example, such devices are incorporated in the design of modern revolvers so that they cannot be fired except by pulling the trigger (older designs may be fired by a substantial blow to the rear of the hammer when in the uncocked position).

- An examination of the condition of the safety devices and the firing mechanism with an evaluation of whether a malfunction could have occurred within these systems, allowing the firearm to be unintentionally discharged.

- Jarring tests in which the weapon is dropped in a controlled manner onto a suitably hard but cushioned surface from a variety of heights and in which

Table 9.2 Typical trigger pull weights

Type of firearm	Typical trigger pull weights in kg	in lb
.22" indoor precision target shooting rim-fire firearms	approx. 1	approx. 2
Sporting rifles, also revolver single-action pull* and other pistols	1.4 to 1.8	3 to 4
Sporting shotguns	1.6 to 2.3	3.5 to 5
Military weapons	2.7 to 3.6	6 to 8

*Revolver double-action pull is significantly heavier.

the hammer (if present) may be struck with a soft mallet. The purpose of these tests is to see if a blow to the gun could make the firing pin contact the primer-containing portion of a cartridge with sufficient force to fire the gun without the trigger being pulled. When interpreting the results of such tests, the examiner will be mindful of the fact that the sensitivity to impact of the primer will, in many cases, differ from one brand of cartridge to the next and even from one batch to the next.

- ■ Tests to establish whether the action of closing the breech could cause the weapon to fire.

- ■ Inspection of the spur of the hammer (in guns with such features) in order to evaluate whether it may be prone to slipping from under the thumb of the shooter during uncocking.

9.3.4 Could the intentional discharge of this firearm have caused unintentional injury?

In court, it may be attested that, although the defendant deliberately discharged the firearm concerned, any injury or death that resulted was not intended as the weapon was aimed clear of the victim. There are indeed a number of circumstances in which this could occur. While in any given case, it is up to the court to decide how credible such an explanation is and the importance that may be attached to it, the firearms examiner may be able to provide information that allows the credibility of such an argument to be properly assessed. For example, consider a case in which it is argued that a pistol was fired at the ground but that the force of the recoil caused the barrel of the gun to rise so that it was aligned with the victim's chest, resulting in death or injury. This is not a likely explanation as not only does the bulk of the movement caused by recoil occur after the bullet has left the gun but also pistols are commonly fitted with sights that are arranged so as to compensate for the effect of recoil when the weapon is used under normal circumstances. In any case, inspection of the weapon concerned will establish whether such a sighting arrangement is present and test firing will provide information on the effect of recoil on the direction of shooting.

Another category of this type of explanation warrants mention here, even though in this instance, examination of the firearm itself cannot establish its credibility. This is that the death or injury was caused by a bullet that had ricocheted (i.e. been altered in its flight path by impact). However, as described in Section 9.2, the incidence of ricochet may be established by the examination of the scene and, in some instances, by the condition of the projectile.

9.3.5 Could this firearm have been used in the commission of an act of suicide?

During the investigation of a fatal shooting, it is crucially important to establish, if at all possible, whether it was as the result of suicide. This determination has to be made with great care not least because, in a given case, a murder may have been perpetrated but been engineered so as to appear to have been suicide.

In order to establish that suicide has been committed, all the known circumstances of a given case will be taken into account. In firearms-related deaths that may be suicide, the weapon that fired the fatal shot will, almost without exception, be found at the scene, although recoil may have flung it clear of the body. Also, depending on the severity of the injuries sustained, it is possible that the fatally wounded victim may have moved the gun, and/or himself or herself after the shooting. The role of firearms examination in cases of suspected suicide is explored further in Box 9.3.

Further information

Box 9.3

The role of firearms examination and the establishment of the manner of death in cases of fatal shootings

In the case of a fatal shooting, the manner of death may be homicide, accident or suicide. It is imperative that, if at all possible, the investigation into each such shooting reveals which of these has occurred. Ultimately, in England and Wales, it is the role of the coroner to establish the manner of death (Chapter 12, Section 12.3.2). However, in cases of fatal shooting, the firearms examiner can play an important part in helping the coroner to complete this task. He or she, often working in close conjunction with others involved in the case (e.g. the pathologist, fingerprints examiners, forensic biologists), may well be able to help to answer important questions. Key among these are those discussed below.

Is this firearm the one that fired the fatal shot?
In virtually every case of suicide by shooting, the weapon involved will be found at the scene. The same will be true of self-inflicted accidental fatal shootings. Therefore, in cases in which a weapon is not found at the scene, homicide or non-self-inflicted accident must be suspected. However, even in cases in which a weapon is located at the scene, this does not necessarily mean that suicide has occurred and it remains imperative to establish whether the weapon found was indeed the one which killed the victim.

The nature of the damage caused by the fatal discharge may enable certain weapons to be ruled out or deemed unlikely to have been responsible. For example, as a bullet passes through bone it will either shatter it or produce a hole, the dimensions of which may provide evidence of the calibre of the weapon involved (although great care needs to be exercised in the interpretation of such evidence). If the projectile(s) from this discharge are retained within the body, they can be recovered and may be compared with spent bullets or shotgun wadding (as appropriate) generated during the test firing of the weapon (Section 9.4). If the wound contains unburned grains of propellant, these can be compared with any others recovered from the barrel of the gun and/or those obtained from any live cartridges taken from the scene. Also, any gunshot residues discovered on the victim can be compared with control samples taken from the inside of the gun and/or the spent cartridge case that is believed to have been involved in the fatal shooting (Section 9.5).

The condition of the gun may also indicate whether it could have fired the fatal shot. For example, as described in Section 9.3.2, the presence of swarf in the inside of the barrel (or barrels, if it has two) of a sawn-off shotgun can indicate that it has not been fired since it was shortened. It follows therefore, that if such a shotgun were found at the scene of an apparent suicide, it is most unlikely to have been the weapon responsible.

Is it probable that the victim shot himself or herself and, if so, was this act intentional or accidental?
Clearly, the firearms examiner cannot provide all of the evidence needed to answer these questions (e.g. he or she will not necessarily have knowledge of any possible

▶

Box 9.3 continued

motive for suicide). However, he or she may well be able to provide key pieces of information and opinion. Importantly, the examiner will usually be able to give an indication of the range of the shot (Section 9.2). This information, when coupled with a knowledge of the distance from the muzzle to the trigger and the reach of the victim, will allow it to be established whether he or she could have pressed the trigger without the help of some device. If, in a given case, such a device was necessary and none was present, this is an extremely strong indication that death was not due to suicide but as a result of either accident or homicide. Also, as outlined in Section 9.3.3, the firearms examiner will be able to establish whether the gun concerned is prone to unintentional discharge.

Significantly, both suicide and accidental shootings that result in self-injury necessarily involve contact between the gun and the victim. Therefore, in such cases, it is quite possible that trace evidence, such as fingerprints and/or DNA, from the victim will be found on the gun and/or its ammunition. Also, except in cases involving air weapons (including gas-powered guns), gunshot residues would be expected to be found. These would occur not only in and around the wound but also on the hand(s) of the victim. Furthermore, these would match residues recovered from the gun barrel and the spent cartridge case believed to have delivered the fatal shot.

It is worth noting that the pathologist, often working with the firearms examiner, will evaluate whether the site of the entrance wound is consistent with what is known about the sites on the body where suicides elect to shoot themselves. Common among such sites are the temples, forehead, mouth and the front portions of the neck and chest. The abdomen and eye are extremely rare targets for the act of suicide by shooting as are, for obvious reasons, locations that are difficult to reach (e.g. the back). Also, in many countries, including Britain, women are rarely victims of accidental or suicide shootings.

Finally, while it might appear to be improbable, many suicide victims shoot themselves repeatedly. Therefore, although multiple gunshot wounds would suggest homicide, this evidence alone is not enough to prove that it has occurred.

9.4 The examination of spent cartridge cases, bullets and wads

The examination of spent cartridge cases, bullets and shotgun plastic cup wads can reveal both class and individualising characteristics. Let us consider each of these types of item in turn.

9.4.1 The examination of spent cartridge cases

A spent cartridge case may carry a great deal of evidence. In the absence of a suspect firearm, it has the potential to reveal a number of important facts, including:

- the probable identity of the firm which made it (most cartridges carry identifying marks, referred to as headstamps, that are impressed onto the head by the manufacturer (for example, see the photograph in Box 9.4));
- the identity of anyone who has handled it and left their fingerprints on it;
- the make and, in some cases, the model of firearm that discharged it.

Importantly, if a suspect weapon is available, then a skilled firearms examiner will be able to establish whether the gun concerned did indeed fire the cartridge involved.

In order to maximise the information available from a spent cartridge case, the examiner will work methodically. If fingerprints are to be developed from the case, it is vitally important that this is done before they are smudged by subsequent handling. Once the case has been checked for the presence of fingerprints and any such prints have been recorded, then the examiner can note the calibre, shape and type of cartridge involved. For example, he or she will be able to readily establish whether the cartridge that was fired was one designed for use in a shotgun, handgun, rifle, etc.; whether it is rimmed or rimless and whether it is centre-fire or rim-fire. On the basis of such information, it will often be possible to specify the class of weapon that is likely to have fired it. For example, a 12-bore shotgun cartridge may well have been fired in a shotgun and will not have been discharged in a conventional handgun. However obvious this type of connection may appear, it is important to realise that:

- some weapons are manufactured to be able to fire more than one type of ammunition (e.g. some revolvers are made such that they can fire both revolver and self-loading pistol ammunition);

- some types of ammunition can be fired in more than one type of weapon (e.g. sub-machine guns fire self-loading pistol cartridges);

- some weapons will fire ammunition of a type other than that intended for them (e.g. some self-loading pistols may fire certain revolver cartridges, although weapon malfunctions may occur);

- it is possible to adapt a gun to fire ammunition that, in its unaltered state, it cannot fire (e.g. the barrel of a shotgun can be exchanged to enable it to fire handgun cartridges) – such adaptations may be permanent or reversible; and

- desperate people will, on occasion, go to extraordinary lengths to enable the weapon at their disposal to fire the ammunition that they have to hand (e.g. by filing down oversized cartridges or by wrapping paper around undersized cartridges).

Information based on calibre, shape and type will be supplemented by class characteristics revealed in the marks left on the cartridge by the gun. For example, as described in Box 9.4, the actions of self-loading weapons usually create extractor, ejector and possibly chambering marks on cartridge cases, as do those of automatic weapons. The exact relative positions of such marks can be used to establish the probable make and, in some cases, model of the gun involved; as can, for example, the positions, shapes and sizes of firing pin marks.

In cases in which a suspect firearm is available, comparison macroscopy (Figure 9.7) can be used to establish whether detailed features of the marks found on the questioned cartridge case match those created when a similar cartridge is test fired with the firearm concerned. These detailed features arise because of impact or abrasion between specific parts of both the gun and the cartridge (e.g. the firing pin of the gun and the primer cup of the cartridge). The exact pattern revealed in these detailed features will be a function of the shape and arrangement of grooves, pits and projections on the surface of the part of the gun involved. As the shape and

((a) Leica Microsystems (UK) Ltd);
((b) and (c) Reproduced by kind permission of Philip Boyce, Forensic Alliance, UK)

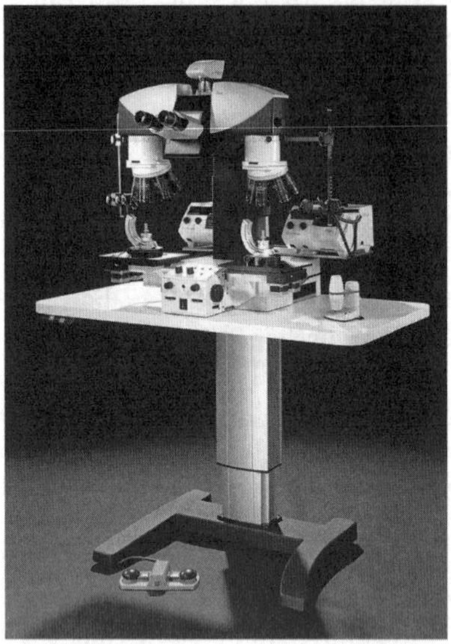

(b) Questioned sample   Control sample

A portion of the external surface of the primer cup of each cartridge case

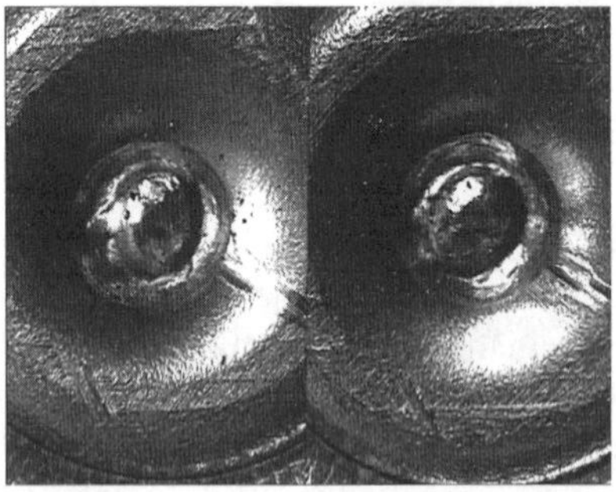

Note that the matching marks on these two cartridge cases were, in each instance, caused by both the firing pin and the forcing back of the cartridge into the face of the breech on firing. Such matches show that both cartridge cases have been forced into contact with the same firing pin and same breech face

(c) Questioned sample   Control sample

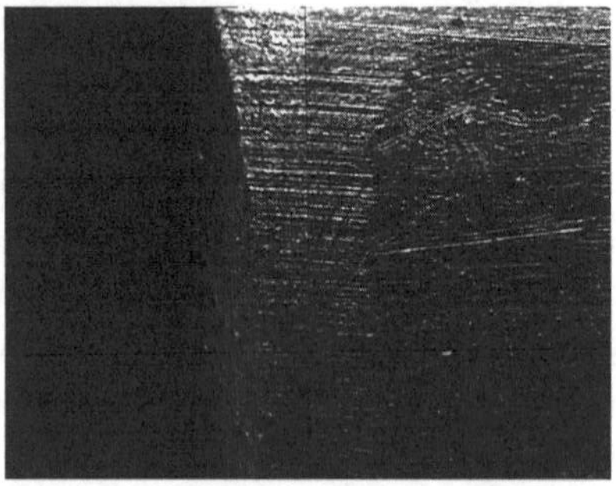

Mark made by a rifling land on the samples

Note the parallel striations of the rifling mark on the control sample match those of the questioned sample, demonstrating that both bullets were fired from the same barrel

Figure 9.7 (a) A comparison macroscope used to observe questioned and control samples under identical conditions, allowing any marks to be compared. Matching marks, as observed using a macroscope, on (b) questioned and control cartridge cases and (c) questioned and control bullets

arrangement of these attributes vary from gun to gun, a match is strong evidence that the questioned cartridge has, at some time, been in the gun concerned.

However, care does need to be exercised in drawing conclusions based on this evidence. For example, if a cartridge has been manually passed through the action of a self-loading weapon but not fired, the details on the extractor, ejector and chambering marks that it bears may well match those on a cartridge case that *has been* fired in the gun. Also, it is possible for a fired cartridge case to be reloaded with a fresh primer, propellant and bullet and reused. Under these circumstances, many of the marks present from the first firing of this cartridge case will be present after the second firing. In either case, the cartridge case concerned may bear the marks of one gun after having been fired in a different weapon. Fortunately, there are marks that can be used to definitively link a spent cartridge case to the gun that fired it last, or on the only occasion that it has been fired. These are those caused by the firing pin and the face of the breech that appear on the primer cup. They can be used to make such a linkage because they are both individualising and are made only when the cartridge is fired (i.e. not merely passed through the gun's action). Furthermore, the primer is replaced whenever a cartridge is reloaded.

9.4.2 The examination of fired bullets

The examination of a bullet recovered from a crime scene may provide evidence of what it has passed through and/or ricocheted off from the time that it left the muzzle of the gun to the moment at which it came to rest. Such evidence may be embodied in impressions made in the bullet of objects with which it has collided. For example, a bullet that has passed through or impacted on clothing may have the weave pattern of the material from which the clothing was made embossed in its nose (Figure 9.8).

However, it may also take the form of items of trace evidence either on the bullet's surface or embedded into it. For example, such items may include traces of:

■ garment fibres, blood, bone and/or hair (as may occur in the case of a bullet that has passed through a victim);

■ wood, glass and/or paint (as may be found if the bullet had struck a wooden door or window);

■ brick, sand and/or cement (as could be seen if it had hit a wall).

(Reproduced by kind permission of Philip Boyce, Forensic Alliance, UK)

Figure 9.8 Weave pattern on the noses of two bullets
Such patterns may be visible on bullets that have either passed through or been stopped by textile fabric. The projectiles shown in this figure were stopped by impact with armoured vests

Clearly, as such trace evidence may be easily lost, it is wise to look for it before any other aspect of the bullet is examined.

A bullet that has suffered little damage will reveal the calibre of its cartridge, as this is evident from the bullet's shape and dimensions. In the case of a damaged but intact bullet, its weight will give an indication of its calibre and allow certain calibres to be excluded as possibilities.

A knowledge of the calibre of the cartridge, coupled with an observation of the overall features of rifling marks present on the bullet, can enable a skilled firearms examiner to narrow down the types of gun that could have fired the cartridge concerned. The features of the rifling marks that may be used in such an assessment include the number of land impressions, and their direction of twist (i.e. right-hand or left-hand – see Figure 9.9), width and angle of inclination. However, some care needs to be taken in this work. For example, in many cases, it is quite possible to

(Reproduced by kind permission of Philip Boyce, Forensic Alliance, UK)

Figure 9.9 (a) Left-hand rifling marks and (b) right-hand rifling marks on three different types of bullet

fire ammunition of an incorrect calibre in a given gun – although in instances where the bullet is recovered in a fairly undamaged state, such an occurrence will normally be evident from the state or lack of the rifling marks engraved upon it. Furthermore, it is quite possible that the firearm that discharged the cartridge had been altered in some way (e.g. re-chambered or re-rifled) so that the calibre and/or rifling marks are not those expected.

In cases in which both a questioned bullet and a suspect firearm have been recovered, it is often possible to establish whether the gun concerned did indeed fire the questioned bullet. Firstly, the gun's calibre and the class characteristics of its rifling are compared with those established from the bullet. If these are consistent with the bullet having been fired by the gun, then comparison macroscopy (Figure 9.7) is used to compare the rifling marks on the questioned bullet with those on similar bullets that have been test fired using the weapon concerned. In this case, the features that are compared are the minute parallel lines (i.e. striations) that form on the relatively soft bullet as it passes down the barrel. The features of the barrel that cause these lines are those imperfections in the barrel's internal surface that were introduced during manufacture, or caused by the abrasive action of previous bullets or cleaning activities, or introduced by corrosion. The striations that a given barrel produces are believed to be unique to it, i.e. such marks are individualising. Therefore, matches between the striations that are found on the questioned bullet with those found on the test bullet can conclusively demonstrate that the same gun fired both bullets.

However, there are reasons why the striations on two bullets fired by the same gun may not match. A number of these are considered below.

- The striations alter as the gun is used and the barrel wears. However, these alterations due to wear are rarely significant except in automatic weapons and firearms constructed from inferior materials.
- If the weapon is recovered in a rusty state, the corrosion products on the inside of the barrel may cause the striations it makes to differ from those formed by the previously clean gun.
- If the barrel has been damaged in an attempt to thwart the forensic linking of the bullet to the gun, this may alter the striations that it produces.
- The barrel of the gun may have been replaced since the questioned bullet was fired (the barrels of many self-loading pistols are readily changed).

Therefore, when interpreting evidence based on the match, or otherwise, between questioned and test-fired bullets, it may be possible either to state that the gun under examination:

- fired both bullets, i.e. the class characteristics (calibre and the large-scale features of the rifling marks) show that it is possible for the gun to have fired both bullets *and* the striations on one bullet match those on the other;
- may have fired both bullets, i.e. the class characteristics (calibre and the large-scale features of the rifling marks) show that it is possible for the gun to have fired both bullets *but* the striations on one bullet *do not* match those on the other; or

■ at least in its current form, could not have fired both bullets, i.e. the class characteristics (calibre and the large-scale features of the rifling marks) do not match.

Finally, while air weapons do not fire cartridges, the projectiles that they discharge will often carry directly analogous information to that of bullets fired from other types of gun. Like such bullets, lead pellets shot from air weapons will normally carry rifling impressions on their flanks that can provide both class and individualising characteristics. Similarly, these pellets can provide information about the calibre of the weapon from which they were discharged and they may bear marks or trace materials that reveal details of objects with which they have impacted.

9.4.3 The examination of shotgun plastic cup wads

Figure 9.2(e) shows an illustration of a modern shotgun cartridge containing a plastic cup wad. When a shotgun is fired, the wadding leaves the muzzle of the weapon with the pellets and travels some distance in the general direction of travel of the shot. Plastic cup wads are used in many modern shotgun cartridges and may therefore be recovered from the scene of a crime in which a shotgun was discharged.

There are a large number of designs of plastic cup wad in use; a fact that can help in the identification of the brand of cartridge from which a given wad was fired. However, although the details of the design of such wads vary, they are all essentially two cups joined back to back. One cup contains the shot and the other acts as a cap over the propellant.

The diameter of the wad indicates the bore of the weapon designed to fire the cartridge that contained the wad. Furthermore, the surface of the plastic cup wad that faces the shot can hold indentations that give an indication of the size of the pellets that were fired.

The high muzzle pressures that are generated in sawn-off shotguns can mean that the cup-shaped portion of the wad that faces the propellant in the live cartridge is turned inside out on firing. The presence of this feature can therefore indicate that such a weapon was used. Additionally, when a sawn-off shotgun is created, inept workmanship may mean that burs of metal are left on the inside of the barrel. These can leave individualising marks on plastic cup wads that are fired from the gun concerned.

Further information
Box 9.4

The creation of marks on cartridge cases by self-loading firearms

Within a fraction of a second of firing, the action of a self-loading gun will have removed the spent cartridge case from the weapon and, provided that the magazine was not empty at the time of firing, placed a live cartridge in the chamber. The firing mechanism will also have been re-cocked. The energy required to undertake these processes is obtained from the firing of the gun in the first instance. The shooter may then fire the weapon again by re-pulling the trigger.

Pulling the trigger causes the firing pin of the weapon to be forced into the metal primer cup, where it leaves an impression of its tip. Immediately after this, the process of firing makes the cartridge case expand and may thereby result in the formation of marks on its sides owing to voids or imperfections within the chamber. Importantly, firing also forces the case backward into the face of the breech. In most cases, this results in the creation of an impression

Box 9.4 continued

of the breech face on the primer cup and, normally, elsewhere on the head of the cartridge case.

Once the gas pressure within the barrel has dropped to a safe level, the breech will be made to open by the action of the weapon. In some cases, this causes the tip of the firing pin to be pulled slightly across the primer cup, leading to the formation of a drag mark (see figure (a) below).

In the majority of self-loading weapons, the spent cartridge case is pulled from the chamber by an extractor claw engaged in the case's extractor groove (Figure 9.2(d)). As the empty case travels towards the rear of the gun, it is made to strike an ejector-rod, which is positioned so as to cause the case to be flung out of the weapon via the gun's ejection port. Note that if the firing pin is still protruding into the primer cup at the time of ejection, this too can cause a drag mark to be formed similar to that shown in figure (a). Immediately after the ejection of the empty case, the action picks up a live cartridge (if present) from the magazine and pushes it into the chamber. These processes typically result in the formation of marks on the flanks of the case made when the cartridge was pushed

into the chamber (known as chambering marks), and where the extractor claw engaged in the extractor groove and the cartridge head struck the ejector-rod. The general locations of these marks are shown in figure (b) below.

There are other ways in which a self-loading gun can mark cartridge cases. For example:

■ to warn the shooter of the gun's condition, Walther PPK pistols have a pin that protrudes from the weapon when a cartridge is in the chamber – the presence of this pin causes an indentation to appear in the head of spent cartridge cases;

■ guns fitted with box magazines may produce marks on the flanks of the cartridge cases that they use because of the abrasion that occurs between each cartridge case and the lips of the magazine when the action of the gun withdraws a live cartridge from it;

■ in some weapons, the cartridge cases can glance off the edge of the ejection port as they leave – so producing marks on the flanks of the spent cases of fired cartridges.

(a)

(b)

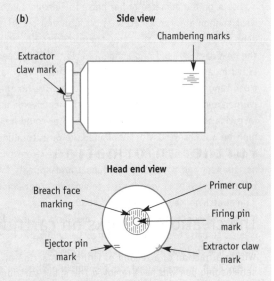

(a) The head of a fired cartridge case showing the impression of the breech face (i.e. in this case, striations from top to bottom) and firing pin, together with a drag mark. (b) The marks commonly made on a cartridge case by the action of a self-loading firearm

(Photograph reproduced by kind permission of Philip Boyce, Forensic Alliance, UK)

9.5 Gunshot residues

The discharge of a firearm results not only in the ejection of the intended projectile(s) but also secondary ejecta. These secondary materials include partially combusted and unburned propellant, the combustion products of both the propellant and the primer, and matter derived from the barrel, cartridge case and projectile(s). When a gun is fired, these materials form a heterogeneous cloud of finely divided particles, known collectively as gunshot residues (GSR), firearms discharge residues (FDR) or cartridge discharge residues (CDR). These residues settle on all nearby surfaces. These include the insides of the barrel and cartridge; where exposed, the hand(s), clothes, hair and face of the shooter; and the target (provided that it was sufficiently close to the firearm when it was fired).

As illustrated by the Jill Dando case (Box 9.5), gunshot residues can provide important evidence linking a suspect to a crime scene.

Case study

Box 9.5

The Jill Dando case

On 26 April 1999, the UK television presenter Jill Dando was shot on the doorstep of her home in Fulham, southwest London at approximately 11.30 a.m. and certified dead just after 1 p.m. at nearby Charing Cross Hospital. The next day, Scotland Yard announced that she had been killed by a single shot to the side of her head, fired at close range. One theory concerning the motive for this murder, and one that gained weight as the massive police investigation progressed, was that the killer could be a fan who was obsessed with Miss Dando. Rewards totalling a quarter of a million pounds were offered (from two newspapers and a private individual) and appeals for information were staged by the television programme 'Crimewatch' in May 1999 and April 2000.

Thirteen months after Miss Dando's murder, a 41-year-old man called Barry George (also known as Barry Bulsara) from the Fulham area was arrested by police. Four days later, on 29 May 2000, he was charged with the murder of Miss Dando at West London Magistrates' Court. Almost a year later, on 4 May 2001, the trial of Barry George at the Old Bailey finally got under way after a number of adjournments. Eight weeks later, after a period of deliberation lasting over 30 hours, the jury returned a verdict of guilty, by a majority of ten to one. Barry George was sentenced to life imprisonment on 2 July

2001. When the verdict was returned, his defence team immediately announced their intention to appeal.

A pivotal part of the prosecution's case concerned trace evidence in the form of gunshot residue. A microscopic particle of this material (approximately 11 μm in size) was recovered from the pocket of a coat belonging to Barry George. According to a firearms examiner from the Forensic Science Service (FSS) called to appear in court as an expert witness, this could have originated from the fired cartridge case recovered from the crime scene. Although the murder weapon was never found, the examination of the recovered cartridge case by another firearms expert indicated that the gun used was a short, self-loading 9 mm pistol. Marks present on the bullet showed that it had been fired from a gun with a smooth-bored barrel and not from a rifled barrel, as would be expected with a conventional pistol. A possible explanation for this anomaly was that the gun used was a deactivated* gun that had subsequently been reactivated.

Aside from the matter of the gunshot residue described above, the prosecution's case was composed mainly of circumstantial evidence, including that of eyewitnesses. An appeal by Barry George against his conviction was dismissed on 29 July 2002. Later that same year, in December 2002, permission to take his appeal to a higher court was turned down by the House of Lords. At the time of writing

Box 9.5 continued

(November 2006), the Criminal Cases Review Commission (CCRC) is examining new evidence in the case, submitted by Barry George's lawyers. This independent body is responsible for the investigation of suspected miscarriages of justice in England, Wales and Northern Ireland and has the power to refer cases to the appropriate court of appeal (Chapter 14, Section 14.1.3).

*In the wake of the Dunblane school shootings of 1996, legislation was introduced that effectively outlawed the possession of handguns. However, these could still be legally owned, e.g. as collectors' items, if they had the necessary official certification to show that they had been rendered incapable of firing projectiles.

A number of techniques have been devised to analyse for the presence of gunshot residues. These are based on the detection (and in some cases the quantification) of either:

■ the organic fraction, which is dominated by the materials derived from the propellant; or

■ the inorganic fraction, which is made up of materials formed from the combustion products of the primer and metals from the cartridge case, barrel and bullet.

To date, the most successful of these techniques is the application of SEM-EDX (Box 9.6), which concentrates on the inorganic fraction. This technique not only allows much of the elemental composition of individual microscopic particles to be established but also enables images that show their morphology (i.e. shape) to be obtained. This is important because, in many cases, knowledge of these two attributes will allow gunshot residue particles to be uniquely identified as such and the

Forensic techniques

Box 9.6

Scanning electron microscopy (SEM) and energy dispersive X-ray analysis (EDX) (together known as SEM-EDX)

SEM compared with light microscopy

SEM is a technique that uses a beam of electrons to produce magnified images of samples. It has three main advantages over microscopy that uses light to carry out this function. First, SEM can produce images with a much higher degree of spatial resolution than can light microscopy. Spatial resolution is a measure of the ability to tell apart features that are physically close together.

SEM is capable of distinguishing between adjacent features that are only 4 nm apart. That is, SEM is capable of a spatial resolution of 4 nm. This compares extremely favourably with the best spatial resolution that can be obtained by light microscopy, which is 200 nm.

Second, SEM has a much greater depth of field, especially at high levels of magnification, than does light microscopy. Depth of field is an expression of the

Box 9.6 continued

distance along the path taken by the beam that impacts with the sample either side of the ideal focal point of that beam that still produces an image with an acceptable level of spatial resolution. Taken together, these first two points mean that SEM is much better than light microscopy at producing images of the surfaces of three-dimensional objects at high levels of magnification.

The third main advantage of SEM is its ability – when coupled with a technique known as energy dispersive X-ray analysis (EDX) (described below) – to provide information about the elemental composition of a sample and the spatial distribution of the elements within it. This is something that light microscopy cannot do.

It is important to realise, however, that light microscopy has advantages over SEM. For example, SEM cannot provide information about refractive index, bi-refringence (Chapter 3, Box 3.3) or colour. For many applications, therefore, SEM and light microscopy are complementary techniques.

The generation of SEM images and the nature of EDX

A scanning electron microscope consists of:

■ a source of a stream of electrons;
■ a system to focus this stream into an extremely narrow beam (called the primary beam);
■ a means of causing this beam to repeatedly scan a portion of the surface of the sample in a series of parallel lines – thereby scanning a rectangular area of the sample's surface;
■ a means of detecting variations in the intensity of a signal produced by the interaction of the beam with the sample's surface;
■ a means of displaying these variations as alterations in the intensity of light and shade of a series of parallel lines that thereby form a rectangular image of a scanned portion of the sample's surface.

When the primary beam of electrons hits the sample's surface, the energy that it imparts to that surface is dissipated by a number of processes. Importantly, these include the ejection of both secondary and back scattered electrons, and the production of characteristic X-rays. Each of these phenomena produces a signal that can be used to generate an image of the surface of the sample.

Secondary electrons (SE) are those that are ejected from the atoms of the sample during interactions with the primary beam of electrons. Secondary electrons are not highly energetic and so can only escape from those regions of the sample that are very near to the surface. For this reason, and because the area from which these electrons emanate is essentially the same as the area irradiated by the primary beam, secondary electrons provide the images with the best spatial resolution. These images are also readily interpreted to give information about the surface topography of the sample. This is because protruding parts of its surface appear as bright areas, while indented areas are dark – just as they would appear if the sample were illuminated with light.

Back-scattered electrons (BSE) arise when the electrons of the primary beam rebound after interactions with the nuclei of the atoms that make up the sample. BSE are typically much more energetic than secondary electrons and therefore can originate from deeper within the sample and produce images that show poorer spatial resolution. The interactions that produce the BSE are strongly influenced by the sizes of the charge on the nuclei of the atoms involved. The atomic number of a nucleus is equal to the number of positively charged particles that it contains. Consequently, the BSE image of a flat surface is brighter in those areas that represent parts of the sample with a relatively high average atomic number (i.e. high average nuclear charge) than those that correspond to regions of low average atomic number (i.e. low average nuclear charge). As all atoms that have the same atomic number are atoms of the same element, the BSE image conveys some, albeit highly qualitative, information about the elemental composition of the sample. If the sample is not flat, the BSE image is harder to interpret because, in addition to information about the elemental composition of the sample, it also exhibits changes in brightness with variations in surface topography.

The bombardment of a sample with the primary electron beam will induce it to produce characteristic X-ray photons (a photon is a particle of electromagnetic radiation). Each such photon is released from the sample as a consequence of the ejection of an electron from an inner shell of an atom. This happens within the sample as a result of interactions between the atoms concerned

Box 9.6 continued

and electrons from the primary beam. An ejection such as this leaves a gap in the inner shell involved. If this gap is filled by an electron from an outer shell of the same atom, an X-ray photon is released with an energy that is characteristic of the atomic number of the atom. This means that an analysis of the energy of the photons released by this process can be used to establish the elemental composition of that part of the sample that is immediately under the portion of its surface that

is radiated with the primary electron beam. Alternatively, the system used to detect these photons can be tuned to the energy of one of the characteristic X-rays of an element of interest. This enables an image of the distribution of this element in the surface portion of the sample that is irradiated with the primary beam to be established. Such images, which are usually referred to as maps, do not have the spatial resolution of SE or BSE images.

discovery of these particles on a suspect may therefore be incriminating. In other cases, particles will be either identified as possibly being gunshot residues or shown not to have arisen from the firing of a gun.

Figure 9.10 is the result of an SEM-EDX analysis of a particle of gunshot residue. Note that it has the spheroidal (ball-like) morphology that is typical of most such particles. Note also that this example contains lead (Pb, which may be from the primer or the bullet), and barium (Ba), antimony (Sb) and potassium (K) (from the primer). Other typical elements that may be found in particles of gunshot residue from modern cartridges are calcium and silicon (from the primer), copper and zinc (from the cartridge case) and iron (from the barrel). As mentioned before, gunshot residues are heterogeneous. Consequently, the particles in a given sample will not necessarily share exactly the same elemental composition. However, the elements that they do contain will represent those derived from the cartridge that was fired and the gun that fired it. Interestingly, there are a number of different primer compositions in use. It may therefore be possible to distinguish between cartridges on the basis of the elemental composition of the gunshot residues that they produce.

Gunshot residues can be recovered from the surfaces on which they have alighted using a number of techniques. These include the application of an aluminium stub that is topped with a sticky, electrically conducting tab (Figure 9.11). This has the advantage that the stub and tab can be directly placed into the SEM-EDX machine without further sample pre-treatment.

In addition to analysing for the inorganic part of gunshot residues, it is common practice to determine whether there are also organic materials present that are consistent with the discharge of a firearm. Some laboratories routinely carry out such analysis for organic compounds, while others do so only if the analysis for inorganic materials produces a positive result. Sampling for the organic fraction is conveniently carried out by using a vacuum to draw air from over the surface to be analysed and thence onto a suitable filter.

(a)

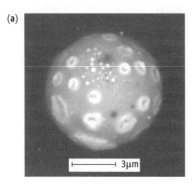

(b)

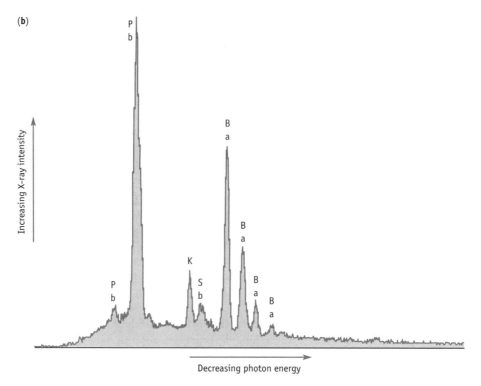

Figure 9.10 SEM-EDX analysis of a particle of gunshot residue
(a) The morphology of the particle as revealed by SEM. (b) The elemental composition of this particle as revealed by EDX

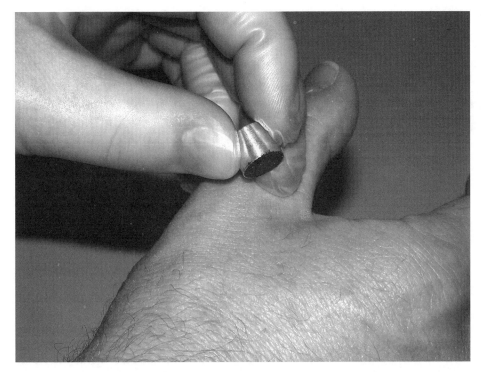

Figure 9.11 The use of an aluminium stub that is topped with a sticky, electrically conducting tab to collect gunshot residues

9.6 Summary

■ Under English law, a firearm, as defined in Section 57 of the Firearms Act 1968 (as currently amended) is '... a lethal barrelled weapon of any description from which any shot, bullet or other missile can be discharged...'. The categories of non-air weapon firearms most commonly encountered by forensic examiners are handguns, shotguns, rifles and sub-machine guns. Of these, the first is of particular importance as they are the most common category of non-air weapon firearm to be identified as being involved in offences recorded in England and Wales. Most handguns are either revolvers or self-loading firearms. Unlike the other types of firearm listed above, shotguns are designed to fire multiple projectiles (pellets) with each discharge.

■ Ballistics is the scientific study of projectile motion. When considering small arms, distinction is drawn between internal ballistics (concerned with projectile motion within the barrel), external ballistics (concerned with the flight of the projectile after it leaves the firearm) and terminal ballistics (the study of the interaction of the projectile with the target). Knowledge of ballistics, often linked with the test firing of the suspect weapon, can help in crime scene reconstruction by providing information about, for example, the range of fire and the likelihood of ricochet.

■ The examination of a suspect firearm will often provide the answers to important questions. These may include:

– Whom or what has this firearm been in contact with?

– Could this firearm be responsible for firing the shots that were discharged at a given shooting incident?

– Could this firearm have been unintentionally discharged?

– Could the intentional discharge of this firearm have caused unintentional injury?

In cases of fatal shootings, it also has an important role to play in the establishment of the manner of death whether homicide, accident or suicide.

■ The examination of any given spent cartridge case has the potential to establish the identity of anyone who has handled it and left their fingerprints on it and the weapon that fired it. Similarly, the marks left on a bullet when discharged from a gun can, in many cases, be used to uniquely match it to the weapon concerned. A spent bullet may also reveal evidence of what it passed through and/or ricocheted off from the time it left the muzzle of the gun to the moment at which it came to rest. Plastic cup wads fired from sawn-off shotguns along with the charge of pellets may also carry individualising marks that enable the gun concerned to be unambiguously identified.

■ When a person discharges a firearm, gunshot residues will normally settle on their hands, face, hair and clothes. These residues can be recovered after the event and, in some cases, be clearly identified as having been generated when a gun was fired. Under favourable circumstances, the gunshot residues from different cartridges may be distinguished on the basis of their elemental composition.

Problems

1. During a fatal shooting incident, three shots were fired: two from one gun and one from another. However, only one bullet struck the deceased. Furthermore, this bullet passed right through the victim. All three spent cartridge cases and all three bullets were recovered from the scene, as were both of the guns. Would it be possible to establish which gun had fired the fatal shot?

2. When confronted with evidence that she fired a fatal shot, a suspect in a homicide case admitted to firing the gun but asserted that the gun was accidentally discharged and that, in any case, it was not pointing at the victim when it was fired. Under ideal circumstances, what types of evidence could the firearms examiner produce that would corroborate or refute the suspect's assertion?

3. If you were to be asked to design the firearms examination provision for a major supplier of forensic science services, what advantages and disadvantages would you see in building one laboratory compared with two separate laboratories? In the latter case, one laboratory would only carry out gunshot residue analysis, whereas the other would be restricted to the examination of suspect firearms and spent cartridge cases, bullets, wads and shot.

4. Consider two bullets fired from the same gun, using identical cartridges from exactly the same place, in precisely the same direction, through the canopy of a tree in quick succession under identical conditions. The first bullet ricocheted off a twig. This caused the bullet to deviate by one degree from its original path. It also broke the twig clear of its branch so that the second bullet hit no part of the tree. How far apart would the impact sites of the two bullets be? Assume that the target is, to a good approximation, at right angles to the flight path of both bullets and that it is 50 metres from the twig in question.

5. Compare and contrast the evidential implications of:
   (a) finding gunshot residues on someone's hand and
   (b) finding someone's fingerprints on a spent cartridge case.

6. Discuss the evidence that may be available from spent cartridge cases, bullets and wads.

Further reading

Byers, S. N. (2005) *Introduction to forensic anthropology: a textbook* (2nd edn). Boston: Allyn & Bacon. (Chapter 12 of this book is concerned with the characteristics of damage to skeletal remains caused by bullets and other projectiles.)

Coleman, K., Hird, C. and Povey, D. (2006) *Violent crime overview: homicide and gun crime 2004/2005*. Supplementary volume to *Crime in England and Wales 2004/2005*. Home Office Statistical Bulletin. London: Home Office Research, Development and Statistics Directorate.

Heard, B. J. (1997) *Handbook of firearms and ballistics: examining and interpreting forensic evidence*. Chichester: John Wiley & Sons Ltd.

Home Office (2001) *Criminal statistics: England and Wales 2000*. London: HMSO. Crown copyright. (Chapter 3 of this report is concerned with crime involving firearms.)

Rowe, W. F. (1988) 'Firearms identification', in R. Saferstein (ed.) *Forensic science handbook*, Volume II. Upper Saddle River, NJ: Prentice Hall.

Shepherd, R. (2003) *Simpson's forensic medicine* (12th edn). London: Arnold. (Chapter 11 of this book is concerned with firearm and explosive injuries.)

Warlow, T. A. (2004) *Firearms, the law and forensic ballistics* (2nd edn). London: Taylor & Francis Ltd. (A detailed and comprehensive text, written from a UK perspective.)

Fires

10

10

Chapter objectives

After reading this chapter, you should be able to:

> Understand what is meant by the term fire and the conditions that are required for fire to occur.

> Distinguish between the natures of smouldering combustion and flaming combustion and why one of these may become the other.

> Describe how fire behaves in rooms and similar compartments, and outdoors.

> Appreciate why fires are investigated.

> Explain why it is wise to approach a fire scene as if it were a crime scene until and unless it is known not to be.

> Understand the principles that allow fire scene investigations to establish the seat and cause of a fire and whether or not it was intentionally started.

> Recognise the role of laboratory chemical analysis in the investigation of suspicious fires.

Introduction

Throughout the populated world, fire causes considerable damage, loss of life and human misery. Unfortunately, a significant proportion of this destruction and distress results from deliberately ignited fires. For example, in 2004, 442 700 fires were attended by local authority fire brigades in the United Kingdom, of which there were 91 200 fires (i.e. more than one-fifth of the total) that were either known to be or suspected of being deliberately started. Of these 91 200 fires, 28 044 occurred in buildings and led to an estimated 60 fatal and 2533 non-fatal casualties.

In this chapter, the nature of fire is described (Section 10.1), as is its behaviour in both rooms and similar compartments, and outdoors (Section 10.2). The means by which fire scenes are investigated are discussed (Section 10.3) and the laboratory analysis of samples for materials that might have been used by an arsonist in an attempt to accelerate the spread of fire is explored (Section 10.4).

10.1 The nature of fire

Fire is that condition, characterised by the evolution of heat and light, that occurs as a consequence of a chemical process known as combustion. Combustion is an exothermic (i.e. heat-evolving) redox reaction. Redox reactions are those that involve the complete transfer of electrons from one chemical species to another. The chemical species that loses electrons is referred to as the reductant or reducing agent, whereas the species that gains them is known as the oxidant or oxidising agent. In combustion reactions, the reductant is referred to as the fuel.

In the vast majority of fires, the oxidant is the molecular oxygen ($O_{2(g)}$) that makes up 20.95 per cent by volume of dry, normal air at sea level. Such fires are referred to in this book as conventional fires. In contrast, under unusual circumstances, other oxidants may be involved. For example, fires involving fireworks will be sustained, at least in part, by the oxidising agents (such as the nitrate ion, NO_3^-) present within the formulations of the contents of the fireworks themselves.

There are four conditions that must be met in order for a fire to start and to be self-sustaining. Two of these have already been mentioned. These are the presence of both a fuel and an appropriate oxidant, which must be brought together in suitable proportions. In addition, sufficient, suitable energy must be supplied (usually as heat) for the ignition of the fire. Once a self-sustaining fire has started, the heat that it generates is more than enough for this purpose, thereby allowing continuous re-ignition to occur. Finally, the fuel and oxidant must have the ability to react in a chain reaction that is self-sustaining. The absence of any one of these conditions means that a fire will not start. Furthermore, removal of one or more of them will put out an established fire. This is the basis of all fire-fighting techniques.

Distinction can be made between fires that have flames (i.e. plumes of burning gas) and fires that smoulder (i.e. produce heat and light without the presence of flames). In conventional fires, the flammable gas necessary for the presence of flames may arise from the pyrolysis (i.e. the chemical breakdown under the influence of heat) of a solid fuel, such as wood or coal. Alternatively, it may be present as the result of the vaporisation of a liquid fuel, such as petrol, or the fuel itself may be a gas, such as methane (the dominant component of natural gas).

Smouldering can take place when solid fuels burn. This mode of combustion is frequently observed in conventional fires and, when it occurs, takes place at the interface between the solid fuel and the air. Many organic solid fuels (i.e. solid fuels based on carbon compounds), including wood, pyrolyse in conventional fires to produce not only flammable gases but also a char. In many instances, this char – which is impure carbon – remains after the gaseous pyrolysis products have ceased to form and undergoes smouldering combustion.

Well-ventilated char that is undergoing smouldering combustion, and which may be very hot, can produce small flames that are mainly due to the gaseous combustion of carbon monoxide (CO). Notwithstanding this, completely pyrolysed smouldering char will not support the full flaming combustion frequently observed during the char-producing pyrolysis process, unless fresh fuel is supplied to the fire.

Smouldering can also arise in solid fuels that are still capable of forming flammable gases by pyrolysis. This can occur if the ventilation and/or the heat supply is insufficient to support flaming combustion. If such a fire is allowed to spread, it

Fire

The phenomenon in which heat and light are liberated by the process of combustion.

may become sufficiently hot and ventilated to allow flaming combustion to ensue (i.e. the fire may burst into flames). In the normal course of events, the flaming fire will then spread at a much faster rate than the preceding smouldering combustion.

Unusually, a conventional fire may be preceded by an explosion or explosions. This may occur because of the deliberate or accidental discharge of an explosive device. It may also occur when a mixture of air and a flammable gas (e.g. natural gas), dust (e.g. flour or coal dust) or vapour (e.g. petrol vapour) is ignited. For example, an arsonist who douses the inside of a property with petrol prior to setting it alight may well blow himself up when striking the match. As shown in Chapter 11, Figure 11.1, flammable vapour explosions can be highly destructive.

On occasion, an explosion or explosions may accompany a conventional fire. This can happen if, during the course of a fire, a container of flammable liquid or gas is heated. This will cause the pressure in the container to rise and, if it bursts, a cloud of flammable gas or rapidly vaporising flammable liquid may be discharged into the vicinity of the fire. An explosion will then occur if the gas or vapour mixes with sufficient oxygen from the air and is then set alight, most commonly by the fire. Also, there are circumstances in which smouldering combustion occurring within a vigorous fire can lead to flaming combustion that spreads with sufficient rapidity to cause an explosion. This can happen if solid fuel that is capable of sustaining flaming combustion is made to smoulder because the fire is held within a compartment, such as a room, that is poorly ventilated. Under these circumstances, the fuel will pyrolyse and the concentration of flammable gaseous pyrolysis products will rise within the compartment. If the compartment is then breached by, for example, a fire-fighter breaking a window, the sudden ingress of fresh air may fulfil the remaining condition for intense flaming combustion, namely the presence of an oxidant in sufficient amounts. If this occurs, an explosion can result that is variously known as a smoke explosion, **flashback**, backdraft or ventilation-induced flashover.

The nature of explosives and explosions, and the means by which explosion scenes may be investigated are discussed in Chapter 11.

Flashback
An explosion occurring during a fire when fresh air is suddenly allowed to mix with air in a compartment that is both oxygen-depleted and rich in flammable, volatile pyrolysis products.

10.2 The behaviour of fire

10.2.1 Fires in rooms and similar compartments

If allowed to burn unhindered, a fire taking place in a room that has a typical fuel load will, in most cases, proceed in a fairly predictable fashion, although the time taken from the start of a room fire to its end may vary significantly from one such incident to another. For ease of understanding, it is possible to divide the sequence of events that occurs in a room fire into a number of stages, namely: ignition, growth, flashover, post-flashover steady-state burning (also referred to as a fully developed fire) and decay. The last of these stages ends when the fire stops burning. As shown in Figure 10.1, once ignition has occurred, the heat release rate of a given room fire (which is the power transmitted out of the fire as heat) typically follows a pattern of increase, plateau and decline. These three phases correspond to growth culminating in flashover, post-flashover steady-state burning and decay respectively.

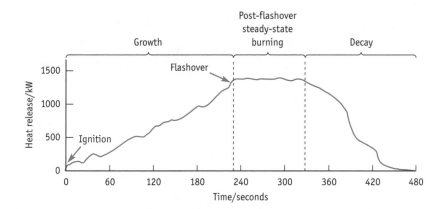

Figure 10.1 A typical graph showing the total heat release rate of a normal fire in a furnished room plotted as a function of time

Note that a similarly shaped graph is produced when the average temperature of the layer of hot gas within the room is plotted as a function of time

Each of the stages of a typical room fire listed in this paragraph are considered in turn below.

Ignition

Ignition occurs when all four of the conditions that are required for a fire to start – as set out in Section 10.1 – occur simultaneously in the same place. The newly ignited fire may produce flames from the start. However, even in fuels that are capable of sustaining flaming combustion, the fire may smoulder at the outset, bursting into flames only once the heat release rate and ventilation are adequate for it to do so. Indeed, some smouldering fires never reach these conditions and so do not burst into flames, and do not proceed through the sequence of events described here but smoulder until they self-extinguish.

In the vast majority of conventional fires, whether flaming or smouldering, ignition happens when heat supplies energy at a sufficient rate to a suitable fuel that is already in contact with the oxygen in the air. The heat that ignites the fire may be liberated by a number of processes. The most notable of these are listed below.

■ *Friction*, as is the case when the head of a 'strike anywhere' match is rubbed against a suitably rough surface or when a mechanical bearing overheats due to insufficient lubrication.

■ *Exothermic chemical reactions*, such as occur during the self-heating of fuels (as happens in cases of spontaneous combustion and fires caused by pyrophoric carbon, Box 10.1), and, much more commonly, in cases in which an established fire causes another portion of fuel to ignite. Such an established fire may be small, as in the case of a burning match, or large, for example a raging house fire.

Further information
Box 10.1

Spontaneous combustion and pyrophoric carbon

Spontaneous combustion

There are a number of fuels that, under certain circumstances, are known to ignite without the application of an external source of energy. In other words, they undergo spontaneous combustion. Such fires start when exothermic (i.e. heat-releasing) chemical reactions occurring within the fuel produce heat at a more rapid rate than can be removed from the fuel by the processes of thermal conduction, convection and heat radiation (Box 10.3). These circumstances lead to an increase in the temperature of the fuel (i.e. the fuel is self-heating). This, in turn, causes the rate of the exothermic reaction to increase, thereby enhancing the heat release rate and speeding up the reaction still further (for many reactions, the temperature rise that is required to cause a doubling of rate is approximately 10°C). If this process continues unchecked, the ignition temperature of the fuel will eventually be reached and spontaneous combustion will ensue.

In most cases of spontaneous combustion, the exothermic reaction involved is the aerial oxidation of the fuel. As this takes place at the fuel–air interface, it is best facilitated if the surface area to volume ratio of the fuel is high, as in the case of finely divided solid fuels or liquid fuels soaked onto an absorbent matrix. Furthermore, in order to allow the temperature to build up, the fuel will,

in most cases, have to be in a thermally insulated environment that, nonetheless, is permeable to the air. These observations are entirely in keeping with the properties of the common fuels that are known to be susceptible to spontaneous combustion. These include crumpled rags soaked in a drying oil (such as 'boiled' linseed oil), stacked hay or other similar vegetable matter, and coal when stored in large stockpiles.

Pyrophoric carbon

The prolonged heating of significant amounts of wood at temperatures in excess of 105°C, but more typically 120–200°C, under conditions in which ventilation is severely restricted can cause the production of sufficient flammable char to lead to a fire if enough air is subsequently admitted. The char forms because of the slow pyrolysis of the wood. Weeks, months or years may be needed for sufficient char to build up to pose a fire hazard. The char itself is known as pyrophoric carbon or pyrophoric charcoal. The adjective pyrophoric means 'will spontaneously combust on exposure to air or oxygen'. It is used in this context because once air is allowed to gain access to the char at the elevated temperatures that formed it, it will undergo a self-heating, exothermic reaction, thus allowing ignition to occur.

■ *Electrical heating*, as occurs when an electric current passes through a resistor. All normal materials through which electricity passes offer some resistance[1] and so will produce heat. The standard electrical wiring systems used to supply electricity to households, industry and commerce are no exception to this. However, they are designed such that, when they are installed and used correctly, the rate at which they produce heat is sufficiently low that it will be safely dissipated. There are nevertheless conditions

---

1 Superconductors are the only exception to this. They are rare materials, the use of which is currently confined to highly technical applications and which will not be encountered in the vast majority of fire investigations.

under which electrical heating can cause ignition temperatures to be reached. For example, this may happen when electricity passes through:

- a gas (in which case the current flow is referred to as an arc) (Box 10.2);
- a poor electrical contact in a wiring system;
- a heating element (e.g. as found in an electric cooker);
- the incandescent wire in a conventional light bulb;
- a conductor (such as an electrical wire) at a current that is in excess of that which it is designed to withstand;
- a failing organic insulating material.

■ *The nuclear reactions that occur in the Sun.* These lead to the production of heat radiation (Box 10.3), which moves out into space in all directions from the Sun. This radiation delivers an insolation rate (i.e. the rate at which solar radiation delivers energy per unit horizontal area of the Earth's surface) with a maximum of about $1\,\text{kW}\,\text{m}^{-2}$. This is insufficient to ignite frequently encountered fuels. However, the action of a reflective concave surface or a transparent object capable of acting as a converging (i.e. convex) lens may focus the Sun's rays. This may produce a maximum energy delivery rate of $10\text{–}20\,\text{kW}\,\text{m}^{-2}$, which is capable of heating cellulose-based fuels (e.g. newspaper) to their ignition temperatures.

With the exception of fires caused by the self-heating of fuels, before ignition can occur energy must be transmitted to the fuel that is to be involved in the fire. This energy is usually supplied by heat, in which case, mechanisms by which it may be transmitted are thermal conduction, convection and heat radiation (Box 10.3). In some instances, one of these mechanisms dominates, while in others two or all

Case study
Box 10.2

An unusual case of an arc as a source of ignition

An arc is the discharge of electricity through a gas. Arcs vary considerably in scale, including both lightning bolts and the comparatively minute discharges of static electricity that may occur when a person walks across a dry carpet and reaches towards an earthed conductor. While arcs can ignite solid fuels, flammable vapours and gases are much more susceptible to this form of ignition and, as shown in the case described below, may be set on fire by small-scale arcs.

In 1922, there was an explosion in New York that was caused by the discharge of static electricity through a mixture of coal gas (a poisonous, highly flammable sub-

stance that is predominantly made up of hydrogen and methane) and air. The mixture was held in a tank made of iron and was being employed in the destruction of unwanted cats. The static electricity involved had built up on the fur of one of the tomcats as a direct consequence of his struggles to avoid being placed in the tank. When he eventually was dropped into the tank, the explosion that occurred scattered dead cats (including the tom) and injured the three people employed in disposing of the cats. All the injured people were lacerated and burnt to some extent and one of them sustained a suspected skull fracture.

Further information

Box 10.3

Heat, thermal conduction, convection and heat radiation

Heat (which is measured in joules, symbol J) is the name given to the interaction that occurs spontaneously when two objects at different temperatures are brought into thermal contact with one another. During this process, energy is spontaneously transferred by the heat inter-action from the hotter object to the cooler one. In this context, the term interaction denotes an observable change that occurs in one part of the universe that is cor-related with a corresponding change in another. For example, if a block of steel at 10°C is brought into ther-mal contact with another at 20°C, the cooler block will be observed to rise in temperature as thermal energy is transferred into it, while the warmer block's temperature will fall as thermal energy flows from it.

There are three means by which thermal contact may be achieved, namely thermal conduction, convection and heat radiation.

Thermal conduction is the transmission of heat through matter via the thermal excitation of the motion of its constituent particles (molecules, atoms, ions, etc.) and without the occurrence of macroscopic movement within the matter concerned. Note that the term thermal conduction is often shortened to *conduction* where the context makes it clear that it is heat, and not electricity, that is being discussed.

Convection is the transmission of heat as a consequence of the macroscopic movement of a fluid medium. Flows that are created in the fluid by this heat transfer mecha-nism are called convection currents. Clearly, convection will not happen within solids but can take place in both liquids and gases. The elevated temperatures that occur in a fire lead to the establishment of convection currents because of the heating and concomitant expansion of the immedi-ately surrounding air that fires cause. This hot air, together with any hot gaseous combustion products, is significantly more buoyant than the comparatively cool air around it and so rises rapidly. This produces a decrease in the atmos-pheric pressure in the immediate vicinity of the fire, creating a horizontal pressure gradient. A force is therefore established along this gradient that accelerates cool air from the relatively high-pressure zone around the fire towards the fire itself. As this cool air approaches the fire, it too is heated and so becomes buoyant, thereby perpetu-ating the process. A portion of the thermal energy that is borne aloft in the plume of buoyant gas so created will be transferred by heat interactions with objects in its path. It is this form of convection that is responsible for the bulk of the movement of thermal energy that occurs in normal fires, such as may be encountered in buildings. In many cases, it is therefore largely, but not wholly, responsible for the spread of a normal fire and the pattern of damage that it leaves behind.

Heat radiation (also called *radiant heat* or, where the context makes it clear that it is heat that is being dis-cussed, simply *radiation*) is the only means by which the heat interaction can occur through a vacuum. It refers to the transmission of heat in the form of electromagnetic radiation. The total amount of energy that is emitted in this form by an object per unit time per unit area (symbol E, measured in joules per second per square metre, i.e. $J s^{-1} m^{-2}$ [which is the same as the total power emitted in this form per unit area in watts per square metre, $W m^{-2}$]) is given by:

$$E = e\sigma T^4$$

where e is the total emissivity of the object, σ is Stefan's constant ($5.7 \times 10^{-8} J s^{-1} m^{-2} K^{-4}$) and T is the temperature of the object in kelvin, symbol K (i.e. its temperature in °C plus 273.15).

Consider an object that is completely enclosed and that is in thermal equilibrium with its enclosure (i.e. at the same temperature as its enclosure). Under these con-ditions, the energy emitted as heat radiation by the object per unit time per unit area will be identical to the heat radiation energy that it absorbs from its surround-ings per unit time per unit area.

If, however, the object is at a lower temperature than its enclosure, it will radiate less energy than it absorbs per unit time per unit area. Consequently, it will be a net importer of power and its temperature will therefore increase with time until thermal equilibrium is attained. In a similar fashion, during a fire, fuel that is below its ignition temperature may also act as a net importer of power in the form of heat radia-

tion from actively combusting materials that are at higher temperatures than it. By this means, the fire may be spread if the relatively cool fuel is heated above its ignition temperature. This can be an important mechanism of fire spread, particularly in intense conflagrations.

three of them play a significant role. For example, the ignition of a property that is adjacent to a house that is on fire may occur principally because of heat radiation from the fire. In contrast, when the flame of a cigarette lighter is held under a piece of paper to set it on fire, the heat transfer will occur by all three mechanisms.

In many cases, a fire is ignited when a source of heat is physically moved into a position where it can supply energy at a high enough rate to cause the ignition temperature of a fuel to be reached. This physical movement may be deliberate, such as when an arsonist throws a lighted match onto a petrol-soaked carpet. However, this is not always the case. It may occur, for example, when convection currents carry a smouldering spark from an established fire into the air and it is then transported by the wind to a new batch of fuel.

Growth

During the early stages of a fire in a room, the combustion is normally limited to the fuel item that was originally ignited. This will burn freely, producing a plume of hot gas that is carried upward by convection until it meets the ceiling, whereupon it will spread outwards until the walls are reached. At this point, the hot gas, which is depleted of oxygen and laden with the products of pyrolysis and combustion, forms a layer at the top of the room that will become thicker with time. Beneath this layer of hot gas, the air remains relatively fresh and cool. Typically, during the development of this layer, the fire will spread. The exact pattern that this spread takes varies from fire to fire and is dependent on the position of items of fuel relative to the fuel item that initially caught fire. If there is fuel above this item, it will typically ignite, allowing the fire to spread upwards and outwards, producing a characteristic V-shaped char pattern. Heat radiation from the combustion of the first fuel item to burn will often elevate neighbouring fuel items to their ignition temperatures, allowing the fire to spread horizontally. During the growth stage, fire development is not usually limited by the air supply but by the rate at which new fuel items become involved. Consequently, as the progress of the fire is limited by the availability of fuel, the fire is referred to as being **fuel-controlled**.

The flames in the plume of hot gas that rises from burning fuel items vary in length. If a given fuel item, for example an armchair, were to burn on the floor of a room, its position in that room will influence the length of the flames that it produces. Flames produced by the item burning against a wall will typically be longer than if the item were burning in the centre of the room. If the item were to burn in a corner, its flames would normally be longer still. The explanation for this phenomenon lies in the rate at which air can be entrained in the rising plume of hot gas

Fuel-controlled fire
A fire that is limited by the supply of fuel, not the availability of oxygen.

within which the flames occur. A fire that occurs in an item resting on the floor in the middle of the room can draw in air from all sides. This air supplies oxygen that allows the gaseous pyrolysis products to burn shortly after their formation and cools the plume of gas. Both of these effects will tend to keep the flames short. The plume of hot gas rising from the same fire occurring near to a wall is more restricted in the directions from which it can entrain air. Consequently, the rate of air entrainment is comparatively low, meaning that the hot gases are not cooled to the same degree and the pyrolysis products take longer to burn, resulting in flame elongation. For the same reasons, the fire burning in the corner will have flames that are longer still.

As the fire grows, the heat release rate due to combustion will normally exceed the rate at which heat is transferred out of the room. As a consequence, the temperature of the room will rise. However, throughout the growth stage, the temperature differential between the hot gases in the upper part of the room and the relatively cool, relatively normal air in the lower part will be maintained.

Often the temperature in the layer of hot gas in the upper part of the room will become high enough to allow the pyrolysis products and partially combusted material that it contains to ignite. This ignition may happen due to flames, which may have become elongated because of their proximity to a wall or corner, reaching the hot gas layer from below. Once the hot gas layer ignites, the flame within it spreads at a very high rate (up to 3 to $5\,m\,s^{-1}$). Consequently, within a period of a few seconds, all the room just beneath the ceiling may become engulfed in flame and the temperature of the hot gas zone will increase appreciably. The spread of flames through such flammable products of combustion, during the progress of a fire, is known as **rollover** or **flameover**. It may also be observed whenever these products escape from a zone of oxygen depletion into more normal air, so long as they are hot enough to ignite in their new environment.

Rollover or flameover
The ignition of, and rapid spread of flame within, the hot gases that have accumulated in, or are venting from, the upper part of a burning room or similar compartment.

Flashover

As the temperature of the hot gases in the upper part of the room increases, so does the rate at which these transmit heat in the form of heat radiation (Box 10.3). In a room of normal dimensions, irrespective of whether or not flameover occurs, if this gas reaches a temperature of about 600 °C, the radiant heat that it produces reaches floor level at a rate of approximately $20\,kW\,m^{-2}$. This is sufficient to ignite cellulose-based fuels, such as wood and cotton. Consequently, at this point, all fuel items in the room will burst into flames within a very short period of time. This phenomenon, in which all combustible items become involved in the fire, is known as **radiation-induced flashover**, or just flashover. The high level of turbulent mixing that accompanies this generalised burning disrupts the layered structure of the gases in the room that developed during the growth stage of the fire.

Flashover does not happen in all room fires. In order for it to occur, it is necessary for a layer of hot gases to accumulate in the upper part of the room and for these gases to reach a sufficiently high temperature. These conditions may not be met for a number of reasons. Flashover will not occur if:

Radiation-induced flashover
The involvement in a fire, over a very short time span, of essentially all of the fuel items in a room or similar compartment as radiation from hot gases present in the upper parts of the compartment causes the ignition of the exposed surfaces of fuel items.

- the room contains insufficient fuel;
- the fuel present releases heat at an insufficient rate;

- the level of ventilation is too low (insufficient ventilation will slow both the combustion process and the heat release rate – in extreme cases, poor ventilation may even extinguish the fire);
- the flow of heat and/or gases out of the room is too great.

Post-flashover steady-state burning (also referred to as a fully developed fire)

Once flashover has occurred, all of the fuel present in the room is involved in the fire and its heat release rate is maximal (Figure 10.1). At this stage, the fuel in the room will continue to burn at a rate that is determined by the amount of air available (i.e. it is **ventilation-controlled**) until most of this fuel has been used up. During this phase, because of the limited supply of oxygen, more gaseous fuel will normally be produced by pyrolysis and partial combustion than can be consumed within the room. Consequently, rollover flames are likely to occur as the hot smoke leaves the room.

Ventilation-controlled fire
A fire that is limited by the supply of oxygen, not the availability of fuel.

Decay

As the available fuel is consumed, a point will be reached where the rate of air supply outstrips the fuel supply rate and the fire again becomes fuel-controlled. Consequently, during this phase, as the fuel supply drops, so does the heat release rate (Figure 10.1). At the same time, the amount of flaming combustion present will decrease as the ability of the remaining fuel to form flammable pyrolysis products diminishes. Eventually, the fire will be dominated by smouldering combustion and, ultimately, the fire will self-extinguish.

In a room fire, decay can also occur under ventilation control if the air supply is so low that the flames die down. Under these conditions, the concentration of flammable pyrolysis products may build up sufficiently to create the conditions necessary for flashback to ensue if air is suddenly admitted to the room (Section 10.1).

10.2.2 Outdoor fires

Outdoor fires ignite for the same reason and in essentially the same way as do fires within rooms and similar compartments. However, once lit, the behaviour of outdoor fires is, in the main, much simpler than that of fires that occur in rooms.

Consider a small flaming fire that is lit in an open space, on flat, horizontal ground, on a still day. The high temperatures of the fire will cause convection currents to be established (Box 10.3) that involve a plume of hot gases rising above the fire and a flow of air from surrounding areas into the base of the fire. The fire will move outward in the direction of available fuel. This process will occur fairly slowly because the convection-driven stream of air that is moving towards the base of the fire almost exclusively transports heat away from the direction of fire propagation, leaving conduction and radiation as the only means of raising surrounding fuel items to their ignition temperatures. Under these circumstances, if the fire is evenly surrounded by sufficient fuel with identical burning characteristics, a circular fire-spread pattern will result (Figure 10.2).

(Photograph by Andrew
Jackson, Staffordshire
University, UK)

Figure 10.2 Outdoor burn pattern left by circular fire spread

If this same fire were to occur on a slope, however, the convection currents would cause hot gases to heat any fuel on its up-hill side, thereby facilitating the much more rapid spread of fire in this direction. This will typically produce a fan-shaped fire spread pattern (Figure 10.3). Note that slow down-hill burning will also occur due to the mechanisms described in the previous paragraph. In addition, any burning items, such as the branches of trees, that fall down-slope out of the burning zone, may well create new centres of ignition, each of which will typically produce its own fan-shaped burn pattern.

Ambient wind has the effect of pushing the plume of hot gases that arise from the top of a fire towards the ground. This, like the effect of a slope, will help the spread of fire, in this case in a downwind direction. On flat, horizontal land, that is evenly covered in fuel of similar burning characteristics, wind that is blowing strongly in one direction will typically produce a burn pattern that is significantly longer than it is wide. It is noteworthy that wind-driven sparks from one fire can kindle a new fire in a downwind location.

Fierce fires produce significant amounts of radiant heat. This can cause fire to move from one place to another, even though the intervening space contains no fuel. This can result in one burning building setting another on fire.

10.3 Fire scene investigation

Seat of fire
*The location where
the fire started. Also
known as its point
of origin.*

A fire investigation will have a number of aims. Typically these include:

■ the identification of where the fire started (known as the **seat of fire** or point of origin);

(Photograph by Andrew
Jackson, Staffordshire
University, UK)

(a)

(b)

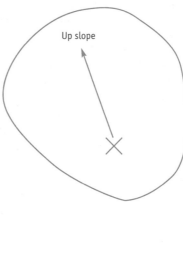

Figure 10.3 The result of a fan-shaped fire spread pattern
(a) A photograph of the scene and (b) a drawing showing the position of the fan-shape and the probable location of the seat of the fire (marked with an X)

- the determination of the cause of the fire (the meaning of this term is described below) and whether it was intentionally started;
- the establishment of legal liabilities associated with the fire;
- the determination of the factors that contributed to and controlled both the fire's spread and the production of heat, flame and smoke during its progress;
- the identification of any health and safety issues that arose during the fighting of the fire;
- the identification of dangerous practices, materials and manufactured items that contributed to the start or progress of the fire;
- the collection of data for use by policy makers.

In addition, in cases in which claims are to be made against insurance policies, loss adjusters will be instructed by the insurance companies involved to assess the extent and monetary value of fire damage.

Fire scene investigations will achieve their optimum effectiveness only if they are carried out with due care, diligence and expertise, and in an ethically and legally acceptable fashion.

As explained in Section 10.1, a fire will start whenever a suitable fuel and oxidant, which are capable of a self-sustaining chain reaction, are brought together in appropriate proportions and provided with sufficient energy for ignition to occur. A statement of how these conditions arose at the start of a particular fire is a statement of the **cause of fire**.

Throughout the populated world, a disturbingly high proportion of fires are deliberately started. For example, in the United Kingdom, approximately 20 per cent of fires attended by local authority fire brigades are either known to be or suspected of being intentionally ignited. However, prior to the commencement of the investigation of any one fire, it is usually not clear whether the fire concerned was deliberately started and, if so, that arson has been committed (see Box 10.4 for a definition of arson and a description of the motives of arsonists). This means that each fire scene that is investigated should be treated as if it were a crime scene until and unless it is established that this is not the case. This precautionary approach is wise for the following reason. If an investigation establishes that it is likely that arson has occurred, and the processing of the site has *not* been carried out as if it were a crime scene, then the value to any subsequent prosecution case of evidence obtained from the scene may be severely limited. Consequently, the principles of crime scene processing (including those relating to the preservation and recording of the scene and the recovery of items of physical evidence), as set out in Chapter 2, are also relevant to fire scene processing. However, in the United Kingdom, while non-fire crime scenes are handled exclusively by the police, police scientific support professionals and experts that may be called to the scene by the police, fire scene processing also involves Fire Scene Investigators (who are employees of the Fire Service). Indeed, unless the examination of a fire incident reveals that a crime may have been committed, the entire investigation, except that undertaken by loss adjusters, will be carried out by such Fire Investigation Officers and any experts that they may call in.

Cause of fire
The act, omission or defect that allowed the conditions necessary for the ignition of the fire to occur and the fire to be started.

Further information
Box 10.4

Arson

Arson may be defined as the deliberate, malicious setting on fire of property, either one's own with the intent to defraud (e.g. by making a fraudulent insurance claim) or someone else's. In the United Kingdom, law concerning arson is set down in Section One of the Criminal Damage Act 1971. For the police to record a particular incident of fire as arson, they must have sufficient proof of intent, recklessness and the involvement of property.

Adults
There are a number of motives that lead adults to commit arson. As indicated in Table 10.1, in some cases, the nature of the motive will help shape the arsonist's modus operandi (MO). (The MO of a criminal is the manner in which he or she carries out the crime concerned.) It must be stressed that the connection between motive and MO is tentative; there is no guarantee that a given motive will lead to a particular MO in each case.

Box 10.4 *continued*

Table 10.1   Why and how adults commit arson

Class of motive	Subclass (where applicable)	Typical MO and related traits that may be observed	Illustrative examples of specific motives
Revenge	Revenge against individuals	Perpetrator known to the victim, little sign of forward planning, damage to the personal property of the victim intended and/or occurs (often by a combination of non-fire vandalism and arson).	Revenge against an unfaithful spouse.
	Revenge against institutions	Buildings in which the institution is located (e.g. bank, law court, company premises) may be targeted, as may senior staff of the institution concerned. Commonly, multiple attempts are made to set the same target alight. Such attempts may be simultaneous and/or perpetrated over a protracted period of time.	Revenge by an aggrieved former employee or customer of the institution concerned.
	Revenge against groups	Arson perpetrated against the individual members of a group (e.g. race, religion, club, gang), and/or buildings (e.g. places of worship) and/or symbols (e.g. a cross) associated with the group. Pre-planning may be evident with devices – especially Molotov cocktails – employed in many cases. Non-fire vandalism may occur in addition to the arson.	Racist hate.
	Revenge against society	A series of fire sets, frequently aimed at apparently random targets. Attacks often premeditated but using materials available at the scene lit with a match or a cigarette lighter.	Perpetrator feels wronged by society and powerless.
Vandalism		Opportunistic rather than premeditated. Unsophisticated with devices uncommon (although Molotov cocktails may be encountered). Schools, motor vehicles, outdoor vegetation and unused buildings are frequent targets. Non-fire vandalism and/or petty theft may occur in addition to the arson. Perpetrator may act alone or as part of a gang. Peer pressure is often part of the motive. More commonly committed by juveniles than adults. Typical adult perpetrator would be an unskilled worker of average or below average intelligence.	Boredom and the desire for entertainment.

▶

Box 10.4 *continued*

Table 10.1 Continued

Class of motive	Subclass (where applicable)	Typical MO and related traits that may be observed	Illustrative examples of specific motives
Profit	Arsonist owns the property targeted	Premeditated. Use of incendiary devices (often with a delayed action) is common. Attempts made to maximise the amount of damage by:	Fraudulent insurance claim.
		■ facilitating the rapid spread of fire (e.g. by increasing ventilation, the use of flammable liquids as fire accelerants, placing of lines of flammable material (called trailers) to take fire from one place to another in the structure, the lighting of multiple fires essentially simultaneously in the same property); and/or	Destruction of property that has become a financial liability or which lowers the value of other property owned by the perpetrator.
		■ hindering/slowing fire-fighting activities (e.g. by disabling fire alarm systems or sprinklers and/or blocking the approach of the fire brigade to the scene).	
		The establishment of plausible alibi by the arsonist. The over-insurance of the property. The removal or replacement of valuable items. The owner of the damaged property in financial difficulties and/or with a history of previous property fires.	
	Arsonist does not own the property	Premeditated. However, in the main, the preparations to optimise the conditions for the fire are not as elaborate as in cases in which the arsonist owns the property targeted. This is because the arsonist is unlikely to have uncontrolled access to the property. In cases in which the property is set light from within, the arsonist will usually have to break in.	Finding/ensuring employment as, e.g. a fire-fighter, a security guard, building contractor. Eliminating business competition. As part of attempts to intimidate and/or extort money.
Concealment of a previous crime		In cases of murder, attempts may be made to burn the body so as to hide the identity of the victim, destroy evidence that links the victim to the murderer and/or disguise the manner and cause of death. In many	Destruction of evidence.

Box 10.4 continued

Table 10.1 Continued

Class of motive	Subclass (where applicable)	Typical MO and related traits that may be observed	Illustrative examples of specific motives
Concealment of a previous crime (continued)		such cases, flammable liquids are used to increase the destructive ability of the fire. Body often located at the seat of the fire.	
		In cases of burglary combined with arson, the fire is often lit in an attempt to destroy evidence that the criminal did not intend to leave behind at the scene (e.g. blood). Consequently, arson is not premeditated and is, in the main, carried out using fuels available at the scene. These are commonly lit at the point of entry and/or at locations from where articles were stolen.	
		Fire may be used to destroy evidence left on stolen property and/or equipment used in the commission of a crime (e.g. a 'get-away car'). In such cases, the fire will typically be centred on the object(s) concerned.	
		Arson is also used to destroy paper evidence of wrongdoing, such as may happen in cases of tax fraud. In such cases, efforts will be made to ensure that the incriminating papers are destroyed (e.g. by leaving filing cabinet drawers open, using the papers as fuel, using flammable liquids to increase fire damage). The papers are often at the seat of the fire.	
Excitement and/ or vanity		Usually unplanned and therefore fuels employed are typically those present at the scene. However, in serial arson cases of this type, patterns of behaviour may emerge. These may include preferences exhibited by the arsonist for particular times of the day, days of the week, specific dates, method of fire lighting, target objects (e.g. empty buildings) and/or places where fires are lit (e.g. basements).	Feelings of power to cause the emergency services to act. Self-aggrandisement by appearing to detect the fire and/or helping to fight it.
		Arsonists of this type may well observe the fire-fighting activities or even report the fire and/or attempt to help in fighting it.	

▶

Box 10.4 continued

Table 10.1 Continued

Class of motive	Subclass (where applicable)	Typical MO and related traits that may be observed	Illustrative examples of specific motives
Terrorism and social unrest		Terrorist arson is premeditated and often involves incendiary devices, which may be relatively simple (e.g. Molotov cocktails) but can be highly sophisticated. The group involved seeks publicity and so will usually claim responsibility for the act by some means (e.g. graffiti at the scene, phone calls to radio stations). Targets chosen are typically one or more of: ■ structures of political significance (e.g. political party headquarters); ■ structures of economic significance (e.g. company offices); ■ the property of individuals, who may be randomly selected members of the public (in order to terrorise a community). Social unrest that leads to rioting often involves arson. This type of arson is accompanied by other forms of physical damage to property and, in many cases, looting. The arson may not be premeditated, in which case, the fuels used are typically those that are found at the scene. If incendiary devices are employed, these are usually Molotov cocktails or similarly unsophisticated instruments.	Political extremism.
Pyromania		This form of arson is rare. Pyromania is a medical condition and its sufferers tend to be serial fire setters, often initially causing small fires in rubbish or outdoor vegetation but may later set unoccupied structures and ultimately occupied buildings alight. While the fire setting is premeditated, flammable liquids and incendiary devices are not usually employed. Instead, the initial fuel is usually piled-up paper or similar material. Pyromaniacs rarely set fires during daylight. They are typically males with Intelligence Quotients (IQs) of around 70 and retiring personalities.	The pathological easing of mental tension. Response to 'commands' given by 'voices' heard in the head of the pyromaniac.

Box 10.4 continued

Children

Children as young as 3 years old may deliberately start fires. They do this out of curiosity (carried out by younger children who are essentially 'playing with fire'), in order to vandalise property (typically by older children), as a response to a crisis or abuse, to seek attention and/or as an expression of anger.

In the case of curiosity-motivated fires, the child concerned may be unaware of the consequences of fire setting. In other cases, the fire may be intended to be small or confined to targets of limited economic value (e.g. rubbish bins). Regrettably, some older children set fires with the intent of causing extensive destruction. Inevitably, the nature of fire means that even those started out of curiosity or intended to remain small may result in a large-scale conflagration with significant loss of property and possible injury and/or the loss of life.

Clearly, from a forensic science perspective, it is of paramount importance to investigate a fire scene with a view to establishing whether the fire was caused intentionally. In order to do this, it is normally necessary to determine both the seat and the cause of the fire. The remainder of this section is dedicated to a review of the principles that allow this to be done.

10.3.1 Witnesses and background information

Eyewitnesses to the fire can provide valuable information that will help the fire investigator rationalise the observations that he or she makes at the scene once the fire has been extinguished. Fire-fighters in attendance will be able to provide facts such as the times at which the alarm was raised and of their arrival on the scene. They will also be able to supply information about the progress of the fire and the methods that they employed in tackling it. This could include, where applicable, where the fire appeared to have spread from, whether or not it was accompanied by explosions, whether radiation-induced flashover occurred and the location of any windows that were broken as a consequence of the fire. It may also include how and where the fire-fighters gained access to the premises, which, if any, windows they broke, any actions taken by the fire-fighters to ventilate a building that was on fire and where they applied water.

Eyewitnesses among the public, although likely to be less reliable than fire-fighters in their recollections, can nonetheless provide useful insights. For example, they may be able to recall the region of the premises in which the fire was first seen, whether the fire was preceded by apparent interruptions to any electricity supply and whether the fire appeared to be preceded by or accompanied by an explosion or explosions.

The owner or tenant of any building damaged by fire should be able to provide details of the contents of its rooms immediately prior to the fire. Ideally, this will include the locations of pieces of furniture, appliances, machines, any flammable liquids or gases held on the property and any particularly valuable items. Furthermore, the owner or tenant should be able to give information about the security of the building, in particular whether all of the external doors and windows were locked prior to the fire (which may or may not be corroborated by evidence supplied by the fire-fighters). Later in the investigation, laboratory tests may be carried out on items or materials that were involved in the fire (e.g. electrical appliances or, in the case of industrial premises, process chemicals). Under these circumstances, a detailed inventory of the pre-fire contents of the building may be very helpful as it could provide information that allows undamaged control samples to be obtained for comparative purposes.

In order to obtain the maximum amount of reliable information, the interviewing of witnesses is best performed in a highly objective way by appropriately trained and experienced personnel. Such interviews should be approached with appropriate sensitivity, be properly recorded and the procedures adopted must be legally acceptable. It should be borne in mind that one of the interviewees might be the person who set the fire in the first place.

Background documentation, such as photographs or videotapes taken of the scene either before or during the fire (including any taken of the onlookers during the tackling of the fire) can be of value. Architect's drawings/plans of any building involved in the fire can also be useful in this respect.

It is useful to know of any history of previous fires at the same location and/or in the neighbourhood. Some premises have a legitimate history of fires, as may be the case in certain industrial plants. However, it is not unknown for an arsonist either to attempt to burn down a facility with such a history or to repeatedly set fire to the same structure.

10.3.2 Processing the scene

As stated earlier, it is wise to treat all fire scene investigations as if they are crime scene investigations until there is reason to know otherwise. With this in mind, attention should be paid to the preservation and recording (using notes, sketches, photographs and video, as appropriate) of the scene, and the recovery of items of physical evidence from the scene (Chapter 2).

As a part of the preservation of the scene, a cordon should be placed around the scene at the earliest practicable opportunity, in order to restrict access to the site to authorised personnel only. Once the scene has been secured, it can be systematically searched, a process that often progresses from the least damaged to the most damaged areas. The aims of the search include the identification of indicators that help to locate the seat of the fire and those that provide evidence of the cause of the fire (see below for more details).

In cases of suspected arson, items of physical evidence that may link the scene, and/or the events that took place during the setting of the fire, to any perpetrator will also be searched for. These items will be treated in the same manner as those taken from any other crime scene (Chapter 2).

Fire accelerant
A flammable material (most commonly liquid) used to facilitate and/or increase the rate of spread of fire and/or increase the intensity of fire.

The search of a site at which there has been a building fire will normally commence with an inspection of the outside of the building and a systematic examination of the grounds in which it stands (which will be inside the cordon). The search of the grounds will focus on finding items of physical evidence. These could include tools that might have been used by an arsonist to break into the property, containers that may have held flammable liquids used by an arsonist to accelerate the spread of the fire (such liquids are examples of **fire accelerants**) or footprints that he or she left at the scene. In cases in which an explosion (or explosions) took place in addition to the fire, this search will also be used to locate any items of debris that were distributed outside the building by the blast.

An inspection of the exterior of the building will normally be of value as it may help the investigator to ascertain:

- safety issues associated with entering it (e.g. the presence of harmful materials released by the fire (e.g. smoke, hazardous building materials such as asbestos) or structures in danger of collapse);
- any signs that the building might have been forcibly entered before the fire took place;
- indications of the region of the building that contains the seat of the fire.

In outdoor vegetation fires, an indication of the likely location of the seat of the fire can be gained from the burn pattern, the topography of the land, knowledge of the weather conditions at the time of the fire and eyewitness accounts. In such cases, the search will normally start in those areas that are most remote from the seat, systematically moving towards the seat with an ever-increasing degree of thoroughness as the seat is approached.

10.3.3 Finding the seat of a fire

In order to find the seat of a fire, an investigator will normally make use of any eyewitness accounts of the spread of the fire and interpret the pattern of damage created by the fire. This interpretation requires knowledge of the nature and behaviour of fire, and is the subject of this section. Unfortunately, there is no single indicator within the patterns that are left by fires that can be used to unequivocally locate fire seats in all circumstances. In most cases, the investigator will use multiple indicators that, when considered together, enable the seat to be found. This is not a simple matter and, while the description provided here cannot be comprehensive, it serves as an introduction to this topic.

Consider a matrix of solid fuel that is in contact with the air, such as dry vegetation in an outdoor fire or the flammable furniture and fittings of a house on fire. If an adequate air supply is maintained, once a fire is started, it will spread through this matrix – provided that the portions of the fuel that are on fire can supply heat at a sufficient rate to bring new parts of the fuel to their ignition temperatures.

As explained in Box 10.3, heat may be transferred by three mechanisms, namely conduction, convection and radiation. In a fire that is burning without the constraint of physical barriers:

- convection moves heat upwards;
- conduction moves heat away from its source via the material through which it is travelling;
- radiation allows heat to travel in all directions from its point of origin, unless it is absorbed or reflected.

Importantly, under most circumstances, convection is the most efficient of these three mechanisms at transferring heat from burning fuel to fuel that is yet to ignite. Consequently, fire will tend to move upwards through a three-dimensional matrix of solid fuel much more rapidly than outwards or downwards. This will tend to produce a conical pattern of fire development, which is narrowest at the bottom and widest at the top and which has the seat of the fire at or very near to its base. Any vertical, or near vertical, flat surface (e.g. a wall) that comes into contact with this will tend to have a burn pattern on it that is approximately V-shaped. In objects that are partially burnt through, these V-shaped patterns may also be evident, either in full or in part (Figure 10.4).

Such V-shapes are useful as, in the main, they become narrower as the initial ignition point is neared. Note that, as illustrated in Figure 10.5, such V-shaped patterns may be evident when a burnt building is viewed as a whole from the outside. Also, as described before in this chapter, for reasons similar to those previously outlined in this paragraph, outdoor vegetation fires on slopes tend to be fan-shaped with the seat of the fire located near to, but above, the bottom of the pattern (Figure 10.3). Note also that the smoke patterns seen in fire-damaged buildings also tend to show approximately V-shaped patterns, which point towards the initial point of ignition at their base.

There are some important modifying factors that can alter the shape of these V-shaped patterns. Wind, or other externally generated airflows, may alter the path of the convection currents that are largely responsible for the upward movement of heat and smoke through the fuel matrix, thereby modifying the burn and smoke

(Reproduced by kind permission of Dave Bott, Staffordshire Fire & Rescue Service, UK)

(a)

(b)

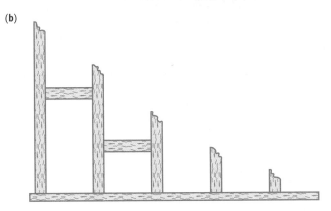

Figure 10.4 Examples of V-shaped burn patterns as shown in objects that are partially burnt through

(a) An entire V-shaped pattern in wood and (b) a drawing of a partial V-shaped pattern as revealed in the wooden supports left after the plasterboard cladding of a partition wall has been destroyed by fire

(a)

(b)

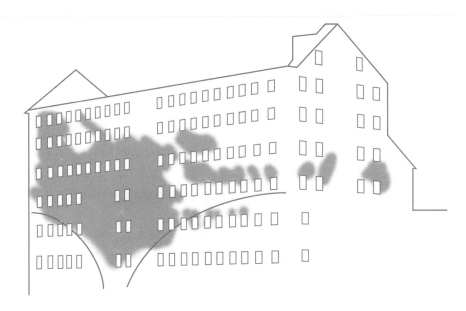

Figure 10.5 V-shaped smoke damage evident when a burnt building is viewed as a whole from the outside

(a) A photograph of the scene and (b) a drawing showing the position of the V-shape patterns that remain after the fire has ceased. The top of V-shaped patterns may become dramatically broader beneath horizontal obstructions to vertical flow (especially ceilings). In room fires, this will often lead to the development of a progressively deepening layer of hot gas immediately beneath the ceiling. This will produce charring and smoke deposition on the entire ceiling and the walls that it has contact with. If the fire is intense enough, this situation may lead to radiation-induced flashover (Section 10.2) which may cause the large-scale disruption of any V-shaped patterns produced in the room up until that point. Also, when a room is on fire, objects such as curtains, pictures and light fittings may catch alight and drop onto fresh fuel from above, thereby spreading the fire. This **dropdown** (as it is called) will often cause what appear to be multiple seats of the fire. This can be highly misleading, as the genuine presence of multiple seats is a strong indicator of a deliberately ignited fire (Box 10.4). Finally, it should be noted that fire can lead to the formation of an *inverted* V-shaped pattern on a wall, or similar vertical object. For example, this can happen in a room when a fire occurs in a relatively small amount of fuel that is near to the vertical object concerned but does not directly lead to the spread of fire up it. The contents of a waste-paper bin, a dropdown and a pool of flammable liquid are all examples of fuel items that may cause this effect.

In many fires, the area of most intense destruction corresponds with the region that contains its seat, as it is here that the fire usually has had longest to become established and to act. There are a number of indicators that can be used to discern patterns in the degree of destruction, including the comparison of depths of char formed on wooden items (Figure 10.6). The depth of char that is formed depends on a number of factors. These include the species of the wood, whether the wood is cut with or across the grain, the length of time that the wood has been exposed to heat,

Dropdown
The falling of burning materials during a fire, thereby producing secondary ignition at low elevation.

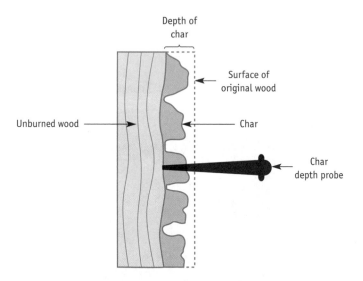

Figure 10.6 Char depth measurement
Note that the probe used (e.g. tyre tread depth gauge) is one with a small cross-section but that is blunt-tipped and that the depth is measured from the original surface of the wood and not the surface of the char

the rate at which heat is supplied to each unit area of the wood, and the shape and thickness of the item concerned. Nonetheless, the measurement of char thickness on items made of the same type of wood that are found at the same vertical height but at different locations within the fire scene can give a comparative indication of the intensity of destruction at those locations. Under these circumstances, the char tends to become deeper as the intensity of destruction becomes greater. It is important to note, however, that interpretation of observations designed to reveal the intensity of destruction needs great care. This is because factors such as the degree of ventilation, fuel loading and fire-fighting activities can have a significant impact on the intensity of destruction that is wrought at any one location within a given fire scene.

A number of materials that are commonly encountered in fire-damaged areas and structures are both marked by fire and are poor conductors of heat. These include common fuel materials (e.g. wood), as well as non-flammable substances (e.g. concrete). Objects made of such materials – such as wooden doors or concrete pillars – are frequently marked to a greater degree on the side facing the fire than on the side facing away from it (Figure 10.7). Therefore, if the position of such objects at the time of the fire is known, the markings on them may be useful in establishing the direction from which the fire came. Ultimately, this may lead to the seat of the fire.

(a)

(Reproduced by kind permission of Dave Bott, Staffordshire Fire & Rescue Service, UK)

(b)

Figure 10.7 A pair of fire-resistant doors showing (a) extensive damage on the side facing the fire and (b) the relatively undamaged side facing away from the fire

Certain fire alarm and/or sprinkler systems can be interrogated after a fire to show the order in which different parts of the system concerned were activated by the spread of the fire. This can be used to work out the region in which the fire first started.

Heat may bring about physical and/or chemical changes in a number of non-flammable materials – including glass, concrete, plaster and many metals. These changes can also produce features that help to indicate where the seat of the fire is likely to be located. For example, light bulbs that are filled with inert gas tend to extend towards, and then burst in, the direction of maximum heating.

10.3.4 Establishing the cause of a fire

Most fires start when a source of ignition supplies sufficient energy, usually as heat, to light a fuel that is already in contact with a suitable oxidising agent (in the vast majority of cases, this oxidising agent is oxygen (O_2), provided by the air). Under these circumstances, the key to establishing the cause of the fire is normally the finding of its seat (see above). Doing this will often enable the identity and/or location of the fuel item in which the fire started to be established.

Once the seat has been located, it should be examined with great care, with particular attention being paid to likely initial fuel items and possible sources of ignition. In some instances, direct evidence of such sources may be present. For example, there may be an electric heater that is clearly dangerously close to what is likely to be the remnants of the initial fuel item. However, in others this may not be the case, as when an arsonist starts a fire with a cigarette lighter that he or she subsequently takes away when they leave the scene.

From a forensic science point of view, the most important feature to be established concerning the cause of a fire is whether the fire was deliberately started, as the crime of arson necessarily involves this act (Box 10.4). There are many indications of deliberate fire setting, some of which are essentially unequivocal (e.g. finding the remains of an incendiary device at the seat of the fire) while others are circumstantial. Some of these indicators may be found at the scene and others elsewhere. Clearly, no two instances of deliberately set fires are the same and the exact nature and number of indicators left by the fire setter will vary from case to case. However, there are a number of more commonly encountered classes of indications of the deliberate starting of fire. Notably these include the following:

- ■ Lack of evidence for a natural or accidental cause of the fire (note that this in itself is not normally sufficient to establish that the fire was deliberately started; also, attempts may be made to make deliberate fires appear to be accidental by, e.g., starting them with, or near to, heating appliances, cookers, machinery, etc.).
- ■ Evidence that a flammable liquid was among the first fuels to be ignited; such evidence may include:
  - burning at low elevations within the fire-damaged area (Figure 10.8);
  - burn patterns that are localised (Figure 10.8);
  - burn patterns that show sharp, curved edges (Figure 10.8);
  - the presumptive detection of vapours of hydrocarbon (or other) liquid fuels from locations (e.g. cracks between floorboards) and materials (e.g. carpet underlay) that may have offered the liquid protection from being

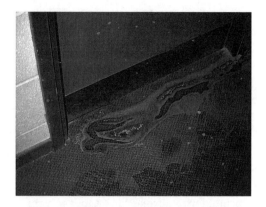

(Reproduced by kind permission of Dave Bott, Staffordshire Fire & Rescue Service, UK)

Figure 10.8 A localised, low-elevation burn pattern with sharp, curved edges
These characteristics provide evidence for the prior presence of burning flammable liquid

burnt (such presumptive detection may be achieved by using the human sense of smell, trained 'sniffer' dogs (known as hydrocarbon search canines) and/or portable electronic detectors);

– detection and identification of liquid fuel by the laboratory analysis of samples retrieved from the scene (this is the only definitive evidence for the presence of flammable liquids and is discussed further in Section 10.4).

Note that other materials (such as burning plastics and dropdowns) can mimic the burn patterns produced by flammable liquids; also the presence of flammable liquid does not prove deliberate fire setting as such liquids may have been innocently stored at the scene prior to the fire.

■ Evidence of the presence of an unusually high quantity and/or quality of fuel at the seat of the fire (which may be exhibited, for example, in unexpectedly severe destruction).

■ Objects suspiciously out of place, for example:
  – piles of fuel items (which may be evidenced by the presence of otherwise inexplicably high numbers of hinges, drawer locks, furniture springs, etc. within the ash);
  – containers that may have held flammable liquids found in unexpected places;
  – tools or other equipment that might have been used to break into a property or to perpetrate sabotage;
  – filing cabinet or desk drawers left open (to aid the combustion of documents);
  – the substitution of good furniture for poor-quality items; the prior removal of objects of sentimental or monetary value (e.g. photographs, jewellery or share certificates);
  – otherwise inexplicable escape of pets;
  – doors, windows or roof space access hatches wedged or left open;
  – electrical switches left on that would normally be expected to be off;
  – heating system thermostats set unusually high (to improve ventilation);
  – objects placed so as to hinder the activities of the fire brigade;

- transparent or reflective objects that are capable of focusing the Sun's rays left in a position where they could lead to the ignition of fuel.

■ Unusual damage, for example:
  - partition walls/ceilings/floors broken through to improve ventilation and aid the spread of the fire;
  - signs of break-in;
  - disabled fire and/or intruder alarms;
  - indications of sabotage (e.g. cut fuel pipes, electrical supply systems that have been tampered with).

■ Evidence that a crime was committed at the scene prior to the fire.

■ A history of fires in the building or neighbourhood concerned and/or a similar history associated with anyone who stands to gain from the fire.

■ A familiar face in the crowd watching the fire or someone leaving the scene (most people are attracted by the spectacle of a fire and will want to observe it).

■ The presence of one or more incendiary devices or their remains; examples of such devices include:
  - incendiary devices with a time-delayed action (which may be very simple, such as a balloon, or similar container, filled with flammable liquid and left above an ignition source);
  - Molotov cocktail (i.e. a container filled with a flammable liquid and equipped with an ignition device designed to light the liquid when the container is broken – Molotov cocktails are usually thrown);
  - a purely chemical means of causing ignition.

■ Fire safety systems such as automatic fire detection systems and/or sprinkler systems turned off or made inoperative.

■ Multiple fire seats (if this occurs, intact but failed incendiary devices may be found elsewhere on the premises).

■ Evidence of lines of flammable material (known as trailers) deliberately placed so as to spread the fire from one location to another.

■ Mismatches between statements made by, for example, the owner of the fire-damaged property (including any contents inventory provided) and the sequence of events known to have taken place during the incident and/or the physical evidence left after the fire.

■ Indications of a motive for arson among any people who had the potential to start the fire (Box 10.4).

■ Patterns of destruction in any one fire or patterns that emerge when the characteristics of several fires are compared that suggest that an arsonist may be at work (Box 10.4).

In cases of arson, these indicators not only help establish the cause of the fire, they may also give an insight into the possible motives of the arsonist. For further information on this important topic, see Box 10.4.

10.4 The analysis of fire accelerants

Laboratory-based chemical analysis of samples connected with cases of suspected illegal fire setting (whether successful or attempted) can provide valuable evidence. Such samples may be those recovered from the scene of a fire (whether actual or apparently intended), any suspects involved in the case and/or the possessions of those suspects.

The initial purpose of such analysis is to establish whether the sample contains a substance that may have been used with the aim of increasing the rate of fire spread (i.e. a potential fire accelerant). Furthermore, laboratory analysis may:

- identify the chemical nature of any fire accelerant detected;
- allow the amount of any such material present in the sample to be established; and/or
- provide points of comparison between samples taken from different locations.

The last of these may be of particular importance in helping to establish a link between a suspect and an apparent crime scene.

During analytical work of this type, distinction is made between trace and bulk quantities of questioned material. As a rule of thumb, trace quantities are those that are too small to be seen with the naked eye and, conversely, anything that can be seen under these conditions is present in bulk amounts. An example of the former of these is the low level of petrol that may remain on an arsonist's clothing after he or she used this fuel as a fire accelerant.

This distinction between trace and bulk amounts of questioned material is important for a number of reasons. These include the great potential that bulk samples have for contaminating items that are suspected of containing trace quantities of incriminating material. It is vital therefore that rigorous systems are in place that ensure that such items can never be brought into contact with bulk samples or traces of material that have come from those bulk samples. The necessity for the avoidance of cross-contamination of this type increases with the sensitivity of the technique employed for the analysis of the items concerned.

In cases of arson, the fire accelerants most commonly detected by laboratory analysis are liquid fuels. Among these, liquid petroleum distillates are the most frequently encountered, although other flammable liquids, such as short-chain alcohols (e.g. ethanol), may also be used as accelerants. The most prevalent petroleum distillate found in this context is petrol but others, such as paraffin or diesel oil, may be employed by an arsonist. Each of these distillates is a complex mixture of volatile hydrocarbons (a hydrocarbon is a compound that contains only hydrogen and carbon).

Gas chromatography (GC, see Chapter 11, Box 11.5) is the main technique used to analyse samples suspected of containing liquid fire accelerants. This is because not only is GC a means of analysing volatile compounds that is highly sensitive (and so can be used for the analysis of trace as well as bulk samples), it is also capable of isolating, and potentially identifying, individual components of mixtures of such compounds. Furthermore, in cases of complex mixtures, it can produce a pattern that is characteristic of the mixture concerned. This pattern acts as a class characteristic of the mixture, allowing, for example, petrol to be distinguished from diesel oil (Figure 10.9). Also, if a pattern obtained from a sample taken from one location is found to match that generated by a sample taken from another, this establishes that the two samples could have had the same origin. Therefore, if such a match were to be found between samples of liquid taken from the floor of a fire-damaged house and a largely empty petrol can found in a suspect's possession, this would mean that the liquid in the house *could* have come from the can.

When carrying out the laboratory analysis of samples that are suspected of containing fire accelerants, the parallel analysis of appropriate control samples may be of utmost importance. In this context, the control samples chosen will be ones intended to replicate the matrix within which the accelerant is believed to reside in the questioned samples. Such controls may aid the interpretation of the results of the analysis of the questioned samples and be of fundamental importance in ensuring that the findings are truly rigorous. For example, during a fire investigation, fire-damaged carpet may be found that exhibits signs (e.g. odour and burn pattern) that indicate the presence of liquid hydrocarbon fuel. This carpet would be sampled and sent for analysis. If, at the same time, control samples of that same fire-damaged carpet were taken from an area that shows no evidence of containing liquid fuel, this would aid the interpretation of GC analysis carried out in the laboratory. This is because GC alone cannot distinguish the origin of the compounds that it detects. If the questioned sample of carpet were to contain petrol, volatile combustion products and volatile chemicals that were present in it before the fire, all three classes of material would be represented in the GC results. However, GC analysis of the control sample would only show the latter two classes. Subtraction of the results of the analysis of the control sample from those of the questioned sample will help the analyst to discern the data relating to the petrol. Furthermore, the analyst will be able to demonstrate to a court that the results that he or she has attributed to petrol have not originated either from the carpet or from the combustion products of the fire.

It is vitally important to realise that analytical data that show the presence of flammable liquid are not proof that a crime has been committed. For example, petrol may be found on the floor of a fire scene because it was stored at that scene for legitimate purposes and the container in which it was held burst during the fire. Similarly, analytical data that show a match between an accelerant recovered from an arson scene and flammable liquid found in the possession of a suspect do not provide proof that the individual concerned perpetrated the crime in question. This is because the analysis of flammable liquids reveals class characteristics and not individualising ones (see Chapter 1, Section 1.2.1).

(a)

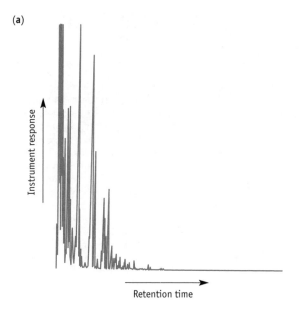

(Supplied by Neil Lamont, Staffordshire University, UK)

(b)

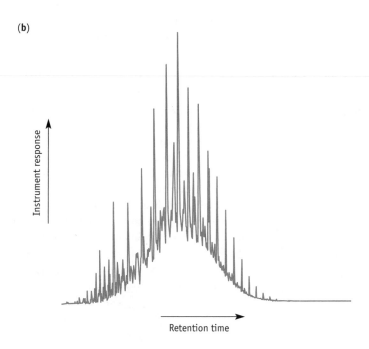

Figure 10.9 Typical gas chromatograms of (a) petrol and (b) diesel oil; note that these were recorded under identical conditions

10.5 Summary

■ Fire will occur whenever a suitable fuel and oxidant, which are capable of undergoing a self-sustaining chemical chain reaction, are in contact and exposed to sufficient energy (usually in the form of heat) to cause ignition to occur. In the absence of fire-fighting activities, once ignited, a normal fire within a typical room or similar compartment can be described as passing through each of four stages before self-extinguishing. These stages are called growth, flashover, post-flashover steady-state burning and decay. The behaviour of fires in the open is somewhat simpler, but is influenced by the slope of the land and wind direction.

■ Fire scene investigations are carried out for a number of reasons. Important among these are, for a given fire, the establishment of both where it started (i.e. finding its seat)

and its cause. The deliberate ignition of fires is a significant problem in both the UK and elsewhere. Given that at the outset of the investigation of any one fire, it is not necessarily clear whether it was intentionally ignited, it is wise to treat each fire scene as if it were a crime scene until it is established that it is not. The identification of a fire as one that has been deliberately started is based on the observation of one or more indications, such as the presence at the scene of incendiary devices (or their remains) or evidence that flammable liquids have been used to accelerate the spread of fire. The presence of flammable liquids can only be unequivocally established if they are found during the laboratory analysis of samples taken from the scene. Such analyses may reveal class characteristics that help to establish links between items, scenes and/or individuals.

Problems

1. Describe the means by which heat is transmitted from a flaming match to a piece of newspaper that is ignited by that match. Explain why it is easier to light a piece of crumpled newspaper in this way if the match is held underneath the paper rather than above it.

2. Discuss whether a small outdoor fire in the early stages of its development would normally be ventilation-controlled or fuel-controlled.

3. An arsonist who wishes to make money from his or her crime by submitting a subsequent claim to an insurance company is faced with a fundamental dilemma. On one hand, if this crime is to be successful, the fire must do as much damage as possible. However, on the other, the types of measure that he or she could take in order to ensure that damage is maximal (e.g. the use of a fire accelerant, the disarming of automatic fire-fighting systems) will leave evidence that the fire was deliberately set. Review the various means by which the arsonist might attempt to overcome this dilemma. For each such means, describe the evidence that might be left by the arsonist that may be uncovered by a skilful investigator.

4. During a fire scene investigation, it is of great importance to be able to establish whether the fire was started deliberately or accidentally. Discuss the features of a scene that would indicate to you that it was the scene of a deliberately set fire and how these features would contrast with those that may be observed at the scene of a fire of accidental cause.

5. When collecting, storing and transporting samples from fire scenes for subsequent laboratory-based forensic analysis, what steps would you take to ensure that:

   (a) adequate control samples are taken;

   (b) all samples can be uniquely identified; and

   (c) contamination of the samples cannot occur.

Note that before answering this question, you might find it useful to read Chapter 2.

6. Review the means by which crime scenes are preserved and recorded and the methods used to recover items of physical evidence from them (see Chapter 2). Describe any specific issues that may need to be addressed when applying these means and methods to fire scenes.

7. Arsonists have been known to set fire to their own commercial premises during a riot in an attempt to blame the act on the rioters and claim compensation. How might a detailed examination of such a fire scene reveal that the premises were set on fire by someone with a profit motive rather than a rioter?

8. Write an account entitled 'The roles of thermal conduction, convection and heat radiation in shaping the behaviour of fire in (a) typical room fires and (b) outdoor fires'.

9. Some flammable liquids have virtually no odour. Does this mean that their presence at a fire scene would remain undetected?

Further reading

Daéid, N. N. (2004) *Fire investigation*. Boca Raton, FL: CRC Press LLC.

DeHaan, J. D. (2006) *Kirk's fire investigation* (6th edn). Upper Saddle River, NJ: Prentice Hall, Inc.

Drysdale, D. (1998) *An introduction to fire dynamics*. Chichester: John Wiley & Sons Ltd.

Faith, N. (2000) *Blaze: the forensics of fire*. New York: St Martin's Press.

Hall, R., Brakhage, C. S., Murnane, L. and Ruane, T. P. (eds), validated by the International Fire Service Training Association (IFSTA) (2005) *Introduction to fire origin and cause* (3rd edn). Oklahoma: Oklahoma State University.

Noon, R. K. (1995) *Engineering analysis of fires and explosions*. Boca Raton, FL: CRC Press LLC.

Office of the Deputy Prime Minister (2006) *Fire statistics, United Kingdom, 2004*. London: Home Office Research, Development and Statistics Directorate.

Petrovich, W. P. (1998) *A fire investigator's handbook: technical skills for entering, documenting and testifying in a fire scene investigation*. Illinois: Charles C Thomas Publishers Ltd.

Weiner, M. (2001) *The economic costs of fire. Home Office Research Study 229*. London: Home Office Research, Development and Statistics Directorate.

Chapter objectives

After reading this chapter, you should be able to:

> Define what is meant by the terms explosion and explosive.

> Describe how explosions and explosives may be classified.

> Understand the basic principles of explosion scene investigation.

> List the means by which samples may be analysed for the presence of explosives.

> Recognise the forensic value of the detection and/or identification of explosives, whether by chemical analysis or other means, and the steps that need to be taken to ensure that the interpretation of such information is valid.

Introduction

Regrettably, the destructive nature of explosions has been used by a number of terrorist organisations and criminals as a means of furthering their particular aims. Explosions have been used to terrorise communities, murder individuals, damage property and facilitate theft (as in the case of safe-breaking).

This chapter describes what is meant by the terms explosion and explosive. It explores the means by which explosion scenes can be investigated and the role of laboratory-based techniques in the analysis of samples that are suspected either of being explosives or being contaminated with them.

11.1 The classification of explosions and explosives

Explosion
The violent effect produced due to the rapid build-up of gas pressure at a location because of the sudden liberation of energy and, in most cases, gas at that location.

An **explosion** is a manifestation of a sudden release of energy. It may be defined as the violent effect produced due to the rapid build-up of gas pressure at a location because of the sudden liberation of energy and, in most cases, gas at that location. The process that leads to a given explosion may be chemical, mechanical, thermal, electrical or nuclear in nature. In the forensic context, explosions directly caused by chemical reactions are the most interesting and are described later in this section.

Mechanical explosions occur when containers of pressurised gas and/or liquid burst to liberate gas. Such explosions may happen, for example, in a fire or when a system that is designed to be pressurised from within becomes over-pressurised (e.g. a vehicle tyre that is over-inflated). Thermal explosions may be produced when a liquid is rapidly brought to its boiling point by contact with another liquid that is significantly hotter than it, such as may happen if water and molten steel are allowed to meet. An electrical explosion results if the heating effect of the discharge of electricity through an electrically insulating material is sufficiently intense. Nuclear explosions are beyond the scope of this book and will not be discussed here.

Any substance that is capable of producing an explosion is known as an **explosive**. However, most commonly, and in this book, the term explosive is used to denote any one of those materials that can produce explosions as a consequence of chemical reactions. Clearly, any substance of this type must be able to undergo a chemical process that rapidly releases energy and, ideally, gas. To trigger an explosion, this process must be initiated. Initiation requires the supply of sufficient energy, in a utilisable form, to at least some part of the explosive[1]. In order to be an explosive, a material must therefore be capable of propagating the explosive chemical process through itself from the site of initiation.

There are many explosives known that consist of suitable **oxidising** and **reducing agents** that are present in intimate combination and in appropriate proportions. This combination may be achieved by the physical mixing of materials that have oxidising properties with those that have reducing ones. Typical oxidising materials used for this purpose include inorganic nitrates, perchlorates and chlorates. Suitable reducing materials, which may be thought of as fuels, include carbon, sulphur, hydrocarbons, carbohydrates (e.g. sugar) and finely divided metals (e.g. aluminium). Gunpowder (also called black powder) is the archetypal explosive of this sort. It is a mixture of saltpetre (potassium nitrate), charcoal (carbon) and sulphur. Another commonly encountered explosive mixture is ammonium nitrate and fuel oil (ANFO), which is used as a blasting agent in quarries.

An alternative means of achieving the intimate combination of oxidising and reducing agents is to synthesise a compound, parts of which are oxidising in nature while others are reducing. Such compounds tend to produce a more dramatic explosive effect than do physical mixtures of oxidising and reducing materials. They include:

- 2,4,6-trinitrotoluene (TNT);
- cyclotrimethylenetrinitramine (RDX);
- glyceryl trinitrate (nitroglycerine);
- 2,4,6-trinitrophenylmethylnitramine (tetryl);
- cyclotetramethylenetetranitramine (HMX); and
- pentaerythritol tetranitrate (PETN).

It is important to realise, however, that many explosive formulations that contain explosive compounds are, in fact, blended products. These blends are made in order to modify the characteristics of the pure materials from which they are formulated. For example, nitroglycerine is rendered much safer to handle by combining it with

Explosive
Any substance that is capable of producing an explosion (although this term is commonly restricted to those substances that can produce explosions due to chemical reactions).

Oxidising agent
A chemical species that is capable of accepting electrons from another chemical species. Also known as an oxidant.

Reducing agent
A chemical species that is capable of donating electrons to another chemical species. Also known as a reductant.

---

1 Some explosive materials may liberate sufficient energy by internal chemical reactions to cause an explosion to be initiated without the input of energy from outside. That is, they spontaneously explode (for example, mixtures containing sulphur and a chlorate are notorious for doing this). Clearly, this is not a desirable characteristic in useful explosives.

Deflagration

A type of chemical explosion in which the speed at which the reaction front moves through the explosive is less than the speed of sound in that material.

Detonation

A type of chemical explosion in which the speed at which the reaction front moves through the explosive is greater than the speed of sound in that material.

High explosive

An explosive that normally detonates rather than deflagrates

(Reproduced by kind permission of Dave Bott, Staffordshire Fire & Rescue Service, UK)

an inert absorbent such as kieselguhr (a diatomaceous earth – a geological material produced by the sedimentary deposition of diatoms' skeletons) to form dynamite (known as straight dynamite in the United States).

Explosions due to chemical reactions can be subdivided into two types, namely deflagrations and detonations. During a **deflagration**, the speed at which the reaction front moves through the explosive is less than the speed of sound in that material. In a **detonation**, the speed at which the reaction front moves through the explosive is greater than the speed of sound in that material.

High explosives are ones that normally detonate, and thereby produce a shattering effect. They are used in both military and industrial applications where blast is required. High explosives do not normally need to be confined in a container in order to explode. However, a number of military munitions are normally filled with this type of explosive, including shells, mines, bombs and grenades. When they explode, such munitions produce both blast and rapidly moving fragments of their casings. PETN- and RDX-based formulations are commonly used in military blasting applications. Frequently encountered industrial blasting formulations may be based on ammonium nitrate and/or nitroglycerine. These include ANFO and dynamite (both described earlier) and blends based on mixtures of either nitroglycerine and nitrocellulose, or nitroglycerine, nitrocellulose and ammonium nitrate. Unsurprisingly, high explosives are also called detonating explosives.

Deflagrating explosives (formerly known also as low explosives) are those that will not normally detonate. Furthermore, in order to explode – rather than burn – they need to be confined or contained. Also, when they do explode, their action is better described as pushing rather than shattering. Nonetheless, as illustrated by the example shown in Figure 11.1, their action can be devastating. Examples of such explosives include the propellants used in firearms (Chapter 9) and explosive mixtures of air and fuel gases (e.g. natural gas or petrol vapour) or flammable dusts (e.g. flour or coal).

Figure 11.1 A two-storey brick-built property that was demolished by a deflagrating explosion caused by the ignition of petrol vapours within the building

In many applications, a distinction can be drawn between primary and secondary explosives. In such applications, the former of these materials is significantly more easy to initiate than the latter. The devices used in these applications contain a small amount of primary explosive and a main charge consisting of a larger quantity of secondary explosive. During use, initiation of the primary explosive liberates a sudden burst of energy that is sufficient to initiate a reaction in the main charge. This arrangement is used in firearms cartridges in which a percussion-initiated primary explosive (the primer) is used to set off the main charge (the propellant) (Chapter 9). It is also used in devices in which a main charge of high explosive (secondary explosive) is initiated with a detonator, which contains primary explosive.

It is also useful to recognise a distinction between **condensed explosives** and **dispersed explosives**. This is described in Box 11.1 together with the patterns of damage caused by an explosive that indicate which of these two forms was involved in a given incident and whether a detonation or a deflagration had occurred.

Condensed explosive
An explosive that is either a solid or a liquid.

Dispersed explosive
An explosive that is either a gas or an aerosol.

Further information

Box 11.1

Explosions in condensed and dispersed explosives

Liquid and solid explosives are both referred to as condensed; an explosive that is either a gas or an aerosol is described as being dispersed. (An aerosol is a solid or liquid that is finely dispersed in a gas, such as flour [a solid] in air [a gas].) Both detonations and deflagrations can occur in explosives of either type, although detonations are rare in dispersed explosives. Importantly, as outlined in Table 11.1 below, the patterns of damage resulting from an explosion give strong indications as to whether the explosive was condensed or dispersed and whether it detonated or deflagrated.

Terrorists have been known to use a small charge of high explosive to disperse and ignite a quantity of flammable liquid (e.g. petrol). As might be expected, the aftermath of an explosion caused by such a device will show the characteristics of both the detonation of the condensed high explosive and the deflagration of the dispersed material. In such cases, the effects of the detonation are most evident near to the location of the device at the time at which it exploded, while the characteristic damage caused by the deflagration is more clearly observed further away from this point. Note that the explosion of such devices is likely to also result in a fire, which will cause its own pattern of damage. Fires and the damage they cause are explored in Chapter 10.

Table 11.1   Typical characteristic damage patterns observed in detonations and deflagrations of condensed and dispersed chemical explosives

Type of chemical explosive	Type of explosion	Typical characteristic patterns of damage
Condensed	Detonation	Severe blast effects with the cutting (even of steel springs)/shattering/pulverising of objects near to the location of the explosive charge. When detonated on a surface, condensed explosives typically form a crater in that surface (see the photograph overleaf). The explosion centre* (i.e. the place where the explosion started) and the region of maximum damage usually coincide. Explosion pressure becomes lower with increasing distance from the explosion centre.

▶

Box 11.1 *continued*

Table 11.1   Continued

Type of chemical explosive	Type of explosion	Typical characteristic patterns of damage
Condensed	Deflagration	Damage caused by intense heat is near to the location of the explosive charge. Blast damage is less severe than in detonations of condensed explosives. Bending as opposed to cutting effects is observed in objects near to the charge at the time of the explosion. The explosion centre* and the region of maximum damage usually coincide. Explosion pressure becomes lower with increasing distance from the explosion centre.
Dispersed	Detonation	Rare but can occur in pipelines, lift shafts or other elongated enclosures. Shattering effects seen. The explosion centre* and the region of maximum damage do not coincide. Explosion pressure becomes higher with increasing distance from the explosion centre towards the region of maximum damage.
Dispersed	Deflagration	The displacement (as opposed to shattering) of surrounding objects (e.g. the walls of a room in which such an explosion occurred might well have been pushed outward). Objects *within* the explosion are often little damaged (e.g. in one case, a natural gas explosion occurred in the basement of a bungalow with sufficient ferocity to blow a settee vertically out of the building and yet two people who were in the basement at the time of the explosion sustained only superficial burns). Craters are not produced. The explosion centre* and the region of maximum damage frequently do not coincide. Explosion pressure shows little discernible pattern and/or reaches a maximum some distance from the explosion centre.

*See Box 11.3 for information about how, in any given case, the explosion centre may be found.

The crater left by the detonation of a condensed explosive

(Reproduced by kind permission of Andy Kirby, Staffordshire Police, UK)

11.2 Explosion scene investigation

The investigation of the scene of an explosion has, in most cases, the potential to become the investigation of the scene of a serious crime. Consequently, until and unless there is a reason to treat it otherwise, it is wise to process the scene of an explosion as if it were that of a serious crime. The methods used in the processing of serious crime scenes, and the underlying principles on which these methods are based, are described in detail in Chapter 2.

Nevertheless, explosion scene investigations differ from those of other scenes in a number of important respects. These principally arise out of:

- the unusual risks to the investigators, the emergency services and the public that are frequently posed by explosion scenes (although it should be noted that fires and other large scenes often also pose significant risks);
- the immense destruction that is often wrought by an explosion and any subsequent fire;
- the need to establish the cause of the explosion (i.e. what exploded and why it did so).

The principles, methods and management structures used to examine an explosion scene are, in essence, the same as those used to process any other major crime scene. As is the case with all major crime scenes, the management system incorporates mechanisms to allow experts to be called to the scene of an explosion as required. In the United Kingdom, in cases in which an explosive device may have been responsible for the explosion, the scene will be attended by both the emergency services and Explosives Ordnance Disposal (EOD, i.e. Army Bomb Disposal) personnel. Furthermore, in cases in which a terrorist organisation is suspected of involvement, the Metropolitan Police Anti-Terrorist Branch will normally be asked to assist the local police force in the processing of the scene.

Irrespective of the likely cause of the explosion, the preservation of life and the maintenance of safety are of paramount importance and there are systems in place to facilitate this. For example, in scenes that may involve explosive device(s), the site is not entered for the purposes of examination until it is declared safe by EOD personnel. Whether or not the explosion is suspected to have been caused by an explosive device, it is highly likely that an explosives expert will be called to attend the scene. His or her aim is to establish the cause of the explosion. However, he or she may also be called upon to assist the emergency services and/or military in the minimisation of the risk of subsequent explosions.

At some point, it will be necessary to approach the explosion scene for the first time. This will normally be part of the emergency response process in a bid to rescue any injured people from the devastation. However, if it is known beyond doubt that there are no injured persons present, this approach will be made part of the more controlled process of explosion investigation. When approaching the scene, it is vitally important to take into account the risks posed by the scene itself and any rescue operations to the health and safety of all those involved. These risks may arise as a consequence of damage caused by the explosion and could include, for example, the exposure of hazardous materials (e.g. asbestos, body fluids), the presence of potentially explosive gases or structures in imminent danger of collapse. In the case of deliberate bombings, extreme caution must be exercised in case another bomb has been placed nearby with the express purpose of killing or injuring those who respond to the first explosion.

As is the case for all crime scenes, the recording of the scene is of great importance (Chapter 2, Section 2.3). As part of this, all actions carried out at the scene should be properly logged from the earliest opportunity. Also, the establishment of a cordon around the scene of an explosion is a vital early step in its preservation. The debris from the explosion may be of great forensic significance. This is especially true of debris from any explosive device involved (Box 11.2). The violent and destructive nature of an explosion means that debris is likely to be scattered over a large area and evidentially significant pieces of material may be very small compared with the scale of the scene. On initial arrival at the scene, it may not be possible to be certain how far evidentially valuable material has been scattered from the location of the explosion. However, it is usually sufficient to place the cordon so that it has a radius from this location that is 1.5 times the distance travelled by the furthest flung piece of obvious debris. It must be borne in mind, however, that this may not be sufficient to encircle all significant items in all cases. For example, end caps from pipe bombs have been known to be blown for very considerable distances from the location of the explosion.

Once the cordon has been established, it is used to control access to the scene. After any emergencies created by the explosion have been brought under control, including those associated with any injured, those steps in addition to the placement of the cordon that are necessary to preserve the scene are carried out (Chapter 2, Section 2.2). The scene is then systematically searched for items of physical evidence and examined for features, such as patterns of damage (Box 11.3), that may help to reconstruct the events of the incident and establish the

Further information

Box 11.2

Evidential value of debris from explosive devices

The debris from any explosive device may include portions of any detonator employed, the wrappings from cartridges of commercial explosive (if used), and/or fragments of any electrical or mechanical timing devices, remote control or victim-actuated mechanism present. The examination of such fragments may reveal a number of valuable facts. Importantly, it may allow:

■ the materials from which the explosive device was made to be identified (e.g. the laboratory analysis for trace levels of explosive not consumed in the incident

can reveal the nature of the explosives involved, as may the presence of trade marks on wrappings);

■ the construction of the device to be deduced;

■ the likely manner in which it was triggered to be established;

■ in some cases, the likely identity of one or more people involved in the incident (e.g. from fingerprints found on one of the device's component parts, such as sticky tape used to hold it together).

cause of the explosion. Other than debris that originates from the explosive device itself and any container that was used to conceal it, the types of physical evidence that are sought are essentially the same as those looked for at any serious crime scene. Such evidence may include both recoverable materials (e.g. body fluids) and marks and impressions (e.g. footprints). For more information on the search for items of physical evidence, and their collection, packaging, labelling and storage, see Chapter 2, Section 2.4.

In order to fully investigate the cause of an explosion, it is necessary to draw upon all the relevant information available. This will include not only observations made at the scene but also the results of any laboratory analyses undertaken

Further information

Box 11.3

Patterns of explosion damage

Explosions due to explosives cause damage by displacing and permanently distorting objects as well as by the heat that they release and the fires that may follow. At the scene of an explosion, the analysis of the patterns of damage can be highly informative. A number of features of the damage are of value. Notably, these include those that provide indications of:

■ the direction in which the blast and/or fragments travelled at any given point in the scene (an example of the former type of feature is the bending of a pipe, while an example of the latter is the penetration of a relatively soft material by a fragment of bomb casing, thereby leaving an elongated hole – extrapolation from this would allow the direction of travel of the fragment to be established);
■ the location of the region of maximum damage;
■ the maximum pressure that was exerted by the explosion at various points in the scene.

The construction of a plan of the scene on which direction indicators are marked will frequently allow the investigator to establish the location of the place where the explosion started, i.e. the explosion centre. This is possible because the explosion centre will be revealed as the place from which blast and/or fragments of any explosive device originated. Locating the explosion centre is of considerable value because:

■ it will coincide with the place where the explosion was initiated, thereby assisting the investigation by indicating where to look for evidence of the means by which initiation occurred;
■ in cases that involve condensed explosives (Box 11.1), the vicinity of the explosion centre is a likely place to find explosive residues in concentrations that may be detected by laboratory analysis (Section 11.3);
■ this is the origin of the trajectory taken by any fragments of any bomb involved (and/or any container used to conceal any bomb) thereby providing information about the likely location of such fragments;
■ when used in conjunction with other observations based on patterns of damage, it will allow experts to discern strong indications as to whether a given chemical explosion was caused by a condensed explosive or a dispersed one, and whether this explosive detonated or deflagrated (see Box 11.1).

In the case of condensed explosives, one of the parameters that may be estimated from an analysis of damage patterns is the weight of the charge. There are a number of ways in which this may be done. For example, for all but small charges, crater dimensions can be used, thus:

$$W \approx \frac{d^3}{16}$$

where W is the weight of the charge in kilograms and d is the diameter of the crater in metres.

(Section 11.3), interviews with witnesses and/or suspects, discussions with other personnel attending the scene (such as members of the emergency services) and those with specialist knowledge of the location (such as the architects and the owners of property that was damaged), and information available from an examination of any injuries sustained by individuals during the explosion.

The investigation of an explosion will normally allow a number of conclusions to be drawn, although the degree of certainty associated with these may vary from conclusion to conclusion and from incident to incident. Importantly, these conclusions will normally include an assessment of whether the explosion occurred as the result of an accident or a deliberate act and the type of explosion involved (i.e. chemical, mechanical, thermal, electrical or nuclear). In instances of explosions caused by chemical reactions, on which this chapter concentrates, the investigation will normally reveal whether the explosive was condensed or dispersed and whether it deflagrated or detonated (Box 11.1). Furthermore, in such cases, strenuous efforts will be made to establish the exact chemical nature of the explosive, the means by which it was initiated and, in the case of a deliberately caused explosion, the motives, modus operandi and identity of the person or persons responsible.

Note that the process of elimination is an important tool in the investigation of explosions as it can reveal truths that are not directly observable. For example, if *all* natural and accidental causes of an explosion can be eliminated, then it must be concluded that the explosion occurred as the result of a deliberate act.

It is important to realise that some explosion scenes are not what they first appear to be. For example, if an explosion were to occur on board an aeroplane, causing it to crash to the ground, then the enormous damage of the impact may initially disguise damage caused by the explosion. Under these circumstances, unless sufficient pains are taken during the crash investigation, its true root cause may never be established. This point is illustrated by the enormous effort that was necessary to establish the cause of the Lockerbie disaster, as described in the case study given in Box 11.4. This case study also illustrates the importance of the process of elimination in explosion scene investigations.

Case study

Box 11.4

The bombing of Pan Am flight 103

On 21 December 1988 at 7.03 p.m. GMT, the Boeing 747 aeroplane (registration N739PA) that was Pan Am flight 103 fell from the sky, disintegrating as it did so. There had been no distress call from the aeroplane, which had been heading for New York, having taken off from London en route from Frankfurt. Large parts of it crashed to the ground in and around Lockerbie, a small town in Dumfries and Galloway, Scotland, with debris scattered over an area of land of approximately 845 square miles (2190 km^2). All 259 people on board the flight and a further 11 on the ground were killed during this tragedy. The financial costs were considerable too, including approximately £17 million spent on aftermath operations, including police enquiries, and the cost of the aircraft (its insurance hull value amounted to approximately US$32 million).

Box 11.4 *continued*

The post-crash operations were extensive and complex. They involved many organisations, including the Fire Brigade, Police, British Air Accidents Investigation Branch (AAIB), the Army, Royal Air Force and Navy in the United Kingdom, and many agencies from other nations – including the US Federal Bureau of Investigation (FBI). To give an indication of the scale of work undertaken, it is worth noting that within one week of the crash, more than 5000 UK police officers had been involved.

As a result of the painstaking search of land on both sides of the border between England and Scotland, in excess of four million individual pieces of debris were located. More than 85 per cent of the structural parts of the aeroplane were retrieved. This enabled the investigators to physically reconstruct the Boeing 747 inside a large hangar. Examination of the wreckage revealed no indication that corrosion or fatigue of the aircraft had caused its failure. What is more, the aeroplane's flight recorder demonstrated that, at the time when disaster struck, its controls had been at appropriate settings for normal flight.

Close inspection of the wreckage revealed evidence of the detonation of an explosive device within one of the containers in which luggage had been stored within the forward baggage hold. Key aspects of this evidence included:

■ the presence of trace levels of explosives;
■ minute fragments embedded in the skin of the aircraft and container parts – including a small piece of printed circuit board that could be identified as having come from a radio-cassette player that had been used to conceal the explosive device;
■ fibres indicating that a brown suitcase had contained the bomb together with clothing.

A range of simulation experiments were carried out in which explosive devices were detonated within luggage containers of the type in which the bomb was thought to have exploded. These demonstrated that the detonation was likely to have occurred in a position within the container that indicated that the bomb had been loaded onto the aeroplane at Frankfurt.

Textile fibres recovered from pieces of the suitcase believed to have held the explosive device were traced to clothing that had been flown to Frankfurt from Malta. During a trial held under Scottish law in Camp Zeist, the Netherlands, a Libyan, Abdel Baset Ali Mohamed Al-Megrahi, was shown to have purchased these clothes from a boutique in Malta. On 31 January 2001, he was found guilty and convicted of the bombing of Pan Am flight 103 and given a life sentence. On 24 November 2003, three judges ruled that he must serve a minimum of 27 years in jail before being considered for parole.

11.3 The analysis of explosives

Laboratory-based chemical analysis of samples connected with cases of suspected illegal use of explosives can provide valuable evidence. Such samples may be those recovered from the scene of an explosion (whether actual or apparently intended), any suspects involved in the case and/or their possessions.

The initial purpose of such analysis is to establish whether the sample contains an explosive. Furthermore, laboratory analysis may identify the chemical nature of any explosive detected. It may also allow the amount of any such material present in the sample to be established and/or provide points of comparison between samples taken from different locations. The last of these may be of particular importance in helping to establish a link between a suspect and an apparent crime scene or between a number of seemingly independent incidents.

During chemical analysis, a distinction must be made between trace and bulk quantities of questioned material. Strictly, bulk quantities are those that may be weighed. However, as a rule of thumb, trace quantities are those that are too small to be seen with the naked eye and, conversely, anything that can be seen under these conditions is considered as being present in bulk amounts. Examples of trace quantities include the explosive residues that may be recovered from a suspect's hands after he or she has handled explosives.

This distinction between trace and bulk amounts of questioned material is important for a number of reasons. These include the potential that bulk samples have for contaminating items that are suspected of containing trace quantities of incriminating material. It is vital, therefore, that rigorous systems are in place to ensure that such items can never be brought into direct contact with bulk samples or with surfaces that have been potentially contaminated by contact with bulk samples. For example, it is good practice to completely separate those facilities that handle and analyse bulk explosives from those that deal with trace samples. In the case of explosives, another reason for this distinction is that great safety precautions need to be taken during the analysis of substantial bulk samples because of both the explosion hazard that they pose and, in many cases, their toxic nature.

A wide range of techniques may be used for the analysis of samples that are suspected of being composed of, or contaminated with, explosives. These include:

■ the physical testing of the explosive properties of the sample;

■ spot tests (i.e. chemical tests devised to produce visible changes in the presence of small amounts of specific types of chemical and that may indicate the presence of an explosive);

■ light and scanning electron microscopy (the latter of which can be coupled with energy dispersive X-ray analysis (EDX), allowing the determination of the elemental composition of the sample (Chapter 9, Box 9.6));

■ infrared spectroscopy – a technique that can allow the detection of the presence of individual chemical species or chemical functional groups, and that provides multiple points of comparison between samples (Chapter 3, Box 3.9);

■ various forms of chromatography (Box 11.5), including:
  - thin-layer chromatography (TLC);
  - gas chromatography (GC) (which may be linked to mass spectrometry (MS) to give GC–MS);
  - high-performance liquid chromatography (HPLC); and
  - ion chromatography (IC);

■ atomic absorption spectroscopy (AAS) – a technique that can be used to quantify most elements that may be present in a sample (Chapter 7, Box 7.5).

The methods that are selected for a given application will depend on a number of factors. Notably, these include:

■ whether the sample is believed to contain bulk or trace amounts of explosive (e.g. the physical testing of the sample's explosive properties can be carried out only on bulk samples);

Forensic techniques

Box 11.5

Chromatography

The term 'chromatography' is applied to any analytical technique that is used to separate the components of mixtures by means of a system containing both a mobile phase and a stationary phase. The mobile phase employed is either a gas, liquid or, less commonly, a supercritical-fluid. The stationary phase may be a solid (usually finely divided), a liquid immobilised onto a solid or a chemical species bonded to a solid. Essentially, the mixture under test is carried through or over the stationary phase by the one-way flow of the mobile phase. Separation is possible if the molecules, atoms or ions that make up the different components of the mixture spend different proportions of their time in the mobile phase. This is because the more of the time that a component's molecules, atoms or ions spend in the mobile phase, the faster the component will migrate through the stationary phase and the components of the mixture will separate if they have differential migration rates.

There are many different chromatographic systems available. The methods used may be classified as either planar chromatography or column chromatography. In the former, the stationary phase is held within the pores of a piece of paper or onto a flat plate. In column chromatography, the mobile phase is made to flow, either by gravity or by pressure, through a stationary phase held in a column or thin tube.

The main chromatographic methods used in forensic analysis are each examined in turn.

Thin-layer chromatography (TLC)

Thin-layer chromatography (TLC) is an example of planar chromatography. In this system, the stationary phase is provided by a thin layer of an appropriate material, such as finely divided silica or alumina, bound onto a flat plate, typically made of plastic or glass. The sample under test is applied as a spot near to the bottom of the plate in a position marked with pencil (the origin). In the most common variant of this technique, the plate is then placed roughly vertically in a closed tank that contains a shallow pool of liquid (the mobile phase, known as the solvent or the developer). Importantly, the solvent pool is

not so deep that it comes into direct contact with the sample spot. As the solvent gradually rises through the stationary phase by capillary action, the components of the sample become separated. This process is called development. After separation, but before the solvent has reached the top of the plate, the plate is taken out of the developing tank. The position of the boundary between the wet and dry portions of the plate (i.e. the solvent front) is marked with pencil and the plate is then dried. The separated components of the mixture appear as individual spots on this record of chromatography (known as a chromatogram). If necessary, these spots are made visible (i.e. visualised), for example, by using an appropriate chemical treatment or by fluorescence examination under ultraviolet light.

TLC cannot provide definitive proof of the identity of a given sample or its constituent component(s). However, in forensic analysis, it can be used to compare questioned samples with known standards (i.e. positive control samples) and thereby facilitate tentative identification. This is best done by placing the questioned sample and the standard on the same TLC plate, and then subjecting both of them to identical treatment. If the questioned sample and the standard behave indistinguishably when developed and, where needs be, visualised, this is evidence that they may be the same material. Figure 8.3 in Chapter 8 gives an example of this type of experiment, as applied to the analysis of ink.

TLC can be used to provide tentative identification of the compound(s) present in a questioned sample. In many applications, it is not practicable to place all of the possible compounds that might be in a given questioned sample on the same TLC plate as the sample itself. Fortunately, information that can narrow down the range of possible compounds can be derived from an initial TLC experiment. This is performed on a plate on which only the questioned sample is placed. From this, the retardation factor (R_f) of the component(s) of the sample can be determined using the following expression:

$$R_f = \frac{\text{distance travelled by the component}}{\text{furthest distance travelled by the solvent from the origin}}$$

▶

Box 11.5 continued

Provided that the same type of TLC plate is used and that it is developed under the same conditions, the R_f value of a given compound is essentially constant. This means that the R_f value(s) obtained from this initial experiment can be compared with tabulated R_f values to find compounds with similar or identical R_f values to those of the questioned sample's component(s). In a second experiment, these compounds can be placed on the same TLC plate as the questioned sample, thereby allowing direct comparison after development and, if required, visualisation. Figure 7.9 (Chapter 7) illustrates the calculation of R_f values for two drugs.

In addition to the analysis of inks, and drugs and other poisons, TLC can be used in forensic science to analyse fibres (Chapter 3, Section 3.1.2) and explosives (Section 11.3).

High-performance liquid chromatography (HPLC)

High-performance liquid chromatography (HPLC) is an advanced type of column chromatography in which a liquid mobile phase is pumped under pressure through a column packed with a stationary phase. This stationary phase is made up of tiny solid particles, in many cases coated with an immobilised organic material. Briefly, the sample under test is injected into the column at one end and carried by a suitable liquid through the solid matrix. Separation of its constituent components occurs and, as they exit the column at the other end, they are detected one at a time by the use of a suitable detector (commonly based on fluorescence or the absorption of ultraviolet light). A record is made of the retention time of each component, that is, the time that each one spends in the column. These retention times are then compared with those of standard compounds in order to establish the likely identity of the components of the sample.

In common with TLC, this type of chromatography does not definitively prove the identity of the sample under test. However, proof of identity may be enhanced by the incorporation of a diode array detector (DAD). This simultaneously detects and records the ultraviolet–visible absorption spectrum of any component that absorbs in this region of the electromagnetic spectrum. It thereby simultaneously provides two different characteristics (the retention time and the absorption spectrum) that can be used when comparing an unknown component of a sample with a standard.

HPLC is performed at, or near, room temperature, which means that it is suitable for compounds that are sensitive to high temperatures. In forensic analysis, it can be used in the separation of complex mixtures of drugs (Chapter 7, Section 7.5.3), inks (Chapter 8, Section 8.5) and explosives (Section 11.3).

Ion chromatography (IC) is a technique that can be used to separate and quantify mixtures of either cations (i.e. positively charged ions) or anions (i.e. negatively charged ions). In the former case, the stationary phase is a cation exchange resin, while in the latter it is an anion exchange resin. In both cases, the stationary phase, in the form of tiny beads, is held in a column. The mobile phase is an aqueous solution, commonly of either dilute acid (in the separation of cations) or dilute base (in the separation of anions) and detection is usually by conductivity. In most applications, the mobile phase is pumped through the column. Therefore, in such cases, IC is considered as a type of HPLC.

Gas chromatography (GC)

Gas chromatography (GC) is another example of column chromatography. In GC, the mobile phase that carries the sample is a gas, usually nitrogen or helium, known as the carrier gas. While in some applications the stationary phase is a solid, this is rare. The norm is for the stationary phase to be a thin film of liquid that is immobilised within the column, and it is this variant of GC that is described here.

There are two main types of GC apparatus used with immobilised liquid stationary phases:

■ *Packed columns*. These are made of metal, glass or Teflon. They are typically 1–6 m long and have inside diameters of 2–4 mm. Packed columns are filled with a finely divided, inert packing material, commonly diatomaceous earth. The surface of this solid support retains the thin film of liquid that constitutes the stationary phase.

■ *Capillary columns* (also known as *open tubular columns*). Capillary columns may be made of glass or, more recently, of fused silica, and are coiled. They range in length from 10 to 100 m and have inside diameters of 0.1–0.75 mm. In capillary columns, the inside wall of the tube is directly coated with the liquid stationary phase.

Box 11.5 continued

In GC, the sample is injected, usually in liquid form, into a heated injection chamber where it is vaporised (unless it is injected as a gas) and carried by the mobile phase through the heated column containing the stationary phase. The components of the sample mixture are separated according to their relative affinities for the mobile and stationary phases. As each emerges from the column, it is detected by, for example, a flame ionisation detector (FID) and recorded as a chromatogram that is a plot of retention time (on the horizontal axis) against detector response (examples of such chromatograms are given in Figure 10.9, Chapter 10).

In GC, the retention time for each individual component of a sample mixture is the time taken from initial injection to emergence from the column. These retention times can be compared with those of known standards, allowing tentative identification of the components. Definitive proof of component identity can be achieved, however, by using one of the 'hyphenated techniques', usually gas chromatography–mass spec-

trometry (GC–MS). GC–MS is used to confirm the analysis, for example, of banned substances in body fluids after immunoassay (Chapter 7, Section 7.5.3) and of explosive compounds present in samples at trace levels (Section 11.3).

It should be noted that it is possible to obtain quantitative, as well as qualitative, information from GC chromatograms. This can be done because the area under each peak is proportional to the amount of the component concerned that is present in the sample.

Finally, a special type of GC, known as pyrolysis-gas chromatography, is worthy of mention. This is used to obtain information about samples of low volatility. In pyrolysis-GC, the sample under test is broken down into various gaseous products by heating it to extremely high temperatures (up to 1000 °C), before the gases are entered into the mobile gas phase of the GC column. In forensic analysis, pyrolysis-GC may be used, for example, to characterise man-made fibres and paints (Chapter 3, Sections 3.1.2 and 3.5 respectively).

■ the nature of the explosive material that is suspected to be present (e.g. if it is believed that the material might contain an ionic oxidising agent, such as nitrate (NO_3^-), ion chromatography might be employed, whereas if it were to contain a relatively volatile organic explosive compound (e.g. nitroglycerine) gas chromatography might be chosen);

■ the sample matrix within which it is believed that explosive may be found (e.g. if the matrix is soil dug from the crater left by a bomb, it is likely that some form of sample pre-treatment – designed to largely separate any explosive present from its original matrix – will be used prior to the application of the main analytical technique(s)).

A range of methods based on GC and HPLC has been devised for the analysis of explosive compounds such as nitroglycerine or PETN. Given the superb sensitivity that may be achieved by these techniques, they are the methods of choice for the analysis of such compounds at trace levels.

When carrying out the laboratory analysis of samples that are suspected of containing explosives, the parallel analysis of appropriate control samples may be of utmost importance. In this context, the control samples chosen will be ones intended to either:

■ replicate the matrix within which the explosive is believed to reside in the questioned samples; and/or

■ check that the environment from which the questioned samples were taken, or in which they were stored or handled, could not produce a falsely positive result.

For example, consider a case in which swabs were used to take samples from the hands of someone suspected of handling explosives. If these were analysed and shown to contain traces of explosive and the case were to go to court, defence lawyers could argue that the traces of explosive could have arisen because of contamination from:

■ the swabs themselves;

■ any solvents or reagents used to damp the swabs prior to their contact with the hands of the suspect or during the subsequent processing of the swabs; and/or

■ any surfaces (laboratory bench tops, the gloves worn by the analyst, etc.) with which the swabs could have been brought into contact during their processing.

However, the defence's argument could be shown to be invalid if the laboratory had also:

■ analysed the following control samples:
  - swabs that were identical in all respects (including being damped with any solvent or reagent employed) to those used to take samples from the suspect except that they had not been in contact with the suspect's hands; and
  - swabs taken from all surfaces from which contamination could have occurred;

■ carried out this analysis of control samples, using techniques, solvents, reagents and equipment identical to those used for the questioned samples, and by this means established that none of the control samples showed any traces of the explosive found in the questioned samples.

It is vitally important to realise that analytical data that show the presence of explosive material are not in themselves proof that a crime has been committed nor are they proof that a given individual participated in a proven crime. For example, explosives may be found on farmland because that land had previously been used as part of a military firing range. In a similar vein, seemingly incriminating traces of explosive may be innocently present on the hands of an individual. This may occur, for example, either because he or she had encountered such material as part of his or her work (e.g. as a quarry worker or a member of the armed forces) or because that person had shaken hands with someone who had recently handled explosives. Also, apparently incriminating chemicals that may be part of an explosive formulation often have other legitimate uses (e.g. ammonium nitrate is both a component of the explosive ANFO and used as a plant fertiliser).

11.4 Summary

■ An explosion is the violent effect produced due to the rapid build-up of gas pressure at a location because of the sudden liberation of energy and, in most cases, gas at that location. In the forensic context, the most important type of explosion is one produced by a chemical explosive. Such explosives may be formed by the combination of suitable oxidising and reducing agents in appropriate proportions.

■ Explosions may be divided into those that are deflagrations and those that are detonations. High explosives are those that normally detonate when they explode, whereas deflagrating explosives will not ordinarily do so. An explosive device will often be constructed using a small amount of relatively easily initiated primary explosive, the explosion of which is designed to set off a larger charge of a secondary explosive. Explosives may be classified on the basis of their physical form: condensed explosives are solids or liquids, while explosive gases and aerosols are said to be dispersed.

■ Many of the principles and methods used in the investigation of an explosion scene are those employed during the processing of any serious crime scene. However, explosion scene investigation differs from normal serious crime scene investigation to allow for the unusual risks posed by the aftermath of an explosion, the immense destruction that often accompanies an explosion and the need to establish the cause of the explosion.

■ A wide range of laboratory-based analytical techniques can be used to detect, identify and/or quantify explosive materials, whether present in bulk or trace amounts. The information provided may be of value, for example, in establishing a link between a suspect and an apparent crime scene. When analysing samples for trace levels of explosive, great care has to be taken to avoid the possibility of contamination. Appropriate control samples must be used to show that such contamination has not occurred.

Problems

1. Consider a case in which an explosion occurred immediately after a fire-fighter broke a window of a room in a burning house. List the possible causes of such an explosion. Decide which of the causes on your list you believe to be the most probable explanation of what happened. Describe the evidence that would be collected by an explosion scene investigator in order to test whether this cause does indeed explain the occurrence of the explosion. Before answering this question, you may find it useful to read Chapter 10.

2. During an explosion scene investigation, it is of great importance to be able to establish whether the explosion was deliberate or accidental. Discuss the features of a scene that would indicate to you that it was the scene of a deliberate explosion and how these features would contrast with those that may be observed at the scene of an accidental explosion.

3. When collecting, storing and transporting samples from explosion scenes for subsequent laboratory-based forensic analysis, what steps would you take to ensure that:

   (a) adequate control samples are taken;

   (b) all samples can be uniquely identified; and

   (c) contamination of the samples cannot occur?

   Note that before answering this question, you might find it useful to read Chapter 2.

4. Review the means by which crime scenes are preserved and recorded and the methods used to recover items of physical evidence from them (see Chapter 2). Describe any specific issues that may need to be addressed when applying these means and methods to explosion scenes.

5. Consider a case in which an individual is detained by the police on suspicion of causing explosions. This person's vehicle is examined and is found to contain traces of ammonium nitrate (NH_4NO_3). Is this incriminating evidence?

6. What is meant by each of the following terms?

    (a) explosion;

    (b) explosive;

    (c) deflagration;

    (d) detonation;

    (e) high explosive;

    (f) deflagrating explosive;

    (g) primary explosive;

    (h) secondary explosive;

    (i) condensed explosive;

    (j) dispersed explosive.

7. Write an account entitled 'How the location of the explosion centre within the scene of an explosion may be found and the value of this information to the explosion scene investigation'.

8. A bomb produced a crater with a mean diameter of 14.75 m. Approximately, what weight of explosive did it contain? Express your answer in kg (for answer, see footnote[2]).

Further reading

Akhavan, J. (2004) *The chemistry of explosives* (2nd edn). Cambridge: Royal Society of Chemistry.

Beveridge, A. (ed.) (1998) *Forensic investigation of explosions*. London: Taylor & Francis.

Noon, R. K. (1995) *Engineering analysis of fires and explosions*. Boca Raton, FL: CRC Press LLC.

Yallop, H. J. (1980) *Explosion investigation*. Jointly published by Harrogate: The Forensic Science Society and Edinburgh: Scottish Academic Press Ltd.

Yinon, J. (1999) *Forensic and environmental detection of explosives*. Chichester: John Wiley and Sons Ltd.

---

2. Answer = 200 kg

Chapter objectives

After reading this chapter, you should be able to:

> Describe the main changes that occur in the human body in the early stages after death and understand how these may be utilised to help estimate the post-mortem interval.

> Discuss how forensic entomology may be used to establish the post-mortem interval, the circumstances surrounding the death and any change in location of the body after death.

> Outline the process of post-mortem decomposition and appreciate how the rate at which it proceeds is influenced by certain factors (both external and internal in origin).

> Explain what is meant by the terms skeletalisation, mummification and adipocere formation, and how these processes are related to ambient conditions.

> Appreciate the role of the coroner in England and Wales in the investigation of reported deaths.

> Understand the procedure involved in medico-legal post-mortem examinations.

> Recognise the characteristics that may be used to identify unknown individuals from their remains.

Introduction

When the death of an individual cannot be attributed to natural causes, further investigation into the death, and the circumstances surrounding it, is required. This often involves a medico-legal post-mortem examination of the body, the exact nature of which will depend on the condition of the corpse. In circumstances where the body is fresh or, at least, has not yet lost its soft tissues through the natural process of decomposition, post-mortem examination should include both external examination and internal dissection of the cadaver. Ideally, this procedure should be carried out by a **forensic pathologist**. In cases where the human remains consist only of the bony skeleton (or parts thereof), post-mortem examination will benefit

Forensic pathologist
A medically trained specialist who, through the performance of forensic autopsy, provides legally required information concerning the death of an individual.

Forensic anthropologist
A person who specialises in the study of human skeletal remains within a legal context, particularly in relation to establishing personal identity.

from the specialist knowledge of the **forensic anthropologist**. In this context, and in other situations where the soft tissues of the body have been degraded, the expertise of the forensic odontologist may prove invaluable in eliciting important information. It should be noted that in the past 15 years or so, another type of specialist, the forensic archaeologist, has increasingly brought valuable knowledge and expertise from a traditional discipline into the forensic arena, especially in the location (Box 12.1), excavation and recovery of buried human remains.

Whatever the condition of the human remains under investigation, the purpose of the post-mortem examination is to establish a number of relevant facts. Importantly, these include:

- the time of death;
- the cause of death;
- the identification of the deceased.

These three topics, plus a discussion of the natural process of post-mortem decomposition, form the basis of this chapter. The forensic examination of evidential items that may be found in association with human remains, such as fibres and body fluids, is dealt with elsewhere in this book (particularly in Chapters 3 and 5).

Further information

Box 12.1

The role of the forensic archaeologist in the search and location of buried human remains

It is only since the late 1980s/early 1990s that specialists from the traditional discipline of archaeology have become involved in criminal investigation. Skilled archaeologists are experienced in a wide variety of techniques, including map analysis, aerial photography and geophysical survey, which can be usefully applied to the search for, and recovery of, hidden bodies (see below). On occasion, forensic archaeologists are called to give expert testimony in court, either for the prosecution or the defence (Chapter 14, Section 14.3). In this capacity, and indeed at all stages of an investigation, the forensic archaeologist must remain entirely impartial.

The decision to call in a forensic archaeologist, and the level of involvement required of that individual in any particular case, rests with the Senior Investigating Officer (SIO) (Chapter 2, Section 2.1). In the UK, there are currently about 10 forensic archaeologists who assist the police on a regular basis, although there are about three times this number whose services are available. Registration with the Council for the Registration of Forensic Practitioners (CRFP) (Chapter 1, Section 1.4.2) assures the quality and competence of accredited practitioners of forensic archaeology. In some instances, the services of a forensic archaeologist are required in the

Box 12.1 continued

periodic re-investigation of old, unresolved crimes, a process known as cold case review.

Search methods

Archaeological search methods, any or all of which may be utilised in the hunt for buried human remains, are listed below. These are placed in order from non-invasive to invasive techniques. Clearly, the sequence in which these techniques are applied is of great importance in maximising the amount of information and forensic evidence gathered.

■ *Map analysis*. Maps of various types (including, in the UK, Ordnance Survey maps) constitute a key resource for forensic archaeologists in the design of suitable search methods. Geological maps and those detailing land use may also give valuable information.

■ *Aerial photography*. The examination of aerial photographs, including infrared photographs, used in conjunction with map resources, may help to pinpoint anomalies of the vegetation and/or ground surface that could be usefully investigated further in the field.

■ *Field observation*. In the field, identifying changes in vegetation and topography that may indicate the presence of buried remains requires skilled observation. For example, the presence of a slight hollow may be the result of settlement of the material used to infill a grave and, possibly, the decomposition of a corpse underneath. Fieldworkers must also be aware of their physical impact on the surroundings and the need to avoid or minimise damage to evidence wherever possible.

■ *Geophysical survey techniques*. Some of the techniques of geophysical survey used in traditional archaeology can be effectively applied, by suitably experienced individuals, in forensic investigation. These non-invasive techniques have the advantage of providing on-the-spot information about areas below ground. For example, magnetic survey methods using a magnetometer (*magnetometry*) can detect minor changes in the Earth's magnetic field, while *resistivity* survey methods can detect changes in electrical resistance in the ground when an electrical current is passed through it. Both of these techniques can alert the operator to the presence of below-ground anomalies, which may be due to the presence of buried remains, and therefore help identify hot-spots within a gridded area that warrant further investigation. Another geophysical survey technique, *ground penetrating radar* (GPR), may be useful in detecting bodies in the built environment, e.g. within buildings or below areas of tarmac or concrete.

■ *Manual techniques*. Once areas of potential interest have been identified, manual techniques, which by their very nature are destructive, can be applied, usually within a grid system. These may involve the use of ground probes or augers (boring devices used for taking soil samples). Specially trained dogs, known as cadaver dogs, may also be usefully employed in the detection of buried corpses. Vent holes are created within the search area to allow the 'body dogs' to sniff out any decomposition gases issuing from human remains buried below.

As well as their role in the search for, and recovery of, (usually) individual bodies, forensic archaeologists may be involved in the location of mass graves under the auspices of organisations such as INFORCE (International Forensic Centre of Excellence for the Investigation of Genocide). Investigative teams are often initially directed to mass burial sites by witness statements and/or the results of satellite photography. Such sites of mass burial have been identified in a number of countries in recent years, including Iraq, Rwanda, and Kosovo in the former Balkans.

For detailed information on the role of the forensic archaeologist in the excavation of mass and individual graves, and the recovery of forensic evidence, the interested reader is referred to the excellent book by John Hunter and Margaret Cox (see Further reading).

12.1 Early post-mortem changes and the estimation of time of death

When a human body is discovered, one of the key questions to be asked is 'When did the person die?' The answer to this question is particularly important in cases of suspicious death. The accuracy of estimating the time since death is negatively correlated with the time that has elapsed since death occurred. In this section, the main early post-mortem changes – i.e. changes in temperature, hypostasis, rigor mortis and changes in the eyes – are each examined in turn, with particular reference to their utility in estimating the time since death (known as the **post-mortem interval**). After the first few days, and up to several months after death, the study of insects (and, to some extent, other invertebrates) present on and around the decomposing corpse may yield valuable information about the post-mortem interval (Box 12.2).

Post-mortem interval
The period of time that has elapsed since death occurred.

12.1.1 Changes in body temperature

During life, the core temperature of humans (i.e. that within the abdominal organs and skull) is normally maintained at a constant value of around 37 °C. After death, the mechanisms that regulate this temperature cease and the body ultimately attains the temperature of its environment. In those parts of the world where the ambient environmental temperature is below 37 °C, this means that the body cools. During the cooling of the core, the drop in temperature is approximately exponential. If the temperature of the environment is in the range 16–20 °C, the temperature of the core at 6, 10 and 15 hours after death may be 30–34 °C, 28 °C and 24–26 °C respectively. However, it is important to realise that a number of factors can affect the rate of cooling of a corpse, including atmospheric conditions (e.g. air temperature, humidity and precipitation), the initial temperature of the body, the amount of clothing worn by the victim and/or the body weight to surface area ratio of the deceased. It should be noted that after about 42 hours, when the process of decomposition is well established, the temperature of the core of the body may be expected to rise slightly.

Based on observations of the type outlined in the previous paragraph, a number of methods have been devised that use one or more measurements of core body temperature to *estimate* the time of death by back-calculation. Although such methods may be subject to sizeable errors, body temperature represents the best measure available for estimating the time of death, especially within the first 18 hours after death.

12.1.2 Hypostasis

Hypostasis
A post-mortem condition, similar in appearance to bruising, caused by the settlement of blood in the lowermost parts of the body during the early stages of decomposition. Also known as post-mortem lividity or livor mortis.

Hypostasis, also known as post-mortem lividity or livor mortis, develops shortly after death, becoming apparent within one hour, fully developed after three or four and usually persisting until decomposition (Section 12.2). Hypostasis is caused when the blood, whose normal circulation has ceased at the point of death, passively flows and settles in the blood vessels of the lowest parts of the body, under the

Further information

Box 12.2

The application of forensic entomology to the study of human remains

Entomology is the study of insects. In the forensic context, this discipline is primarily concerned with the interpretation of insect evidence found in association with decomposing corpses discovered under suspicious circumstances. Perhaps rather surprisingly, although there is documented evidence that entomology has assisted in the solution of violent crimes over several centuries, it has only recently become an integral part of the forensic investigation of major crime cases. In such instances, entomological samples are usually collected at the scene by a Scenes of Crime Officer (SOCO) or, if present, by an entomologist (who will then pass the material to a SOCO to document as an exhibit).

In the hands of a suitably qualified and experienced forensic entomologist (e.g. an expert from the Natural History Museum in London, or from an institute of higher education), evidence from insects and other invertebrates may yield valuable information regarding:

■ the post-mortem interval;
■ the circumstances surrounding the death;
■ any change in the location of the body after death.

The colonisation of dead bodies

In the case of bodies left above ground, the first colonisers to arrive are the true flies (order Diptera) belonging to the families Sarcophagidae (flesh-flies) and Calliphoridae (blowflies, also known as bottleflies). These can arrive at the body within minutes of death to lay their eggs (in the case of blowflies) or deposit their maggots (in the case of flesh-flies) in natural orifices – such as the eyes, mouth or nostrils – or in wounds. These initial colonisers are joined a little later by species of houseflies (family Muscidae, order Diptera).

True flies are holometabolous, i.e. they undergo full metamorphosis with a life cycle comprising four distinct stages – egg, larva (or maggot), pupa and adult (see figure opposite). Within the larval stage, there are three recognisable substages known as the first, second and third instars. Entry to the second and third instar stages is preceded by the shedding of the tough larval skin to allow for subsequent growth (a process known as ecdysis). The larvae are necrophagous (i.e. they feed directly on dead tissue) and can reduce the corpse to skin, bone and cartilage within about two weeks (depending on conditions). At this stage, species from other insect groups, notably beetles (order Coleoptera), start to arrive, while the number of fly larvae present progressively declines. Both the fly larvae and the beetle species have invertebrate parasites and predators associated with them.

The successive colonisation by insects described above is characteristic of bodies left to decompose above ground. Such insects will be excluded from bodies found in certain other situations, such as buried deep underground or submerged underwater. These will be colonised instead by other invertebrate species (including insects) characteristic of that particular environment. In certain situations, for example if a body were hidden in a sealed trunk, it may be impossible for *any* species to gain access to the body.

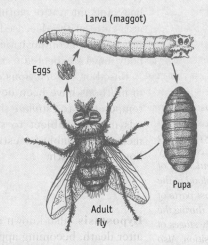

Life cycle of the bluebottle
(From Cacutt, L. (1988) *Complete book of fishing: the angler's guide to coarse, sea and game fishing.* London: Colour Library Books Ltd.)

▶

Box 12.2 *continued*

Collection of entomological samples

It is important that entomological samples taken from the body at the scene, and later at autopsy, are collected, preserved and analysed correctly. In addition, live specimens should be collected to rear through to their adult stage, to assist in the identification of the species present. It should be noted that third instar larvae ready to pupate leave the body and bury themselves in the ground nearby. Pupae constitute valuable entomological evidence, even after the adult flies have emerged and the tanned pupal cases are empty. Consequently, it may be profitable to search the ground near to the body for their presence.

Post-mortem interval

In the early days after death, examination of the development stages of the insects present can be used to estimate the period of time since the eggs were laid, and thus the post-mortem interval. This procedure was first used in the Ruxton case (Box 12.4). Information from other sources, such as the state of decomposition of the body itself, is also valuable in this respect. As insects are cold-blooded animals, their rate of development is affected by environmental conditions, particularly temperature. Consequently, if a body is found outside, knowledge of the climatic conditions (both before and after the approximate time of death) is necessary when estimating the time required for the species in question to reach the development stage(s) observed.

Other factors can influence the rate of development of individual insect species. For example, the larvae usually form a 'maggot-mass' and move around the body in this collective fashion to feed. This behaviour raises the temperature of their microenvironment, particularly in the late second and third instar stages, and needs to be considered when estimating development rate.

After the flies leave, the succession patterns of species arriving to colonise the body, each associated with a particular stage of its decomposition, can be used to estimate the post-mortem interval.

Circumstances surrounding the death

The concentration of insects on particular parts of a body in the early stages of decomposition may indicate the location of injuries. Insects are particularly attracted to wounds that have been inflicted prior to death (i.e. ante-mortem) because these bleed more profusely than those made after death. This may therefore provide information relevant to the circumstances of death. In certain situations, eggs may be laid in wound sites before the death of the individual concerned. The consumption of living tissues by the emergent insect larvae is known as myiasis and has important implications for calculating the post-mortem interval. (Myiasis is also associated with cases of abuse and neglect, particularly of vulnerable individuals, such as the elderly and the very young.)

In certain situations, the insects themselves may be used to provide relevant information about the individual whose body they have been using as a food source. For example, maggots have been used as specimens for toxicological analysis where no suitable human body tissues were available. Drugs such as phenobarbital and cocaine have been successfully detected in insect tissues, thus demonstrating the exposure to these substances by the persons concerned. It is also worth mentioning the recent research interest in the analysis of parasitic insect taxa for human DNA. If successful, this type of analysis could be of great potential importance in linking a suspect with a scene and/or a victim, especially in cases of violent crime.

Movement of the body after death

Entomological evidence may provide information about a change in the location of a body after death. For example, insect species present on a body discovered in a rural area may include those usually associated with an urban location. This indicates that the person was initially killed in a town or city and his or her body subsequently dumped in the countryside. Knowledge of the geographical distribution of insect species, as well as their life cycles, is of particular use in this respect.

influence of gravity. In cases of hanging, for example, this occurs in the lower legs and forearms. Hypostasis is normally apparent as a dark pink or dark purple-blue discoloration, similar in appearance to bruising. However, it does not occur in those areas of the body where pressure is exerted, either through contact with a firm surface or by clothing. The flow of blood into the capillaries is prevented and the areas thus affected are characteristically pale in appearance.

The degree of post-mortem lividity present in a body can give some indication of the time of death, if observed shortly after death has occurred. However, this phenomenon is now considered a less reliable indicator of time of death than rigor mortis (Section 12.1.3). The main use of hypostasis is in demonstrating that the position or location of a body has been changed since death. If a body is moved within a few hours of death, the original areas of lividity tend to disappear and re-form in new areas, consistent with the new position of the body. However, if the post-mortem interval is several hours, the original areas of lividity tend to persist. If these are inconsistent with the position of the body when discovered, this strongly indicates that the body has been moved from its original position several hours after death.

It should be noted that injuries caused by strangulation or crushing may give the appearance of hypostasis. However, these can be distinguished from hypostasis by the presence of tiny haemorrhages under the surface of the skin (known as petechiae), especially on the eyelids. One final point worth making is that in certain types of poisoning, the colouring of post-mortem lividity is markedly different from the dark pink or dark purple-blue colour normally observed. For example, a cherry-pink coloration is indicative of carbon monoxide poisoning (Chapter 7, Section 7.1.3).

12.1.3 Rigor mortis

Rigor mortis is the characteristic stiffening of the body that occurs in the early stages after death. It is caused by temporary rigidity within both the voluntary and involuntary muscle systems brought about by complex post-mortem biochemical changes in the body. Immediately after death, the body is flaccid. However, within about 4–6 hours, the process of rigor mortis begins. This invariably starts in the face, jaw and neck muscles and extends downwards to affect the arms, trunk and then legs. Within between 12 and 18 hours, the entire body is rigid. Rigor mortis usually disappears between 24 and 36 hours after death (in the same order as it appeared), leaving the body flaccid again. Like hypostasis, rigor mortis can provide information suggestive of a change in location of the body after death. This will be apparent if the attitude of the rigid body is inconsistent with its surroundings, e.g. where a body dumped in a ditch exhibits a position that is consistent with the individual having died sitting in a chair.

The use of rigor mortis in estimating the time since death is highly unreliable as this process is so variable. The times given above for the onset and disappearance of rigor mortis should be viewed, therefore, as rough guidelines only. The process of rigor mortis is highly influenced by temperature. For example, in hot climates, rigor mortis commences early, progresses quickly and disappears rapidly compared with cooler climes. In addition, the intensity of rigidity found is affected by the level of muscular development of the individual concerned. Elderly people and the very young may exhibit little or no rigor mortis owing to their lack of muscular development.

Rigor mortis
The stiffening of the body after death, a temporary condition that begins a few hours after death and wears off approximately two or three days later.

It should be noted that, in rare instances, a condition known as cadaveric spasm, or cadaveric rigidity, occurs immediately after death, which may be mistaken for the very early onset of rigor mortis. The underlying mechanism for this is unknown, but it is apparently associated with extreme fear or tension experienced by the individual just before death. For example, it may be observed in some suicide cases, where the gun or knife used for self-destruction is found locked in the hand of the deceased immediately after death.

12.1.4 Changes in the eyes

Early post-mortem changes that occur in the eyes of the deceased can also be used to estimate the time since death. The most important of these is the level of potassium present in the vitreous humour of the eye (i.e. the clear gelatinous material that occupies the bulk of the eyeball and is located behind the lens). Potassium is slowly released into the vitreous humour from the blood cells of the retina, which break down after death. Knowledge of the rate of potassium release can be used to calculate the post-mortem interval.

Another change that may occur in the eyes in the early stages after death is the development of cloudiness. During life, the crystalline structure of the cornea, and, to some extent, the lens, is dependent on hydration (i.e. the level of water present). After death, the water of crystallisation is lost and, as a result, the eye desiccates and becomes opaque in appearance. However, the time taken for these changes to appear is affected by environmental conditions, e.g. of air temperature and humidity, and whether the eyes are closed or open. Consequently, this is not regarded as a reliable means of estimating the time since death.

12.2 Post-mortem decomposition and related phenomena

12.2.1 The process of post-mortem decomposition

In general terms, the process of decomposition may be defined as the gradual breakdown of dead organic matter (both animal and vegetable) and the resultant release of elements and compounds to the environment. In humans, post-mortem decomposition (also known as **putrefaction**) usually begins directly after death, although indicative signs may not appear for a few hours, or even two or three days, depending on circumstances. Post-mortem decomposition is brought about by a combination of factors, namely the action of bacteria and fungi and the chemical breakdown of the body tissues through autolysis (i.e. the enzymatic self-destruction of the body cells). Scavenging animals may also attack the corpse, thus contributing to the decomposition process. Among these are certain insect species whose presence may provide some indication of the conditions under which decomposition has occurred, and of the time since death (Box 12.2).

In humans, the process of post-mortem decomposition is generally characterised by a number of identifiable changes in the appearance of the body, which arise in roughly chronological order. In the case of bodies not immersed in water, the first

Putrefaction
Another term used for the natural process of post-mortem decomposition.

sign to appear, usually within two or three days of death, is a greenish staining of the skin. This begins on the right flank of the abdomen and spreads to cover the entire abdominal region. This change in colour is due to the breakdown of haemoglobin in the red blood cells by the action of intestinal bacteria. After about three days, visible swelling of the body begins to occur. This distension is due to the gases produced by decomposition and is particularly noticeable in areas such as the face, genitals and abdomen. The next noticeable change is the greenish or reddish delineation of the veins near the surface of the skin, producing the characteristic effect of 'marbling'. Blisters, filled with gas or fluid, then start to form on the skin. When these burst, significant areas of the epidermis become detached from the body and are lost. The tongue swells, the eyeballs liquefy and decomposition fluids escape from the mouth and nose. Within approximately a month of death, the thoracic and abdominal cavities burst while the body tissues start to soften, liquefy and gradually dissolve.

The succession of post-mortem changes, described above, is of limited value in estimating the length of time that has elapsed since death occurred. This is due to the high variability of the decomposition rate, which is influenced by a number of different factors. These are associated with environmental conditions and with certain attributes of the deceased. Lower temperatures, restricted air access and the absence of scavenging animals are among the environmental factors that will tend to retard decomposition. Thus, a body buried in the ground where all three of these conditions exist will decompose more slowly than one exposed to the air. The medium in which decomposition takes place therefore has a significant effect on the rate of decomposition. As a rough guide only, the decomposition rate of a body in air is approximately twice as quick as one immersed in water and between four and eight times as rapid as one buried in earth. Characteristics of the individual that may influence decomposition rate include the level of fluids and fat present in the body and the health of the individual concerned. Thus, people who are overweight and/or who are suffering from an infectious disease tend to decompose more rapidly.

12.2.2 Skeletalisation

The normal process of post-mortem decomposition eventually leads to the complete dissolution of the soft tissues of the body and the revelation of its bony framework. This transformation from dead body to skeleton is known as **skeletalisation**. As outlined in Section 12.2.1, the rate of decomposition is affected by a variety of different factors. Climate has a major influence on decomposition rate and, therefore, the process of skeletalisation. Consequently, in temperate climates, in the majority of cases, skeletalisation will take place within about two years, while in tropical zones, the process may be concluded within a matter of weeks.

From a medico-legal perspective, forensic interest in skeletal remains is restricted to those that are less than about one hundred years old. This is because, after this length of time, the perpetrator of any suspected crime is unlikely to be still alive. Unfortunately, the technique of radio-carbon dating, which is used to date artefacts of archaeological interest, cannot be effectively applied to bones that are less than about one hundred years old. However, it may be helpful in demonstrating that the origin of a particular skeleton is not sufficiently recent to warrant further forensic investigation. One indicator that may be useful in dating a more recent skeleton involves the presence, or absence, of strontium-90 in the bones. This radionuclide (half-life 28 years) is present in the fall-out from nuclear explosions and, as it is

Skeletalisation
The post-mortem process whereby a fleshy corpse is gradually reduced to skeletal form through the natural process of decomposition.

chemically similar to calcium, becomes incorporated into the bones of living persons. Its presence in a skeleton, therefore, demonstrates that the individual concerned was alive post-1945, when the first atomic bomb tests were carried out.

12.2.3 Mummification and the formation of adipocere

Under certain conditions, the normal process of decomposition, outlined in Section 12.2.1, does not occur. This may happen either because of mummification or because of the formation of adipocere (a greyish, waxy substance formed by the hydrolysis of body fat). Both of these processes result in bodies that are relatively well preserved.

Mummification | **Mummification** is the desiccation of the body under warm, dry conditions. This
The preservation of | process results in a shrivelled, brownish corpse whose shrunken, leathery skin is
a corpse through | pulled tightly over the framework of the body. The process of mummification occurs
desiccation – a | naturally in hot, dry climates and is seen, for example, in bodies buried in the sand.

Mummification

The preservation of a corpse through desiccation – a process that may occur naturally in warm, dry conditions.

Mummification is the desiccation of the body under warm, dry conditions. This process results in a shrivelled, brownish corpse whose shrunken, leathery skin is pulled tightly over the framework of the body. The process of mummification occurs naturally in hot, dry climates and is seen, for example, in bodies buried in the sand. It may also occasionally happen in temperate regions, if conditions conducive to mummification are met locally. For example, new-born babies concealed after death may become mummified, mainly because of the very low levels of bacteria their bodies contain. Mummification of adults in temperate climates is rare but may be found in bodies that have lain concealed for long periods in places, such as cupboards or under floorboards, where there is circulation of dry air.

Adipocere formation

The hydrolysis of body fats into a waxy, grey substance (adipocere); a post-mortem process that may occur in corpses found in damp locations.

In contrast to mummification, **adipocere formation** is generally favoured by damp conditions. It may occur, for example, in bodies buried in wet soil or submerged in water. The formation of adipocere generally begins within a few weeks or months of death and may take a couple of years to complete. The presence of adipocere helps to maintain the integrity of the contours of the body, possibly for many decades, although it becomes progressively more brittle over time.

It should be noted that mummification or adipocere formation may affect the entire body of an individual. However, it is not uncommon for a particular body to show evidence of more than one post-mortem process. This occurs when the environmental conditions surrounding a body are not uniform. For example, a body half-buried face down in damp woodland may show adipocere formation on its front but evidence of normal decomposition elsewhere. Importantly, if there is a mismatch between the type of post-mortem process (or processes) observed and the conditions immediately surrounding the body, this may indicate that death did not take place *in situ* but that the body was dumped after death.

12.3 The establishment of cause of death

When an individual dies, it is essential that the medical 'cause of death' be established by a qualified medical practitioner. As circumstances dictate, this may occur either at the scene of death or, in the case of deaths reported to the coroner (Section 12.3.2), at a later stage, usually after the performance of a post-mortem examination (Section 12.3.3). The information concerning the medical cause of death is then entered on the death certificate in accordance with international standards recommended by the World Health Organization.

As well as the medical cause of death, the 'manner of death' – i.e. accident, homicide, natural causes or suicide – is also required (both legally and statistically). In some countries, this may be entered on the death certificate by the doctor. In others, including England and Wales, the manner of death is a matter for the coroner (Section 12.3.2). It should be noted that in England and Wales, the doctor is required to enter on the death certificate whether he or she is of the opinion that a death, although due to natural causes, resulted from an industrial disease process. Thus, for example, exposure to asbestos during employment may have contributed to a death whose natural cause is mesothelioma.

12.3.1 The circumstances under which deaths are reported by medical practitioners to the coroner

When the death of an individual is judged by the medical doctor attending the body to be due to natural causes, he or she can issue a death certificate (i.e. a certificate of the medical cause of death). Whether or not the doctor can then proceed to release the body to the next-of-kin for burial, or cremation, will depend on the exact circumstances of each case. If the medical practitioner requires guidance of how best to proceed in a particular case, he or she may consult informally with a coroner's officer (who is usually a police officer). This type of informal consultation does not constitute an official 'death reported to the coroner'.

There are a number of specific situations where the doctor must report the death of an individual to the coroner even though that death is due to natural causes and has, therefore, been certified. Examples include:

- deaths due to food poisoning;
- deaths where the individual has undergone an operation in the last three months of life;
- deaths where the doctor has not seen the deceased in the two weeks prior to his or her death;
- deaths due to industrial disease or toxicity;
- deaths where the individual was an alcoholic;
- deaths of persons in legal custody, even if he or she died in hospital during the serving of a sentence.

However, if the death of an individual is due to natural causes *and no referral to the coroner is necessary*, the body can be released to the family for burial or cremation. In cases where the body is destined for cremation, a second medical examination is required before a death certificate can be issued. This must be carried out by an independent, medically qualified doctor who has been fully registered for over five years. This procedure is extremely important as it provides a last protection for the deceased individual. It was through its implementation that the criminal activities of Dr Harold Shipman were eventually discovered (Chapter 7, Box 7.2).

In all cases where the death of an individual is unnatural, sudden, unexpected or suspicious in any way, the medical practitioner will not issue a death certificate but will report the uncertified death to the coroner as soon as possible. The role of the coroner in the investigation of reported deaths is examined in the next section.

12.3.2 The role of the coroner in the investigation of reported deaths

In England and Wales (and in many Commonwealth countries), the coroner's system represents the authority responsible for the medico-legal investigation of reported deaths (in Scotland, this role is fulfilled by the Procurators Fiscal). Coroners are independent judicial officers. They may be either lawyers or doctors by training, but are often both. Each coroner has his or her own geographical area of jurisdiction and is required to hold investigations into the reported deaths of any individuals whose bodies lie within their district (even if the actual death took place outside their area of jurisdiction). As well as receiving reports from medical practitioners (Section 12.3.1), coroners are also notified of certain types of death (i.e. deaths whose cause is unnatural, violent or unknown) by hospital authorities, Registrars of Births and Deaths, and the police.

Once a death has been reported to the coroner, he or she must decide whether further investigation is required. If the coroner decides that the death was due to natural causes, no further enquiry is necessary. In such circumstances, a death certificate is issued by a doctor at the coroner's behest and the Registrar of Births and Deaths notified accordingly. However, if the coroner deems that further investigation is necessary, he or she can request a pathologist to perform a post-mortem examination (Section 12.3.3). If the findings of this examination demonstrate that death was due to natural causes, and the case is not one in which the coroner is legally required to hold an inquest, the coroner's investigation is concluded and appropriate steps taken to release the body for burial or cremation.

If the pathologist's examination shows that the death of a particular individual was not due to natural causes, the coroner will hold an inquest. The purpose of this public inquiry is not to apportion blame but to establish the facts that surround the death. These include the identification of the deceased, the medical cause of death and where, when and how the deceased met his or her death. In addition, those particulars needed to register the death are also obtained. (It should be noted that if, during the course of an inquest, an individual is charged with causing the death of the subject of the inquiry, the inquest will be adjourned. Once the trial is completed, the inquest is not usually resumed.) The majority of inquests are conducted without the presence of a jury and the verdict returned by the coroner. However, in certain circumstances, e.g. where a death has happened in prison, the inquest is held with a jury. In such cases, the jurors are responsible for returning the verdict of the inquest.

The main categories of verdicts returned at inquests are:

■ death by accident or misadventure;

■ suicide;

■ death from natural causes;

■ death from industrial diseases;

■ open verdict (where not enough evidence is available to categorise it otherwise);

■ drug-related;

■ homicide (either lawful killing, or unlawful killing).

Further information

Box 12.3

Facts and figures concerning deaths reported to coroners in England and Wales (2005)

The number of registered deaths in England and Wales for the year 2005 stands at 513 000 (provisional figure). Of these registered deaths, 232 400 (i.e. 45.3 per cent) were reported to the coroner, the higher number to date. This represents a rise of 6900 (i.e. 3.1 per cent) on the previ-ous year's figures, where 225 500 (i.e. 43.9 per cent) of the 514 300 registered deaths were reported. Statistics show that deaths reported to coroners as a percentage of registered deaths have risen steadily since 1920. Figure (a) illustrates this trend for the period 1995–2005.

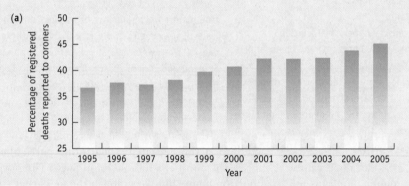

(a)

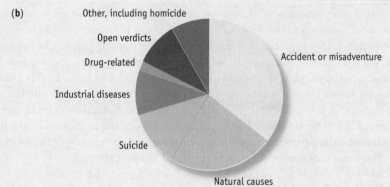

(b)

(a) Percentage of registered deaths reported to coroners for the period 1995–2005. (Note that these figures include NFA (No Further Action) cases, which are deaths notified to coroners that required neither an inquest nor a post-mortem, and where no certificate of any kind was issued. From 2005, they comprise only those cases where the sex of the deceased was not known.) (b) Verdicts returned at inquests in England and Wales in 2005

Source of data: Allen, R. (2006) *Statistics on deaths reported to coroners, England and Wales, 2005*. London: Department for Constitutional Affairs.

Box 12.3 continued

Of the 232 400 deaths reported to coroners in 2005, post-mortem examinations were held in 114 620 (i.e. less than half (49.3 per cent) of cases). This represents the lowest point yet in a continuing downward trend over the past 25 years in which the proportion of cases necessitating a post-mortem examination has decreased. Inquests were held in 29 300 cases of reported deaths (i.e. 12.6 per cent), a rise of about 1000 compared with 2004. In the vast majority of cases where inquests were held (i.e. 94 per cent), post-mortem examinations were carried out.

Of the verdicts returned at inquests in England and Wales in 2005, the commonest category was death by accident or misadventure (35.4 per cent), followed by death from natural causes (23 per cent), suicide (12.1 per cent), industrial diseases (9.6 per cent) and open verdicts (9.4 per cent) (figure (b)). Annual statistics dating back to 1988 show that death by accident or misadventure consistently formed the largest category of verdicts returned at inquests. However, the overall trend since 1988 shows a decrease in the size of this category, with the lowest percentage yet (35.4 per cent) recorded in 2005. For the years 1988 to 1999, annual statistics show that suicide formed the next largest category, ranging from 16.2 to 20.1 per cent. However, in the year 2000, suicide accounted for 15.7 per cent of the verdicts returned at inquests, which was 0.1 per cent *less* than the category 'death from natural causes'. In each of the five subsequent years (2001–05 inclusive), 'death from natural causes' has remained the second-largest category, with suicide in third position. For the year 2005, a verdict of homicide was returned in 252 cases, i.e. 0.94 per cent of the verdicts returned (figure (b)). This accounts only for those cases that have gone to inquest and for which nobody has yet been prosecuted. Therefore, it is not a true picture of the number of homicides in England and Wales. For example, in the year 2004–05, there were 839 deaths that were initially recorded as homicides in England and Wales (source of information: Coleman, K., Hird, C. and Povey, D. (2006) *Violent crime overview: homicide and gun crime 2004/2005* (2nd edn). Supplementary volume to *Crime in England and Wales 2004/2005*. London: Home Office Research, Development and Statistics Directorate.

(Please note that the figures given are quoted to the nearest hundred.)

Other categories of verdict that may be returned at inquest include:

- attempted or self-induced abortion;
- cause of death aggravated by lack of care or self-neglect;
- want of attention at birth;
- stillborn.

Factual information concerning the deaths reported to coroners in England and Wales in 2005, including verdicts returned at inquests, is presented in Box 12.3.

12.3.3 Post-mortem examination

Post-mortem examination means examination of a body after death. In Britain, this term is usually taken to be synonymous with the word 'autopsy'. Autopsy is the dissection of a corpse for investigative purposes and the procedure involves both external and internal examination of the deceased. It should be noted, however, that in some countries, examinations that are restricted to the exterior of the body are also referred to as post-mortem examinations.

There are two types of autopsy: clinical and medico-legal. Clinical autopsies may be performed in cases where an individual has received treatment for a particular disease before his or her death and, consequently, the cause of death is believed to be known. The purpose of this type of autopsy is to verify the diagnosis and, by doing so, give reassurance to the relatives of the deceased. However, very strict rules are now in force and a clinical autopsy cannot be performed without the consent of the next-of-kin. Any information gained through clinical autopsies may be used for research and educational purposes.

Medico-legal autopsies (sometimes referred to as forensic autopsies) are carried out when the cause of death is unknown or suspicious, at the request of the appropriate legal authority. In England and Wales, this is represented by the coroners' system (Section 12.3.2). Medico-legal autopsies are only performed by pathologists who appear on the Home Office list. In order to be included on this approved list, individuals must undergo extensive forensic training (including considerable on-the-job training) and gain the necessary qualifications.

The procedure used for medico-legal autopsy tends to follow a general pattern, although it necessarily differs in detail according to the particular circumstances of death. Naturally, the condition of the corpse will influence the effectiveness of the autopsy. Since decomposition of the body begins immediately after death (Section 12.2), the shorter the time interval between death and autopsy, the better from the pathologist's point of view. However, useful information has been obtained from the autopsy of bodies exhumed from graveyards several months after burial.

In certain cases, such as suspected murder, the pathologist usually attends the suspected crime scene to view the body *in situ*, prior to its removal to a mortuary for autopsy. He or she may take photographs of the deceased at the scene to include in the autopsy report. In some instances, the pathologist may be able to give an opinion as to the apparent manner of death (i.e. natural, accident, suicide or homicide) based on his or her observations at the scene. (In suspicious cases, the body is treated as a crime scene in its own right and details concerning its preparation for removal to the mortuary, and the recovery of physical evidence associated with it, are given in Chapter 2, Section 2.4).

Ideally, the body of an individual should be identified before autopsy takes place; a task usually performed by a relative or a close friend of the deceased. However, identification is not possible in every case. For example, the body may be unrecognisable, perhaps as a result of decomposition or mutilation. In such cases, autopsy will proceed in the absence of identification, which must be established by other means (Section 12.4).

If the body is clothed, the pathologist will make a preliminary examination of the clothing, especially for any damage marks present (such as knife cuts or bulletholes) and bloodstains, and note how these are related to any injuries present on the body. After examining the clothed body, the clothing is removed and each item stored separately. It should be noted that traces of physical evidence, e.g. scrapings from underneath the fingernails, are routinely recovered from the body in the mortuary, both before and after the clothing is removed, for subsequent forensic analysis. This task is performed by appropriate personnel, such as SOCOs or forensic scientists. The various stages of the autopsy procedure are recorded using both photographs (including close-ups, e.g. of injuries) and observational notes.

Medico-legal autopsy
A post-mortem examination performed as part of the investigative procedure into the death of an individual whose demise cannot be attributed to natural causes.

External examination

In medico-legal autopsies, especially where death has been traumatic, the external examination of the body usually yields more evidence than the internal dissection that follows it. External examination should therefore be most thorough and all relevant features noted. These typically include:

- characteristics of race, sex and age;
- body length;
- body weight (including state of nutrition);
- any abnormal skin coloration (including presence of hypostasis – Section 12.1.2);
- the presence of any marks, e.g. tattoos, old burns, injury scars (these may be important for identification purposes – Section 12.4);
- the degree of rigor mortis;
- the presence of any discharged body fluids, e.g. blood and urine;
- the condition of the anus and external genitals;
- the presence of any injuries of recent origin, e.g. incised wounds, burns, bruises or gunshot wounds (recorded by marking on pre-printed body diagrams (Figure 12.1), detailed description and photographs).

(From Knight, 1997)

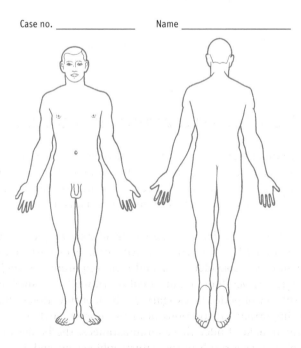

Case no. _____   Name _____

Figure 12.1 Pre-printed body diagram
A typical body chart for marking injuries, in living or dead. More detailed and different aspects of the body surface can be depicted in a range of such charts

In some cases, for example, where explosives or gunshots have been involved, the body may be examined using radiological techniques before proceeding to the next stage – the internal examination.

Internal examination

After a thorough evaluation has been made of all relevant external features, the body is opened up for internal examination. This is usually performed by making an incision down the front of the body from just below the larynx to the pubic region, avoiding the navel. In cases of hanging or strangulation, a Y-shaped incision is favoured. This extends from behind each ear, converges above the breastbone and proceeds in a downward direction.

The internal examination of a body should include all major body organs. Samples of body fluids (e.g. urine, blood and cerebrospinal fluid), stomach and intestinal contents, and organs (particularly the liver) are collected for analysis, mainly of a toxicological nature (Chapter 7, Section 7.5). In addition, tissue samples, e.g. brain, lung and heart, should also be taken, wherever possible, in order to study their structure in detail, especially with reference to signs of natural disease. After the internal examination is concluded, the cadaver is sewn up. For a detailed description of the internal examination of the body during autopsy (a task far beyond the remit of this book), the interested reader is referred to Bernard Knight's excellent text on forensic pathology (see Further reading).

The findings of the autopsy, including (where possible) their relationship to the cause of death, should be written up in the form of a comprehensive and detailed report as soon as possible after completion of the examination. This final report, accompanied by relevant photographs and documents, is then submitted to the coroner (Section 12.3.2).

12.4 The identification of human remains

In most cases, human remains are identified by a close relative or friend who is asked to view the body for this purpose. Where identity cannot be established by these means, at least in the first instance, other methods must be employed. This section outlines those characteristics of human remains upon which these methods are based.

The identification of the deceased person is an integral part of the post-mortem examination (Section 12.3.3). Correct identification is essential for several reasons, including humanitarian considerations and legal requirements, and is of particular importance where the death of an individual is criminal or suspicious in nature and therefore the subject of police investigation. The identification of human remains is also especially important in situations of mass disaster, such as caused by a severe explosion or earthquake. Under these circumstances, the bodies of the victims are often unrecognisable as a result of the catastrophic event and, in many cases, badly fragmented. It is therefore necessary to both assign the separate body parts to specific individuals and to identify the people concerned; this may be achieved through DNA profiling (Chapter 6).

The characteristics that are used to establish the identity of a dead person depend on the physical state of the body. In the absence of severe disfigurement, through, for example, exposure to intense heat, the state of the body will depend mainly on the degree to which it has decomposed. Post-mortem decomposition is a natural process whereby the dead body gradually disintegrates over time until only the skeletal components remain (Section 12.2). Identification of the individual by visual cues becomes progressively more difficult as the decomposition process advances. Furthermore, identification may be hindered if the corpse has been subjected to dismemberment or mutilation.

It should be noted that, on occasion, it may be necessary to identify *living* persons who are not able to provide their own personal details. This may occur if, for example, they are suffering from memory loss or are too young to articulate the information. Although this aspect is not dealt with specifically in this chapter, much of the information gathered from fresh corpses is equally applicable to the identification of living individuals.

12.4.1 The identification of non-skeletalised bodies

A number of characteristics may be used, in combination, to identify the body of an individual before it becomes skeletalised (i.e. reduced to a skeleton). Usually, as the body decomposes, the availability and clarity of these features become progressively less. Therefore, the fresher the corpse, the greater the chance of obtaining accurate information that will lead, potentially, to the identification of the deceased. As well as advanced putrefaction, extensive mutilation of the body also increases the difficulty of making a positive identification. This is illustrated by the case of Dr Buck Ruxton who murdered his wife and maid in 1935 and sought to prevent their identification by dismemberment and extensive mutilation of their bodies (Box 12.4).

Many of the features used in the identification of non-skeletalised bodies are morphological. They include the following:

■ *Height* (*stature*). This is recorded by measuring the length of the body from the heel to the crown of the head. It should be noted that this may differ slightly from the height of the live individual because of post-mortem changes.

■ *Weight*. Care should be taken in using the weight of the corpse to estimate that of the live individual. For example, bloating associated with decomposition may lead to an overestimation of the weight of the individual before death.

■ *Eye colour*. This may be a useful morphological feature in the identification of Caucasians (where the colour of the iris varies) but only in the first day or two after death. After this time, all irises appear brownish as a result of decomposition.

■ *Hair colour, structure and distribution*. Hair has the advantage that it is practically indestructible and will usually persist long after the soft tissues of the body have dissolved. The colour of hair may be useful in identification, although it can be affected by decomposition, e.g. fair hair tends to become darker. The natural colour of head hair may have been altered during life by dyeing or bleaching and this should be taken into account when making a possible identification. In addition, the structure of head hair may indicate racial origin of the decedent while the distribution of facial hair, for example the presence of a beard, may assist in personal identification.

Case study

Box 12.4

The Ruxton case

On the morning of 29 September 1935, several bundles, including one from which a human arm protruded, were sighted by a young woman on holiday. These were scattered along the banks of the Gardenholme Linn, a tributary of the River Annan, near Moffat in Scotland. Subsequent police investigations led to the eventual recovery of 70 body fragments, including some recovered downstream and others found in different localities. These fragments were sent to the Anatomy Department of Edinburgh University for examination. It was obvious to the pathologists involved, Professor John Glaister and Professor James Couper Brash, that the person responsible for the dismemberment, of what they believed to be two bodies, had considerable medical and anatomical knowledge. Moreover, the perpetrator had deliberately sought to prevent identification of the two victims by extensive mutilation, including, in each case, the removal of their eyes, nose, ears, lips and facial skin and, in one case, the removal of the fingertips.

Through painstaking reconstruction of the body pieces, the pathologists concluded that one of the corpses belonged to a female, probably between 20 and 21 years of age, and between 4 feet 10 inches and 4 feet 11$^1/_2$ inches (1.47–1.51 m) in height. The other body proved more problematic because of the more extensive mutilation of the face. Initially, it was identified as a man of about 60 years of age and around 5 feet 6 inches (1.68 m) in height but was later revised to that of a strongly built woman, probably between 35 and 45 years of age and about 5 feet 3$^1/_2$ inches (1.61 m) tall.

Meanwhile, insect larvae (maggots) infesting the decomposing remains were identified, by Dr Alexander Mearns, as those of the bluebottle *Calliphora vicina*. From the developmental stage of the maggots present, he estimated that the minimum time between death and the discovery of the remains was 12–14 days. Further information relevant to estimating the time of death was provided by one of the newspapers used to wrap some of the body fragments. This was dated 15 September 1935, thus corroborating the entomological evidence. The newspaper in question, the *Sunday Graphic*, also played a key role in establishing a connection between the parcelled human remains found in Scotland and the Morecambe/Lancaster area in England. Examination of its printed contents revealed that it was a local edition distributed only in Morecambe, Lancaster and the surrounding area.

The disappearance of Mrs Isabella Ruxton (aged 34 years and 7 months) and of her children's nursemaid Mary Jane Rogerson (aged 20 years) from the family home in Lancaster was linked with the discovery of the human remains in Scotland. Both were last seen on 14 September 1935. The physical characteristics of the two missing individuals were found to be similar to those attributed to the corpses reassembled, as far as possible, from the parcels of human remains. In Mrs Ruxton's case, the use of photo-superimposition (Box 12.6) demonstrated a close match between her bare skull and a photographic portrait taken when she was alive. In each case, mutilation of specific parts of the corpses coincided with those parts of the missing individuals that were either known to bear identifying features (such as operation scars or birthmarks) or were particularly characteristic of that individual. However, the fingertips had not been removed from the younger woman and fingerprints taken from her corpse were found to match those present on objects in the Ruxton's Lancaster home.

As a consequence of mounting evidence against him, Dr Buck Ruxton was arrested and tried for the murder of his common-law wife, Isabella, and that of Mary Jane Rogerson, the nursemaid. He was found guilty and hanged on 12 May 1936.

Readers interested in reading an account of the case by the pathologists involved are referred to Glaister, J. and Brash, J. C. (1937) *Medico-legal aspects of the Ruxton case*. Churchill Livingstone.

■ *Skin pigmentation*. Pigmentation of the skin may be of some use in ascribing racial origin. However, caution should be exercised as the process of decomposition can significantly alter skin colour.

■ *Facial appearance*. The possession of certain characteristic facial features may be useful in determining racial origin. If the body is not noticeably decomposed, photographs of the face – both full face and profile – may be circulated to obtain a possible identification of the deceased.

■ *Fingerprints*. The use of fingerprints in the identification of individuals is discussed in detail in Chapter 4, Section 4.1. In the early post-mortem stages, fingerprints may be obtained from a corpse in much the same manner as from a live individual, i.e. by inking or powdering them. However, they may also be successfully taken where the body has deteriorated through, for example, decomposition or prolonged immersion in water, provided that appropriate preparatory steps are taken. The fingerprinting of deceased individuals is usually performed at the end of the post-mortem examination, in order to avoid contamination of any other evidence present on the body. This process usually involves inking or powdering the fingers directly but, in some cases, may require the removal of the skin.

As described above, some morphological features, such as skin pigmentation and hair characteristics, may help to identify the racial origin of the deceased. Establishing the sex of the individual (an essential factor in personal identification) is straightforward in the early stages of decomposition. Indeed, the persistence of the uterus in females, and, to a lesser extent, the prostate gland in males, means that this is still feasible even when decomposition has reached an advanced state. However, if it is not possible to determine the sex of the deceased through direct observation, DNA profiling can normally be used (Chapter 6, Section 6.3). Much harder to establish is the age of the deceased, although the presence of certain features is indicative of advancing years. These include the red Campbell de Morgan spots found on the skin and a white or grey ring surrounding the iris of the eye, known as the arcus senilis. However, the arcus senilis is also an indicator of raised cholesterol in the bloodstream and care should therefore be taken in interpreting its presence as a sign of old age. Below the age of about 25, the pattern of eruption of the teeth (both 'milk' and permanent sets) can be used to estimate the age of the decedent.

External examination of the corpse may reveal the presence of certain features specific to that individual that are potentially useful in establishing a positive identification. These include the following:

■ *Tattoos*. Tattoos are essentially permanent marks on the skin. They are made by pricking the skin and inserting one or more pigments to form the desired design. The nature and location of the tattoo and, in particular, the inclusion of specific names (often the first name of a boy- or girlfriend) may be useful to the police in identifying the decedent. In some cases, the actual design of the tattoo itself may convey useful information about the activities of the deceased during life. Tattoos are especially useful as identifying features as they are relatively persistent and may be clearly seen, even after the outer layer of the epidermis (the stratum corneum) has been lost during the decomposition process.

- *Scars.* Scars are healed wounds and, as such, represent sites of *past* injury. They are commonly caused by surgery or by accident, or, less frequently, by deliberate assault. The presence of a scar, or scars, on the skin may be useful in identifying an individual, provided that they can be verified by relatives or friends, or checked against relevant medical records.
- *Skin blemishes*, e.g. moles and birthmarks.
- *Pierced body parts*, e.g. nose, ear lobes and eyebrows.
- *Circumcision.*
- *Amputated limbs* or *digits*.

In addition to the external features outlined above, the dissection of the body during post-mortem examination may reveal the presence of certain medical conditions, such as stomach ulcers or gallstones, or evidence of previous surgery or injury. Damage to bony structures may also be revealed prior to dissection through the use of radiography. Such internal findings may be useful in assisting identification, through comparison with ante-mortem records of possible matches.

Importantly, the techniques of DNA profiling (Chapter 6), which are used to identify living individuals, may also be successfully applied to post-mortem tissues.

12.4.2 The identification of skeletalised remains

Through the natural process of decomposition, the soft tissues and organs of the body gradually disappear to reveal the bony skeleton underneath (Section 12.2). Identification of the individual when only the skeletal components remain is more difficult than when a fresh (or even decomposing) body is available, and even more so if the skeleton is incomplete or fragmented.

In cases where the skeletal remains consist of a collection of bones and/or bone fragments, it is necessary to establish whether they are human in origin before investigating further. If the bones are wholly, or largely, intact, a working knowledge of anatomy is usually sufficient to distinguish human bones from those of other animals, although some of the smaller bones may be more difficult to assign. (Anatomical knowledge is also useful when other materials, such as plastic, stone or wood, are (mistakenly) thought to be bones.) However, if only fragments of bone are available, other techniques are required to identify their origin. Species-specific serological tests (Chapter 5, Section 5.1.3) may be applied if the bones in question are recent enough to still contain the protein necessary for the tests (i.e. less than a decade old) and provided that they have not been severely burnt. Although these tests are usually the preferred option for identifying species of origin, DNA techniques based on mitochondrial DNA can also be used for this purpose (Chapter 6, Section 6.5).

Once it has been verified that the bones in question are human, the difficult task of identifying the individual can begin. As is the case with non-skeletalised bodies, general characteristics are usually established first, followed by those individualising features that may lead to personal identification through comparison with ante-mortem information (if available).

Class characteristics

The degree to which it is possible to establish class characteristics – of height, sex, age and race – is dependent on a number of factors, including the types of bones available (if the skeleton is incomplete) and their condition. Each of these class characteristics is now briefly examined in turn:

■ *Height* (*stature*). In cases where the skeleton is complete, the height of the live individual may be estimated by direct measurement. However, when taking this measurement, the lack of tissue, for example between the vertebrae of the backbone, must be taken into account. In the absence of a whole skeleton, measurement of the length of the **long bones** (also referred to colloquially as the major limb bones) may be used to calculate the stature of the individual, by reference to appropriate stature tables. The long bones of the leg, i.e. the femur (thighbone), fibula and tibia (shinbones), are usually preferred for this purpose over the long bones of the arm (i.e. the humerus, radius and ulna).

■ *Sex*. The sex of a skeleton can be determined, with a high degree of accuracy, by an individual who is suitably experienced in anatomy. Morphological differences between the sexes are particularly noticeable in the pelvis, skull and, to a lesser extent, the long bones (and, of these, the femur in particular). However, it should be noted that both race and age may have an effect on the appearance, including size, of these features.

■ *Age*. Estimating the age of an individual at the time of death, through an examination of his or her skeletal remains, generally becomes more difficult the greater the age of the person concerned (especially after the middle of the third decade). Up to the age of about 5 years, the appearance of the major ossification centres (where bone is formed to replace cartilage) can be used to estimate age, since each of these appear at a particular time during the early years of life. Between the ages of 5 and 25 years, another process of bone growth, the fusion of the epiphyses (singular: epiphysis), can similarly be used to estimate the age of an individual at the time of his or her death. To understand what is meant by the term 'epiphysis' and the process of its fusion, it is useful to use the femur as an illustrative example (as its major structural components are typical of those found in all long bones). As can be seen from Figure 12.2, the diaphysis (i.e. the central shaft of the long bone) terminates in a growing region called the metaphysis at each end. At the proximal end of the femur (i.e. the end nearest to the trunk of the body), the metaphysis is capped by two epiphyses, while at its distal end it is capped by one epiphysis. In each case, the epiphysis is formed from a separate centre of ossification and eventually fuses with the end of the long bone with which it is associated. The process of fusion, known as epiphyseal union, takes several years to complete and occurs at a number of specific locations within the body (Figure 12.3). For each such location, epiphyseal union occurs over a known age range. Available data take into account variations in the exact timing of this range due to factors such as gender and the climate experi-

Long bones
A collective term applied to the femur, fibula and tibia of the leg and the humerus, radius and ulna of the arm.

enced during development. For example, epiphyseal union for the head of the femur (thighbone) for a male in a non-tropical climate is partial at the age of 16 years and complete by the age of 19 (Figure 12.3). It should be noted that tooth eruption can also be utilised in estimating the age of individuals who die before the age of about 25 years.

■ *Race.* It is much more difficult to identify the possible racial origin – white (Caucasian), Negroid or Mongoloid – of skeletal remains than either to determine sex or to estimate age. However, there are some features, especially of the skull, that can be used to indicate racial origin. For example, 'shovel-shaped' upper incisors (i.e. those with raised edges on their lingual surface) have a high frequency of occurrence in a number of Mongoloid races, such as the Chinese and Japanese, but a low frequency of occurrence (i.e. <15 per cent) in Caucasians and Negroids. The lingual surface of the upper incisors of the latter two groups is usually flat.

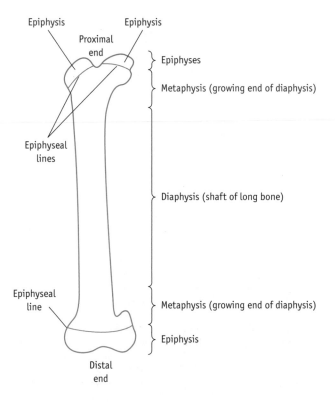

(From original drawing by Julie Jackson)

Figure 12.2 Major structural features of the femur (thighbone)
Note that each epiphyseal line shows where the epiphysis and metaphysis concerned fuse during epiphyseal union

(From Knight, B. (1996)
Forensic pathology (2nd
edn). London: Arnold.
Reproduced by permission
of Arnold.)

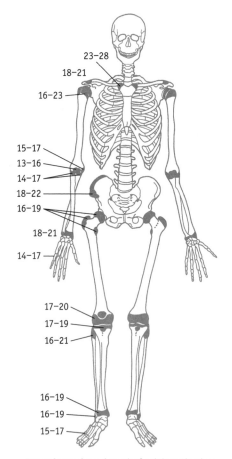

Approximate dates (years) of epiphyseal union

The commencement and completion of union takes several years. The table is only a guide for male subjects (female slightly earlier) in non-tropical climates; the two dates are partial and complete union (years).

Head of femur	16–19	Acromion	17–19
Greater trochanter	16–19	Distal femur	17–20
Lesser trochanter	16–19	Proximal tibia	17–19
Head of humerus	16–23	Proximal fibula	16–21
Distal humerus	13–16	Distal tibia	16–19
Medial epicondyle	16–17	Distal fibula	16–19
Proximal radius	14–17	Metatarsals	15–17
Proximal ulna	14–17	Iliac crest	18–22
Distal radius	18–21	Primary elements pelvis	14–16
Distal ulna	18–21	Sternal clavicle	23–28
Metacarpals	14–17	Acromial clavicle	18–21

Figure 12.3 A guide to the age of epiphyseal union in the major centres

Individualising features

Once the class characteristics of the individual have been established (as far as is possible), attention is then focused on those features of the skeletal remains that may be of use in making a personal identification. This is only possible if reliable ante-mortem information for potential matches is available for comparison. Features that may be used for identifying purposes include the following:

■ *Dentition.* As a consequence of their practical indestructibility, teeth can provide the best means of personal identification, not only for skeletal remains but also in cases where the body is otherwise unrecognisable, for example severely disfigured through exposure to intense heat. The arrangement and characteristics of the teeth and the treatment to which they have been subjected during life (e.g. repairs, restoration, extractions) mean that human dentition is, potentially, uniquely identifiable. The post-mortem examination of teeth and their comparison with ante-mortem dental records requires the expert knowledge of the forensic odontologist. An example of how ante-mortem dental records were successfully used to identify a victim of murder is given in Box 12.5.

Case study

Box 12.5

The use of forensic dentistry in the identification of Rachel Dobkin

In July 1942, workmen demolishing the wreckage of a Baptist chapel in Kennington, southeast London, discovered a corpse beneath a stone slab in the cellar. Although the body was almost fully skeletalised, it had clearly been dismembered and was not, as initially thought, a victim of the German bombing raids. Moreover, slaked lime (calcium hydroxide) had been spread over the body, ostensibly to accelerate its decomposition (although, in fact, it has the reverse effect) and there was evidence that the body had also been burnt.

The Home Office pathologist Dr Keith Simpson was called in to examine the remains. He established that the victim was female and noted that her hair, which was dark brown, was starting to turn grey. He estimated her age as somewhere between 40 and 50 years, her height as around five feet (1.52 m) and that she had been dead for between 12 and 18 months. The presence of a blood clot associated with the remains of the victim's larynx (voice box) strongly pointed to manual strangulation as the cause of death. Post-mortem examination of the remains also showed that the uterus of the victim was enlarged due to the presence of a fibroid tumour.

After consulting the record of missing persons, the police came up with a potential match; that of Mrs Rachel Dobkin, aged 47 years, who had been reported missing about 15 months earlier (on 11 April 1941). As well as concurrence between her age, height and the date of her disappearance, ante-mortem medical records revealed that she had indeed suffered from a fibroid tumour. However, odontological evidence was to prove crucial in positively identifying the corpse as that of Mrs Dobkin. Although the lower jaw of the skeletalised victim was not recovered, a comparison between the teeth of the upper jaw, which had undergone extensive dental treatment, and the meticulous ante-mortem dental records held for Mrs Dobkin demonstrated an exact match. In particular, it was known that the extraction of two specific teeth had left parts of the roots embedded in Mrs Dobkin's jaw. X-ray examination of the corpse's jaw revealed the presence of these two residual roots.

Mr Harry Dobkin, the estranged husband of the deceased, who worked as a fire-watcher in the vicinity of the Baptist chapel in Kennington, was arrested and charged with her murder. He was found guilty and hanged.

Photosuperimposition
A forensic technique in which a photographic image of the bare skull of the decedent is superimposed onto a photographic portrait, taken during life, of a possible match.

Facial reconstruction
A forensic technique aimed at reconstructing the facial appearance of an individual based on the features of his or her skull.

■ *Anatomical structure.* Certain parts of the skeleton can be used for identification purposes if suitable ante-mortem radiological (X-ray) information from possible victims is available. The skull is especially useful in this respect. In particular, the pattern of the frontal sinus is unique to each individual and can be used to exclude or confirm a potential match. The techniques of **photosuperimposition** and **facial reconstruction**, which make specific use of the skull to identify individuals, are discussed in Box 12.6.

■ *Bone injury.* Evidence of *past* injury to the bone, such as a fracture, may prove useful in identification. However, this may not be evident if sufficient time has elapsed to allow the injury to heal completely.

■ *Bone disease.* There are a number of disorders affecting bone structure that may be apparent in skeletal remains. The four common ones are Paget's disease (osteitis deformans), osteitis fibrosa, osteomalacia (adult form of rickets) and osteoporosis. Each of these diseases has a characteristic histological appearance under the microscope that any suitably qualified forensic pathologist could easily identify.

■ *Surgical implants.* The presence of a surgical implant, such as an artificial hip joint, bearing a unique serial number may allow definitive identification of the individual concerned (Figure 12.4).

■ *Material suitable for DNA analysis.* It may be possible to make a personal identification of skeletal remains through the technique of DNA analysis (Chapter 6, Section 6.3). Good sources of DNA include dental pulp and bone marrow but even bone itself can be used if necessary.

Forensic techniques

Box 12.6

Personal identification: the role of photosuperimposition and facial reconstruction

Photosuperimposition

In some cases, photosuperimposition has been used successfully to match a skull with a photograph of the suspected victim. One of the most notable examples is that of Isabella Ruxton, who was murdered by her husband, Dr Buck Ruxton, in 1935 (Box 12.4). Traditionally, the technique of photosuperimposition involved photographing the skull and then superimposing the resultant image, printed on transparent film, over a photographic portrait of the individual in question. During this procedure, both the orientation and size of the photograph of the skull were matched as closely as possible to that of the portrait. In recent years, video techniques have been used to superimpose images of the skull onto a picture of the individual concerned. Correspondence of major anatomical features, such as the teeth, supraorbital ridges and nasal aperture, indicates that the skull could belong to the individual in the portrait, while no agreement excludes the individual as a possible match.

Facial reconstruction

Facial reconstruction is a highly skilled procedure that involves building-up the facial appearance of an individual from his or her bare skull (see figure opposite). This

Box 12.6 continued

technique was pioneered towards the end of the nineteenth century by Wilhelm His (a Swiss anatomist) and later developed by others, notably the Russians A. D. Grigoriev and Mikhail Gerasimov. Historically, facial reconstruction has largely been of interest to historians and archaeologists. However, in recent years, this technique has become recognised as an important forensic tool in the identification of skeletal remains.

Facial reconstruction uses, as its basis, compiled data concerning the average thickness of soft tissue over many different points on the skull. Using a cast of the skull, layers of suitable material, usually modelling clay, are built up to cover the skull to the requisite depth. This is achieved by first inserting, for example, rods or cocktail sticks into the cast to predetermined depths and then just covering them with the clay. The clay is then smoothed over to resemble human skin. Prosthetic eye-

balls are inserted into the eye sockets to give the reconstruction a more life-like appearance.

Reconstruction of other aspects of the individual's appearance, such as the nose, ears, lips and hair (colour, length, style, etc.) relies on the skill and experience of the sculptor, since the underlying bone structure provides little or no relevant information.

However, despite these difficulties, facial reconstruction has led, on occasion, to the identification of skeletal remains. For example, reconstruction of the facial appearance of an unknown female by Richard Neave (of the Department of Art in Medicine, Manchester University) led to the recognition and identification of Karen Price, whose body was found buried in a Cardiff garden in 1989. In recent years, techniques based on computer graphics have been developed for the purpose of facial reconstruction.

(a) 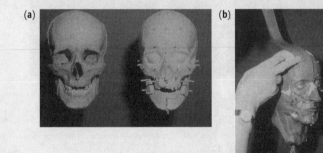 (b) (c)

The process of facial reconstruction

(a) *A cast of a bare skull;* (b) *the application of layers of clay and* (c) *the finished sculpture*

(Reproduced by kind permission of Richard Neave, Forensic/Medical Artist, RN-DS Partnership and Honorary Medical Artist, University of Manchester)

(Joint kindly supplied by
Orthodynamics, UK;
photographs taken by
Derek Lowe, Staffordshire
University, UK)

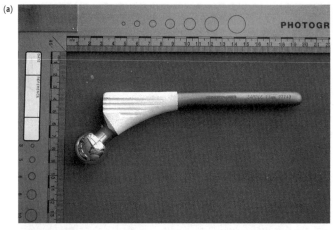

Figure 12.4 The part of an artificial hip joint that is fitted to the femur
(a) The entire item. (b) A close-up showing the serial number and the manufacturer's name which, in combination, can be used in conjunction with records kept by the manufacturer and the hospital to identify the individual fitted with the joint

12.5 Summary

■ When the death of an individual is sudden, violent, unnatural, of unknown cause or suspicious in any way, forensic examination of the human remains can yield much valuable information concerning the death and the circumstances that surround it. In England and Wales, deaths that cannot be attributed to natural causes are reported to the coroner for further investigation. Sources of reported deaths include medical doctors, hospital authorities, the police and Registrars of Births and Deaths.

■ In each case of reported death, the coroner must decide whether it is necessary to order a post-mortem examination of the body (figures for the year 2005 show that this occurred in approximately 49 per cent of cases). Post-mortem examination for medico-legal purposes is usually carried out by a forensic pathologist. However, in cases where the human remains are in skeletal form, or are otherwise unrecognisable, forensic anthropologists and/or forensic odontologists may provide the necessary expertise.

■ The purpose of the post-mortem examination is to establish certain facts concerning the decedent and the circumstances surrounding his or her death. Notable among these are the time of death, the cause of death and the identification of the individual. In cases of suspicious deaths, such facts are critical to the police investigation.

Problems

1. In the early stages after death, certain changes are usually observable or detectable in the human body. With reference to *three* of these, describe how each may be used to help estimate the post-mortem interval and compare their relative utility in this respect.

2. How might entomological evidence collected from a murder scene help to establish the following:

   (a) the time since death;

   (b) the circumstances surrounding the death;

   (c) any change in location of the body after death?

3. Describe the changes in appearance of a dead body that occur during the normal process of post-mortem decomposition. Explain how certain features of the body itself and the particular environmental conditions that surround it may affect the rate of normal post-mortem decomposition.

4. Describe the processes of mummification and adipocere formation and the environmental conditions that favour each of these.

5. This question concerns a fictitious scenario. The bodies of an elderly man and his wife are found together in the living room of their house. Although there are no obvious signs of violence, circumstances decree that the medical doctor in attendance report the deaths to the coroner. Describe, step-by-step, how the coroner would conduct an investigation into these uncertified deaths. Include in your answer the main categories of verdict that may be returned at inquest.

6. Describe the general procedure used in medico-legal post-mortem examinations, with particular reference to those aspects that may provide information relevant to the cause of death.

7. Imagine that the skeleton of an unknown individual is found buried in a disused quarry and needs to be identified.

   (a) What class characteristics of the individual may be established through an examination of the skeletal remains, and how might each of these be deduced?

   (b) What types of individualising features would the pathologist look out for and how might these potentially lead to the identification of the individual?

8. Describe how the processes of (a) photosuperimposition and (b) facial reconstruction may assist in the identification of individuals from bare skulls.

Further reading

Byers, S. N. (2005) *Introduction to forensic anthropology: a textbook* (2nd edn) Boston, MA: Allyn & Bacon.

Catts, E. P. and Haskell, N. H. (1990) *Entomology and death: a procedural guide.* Clemson, SC: Joyce's Print Shop, Inc.

Goff, M. L. (2000) *A fly for the prosecution: how insect evidence helps solve crimes.* Cambridge, MA: Harvard University Press.

Gunn, A. (2006) *Essential forensic biology: animals, plants and microorganisms in legal investigations.* Chichester: John Wiley & Sons Ltd.

Hunter, J. and Cox, M. (2005) *Forensic archaeology: advances in theory and practice.* Abingdon: Routledge.

Knight, B. and Saukko, P. (2004) *Knight's forensic pathology* (3rd edn) London: Arnold.

Shepherd, R. (2003) *Simpson's forensic medicine* (12th edn) London: Arnold.

Statistics and the analysis, interpretation and evaluation of evidence

13

Chapter objectives

After reading this chapter, you should be able to:

> Recognise different types of data.
> Describe the defining characteristics of normally distributed data.
> Understand the measures of location and dispersion of data that are commonly used in the context of statistics.
> Understand the concepts of probability and odds.
> Calculate confidence limits and confidence intervals.
> Understand what is meant by each of precision, accuracy and error within the context of analytical science.
> Conduct linear regression analysis to find the best-fit straight line for any given scatter graph.
> Understand and conduct t-tests.
> Understand the difference between parametric and non-parametric statistical tests.
> In the context of evidence interpretation and evaluation:
>   − construct likelihood ratios using appropriately chosen hypotheses;
>   − apply Bayes' theorem.
> Understand the hierarchy of propositions and the importance of this concept.
> Recognise and avoid both the prosecutor's fallacy and the defence attorney's fallacy.
> Appreciate that it has been judged that, in jury trials, there are limits to the usefulness of the Bayesian approach.

Introduction

Arguably, the work undertaken by a forensic scientist on any one particular piece of evidence that is used in court is a seamless process from the arrival of the item concerned in the scientist's possession to the presentation of the scientist's findings to the court. However, in order to understand this process better, there is value in thinking of it as having three stages. These shall be referred to here as analysis, interpretation and evaluation. Do keep in mind, however, that the division between these three phases is somewhat artificial, that the boundaries between them are blurred, and that the emphasis placed on each will vary from case to case and from one type of evidence to the next.

The analysis stage is concerned with the characterisation of the item of evidence by noting its properties. For example, examination of a shard of glass recovered from a crime scene will reveal its apparent colour and, by means of the measurements described in Chapter 3, Section 3.2.2, its refractive index.

Interpretation is concerned with what can be established about the nature of the item of evidence from the data obtained by analysis. For example, consider an instance in which the analysis of a shard of glass shows it to be green and to have a refractive index in the range expected for both glass commonly used to make bottles and that used to manufacture windowpanes. From this information, it would be reasonable to conclude that this shard could have originated from either of these sources. Furthermore, as green glass is rarely used to make windowpanes but bottles made of green glass are common, it might be reasonable to interpret the results of the analysis to mean that it is more likely that the shard came from a bottle than from a windowpane.

However, great care must be taken not to jump to conclusions during the interpretation process. To return to our example, it must be borne in mind that the shard may be from neither a bottle nor a windowpane, as green glass is made into other objects as well.

Evaluation is the placing of the work within the context of the case in question. If, in the course of a burglary, a windowpane is broken with a hammer held in the right hand of the perpetrator who was wearing a long-sleeved jacket, the person's right sleeve will be showered in minute pieces of glass from the window. If a suspect were arrested 30 minutes after the incident, it would be prudent to examine his or her clothing for small fragments of glass. Consider what would occur if it were found that the suspect had multiple tiny fragments of glass on his or her jacket's right sleeve but the suspect claimed that these must have originated from a beer bottle that he or she had broken while working in a bar that evening. Under these circumstances, the forensic scientist is likely to be asked to examine glass taken from the broken window, that from the sleeve and, if it is available, that from the bottle. The scientist might well be asked for an evaluation of the likelihood of the glass on the sleeve originating from the bottle, the broken pane or both of these sources. To do this, the scientist must compare the characteristics of glass samples taken from all three locations with each other and with what is known about glass in general. This is an example of evidence evaluation.

It is important to realise that although a forensic scientist might be asked to evaluate the evidence that he or she has scrutinised, it is not the job of the scientist to establish the guilt or innocence of the accused. This is the task of the court. This distinction between the roles of the scientist and the court is of fundamental importance and is returned to in Chapter 14.

Statistical methods exist that can help the forensic scientist in each of the analysis, interpretation and evaluation phases of work. This chapter is intended to introduce key aspects of these methods. However, the reader is encouraged to extend their learning beyond its contents by reading the books listed at the end of this chapter.

13.1 Data

The discipline of statistics is concerned with the collection of data and the measurement of uncertainty. In order to appreciate how this can be of value within the context of forensic science, it is necessary to understand something of the nature of data and uncertainty.

13.1.1 Types of data

Data are facts and figures that convey information. The feature of data that distinguishes them from other forms of information is normally taken to be that data are gathered in order to conduct analysis, interpretation or evaluation, or to help make decisions.

As illustrated in Figure 13.1, different types of data are recognised. As the name suggests, **qualitative data** convey information about the qualities of the things being studied and do not directly convey information about quantity or size. A piece of qualitative data conveys which of a number of separate categories (also known as classes or groups) of the same feature a given thing belongs to. For example, a drug (the thing) may be described as being one of cocaine, heroin, marijuana, etc. (the categories) – the feature here is the type of drug. The drugs in each of these categories have attributes in common and have attributes that are different from all other categories of drug. Qualitative data are useful as they sort things into categories (a process called classification); because they do this, qualitative data can also be called categorical data.

In the forensic context, attributes that allow an item or person to be assigned to a category that contains two or more items or people are known as class characteristics. For example, examination of a bullet that has been fired from a rifled firearm may reveal characteristics (calibre, direction of rifling, etc.) that may allow the possible makes and models of the firearm to be established. Even if it were possible to narrow the firearm to a particular make and model, these details would still be class

Data
Facts and figures that convey information.

Qualitative data
Data that convey information about the qualities of the things being studied and that do not directly convey information about quantity or size.

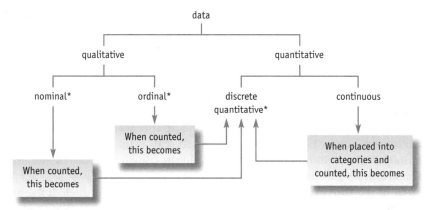

* Each of these is a discrete data type.

Figure 13.1 A classification of data

characteristics, as a manufacturer will make many firearms of the same make and model. In contrast, attributes that allow an item or person to be assigned to a category that contains only one item or person are known as individualising characteristics. As described in Chapter 9, Section 9.4.2, the striation markings in the land impressions made on a fired bullet by a rifled barrel can, under many circumstances, be used to individualise the barrel concerned as it is believed that each barrel will produce a unique pattern of these striations. Note that, in theory at least, it is possible for a combination of class characteristics to be individualising. Although each such characteristic places the item or individual into a group with others, the exact combination of these characteristics may be unique to that item or person. For example, the SGM+ DNA profiling system examines ten loci. It is quite possible for a person to have a relatively common genotype for each of these loci (i.e. each locus will place that person into a group that contains many other people) and yet have a unique DNA profile. This will occur if the combination of these relatively common attributes is found only in that person. Information on how DNA profiles are interpreted is given in Chapter 6, Section 6.4.

Ordinal and nominal
Qualitative data that have an underlying order are said to be ordinal, while those that do not are termed nominal.

Another example of data that are qualitative are the growth stages of true flies – egg, larva (with its three growth substages: the first, second and third instars), pupa and adult (Chapter 12, Box 12.2). In contrast to categories of illicit drugs, these data have an underlying order. Qualitative data that have such an order are said to be **ordinal** while those that do not are termed **nominal**.

Quantitative data
Data that convey information about size or quantity.

Unlike qualitative data, **quantitative data** convey information about size or quantity. As shown in Figure 13.1, two forms of quantitative data are recognised, continuous and discrete. **Continuous data**, also called measurements, are those that can have any value in a range of allowed values. For example, the percentage of diamorphine in street heroin, can, in theory at least, have any value between 0 and 100 per cent. In contrast, **discrete quantitative data** (also known as counts) can have only integer (i.e. whole number) values and are generated by counting the number of observations that occur within different nominal or ordinal categories. For example, if a corpse were discovered and the number of true flies found on it in each of their growth stages were known, then this numerical information would be discrete quantitative data. As described in Section 13.1.2, it is possible to transform continuous data into discrete quantitative data by classifying the data into discrete categories and counting the number of data points in each category. Note that, as indicated in Figure 13.1, qualitative data, whether nominal or ordinal, are also classified as discrete.

Continuous data
Quantitative data that can have any value in a range of allowed values. Also called measurements.

Discrete quantitative data
Quantitative data that can have only integer values. Also called counts.

In addition to the classification summarised in Figure 13.1, it is useful to differentiate between constants and variables. **Constants** are items of data that have one fixed value each – although for constants with units, the number used to express that value will change if the units are changed. For example, the speed of light in a vacuum is a constant with a value of $299\,792\,458$ m s^{-1}, which, on the basis of there being 3600 seconds in an hour and 1609.344 metres in a mile, is the same as $670\,616\,629$ miles per hour. In contrast to a constant, a **variable** is data of any of the types shown in Figure 13.1 and that can have any one of a number of values, although often within certain limits. For example, the angle of impact between a drop of blood and a wall is a variable that can have any positive value that is $\leqslant 90°$. Both constants and variables are commonly represented by symbols. These are normally either letters of the English or Greek alphabets and are conventionally written

Constant
An item of data that has one fixed value.

Variable
An item of data that can have any one of a number of values.

in italics. For example, the speed of light in a vacuum is conventionally symbolised as c, whereas, most commonly, an angle is represented as θ.

In the analytical aspects of forensic science in particular, as well as in science in general, it is common to plot graphs to show how variations in one variable alter the values of another variable. To create these graphs, the scientist repeatedly alters one of these variables from one known value to the next while recording the value of the other variable. The variable that is under the direct control of the scientist is called the *independent variable*, while the other is termed the *dependent variable*. Conventionally, the independent and dependent variables are plotted on the x (i.e. horizontal) and y (i.e. vertical) axes, respectively. An important application of this is the creation of the calibration graphs that are central to the quantification of a wide range of analytes of forensic interest. In these, the independent variable is the concentration of the analyte in question and the dependent variable is the response of the instrument being used to perform the analysis. An example of this is given in Chapter 7, Box 7.5, in which the creation and use of a calibration graph is described within the context of atomic absorption and emission spectroscopies, which can be used to quantify metallic poisons. The creation of calibration graphs is returned to in Section 13.3, where a statistical method for establishing where it is best to draw the line on a straight-line graph is described.

13.1.2 Normally distributed data

Frequency is the name given to the number of times that a given event happens or value occurs. Under certain circumstances, a study of the frequency of past events or occurrences can lead to knowledge of how common these events or occurrences are, have been and will be. This is probability information (see Box 13.1 for a definition of probability), and it is powerful in a number of ways. For example, it can also be used to assess the confidence that should be placed in a given interpretation of experimental results. Also, this information allows the relative probabilities of the observed evidence occurring given the alternative explanations proposed by the prosecution and defence in court. These applications of probability information are explored later in this chapter, while this section is concerned with an important illustration of how this information can be obtained from a study of frequency data.

> **Frequency**
> *The number of times that a given event happens or value occurs.*

Take, for example, a hypothetical case involving the analysis of a sample of blood for its ethanol concentration, the true value of which (symbolised as μ) is exactly 81 mg of ethanol per 100 ml of blood. Assuming the absence of systematic or gross errors, the measurement of this continuous variable would still be the subject of random error (see Section 13.2 for a discussion of the various types of error and Section 13.1.1 for the meaning of the terms 'continuous' and 'variable'). The consequence of this random error is that the result (symbolised as x) of any one single analysis is unlikely to be a figure that exactly equals μ. Assume that a data set (i.e. a group of data points) has been created by performing a number of repeated analyses on the same sample of blood, using the same analytical procedure. The data set produced contains a range of results many, but not all, of which are close to μ. Half of these data points are larger than μ and half are smaller. Note that n is the symbol used for the number of data points in a data set and, in this case, n is very large.

To explore further the pattern of dispersal that the n values of x have about μ, it would be valuable to generate a graph showing the frequency of different values of x.

Further information

Box 13.1

Probability and odds

In the context of forensic science, *probability* is a rationally assessed measure of how certain it is that a given assertion is true. Such assessments can be made only if the assertion concerned is one that is either true or false. This is exemplified by the statement that 'the person observed at the scene was male'. However, the degree of certainty with which we can state that the assertion is true will depend on the available evidence. In other words, the probability is conditional on the evidence that is both available and taken into account.

Two different but equivalent scales are used to express probabilities. One of these extends from 0 to 1, and the other, which is derived from the first by multiplying by 100, runs from 0 to 100 per cent. On either scale, 0 means that, on the basis of the evidence used, it is certain that the assertion is *not* true. At the opposite extreme, a probability of 1 (i.e. 100 per cent) means that, based on the evidence used, it is known with absolute certainty that the assertion is true. In the example given in the previous paragraph, if the only evidence available is that half of the population is male, then the probability that the assertion is true is 0.5 (i.e. 50 per cent).

Odds are another means of expressing the same information as that embodied in probability. Using the scale of probability that ranges from 0 to 1, and letting A stand for the assertion concerned and P(A) stand for the probability that A is true, then:

$$\text{The odds in favour of } A = \frac{P(A)}{(1-P(A))}$$

For example, in the case in question, on the basis of the available information, the odds in favour of the assertion that the person seen at the scene was male are:

$$\frac{0.5}{(1-0.5)} = \frac{0.5}{0.5} = \frac{1}{1}$$

i.e. odds of 1 to 1.

Odds can be converted to probability, thus: if the odds in favour of x are a to b, then

$$\text{probability of } x = \frac{a}{(a+b)}$$

For example, the odds in favour of the assertion that the person seen at the scene was male are 1 to 1, and therefore the probability of this is $1/(1+1) = 0.5$ or 50 per cent.

In this case, the data are continuous. Consequently, even though n is large, it is most probable that each value of x would be unique. This means that, in this case, simply plotting x on the horizontal axis and the frequency of x (symbolised by f_x) on the vertical axis would not generate a useful graph. Instead, all that this would produce is a straight horizontal line at a frequency of 1. Therefore, to produce a meaningful plot from continuous data such as this, it is necessary to group the data into discrete categories, called classes or bins. Each of these classes (which may be symbolised g) spans a range of values (i.e. it has a width, w), which touches but does not overlap the range of values of its nearest neighbour classes. Each data point (i.e. each value of x) within the data set is then allocated to one of these categories, a process that may be referred to as classification. This is done such that each data point within any one class will have a value that falls within the range of the class concerned. The number of data points in each class can now be counted and is called the class frequency (f_g). By this means, the data have been transformed from measurements into counts. That is, the data have been changed from continuous quantitative data to discrete quantitative data. Provided that the value for w was chosen to be the same for all classes (which it was in this case), Equation 13.1 can be used to calculate the relative frequency (rf_g) of a given class from its value of f_g:

$$rf_g = \frac{f_g}{w \times n}$$
Eq 13.1

This calculation can then be repeated for each class and a histogram can be plotted with the classes on the horizontal axis, each touching its nearest neighbour(s), and the relative frequency on the vertical axis. Figure 13.2 shows such a histogram for the case in question.

If n is very large, as it is in this instance, this allows a large number of classes, each of narrow width, to be used when plotting the histogram. The larger the value of n, the narrower and more numerous the classes can be and the smoother and less step-like the line made by the tops of the columns becomes. Ultimately, it will become a smooth line as shown, for the case in question, in Figure 13.3.

At this point it is useful to introduce the concepts of populations and samples. In the statistical sense, the word **population** refers to all of the observations of the type being made, whether measurements or counts, that could be made on the item or group of related items under study. It is a self-contained and complete data set. For example, in the case in question, the population would be the results of the

Population
In statistics, the complete data set that is all of the observations of the type being made that could be made on the item or group of related items under study.

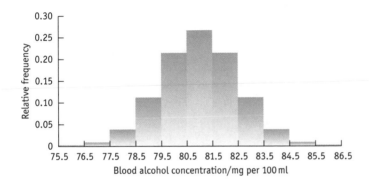

Figure 13.2 Relative frequency data generated from a large sample

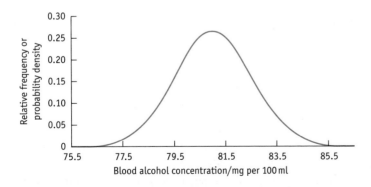

Figure 13.3 An example of normally distributed data

largest conceivable number of repeated analyses on the same sample of blood, using the same analytical procedure. In the context of statistics, the word **sample** means a collection of measurements or counts that is a subset of the population. In analytical science, the term sample has a slightly different meaning as it refers to the item being analysed. In many instances, this will be a part of a larger bulk of material (e.g. part of a paint flake recovered from a crime scene). Clearly, some care is needed in order to avoid confusion between these two meanings, although from the context in which the term is used the meaning is generally clear.

The data presented in Figure 13.2 are derived from a sample, albeit an unusually large one, whereas those shown in Figure 13.3 are from the population. Notice that although the vertical axis in Figure 13.2 is relative frequency, the same axis in Figure 13.3 is labelled as either relative frequency or probability density and, hence, Figure 13.3 is a probability density curve. Such curves are important because they can be used to establish the probability of a given event happening or a given value occurring. To illustrate how this is done, the probability in the case in question of any one single analysis result being 80 mg or less of ethanol per 100 ml of blood is described below.

The total area under a probability density curve is 1. This is the total probability of all possibilities represented on the graph occurring. Therefore, the shaded area in Figure 13.4 is the probability that any one single measurement, taken at random from all possible such measurements, has a value of ≤ 80 mg/100 ml. As this shaded portion has an area of 0.2514, there is a 25.14 per cent probability of this event occurring.

Importantly, the curve shown in Figures 13.3 and 13.4 is a normal distribution curve. A normal distribution curve is one that is defined as conforming to Equation 13.2

$$\text{Probability density} = \frac{1}{\sqrt{2\pi\sigma^2}} \exp\left\{-\frac{(x-\mu)^2}{2\sigma^2}\right\} \qquad \text{Eq 13.2}$$

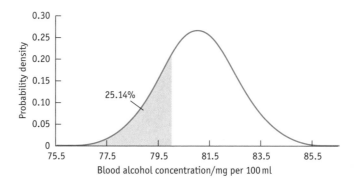

Figure 13.4 A graph of population data for the analysis of blood alcohol concentration, showing the probability that any one single measurement, taken at random from all possible such measurements, has a value of ≤ 80 mg/100 ml. Note that in this instance, the value of the population mean is 81 mg per 100 ml and that of its standard deviation is 1.5 mg per 100 ml

in which there are two variables other than x. These are μ, which is the mean of the population, and the population's standard deviation, σ; which are defined in Boxes 13.2 and 13.3, respectively. (Note π is the constant 3.14159....) In the example under consideration, the value of μ is 81 mg per 100 ml and that of σ is 1.5 mg per 100 ml.

All normal distribution curves are bell-shaped, with the value of x equal to μ at that point on the curve where the probability density is at its maximum value. Normal distribution curves vary in their heights and widths, depending on their values of σ. Those with small values of σ are tall and narrow, while those that are short and wide have large σ values. To illustrate these effects, Figure 13.5 shows two normal distribution curves, both with $\mu = 10$ but one with $\sigma = 1$ and the other with $\sigma = 3$. From this it can be seen that for normally distributed data, μ determines the location of the data and σ is a measure of its dispersion (see Boxes 13.2 and 13.3, respectively, for more information about these and other measures of location and dispersion).

One of the key features of a normal distribution curve is that the area under it between any two values of x can be calculated. For example, as shown in Figure 13.6, between $x_1 = \mu - 1.00 \times \sigma$ and $x_2 = \mu + 1.00 \times \sigma$, the area has been calculated to be 0.682. As this area is the probability of any one data point taken at random from the population having a value between x_1 and x_2, this means that 68.2 per cent of the data points of the population reside within $\pm 1.00\sigma$ of the mean. Furthermore, the remainder of the data points must reside in the two tails of the curve that are more than one standard deviation from the population mean. As the normal distribution curve is symmetrical about the population mean, this implies that each tail contains $(100 - 68.2)/2 = 15.9$ per cent of the data points. Further commonly encountered examples of known areas under the normal distribution curve are given in Table 13.1.

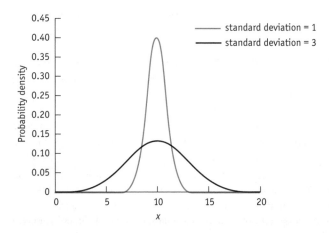

Figure 13.5 A graph showing two normal distribution curves, both with $\mu = 10$ but one with $\sigma = 1$ (blue line) and the other with $\sigma = 3$

Further information

Box 13.2

Measures of location

In many instances, a quantitative data set (whether made up of measurements or counts) can be thought of as containing data that are distributed in some way about a central point. This central point can be envisaged both as being an expression of the typical value of the variable that is being measured and as defining the location of the data set concerned. Several types of central points, all known as averages, may be defined. Those in common use are the arithmetic mean, the median and the mode. These are defined and discussed briefly below.

Arithmetic mean (known as the mean)

This is the most commonly calculated average and what is most often meant when the word 'average' is used. It is the sum of all of the individual data points (x) in the data set divided by the number of data points (n) that it contains. That is:

$$\text{Mean} = \frac{\Sigma x}{n}$$

For example, if the refractive indices of four fragments of glass recovered from the coat of a suspect were found to be 1.511 56, 1.511 50, 1.511 62 and 1.511 60, the mean value would be:

$$\frac{1.511\,56 + 1.511\,50 + 1.511\,62 + 1.511\,60}{4} = 1.511\,57$$

Note that distinction is drawn between the mean of a population and the mean of a sample. These are symbolised μ (pronounced 'mu') and $\bar{x}$ (pronounced 'x bar'), respectively. The value of $\bar{x}$ for a sample taken from a given population is an estimate of that population's μ.

Variation of data points away from the mean may be due to random errors (Section 13.2) inherent in the measurement. If this is the sole source of variation, then μ is the true value of the variable being measured. For example, consider the repeated analysis of a single uniform piece of cannabis resin for its Δ^9-tetrahydrocannabinol (Δ^9-THC) concentration. Provided that true population data can be collected and the only error is random error, then the mean value of the analytical results of the repeats will be the true concentration of

Δ^9-THC in that piece. Note, however, that μ is not always the true value, even when the only type of error is random error. This happens when the parameter being measured varies across the population, so no single true value exists. Under these circumstances, μ is a parameter that characterises the population as a whole. For example, consider a population that is made up of assorted pieces of cannabis resin, each of which is analysed for its Δ^9-THC concentration. Even if each piece is uniform in terms of the concentration of this component, random error cannot be the sole source of variation if the actual concentration of Δ^9-THC varies from one piece of resin to the next. Therefore, μ is a property of the population and not a true value of the Δ^9-THC concentration.

Median

This is the central value when the data are placed in order of increasing value (or the mean of the two central values if there is an even number of data points). For example, if the number of minutiae in each of nine fingerprints were found when placed in ascending order to be 16, 17, 18, 20, 20, 25, 26, 28 and 33, the central value is 20, which is therefore the median of this data set. Note that the position of the centre can be found by counting j data points from either end of the list of data points, where $j = (n + 1) \times 0.50$ and n = the number of data points in the data set.

In instances in which the data are skewed (i.e. not distributed symmetrically about the mean), the median is often used instead of the mean to provide an average value.

Mode

This is simply the most common value. For example, if the number of minutiae in each of nine fingerprints were found to be 16, 28, 20, 33, 17, 20, 18, 26 and 25, the mode would be 20. This is because this value, which would be referred to as the modal value, appears twice while each of the others appears only once.

In continuous data, identical values are rarely found. However, in the absence of such values, a mode can be established if the data are grouped into classes (the clas-

Box 13.2 continued

sification of continuous data is described in Section 13.1.2). The mode is now the class that contains the largest number of data points. This class, called the modal class, will span a range of values. For example, in a data set made up of the measurements of the heights of a group of people, the modal class might be one that spans the range 1.76 to 1.78 metres. If it were necessary to identify a specific value as the mode of a continuous data set such as this, this can be taken to be the central value of the modal class. In the example given here, the modal value would therefore be 1.77 metres.

The mode is particularly useful when an average of nominal data is needed, as it is not possible to calculate a mean or a median value in such instances (the term nominal data is defined in Section 13.1.1).

Further information
Box 13.3

Measures of dispersion

In addition to knowing about the location of a central point of a data set (Box 13.2), it is often useful to be able to describe the extent to which the data within that data set are dispersed. There are several parameters that can be calculated to describe this dispersion, included in which are the standard deviation, variance and interquartile range. These are described below.

Standard deviation and variance

The standard deviation can be thought of as an average displacement of the data points from the mean. That is, it is a measure of how wide the data set is. At first glance it would seem that calculation of such an average would involve the subtraction of the mean (μ) from each data point (x) in turn (i.e. $x - \mu$). The results of these calculations would then be added together and divided by the number of data points (n) in the data set, thus:

$$\frac{\Sigma(x - \mu)}{n}$$

However, there is a problem with this. For normally distributed populations, half of the values of x will be $> \mu$ and half will be $< \mu$ and for every value of $(x - \mu)$ that is positive there is one that is the same except that it is negative. Consequently, $\Sigma(x - \mu)/n$ will be zero, no matter how wide or narrow the distribution is. To get around this difficulty, each value of $(x - \mu)$ is squared

before they are added together and then divided by n. This works because the square of $(x - \mu)$ will be positive in all instances. The only difficulty is that the number obtained is the square of the desired value, but this is solved easily by taking the square root. The standard deviation of a population (σ) is therefore given by:

$$\sigma = \sqrt{\frac{\Sigma(x - \mu)^2}{n}}$$

The standard deviation of a sample (s) is given by a slightly different formula, namely:

$$s = \sqrt{\frac{\Sigma(x - \bar{x})^2}{n - 1}}$$

The variance is the standard deviation squared. For a population, it is:

$$\sigma^2 = \frac{\Sigma(x - \mu)^2}{n}$$

and for a sample, it is:

$$s^2 = \frac{\Sigma(x - \bar{x})^2}{n - 1}$$

Interquartile range

This is the difference between the first and third quartiles. In data placed in order of increasing value, the first and third quartiles are the values below which, respectively, one-quarter and three-quarters of all of the data points reside. Once the data set of n values has been

▶

Box 13.3 *continued*

arranged in order of increasing value, these quartiles can be estimated as described below.

The first and third quartiles can respectively be taken to be the values of the data points found by counting j_1 and j_2 data points from the start of the list of data points, where $j_1 = (n + 1) \times 0.25$ and $j_2 = (n + 1) \times 0.75$. For example, if the percentage of diamorphine in six samples of heroin was, in order of increasing value, found to be 25.6 per cent, 27.6 per cent, 30.4 per cent, 31.3 per cent, 32.9 per cent and 36.9 per cent, j_1 would be $(6 + 1) \times$ 0.25 = 1.75 and j_2 would be $(6 + 1) \times 0.75 = 5.25$. The first quartile would be 27.1 per cent as this is three-quarters of the way between 25.6 per cent and 27.6 per cent (i.e. 25.6% + ((27.6% − 25.6%) × 0.75) = 27.1%). Similarly, the third quartile would be one-quarter the way between 32.9 per cent and 36.9 per cent, that is 33.9 per cent (i.e. 32.9% + ((36.9% − 32.9%) × 0.25) = 33.9%). This would establish the interquartile range in this instance to be 33.9% − 27.1% = 6.8%.

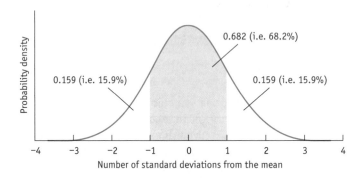

Figure 13.6 The probability density curve of a normal distribution showing the area inside and outside of the region between $x_1 = \mu - 1.00 \times \sigma$ and $x_2 = \mu + 1.00 \times \sigma$

Table 13.1 Commonly encountered examples of known areas under the normal distribution curve

Range of values of *x*	Corresponding percentage of the total area under the normal distribution curve* /%
$\mu \pm 1.00 \times \sigma$	68.2
$\mu \pm 2.00 \times \sigma$	95.4
$\mu \pm 3.00 \times \sigma$	99.7
$\mu \pm 1.96 \times \sigma$	95
$\mu \pm 2.58 \times \sigma$	99

* This is the percentage of the data points in the population that have values of *x* in the range shown (e.g. 99 per cent of data points in a population have values within the range $\mu - 2.58 \times \sigma$ to $\mu + 2.58 \times \sigma$, where μ is the true value or population mean and σ is the standard deviation of the population).

13.1.3 Confidence limits and confidence intervals

Let us return to the hypothetical example concerning blood alcohol concentration that was introduced in Section 13.1.2. In the UK, driving with a blood alcohol concentration of more than 80 mg of ethanol per 100 ml of blood is an offence under current legislation (Chapter 7, Section 7.2.2). It has already been noted that if a single determination of the ethanol content of the blood concerned were performed, then there is a real possibility that the result (x) would be a false negative. That is, it would produce a value of less that 80 mg per 100 ml, despite the fact that the true value (μ) is more than this figure. The probability of this false negative occurring can be reduced by using $\bar{x}$ in place of x as the estimate of the true blood alcohol concentration. In this, the value $\bar{x}$ would be the mean of a sample, consisting of a number (n) of values of x, generated by repeating the measurement several times.

To see why this works, recall that the true value of the blood alcohol concentration is exactly 81 mg per 100 ml and the standard deviation (σ) for the population of measurements of this variable is 1.5 mg per 100 ml. If a very large number (i.e. a population) of values of $\bar{x}$ were established, these would have a normal distribution. This would have the same mean as that of the population of x, i.e. μ. However, the standard deviation of the population of $\bar{x}$ values would be lower than that of the population of x. The standard deviation of a population of means equals the *standard error of the mean* (symbolised *SE*), which is calculated using Equation 13.3:

$$SE = \frac{\sigma}{\sqrt{n}} \qquad\qquad \text{Eq 13.3}$$

where σ is the standard deviation of the population of x and n is the number of values of x in each sample.

From Equation 13.3, and as illustrated in Figure 13.7, it can be seen that the larger the sample size (i.e. the higher the value of n), the taller and narrower the probability distribution becomes. This means that the uncertainty associated with $\bar{x}$ as an estimate of μ decreases as n increases. Figure 13.7 illustrates this using the hypothetical case in question. From this, it can be seen that whereas 25.14 per cent of single measurements will be below 80 mg per 100 ml, the proportion of values of $\bar{x}$ below this figure is decreased to 6.81 per cent if the value of n is 5 and 1.74 per cent if the value of n is 10.

Clearly, in real life, the value of μ is not known. Instead, the best estimate that is available is $\bar{x}$. It would be useful if it were possible to calculate an expression of the uncertainty associated with this estimate. *Confidence limits* and *confidence intervals* are attempts to do this. To set confidence limits, it is necessary to choose a confidence level. Traditionally, such levels are set at either 95 per cent or 99 per cent, although these figures have no particular merit in the general sense and the analyst should decide on the confidence level to be used in a particular case based on the circumstances of that case. For the sake of argument, let us assume that the desired confidence level is 95 per cent. From Table 13.1 it can be seen that 95 per cent of a normally distributed population resides within $\mu \pm 1.96 \times \sigma$ and recall that the standard deviation of a population of means equals its standard error ($= \sigma/\sqrt{n}$). From this, it is argued that the lower 95 per cent confidence limit is given by Equation 13.4, and the upper limit by Equation 13.5.

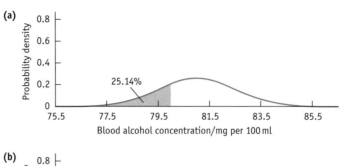

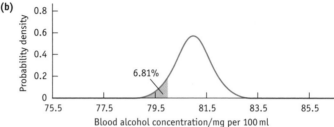

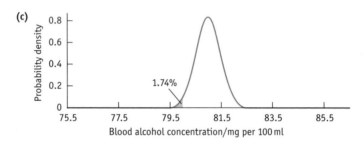

Figure 13.7 The effect of increasing sample size on the distribution of sample means
(a) n = 1; (b) n = 5; (c) n = 10. Each graph relates to the same population of individual
measurements, and this has a population mean of 81 mg per 100 ml and a population
standard deviation of 1.5 mg per 100 ml. Note that for each graph, the shaded area is the
proportion of data points that fall below 80 mg per 100 ml

$$\text{Lower 95 per cent confidence limit} = \bar{x} - (1.96 \times \sigma/\sqrt{n}) \qquad \text{Eq 13.4}$$

$$\text{Upper 95 per cent confidence limit} = \bar{x} + (1.96 \times \sigma/\sqrt{n}) \qquad \text{Eq 13.5}$$

From this, the 95 per cent confidence interval spans from the first of these limits to
the second, that is:

$$\text{95 per cent confidence interval} = \bar{x} \pm (1.96 \times \sigma/\sqrt{n}) \qquad \text{Eq 13.6}$$

Note that the confidence limits and confidence interval at confidence levels other
than 95 per cent can be calculated. This is done by replacing 1.96 in Equations
13.4–13.6 by the number of standard deviations either side of the mean that delimit
w per cent of the data of a normal distribution, where w per cent is the desired
confidence level. For example, using the information provided in Table 13.1, it can
be seen that the confidence interval at a 99 per cent confidence level would be
$\bar{x} \pm (2.58 \times \sigma/\sqrt{n})$.

Notice that when calculating confidence limits or confidence intervals, the standard deviation of the population (σ) has been needed. It is relatively rare that this information is available. More commonly, the only estimate of σ available is s, the standard deviation of the sample. This can be used to estimate the standard error of the mean (SE) of the population by substituting s for σ in Equation 13.3. To differentiate between the SE calculated using σ and its estimate calculated using s, the estimate may be referred to as the *standard uncertainty* (u), which is calculated by Equation 13.7.

$$u = \frac{s}{\sqrt{n}} \qquad \text{Eq 13.7}$$

Note that many authors refer to both SE and u (as defined by Equations 13.3 and 13.7, respectively) as being the standard error of the mean (SE), with the context of its use allowing the reader to discern the meaning.

Using s as an estimate of σ broadens the distribution of $\bar{x}$, so that it is no longer normally distributed. This means that for a given confidence level ($w\%$) and sample size (n), the confidence interval has to broaden too. The statistic t is used to allow for this and the confidence interval (CI) is calculated by means of Equation 13.8; the lower and upper confidence limits being given by Equations 13.9 and 13.10, respectively.

$$CI = \bar{x} \pm (t \times s/\sqrt{n}) = \bar{x} \pm t \times u \qquad \text{Eq 13.8}$$

$$\text{Lower confidence limit} = \bar{x} - (t \times s/\sqrt{n}) = \bar{x} - t \times u \qquad \text{Eq 13.9}$$

$$\text{Upper confidence limit} = \bar{x} + (t \times s/\sqrt{n}) = \bar{x} + t \times u \qquad \text{Eq 13.10}$$

For each of Equations 13.8–13.10, the appropriate value of t is found from tables such as that shown in Table 13.2. To find this value of t, two parameters are required. One of these is the confidence level, which has exactly the same meaning as described before. The other is the number of degrees of freedom (df), which for confidence limit and confidence interval calculations is $n-1$. It is also necessary to know whether it is the one-tailed or the two-tailed value of t that is required. To calculate confidence limits and confidence intervals, the two-tailed value of t is needed. Now, using Table 13.2, the column headed with the chosen confidence level and the correct number of tails is selected, as is the row with $df = n - 1$. At the intersection of this column and row is the value of t required to calculate the confidence interval or confidence limits.

As shown in Table 13.2, the columns may be headed by the significance level (α) in place of the confidence level. Indeed, in many publications that provide tables of t, only the value of α is written at the heads of the columns. It is, therefore, important to know that for a given value of α, on a scale of 0 to 1, the corresponding confidence level in per cent is $(1 - \alpha) \times 100$, or, if α and confidence levels are in per cent, then the corresponding confidence level is $100 - \alpha$. For example, an α of 0.05 or 5 per cent equals a confidence level of 95 per cent.

It is important to understand what confidence limits and confidence intervals represent. Consider a w per cent (e.g. 95 per cent) confidence interval based on a sample of n measurements. What this means is that if a population of samples were taken, each containing n measurements (with each measurement made using the same method), w per cent of the means of these samples would reside within the confidence interval, that is between the w per cent confidence limits. It also means

Table 13.2 Selected values of t (see Appendix 2 for a more extended version of this table)

Degrees of freedom	97.5% 2.5% 95% 5%	99.5% 0.5% 99% 1%	Confidence Significance* Confidence Significance*	One tail One tail Two tails Two tails
1	12.7	63.7		
2	4.30	9.92		
3	3.18	5.84		
4	2.78	4.60		
5	2.57	4.03		
6	2.45	3.71		
7	2.36	3.50		
8	2.31	3.36		
9	2.26	3.25		
10	2.23	3.17		
11	2.20	3.11		
12	2.18	3.05		
13	2.16	3.01		
14	2.14	2.98		
15	2.13	2.95		
16	2.12	2.92		
17	2.11	2.90		
18	2.10	2.88		
19	2.09	2.86		
20	2.09	2.85		
Infinity	1.96	2.58		

* Often symbolised as α

that if one were to predict that for any given sample its mean would reside between these confidence limits, then one would be correct w per cent of the time. This is commonly interpreted as meaning that there is w per cent chance of μ being within the w per cent confidence limits and, although this is strictly speaking incorrect, it is in frequent usage.

13.2 Precision, accuracy and error

In analytical science, the terms 'precision', 'accuracy' and 'error' have specific meanings. These meanings are explored in this section.

Precision

An expression of how reproducible a given measurement is.

Precision is how reproducible a given measurement is. If repeat or replicate measurements[1] produce results that are close together, the data are described as being precise (i.e. having high precision), the opposite being imprecise (i.e. having low precision).

---

1 Repeat measurements are from a series of experiments conducted sequentially, whereas in replicate measurements the experiments are carried out simultaneously. In each type of measurement, as far as is practicable, each experiment is identical to the next.

The standard deviation of a sample of measurements (s) is a gauge of its precision. If the depth of tread on a car tyre was measured repeatedly and the data generated were found to have a standard deviation of 0.1 mm, then this would be more precise than a similar set of measurements of car tyre tread depth that had a standard deviation of 0.9 mm.

However, it is important to keep in mind the size of the mean of the measurements when using standard deviation as a gauge of data quality. For example, consider two different sets of repeated measurements of the depth of tread on a given location on each of two different car tyres. If these two sets of measurements have the same standard deviation but different means, then the data set with the smaller mean is arguably of poorer quality. This is because although the absolute value of the standard deviation is the same in both instances, its value relative to the size of the mean is larger in the case of the measurement set with the smaller mean. In other words, of the two data sets, this one has the lower *relative precision*. The measure of this is the ratio of the standard deviation to the mean.

Two parameters based on this ratio are in common use as alternative gauges of relative precision. These parameters, the coefficient of variation (CV) and the relative standard deviation (RSD), are defined in Box 13.4. For each of these, the larger the value of the parameter (ignoring any negative sign in front of the value), the lower the relative precision. For example, the CV and %RSD of a set of measurements of the depth of tread on one location on a car tyre with a mean of 5.1 mm and a standard deviation of 0.1 mm will be 2 per cent. If the depth of tread on a single location on another car tyre is repeatedly measured, producing a mean

Further information

Box 13.4

Coefficient of variation and relative standard deviation

The *coefficient of variation* (CV) may be defined as:

$$CV = \frac{s}{\bar{x}} \times 100\%$$

The *relative standard deviation* (RSD) is defined by:

$$RSD = \frac{s}{|\bar{x}|}$$

This is often expressed in parts per thousand (ppt), thus:

$$RSD = \frac{s}{|\bar{x}|} \times 1000 \text{ ppt}$$

or as per cent (known as %RSD), thus:

$$RSD = \frac{s}{|\bar{x}|} \times 100\%$$

In the equations given above, s is the standard deviation of the sample, $\bar{x}$ is its mean and $|\bar{x}|$ is the absolute value of its mean. The absolute value of the mean is its value given as a positive number irrespective of whether it is positive or negative, e.g. the absolute value of a mean of 0.43 is 0.43, as is the absolute value of a mean of −0.43.

Note that the CV will always have the same sign as the mean used to calculate it. In contrast, the RSD, as defined above, will be positive irrespective of the sign of the mean.

Unfortunately, there is potential for confusion as there is also another, equally valid, definition of RSD in use. In this alternative definition, $\bar{x}$ is used in place of $|\bar{x}|$ in the equations given above. Although this makes no difference to the RSD of samples that have positive means, the two versions produce RSD values with different signs for samples that have negative means.

measurement of 1.1 mm but the same standard deviation as before, the *CV* and *%RSD* of this second data set is 9 per cent. This higher value of the *CV* and *%RSD* reflects the lower relative precision of the second data set.

Accuracy is how near a given measurement, or average (usually the mean) of several repeat or replicate measurements, is to the true or accepted value. If the difference between the measured and true or accepted value is small, then the measurement (or average measurement) is said to be accurate, the opposite being inaccurate.

Error is an expression of inaccuracy. Both *absolute error* (*E*) and *relative error* (*E_r*) are recognised; these are defined by Equations 13.11 and 13.12, respectively.

$$E = x - x_t \qquad\qquad \text{Eq 13.11}$$

$$E_r = \frac{x - x_t}{x_t} \qquad\qquad \text{Eq 13.12}$$

where x is the measurement that has been made and x_t is the true (or accepted) value. Note that the relative error is usually expressed as a percentage, that is:

$$E_r = \frac{x - x_t}{x_t} \times 100\% \qquad\qquad \text{Eq 13.13}$$

or as parts per thousand (ppt), thus:

$$E_r = \frac{x - x_t}{x_t} \times 1000 \text{ ppt} \qquad\qquad \text{Eq 13.14}$$

In replicate or repeat determinations, the E or E_r of the mean is the error of interest. In which case, x in Equations 13.11–13.14 inclusive is simply replaced by $\bar{x}$. As a consequence of the way in which error is defined in these equations, a negative value of E or E_r means that x (or $\bar{x}$) $< x_t$ and a positive value of E or E_r means that x (or $\bar{x}$) $> x_t$.

As with the concept of relative precision introduced earlier in this section, the advantage of relative error as a gauge of data quality is that the context of the measurement is taken into account. To return to the example of car tyre tread depth measurements, if the mean measurement was 5.1 mm but the true value was 5.0 mm, this mean would have an absolute error of 0.1 mm. This would also be the case if the true value was 1.0 mm and the mean measured value was 1.1 mm. However, the relative errors would be different, namely 2.0 per cent (i.e. 20 ppt) and 10.0 per cent (i.e. 100 ppt). From this, it can be seen that although the absolute error is the same in both cases, the latter is more inaccurate in the context of the size of the true value and so is arguably a poorer-quality item of data.

In analytical science, several different types of error are recognised. These are described below.

Systematic errors (also called *determinate errors*) cause the value of the measurement (or mean of replicate or repeat measurements) to be consistently high or low and so decrease accuracy. Each such error has a specific origin. They can be subdivided into the following:

■ *Personal errors*. These occur because the analyst misjudges the outcome of a test in a way that consistently over- or underevaluates the measurement or count being made. For example, consider the measurement of tyre tread depth by placing a ruler into the tread well and reading the scale where it meets the outermost surface of the tyre. This could be subject to personal determinate error if the person taking the reading does so while looking along a line that it not perpendicular to the ruler. Such errors may be minimised by using equipment that requires little in the way of judgement on the part of the person making the measurement.

■ *Instrument errors*. These occur because the equipment used produces readings that consistently over- or underevaluate the measurement or count being made, e.g., a volumetric pipette that delivers a greater volume than indicated. These can often be eliminated by establishing the true value that corresponds to that indicated by the instrument or by adjusting the instrument such that the indicated value is the true value.

■ *Method errors*. These occur because some aspect of the materials used to conduct the analysis responds in a suboptimal fashion, leading to a consistent over- or underevaluation of the measurement or count being made. For example, presumptive tests, such as those used to indicate the likely presence of blood or certain types of drugs, are often non-specific. That is, they will produce a positive result with substances other than that being tested for. Consider what would happen if a presumptive test for the presence of a particular substance were used to produce a count of the instances of occurrence of that substance. This would tend to lead to a result that was higher than the true value, assuming that the test always produced a positive result in the presence of the substance in question. Detection of, and correction for, method errors is not easy in all cases. However, the appropriate use of control experiments (those designed to establish that the response produced by the test is not spurious) and confirmatory tests (i.e. conducting the analysis using two or more completely different methods and comparing results) can minimise their impact.

Some systematic errors cause the relative error to increase as the quantity being determined gets smaller. These are *constant errors*. Other determinate errors do not cause the relative error to vary as the quantity being measured changes in size. These are *proportional errors*. **Random errors** (also called *indeterminate errors*) cause dispersion of replicate or repeat measurements about the mean measurement. Such errors decrease the precision of a set of replicate or repeat measurements or counts.

Gross errors are due to mistakes or unusual events (e.g. an electrical power surge). Gross errors often produce outliers (i.e. data points that are radically far from the mean value compared with those generated by other replicates or repeats) but can affect all replicates or repeats of a determination.

Random errors
Errors that cause dispersion of replicate or repeat measurements about the mean measurement. Also called indeterminate errors.

Gross errors
Errors due to mistakes or unusual events.

13.3 Regression analysis

As mentioned in Section 13.1.1, there are many analytical techniques that require calibration graphs to be constructed and used. In most applications, in order to construct such a graph, a series of standards is produced, each standard containing a different but known concentration (or, in some instances, amount) of the analyte. (The term 'analyte' means the chemical that is to be analysed for.) The analytical procedure is then conducted on each standard; each time this is done, the response of the analytical system is noted. In most cases, this response is a number produced by the analytical equipment being employed.

The calibration graph is then constructed by plotting the analyte concentration (or amount) on the horizontal (x) axis against the system's response, which is plotted on the vertical (y) axis. A best-fit line is then drawn through the data points.

This graph can then be used to find the concentration (or amount) of analyte present in a sample. To do this, the analytical procedure is carried out on the sample and the system's response is noted. The point on the y-axis where this response lies is found and a line parallel to the x-axis is drawn from this point until it intersects with the line of best fit. A line that is parallel to the y-axis is then drawn from this point of intersection to the x-axis. The value of x where this vertical line crosses the horizontal axis is noted as the concentration (or amount) of analyte in the sample. This process is exemplified by the calibration procedure described in Chapter 7, Box 7.5.

The accuracy of this process is clearly reliant on establishing exactly where the line of best fit lies. Regression analysis is a statistical method for finding this. It quantifies the relationship between one variable and another on which it depends. There are a number of types of regression analysis. However, the one described here is linear regression. This calculates the position of the straight line of best fit through a scatter graph and so is not applicable to situations in which it is believed that the best-fit line is curved. There are non-linear forms of regression analysis that can be used in such situations, although these are not discussed here.

All straight lines have the equation:

$$y = mx + c \qquad \qquad \text{Eq 13.15}$$

in which x is the independent variable, y is the dependent variable, m is a constant that is the slope of the line and c, which is also a constant, is the value of y when $x = 0$.

In the case of the general calibration graph that is described above, x is the concentration (or amount) of analyte and y is the system's response.

During linear regression analysis, the following are calculated:

■ The regression coefficient. This is m for the straight line of best fit. It is calculated using Equation 13.16:

$$m = \frac{\Sigma(x - \bar{x})(y - \bar{y})}{\Sigma(x - \bar{x})^2} \qquad \qquad \text{Eq 13.16}$$

■ The regression constant. This is c for the straight line of best fit. It is calculated using Equation 13.17:

$$c = \bar{y} - m\bar{x} \qquad\qquad \text{Eq 13.17}$$

Once the values of m and c have been found, the straight line of best fit has been defined for the scatter graph in question. Now, for any given value of y, the corresponding value of x can be calculated by rearranging Equation 13.15 to give Equation 13.18:

$$x = \frac{(y - c)}{m} \qquad\qquad \text{Eq 13.18}$$

This removes the need to construct those lines that are parallel to the x- and y-axes and that are described earlier in this section, as the concentration (or amount) of analyte in the sample can be found directly by calculation.

An example of the use of linear regression analysis in this context is given in Box 13.5, as is the corresponding scatter graph with the straight line of best fit shown.

Forensic techniques

Box 13.5

An example of linear regression analysis

Flame photometry is an analytical technique that can be used to determine the concentration of certain metals in solution. It requires the calibration of the instrument used (a flame photometer) each time an analysis is performed.

Consider a hypothetical case in which a flame photometer was to be used to analyse the calcium content of water found in a drinking glass at a crime scene. Before use, the photometer was calibrated using standards that were samples of water containing calcium of known concentration (which in this case was measured in parts per million, ppm). These standards were entered into the photometer sequentially and, for each one, the reading given by the instrument was noted. These instrument readings have no units. The data generated are given in the table below.

A table of the calibration data

Calcium concentration/ppm	Instrument reading
0	0
5	26
10	50
15	81
20	103

The water from the crime scene was found to give an instrument reading of 31. A scatter graph of the calibration data was drawn (see below), which clearly indicated that the optimum shape for the best-fit line through the data would be a straight line.

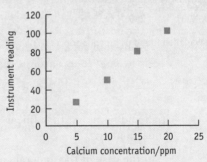

Calibration data shown as a scatter graph

As described in Section 13.3 of the main text, all straight lines accord with the equation $y = mx + c$. Linear regression was used to establish the values of m and x in this case, as described below.

Equation 13.16 (see Section 13.3) allows m to be calculated:

$$m = \frac{\Sigma(x - \bar{x})(y - \bar{y})}{\Sigma(x - \bar{x})^2} \qquad\qquad \text{Eq 13.16}$$

▶

Box 13.5 continued

As in this case, the calcium concentration is the independent variable and the instrument reading is the dependent variable; these were designated as x and y, respectively (see Section 13.1.1 for definitions of independent and dependent variables). The means $\bar{x}$ and $\bar{y}$ were then calculated to be 10 ppm and 52, respectively, and the calculations indicated in the following table were carried out:

A table showing calculations carried out to find m

$x - \bar{x}(=a)$ (units = ppm)	$y - \bar{y}(=b)$ (no units)	$a \times b$ (units = ppm)	a^2 (units = ppm²)
−10	−52	520	100
−5	−26	130	25
0	−2	0	0
5	29	145	25
10	51	510	100
	Total	1305	250

As indicated above, the totals of the last two columns were then calculated as these are, respectively, the numerator and denominator of Equation 13.16, and m was found, thus:

$$m = \frac{\Sigma(x - \bar{x})(y - \bar{y})}{\Sigma(x - \bar{x})^2} = \frac{1305}{250} = 5.22 \text{ ppm}^{-1}$$

The value of c was then found using Equation 13.17:

$$c = \bar{y} - m\bar{x} \qquad \text{Equation 13.17}$$

thus:

$$c = \bar{y} - m\bar{x} = 52 - 5.22 \times 10 = -0.2$$

The equation of the regression line is therefore:

$$y = 5.22x - 0.2$$

A plot of this line is shown in the graph given below. This illustrates that this line does indeed fit the data shown in the scatter graph that is given earlier in this box.

Rearranging the previous equation gives:

$$x = \frac{y + 0.2}{5.22} \text{ ppm}$$

From this, the concentration of calcium in the crime scene sample of water can be calculated as:

$$x = \frac{31 + 0.2}{5.22} = 5.98 \approx 6.0 \text{ ppm}$$

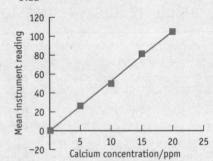

A graph of the calibration data together with the line of best fit that was established by linear regression analysis

It should be noted that linear regression analysis is based on a number of assumptions, namely:

1. the values of x are known with complete accuracy (i.e. no error);
2. if the values of y that correspond to each value of x were also known without error, then the points on the graph would fall on a straight line;
3. that multiple measurements of the value of y for a given value of x would be normally distributed about the true mean of y at that value of x;
4. that as x alters, the variance associated with each of the values of y remains constant.

Finally, a calibration graph that is one shape (e.g. a straight line) in one range of concentrations (or amounts) of analyte may become another shape at other concentrations. This cannot be seen unless the scatter graph is extended into those regions where the shape changes. For this reason, the regression line should not be extended beyond the range of the data points that were used to calculate it.

13.4 Hypothesis testing using *t*-tests

The ideas in this section are founded on those introduced in Section 13.1.3. Therefore, it might be advisable to read that section before tackling this one.

A hypothesis is a reasoned explanation of observations. Consider two samples, each made up of measurements of the same variable. One of these samples could be, for example, made up of measurements of the refractive indices of a number (n_1) of fragments of glass from a crime scene. Similarly, the other sample could be the refractive indices of a number (n_2) of glass fragments recovered from the clothing of a suspect. (Note that the subscripted numbers in the symbols n_1 and n_2 are there to differentiate between the two data sets.) If the means of these samples are different, then there are two possible hypotheses to explain this, namely:

■ that this observation is due to chance alone;

■ that this observation is *not* due to chance alone.

The first of these is the **null hypothesis** (H_0), and the second is the **alternative hypothesis** (H_A). In this case, if we knew the true values for the means and H_0 were correct, then $\mu_1 - \mu_2 = 0$ but if H_A were correct, then $\mu_1 - \mu_2$ 0. Hence, in this case the equations $\mu_1 - \mu_2 = 0$ and $\mu_1 - \mu_2$ 0 can be considered as statements of H_0 and H_A, respectively. A *t*-test can be used to establish whether, at a particular confidence level, there is sufficient evidence to reject $\mu_1 - \mu_2 = 0$ and accept $\mu_1 - \mu_2 \neq 0$. In other words, a *t*-test is a test to establish the significance that can be placed on the observation that there is a difference between two sample means.

To see how this can be done, consider two fairly large samples of n_1 and n_2 observations respectively (to continue with the earlier example, these could be the refractive indices of n_1 fragments of glass from a crime scene and n_2 from a suspect). These samples will each have a mean ($\bar{x}_1$ and $\bar{x}_2$) and a standard deviation (s_1 and s_2). Assuming that the populations from which n_1 and n_2 originate are normally distributed, as the number of observations in each sample is quite large, $\bar{x}_1$ and $\bar{x}_2$ will be reasonably good approximations for μ_1 and μ_2 respectively. Similarly, s_1 and s_2 will be fairly accurate estimates of σ_1 and σ_2 respectively. These estimates can be used to generate good approximations of the normal distributions for each population.

Recall from Section 13.1.3 that if a population-sized number of samples is taken from a normally distributed population, then the distribution of the means of these samples will itself be normal. This second normal distribution (i.e. the distribution of the means) will have a standard deviation that is the standard error of the mean (*SE*, given by Equation 13.3) and a mean that is the same as that of the population from which the samples are taken (i.e. μ). As, in this example, n_1 and n_2 are large, in each case the standard uncertainty (*u*, given by Equation 13.7) will be a good estimate of the standard error of the mean. Figure 13.8 shows the estimated distributions of the populations from which n_1 and n_2 have been drawn and the estimated distribution of the means of repeated samples taken from these populations.

Null hypothesis (H_0)
The hypothesis that the observed difference between the samples (e.g. an observed difference between their means) is due to chance alone.

Alternative hypothesis (H_A)
The hypothesis that the observed difference between the samples (e.g. an observed difference between their means) is not due to chance alone.

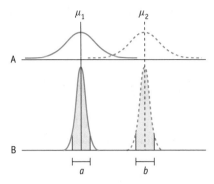

A = The distribution of the populations
B = The distribution of the means of n_1 and n_2 observations

$a = \bar{x}_1 \pm 1.96 \times SEM_1$ ⎫ and therefore, for each distribution of means, the shaded area shows where
$b = \bar{x}_2 \pm 1.96 \times SEM_2$ ⎭ 95% of the data points will reside; where each data point is a mean.

Figure 13.8 The estimated distributions of two populations (A) from which two samples have been drawn of sizes n_1 and n_2 and the estimated distributions that the means of repeated samples of sizes n_1 and n_2 taken from these populations would have (B)

The 95 per cent confidence intervals, calculated using Equation 13.8, of the two data sets are shown as shaded areas on Figure 13.8. Notice that in this case these do not overlap. This means that at a confidence level of more than 95 per cent, it is possible to reject the null hypothesis in favour of the alternative hypothesis. If the shaded areas had overlapped, it would have meant that it would *not* be possible to reject the null hypothesis in favour of the alternative hypothesis at a 95 per cent confidence level.

It is quite possible to test for the difference between sample means as described above. However, it is more convenient to do this by examining the distribution of the differences between the means. Just as the confidence interval for the mean $\bar{x}$ is given by $\bar{x} \pm t \times u$ (Equation 13.8), the confidence interval for the difference between the means, $\bar{x}_1 - \bar{x}_2$, is given by $(\bar{x}_1 - \bar{x}_2) \pm t \times SE_{\bar{x}_1-\bar{x}_2}$. In this, $SE_{\bar{x}_1-\bar{x}_2}$ is the standard error for the difference between $\bar{x}_1$ and $\bar{x}_2$, as calculated from the variance and the number of data points in each sample (i.e. s_1^2, s_2^2, n_1 and n_2)

To understand how $SE_{\bar{x}_1-\bar{x}_2}$ can be calculated, recall Equation 13.7 for the calculation of the standard uncertainty (u):

$$u = \frac{s}{\sqrt{n}}$$
Eq 13.7

Just as u is an estimate of the standard deviation of a population of means, u^2 is an estimate of the variance of the population of means concerned and u^2 is given by Equation 13.19:

$$u^2 = \left(\frac{s}{\sqrt{n}}\right)^2 = \frac{s^2}{n}$$
Eq 13.19

The variance of the difference between $\bar{x}_1$ and $\bar{x}_2$ is $SE_{\bar{x}_1-\bar{x}_2}{}^2$. As variances can be combined by addition, this is given by Equation 13.20:

$$SE_{\bar{x}_1-\bar{x}_2}{}^2 = \frac{s_1^2}{n_1} + \frac{s_2^2}{n_2} \qquad \text{Eq 13.20}$$

Therefore, Equation 13.21 gives $SE_{\bar{x}_1-\bar{x}_2}$:

$$SE_{\bar{x}_1-\bar{x}_2} = \sqrt{\frac{s_1^2}{n_1} + \frac{s_2^2}{n_2}} \qquad \text{Eq 13.21}$$

For example, consider two data sets {2, 6, 3, 4} and {6, 7, 5, 4}. Recall from Box 13.3 that sample variance s^2 is given by

$$s^2 = \frac{\Sigma(x - \bar{x})^2}{n - 1}$$

To find s^2 for each data set, the numbers given in bold in Table 13.3 are calculated from those shown in normal font.

Table 13.3 The calculation of sample variance (s^2) for each of the two data sets {2, 6, 3, 4} and {6, 7, 5, 4}

x_1	$(x_1 - \bar{x}_1)^2$	x_2	$(x_2 - \bar{x}_2)^2$
2	**3.06**	6	**0.25**
6	**5.06**	7	**2.25**
3	**0.56**	5	**0.25**
4	**0.06**	4	**2.25**
$\bar{x}$	**3.75**		**5.50**
$\Sigma(x - \bar{x})^2$	**8.74**		**5.00**
s^2	**2.91**		**1.67**

Therefore, in this case:

$$SE_{\bar{x}_1-\bar{x}_2} = \sqrt{\frac{s_1^2}{n_1} + \frac{s_2^2}{n_2}} = \sqrt{\frac{2.91}{4} + \frac{1.67}{4}} = 1.07$$

Recall that the confidence interval for the difference between the means, $\bar{x}_1 - \bar{x}_2$, is given by $(\bar{x}_1 - \bar{x}_2) \pm t \times SE_{\bar{x}_1-\bar{x}_2}$. The value of t needed to calculate this is found for the desired level of confidence and at $n_1 + n_2 - 2$ degrees of freedom from tables of the distribution of t, such as given in Table 13.2. To continue with the example introduced above, it can be seen from Table 13.2 that a confidence level of 95 per cent (i.e. a significance level of 5 per cent or 0.05) and at $4 + 4 - 2 = 6$ degrees of freedom, $t = 2.45$.

Therefore, $(\bar{x}_1 - \bar{x}_2) \pm t \times SE_{\bar{x}_1-\bar{x}_2} = (5.50 - 3.75) \pm 2.45 \times 1.07$

$$= 1.75 \pm 2.62 = -0.87 \text{ to } 4.37 \qquad \text{Eq 13.22}$$

This includes zero; therefore, it is not possible to *exclude* the possibility at a 95 per cent level of confidence that the null hypothesis (i.e. $\mu_1 - \mu_2 = 0$) is correct (let us call this conclusion 1). In other words, it is *not* possible to reject the null hypothesis in favour of the alternative hypothesis at a 95 per cent confidence level. If the range found by Equation 13.22 had not included zero, then this would mean that at a confidence level of more than 95 per cent it would be possible to reject the null hypothesis in favour of the alternative hypothesis.

There is another equivalent, but more convenient, way of deciding whether the null hypothesis can be rejected at a given confidence level.

Recall that the confidence interval (*CI*) of a sample at a given level of confidence (e.g. 95 per cent) is given by

$$CI = \bar{x} \pm t \times u$$

In this, $t \times u$ is the deviation (*d*) either side of the mean, i.e. $d = t \times u$. Therefore, for a given deviation from $\bar{x}$, t could be calculated thus:

$$t = \frac{d}{u} \qquad \text{Eq 13.23}$$

By extension of this logic, when considering the difference between means, $\bar{x}_1 - \bar{x}_2$, t can be calculated from:

$$t = \frac{\bar{x}_1 - \bar{x}_2}{SE_{\bar{x}_1 - \bar{x}_2}} = \frac{\bar{x}_1 - \bar{x}_2}{\sqrt{\dfrac{s_1^2}{n_1} + \dfrac{s_2^2}{n_2}}} \qquad \text{Eq 13.24}$$

Let us call this calculated t, t_{calc}. For the above example,

$$t_{calc} = \frac{3.75 - 5.5}{\sqrt{\dfrac{2.91}{4} + \dfrac{1.67}{4}}} = \frac{-1.75}{1.07} = -1.63 \qquad \text{Eq 13.25}$$

This can be compared with the value of t obtained from a table of t (such as that given in Table 13.2) at $n_1 + n_2 - 2$ degrees of freedom and the chosen level of confidence. Such a value taken from a table of t is often referred to as the critical value of t and is frequently symbolised t_{crit}. *If $t_{calc} < t_{crit}$, the null hypothesis cannot be rejected at the chosen level of confidence. However, if $t_{calc} > t_{crit}$, the null hypothesis can be rejected in favour of the alternative hypothesis at the chosen level of confidence.* When making such comparisons, t_{calc} is treated as if it had a positive value, irrespective of whether it is positive or negative (i.e. the absolute value of t_{calc} (symbolised $|t_{calc}|$) is used in place of t_{calc} itself).

To return to the example discussed above, at 6 degrees of freedom and at a 95 per cent level of confidence, the tabulated value of t (i.e. t_{crit}) = 2.45. As $t_{calc} < t_{crit}$, the null hypothesis cannot be rejected at the 95 per cent confidence level. This is exactly the same conclusion as conclusion 1.

Note that the calculation given above that is based on Equation 13.24 is an example of a two-sample t-test in which it is assumed that the variances of the two populations are not equal. Table 13.4 summarises the salient features of this and some other common forms of the t-test.

In Table 13.4 mention is made of both one- and two-tailed versions of the t-test. Which of these is performed will depend on the nature of the alternative hypothesis, H_A. A one-tailed t-test would be carried out when the experiment is designed to test the null hypothesis against an alternative that implies direction. That is, H_A would equal one of the following:

$\mu_1 - \mu_2 > 0$ or $\mu_1 - \mu_2 < 0$ in the case of two-sample tests, or

$\mu - \nu > 0$ or $\mu - \nu < 0$ in the case of one-sample tests.

Table 13.4 Some common forms and applications of the *t*-test

Name	Two-sample *t*-test assuming unequal variances	Two-sample *t*-test assuming equal variances	One-sample *t*-test	Paired *t*-test
Application	Testing whether the observed difference between the means of two samples is significant	Testing whether the observed difference between the means of two samples is significant when there is reason to believe that both samples are from populations with the same variance	Testing the significance of the observed difference between the mean of the experimental data and a given value (v)	Testing the significance of the observed difference between two means obtained from the same sample subjects on two occasions
Hypotheses	H_0 is $\mu_1 - \mu_2 = 0$ H_A is $\mu_1 - \mu_2 \neq 0$ or	H_0 is $\mu_1 - \mu_2 = 0$ H_A is $\mu_1 - \mu_2 \neq 0$ or	H_0 is $\mu - v = 0$ H_A is $\mu - v \neq 0$ or	H_0 is $\mu_1 - \mu_2 = 0$ H_A is $\mu_1 - \mu_2 \neq 0$ or
	H_0 is $\mu_1 - \mu_2 = 0$ H_A is $\mu_1 - \mu_2 > 0$ or	H_0 is $\mu_1 - \mu_2 = 0$ H_A is $\mu_1 - \mu_2 > 0$ or	H_0 is $\mu - v \leq 0$ H_A is $\mu - v > 0$ or	H_0 is $\mu_1 - \mu_2 = 0$ H_A is $\mu_1 - \mu_2 > 0$ or
	H_0 is $\mu_1 - \mu_2 = 0$ H_A is $\mu_1 - \mu_2 < 0$	H_0 is $\mu_1 - \mu_2 = 0$ H_A is $\mu_1 - \mu_2 < 0$	H_0 is $\mu - v \geq 0$ H_A is $\mu - v < 0$	H_0 is $\mu_1 - \mu_2 = 0$ H_A is $\mu_1 - \mu_2 < 0$
Calculation of t_{calc}	$t_{calc} = \dfrac{\bar{x}_1 - \bar{x}_2}{\sqrt{\dfrac{s_1^2}{n_1} + \dfrac{s_2^2}{n_2}}}$	$t_{calc} = \dfrac{\bar{x}_1 - \bar{x}_2}{s'\left(\sqrt{\dfrac{1}{n_1} + \dfrac{1}{n_2}}\right)}$ in which $s' = \sqrt{\left[\dfrac{1}{n_1 + n_2 - 2}\right]\left[\Sigma x_1^2 - \dfrac{(\Sigma x_1)^2}{n_1} + \Sigma x_2^2 - \dfrac{(\Sigma x_2)^2}{n_2}\right]}$	$t_{calc} = \dfrac{\bar{x} - v}{u}$	1. For each subject, calculate the difference (d) between the value of the variable in question on the first occasion with its value on the second 2. Subject the data set created by step 1 to a one-sample *t*-test, in which $\bar{x}$ is the mean of the d values, $v = 0$ and $n =$ the number of values of d

(continued overleaf)

Table 13.4 *Continued*

Name	Two-sample t-test assuming unequal variances	The two-sample t-test assuming equal variances	One-sample t-test	Paired t-test
Parameters used when looking up t_{crit} from tabulated values of t such as provided in Appendix 2	The chosen significance level $= \alpha = 1 - \dfrac{w\%}{100}$, $df = n_1 + n_2 - 2$ and, if H_A is $\mu_1 - \mu_2 \neq 0$ number of tails = 2 but if H_A is $\mu_1 - \mu_2 > 0$ or if H_A is $\mu_1 - \mu_2 < 0$ then number of tails = 1	The chosen significance level $= \alpha = 1 - \dfrac{w\%}{100}$, $df = n_1 + n_2 - 2$ and, if H_A is $\mu_1 - \mu_2 \neq 0$ number of tails = 2 but if H_A is $\mu_1 - \mu_2 > 0$ or if H_A is $\mu_1 - \mu_2 < 0$ then number of tails = 1	The chosen significance level $= \alpha = 1 - \dfrac{w\%}{100}$, $df = n - 1$ and, if H_A is $\mu - \nu \neq 0$ number of tails = 2 but if H_A is $\mu - \nu > 0$ or if H_A is $\mu - \nu < 0$ then number of tails = 1	The chosen significance level $= \alpha = 1 - \dfrac{w\%}{100}$, $df = n - 1$ and, if H_A is $\mu_1 - \mu_2 \neq 0$ number of tails = 2 but if H_A is $\mu_1 - \mu_2 > 0$ or if H_A is $\mu_1 - \mu_2 < 0$ then number of tails = 1
If $|t_{calc}| \geq t_{crit}$	Reject H_0 in favour of H_A at a confidence level of $> w\%$ (if $|t_{calc}| > t_{crit}$) or exactly $w\%$ (if $|t_{calc}| = t_{crit}$)			
If $|t_{calc}| < t_{crit}$	Cannot reject H_0 in favour of H_A at a confidence level of $w\%$			

H_0 = null hypothesis; H_A = alternative hypothesis; μ = population mean; $\bar{x}$ = sample mean. Subscripts 1 and 2 refer to populations 1 and 2 (e.g. $\bar{x}_1$ is the mean of the sample of population 1). s^2 = sample variance (see Box 13.3); n = number of data points in a sample; $w\%$ = chosen confidence level (commonly 95 per cent (i.e. $\alpha = 0.05$) or 99 per cent (i.e. $\alpha = 0.01$)); df = degrees of freedom; $|t_{calc}|$ = absolute value of t_{calc}. Note that tests in which the number of tails = 1 are called one-tailed tests, whereas those in which the number of tails = 2 are called two-tailed tests.

However, a two-tailed test would be carried out when the experiment is designed to establish whether there is merely a significant difference between the means (i.e. $\mu_1 - \mu_2 \neq 0$ or $\mu - \nu \neq 0$).

For example, if the diamorphine concentration of street heroin that was seized in any one year was found to be normally distributed, then a *t*-test could be used to test the significance that could be ascribed to a change in the mean diamorphine concentration observed from one year to another. A one-tailed test would be appropriate if the alternative hypothesis were that the concentration of diamorphine in street heroin seized in year one (e.g. 2006) is higher than that seized in year two (e.g. 2004), as in this case the alternative hypothesis would be $\mu_1 - \mu_2 > 0$. In contrast, a two-tailed test would be employed if the alternative hypothesis were that the concentration of diamorphine in street heroin seized in year one is different from that seized in year two (i.e. H_A is that $\mu_1 - \mu_2 \neq 0$). In both cases, the null hypothesis would be that the mean diamorphine concentration was the same in both years (i.e. H_0 is that $\mu_1 - \mu_2 = 0$).

Finally, it is important to realise that the level of confidence, in the context of a *t*-test, is the probability of not rejecting H_0 in those instances in which H_0 is true. For example, if the level of confidence is 95 per cent and if H_0 is true, then in the long run 95 per cent of the times that the test is carried out H_0 will not be rejected; however, on 5 per cent of occasions it will be wrongly rejected. This is not a particularly easy concept and, because of this, great care needs to be exercised when stating the outcome of a *t*-test. As outlined in Table 13.4, there are three possible outcomes, namely:

- if $|t_{calc}| > t_{crit,}$ H_0 is rejected in favour of H_A at a confidence level of $> w$ per cent;
- if $|t_{calc}| = t_{crit,}$ H_0 is rejected in favour of H_A at a confidence level of w per cent;
- if $|t_{calc}| < t_{crit,}$ H_0 cannot be rejected in favour of H_A at a confidence level of w per cent.

where w per cent is the confidence level at which the test was carried out. To illustrate how easy it is to make a mistake in this area, consider a case in which the correct statement is 'H_0 cannot be rejected in favour of H_A at a confidence level of 95 per cent'. This could be *wrongly* interpreted to mean that there is a 95 per cent probability that H_0 is correct. If in doubt, proceed as follows:

1. Define what is meant in the case in question by each of H_0 and H_A.
2. Perform the appropriate *t*-test (see Table 13.4).
3. Select the one of the three bullet points given above that is applicable in the case in question and use the wording given, substituting the chosen level of confidence in place of w per cent.

13.5 Parametric and non-parametric tests

The *t*-test described in the previous section makes use of the actual values of the data points in the data sets that are being compared. Statistical tests that make use of actual values are called parametric tests. There are a number of such parametric tests, each designed to address different statistical needs.

Parametric tests are applicable to normally distributed data or data sets that can be made to be normally distributed by transformation (e.g. by taking logarithms of each of the values in the data set). However, there are types of data, including ordinal data (Section 13.1.1), that cannot be analysed by such tests. A range of non-parametric tests have been devised for cases in which parametric tests are not applicable, and for many parametric tests there is a non-parametric equivalent. For example, the Mann–Whitney test is a non-parametric equivalent of the unpaired two-sample *t*-test. Likewise, the Wilcoxon test is a non-parametric equivalent of the paired *t*-test and the one-sample *t*-test.

In general, in non-parametric tests the data are placed in ascending order and then each data point is assigned a rank number that denotes its position in that order. The non-parametric test in question then uses this rank and not the actual value of the data point. Note that as nominal data (Section 13.1.1) does not have values and cannot be placed in ranks, such data cannot be tested by either parametric or non-parametric tests.

Although it is generally true that data that can be subjected to parametric testing can also be analysed using the non-parametric equivalents, the former of these is chosen wherever possible. This is because parametric tests are, in most cases, more powerful than non-parametric tests.

Further discussion of the range of parametric and non-parametric tests available is beyond the scope of this text, and the interested reader is directed to the further reading section of this chapter for more information on these topics.

13.6 Likelihood ratios and the Bayesian approach

Under cross-examination, the interpretation and evaluation of the scientific test results by the forensic scientist are likely to constitute the most significant area of contention (Chapter 14, Section 14.4). The opinion of the forensic scientist is formed by what he or she considers to be the most probable explanation of the results. However, the forensic scientist must be careful in the way that he or she expresses opinions. In particular, the forensic scientist should not make any statements that directly imply the guilt, or otherwise, of the defendant standing trial. Such decisions are the province of the jurors or magistrates hearing the case.

One means by which a forensic scientist can express opinion is via the statement of a likelihood ratio. This can, by the application of Bayes' theorem, help those hearing the case to establish the odds of the accused being guilty (the concept of odds is explained in Box 13.1, as is its relationship to probability). Unfortunately, this is not a particularly easy topic. In order to approach it, let us first consider what is meant by the term **likelihood ratio** (*LR*). This is defined as follows:

$$LR = \frac{\text{The probability of the evidence occurring given that a hypothesis is correct}}{\text{The probability of the evidence occurring given than an alternative hypothesis is correct}} \qquad \text{Eq 13.26}$$

or, using symbols:

$$LR = \frac{P(E|H_1)}{P(E|H_2)} \qquad \text{Eq 13.27}$$

in which P stands for 'the probability of', E stands for 'the evidence occurring', | stands for 'given that', H_1 is the hypothesis under test and H_2 is the alternative hypothesis.

As shown in Table 13.5, a likelihood ratio of 1 means that the evidence supports neither the hypothesis nor the alternative hypothesis, and such evidence is said to have no probative value. Likelihood ratios greater than 1 support the hypothesis, whereas those less than 1 support the alternative hypothesis. The further the likelihood ratio is from 1, the greater is the probative value of the evidence.

Likelihood ratio
The probability of the evidence occurring given that a hypothesis is correct divided by the probability of the evidence occurring given that an alternative hypothesis is correct.

Table 13.5 Likelihood ratios and the strength of evidence

		Likelihood ratio $(LR) = \dfrac{P(E|H_1)}{P(E|H_2)}$	A verbal scale of strength of evidence*
Increasing probative value	Increasing support for the hypothesis (H_1) being correct	10 000 < LR	Very strong support for H_1
		1000 < LR ≤ 10 000	Strong support for H_1
		100 < LR ≤ 1000	Moderately strong support for H_1
		10 < LR ≤ 100	Moderate support for H_1
		1 < LR ≤ 10	Limited support for H_1
No probative value	Evidence has no ability to support H_1 over H_2 or vice versa	1	
Increasing probative value	Increasing support for the alternative hypothesis (H_2) being correct	1 > LR ≥ 0.1	Limited support for H_2
		0.1 > LR ≥ 0.01	Moderate support for H_2
		0.01 > LR ≥ 0.001	Moderately strong support for H_2
		0.001 > LR ≥ 0.0001	Strong support for H_2
		0.0001 > LR	Very strong support for H_2

*Evett, I. W., Jackson, G., Lambert, J. A. and McCrossan, S. (2000) 'The impact of the principles of evidence interpretation and the structure and content of statements', *Science and Justice* **40**, pp. 233–239.

In the forensic context, the convention that is followed is that:

■ the hypothesis is an account of the evidence that would be true if the prosecution's case is correct;

■ the alternative hypothesis is an account of the evidence that would be true if the defence's case is correct.

As discussed in Section 13.6.1, there are specific rules that govern the choice of the hypothesis and the alternative hypothesis. One possibility that these rules allow is that the alternative hypothesis may simply be that the hypothesis referred to in the numerator (i.e. the upper part of the fraction) is not correct. In this case, the likelihood ratio is as given by Equation 13.28:

$$LR = \frac{\text{The probability of the evidence occurring given that}}{\text{The probability of the evidence occurring given than the}} \qquad \text{Eq 13.28}$$
a particular hypothesis is correct / same hypothesis is *not* correct

Using symbols, this becomes:

$$LR = \frac{P(E|H)}{P(E|\bar{H})} \qquad \text{Eq 13.29}$$

in which P, E and $|$ have the same meanings as in Equation 13.27 and H is the hypothesis under test. The bar in the symbol $\bar{H}$ stands for 'not'. Hence, $\bar{H}$ means 'the hypothesis, H, is not correct' and is termed the 'not hypothesis'.

In order to establish why the likelihood ratio is a useful concept, let us consider a hypothetical example:[1] consider a case in which an adult is known to have been at a crime scene. In this case, in order to establish the guilt or innocence of the accused, it is important to ascertain whether this person was a man.

Before hearing any evidence, the jury (or magistrates) will know that, to a very good approximation, half of the population is male. Therefore, the probability of any one adult selected at random being a man is 0.5. On the basis of this information alone, the odds that the person at the scene was a man can be worked out as:

$$\frac{0.5}{(1 - 0.5)} = \frac{0.5}{0.5} = \frac{1}{1} \qquad \text{Eq 13.30}$$

i.e. 1 to 1.

Useful though this information is, it is not particularly discriminating. However, if an eyewitness were available who could testify that the person concerned was at least six feet (1.8 m) tall, then this might suggest that it is more likely that the individual at the scene was a man than a woman. This suggestion is based on the observation that the proportion of adult males who are at least six feet tall is greater than that of adult females. In an attempt to quantify the value of this evidence, an expert witness could be asked to inform the court of the percentage of the adults of each sex with a height of at least six feet. For argument's sake, let us

---

1 This example is modelled on a hypothetical case described by Robertson and Vignaux (1995); see the Further reading section at the end of this chapter for full bibliographic details.

assume that 5 per cent of men and 0.5 per cent of women fall into this category. In other words, the probability that a man who was selected randomly from all of the men in the population would be at least six feet tall is 5 per cent, whereas the equivalent probability among women is 0.5 per cent. This information can be used by the expert witness to generate a likelihood ratio to help the court test the hypothesis that the person at the scene was a man, thus:

$$LR = \frac{\text{The probability of a person being} \geq 6\,\text{ft tall given that the person is a man}}{\text{The probability of the person being} \geq 6\,\text{ft tall given that the person is not a man}}$$

$$= \frac{5}{0.5} = 10 \qquad\qquad \text{Eq 13.31}$$

This, in turn, can be used by those hearing the case to modify the 1-to-1 odds that they had calculated previously, thus:

$$\frac{1}{1} \times 10 = \frac{10}{1} \qquad\qquad \text{Eq 13.32}$$

i.e. the odds are 10 to 1 in favour of the person at the scene being a man. This figure is much more discriminating than the earlier 1-to-1 odds.

In the language of the Bayesian approach, the original 1-to-1 odds are an example of **prior odds** and the final 10-to-1 odds are an example of **posterior odds**. Both prior odds and posterior odds are mathematical statements of what is known about the hypothesis being tested (in this case, that the person at the scene was a man). However, the prior odds represent what is known before the new evidence is taken into account, whereas the posterior odds embody what is known after this new evidence, expressed as a likelihood ratio, has been incorporated. According to **Bayes' theorem**:

$$\text{Prior odds} \times LR = \text{posterior odds} \qquad\qquad \text{Eq 13.33}$$

Note that the prior odds are written as odds in favour of the hypothesis, producing posterior odds that are also expressed as odds in favour of the hypothesis. Posterior odds are a mathematical statement of what is known about the hypothesis being tested after the implications of the new evidence have been taken into account.

It is important to realise that the expert witness provides the likelihood ratio and not the prior odds. It may be argued that this is all that an expert witness can and, indeed, should do. In order to assist the jury in its understanding of the significance of a given likelihood ratio, the forensic scientist may express it verbally in terms of strength of evidence, according to a scale such as that given in Table 13.5. The prior odds are established either by the prior knowledge of those hearing the case or as a consequence of evidence presented during the trial. The expert witness will not necessarily have all of this information; nor is it his or her job to establish the guilt or innocence of the accused but to assist the court in arriving at the correct decision.

In the case in question, for example, evidence presented during the trial might have established that the person at the scene was a nurse. If it is assumed, for the sake of argument, that only 2 per cent of nurses are men, then this will, in effect, radically alter the prior odds. Instead of being 1 to 1, they would become:

Prior odds
A mathematical statement of what is known about the hypothesis being tested before the implications of the new evidence have been taken into account.

Posterior odds
A mathematical statement of what is known about the hypothesis being tested after the implications of the new evidence have been taken into account.

Bayes' theorem (also called Bayes' rule)
The posterior odds equal the prior odds multiplied by the likelihood ratio.

$$\frac{0.02}{(1-0.02)} = \frac{0.02}{0.98} = \frac{0.02 \div 0.02}{0.98 \div 0.02} = \frac{1}{49} \qquad \text{Eq 13.34}$$

i.e. 1 to 49 in favour of the hypothesis.

This would mean that the posterior odds would become:

$$\frac{1}{49} \times 10 = \frac{10}{49} \approx \frac{1}{5} \qquad \text{Eq 13.35}$$

i.e. odds of 5 to 1 *against* the person at the scene being a man.

If the expert witness had attempted to establish the posterior odds for the court, without knowing that the person was a nurse, then he or she would have given misleading testimony. The expert witness would have given the impression that the person at the scene was more likely to be a man. However, knowing that this person is a nurse would lead the court to the conclusion that the opposite was true.

Arguably, the Bayesian approach is of particular value when considering transfer evidence (also referred to as trace evidence). This occurs in accordance with Locard's exchange principle, which states that 'every contact leaves a trace'. Thus, between any victim and perpetrator of a particular crime, or between any crime scene and individual present at that scene, a transfer of evidence is likely to occur that could, potentially, link the two together. As demonstrated by the variety of topics dealt with in this book, the range of materials that may constitute transfer evidence is wide and includes fibres, glass fragments and body fluids (on which DNA analysis may be performed), to name but a few. The Bayesian approach may also be applied to evidence based on marks and impressions.

13.6.1 The choice of hypotheses and the hierarchy of propositions

Recall from Equation 13.27 that a likelihood ratio (*LR*) may be written thus:

$$LR = \frac{P(E|H_1)}{P(E|H_2)} \qquad \text{Eq 13.36}$$

in which P stands for 'the probability of', E stands for 'the evidence occurring', | stands for 'given that', H_1 is the hypothesis under test and H_2 is the alternative hypothesis.

In order for a likelihood ratio to be meaningful, H_1 and H_2 must be statements that are either true or false. Furthermore, they must be mutually exclusive; in other words, in order to create a meaningful likelihood ratio, it must be impossible for both of the propositions to be true. For example, if H_1 is that the perpetrator of the crime is male, then an acceptable H_2 would be that the perpetrator of the crime is not male. However, if H_2 were that the perpetrator of the crime was an adult, then this would not be appropriate, as it is entirely possible to be both male and adult.

In the example in which H_1 is that the perpetrator of the crime is male and H_2 is that the perpetrator of the crime is not male, then H_1 and H_2 are not only mutually exclusive but also exhaustive. Two hypotheses are exhaustive when between them they account for all possibilities. In the example under consideration, H_2 could be written as 'H_1 is not correct'. If H_1 and H_2 are mutually exclusive, then defining H_2 as being not H_1 ensures that H_1 and H_2 are exhaustive. However, it is not necessary for the two hypotheses of a likelihood ratio to be exhaustive. Indeed, there are scenarios in which an accurate reflection of the probative value of the evidence can be achieved only if H_1 and H_2 are not exhaustive.

For example, take a case in which human blood is found at a murder scene of a type that, for argument's sake, is found in 1 in every 200 people in the general population. Given this scenario, let us consider what the likelihood ratio would be associated with finding that the blood of the accused was of the same type as found at the crime scene. In doing this, it will be assumed that it is not possible for a person's blood type to change and that the test for blood types is error-free. On this basis, if H_1 is that the blood found at the scene was from the accused and H_2 is that the blood found at the scene was from not from the accused (i.e. H_2 = not H_1), then the likelihood ratio generated by this evidence is:

$$LR = \frac{P(E|H_1)}{P(E|H_2)} = \frac{1}{\left(\frac{1}{200}\right)} = 200 \qquad \text{Eq 13.37}$$

If you have difficulty in understanding why the denominator is 1/200, note that H_2 could equally have been written as 'that the blood found at the scene was from any one person other than from the accused'. As this person is taken at random from the general population, there is a 1 in 200 probability that his or her blood type will be the same as that of the accused. Note that in this example H_1 and H_2 are both mutually exclusive and exhaustive.

Using the verbal scale given in Table 13.5, the likelihood ratio given by Equation 13.37 is moderately strong evidence in support of the blood at the scene originating from the accused.

Let us now imagine that the murder was committed by stabbing the victim to death and that the victim's blood type was the same as that of the accused. Now, the two most likely hypotheses are that the blood found at the scene was from the accused (H_1) and that the blood found at the scene was from the victim (H_2).

$$\frac{P(E|H_1)}{P(E|H_2)} = \frac{1}{1} = 1 \qquad \text{Eq 13.38}$$

which, as shown in Table 13.5 has no probative value. Note that, as before, H_1 and H_2 are mutually exclusive. However, they are no longer exhaustive. Nonetheless, they more accurately portray the full situation than do the H_1 and H_2 of Equation 13.37.

It is useful to draw a distinction between explanations and propositions.[2] An **explanation** is any statement that accounts for the existence of the evidence in the state in which it was discovered. For example, 'The DNA profile obtained from the semen found on the knickers was identical to that from the suspect because the semen originated from the suspect.' Let us refer to this as Explanation A. An alternative explanation would be 'The DNA profile obtained from the semen found on the knickers was identical to that from the suspect because the semen originated from another man with an identical DNA profile to that of the suspect.' This alternative will be denoted Explanation B. For each of these explanations, the probability of the

Explanation
Any statement that accounts for the existence of the evidence in the state in which it was discovered.

---

2 Evett, I. W., Jackson, G. and Lambert, J. A. (2000) 'More on the hierarchy of propositions: exploring the distinction between explanations and propositions', *Science and Justice* 40, pp. 3–10.

evidence occurring given that the explanation is correct is 1. This means that a likelihood ratio constructed using these explanations would also be 1. As shown in Table 13.5, this has no probative value. This is despite the fact that the DNA evidence does provide information about the origin of the semen, clearly implying that this evidence should have probative value.

To reveal this probative value, it is necessary to use propositions, not merely explanations, as the hypotheses when constructing the likelihood ratio. In this context, **propositions** are statements that are designed in pairs by carefully taking into consideration the circumstances of the case. To illustrate this, consider Explanation A. If this were a statement of the prosecution's contention, then a meaningful alternative could be created by re-wording Explanation B to give 'The DNA profile obtained from the semen found on the knickers was identical to that from the suspect because the semen originated from some other unknown man.' Unlike Explanation B, the probability of the evidence occurring given that this alternative is correct is not 1. Instead, it equals the frequency in the relevant population of men of the DNA profile that was identified from the semen. For argument's sake, assume that the profile in question has a frequency of 2.0×10^{-14} (the method used to calculate DNA profile frequencies is described in Chapter 6). Note that, as before, the probability of the evidence occurring given that Explanation A is correct is 1. This means that the likelihood ratio constructed using Explanation A and the meaningful alternative would have a value of $1/(2.0 \times 10^{-14}) = 5 \times 10^{13}$, indicating correctly that this DNA evidence has very great probative value indeed. In replacing Explanation B with the meaningful alternative given above, a pair of propositions has been created. This has happened because the re-wording of Explanation B has taken into account the circumstances of the case and the wording of Explanation A.

Arguably, for any given piece of evidence, the likelihood ratio that is most pertinent to the task of the court is the one in which H_1 is that the accused is guilty of the crime in question and H_2 is that the accused is not guilty of that same crime. However, in many instances, the forensic scientist does not have all of the information that is necessary in order to formulate this likelihood ratio.

Take, for example, a crime in which the perpetrator broke a window. Consider a situation in which the scientist has been provided with fragments of glass recovered from a suspect's clothing (the questioned sample) and control pieces of glass taken from that which remains within the window frame at the crime scene. The scientist then measured the refractive indices of the questioned and control samples and found them to be indistinguishable. If the scientist had at his or her disposal a suitable database of the frequency distribution of the population of glass refractive indices, then he or she could evaluate the following likelihood ratio:

$$LR = \frac{P(E|H_1)}{P(E|H_2)}$$

Eq 13.39

in which E is that the refractive indices of the questioned and control samples are indistinguishable, H_1 is that the questioned sample originated from the broken window at the crime scene, and H_2 is that the questioned sample did *not* originate from the broken window at the crime scene.

Notice that the H_1 and H_2 of Equation 13.39 are not worded in terms of any crime, or the guilt or innocence of the accused. This is because the scientist does not have the necessary information on which to assess a likelihood ratio based on

Propositions
Statements that are designed in pairs by carefully taking into consideration the circumstances of the case.

such concepts. Instead H_1 and H_2 of Equation 13.39 are worded in terms of the source of the questioned sample. They are, therefore, examples of source-level propositions (also called level I propositions). Other examples of pairs of source-level propositions are given in Table 13.6. As can be seen from this table, two other levels of proposition are also recognised, namely the activity level (level II) and the offence level (level III, which is also referred to as the crime level).

As it is the task of the court to establish whether the accused is guilty, level III propositions are more pertinent to its deliberations than are level II propositions, which, in turn, are of greater pertinence than level I propositions. It is for this reason that Table 13.6 represents a hierarchy of propositions.

With this in mind, returning to the example of the crime in which a window was broken, it is now clear that it would be more useful to the court if H_1 and H_2 of Equation 13.39 could be worded as level II propositions. Such propositions are termed activity-level propositions as they are worded in terms of actions. Ideally, in this case, as in others, these activity-level propositions would reflect the competing scenarios presented by the prosecution and the defence. H_1 could be that the accused broke the window and H_2 could be that the accused was not present when the window was broken. These are not the only possibilities, however. For example, the defence might concede that the accused was present when the window was broken but propose that he was not the person who broke the window. In this case, H_1 might well remain as defined earlier in this paragraph, but H_2 would become that the accused was present when the window was broken but did not break it. In order to assess such activity-level propositions, the scientist would require more information than was needed to calculate the likelihood ratio presented in Equation 13.39. For example, data on the transfer of glass fragments to clothing and persistence of these fragments on clothing would be required. Similarly, information on how the window was broken (e.g. was a stone thrown through it or was it kicked in?), and the time that had elapsed between the incident and the recovery of the fragments from the suspect's clothing, would be needed. Also of value would be knowledge of the distribution of the glass fragments on the suspect's clothing. Given the enhanced pertinence to the job of the court that level II propositions have over their level 1 counterparts, it can be argued that, wherever possible, the forensic scientist should base his or her assessment of the probative value of the evidence on activity-level propositions.

Level II propositions have a further advantage over level 1 propositions; that is, they can also be used to assess the probative value of the absence of evidence. To continue with the example of the case involving the broken window, not finding any fragments of glass on the clothing of the suspect may well be evidentially significant. However, source-level propositions cannot be used to assess this. In contrast, provided that there is enough background information available, the following likelihood ratio could be calculated:

$$LR = \frac{P(E|H_1)}{P(E|H_2)}$$

Eq 13.40

in which E is that no fragments of glass were recovered from the suspect's clothing, H_1 is that the suspect broke the window at the crime scene, and H_2 is that the suspect was not near the window when it was broken. The types of information that would be needed to calculate this likelihood ratio would include transfer and

Table 13.6 The hierarchy of propositions

Level	Examples of pairs of propositions, H_1 and H_2	Typical information required	Pertinence to the task of the court
level I (source level)	H_1 The fibres on the deceased came from Mr X's jacket H_2 The fibres on the deceased came from a textile item other than Mr X's jacket H_1 The blood on Mr Y came from Miss Z H_2 The blood on Mr Y came from some person other than Miss Z H_1 The paint on the deceased's clothes came from the vehicle in question H_2 The paint on the deceased's clothes came from some other vehicle	1. Characteristics of the questioned and control items 2. Frequency of occurrence of items with the same characteristics as that of the control within the population of similar items 3. Data that inform the selection of the appropriate population when assessing the frequency referred to in 2	Increasing pertinence
level II (activity level)	H_1 Mr W punched Mr Z H_2 Someone other than Mr W punched Mr Z H_1 Mr P broke the window at the crime scene H_2 Someone other than Mr P broke the window at the crime scene H_1 The vehicle in question struck the deceased H_2 A vehicle other than the one in question struck the deceased	1 to 3 plus: 4. Circumstances of the case as these will, for example, influence the transfer and persistence of trace evidence such as fragments of glass	
level III (offence level; also called crime level)	H_1 Mrs V murdered Mr U H_2 Someone other than Mrs V murdered Mr U H_1 The arson was committed by Mr B H_2 Mr B did not have anything to do with the arson H_1 Miss C committed the criminal damage H_2 The criminal damage was committed by someone other than Miss C	1 to 4 plus: 5. Information from outside the scientific domain, such as the legal definition of an offence or knowledge of the truthfulness of an alibi	

persistence data, the alleged means by which the window was broken, and the alleged actions of the suspect between the time of the incident and that of the attempted collection of glass fragments from his or her clothing.

In order to assess the evidence using level III propositions, yet more information is required than is needed in the case of level II propositions. Importantly, this additional information includes knowledge that is not scientific in nature, such as the legal definitions of crimes. Arguably, such knowledge is outside the forensic scientist's field of expertise and is, therefore, the domain of the court. If this argument is accepted, then a forensic scientist cannot properly assess many if not all level III propositions.

Finally, it is noteworthy that in Table 13.6, none of the alternative hypotheses (i.e. the propositions labelled H_2) given as examples is written as a not hypothesis.[3] This is for a good reason. To understand this, let us consider the process that the scientist would go through in order to calculate the likelihood ratio that is given by Equation 13.39. On the basis that the refractive indices of the questioned and control samples would be indistinguishable if they originated from the same piece of glass, $P(E|H_1) = 1$. To establish the value of the denominator of Equation 13.39, the scientist would examine the database to find out the frequency with which glass of the refractive index of interest is found in the population. This frequency would equal $P(E|H_2)$. Notice that to find the value for $P(E|H_2)$, the scientist in fact equated H_2 with 'the questioned sample originated from a broken glass item other than the broken window at the crime scene'. Although this is equivalent to the statement of H_2 given in the paragraph that contains Equation 13.39, it is arguably more useful as it informs the reader how an assessment of $P(E|H_2)$ would be arrived at. For this reason, a case can be made that it is good practice to avoid wording the alternative hypothesis as simply the not hypothesis but instead to phrase it in a way that reflects the process that was used to evaluate $P(E|H_2)$.

13.6.2 The prosecutor's fallacy and the defence attorney's fallacy

One of the advantages of being conversant with the Bayesian approach is that it heightens the scientist's awareness of certain common but serious errors of thought.

Take, for example, the interpretation of data provided by a chemical test for the presence of a particular controlled substance, e.g. heroin. For argument's sake, imagine that exhaustive studies have shown that this test gives a positive result in 99 per cent of cases in which it is applied to samples that contain this controlled substance. Consider a case in which a forensic scientist has performed this test and is presenting her findings in court. The barrister asks: 'To avoid any confusion, please will you confirm that this evidence means that there is a 99 per cent probability that the substance is, or at least contains, heroin?'

At first glance, it might appear that the answer to this should be 'Yes, I can confirm that.' However, this would be wrong. To explore this further, it is useful to introduce the following:

---

3 If the reader is unsure what is meant by the phrase 'not hypothesis', see Equation 13.29 for an explanation.

$$P(A|B) = C\%$$ Eq 13.41

This stands for the probability (P) of a specific assertion (A) being true given that ($|$) another specific assertion (B) is also true is $C\%$. In this instance, A is the positive test result and B is that the substance is, or at least contains, heroin. The exhaustive studies referred to above concluded that:

$$P(A|B) = 99\%$$ Eq 13.42

The statement represented by Equation 13.42 is called a *conditional*. At this stage it is important to realise that:

$$P(A|B) \neq P(B|A)$$ Eq 13.43

Transpose the conditional

To equate $P(A|B)$ with $P(B|A)$, which is an error of thought. This error is also known as the prosecutor's fallacy.

To claim otherwise is to **transpose the conditional** and is a serious error.[4] In the example cited earlier, that concerned the barrister's question, the statement that the witness is being invited to confirm is a transposition of the conditional and is therefore wrong. As in this case, transposing the conditional within the forensic context normally artificially bolsters the prosecution's case. For this reason, this error is also referred to as the *prosecutor's fallacy*.

As introduced earlier in this chapter, the likelihood ratio (LR) defined by Equation 13.26 can be written using symbolism of the type given in Equation 13.41, by substituting the A and B of Equation 13.41 with more specific symbols, thus:

$$LR = \frac{P(E|H_1)}{P(E|H_2)}$$ Eq 13.27

in which P stands for 'the probability of', E stands for 'the evidence occurring', $|$ stands for 'given that', H_1 is the hypothesis under test and H_2 is the alternative hypothesis.

From Equation 13.27, it is clear that each likelihood ratio presents two opportunities to transpose the conditional, as this could occur in either the numerator (i.e. the upper part of the fraction) or the denominator. In forensic applications, likelihood ratios are normally written such that H_1 is the hypothesis that is being put forward by the prosecution and H_2 is the hypothesis propounded by the defence. With this in mind, the example concerning the chemical test for controlled substances is an example of the potential for this error to occur in the numerator. Let us now consider an example of such a mistake in the denominator.

Consider a case in which a bloodstain was left at the scene and that this had a blood type that was the same as the defendant's, and that this is found in 1 in 200 people in the general population. Let H_1 be that the bloodstain came from the defendant and H_2 be that it came from some other unknown person (i.e. anyone except the defendant). Assuming that a person could not change their blood type and that the test for the blood type is free of errors, $P(E|H_1)$ of Equation 13.27 would equal 1 (i.e. 100 per cent) in this case, and $P(E|H_2)$ would be given by:

$$P(E|H_2) = \frac{1}{200} = 5 \times 10^{-3}$$ Eq 13.44

---

4 To see that transposing the conditional is a mistake, let us consider an obvious example. Let A be that the animal is a bird and B be that the animal is a robin. Then, as the only animals that are robins are birds, $P(A|B) = 100\%$. However, not all birds are robins and so $P(B|A) \neq 100\%$.

So the overall likelihood ratio would be:

$$\frac{P(E|H_1)}{P(E|H_2)} = \frac{1}{5 \times 10^{-3}} = 200 \qquad\qquad \text{Eq 13.45}$$

which is moderately strong evidence in support of the prosecution's case (Table 13.5).

In terms of odds (see Box 13.1), the denominator in Equation 13.45 would be:

$$\frac{5 \times 10^{-3}}{(1 - 5 \times 10^{-3})} \approx \frac{5 \times 10^{-3}}{1} = \frac{1}{200} \qquad\qquad \text{Eq 13.46}$$

That is 200 to 1 against the bloodstain having the same blood type as the defendant if the bloodstain had been left by anyone other than the defendant. Transposing this conditional would lead to the erroneous conclusion that the odds of the bloodstain having been left by anyone other than the defendant are 200 to 1 against. To see that this is wrong, note that there are many millions of people in the world with the same blood type as the defendant. If any one of these were chosen at random, and as blood type evidence is the only evidence under consideration, the odds of this person leaving the stain would be exactly the same as that of the defendant.

Another error of logic that is commonly made is what is known as the **defence attorney's fallacy**. The error committed during this fallacy is to assume that because a feature that links a defendant to a crime could equally well link many other people to that crime, the evidence provided by this feature is worthless. To see why this is an erroneous argument, note that a likelihood ratio is an expression of the probative value of the evidence that generated it. Evidence that either tells strongly for the prosecution or the defence is said to have high probative value. Such items of evidence will have either large likelihood ratios (if they tell for the prosecution's case) or small likelihood ratios (if they tell for the defence's case). Evidence with no probative value will have a likelihood ratio of 1. Note also that likelihood ratios associated with different pieces of independent evidence[5] can simply be multiplied together to generate a likelihood ratio that represents the overall probative value of these pieces of evidence. This means that several pieces of evidence, each of which tells for the prosecution's case but with low individual probative values, may combine to produce a high probative value overall. Evidence that links a defendant to a crime but that could equally well link many other people to that crime has low probative value but is not worthless.

> **Defence attorney's fallacy**
> *It is an error of thought to assume that because a feature that links a defendant to a crime could equally well link many other people to that crime, the evidence provided by this feature is worthless.*

13.6.3 The use of the Bayesian approach in jury trials

In a number of important rulings concerning cases that involved DNA evidence, the Court of Appeal (Criminal Division) has criticised the explicit explanation to jurors in court of the Bayesian approach as a means by which they can combine all of the evidence that they hear in a particular case. Furthermore, the Court of Appeal has recommended that experts presenting DNA evidence do not report a likelihood ratio but instead provide a random occurrence ratio. This is what is commonly

---

5 Two pieces of evidence are independent if knowing about the existence of one of these would not alter the likelihood ratio associated with the other. Likelihood ratios associated with pieces of evidence that are not independent can be combined but not by simple multiplication. Details of this are available in the Further reading section at the end of this chapter.

termed the match probability (Chapter 6, Section 6.4.2) and is the probability of a person chosen at random from the population of interest having the same DNA profile as that of the defendant. Provided that the expert has sufficient knowledge to be able to do so, the Court of Appeal has suggested that the DNA expert might also properly tell the jury how many individuals in a given group of people would have the profile in question. With this in mind, for example, the expert might tell the jury how many people in the population of the UK could be expected to have the same DNA profile as the defendant. However, to be in keeping with the findings of the Court of Appeal, the expert's evidence should stop short of explanations of the use of the Bayesian method for combining evidence.

The Court of Appeal has also provided guidelines to judges for their use when summing up the importance of DNA evidence, providing the following by way of an exemplar:

> Members of the jury, if you accept the scientific evidence called by the Crown this indicates that there are probably only four or five white males in the United Kingdom from whom that semen stain could have come. The defendant is one of them. If that is the position, the decision you have to reach, on all the evidence, is whether you are sure that it was the defendant who left that stain or whether it is possible that it was one of that other small group of men who share the same DNA characteristics.[6]

Clearly, this makes no use of Bayes' theorem.

The Bayesian approach provides a logical framework for evidence evaluation. Therefore, a very strong case can be made for its usefulness to a forensic scientist when he or she is assessing the probative value of a given piece(s) of evidence that has or have been analysed by methods that are within the scientist's field of expertise. However, as has been made clear by the Court of Appeal, at least in England and Wales, there are serious misgivings about its use as a tool by which juries can combine the various items of evidence that are presented to them in a given case.

13.7 Summary

■ Data are facts and figures that convey information. Forensic scientists gather data that provide evidence either for or against the prosecution's case. In order to be able to present the evidence in court, the data on which evidence is based must be analysed, interpreted and evaluated. In this context, analysis can be thought of as the characterisation of the item under consideration. This might involve, for example, the establishment of the concentration of one of the components of a mixture. Interpretation is the step in which the data from the analysis phase are used to establish the nature of the item being examined. Finally, evaluation is the process of placing into the context of the case the data that have been obtained from the other two steps.

■ Statistical tools have been developed that are of value in each of these three aspects of the forensic scientist's work. For example, analysis frequently requires calibration graphs to be constructed, and regression analysis allows the line of best fit to be established for such graphs. Interpretation can be aided by, for example, t-tests. For instance, these can be used to test whether two groups of fragments of glass, one from the crime scene and one from the clothing of a suspect, are significantly different from each other. The evaluation of evidence is arguably well served by the Bayesian approach, as this allows the probative value of the evidence under consideration to be calculated.

6 R. v. Doheny and Adams [1997] 1 Cr. App. R. 369.

Problems

Note that outline answers to these problems are provided on the book's accompanying website.

1. The following data were obtained when a sample of blood was repeatedly analysed for its alcohol content. Is it possible to be 95 per cent confident that this sample was above the drink-drive limit of $80\,mg/100\,ml$?

Measurement number	Alcohol content/mg per 100 ml
1	82
2	81
3	79
4	80
5	83

2. Two analysts, one with considerably more experience than the other, calibrated the same automatic volumetric pipette. This was done by repeatedly using the pipette to deliver samples of water. The temperature of the water was known and the weight of each sample was determined to four decimal places of a gram. Literature values were then used to find the density of water at the measured temperature in g/cm^3 to five decimal places. From this, the volume of water delivered in each sample was calculated. The data generated are given below:

Volume of each sample/ml	
Experienced analyst	Inexperienced analyst
0.2012	0.2021
0.1988	0.2022
0.1985	0.2021
0.2016	0.2023

   (a) Comment on the data given above as far as you are able. Note that the volume that the pipette was designed to deliver was $200\,\mu l$.

   (b) If, after answering part (a) of this question, you were informed that while the experienced analyst changed the disposable tip of the pipette between samples, the inexperienced analyst used the same pipette tip throughout, how would this change your answer to part (a) of this question?

3. A forensic scientist determined the refractive indices of each of four fragments of glass obtained from the crime scene and each of four fragments of glass obtained from the suspect's clothing. This resulted in the data shown in the table overleaf.

Glass from crime scene		Glass from suspect	
Fragment no.	Refractive index	Fragment no.	Refractive index
1	1.51156	5	1.51162
2	1.51149	6	1.51163
3	1.51161	7	1.51160
4	1.51160	8	1.51161

The defence team asked to be supplied with a fragment of glass from the crime scene and a fragment of glass taken from the suspect's clothing. These were subsequently analysed in an independent laboratory. Using the same methods as used by the forensic scientist, an analyst at this independent laboratory determined the refractive index of the two fragments of glass four times each. The data generated are shown in the table below.

Glass from crime scene		Glass from suspect	
Fragment no.	Refractive index	Fragment no.	Refractive index
2	1.51150	6	1.51162
2	1.51149	6	1.51163
2	1.51148	6	1.51162
2	1.51149	6	1.51161

(a) On the basis of the data given in the first table, the forensic scientist stated that this did not provide sufficient evidence to show at a 95 per cent level of confidence that the two samples of glass came from different sources. Is this correct?

(b) The analyst working for the independent laboratory concluded on the basis of the data given in the second table that there was sufficient evidence to show with a confidence level of more than 95 per cent that the two fragments of glass came from different sources. Is this correct?

(c) Which do you believe is more reliable: the work of the forensic scientist or that of the independent laboratory? Justify your answer.

4. To establish the refractive index of a piece of colourless glass, it is immersed in an oil with a refractive index that is slightly higher than that of the glass and it is observed in monochromatic light. The oil and the glass are then heated, causing the refractive index of the oil to fall. At a particular temperature (called the match temperature), the glass will become invisible because, at that temperature, the refractive index of the oil equals that of the glass. If the temperature dependence of the refractive index of the oil is known, its refractive index, and hence that of the glass, at the match temperature can be worked out. To establish the temperature dependence of the refractive index of an oil, its refractive index is measured with a refractometer at a range of different temperatures. This exercise was carried out with an oil, known here as oil Z, and the data generated are given in the table below.

Temperature/°C	Refractive index
20	1.522 00
30	1.518 10
40	1.514 20

(a) A calibration graph could be drawn from the data presented in the table, with temperature (in °C) on the x-axis and refractive index on the y-axis. Use linear regression to find the equation for the straight line of best fit for this graph (you are not expected to draw the graph).

(b) Comment on whether the table contains sufficient data to construct a reliable calibration graph.

(c) Using a different oil from oil Z, the refractive index of a fragment of glass was measured three times. The figures obtained were 1.5464, 1.5460 and 1.5465, with a mean of 1.5463. What is the 95 per cent confidence interval associated with the mean of these data?

5. For the purposes of this question, assume that:

◾ there are only two types of glass, namely glass that is lead crystal and glass that is not lead crystal;

◾ all lead crystal glass has a refractive index greater than 1.5210;

◾ measurement of many thousands of randomly selected glasses that are not lead crystal reveals their refractive indices to be normally distributed with a mean of 1.5180 and with a standard deviation of 0.001 53;

◾ the glass recovered from the crime scene had a refractive index of more than 1.5210;

◾ on average, one in five pieces of glass is lead crystal.

(a) What are the odds in favour of the crime scene glass being lead crystal before the refractive index data are taken into account?

(b) How do the refractive index data alter these odds?

(c) Assume *for the purposes of this question* that although many types of lead crystal have densities in excess of $3.0\,g\,cm^{-3}$, no glass that is not lead crystal has this property. How would the observation that the glass obtained from the crime scene had a density greater than $3.0\,g\,cm^{-3}$ alter the odds that you calculated in part (b)?

6. This question concerns a fictitious crime in which a window was broken and for which a suspect has been arrested.

(a) If there are 10 000 people who could have broken the window, what are the prior odds in favour of the suspect being the person who did so?

(b) Inspection of the suspect's coat revealed a number of minute pieces of glass on it. It is estimated that the probability of this occurring is 0.8 if the suspect had indeed broken the window. The prosecution argue that this means that the odds in favour of the suspect breaking the window based on this evidence is 4 to 1. It has been shown that at any one time there are many people who have a number of minute pieces of glass on their coats. On this basis, the defence team argue that this evidence is of no relevance to the case. Which, if either, of these arguments is correct? To help you answer the question, assume that at any one time 4 per cent of the population have a number of minute pieces of glass on their coats.

(c) New evidence from a security camera then became available, which irrefutably showed that the suspect and one other man were the only people who could have broken the window. Ignoring the information presented in part (b) of this question, this security camera evidence was used to create new odds in place of those odds mentioned in part (a) of this question. What are these new odds in favour of the suspect being the person who broke the window?

(d) Faced with this new security camera evidence, the suspect admitted that he was present when the window was broken and that he had been wearing the coat referred to above at that time. Assume, as before, that the probability of the glass evidence being found on the coat if the wearer of the coat had broken the window is 0.8. Crime scene reconstruction experiments showed that the probability of this same evidence being found was 0.2 if the wearer of the coat had not broken the window but had stood nearby when this event occurred. What is the likelihood ratio associated with this evidence? Comment on any assumptions that you make.

(e) The prosecution now argues that this new evidence (i.e. that presented in parts (c) and (d) of this question) proves that the odds in favour of the suspect having broken the window are indeed 4 to 1. Is this correct?

Further reading

Aitken, C. and Taroni, F. (2004) *Statistics and the evaluation of evidence for forensic scientists* (2nd edn). Chichester: John Wiley & Sons Ltd.

Currell, G. and Dowman, A. (2005) *Essential mathematics and statistics for science*. Chichester: John Wiley & Sons Ltd.

Lucy, D. (2005) *Introduction to statistics for forensic scientists*. Chichester: John Wiley & Sons Ltd.

Robertson, B. and Vignaux, G. A. (1995) *Interpreting evidence: evaluating forensic science in the courtroom*. Chichester: John Wiley & Sons Ltd.

Forensic science in court

14

Chapter objectives

After reading this chapter, you should be able to:

> Describe the hierarchical arrangement of the courts within the criminal justice system and the relationship between them.

> List the general categories of criminal offence and understand how these relate to the trial destination of each category.

> Distinguish between the role of the jury and that of the judge in Crown Court trials.

> Understand how the adversarial system of justice works and the procedure for trials held in the criminal courts.

> Appreciate the importance of the forensic science report prepared for use in court.

> Outline the role of the forensic scientist instructed to appear in court as an expert witness.

> Recognise that the interpretation of evidence by the expert witness is likely to be the most significant area of challenge during cross-examination by the opposing side.

Introduction

In Chapters 3–13, the forensic examination of the different types of evidence that may be recovered from crime scenes has been described in detail. In England and Wales, the forensic analysis of this evidential material is usually carried out at the request of the police by the Forensic Science Service (FSS) (Chapter 1, Section 1.3.2). A forensic scientist from the FSS will usually work closely with the police, particularly in cases of serious crime, such as homicide. If during the course of the police investigation into a particular crime, sufficient admissible evidence is accrued, a prosecution can be brought (usually by the Crown Prosecution Service (CPS) on behalf of the State) against the individual(s) accused of committing the crime in question.

This concluding chapter describes the criminal justice system in England and Wales (Section 14.1) and, within this context, the role of the forensic scientist in particular. Critical to the prosecution's case is the report made by the forensic scientist working in conjunction with the police during the investigation, and compiled from the case notes made during his or her examination of the evidence (Section 14.2). In most cases, the forensic scientist's report is all that is seen by the courts. However, in some instances, the forensic scientist is required to be present in court in person to answer questions concerning the findings contained within his or her report. In this capacity, the forensic scientist appears as an 'expert witness' and, as such, may express opinions, as well as giving factual information, when required to do so, during the trial (Section 14.3). It is worth noting that, as part of the adversarial criminal justice system that exists in England and Wales, forensic scientists may be also be employed by the defence to appear in court as expert witnesses (Section 14.3).

14.1 The criminal court system in England and Wales

In England and Wales, the arrangement of the criminal court system is a hierarchical one (Figure 14.1). The system has two criminal courts where individuals are tried, which are therefore said to have 'first instance criminal jurisdiction'. The lower of the two trial courts is the Magistrates' Court (Section 14.1.1) while the higher tier comprises the Crown Courts where individuals are tried by jury (Section 14.1.2). Further information about the different categories of criminal offence recognised within the criminal justice system is given in Box 14.1.

Above the criminal courts are three courts of appeal – the High Court (Queen's Bench Division), Court of Appeal (Criminal Division) and House of Lords (Figure 14.1 and Section 14.1.3). It should be noted that the Crown Court may itself hear

Further information
Box 14.1

The categorisation of criminal offences in England and Wales

In England and Wales, individuals accused of committing criminal offences may be tried either in the Magistrates' Court (lower criminal court) or in the Crown Court (higher criminal court) after committal from the Magistrates' Court. The type of court in which the trial of a particular individual takes place will depend on a variety of factors, notably the seriousness of the offence of which the defendant is accused.

Within the criminal justice system, three categories of offence are recognised.

Summary only offences

Summary only offences are those that can be tried only in a Magistrates' Court. Such offences are of a less serious nature and include, for example, being drunk and disorderly, shoplifting and minor motoring offences such as careless driving, speeding and taking a vehicle without the consent of the owner. Trials for offences heard in the Magistrates' Courts (i.e. summary only offences and either way offences – see below) account for 95 per cent of all criminal trials.

Either way offences

As the name suggests, this type of offence may be tried in either of the two criminal courts – the Magistrates' Court or the Crown Court – depending on the seriousness of the crime in question. The decision over where the trial will take place is made by magistrates at a 'Mode of Trial' hear-

Box 14.1 continued

ing. If the magistrates decide that a case should be tried in the Crown Court, the defendant has no option in the venue for his or her trial. However, if the magistrates are prepared to accept jurisdiction of the case, the defendant can either consent to being tried summarily in the Magistrates' Court or elect for trial by jury in the Crown Court. The offences that fall within the 'either way' category tend to be ones whose seriousness varies according to the circum-

stances of each individual case. Examples include criminal damage, theft and obtaining property by deception.

Indictable only offences

This category covers the most serious of crimes and includes murder, rape, death by dangerous driving and blackmail. Such cases *must* be tried on indictment in the higher of the two criminal courts – the Crown Court.

appeals against decisions of guilt and/or sentence made by the Magistrates' Court (Figure 14.1). Table 14.1 summarises who sits in the different courts that constitute the criminal justice system and the correct form of address to be used for each.

(From Bond *et al.*, 1999)

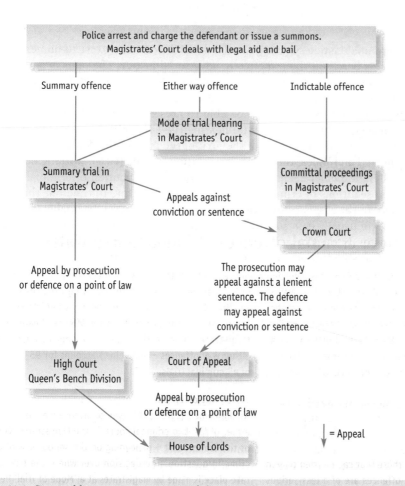

Figure 14.1 Criminal litigation: an overview of the procedure and appeal system

Table 14.1 The criminal courts: the individuals who sit in them and how they should be addressed

Type of criminal court	Who may sit	Correct form of address
The Magistrates' Court	Three lay magistrates Single district judge	'Madam/Sir' 'Madam/Sir'
The Crown Court	A circuit judge A recorder A High Court judge	'Your Honour' 'Your Honour' 'My Lady/My Lord' *or* 'Your Ladyship/Your Lordship'
The Court of Appeal (Criminal Division)	Three judges (or two on occasion) including a minimum of one Lord Justice of Appeal	'My Lady/My Lord' *or* 'Your Ladyship/Your Lordship'
The High Court (Queen's Bench Division)	One Lord Justice of Appeal plus one High Court judge	'My Lady/My Lord' *or* 'Your Ladyship/Your Lordship'
The House of Lords	Between three and seven Lords of Appeal (but normally five)	'My Lady/My Lord' *or* 'Your Ladyship/Your Lordship'

Defendant

The person standing trial in court accused of committing a particular offence, or offences.

The criminal justice system in England and Wales, in contrast to numerous other countries, is based on the principle of adversarial justice. The onus is on the prosecution to prove that the person standing trial (known as the **defendant**) is guilty *beyond reasonable doubt* of committing the crime of which he or she is accused. The prosecution must, therefore, be able to present sufficient admissible evidence to convince either the magistrate(s) hearing the case or, if the trial is being held in the Crown Court, the members of the jury, of the guilt of the defendant.

In England and Wales, the Crown Prosecution Service (CPS), working on behalf of the State, is the chief agency responsible for the prosecution of criminal offences. Private prosecutions of criminal cases do occur from time to time but they are the exception. In the Magistrates' Court, the prosecuting lawyer, invariably employed by the CPS, will usually be a solicitor, although sometimes the prosecuting lawyer will be a barrister. In the Crown Court, the CPS is most likely to be represented by a barrister or a solicitor-advocate (a solicitor with a higher right of audience qualification). It is the role of the lawyer (solicitor or barrister) acting for the defendant (i.e. the defence lawyer) to challenge the evidence put forward by the prosecution. More information on trial procedure and evidence is given in Box 14.2, while Box 14.3 details the case of William Dunlop, the first person to be retried for the same offence, after changes to the law on 'double jeopardy'.

14.1.1 The Magistrates' Court

Practically all criminal cases start in the Magistrates' Court, which constitutes the lower of the two criminal courts (Figure 14.1). The vast majority of these cases (approximately 95 per cent) are tried by the Magistrates' Court and completed there, while the remainder are committed to the higher criminal court – the Crown Court – for either sentencing or trial (Section 14.1.2). Figure 14.2 illustrates, by means of a flow diagram, the various routes that may be followed through the criminal courts (from first court appearance to conviction) for routine cases involving adult defendants.

Further information

Box 14.2

Trial procedure and evidence in England and Wales

The trial forms an essential part of the criminal justice system in England and Wales, which is founded on the principle of adversarial justice. Only individuals who contest their guilt, i.e. plead 'not guilty' at an appropriate stage during their process through the criminal courts, will actually be tried, at either the Magistrates' Court or the Crown Court as appropriate (Figure 14.2). In practice, such individuals are in the minority. In the vast majority of cases, the person concerned will choose to plead guilty to some or all of the charges against him or her. This decision will be made in conjunction with the individual's legal advisor based on his or her assessment of the evidence. On occasion, the CPS will withdraw charges against a defendant either because of a plea-bargaining arrangement (whereby the defendant agrees to plead guilty to a less serious allegation, in exchange for the prosecution not pursuing a more serious allegation) or because, having reviewed the evidence (which may include defence expert witness evidence), the CPS now considers there is insufficient evidence to prosecute the matter.

At trial, a defendant is presumed innocent of the crime for which he or she stands accused until proven guilty beyond reasonable doubt. The onus is on the prosecuting side to present the evidence that will convince the presiding magistrate(s) in the Magistrates' Court, or the jury in the Crown Court, of the guilt of the defendant. The role of the defence is to contest the evidence adduced by the prosecution.

Types of evidence

Evidence presented during the course of a trial may be broadly classified as:

■ real evidence;
■ documentary evidence;
■ witness evidence.

Real evidence (referred to elsewhere in this book as physical evidence) consists of items, known in the court context as exhibits, such as the knife used in a murder. Documentary evidence includes, for example, statements taken from witnesses, hard copy from computers and video recordings. Witness evidence may be presented orally by the following categories of witnesses, who differ from one another in the amount of opinion that they may express:

■ witnesses of fact, who are required to give factual information concerning only what they personally heard or saw and *not* any opinion;
■ professional witnesses, who are people (e.g. police officers) who give evidence that is mostly factual but may contain some opinion, and do so during the discharge of their professional duties;
■ expert witnesses, whose evidence contains both fact and, in areas that are outside the common knowledge of the court, their personal opinion (the role of the forensic scientist as an expert witness is described in Section 14.3).

Trial procedure

The trial of criminal cases are conducted in accordance with the procedure given below:

Opening speech by prosecution outlining case
↓
Evidence called by prosecution
Each witness:
● questioned first by prosecution*
● cross-examined by defence
● re-examined by prosecution (if necessary)
↓
Opening speech by defence (if there is a case to answer)
↓
Evidence called by defence
Each witness:
● questioned first by defence*
● cross-examined by prosecution
● re-examined by defence (if necessary)
↓

Magistrates' Court	Crown Court
Closing speech by defence	Closing speech by prosecution
↓	↓
	Closing speech by defence
	↓
	Summing up by presiding judge to the jury

*The initial examination of a witness by the side who has called them (i.e. either the prosecution or defence) is termed 'examination in chief'.

Case study

Box 14.3

The law on 'double jeopardy' and the retrial of William Dunlop

In accordance with the 'double jeopardy' rule, which dates back over 800 years, an individual acquitted of a crime cannot be tried a second time for that same offence. However, a change in the law on the retrial of serious offences, such as rape and murder, came into force on 4 April 2005 in England and Wales (but not in Scotland) under the provisions of the Criminal Justice Act 2003. This meant that an acquitted person *could* be retried for the same serious crime, provided that 'new and compelling' evidence not available at the time of the original trial (such as DNA evidence, confessions or new witnesses) transpired. Pivotal in bringing about this reform was the enduring campaign of Mrs Ann Ming, the mother of murder victim Julie Hogg, whose killer William Dunlop was the first person to be retried as a result of this change in the double jeopardy law.

Julie Hogg (aged 22) from Billingham, Teesside, was reported missing in November 1989. Several weeks later,

her body was discovered behind a bath panel at her home by her mother. Local man William Dunlop, who had previously been in a brief relationship with the victim, was tried for her murder. Two juries were unable to reach verdicts in his trial, and he was formally acquitted at Newcastle Crown Court in October 1991. Eight years later, in 1999, while serving a seven-year sentence for another assault, William Dunlop confessed to the murder of Julie Hogg to a prison officer. As a result, he received a six-year prison sentence the following year (2000), after pleading guilty to perjury. However, in 2006, William Dunlop became the first person to be retried for the same offence (as a result of the change in the double jeopardy law) after the Director of Public Prosecutions (DPP) referred his case to the Court of Appeal. On 6 October 2006, he was sentenced to life imprisonment at the Old Bailey, London, for Julie Hogg's murder, with a minimum tariff of 17 years.

Home Office statistics for the year 2004 show that 2 022 000 defendants were proceeded against in Magistrates' Courts, comprising 665 000 for summary non-motoring offences, 904 000 for summary motoring offences and 453 000 for indictable offences. In this year, 95.3 per cent of the criminal cases commenced in the Magistrates' Court were completed there, while 4.7 per cent (i.e. 95 300 persons) were committed to the Crown Court for either trial or sentencing. Decisions over issues such as granting bail and the entitlement of the defendant to legal aid are also made by the Magistrates' Court. It should be noted that, as well as dealing with criminal cases, Magistrates' Courts have jurisdiction over a restricted number of civil cases, namely family and licensing matters.

Magistrates' Courts may be presided over either by a panel of three lay magistrates (also known as Justices of the Peace, or JPs) or a single district judge (previously known as a stipendiary magistrate).

Lay magistrates

Unpaid, part-time volunteers who preside (usually in a panel of three) in the vast majority of the Magistrates' Courts in England and Wales. Also known as Justices of the Peace.

Lay magistrates

Around 30 000 **lay magistrates** work in the Magistrates' Courts in England and Wales and account for approximately 99.7 per cent of all magistrates. Lay magistrates are part-time, unpaid volunteers, who are appointed from the local community, in most cases, by the Lord Chancellor (advised by Local Advisory Committees composed of local residents, including magistrates). Ideally, the composition of any one panel of lay magistrates should be representative of the

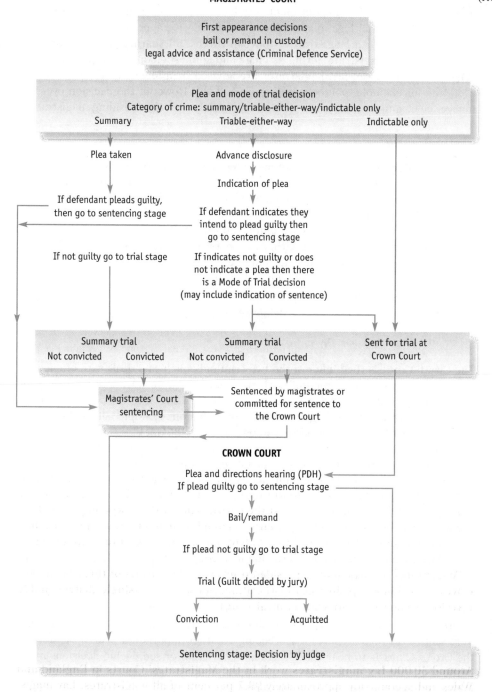

MAGISTRATES' COURT

(From Davies *et al.*, 2005)

First appearance decisions
bail or remand in custody
legal advice and assistance (Criminal Defence Service)

Plea and mode of trial decision
Category of crime: summary/triable-either-way/indictable only

Summary — Triable-either-way — Indictable only

Plea taken

Advance disclosure

Indication of plea

If defendant pleads guilty,
then go to sentencing stage

If defendant indicates they
intend to plead guilty then
go to sentencing stage

If not guilty go to trial stage

If indicates not guilty or does
not indicate a plea then there
is a Mode of Trial decision
(may include indication of sentence)

Summary trial
Not convicted   Convicted

Summary trial
Not convicted   Convicted

Sent for trial at
Crown Court

Magistrates' Court
sentencing

Sentenced by magistrates or
committed for sentence to
the Crown Court

CROWN COURT

Plea and directions hearing (PDH)
If plead guilty go to sentencing stage

Bail/remand

If plead not guilty go to trial stage

Trial (Guilt decided by jury)

Conviction   Acquitted

Sentencing stage: Decision by judge

Figure 14.2 Criminal justice flow chart: the criminal courts – from first court appearance to conviction (for routine cases involving adults)

community it serves and this, as well as personal suitability, should be taken into account when individual appointments are made. Lay magistrates are not required to possess any formal legal qualifications but do receive appropriate training. They usually preside over a Magistrates' Court in threes, all sharing power equally but with the senior magistrate acting as chair and spokesperson of the panel. During the hearing of a case, lay magistrates are advised by a legally qualified Justices' Clerk on, for example, points of procedure and law. However, the decision over the innocence or guilt of the person on trial rests solely with the presiding magistrates.

District judges

District judges
Full-time professional lawyers who preside (alone) in a minority of the Magistrates' Courts in England and Wales. Formerly known as stipendiary magistrates.

District judges (previously known as stipendiary magistrates) constitute only a tiny percentage (0.3 per cent) of the total number of magistrates and are generally associated with the larger urban courts, including, traditionally, the Magistrates' Courts of inner city London. In contrast to lay magistrates, these individuals are paid, professional lawyers who are employed on a full-time basis. A minimum of seven years' experience working either as a barrister or solicitor is required before appointment to the office of district judge can be considered. In comparison with lay magistrates, who usually sit on a panel of three, district judges sit alone to hear cases. Notwithstanding, the sentencing powers of the individual district judge are the same as those of a panel of lay magistrates.

14.1.2 The Crown Court

The Crown Court is the higher of the two criminal courts and deals with offences of a more serious nature, compared with the relatively minor criminal offences sent for summary trial in the Magistrates' Court (Box 14.1). Crown Courts are usually associated with cities and large towns; the most famous example being the Central Criminal Court in London, otherwise known as the Old Bailey.

After initial proceedings in the Magistrates' Court, criminal cases will be sent to the Crown Court directly, in the case of indictable only offences, or after a Mode of Trial hearing in the case of either way offences (Box 14.1). However, if the defendant in question pleads guilty to an either way offence at this stage, and therefore no trial is required, the Magistrates' Court will progress to the sentencing stage (Figure 14.2).

The Magistrates' Court may also send cases to the Crown Court for sentencing after a defendant has been tried and found guilty in the Magistrates' Court. This occurs in instances where the magistrates feel that their powers of sentencing are insufficient for the case in question and referral to the higher criminal court with its greater sentencing powers is necessary. Home Office statistics for the year 2004 show that out of the 95 300 persons sent on to the Crown Court from the Magistrates' Court, 78 400 (82.3 per cent) were committed for trial, while 16 900 (17.7 per cent) were sent to the higher court for sentencing. Another important aspect of the work of the Crown Court is to hear appeals against conviction or sentencing decisions made in the Magistrates' Court (Figure 14.1). Appeals against decisions made by the Crown Court itself are heard in the Court of Appeal (Section 14.1.3).

The Crown Court differs from the Magistrates' Court in that defendants are tried not by magistrates, but by a jury under the auspices of a judge. It is the jury that must decide whether a particular defendant is guilty or not of the crime of which he or she stands accused. In order to return a verdict of 'guilty', there must be agreement between 10 out of the 12 members of the jury hearing the case. The jurors must reach their decision based on the evidence put before them during the trial, which may include that given by an expert witness (Section 14.3). For further information on trial procedure, the reader is referred to Box 14.2.

The jury

A jury is made up of 12 'ordinary' members of the public. The process that leads to their appointment is designed to achieve a random mix of individuals within the jury and is therefore a very important one. For this reason, the selection process is described in some detail below.

Individuals are selected at random from the local register of electors and served with a jury summons. Once summoned, each individual has a duty to declare:

- any ineligibility for jury service (e.g. because he or she is mentally disordered or is a member of the legal profession);
- any disqualification from jury service (e.g. because he or she has been made the subject of a community service order within the last decade, or has received a sentence of imprisonment of five years or more).

Individuals belonging to certain professions, such as the armed forces, may be excused from jury service, as of right, while yet others, including those who are self-employed, may apply to be excused. If not excluded or excused from jury service, all individuals summoned to attend the court must do so, provided that they satisfy the following conditions:

- They have been 'ordinarily resident in the UK for a period of at least five years since the age of thirteen'.
- They are aged between 18 and 70 years.

Having reached this stage of the selection process, the prospective jurors (whose number, usually between 15 and 18, will exceed that required to form a jury) are required to attend the relevant Crown Court Centre. These individuals constitute what is known as the '**jury panel**'. From this panel, 12 persons are selected by random ballot to serve on the jury. At this stage, the defence has a limited right to challenge the selection of any particular individual. Once 12 members of the jury panel have been called unchallenged, the jury is sworn in and the trial of the defendant is able to commence (Box 14.2).

Jury panel
A panel of prospective jurors who are required to attend the relevant Crown Court Centre and from whom the final 12 needed to serve on the jury are randomly selected.

The judges who sit in the Crown Courts

As described previously, the guilt or innocence of a defendant tried in the Crown Court is decided by the jury. However, the entire trial proceedings is overseen by a judge, who will belong to one of the following categories:

- High Court judges.
- Circuit judges.
- Recorders and assistant recorders.

High Court judges (sometimes referred to as 'Red judges' because of the colour of their robes) are the most senior of the categories of judge listed and can try all types of criminal offence, including the most serious ones. Circuit judges have the same jurisdiction as recorders/assistant recorders (who are part-time judicial officers). Both groups can try all but the most serious of the offences committed for trial at the Crown Court (unless, in the case of circuit judges, a 'most serious' case, e.g. of treason, is released by a High Court judge). Appointment to any of these categories of Crown Court judge is made, by the Lord Chancellor's Department, from solicitors or barristers who have a standing of at least a decade.

The role of the judge in the trial proceedings of the Crown Court is an impartial one and includes the following aspects:

- to make sure that the defendant receives a fair trial;
- to deal with all points of law, including the admissibility of disputed evidence;
- to sum up the case to the jury, after the closing speeches of the prosecution and defence;
- to sentence the defendant, if found guilty, or otherwise order his or her acquittal.

14.1.3 The courts of appeal

There are three courts of appeal within the criminal justice system; each of which is briefly described below. Cases may be referred to the appropriate court of appeal by the Criminal Cases Review Commission (CCRC) – an independent body responsible for the investigation of suspected miscarriages of justice in England, Wales and Northern Ireland (Box 14.4).

Case study

Box 14.4

The Sally Clark case

On 23 February 1998, solicitors Sally and Stephen Clark from Wilmslow in Cheshire, UK, were arrested on suspicion of the murder of their second son, Harry, aged 8 weeks, who had died the previous month (on 26 January 1998). Their first son, Christopher, had died 14 months previously (on 13 December 1996) aged 11 weeks. At the time, the Home Office pathologist, Dr Alan Williams, put the cause of Christopher's death as a lung infection. However, in his post-mortem examination of the Clarks' second son, Harry, he found physical signs that could be consistent with death by shaking and, in the light of this, revisited his earlier post-mortem results concerning

Christopher. As a consequence of the pathologist's findings, a murder enquiry was launched into both deaths.

On 2 July 1998, Sally Clark was charged with the murders of her two sons (the Crown Prosecution Service (CPS) having decided to take no further action against her husband). She was sent for trial at Chester Crown Court in October 1999. On 9 November 1999, she was found guilty of murdering her two baby sons and sentenced to two terms of life imprisonment. Mrs Clark always maintained that she was innocent and that her babies had died as a result of sudden infant death syndrome (SIDS), more commonly known as 'cot death'. Her

Box 14.4 *continued*

husband, Stephen, vowed to continue his fight to prove his wife's innocence.

During the trial of Sally Clark, a crucial part of the prosecution's case concerned the evidence given by expert witness, Professor Sir Roy Meadow, an experienced paediatrician. He informed the court that the chance of cot death occurring twice within the same family was 1 in 73 million. He arrived at this figure by squaring the estimated chance of a single cot death occurring in a family such as the Clarks (i.e. non-smokers, relatively affluent) – a probability of 1 in 8543. However, this calculation did not take into account the possibility that environmental or genetic factors may make the risk of cot death higher in particular families. In other words, the two deaths were treated as if they were entirely unrelated to each other.

In July 2000, Sally Clark appealed against her sentence to the Court of Appeal, primarily on the basis that the statistical evidence presented at the original trial was flawed. Although this was accepted by the appeal judges, they were still of the opinion that the evidence of her guilt was 'overwhelming' and, in October 2000, her appeal was rejected.

In July 2002, fresh evidence concerning Sally Clark's case was brought to the attention of the Criminal Cases Review Commission (CCRC). It emerged that essential medical evidence concerning the Clark's second son, Harry, had been known to the pathologist since February 1998 but not disclosed at the original trial. It transpired that Harry had been suffering from an infection caused by the bacterium *Staphylococcus aureus*, which could have been responsible for his death.

As a result of this new evidence, Sally Clark's case was returned by the CCRC to the Court of Appeal. The appeal judges ruled that, because of the withholding of vital medical evidence, her convictions for the murders of Christopher and Harry were unsafe and must be set aside. On 29 January 2003, Sally Clark was finally freed from her life sentence.

Subsequently, Sally Clark's father, Frank Lockyer, brought a complaint against Professor Sir Roy Meadow to the General Medical Council (GMC), the professional regulatory body for doctors practising medicine in the UK. On 15 July 2005, the Fitness to Practise Panel (FPP) of the GMC found Professor Sir Roy Meadow guilty of serious professional misconduct, for presenting 'erroneous' and 'misleading' evidence in the 1999 trial of Sally Clark, and ordered that his name be removed from the medical register.

In response, Professor Sir Roy Meadow appealed to the High Court against the finding of the GMC's FPP and the penalty that it consequently imposed. On 17 February 2006, the High Court judge allowed his appeal, finding him not guilty of serious professional misconduct and quashing the penalty of his erasure from the medical register. The judge also ruled that expert witnesses should have immunity from disciplinary action from their respective regulatory bodies. As a consequence, the GMC warned: 'the ruling would place doctors acting as expert witnesses in court cases beyond the reach of its scrutiny.'

A subsequent appeal brought by the GMC to the Court of Appeal led to the overturn of this High Court ruling on expert witness immunity from disciplinary action, on 26 October 2006. However, the Court of Appeal upheld the previous High Court finding that Professor Sir Roy Meadow was not guilty of *serious* professional misconduct. It should be noted, that in its appeal, the GMC did not seek to reinstate the penalty of removal from the medical register for Professor Sir Roy Meadow.

The High Court (Queen's Bench Division)

The High Court has jurisdiction in both criminal and civil matters. It is divided into three divisions: the Family Division, the Chancery Division and the Queen's Bench Division. It is the last of these, the Queen's Bench Division, that deals with appeals concerning criminal cases. These may emanate from either of the criminal courts, i.e. the Magistrates' Court or the Crown Court. Appeals from the Magistrates' Court, for example, are usually connected with points of law and may be made by either the prosecution or the defence (Figure 14.1). Appeals in the High Court are heard by one High Court Judge and one Lord Justice of Appeal (Table 14.1).

The Court of Appeal (Criminal Division)

The Court of Appeal has jurisdiction in both civil and criminal matters and is composed of a Civil Division and a Criminal Division. The Criminal Division hears appeals from the Crown Court (Figure 14.1). These may be made by the defence against conviction and/or sentence, or by the prosecution in cases where the sentence given to a defendant is felt to be unduly lenient. Normally, three judges sit in the Criminal Division of the Court of Appeal (Table 14.1). This panel may consist of three Lord Justices of Appeal (which may include the Lord Chief Justice); one Lord Justice of Appeal plus two High Court judges; or a combination of one Lord Justice of Appeal, one High Court judge and one circuit judge.

The House of Lords

The House of Lords represents the highest court in the criminal justice system. It receives appeals concerning publicly important points of law from the Criminal Division of the Court of Appeal and also, on occasion, from the Queen's Bench Division of the High Court (Figure 14.1). Such appeals may be made by either the prosecution or the defence and are heard in the House of Lords by several Lords of Appeal (who number between three and seven, but are normally five).

14.2 The forensic scientist's report for use in court

During the processing of a crime scene, any material, such as hairs, fibres, fingerprints or samples of body fluids, that may be of evidential value to the police investigation is recovered and sent for forensic analysis (Chapter 2). In England and Wales, the police have access to the necessary forensic expertise mainly through the comprehensive range of services offered by the Forensic Science Service (FSS). A forensic scientist from the FSS usually works in close association with the police during the course of their investigation, especially in cases of a more serious nature, such as murder. He or she will either personally examine the various types of forensic evidence submitted by the police, or arrange for colleagues with relevant expertise to perform the necessary tests. The results of this forensic examination are written up as case notes. These case notes will form the basis of the forensic scientist's report for use by the prosecuting side in court.

The forensic scientist's report is a very important document, representing, as it does, the culmination of all the labour that has been expended during the conduct of a criminal investigation. It is often instrumental in persuading a defendant to plead guilty, thus obviating the need for a trial. Many factors must be taken into account when preparing such a report for use in court. For example, it is vital that the report is both comprehensive and written in a manner that makes its contents easily understandable to non-scientists, such as lawyers, the police, and the jury or magistrates hearing the case. This is necessary because the report is usually admitted for use in court unaccompanied by the forensic scientist who compiled it. It is only in a tiny minority of cases that the forensic scientist is required by the court to appear in person as an expert witness (Section 14.3).

The content of the report prepared for use in court by the forensic scientist is prescribed by new rules concerning expert evidence set out in the Criminal Procedure (Amendment No. 2) Rules 2006, which came into force on 6 November 2006. The relevant extract is given below:

33.3 – (1) An expert's report must –

(a) give details of the expert's qualifications, relevant experience and accreditation;

(b) give details of any literature or other information which the expert has relied on in making the report;

(c) contain a statement setting out the substance of all facts given to the expert which are material to the opinions expressed in the report or upon which those opinions are based;

(d) make clear which of the facts stated in the report are within the expert's own knowledge;

(e) say who carried out any examination, measurement, test or experiment which the expert has used for the report and –

(i) give the qualifications, relevant experience and accreditation of that person,

(ii) say whether or not the examination, measurement, test or experiment was carried out under the expert's supervision, and

(iii) summarise the findings on which the expert relies;

(f) where there is a range of opinion on the matters dealt with in the report –

(i) summarise the range of opinion, and

(ii) give reasons for his own opinion;

(g) if the expert is not able to give his opinion without qualification, state the qualification;

(h) contain a summary of the conclusions reached;

(i) contain a statement that the expert understands his duty to the court, and has complied and will continue to comply with that duty; and

(j) contain the same declaration of truth as a witness statement.

Crown copyright material is reproduced with the permission of the Controller of HMSO and the Queen's Printer for Scotland.

Although the discussion to date has concentrated on the forensic scientist's report as prepared for the prosecution, in some cases independent forensic reports may also be commissioned by lawyers acting for the defendant. If such a report is to be relied on in court, the defence must disclose it to the prosecution before trial. (The process whereby documentary evidence is shown by one party (i.e. defence or prosecution) to the other before trial is known as **pre-trial disclosure**.) However, if it transpires that the contents of the report commissioned by the defence prove to be unhelpful to the defendant, and it is therefore decided not to make use of the report in court, the defence does not have to disclose it to the opposing side. In contrast, the law requires the prosecution to make pre-trial disclosure of evidence (including forensic evidence), both advantageous and disadvantageous to the prosecution's case, to the defence.

Pre-trial disclosure
The disclosure of documentary evidence by one side (i.e. the defence or the prosecution) to the other side prior to the trial.

It should be noted that the circumstances under which a forensic scientist's report is prepared for the defence differ in several important respects from that compiled for the prosecution. Although the police purchase their forensic services largely from the FSS, defence lawyers usually obtain the necessary expertise through small, independent companies (although these boundaries are beginning to become less clear cut). In the case of a legally aided defendant, the prior authorisation of the Criminal Defence Service will normally be sought in order to 'purchase' independent expertise. The forensic scientist working for the prosecution is usually involved in a criminal case from the start of the investigation and consequently has first sight of the various items of evidence recovered from the crime scene. The forensic scientist engaged by the defence will therefore only have access to the evidence second-hand and will not be able to view the material in its original state.

The difference in the condition of the evidence before and after forensic examination can be significant. For example, the forensic examination of 'foreign' fibres from an article of clothing will necessitate their removal from that garment. When seen by the forensic scientist working for the defence, the evidence will consist of the garment plus the tape lifts of the recovered fibres. In practice, the second forensic scientist (i.e. the one working for the defence) usually compiles his or her report using information and the test results obtained by the first (i.e. the prosecution) forensic scientist, who must disclose this information to them. It is not usual for the defence forensic scientist to carry out his or her own scientific tests. The time available to the second forensic scientist is relatively short compared with that available to the first. However, the second forensic scientist does have the advantage of having access to the defendant's version of events, which may be germane to the interpretation of the evidence assembled by the prosecution side.

It is worth emphasising that the role of the forensic scientist in preparing the report and, if required, appearing in court as an expert witness, is an impartial one. This means that if any of his or her findings are inconsistent with the aims of the side (either prosecution or defence) for which the report was commissioned, such information should not be withheld by the forensic scientist. Thus the obligations to make pre-trial disclosure of evidence on the part of the forensic scientist extend to all experiments and tests that tend to cast doubt on the opinion the scientist is expressing, and he or she must bring such information to the attention of the party instructing him or her. However, as previously stated, there is no obligation on the defence to disclose an unfavourable report, provided no reliance is being placed on that report in court.

14.3 The role of the forensic scientist as expert witness

Expert witness
An individual who is required to appear in court in order to give factual information, and opinion based on fact, from within his or her area of expertise.

As mentioned in the previous section, it is only in a very small number of cases that the forensic scientist is required to appear in court in person and give oral evidence as an **expert witness**. The term 'expert witness' may be defined as a non-lawyer who has expertise in a particular area that is outside the common knowledge of the court and who gives evidence of opinion as well as of fact. Examples other than forensic scientists include doctors, psychiatrists, forensic archaeologists, document examiners and structural engineers. Expert witnesses, like all other witnesses, are immune from civil lawsuits in respect of the evidence they give in court. However, this protection does not extend to immunity from disciplinary action from their respective professional regulatory bodies, for example the General Medical Council in the case of doctors in the UK (for details of the case concerning Professor Sir Roy Meadow, please see Box 14.4).

Support and training for expert witnesses is provided by the Expert Witness Institute (EWI), an independent body launched in 1996. Expert witnesses are involved in civil cases, as well as in criminal ones. However, the forensic scientist as expert witness is more likely to be involved in the trial of criminal offences. The expert's duty to the court as prescribed in the Criminal Procedure (Amendment No. 2) Rules 2006 is given in Box 14.5 and discussed more generally in the main text below.

A forensic scientist may be called to appear in court as an expert witness by either the prosecution or the defence. In cases where such an expert is instructed by the prosecuting side, it is likely that the defence will also bring in their own independent forensic expert in order to test the strength of the scientific evidence presented by the prosecution. Regardless of which side has instructed him or her to give an expert opinion, the forensic scientist must remain impartial and objective at all times. It is the duty of the forensic scientist to help the court to come to its decision by giving independent evidence of fact and of opinion based on fact from within his or her field of expertise. It is the task of the lawyers from each side to win the case on which they are engaged (provided that they operate in accordance with the proper procedure expected of them) and for those charged with decision-making (i.e. the jury or magistrates, depending on the court) to determine the guilt or innocence of the defendant.

In court, the expert witness is permitted to view the proceedings of the case with the permission of the court. When called to the witness box, he or she is allowed to bring a clean copy of the report they have compiled (i.e. one that is without annotation), in order to make reference to relevant parts of it when answering questions. After taking the oath or affirmation, the **examination in chief** of the expert witness (i.e. by the side that has instructed the expert witness) begins. After giving his or her name and work address, the expert witness is usually asked questions concerning his or her qualifications and, sometimes, about relevant experience. Successive questioning often follows the progression of the report and allows the

Examination in chief
The initial examination of a witness by the side (i.e. either the prosecution or defence) responsible for calling him or her.

Further information

Box 14.5

Expert's duty to the court

33.2 – (1) An expert must help the court to achieve the overriding objective by giving objective, unbiased opinion on matters within his expertise.

(2) This duty overrides any obligation to the person from whom he receives instructions or by whom he is paid.

(3) This duty includes an obligation to inform all parties and the court if the expert's opinion changes from that contained in a report served as evidence or given in a statement under Part 24 or Part 29.

Extract taken from The Criminal Procedure (Amendment No. 2) Rules 2006. Crown copyright material is reproduced with the permission of the Controller of HMSO and the Queen's Printer for Scotland.

forensic scientist to demonstrate the strengths of his or her expert opinion.

This stage is followed by **cross-examination** by the opposing side, during which the evidence of fact and opinion of the forensic scientist in the witness box is rigorously tested and, if possible, discredited. The conclusions presented in the written report are based on what the forensic scientist considers the most likely interpretation of the results of the scientific tests. It is highly probable that the opposing side will attack both the accuracy of the test results and the interpretation of these findings by the forensic scientist. For example, it may try to persuade the court that other interpretations of the evidence are more likely than the one put forward by the expert instructed by the opposition. The forensic scientist under cross-examin-ation must therefore be prepared to defend the conclusions that appear in his or her report. However, the forensic scientist, as an impartial participant in the court proceedings, should concede if he or she feels that an alternative explanation could be possible. Ultimately, it is for the jury or magistrates to decide which interpretation of the findings is most probable in the context of the case. (For further information on the interpretation and evaluation of scientific evidence, see below and Chapter 13.)

Cross-examination forms a necessary part of the adversarial system of criminal justice and it is important that the expert witness remains calm and professional throughout his or her court appearance, especially during this stage of the proceedings. The manner in which the expert witness delivers his or her evidence in court has been shown to have a direct bearing on the way it is perceived by those involved in the decision-making. Clear and effective communication is therefore essential. Ideally, answers should be concise yet detailed enough to enable the jurors or magistrates to understand their content and therefore comprehend their relevance to the case in hand. The expert witness should address his or her answers directly to the magistrate(s) in a Magistrates' Court, or, in criminal cases in the Crown Court, to the jury and judge.

Cross-examination may be succeeded by re-examination of the expert witness by the side that instructed him or her (Box 14.2). It should be noted, however, that it is not permissible for new evidence to be introduced at this stage. At the end of giving evidence, the expert witness is usually released by the court and is therefore free to leave.

14.4 The interpretation and evaluation of evidence

The role of the forensic scientist as expert witness is to assist the court in reaching its decision over the guilt or innocence of the defendant standing trial (Section 14.3). He or she gives evidence of fact and, importantly, of opinion based on fact when required to do so by the court. Such opinion evidence should be confined to within the expert's region of knowledge and, if questions fall outside this area, the expert witness should make this clear to the court. As mentioned previously, the expert witness, whether appearing for the prosecution or the defence, should be impartial and objective throughout the court proceedings.

The forensic scientist instructed by the prosecution may be the only forensic scientist to appear in court as an expert witness during the hearing of a particular criminal trial. However, the defence side may also instruct its own independent forensic scientist, especially where the case to be made by the prosecution places a heavy reliance on scientific evidence. The forensic scientist engaged by the defence scrutinises the scientific work undertaken by the prosecution and makes sure that it is clearly understood by the defence lawyers. This will enable the defence to challenge the prosecution's case more effectively. Furthermore, the forensic scientist concerned may be called by the defence to appear in court as an expert witness.

When facing cross-examination by the defence, the prosecution's scientific expert witness is likely to be challenged in two key areas. These are:

■ the accuracy (defined in Chapter 13, Section 13.2) of the test results obtained from the forensic examination of evidential objects;

■ the interpretation and evaluation of the scientific test results thus obtained (see Chapter 13).

With regard to the accuracy of the test results, the defence may raise the possibility of cross-contamination during the collection, transportation, storage and/or testing of the evidence concerned. However, the risk of cross-contamination of evidence has been significantly decreased by the training of Scenes of Crime Officers (SOCOs), and the establishment of a clear chain of custody for items of physical evidence (Chapter 2).

Under cross-examination, the interpretation and evaluation of the scientific test results by the forensic scientist is likely to constitute the most significant area of contention. As mentioned previously, the opinion of the forensic scientist is formed by what he or she considers to be the most probable explanation of the results. However, the forensic scientist must be careful in the way that he or she expresses his or her opinions. In particular, the forensic scientist should not make any statements that directly imply the guilt, or otherwise, of the defendant standing trial. Such decisions are the province of the jurors, or magistrates, hearing the case.

14.5 Summary

■ In England and Wales, the courts within the criminal justice system are arranged in a hierarchy. There are two criminal courts where individuals are tried, i.e. the Magistrates' Court (lower criminal court) and the Crown Court (higher criminal court), and three courts of appeal, namely the High Court (Queen's Bench Division), the Court of Appeal (Criminal Division) and the House of Lords. The trial destination of any particular criminal offence will depend on its classification. Three broad categories of criminal offence are recognised, i.e. summary only offences (tried only in the Magistrates' Court), either way offences (tried either in the Magistrates' Court or the Crown Court) and indictable only offences (tried only in the Crown Court).

■ The trial of criminal offences in England and Wales is based on the principle of adversarial justice. Briefly, this means that in court, the prosecution adduces evidence intended to prove *beyond reasonable doubt* that the defendant is guilty of the crime for which he or she stands accused. In response, the defence lawyer challenges by attempting to raise reasonable doubt about the prosecution's case. The aim of each side, therefore, is to win the case in hand. However, it is the task of the decision-makers (represented by the magistrate(s) in the lower criminal courts or the jury in the Crown Court) to decide whether the defendant is guilty or not guilty.

■ The role of the forensic scientist within the criminal justice system is a very important one. A forensic scientist is often closely involved in the police investigation of criminal offences, especially where these are of a more serious nature. He or she will be responsible for carrying out (or arranging for others to perform) the necessary scientific tests on the forensic evidence recovered from the crime scene and for the preparation of a comprehensive report for use in court. In a tiny minority of cases, the forensic scientist is obliged to appear personally in court as an expert witness and to give evidence of fact and, when required, of opinion based on fact from within his or her area of expertise. When facing cross-examination, the forensic expert is likely to be challenged by the opposition over the accuracy of the scientific test results and, in particular, the interpretation and evaluation he or she has made of these results within the context of the case. It should be emphasised that he or she must remain impartial at all times; it is not the role of the forensic scientist to ascribe the guilt or innocence of the individual on trial.

Problems

1. With reference to the criminal courts in England and Wales, and by use of examples, explain what is meant by each of the following:

   (a) summary only offences;

   (b) either way offences;

   (c) indictable only offences.

2. The criminal justice system in England and Wales is based on the principle of adversarial justice. How is this enacted through the trial procedure of the criminal courts?

3. Compare and contrast the role of:

   (a) lay magistrates and district judges (Magistrates' Court);

   (b) the judge and jurors (Crown Court).

4. Which individuals act as decision-makers in (a) the Magistrates' Court and (b) the Crown Court? In each case, outline the selection process involved. How representative do you think the selected individuals are of the lay population?

5. The forensic scientist's report prepared for use by the prosecution in court is an extremely important document. Discuss the main features that should be covered by a report of this type. Why is it important that it is written in a style that is readily comprehensible to non-scientists?

6. What is an expert witness? With reference to a forensic scientist acting in this capacity, describe the role of the expert witness in court.

7. Under cross-examination, which aspects of the evidence presented by the forensic scientist (appearing as an expert witness) are likely to be challenged by the opposition? How might the forensic expert respond to such attacks?

Further reading

Bond, C., Solon, M. and Harper, P. (1999) *The expert witness in court: a practical guide* (2nd edn, updated and edited by Suzanne Burn). Kent: Shaw & Sons Ltd.

Crown Prosecution Service (2006) *Disclosure: experts' evidence and unused material: guidance booklet for experts.* London: Crown Prosecution Service: CPS Corporate Communication Team. (An instruction booklet containing guidelines on disclosure obligations for expert witnesses instructed by the prosecuting side.)

Davies, M., Croall, H. and Tyrer, J. (2005) *Criminal justice: an introduction to the criminal justice system in England and Wales* (3rd edn). Harlow: Longman.

Hannibal, M. and Mountford, L. (2005) *Criminal litigation.* Oxford: Oxford University Press.

Leadbeatter, S. (ed.) (1996) *Limitations of expert evidence.* London: Royal College of Physicians/Royal College of Pathologists.

Meyer, C. (ed.) (1999) *Expert witnessing: explaining and understanding science.* Boca Raton, FL: CRC Press LLC.

RDS Office for Criminal Justice Reform (2005) *Criminal Statistics 2004 England and Wales* (2nd edn). Home Office Statistical Bulletin. London: Home Office Research, Development and Statistics Directorate. (An annual government publication (available online) giving extensive statistical data about the number and type of offences dealt with by the police and the court system; used in this chapter to provide information on the latter.)

Sprack, J. (2006) *A practical approach to criminal procedure* (11th edn). Oxford: Oxford University Press.

Appendix 1: Sign of elongation and typical birefringence values for man-made fibres

Birefringence	Sign of elongation	Type of fibre	Source
0	Not applicable	Glass	2
0.000 to 0.001	Positive, negative	Triacetate (type of acetate)	1, 2
0.000 to 0.001	Negative*	Verel® (type of modacrylic, which is a type of acrylonitrile)	1
0.001 to 0.005	Negative	Acrylic (type of acrylonitrile)	1, 2
0.002 to 0.005	Positive	Diacetate (type of acetate)	1
0.002 to 0.005	Positive*	Dynel® (type of modacrylic, which is a type of acrylonitrile)	1, 2
0.002 to 0.005	Positive	Vinyon (chlorofibre)	1, 2
0.007 to 0.010	Negative	Saran	2
0.010	Positive	Spandex	1
0.020 to 0.028	Positive	Rayon (viscose) (type of cellulosic)	1, 2
0.021 to 0.037	Positive	Cupro (type of cellulosic)	1, 2
0.025 to 0.030	Positive	Vinal	1, 2
0.028 to 0.034	Positive	Polypropylene (type of polyolefin)	1, 2
0.035 to 0.039	Positive	HT viscose (type of cellulosic)	1, 2
0.039	Positive	Fluorocarbon	1
0.044	Positive	Lyocell (type of cellulosic)	1
0.049 to 0.061	Positive	Nylon 6	1, 2
0.050 to 0.052	Positive	Polyethylene (type of polyolefin)	1, 2
0.056 to 0.063	Positive	Nylon 6.6	1, 2
0.098 to 0.102	Positive	PCDT (type of polyester)	1, 2
0.111	Positive	Sulfar	1
0.120 to 0.230	Positive	Nomex (type of aramid)	1, 2
0.147 to 0.175	Positive	PET (type of polyester)	1, 2
0.148 to 0.150	Positive	PBT (type of polyester)	1
0.200 to 0.710	Positive	Kevlar (type of aramid)	1, 2
0.273	Positive	PEN, e.g. Pentex® (type of polyester)	1

*Modacrylic fibres exhibit variable sign of elongation.[1]

References

1 Robertson, J. and Grieve, M. (eds) (1999) *Forensic examination of fibres* (2nd edn). London: Taylor & Francis.
2 Gaudette, B. D. (1988) 'The forensic aspects of textile fiber examination' in R. Saferstein, (ed.) *Forensic science handbook*, vol. II. Upper Saddle River, NJ: Prentice Hall, pp. 209–272.

Appendix 2: Values of t

Degrees of freedom	90% 10% 80% 20%	95% 5% 90% 10%	97.50% 2.50% 95% 5%	99% 1% 98% 2%	99.50% 0.50% 99% 1%	99.90% 0.10% 99.80% 0.20%	99.95% 0.05% 99.90% 0.10%	Confidence Significance Confidence Significance	One tail One tail Two tails Two tails
1	3.078	6.314	12.71	31.82	63.66	318.3	636.6		
2	1.886	2.920	4.303	6.965	9.925	22.33	31.60		
3	1.638	2.353	3.182	4.541	5.841	10.21	12.92		
4	1.533	2.132	2.776	3.747	4.604	7.173	8.610		
5	1.476	2.015	2.571	3.365	4.032	5.894	6.869		
6	1.440	1.943	2.447	3.143	3.707	5.208	5.959		
7	1.415	1.895	2.365	2.998	3.499	4.785	5.408		
8	1.397	1.860	2.306	2.896	3.355	4.501	5.041		
9	1.383	1.833	2.262	2.821	3.250	4.297	4.781		
10	1.372	1.812	2.228	2.764	3.169	4.144	4.587		
11	1.363	1.796	2.201	2.718	3.106	4.025	4.437		
12	1.356	1.782	2.179	2.681	3.055	3.930	4.318		
13	1.350	1.771	2.160	2.650	3.012	3.852	4.221		
14	1.345	1.761	2.145	2.624	2.977	3.787	4.140		
15	1.341	1.753	2.131	2.602	2.947	3.733	4.073		
16	1.337	1.746	2.120	2.583	2.921	3.686	4.015		
17	1.333	1.740	2.110	2.567	2.898	3.646	3.965		
18	1.330	1.734	2.101	2.552	2.878	3.610	3.922		
19	1.328	1.729	2.093	2.539	2.861	3.579	3.883		
20	1.325	1.725	2.086	2.528	2.845	3.552	3.850		
21	1.323	1.721	2.080	2.518	2.831	3.527	3.819		
22	1.321	1.717	2.074	2.508	2.819	3.505	3.792		
23	1.319	1.714	2.069	2.500	2.807	3.485	3.768		
24	1.318	1.711	2.064	2.492	2.797	3.467	3.745		
25	1.316	1.708	2.060	2.485	2.787	3.450	3.725		
26	1.315	1.706	2.056	2.479	2.779	3.435	3.707		
27	1.314	1.703	2.052	2.473	2.771	3.421	3.689		
28	1.313	1.701	2.048	2.467	2.763	3.408	3.674		
29	1.311	1.699	2.045	2.462	2.756	3.396	3.660		
30	1.310	1.697	2.042	2.457	2.750	3.385	3.646		
32	1.309	1.694	2.037	2.449	2.738	3.365	3.622		
34	1.307	1.691	2.032	2.441	2.728	3.348	3.601		

Degrees of freedom	90% 10% 80% 20%	95% 5% 90% 10%	97.50% 2.50% 95% 5%	99% 1% 98% 2%	99.50% 0.50% 99% 1%	99.90% 0.10% 99.80% 0.20%	99.95% 0.05% 99.90% 0.10%	Confidence Significance Confidence Significance	One tail One tail Two tails Two tails
36	1.306	1.688	2.028	2.434	2.719	3.333	3.582		
38	1.304	1.686	2.024	2.429	2.712	3.319	3.566		
40	1.303	1.684	2.021	2.423	2.704	3.307	3.551		
45	1.301	1.679	2.014	2.412	2.690	3.281	3.520		
50	1.299	1.676	2.009	2.403	2.678	3.261	3.496		
55	1.297	1.673	2.004	2.396	2.668	3.245	3.476		
60	1.296	1.671	2.000	2.390	2.660	3.232	3.460		
70	1.294	1.667	1.994	2.381	2.648	3.211	3.435		
80	1.292	1.664	1.990	2.374	2.639	3.195	3.416		
90	1.291	1.662	1.987	2.368	2.632	3.183	3.402		
100	1.290	1.660	1.984	2.364	2.626	3.174	3.390		
120	1.289	1.658	1.980	2.358	2.617	3.160	3.373		
140	1.288	1.656	1.977	2.353	2.611	3.149	3.361		
160	1.287	1.654	1.975	2.350	2.607	3.142	3.352		
180	1.286	1.653	1.973	2.347	2.603	3.136	3.345		
200	1.286	1.653	1.972	2.345	2.601	3.131	3.340		
300	1.284	1.650	1.968	2.339	2.592	3.118	3.323		
1×10^{10}	1.282	1.645	1.960	2.326	2.576	3.090	3.290		

Glossary

Note that in addition to those definitions relating to firearms that are given in this glossary, a more extensive list is provided in Chapter 9, Box 9.1.

AAIB	Air Accidents Investigation Branch (British).
accuracy	An expression of how near a given measurement, or average (usually the mean) of several repeat or replicate measurements, is to the true or accepted value.
ACPO	The Association of Chief Police Officers of England, Wales and Northern Ireland.
active bloodstains	Bloodstains caused by blood that has been made to travel by a force other than that of gravity.
acute	Occurring over a short time period.
adipocere formation	The hydrolysis of body fats into a waxy, grey substance (adipocere) – a post-mortem process associated with damp conditions.
aerosol	A suspension of solid or liquid particles within a gas.
alkaloid	Any of a group of nitrogen-containing organic bases that occur in plants and fungi; many of which are potentially toxic.
allele	A particular gene can have a number of forms, which differ in the base sequence of the DNA; each of these is an allele.
allele frequency	How common a particular allele is in a population.
alternative hypothesis (symbol H_A)	The hypothesis that the observed difference between the samples (e.g. an observed difference between their means) is *not* due to chance alone.
anagen phase (of hair)	The phase in the growth cycle of an individual hair in which the hair is actively growing.
analyte	The component of the sample targeted by the analysis.
antibodies	Proteins produced by the lymphocytes (a type of white blood cell) in response to the introduction of foreign substances (known as an antigens) into the body.
antigens	Foreign substances that trigger the production of specific antibodies as part of the body's immune response.
associative evidence	Evidence that links, for example, an individual with another individual or with a location.
autopsy	The dissection of a corpse for investigative purposes; a procedure that involves both external and internal examination of the deceased. In Britain, this term is synonymous with 'post-mortem examination'.

ballistics	The scientific study of projectile motion.
base pairs	The unit of length for DNA. There are two types of base pairs in DNA, A–T and G–C.
bloodstain pattern analysis	The interpretation of bloodstain patterns present at violent crime scenes to help reconstruct the events that took place during the commission of a crime.
bulk sample	A sample that is large enough to weigh.
cadaveric spasm	A condition in which the body becomes rigid immediately after death; thought to be associated with extreme fear or tension experienced just before death.
cast-off stain	A type of active bloodstain produced when blood is flung off a blood-soaked object, either as it is moving or as a result of a sudden cessation in its movement.
cause of fire	The act, omission or defect that allowed the conditions necessary for the ignition of the fire to occur and the fire to be started.
chemical species	Any collection of atoms, ions or molecules that share an identical set of chemical properties.
chromosome	A thread-like structure present in the cell nucleus, consisting of a long strand of DNA, carrying many genes, in a complex with protein.
chronic	Occurring over a long time period.
class characteristics	Characteristics that enable an object to be placed into a particular category, for example identifying a trainer as belonging to a certain brand.
common approach path (CAP)	A path that runs from the police cordon to the focal point of a crime scene, designed to allow early and controlled access to the focal point while minimising impact on the scene as a whole.
condensed explosive	An explosive that is either a solid or a liquid.
constant	An item of data that has one fixed value.
continuity of evidence	The provision of a complete, documented account of the progress of an item of evidence from crime scene to court.
continuous data	Quantitative data that can have any value in a range of allowed values.
controlled drugs	In the UK, drugs that are subject to the Misuse of Drugs Act 1971.
cordon	A physical barrier erected by the police to encompass a crime scene and thus restrict access to authorised personnel only.
coroner	An independent judicial officer who is required to hold investigations into the reported deaths of any individuals whose bodies lie within his or her geographical area of jurisdiction.
corroborative evidence	Evidence that supports other evidence.
Council for the Registration of Forensic Practitioners (CRFP)	An independent regulatory body for the accreditation of individual forensic practitioners.
courts of appeal	Within the criminal justice system in England and Wales, the three courts designated to hear appeals against decisions of guilt and/or sentence – the High Court (Queen's Bench Division), Court of Appeal (Criminal Division) and House of Lords.
Crime Scene Co-ordinator	The person (usually the force's SSM or a senior SOCO) who is given the responsibility for managing the scientific support needs of all of the crime scenes of a given serious crime.
Crime Scene Manager	In the case of a serious crime, the individual whose task it is to oversee the processing of a given crime scene.

crime scene reconstruction	The reconstruction of those events that may have taken place before, during and immediately after the commission of a crime, based on the evidence available.
Criminal Cases Review Commission (CCRC)	An independent body responsible for the investigation of possible miscarriages of justice in England, Wales and Northern Ireland.
cross-examination	The questioning in court of a witness appearing for one side (i.e. the prosecution or defence) by the opposing side.
Crown Court	The higher of the two criminal courts in England and Wales.
Crown Prosecution Service (CPS)	The agency working on behalf of the State that is responsible for the prosecution of the vast majority of criminal offences.
cursive writing	Lower case, joined-up handwriting.
cutting agents	Substances that are deliberately mixed in with drugs of abuse before sale in order to increase their apparent bulk and/or purity.
data	Facts and figures that convey information.
deactivated firearms	Firearms that have been deliberately rendered incapable of firing projectiles, so that they can be sold as non-firearms.
defendant	Term used for an individual standing trial in a court of law.
deflagration	A type of chemical explosion in which the speed at which the reaction front moves through the explosive is less than the speed of sound in that material.
dental stone	A powder that, when mixed with water in the appropriate ratio, is suitable for taking casts of, for example, footwear impressions.
depressant	Any drug that has a depressing effect on the central nervous system, including the inhibition of brain activity.
detonation	A type of chemical explosion in which the speed at which the reaction front moves through the explosive is greater than the speed of sound in that material.
diatomaceous earth	A geological material produced by the sedimentary deposition of diatom shells.
diploid	Having two sets of chromosomes; one from each parent.
discrete quantitative data	Quantitative data that can have only integer values.
dispersed explosive	An explosive that is either a gas or an aerosol.
district judges	Full-time professional lawyers who preside (alone) in a minority of the Magistrates' Courts in England and Wales. Formerly known as stipendiary magistrates.
dropdown	The falling of burning materials during a fire, thereby producing secondary ignition at low elevation.
drugs of abuse	A collective term given to those substances that are used recreationally by individuals in order to induce changes in mood and/or perception.
either way offences	Offences that may be tried in either of the two criminal courts – the Magistrates' Court or the Crown Court.
EOD	Explosives Ordnance Disposal (i.e. Army Bomb Disposal)
error	An expression of inaccuracy.
ESDA	Electrostatic detection apparatus – a piece of equipment used by document examiners, mainly for the visualisation of indented writing.
ESLA	Electrostatic lifting apparatus – a portable device used to transfer impressions, such as a dusty footprint, onto a Mylar sheet, in order to preserve it for future examination.

exons	The parts of genes that carry protein information.
expert witness	An individual who is required to appear in court in order to give factual information, and opinion based on fact, from within his or her area of expertise.
Expert Witness Institute (EWI)	An independent body launched in 1996 to provide support and training for expert witnesses.
explosion	The violent effect produced due to the rapid build-up of gas pressure at a location because of the sudden liberation of energy and, in most cases, gas at that location.
explosive	Any substance that is capable of producing an explosion, although this term is commonly restricted to those substances that can produce explosions due to chemical reactions.
external ballistics	The study of projectile behaviour after discharge from the firearm but prior to impact with the target.
facial reconstruction	A highly skilled technique used to reconstruct the facial appearance of an individual from his or her bare skull, based on knowledge of the average thickness of soft tissue over many different points on the skull.
false negative	A negative result given when the substance being tested for is actually present.
false positive	A positive result given by a substance other than that being tested for.
FBI	Federal Bureau of Investigation (US).
fibre	Any long, thin, flexible, solid object with a high length to transverse cross-section area ratio.
fire	The phenomenon in which heat and light are liberated by the process of combustion.
fire accelerant	A flammable material (most commonly liquid) used to facilitate and/or increase the rate of spread of fire and/or increase the intensity of fire.
first officer attending (FOA)	The first police officer to arrive at a given incident scene.
flameover	See Rollover.
flashback	An explosion occurring during a fire when fresh air is suddenly allowed to mix with air in a compartment that is both oxygen-depleted and rich in flammable, volatile pyrolysis products.
FLINTS	Forensic Led Intelligence System; a computer software package jointly developed by West Midlands Police and the Forensic Science Service (FSS) in the late 1990s.
forensic archaeology	The application of traditional archaeological techniques by a suitably qualified specialist in the search, location, excavation and recovery of recent human remains (either individual or en masse) as part of a criminal investigation.
forensic entomology	The study of insects as applied to legal disputes.
forensic odontologist	A specialist in the scientific study of teeth who provides information germane to the resolution of legal disputes.
forensic palynology	The scientific study of microscopic entities, primarily pollen grains and plant spores, and their distribution, as applied to criminal investigations.
forensic pathologist	A medically trained specialist who, through the performance of forensic autopsy, provides legally required information concerning the death of an individual.

forensic podiatrist	A specialist trained in the treatment and care of the lower limb who is able to use certain aspects of that expertise, e.g. in the interpretation of footprints and gait, to assist the police in the identification of individuals.
Forensic Science Service (FSS)	An executive agency of the Home Office and the biggest supplier of forensic science services in the UK.
forensic toxicology	The scientific study of poisons – their nature and effects – in relation to the law.
friction ridge skin	In humans, and other primates, a special type of thickened, ridged skin that covers the palms of the hands and the soles of the feet.
FSS	*See* Forensic Science Service.
fuel-controlled fire	A fire that is limited by the supply of fuel, not the availability of oxygen.
gametes	The sex cells; sperm in males, eggs in females.
genotype	For a particular gene, the combination of alleles at that genetic locus. More widely, the combination of genes carried by an individual – his or her genetic make-up.
genotype frequency	How common a particular genotype is in a population.
GMC	General Medical Council – the professional regulatory body for doctors practising medicine in the UK.
gross error	Error due to a mistake or an unusual event.
gunshot residues (GSR)	The heterogeneous mix of finely divided particles that is expelled alongside the intended projectile(s) when a firearm (other than an air weapon) is discharged.
hallucinogen	Any drug that alters the perception and mood of an individual, without either stimulating or inhibiting brain activity.
haploid	Having only one set of chromosomes. Usually applies to gametes.
Hardy–Weinberg principle	A mathematical relationship that relates allele frequencies to genotype frequencies; if an allele frequency is known, predictions can be made about how frequent certain genotypes will be. The Hardy–Weinberg principle represents an idealised population, correction factors are applied to represent real populations.
Henry System	A ten-print fingerprint classification system devised by Sir Edward Richard Henry and adopted in England and Wales in 1901.
heterozygous	Having two different alleles for a given gene or DNA sequence.
high explosive	An explosive that normally detonates rather than deflagrates.
HOLMES	Home Office Large Major Enquiry System – the nationally networked computer system used by the police to store and retrieve information obtained during the investigation of serious crimes.
homozygous	Having two identical alleles for a given gene or DNA sequence.
hypostasis	A post-mortem condition, similar in appearance to bruising, caused by the settlement of blood in the lowermost parts of the body during the early stages of decomposition. Also known as post-mortem lividity or livor mortis.
indented writing	Writing that appears in the form of an impression on a surface below that originally written on.
indictable only offences	Offences that *must* be tried on indictment in the higher of the two criminal courts – the Crown Court. This category covers the most serious of crimes, for example murder, blackmail and rape.

individual characteristics	Characteristics that are unique to a particular object (e.g. a tool, tyre or shoe) and, as such, are potentially useful in the identification of scene impressions.
intergenic DNA	DNA sequences between genes; some of this has no obvious function and is considered to be 'junk' DNA.
internal ballistics	The study of what occurs in the span of time between the firing pin striking the primer and the projectile(s) leaving the firearm.
Interpol	The International Criminal Police Organization.
introns	DNA sequences between exons, often considered to be a type of 'junk' DNA.
'junk' DNA	DNA sequences whose function, if they have any, is currently unknown. 'Junk' DNA does not contain genetic information for RNA or proteins.
jury	A panel of 12 individuals who are randomly selected from the general population and whose role is to try defendants in the Crown Court under the auspices of a judge.
Justices of the Peace	See Lay magistrates.
latent fingerprints	Fingerprints that are not visible to the naked eye. Such fingerprints need to be visualised, using appropriate development techniques, before examination.
lay magistrates	Unpaid, part-time volunteers who preside (usually in a panel of three) in the vast majority of the Magistrates' Courts in England and Wales. Also known as Justices of the Peace.
likelihood ratio	How much more likely an event is compared with the alternative event.
Livescan	A recently developed technique, adopted by some police forces, in which fingerprints are recorded by electronic scanning.
livor mortis	See Hypostasis.
Locard's exchange principle	A principle based on the notion that 'every contact leaves a trace' or, in other words, any contact between individuals, or between an individual and a physical location, leads to the transference of trace evidence.
locus	The position of a gene on the chromosome.
Magistrates' Court	The lower of the two criminal courts in England and Wales.
magnetic powder applicator	A special device used to apply magnetic fingerprint powder to a surface suspected of bearing latent fingerprints. Excess powder is subsequently removed by an internal magnet.
manner of death	Whether a death was due to accident, homicide, natural causes or suicide.
match probability	The likelihood that two people selected at random could have an identical DNA profile.
matrix	That part of the sample other than the chemical species being analysed for.
microsatellite DNA	Tandem repetitive DNA that has very short repeats of 2 to 4 base pairs; these are the same as short tandem repeats (STRs).
minisatellite DNA	Tandem repetitive DNA that has repeat lengths of 6 base pairs to about 100 base pairs and are often equated with variable number tandem repeats (VNTRs).
mitochondrial DNA	A small DNA circle that is not in the cell's nucleus but within those parts of the cell known as mitochondria.
modus operandi (MO) of a criminal	The way in which the perpetrator of a crime carries out the act.

mummification	The preservation of a corpse through desiccation – a post-mortem process associated with warm, dry conditions.
mutation	A change in a gene, an alteration in its DNA sequence.
NAFIS	National Automated Fingerprint Identification System; the national fingerprint database used by police forces in England and Wales.
NDNAD	The National DNA Database®, established in 1995 and run by the Forensic Science Service.
NFFID	National Firearms Forensic Intelligence Database, established by the Forensic Science Service in partnership with the Association of Chief Police Officers in 2003.
nuclear DNA	DNA present in chromosomes in the cell nucleus.
nucleotides	Biochemicals, each made up of a base, a sugar and a phosphate group. Nucleotides are the building blocks of DNA and RNA.
null hypothesis (symbol H_0)	The hypothesis that the observed difference between the samples (e.g. an observed difference between their means) is due to chance alone.
oxidant	*See* Oxidising agent.
oxidising agent	A chemical species that is capable of accepting electrons from another chemical species. Also known as an oxidant.
passive bloodstains	Bloodstains that are formed solely under the influence of gravity.
phenotype	The observable characteristics of a person or organism.
photosuperimposition	A forensic technique in which a photographic image of the bare skull of the decedent is superimposed onto a photographic portrait, taken during life, of a possible match.
plastic fingerprints	Fingerprint impressions formed when the fingertips are pushed into some suitably soft material such as soap, fresh paint or candle wax.
plea-bargaining	An arrangement whereby the defendant agrees to plead guilty to a less serious allegation, in exchange for the prosecution not pursuing a more serious allegation.
poison	Any substance that has an injurious or fatal effect when introduced into, or taken up by, a living organism.
polymerase chain reaction (PCR)	An *in vitro* method of amplifying (increasing the amount of) a chosen sequence of DNA. It is extremely sensitive, allowing the detection and analysis of very small amounts of DNA found at crime scenes.
population	In statistics, the population is the complete data set that is all of the observations of the type being made that could be made on the item or group of related items under study.
post-mortem examination	*See* Autopsy.
post-mortem interval	The period of time that has elapsed since death occurred.
post-mortem lividity	*See* Hypostasis.
precision	An expression of how reproducible a given measurement is.
presumptive tests	Tests that are designed to quickly and cheaply indicate the presence of certain analytes. Such tests provide qualitative but not quantitative information and are not definitive.
primary transfer	The direct transfer of trace evidence from one object to another.
qualitative	Concerned only with the nature of the substances under investigation and not their amount or concentration.
qualitative data	Data that convey information about the qualities of the things being studied and that do not directly convey information about quantity or size.

quantitative	Concerned with the amount or concentration of the substances under investigation.
quantitative data	Data that convey information about size or quantity.
questioned document	Any document over which there is some dispute or query, usually concerning its authenticity or origin.
radial loop pattern	A fingerprint pattern in which the loop opens in the direction of the thumb (i.e. towards the radial bone of the forearm).
radiation-induced flashover	The involvement in a fire, over a very short time span, of essentially all of the fuel items in a room or similar compartment as radiation from hot gases present in the upper parts of the compartment causes the ignition of the exposed surfaces of fuel items.
random error	Error that causes dispersion of replicate or repeat measurements about the mean measurement. Also called indeterminate error.
reactivated firearms	Legitimately deactivated firearms that have been illegally converted back into a state in which they are capable of firing projectiles again.
reducing agent	A chemical species that is capable of donating electrons to another chemical species. Also known as a reductant.
reductant	*See* Reducing agent.
refractive index (of a medium)	The ratio of the speed of light in a vacuum to the speed of light in that medium. Symbol n.
ricochet	The deviation in the flight-path of a projectile as a consequence of impact.
rigor mortis	The stiffening of the body after death, a temporary condition that begins a few hours after death and wears off after a period of two or three days.
rollover	The ignition of, and rapid spread of flame within, the hot gases that have accumulated in, or are venting from, the upper part of a burning room or similar compartment. Also known as flameover.
sample	In statistics, a collection of measurements or counts that is a subset of the population.
satellite bloodstains	Bloodstains produced when smaller droplets of blood are thrown off by a larger droplet (known as the parent) impacting on a surface.
satellite DNA	A general term referring to any type of tandem repetitive DNA.
scale cast	A cast made by embedding a hair in a suitable varnish and then removing the hair once the varnish has dried, forming an impression of the pattern of scales on the hair's surface.
scene impression	An impression found at a crime scene (e.g. of a tool, shoe or tyre), which may be of potential forensic importance.
Scenes of Crime Officers (SOCOs)	The title given to those members of police scientific support who specialise in the processing of crime scenes. Note that this title is not universal and some police forces in the UK use other equivalent titles for people who carry out this role.
Scientific Support Manager (SSM)	In most police forces in England and Wales, this is the title given to the individual who has overall responsibility for the management of scientific support staff. Each police force in England and Wales has a Scientific Support Manager or equivalent.
script	Lower case, unjoined handwriting.
seat of fire	The location where the fire started. Also known as its point of origin.

secondary transfer	The indirect transfer of trace evidence from one object to another via an intermediary object.
secretors	Individuals in whom blood-group antigens are present in non-blood body fluids, such as urine, semen and saliva.
serological test	Any test that involves the use of a specific antibody to detect the presence of a specific antigen.
short tandem repeat (STRs)	A type of tandem repeat where the repeat length is short, by definition between 2 and 4 base pairs. These are extremely important in modern DNA profiling.
simulation experiments	A series of experiments designed to simulate a particular aspect of a crime, which, through a process of elimination, may help to pinpoint exactly what happened in that specific aspect.
skeletalisation	The normal process of post-mortem decomposition whereby the soft tissues of the body gradually dissolve to reveal the skeleton within.
SOCOs	*See* Scenes of Crime Officers.
soil profile	A vertical section through a soil showing the different horizons from the surface to the underlying parent material.
soil structure	The arrangement of voids, individual soil particles and aggregates of these particles within a soil.
specimen handwriting	Samples of handwriting obtained from an individual suspected of authorship of a piece of questioned handwriting for the purposes of comparison.
stimulant	Any drug that arouses and stimulates the central nervous system.
stipendiary magistrates	*See* District judges.
summary only offences	Offences that can be tried only in the lower of the two criminal courts – the Magistrates' Court.
Superglue fuming	A visualisation technique for latent fingerprints in which a surface, or object, suspected of bearing prints is exposed to ethyl cyanoacrylate fumes.
systematic error	Error that causes the value of the measurement (or mean of replicate or repeat measurements) to be consistently high or low. Also called determinate error.
tandem repeat	A type of DNA sequence where a short sequence of DNA is repeated consecutively a number of times. These have important forensic applications.
tape lift	A portion of sticky tape that has been brought into contact with the area to be sampled in order to recover trace materials such as hairs and other fibres.
telogen phase (of hair)	The phase in the growth cycle of an individual hair in which the hair is no longer actively growing.
terminal ballistics	The study of the behaviour of projectiles when they strike their targets.
test impression	An impression made, under test conditions, of a suspect item (e.g. a tool, shoe or tyre) in order to compare it with a scene impression.
toxin	Any poisonous substance that is naturally produced by an animal, plant, fungus or microorganism.
trace evidence	Minute amounts of materials (such as glass shards, paint chips, hairs or fibres) that are inevitably transferred through contact between individuals, or between an individual and a physical location, according to Locard's exchange principle.

trace sample	An amount so small that it cannot be weighed – although it may well be possible to establish its weight by means of quantitative chemical analysis.
transfer bloodstains	Bloodstains that have been deposited on surfaces as a result of direct contact with objects contaminated with wet blood.
UKAS	United Kingdom Accreditation Service – a government-recognised national body for the accreditation of calibration and testing laboratories, including those offering forensic services, and for companies offering inspection and certification services.
ulnar loop pattern	A fingerprint pattern in which the loop opens in the direction of the little finger (i.e. towards the ulnar bone of the forearm).
variable	An item of data that can have any one of a number of values.
variable number tandem repeats (VNTRs)	A type of tandem repeat; the length of the repeat is not strictly defined but they are often taken to be 6 base pairs to about100 base pairs.
ventilation-controlled fire	A fire that is limited by the supply of oxygen, not the availability of fuel.
watermark	A distinctive design that is incorporated into paper by reducing the number of fibres present within the patterned area during the manufacturing process.

Index

Note: page numbers of defined terms appear in **bold**.